ESSAYS IN ECONOMICS

The Papers of James Tobin

Volume 1 *Essays in Economics: Macroeconomics* (Chicago: Markham, 1972; reprint, Cambridge, MA: MIT Press, 1987)

Volume 2 *Essays in Economics: Consumption and Econometrics* (Amsterdam: North-Holland, 1975; reprint, Cambridge, MA: MIT Press, 1987)

Volume 3 *Essays in Economics: Theory and Policy*, Cambridge, MA: MIT Press, 1982

Volume 4 *Essays in Economics: National and International*, Cambridge, MA: MIT Press, 1996

Other Books by James Tobin

National Economic Policy, New Haven: Yale University Press, 1966

Welfare Programs: An Economic Appraisal, Washington, D.C.: American Enterprise Institute, 1968 (with W. Allen Wallis)

The New Economics One Decade Older, Princeton, NJ: Princeton University Press, 1974

Asset Accumulation and Economic Activity: Reflections on Contemporary Macroeconomic Theory, Chicago, IL: University of Chicago Press, 1982

Two Revolutions in Economic Policy, The First Economic Reports of Presidents Kennedy and Reagan, Cambridge, MA: MIT Press, 1988 (James Tobin and Murray Weidenbaum, editors)

Policies for Prosperity: Essays in a Keynesian Mode, Cambridge, MA: MIT Press, 1989

Full Employment and Economic Growth: Further Essays in a Keynesian Mode, Cheltenham, UK: Edward Elgar, forthcoming in 1996

ESSAYS IN ECONOMICS
NATIONAL AND INTERNATIONAL

James Tobin

The MIT Press
Cambridge, Massachusetts
London, England

© 1996 Massachusetts Institute of Technology

All rights reserved. No part of this book may be reproduced in any form by any electronic or mechanical means (including photocopying, recording, or information storage and retrieval) without permission in writing from the publisher.

This book was set in Times Roman by Asco Trade Typesetting Ltd., Hong Kong, and printed and bound in the United States of America.

Library of Congress Cataloging-in-Publication Data

Tobin, James, 1918–
 Essays in economics, national and international / James Tobin.
   p. cm.—(The papers of James Tobin ; v. 4)
 Includes bibliographical references and index.
 ISBN 0-262-20101-1 (alk. paper)
 1. Economics. I. Title. II. Series: Tobin, James, 1918– .
Essays. Selections; v. 4.
HB171.T629 1996
330—dc20   95-23522
                                                       CIP

To
BILL B. and BILL N.
my students, my friends, my teachers,
this book is gratefully dedicated

CONTENTS

	Preface	xi
1	A Professional Autobiography	1
I	**MONEY AND FINANCE**	21
2	Money and Finance in the Macroeconomic Process	23
3	A Model of U.S. Financial and Nonfinancial Economic Behavior *with David Backus, William Brainard, and Gary Smith*	67
4	Financial Intermediaries	115
5	Money	139
6	Liquidity Preference, Separation, and Asset Pricing	165
II	**MACROECONOMIC THEORY**	169
7	Price Flexibility and Output Stability: An Old Keynesian View	171
8	Macroeconomics under Debate	203
9	On the Welfare Macroeconomics of Government Financial Policy	237
10	The Macroeconomics of Government Finance *with Michael Haliossos*	253
11	Mandatory Retirement Saving and Capital Formation *with Walter Dolde*	335
12	Inventories, Investment, Inflation, and Taxes	369
13	The Natural Rate as New Classical Macroeconomics	385

| III | **MACROECONOMIC POLICY** | 397 |

14	On the Theory of Macroeconomic Policy	399
15	Stabilization Policy Ten Years After	417
16	Monetary Policy: Rules, Targets, and Shocks	471
17	The Monetary and Fiscal Policy Mix	487
18	The Monetary and Fiscal Policy Mix: Long-Run Implications	507
19	Financial Structure and Monetary Rules	519

| IV | **INTERNATIONAL ECONOMICS** | 537 |

20	On the Internationalization of Portfolios	539
21	Policies and Exchange Rates: A Simple Analytical Framework	583
22	The State of Exchange Rate Theory: Some Skeptical Observations	601
23	Are There Reliable Adjustment Mechanisms?	617
24	Agenda for International Coordination of Macroeconomic Policies	633
25	International Currency Regimes, Capital Mobility, and Macroeconomic Policy	643

| V | **ECONOMICS AND ECONOMISTS** | 659 |

26	A Revolution Remembered	661
27	Neoclassical Theory in America: J. B. Clark and Fisher	673
28	Irving Fisher	699
29	Growth and Distribution: A Neoclassical Kaldor–Robinson Exercise	721
30	Arthur M. Okun	737
31	Robert Triffin	743
32	Walter W. Heller	747
33	The Optimal Cash Balance Proposition: Maurice Allais's Priority *with William J. Baumol*	757

34	William S. Vickrey	763
35	Paul Samuelson: Macroeconomics and Fiscal Policy	769
36	Seymour Harris	787
	Index	791

PREFACE

This is the fourth volume of my professional papers in economics, collected under the general title, *Essays in Economics*. The papers in this collection were written and published during 1980–1994, except for the last chapter, my 1974 memoir of Seymour Harris. I am grateful to the MIT Press for publishing this volume and *Essays, Volume 3*, and for taking over and reprinting the first two volumes, thus keeping the whole set in print.

The *Essays* collections do not include less scholarly essays on economic policy intended for general readers. I have published separately two collections of such papers, and a third one is in the works.

Not surprisingly, most of the articles in this volume concern macroeconomic theory and policy. The introductory chapter is autobiographical. Part I contains five essays on money and finance, beginning with my Nobel lecture in 1981. That lecture describes the theoretical model of the economy's financial sector and its relation to macroeconomic activity developed by me and my colleagues at Yale. The following chapter concerns the empirical implementation of the model. Chapter 5 is my attempt to explain the phenomenon of money to encyclopedia readers.

Part II consists of articles on various aspects of macroeconomics. Chapters 7, 8, and 13 state my Keynesian views, in opposition to the new classical attacks prevalent in recent years. All macroeconomic debates are ultimately about policy, but the essays of part III specifically discuss policy issues, both monetary and fiscal. In the last twenty-five years, international money and finance have become increasingly important aspects of macroeconomics and of my own interests. These are the subjects of part IV.

Continuing a practice begun in *Essays, Volume 3*, the final part reprints some articles and memoirs concerning particular economists whose paths I have crossed, if not personally, then at least intellectually.

James Tobin
New Haven

Acknowledgments

Several of the essays were written jointly with others, as indicated in the table of contents. I thank all the joint authors both for our fruitful and pleasant collaborations, and for their consents to republish our works here.

During the years when the essays collected here were written, I have continued even in retirement to benefit from the logistical support and intellectual stimulus of my environment here at Yale University, its Department of Economics, and especially the Cowles Foundation for Research in Economics. I cannot begin to list my individual debts. For help in preparing this book for publication I am grateful to Marian Daly and to two of my undergraduate students, Serkan Saracoglu and Richard Tashjian, and two graduate students, Kevin Foster and Christine Reynolds.

ESSAYS IN ECONOMICS

CHAPTER 1

A PROFESSIONAL AUTOBIOGRAPHY

Beginning with Keynes at Harvard

Rare is the child, I suspect, who wants to grow up to be an economist, or a professor. I grew up in a university town and went to a university-run high school, where most of my friends were faculty kids. I was so unfailing an A student that it was boring even to me. But I don't recall thinking of an academic career. I liked journalism, my father's occupation; I had put out "newspapers" of my own from age six. I thought of law; I loved to argue, and beginning in my teens I was fascinated by politics. I guess I knew that there was economics at the university, but I didn't know what the subject really was. Of course, economic issues were always coming up in classes on history and government—civics, in those days. I expected economics to be among the social science courses I would someday take in college, probably part of the pre-law curriculum.

I grew up happily assuming I would go to college in my hometown, to the University of Illinois. One month before I was scheduled to enroll as a freshman, I was offered and accepted a Conant Prize Fellowship at Harvard. I should explain how this happened. My father, a learned man, a voracious reader, the biggest customer of the Champaign Public Library, discovered in the *New York Times* that Harvard was offering these new fellowships in eight midwestern states. President Conant wanted to broaden the geographical and social base of Harvard College. Having nothing to lose, I accepted my father's suggestion that I apply. University High School, it turned out, had without even trying prepared me superbly for the obligatory College Board exams. Uni High graduates

---

Reprinted by permission from *Lives of the Laureates*, eds. William Breit and Roger W. Spencer, Cambridge, MA: The MIT Press, 1986, pp. 113–134.

only thirty to thirty-five persons a year, but it has three Nobels to its credit and, once I had broken the ice, many national scholarships.

Thus James Bryant Conant, Louis Michael Tobin, and University High School changed my life and career. Illinois was and is a great university. But I doubt that it would have led me into economics. For several reasons, Harvard did.

Harvard was the leading academic center of economics in North America at the time; only Columbia and Chicago were close competitors. Both its senior and junior faculty were outstanding. Two of the previous lecturers in this series were active and influential members of the community when I was a student, Wassily Leontief on the faculty and Paul Samuelson as a Junior Fellow, a graduate student free of formal academic requirements. Of the senior faculty of the 1930s, Joseph Schumpeter would have been a sure bet for a Nobel, Alvin Hansen, Edward Chamberlin, and Gottfried Haberler likely choices. Haberler, still active, remains a possibility. Naturally, Harvard attracted remarkably talented graduate students. That able undergraduates might go on to scholarly careers was taken for granted.

When I arrived at Harvard, I knew I would want to major—at Harvard the word is *concentrate*—in one of the social sciences or possibly in mathematics. By the end of freshman year I was leaning to economics. But I hadn't yet taken any. In those days even Ec A, the introductory course, was considered too hard for freshmen. As a sophomore all of eighteen years old, I began Ec A in a section taught by Spencer Pollard, an advanced graduate student specializing in labor economics and writing a dissertation on John L. Lewis and the United Mine Workers.

Pollard was also my tutor. A Harvard undergraduate, besides taking four courses, met regularly, usually singly, with a tutor in his field of concentration, generally a faculty member or graduate student associated with the student's residential house. Tutorial was not graded. It was modeled, like the house system itself, on Oxford and Cambridge. Pollard suggested that we devote our sessions to "this new book from England." He had recently been over there and judged from the stir the book was creating even before publication that it was important. The book was *The General Theory of Employment, Interest and Money* by John Maynard Keynes, published in 1936.

Pollard was no respecter of academic conventions; that I was only an Ec A student meant nothing to him. I was too young, and too ready to assume that teacher knows best, to know that I knew too little to read the book. So I read it, and Pollard and I talked about it as we went through it. Cutting my teeth on *The General Theory*, I was hooked on economics.

Like many other economists of my vintage, I was attracted to the field for two reasons. One was that economic theory is a fascinating intellectual challenge, on the order of mathematics or chess. I liked analytics and logical argument. I thought algebra was the most eyeopening school experience between the three Rs and college.

The other reason was the obvious relevance of economics to understanding and perhaps overcoming the great depression and all the frightening political developments associated with it throughout the world. I did not personally suffer deprivations during the depression. But my parents made me very conscious of the political and economic problems of the times. My father was a well-informed and thoughtful political liberal. My mother was a social worker, recalled to her career by the emergency; she was dealing with cases of unemployment and poverty every day.

The second motivation, I observe, gave our generation of economists different interests and priorities from subsequent cohorts dominated by those attracted to the subject more exclusively by the appeal of its puzzles to their quantitative aptitudes and interests.

Thanks to Keynes, economics offered me the best of both worlds. I was fascinated by his theoretical duel with the orthodox classical economists. Keynes's uprising against encrusted error was an appealing crusade for youth. The truth would make us free, and fully employed too. I was already an ardent and uncritical New Dealer, much concerned about the depression, unemployment, and poverty. According to Keynesian theory, Roosevelt's devaluation of the dollar and deficit spending were sound economics after all.

By sheer application, unconstrained by the need to unlearn anything, I came to know Keynes's new book sooner and better than many of my elders at Harvard. Keynes was the founder of what later came to be known as macroeconomics, what his young associate Joan Robinson called at the time "the theory of output as a whole," a phrase I found strikingly apt. The contrast was with the theory of output and price in particular markets or sectors. This—what we now call "micro"—was the main stuff of the theory course we economics concentrators took after Ec A. I liked the methodology of the new subject, modeling the whole economy by a system of simultaneous equations; by now I had calculus to add to my algebra. J. R. Hicks and others showed, more clearly than Keynes himself, how the essentials of *The General Theory*, and its differences from classical theory, could be expressed and analyzed in such models.

Harvard was becoming the beachhead for the Keynesian invasion of the new world. The senior faculty was mostly hostile. A group of them had not long before published a book quite critical of Roosevelt's recovery program. Seymour Harris, an early convert to Keynes, was an exception, especially important to undergraduates like myself, in whom he took a paternal interest. Harris was an academic entrepreneur. He opened the pages of the *Review of Economics and Statistics*, of which he was editor, and the halls of Dunster House, of which he was senior tutor, to lively debates on economic theory and policy.

The younger faculty and the graduate student teaching fellows were enthusiastic about Keynes's book. Their reasons were similar to my own but better informed. A popular tract by seven of them, *An Economic Program for American Democracy*, preached the new gospel with a left-wing slant.

Most important of all was the arrival of Alvin Hansen to fill the new Littauer chair in political economy. Hansen, aged fifty, came to Harvard from the University of Minnesota the same year I was beginning economics. He had previously been critical of Keynes and had indeed published a lukewarm review of *The General Theory*. He changed his mind 180 degrees, a rare event for scholars of any age, especially if their previous views are in print. Hansen became the leading apostle of Keynesian theory and policy in America. His fiscal policy seminar was the focus of research, theoretical and applied, in Keynesian economics. Visitors from the Washington firing lines mixed with local students and faculty; I had the feeling that history was being made in that room. For undergraduates the immediate payoff was that Hansen taught us macroeconomics, though under the course rubric Money and Banking. Hansen was a true hero to me, and in later years he was to be a real friend also.

I wrote my senior honors thesis on what I perceived to be the central theoretical issue between Keynes and the classical economists he was attacking. The orthodox position was that prices move to clear markets, rising to eliminate excesses of demand over supply and falling to eliminate excess supplies. Applied to the labor market, this meant that reductions of wages would get rid of unemployment. Excess supply of labor could not be a permanent equilibrium. Unless wage cuts are prevented by law or by monopolistic trade unions, competition for jobs will lower wages and in turn restore or create jobs for the unemployed. This was just an application of the central thesis of orthodox economics, the Invisible Hand proposition of Adam Smith. Individual agents are selfish and myopic. They respond in their own interest to the market signals locally available to them. Their actions miraculously turn out for the best for the society as a whole. Competition brings this miracle about.

Keynes's heresy was to deny that this mechanism could be counted on to eliminate involuntary unemployment. He didn't say just that the mechanism was slow and needed help from government policy. He said it might not work at all. Instead, the economy would be stuck in an underemployment equilibrium. Orthodox economists thought they could prove that free competitive markets allocate resources efficiently. In saying that willing and productive workers can't get jobs, Keynes was indicting the market system for a massive failure. After all, there is no greater inefficiency than to leave productive resources idle.

My honors thesis found fault with Keynes's logic. That may seem surprising. But I didn't think Keynes needed to insist on so sweeping a theoretical victory on his opponents' home court. His practical message was just as important whether unemployment was an incident of prolonged disequilibrium or of equilibrium. My first professional publication (1941) was an article in the *Quarterly Journal of Economics* based on my senior thesis; the *QJE* is, of course, edited and published at Harvard. The issue is very much alive today. It has also remained an interest of mine, a subject on which I have published several other papers, including my 1971 presidential address to the American Economic Association (1972).

Tools of the Trade, Theoretical and Statistical

By graduation time in 1939 I had forgotten about law and drifted into the natural decision, to become a professional economist. Harvard has a way of keeping its own: my fellowship was extended and I went on to graduate school. The transition was easy; I had taken courses with graduate students while I was a senior. Now I needed to pick up some tools of the trade. One was formal mathematical economic theory, and another was statistics and econometrics. Harvard was just beginning to catch up to the state of these two arts.

I see in retrospect that our professors left most of our education to us. They expected us to teach ourselves and learn from each other, and we did. They treated us as adult partners in scholarly endeavor, not as apprentices. I am afraid our graduate programs today try too hard to convey a definite and vast body of material and to test how well students master what we know. I wrote my undergraduate thesis under the nominal supervision of my senior-year tutor, Professor Edward Chamberlin. He said he knew nothing about my subject and left me on my own. Our tutorial sessions were nonetheless interesting; we argued about Catholic agrarianism, his vision of economic utopia. The faculty adviser for my doctoral dissertation in 1946–47 was, by my choice, Professor Schumpeter, one of the truly great economists, indeed social scientists, of the century. He had no use for Keynes and little for my topic, the consumption function. He read what I wrote and made helpful suggestions, but mostly he kept hands off. When I saw him, we talked of many other things, to my lasting benefit.

The theory we were taught was largely in the Anglo-American tradition, in which mathematical argument was subordinated to verbal and graphical exposition and relegated to footnotes. The great book was *Principles of Economics* by Alfred Marshall, Keynes's own mentor in the other Cambridge. Markets were analyzed mostly one at a time—*partial* equilibrium analysis. Little rigorous attempt was made to describe a *general* equilibrium of the system as a whole, with many commodities, many consumers and producers, many markets interconnected with each other.

Mathematical models of general equilibrium were a stronger tradition in continental Europe, to which the French-Swiss economist Leon Walras had made the seminal contribution in 1870. Though F. Y. Edgeworth at Oxford and Irving Fisher at Yale had written in the same vein, they had not greatly influenced the main line of English-language economics from Adam Smith to David Ricardo to John Stuart Mill to Marshall. But in the late 1930s and 1940s the mathematical general equilibrium approach was coming into vogue, thanks to J. R. Hicks and R. G. D. Allen in

Britain and Wassily Leontief and Paul Samuelson at Harvard. Joseph Schumpeter fostered this development, believing that Walras had provided economics its "magna charta," even though his own theory of the dynamics of capitalism was wholly different.

I liked the general equilibrium approach; that was one of the great appeals of macroeconomics. But those models of output as a whole were small enough and specific enough to understand and manipulate. I have never been an aficionado of formal mathematical general equilibrium theory, which is so pure and general as to be virtually devoid of interesting operational conclusions. Moreover, I have come to think that its elegance gives many economic theorists today an exaggerated presumptive faith that free competitive markets work for the best. I did use the approach in some articles in the late 1940s on the theory of rationing, all but one of them in collaboration with Hendrik Houthakker.

In statistics and econometrics Harvard was further behind the times. The professors who taught economic statistics were idiosyncratic in the methods they used and quite suspicious of methods based in mathematical statistical theory. Until the 1950s Harvard was pretty much untouched by the developments in Europe led by Ragnar Frisch and Jan Tinbergen or those in the United States at the Cowles Commission. Students like me, who were interested in formal statistical theory, took refuge in the mathematics department. For econometrics we squeezed as much as possible from a seminar on statistical demand functions offered by a European visitor, Hans Staehle. We also discovered that regressions, though scorned by professors Crum and Frickey, were alive and well under the aegis of Professor John D. Black's program in agricultural economics. In the basement of Littauer Center we could use his electromechanical or manual Marchands and Monroes.

I did just that for my second published paper (1942), originally written for Edward S. Mason's seminar in spring semester 1941, on how to use statistical forecasts in defense planning; my example was estimation of civilian demands for steel. The paper was one reason Mason recommended me for a job in Washington with the civilian supply division of the nascent Office of Price Administration and Civilian Supply. So I left Harvard in May 1941, having completed all the requirements for the Ph.D. except the dissertation. I would not return until February 1946. After nine months of helping to ration scarce materials, I went in the Navy and served as a line officer on a destroyer until Christmas 1945.

Statistics and econometrics were important in my research after the war. In my doctoral dissertation (1947) on the determinants of household consumption and saving, I tried to marry "cross-section" data from family budget surveys with aggregate time series, the better to estimate effects of income, wealth, and other variables. In a later study of food demand (1950), I refined the method. This, along with my empirical and theoretical work on rationing, took place in England in 1949–50, at Richard Stone's Department of Applied Economics in Cambridge. I hoped that cross-section observations could resolve the ambiguities of statistical inference based on time series alone. Later my interest in cross-section and panel data led me to the work of the Michigan Survey Research Center, where I spent a fruitful semester with George Katona, James Morgan, and Lawrence Klein in 1953.

My work on data of this type led me to propose a new statistical method, which became known as Tobit analysis (1958). Probit analysis, which originated in biology, estimates how the probabilities of positive or negative responses to treatment depend on observed characteristics of the organism and the treatment. In economic applications, Yes responses often vary in intensity; for example, most families in a sample would report No when asked if they bought a car last year, while those who answer Yes spent varying amounts of money on a car. My technique would use both Yes-No and quantitative information in seeking the determinants of car purchases.

The label Tobit was perhaps more appropriate than Arthur Goldberger thought when he introduced it in his textbook. Perhaps not. My main claim to fame, a discovery enjoyed by generations of my students, is that, thinly disguised as a midshipman named Tobit, I make a fleeting appearance in Herman Wouk's novel *The Caine Mutiny*. Wouk and I attended the same quick Naval Reserve officers' training school at Columbia in spring 1942, and so did Willy, the hero of the novel.

Innovative and seminal work in mathematical economics and econometrics took place at the Cowles Commission for Research in Economics in the years 1944–1954. The commission was then affiliated with the University of Chicago. Its research output over that period is one of the most fruitful achievements in the history of organized scientific inquiry.

The leaders were Jacob Marschak and Tjalling Koopmans; Koopmans was awarded a Nobel Prize for his contributions to the theory of resource allocation, including linear programming, during this period. The remarkable teams Marschak and Koopmans assembled included two of the previous speakers in this series at Trinity University, Arrow and Klein, and two other Nobel laureates, Simon and Debreu.

When I was a graduate student at Harvard after the war, I stood in awe of the Cowles Commission and of Marschak and Koopmans. I came to know them at meetings of the Econometric Society. For the December 1947 meeting in Chicago I was asked to be a discussant of a paper by Marschak. I didn't get the paper until a few days before the meeting, indeed a day or so before Christmas. I worked hard on the paper— neglecting my wife, Betty, pregnant with our first child, and holiday festivities with our families. I was able to report some important flaws in Marschak's model and to offer some constructive suggestions. One thing led to another. I was asked to join the commission, and in 1954 I was asked to become its research director, to succeed Koopmans as he had succeeded Marschak.

The offer was flattering, challenging, and tempting. But I was very happy at Yale, and Betty and I had come to like New Haven very much as a place to live and raise a family. It turned out that we could have our cake and eat it too. Koopmans was quite interested in relocating the commission, because of difficulties in attracting staff to Chicago at that time and problems in the relation between the commission and the university. He gave me not the slightest inkling of this interest until I had definitely declined the offer. The founder and financial angel of the commission, Alfred Cowles, was a Yale graduate; he hoped his creation could find permanent hospitality from his alma mater.

In 1955 the commission moved to Yale, renamed the Cowles Foundation for Research in Economics at Yale University. I became its research director after all. Cowles Foundation Discussion Paper 1 (1955) was a precursor of the Tobit analysis mentioned above. The coming of Cowles was an important factor in the rise of economics at Yale to front-rank stature. I broadened the scope of the foundation's research to include macroeconomics. I was particularly eager to make room for the interests and talents of a young Yale assistant professor, Arthur Okun, who was working on macroeconomic forecasting and policy analysis.

Developing Keynesian Macroeconomics; Synthesizing It with the Neoclassical Tradition

My main program of research and writing after the war continued my early interests in Keynes and macroeconomics. I sought to improve the theoretical foundations of macro models, to fit them into the main corpus of neoclassical economics, and to clarify the roles of monetary and fiscal policies. In this endeavor I shared the objectives of many other economists, notably Abba Lerner, Paul Samuelson, Franco Modigliani, Robert Solow, J. R. Hicks, and James Meade. A new mainstream, synthesizing the Keynesian revolution and the classical economics against which it was revolting, was in the making. I am proud that Paul Samuelson called me a "partner in [this] crime."

The building blocks of the Keynesian structure were four in number: the relation of wages and employment; the propensity to consume; liquidity preference and the demand for money; the inducement to invest. I have already referred to my work on the first. I turn now to the other three.

Keynes's "psychological law" of consumption and saving stated that saving would be an ever-larger proportion of income as per capita real incomes became greater. National income data between the two world wars appeared to confirm his law. Statistical equations, fit to those data, extrapolated to much higher incomes, foretold trouble after the Second World War. Investment would have to be a much larger fraction of national income than ever before to absorb the high saving and avoid recession and unemployment. The extrapolation was wrong. Incomes rose as expected, but consumption was no smaller a proportion than before. This forecasting error triggered an agonizing reappraisal of the consumption function, with fruitful results.

My doctoral dissertation (1947) was on this subject. I thought Keynes's law should be interpreted to refer to the relation of lifetime consumption to lifetime income, not to a relation between those variables year by year. The same considerations implied that wealth, not just current income, determines consumption in the short run. As so often happens, this idea was in the air. Milton Friedman's permanent income theory and Franco Modigliani's life-cycle model were elegant explanations of saving behavior in this spirit. They showed how cyclical data could look "Keynesian" even though saving would be roughly proportional to income in the long run. I have written a number of papers on this subject over the years.

The episode is, I believe, an example of how economic knowledge advances when striking real-world events and issues pose puzzles we have to try to understand and resolve. The most important decisions a scholar makes are what problems to work on. Choosing them just by looking for gaps in the literature is often not very productive and at worst divorces the literature itself from problems that provide more important and productive lines of inquiry. The best economists have taken their subjects from the world around them.

The bulk of my work in the 1950s and 1960s was on the monetary side of macroeconomics. I had several objectives.

First, I wanted to establish a firm foundation for the sensitivity of money demand or money velocity to interest rates. Why was this important? The quantity theory of money, later called monetarism, asserted that there was no such sensitivity, that the velocity of money was constant except for random shocks and for slow, secular changes in public habits, banking institutions, and financial technology. The implication was that fiscal stimulus, such as government spending or tax reduction, could not affect aggregate spending on goods and services unless accompanied by money creation. The same implication applied to autonomous changes in private investment. In this sense Milton Friedman and other monetarists were saying not just that money matters, with which I agreed, but also that money is all that matters, with which I disagreed.

In an empirical paper in 1947 I let the data speak for themselves, loudly in favor of Keynes's liquidity preference curve. But I was not satisfied with Keynes's explanation of liquidity preference. He said people preferred liquid cash because they expected interest rates to rise to "normal" prosperity levels of the past, causing capital losses on holdings of bonds. As William Fellner, later to be my colleague at Yale, pointed out in a friendly debate with me in journal pages, Keynes could hardly call "equilibrium" a situation in which interest rates are persistently lower than investors' expectations of them. Fellner was espousing a principle of model building later called "rational expectations," and I agreed with him.

I found and offered two more tenable sources of the interest sensitivity of demand for money. One (1956) was based on an inventory theory of the management of transactions balances. As I learned too late, I had been mostly anticipated by William Baumol, but the model is commonly cited with both names. Maurice Allais anticipated both of us. See Chapter 33. The second paper (1958) gave a new rationalization of Keynes's "speculative motive": simply, aversion to risk. People may prefer liquidity, and prefer it more the lower the interest rate on noncash assets, not because they expect capital losses on average but because they fear them more than they value the equally probable capital gains.

I had been working for some time on portfolio choices balancing such risks against expected returns, and the liquidity preference paper was an exposition and application of that work. Harry Markowitz had already set forth a similar model of portfolio choice, and our paths also converged geographically when he spent a year at Yale in 1955–56. My interest was in macroeconomic implications, his more in advising rational investors.

When my prize was announced in Stockholm in 1981, the first reports that reached this country mentioned portfolio theory. This caught the interest of the reporters who faced me at a hastily arranged press conference at Yale. They wanted to know what it was, so I did my best to explain it in lay language, after which they said "Oh no, please explain it in lay language." That's when I referred to the benefits of diversification: "You know, don't put all your eggs in one basket." And that is why headlines throughout the world said "Yale economist wins Nobel for 'Don't put all your eggs...,'" and why a friend of mine sent me a cartoon he had clipped, which followed that headline with a sketch of next year's winner in medicine explaining how his award was for "An apple a day keeps the doctor away."

The fact that one of the available assets in the model of my paper was riskless turned out to have interesting consequences. I felt somewhat uneasy and apologetic that I was pairing the safe asset with just one risky asset to represent everything else. This aggregation followed Keynes, who also used "*the* interest rate" to refer to the common yield on all non-money assets and debts. I proved that my results would apply even if any number of risky assets were available, each with different return and risk. The choice of a risky portfolio, the relative weights of the various risky assets within it, would be independent of the decision how much to put into risky assets relative to the safe asset, money. This "separation theorem" was the key to the capital asset pricing model developed by Lintner and Sharpe, beloved by finance teachers and students, and exploited by the investment managers and counselors who compute and report the "betas" of various securities.

The debate about fiscal and monetary policy, as related to the interest-sensitivity of demand for money, went on for a long time, too much of it a duel between Milton Friedman and me. In a Vermont ski line a young attendant checking season passes read mine and said in a French-Canadian accent, "Tobeen, James Tobeen, not ze economiste! Not ze enemy of Professeur Friedman!" He was an economics student in Quebec; it made his day. He let me pass to the lift. This debate, I would say, ended for practical purposes when Friedman shifted ground, saying that no important issue of monetary policy or theory depended on interest-sensitivity of money demand. The ground he shifted to was the basic issue between Keynes and the classics, the contention that the economy is always in a supply-constrained equilibrium where neither monetary nor fiscal policy can enhance real output.

Second, I proposed to put money into the theory of long-run growth. In the 1950s one phase of the synthesis of Keynesian and neoclassical economics was the development of a growth theory along neoclassical lines. Some, not all, Keynesians were ready to agree that in the long run employment is full, saving limits investment, and "supply creates its own demand." The short run was the Keynesian domain, where labor and capital may be underemployed, investment governs saving, and demand induces its own supply. Roy Harrod had started modern growth theory in 1939, followed by Evsey Domar in the 1940s and Trevor Swan, Robert Solow, Edmund Phelps, and many others in the 1950s and 1960s.

I was involved too. My 1955 piece, "A Dynamic Aggregative Model," may be my favorite; it was the most fun to write. It differed from the other growth literature by explicitly introducing monetary government debt as a store of value, a vehicle of saving alternative to real capital, and by generating a business cycle that interrupted the growth process. In three subsequent papers (1965, 1968, and 1986) I showed that the stock of capital in a growing economy is positively related to the rates of monetary growth and inflation.

Third, in a long series of papers I developed, together with William Brainard and other colleagues at Yale, a general model of asset markets and integrated it into a full macroeconomic model. In a sense we generalized Hicks's famous IS/LM formalization of Keynes by allowing for a richer menu of assets. As I already indicated, I had been uncomfortable with that unique "*the* interest rate" in Keynes and with the simple dichotomy of money versus everything else, usually described as money versus bonds. I thought nominal assets versus real capital was at least as important a way of splitting wealth, if it must be split in only two parts, and this is what I did in the growth models cited above.

Portfolio theory suggested that assets should be regarded as imperfect substitutes for each other, with their differences in expected yields reflecting their marginal risks. Our approach also suggested that there is no sharp dividing line between assets that are money and those that are not. The "Yale approach" to monetary and financial theory has been widely used in empirical flow-of-funds studies and in modeling international capital movements.

Our approach also explicitly recognizes the stock-flow dynamics of saving, investment, and asset accumulation, as in my 1981 Nobel lecture. These dynamics were explicitly ignored in Keynes, who defined the short run as a period in which the change in the stock of capital due to the flow of new investment is insignificant. Stock-flow dynamics are also ignored in IS/LM models. But flows do add to stocks. Investment builds the capital stock, government deficits enlarge the stocks of government bonds and possibly of money, trade surpluses increase the net assets of the nation vis-à-vis the rest of the world, and so on. Without these effects, macro stories about policies and other events are incomplete.

The bottom line of monetary policy is its effect on capital investment, in business plant and equipment, residences, inventories, and consumer durable goods. The effect is not well represented by the market interest rates usually cited, or by quantities of money or credit. Our approach to monetary economics and macroeconomics led us naturally to a different measure, closer to investment decisions. This has become known as "Tobin's q." It is the ratio of the market valuations of capital assets to their replacement costs, for example, the prices of existing houses relative to the costs of building comparable new ones. For corporate businesses, the market valuations are made in the securities markets. It is common sense that the incentive to make new capital investments is high when the securities giving title to their future earnings can be sold for more than the investments cost, i.e., when q exceeds one. We see the reverse in takeovers of companies whose qs are less than one; it is cheaper to buy their productive assets by acquiring their shares than to construct comparable facilities from scratch. That is why in our models q is the link from the central bank and the financial markets to the real economy.

Policy and Public Service

As must be clear from my narrative, I have always been intensely interested in economic policy. Much of my theoretical and empirical research has been devoted to analyzing and discerning the effects of monetary and fiscal policies. In the 1950s I began writing occasional articles on current economic issues for general readership, some of them in *The New Republic*, *The Yale Review*, *Challenge*, and the *New York Times*.

Some of my friends in Massachusetts were advising Senator Kennedy. They told him and his staff about me. In summer 1960 Ted Sorenson came to see me and arranged for the Kennedy campaign to employ me to write some memoranda and position papers on economic growth. Sorenson signed me up despite the fact that I had felt it necessary to tell him I favored Stevenson for the nomination. I didn't notice any effects of my memos during the campaign, but I was told that they were used by the Kennedy team at the party platform deliberations, mainly to oppose the exaggerated "spend to grow" views of Leon Keyserling and some union economists.

My message at the time was that we needed a tight budget, one that would yield a surplus at full employment, and a very easy monetary policy, one that would get interest rates low enough to channel the government's surplus into productive capital investment. The point was to have full employment, but by a mix of policies that promoted growth in the economy's capacity to produce. Incidentally, my message is similar today.

After the 1960 election I served on a transition task force on the domestic economy chaired by Paul Samuelson. One day in early January 1961 I was summoned from lunch at the faculty club to take a phone call from the president-elect. He asked me to serve as a member of his Council of Economic Advisers. JT: "I'm afraid you've got the wrong guy, Mr. President. I'm an ivory-tower economist." JFK: "That's the best kind. I'll be an ivory-tower president." JT: "That's the best kind." I took a day or two to talk to Betty and to my colleagues and then said Yes. I served for twenty months.

Walter Heller was the chairman of the council, and Kermit Gordon was the other member. We had a fantastic staff, including Art Okun, Bob Solow, Ken Arrow, and a younger generation whose names would also be recognized as leaders in our profession today. We were all congenial, intellectually and personally, and we functioned by consensus without hierarchy or bureaucracy. We were optimistic, confident that our economics could improve policy and do good in the world. It was the opportunity that had motivated me to embrace economics a quarter century before.

The January 1962 *Economic Report* is the manifesto of our economics, applied to the United States and world economic conditions of the day. The press called it "the new economics," but it was essentially the blend of Keynesian and neoclassical economics we had been developing and elaborating for the previous ten years. The report was a collective effort, written mainly by Heller, Gordon, Solow, Okun, and Tobin. It doesn't appear on my personal bibliography, but I am proud of it as a work of professional economics as well as a public document. The January 1982 *Report* is the comparable document of Reaganomics, likewise the effort of professional economists to articulate a radically new approach to federal economic policy. It is interesting to compare the two; we have nothing to fear.

The Kennedy council was effective and influential because the president and his immediate White House staff took academics seriously, took ideas seriously, took us seriously. JFK was innocent of economics on inauguration day. But he was an interested, curious, keen, and able student. He read what we wrote, listened to what we said, and learned a lot.

Our central macroeconomic objective was to lower unemployment, 7 percent in January 1961, to 4 percent, our tentative estimate of the inflation-safe unemployment rate. That goal was achieved by the end of 1965, with negligible increase in the rate of inflation and with a big increase in capital investment. The sweet success turned sour in the late 1960s, when contrary to the advice of his council and other Keynesian advisers President Johnson failed to raise taxes to pay for the escalating costs of the war in Vietnam. Critics looking back on the 1960s accuse the Kennedy-Johnson economists of naïve belief in a Phillips trade-off and of policies explicitly designed to purchase lower unemployment with higher inflation. The criticism is not justified. The council did not propose to push unemployment below what came to be known as the "natural rate." Moreover, beginning in 1961 the council and the administration adopted wage and price policies designed to achieve an inflation-free recovery—"guideposts for noninflationary price and wage behavior" were espoused in the report.

I returned to Yale in September 1962. I loved the job at the council, but I knew my principal vocation was university teaching and research. Fifteen-hour days and seven-day weeks were a hardship for me, my wife, and our four young children. I remained active as a consultant to the council, particularly on international monetary issues that had concerned me as a member. Moreover, I was now more visible outside my profession, so I wrote and spoke more frequently on issues and controversies of the day. But I knew that alumni of Washington often have difficulty getting back into mainline professional scholarship. I determined to accomplish that re-entry, and I believe I did.

Kennedy and Johnson added the war on poverty to their agenda. Walter Heller and the council were very much involved. I became quite interested in the economic disadvantages of blacks and in the inadequacies, inefficiencies, and perverse incentives—penalties for work and marriage—of federal and state welfare programs. I wrote major papers on these matters in 1965 and 1968. This was not macroeconomics, but one implication of the Keynesian-neoclassical synthesis was that welfare and redistributional policies could be, within broad limits, chosen independently of macroeconomic goals. Nothing in our view of the functioning of capitalist democracies says either that prosperity requires hard-hearted welfare policies and small governments or that it requires redistribution in favor of workers and the poor.

I favored a negative income tax. So did Milton Friedman—although his version seemed to me too small to fill much of the poverty gap, and he refused to join a national nonpartisan statement of economists favoring the approach. I helped to design a negative income tax plan for George McGovern in 1972. Unfortunately, he and his staff botched its presentation in the heat of the California primary; I am sure most people to this day think McGovern was advocating a kooky budget-breaking handout. After the election Nixon proposed a family assistance plan pretty much the same as the McGovern scheme he had ridiculed during the campaign.

I have lived long enough to see the revolution to which I was an eager recruit fifty years ago become in its turn a mainstream orthodoxy and then the target of counterrevolutionary attack. The tides of political opinion and professional fashion have turned against me. Many of my young colleagues in the profession are as enthusiastic exponents of the new classical macroeconomics as I and my contemporaries were crusaders against old classical macroeconomics in the 1930s. Many of the issues are the same, but the environment is quite different from the great depression. The contesting factions are better equipped—our profession has certainly improved its mathematical, analytical, and statistical tools. I do not despair over the present divisions of opinion in economics. Our subject has always thrived and advanced through controversy, and I expect a new synthesis will evolve, maybe even in my lifetime. I haven't abandoned the field of battle myself. I hope I learn from the new, but I still think and say that Keynesian ideas about how the economy works and what policies can make it work better are relevant today—not just as Keynes wrote them, of course, but as they have been modified, developed, and refined over the last half-century.

Lecture presented April 30, 1985, at Trinity University, San Antonio, Texas.

Date of Birth
March 5, 1918

Academic Degrees
A.B. Harvard University, 1939
M.A. Harvard University, 1940
Ph.D. Harvard University, 1947

Academic Affiliations
Junior Fellow, Harvard University, 1947–1950
Associate Professor of Economics, Yale University, 1950–1955
Professor of Economics, Yale University, 1955–1957
Sterling Professor Emeritus of Economics, Yale University, 1957–1988

References

Tobin, James. "A Note on the Money Wage Problem," *Quarterly Journal of Economics*, May 1941, 508–516; *Essays*, Vol. 1, Chapter 1.

———. "The Role of Statistical Forecasts in Planning for Defense," in C. J. Friedrich and E. S. Mason, eds., *Public Policy*, III, 1942, 197–223.

———. *A Theoretical and Statistical Analysis of Consumer Saving*, Ph.D dissertation, Harvard University, 1947.

———. "Liquidity Preference and Monetary Policy," *Review of Economics and Statistics*, May 1947, 124–131; *Essays*, Vol. 1, Chapter 3.

———. "A Statistical Demand Function for Food in the U.S.A.," *Journal of the Royal Statistical Society*, Series A, Part II, 1950, 113–141; *Essays*, Vol. 2, Chapter 42.

———. (with H. S. Houthakker). "The Effects of Rationing on Demand Elasticities," *Review of Economic Studies*, Vol. XVII, No. 3, 1–14, 1951; *Essays*, Vol. 2, Chapter 40.

———. "A Survey of the Theory of Rationing," *Econometrica*, October 1952, 521–553; *Essays*, Vol. 2, Chapter 39.

———. "A Dynamic Aggregative Model," *Journal of Political Economy*, April 1955, 103–115; *Essays*, Vol. 1, Chapter 8.

———. "Estimation of Relationships for Limited Dependent Variables," *Econometrica*, January 1958, 24–36; *Essays*, Vol. 2, Chapter 44.

———. "The Interest-Elasticity of Transactions Demand for Cash," *Review of Economics and Statistics*, August 1956, 241–247; *Essays*, Vol. 1, Chapter 14.

———. "Liquidity Preference as Behavior Towards Risk," *Review of Economic Studies*, Vol. XXV, No. 67, 1958; *Essays*, Vol. 1, Chapter 15.

———. "Money and Economic Growth," *Econometrica*, October 1965, 671–684; *Essays*, Vol. 1, Chapter 9.

———. "Money, Capital, and Other Stores of Value," *American Economic Review*, May 1961, 26–37; *Essays*, Vol. 1, Chapter 13.

———. "On Improving the Economic Status of the Negro," *Daedalus*, Fall 1965; *Essays*, Vol. 3, Chapter 13.

———. "Notes on Optimal Monetary Growth," *Journal of Political Economy*, August 1968, 833–859; *Essays*, Vol. 1, Chapter 10.

———. "Raising the Incomes of the Poor," in K. Gordon, ed., *Agenda for the Nation*, Brookings Institution, 1968, 77–116; *Essays*, Vol. 3, Ch. 23.

———. "Inflation and Unemployment," *American Economic Review*, March 1972, 1–18; *Essays*, Vol. 2, Chapter 28.

———. "On the Welfare Macroeconomics of Government Financial Policy," *Scandinavian Journal of Economics*, Vol. 88, No. 1, 1986, 9–24; Chapter 9 below.

PART I

MONEY AND FINANCE

CHAPTER 2

MONEY AND FINANCE IN THE MACROECONOMIC PROCESS

1 Introduction: Analytical Frameworks in Macroeconomics and Monetary Theory

The historic terrain of macroeconomic theory is the explanation of the levels and fluctuations of overall economic activity. Macroeconomists have been especially interested in the effects of alternative fiscal, financial, and monetary policies. With the publication of John M. Keynes's *General Theory* in 1936 and the mathematical formalizations of his theory by John R. Hicks [23] and others, the language of macroeconomic theory became systems of simultaneous equations. These are *general equilibrium* systems of interdependence in the sense that the relationships describe an entire national economy, not just a particular industry or sector. The systems are usually not completely closed; they depend on exogenous parameters including instruments controlled by policymakers. Seeking definite relationships of economic outcomes to policies and other exogenous variables, qualitative and quantitative, these models sacrifice detail and generality, limiting the number of variables and equations by aggregations over agents, commodities, assets, and time.

Theoretical macroeconomic models of one brand or another are very influential. They guide the architects of econometric forecasting models. They shape the thinking of policymakers and their advisers about "the way the world works." They color the views of journalists, managers, teachers, housewives, politicians, and voters. Almost everyone thinks about the economy, tries to understand it, and has opinions on how to

Nobel Lecture delivered in Stockholm on December 8, 1981, published in *Les Prix Nobel,* 1982. Here reprinted by permission from the *Journal of Money, Credit, and Banking* 14(2) (May 1982):171–204.

improve its performance. Anyone who does so uses a model, even if it is vague and informal.

A   The Keynes-Hicks Model and an Alternative Framework

Hicks's [23] *"IS-LM"* version of Keynesian and classical theories has been especially influential, reaching not just professional economists but, as the standard macromodel of textbooks, also generations of college students. Its simple apparatus is the trained intuition of many of us when we confront questions of policy and analysis, whatever more elaborate methods we may employ in further study. But the framework has a number of defects that have limited its usefulness and subjected it to attack. In this lecture I wish to describe an alternative framework, which tries to repair some of those defects. At the same time, I shall argue, the major conclusions of the Keynes-Hicks apparatus remain intact. The reconstruction I shall summarize has engaged me for a long time, and I will of necessity draw on previous work.

The principal features that differentiate the proposed framework from the standard macromodel are these:

Precision regarding time.   A model of short-run determination of macroeconomic activity necessarily refers to a slice of time. It is one step of a dynamic sequence, not a repetitive equilibrium into which the economy settles.

Tracking of stocks.   An essential part of the process is the dynamics of flows and stocks, investment and capital, saving and wealth, specific forms of saving and asset stocks. It is not generally defensible to ignore these relations on the excuse that the analysis refers to so short a time that stocks cannot change significantly.

Several assets and rates of return.   The traditional aggregation of all non-monetary assets into a single asset with a common interest rate does not permit analysis of some important policies, institutional structures, and events. My alternative framework can in principle accommodate as many distinct asset categories as appropriate for the purpose at hand, though the illustrative application set forth below distinguishes only four. Asset disaggregation is essential for analyzing, among other phenomena, financing of capital accumulation and government deficits, details of monetary and debt management policies, international capital movements and foreign exchange markets, and financial intermediation.

Modeling of financial and monetary policy operations. Too often macroeconomic models describe monetary policy as a stock M whose time path is chosen autonomously by a central authority, without clearly describing the operations that implement the policy. In fact money supplies are changed by government transactions with the public in which goods or nonmonetary financial assets are exchanged for money, or by similar transactions between banks and the nonbank public. What transactions are the sources of variation of money stocks makes a difference, depending on how they alter the wealth and portfolio positions of economic agents.

Walras's Law and adding-up constraints. "Walras's Law" says that the excess demand functions of an economic agent must sum to zero for every vector of the variables that are arguments in any of the functions. The "law" imposes the consistency of meeting the budget constraint on the schedules of demand or supply which agents communicate to all the markets in which they participate. For the asset markets modeled below, for example, the implication is that household demands for end-of-period holdings of the several assets sum to household demand for end-of-period wealth, for every set of values of the determinants of asset and wealth demands. This implies that the partial derivatives of asset demands with respect to, say, any interest rate must add up to the partial derivative of wealth demand with respect to the same variable.

As my collaborator William Brainard and I observed [49], this consistency requirement is not always explicitly observed in theoretical and statistical models of financial markets. For example, if demand functions are not explicitly specified for the whole range of assets, the function for the omitted category implied by the wealth demand function and the explicit asset functions may be strange in ways unintended by the model-builders. For example, if money demand is related negatively to an interest rate and total wealth demand is not, the implication is that nonmoney asset functions carry the mirror image of the interest effect on money. The best practice is to write down all the functions explicitly, even though one is redundant, and to put the same arguments in all the functions.

B Microfoundations, Aggregation, and Expectations

John R. Hicks's 1935 article has been an inspiration and challenge to me and many other monetary economists. It stimulated us to look for the properties and functions of money, and of promises to pay money in future, that underlie people's willingness to hold these assets. Understanding these foundations, we could seek the observable determinants of demands for money and money substitutes. This quest for the microfoundations of monetary theory has motivated inventory-theoretic models of the demand for transactions media (Baumol [5], Tobin [40], Miller and Orr [30]) and models of portfolio choice (Tobin [41]). It is still unfinished. The reason, I think, is the difficulty of explaining within the basic paradigms of economic theory why paper that makes no intrinsic contribution to utility or technology is held at all and has positive value in exchange for goods and services. I certainly have no solution to that deep question,[1] nor do I regard one as prerequisite to pragmatic monetary theory.

For this and other reasons, macroeconomic models of the type I am advocating are, I admit, only loosely linked to optimizing behavior of individual agents. Following an older tradition, economy-wide structural equations are an amalgam of individual behavior and aggregation across a multitude of diverse individuals. This is the pragmatic alternative to two other procedures, both with serious disadvantages. One is to preserve the diversity of agents' preferences and endowments allowed in fully general equilibrium models; the weak restrictions that optimization places on individual excess demands imply no restrictions at all on market-wide schedules. The other is to assume that all agents are alike or fall into two or three classes (old and young, for example) internally homogeneous but differing from each other in arbitrarily specified ways. Although setups of this kind (the Samuelson [34] overlapping generation model, for example) are promising and already generate instructive parables, they are still so abstract and arbitrary as to be useless for policy analysis and econometric model building.

Another influential methodological wave in current macroeconomics is the emphasis on information and expectations, and on the desirability of building models in which agents' behavior is grounded on the information about the present and future which, according to the model itself, would be revealed to the agents (Lucas [26]). This is a good principle, but my own efforts to construct an improved framework have had a different purpose and emphasis. The system I shall display in this lecture involves expectations, recognizing, as any analysis of financial behavior must, that the attractiveness of various assets to savers and portfolio managers depends on their estimates of the joint probability distributions of the assets' earnings and capital gains. The consequences of variation of these expectations can be traced if, for example, moods, confidence, and "animal spirits" change exogenously, as Keynes thought they frequently do. In dynamic applications and simulations, Lucas's principles of rational expectations could be respected, but I have not done so in the work I will report here.

C Macroeconomic and Full General Equilibrium

Kenneth Arrow's Nobel lecture of 1972 is an elegant exposition of general equilibrium theory, recognizing both its power and its limitations. Were there a full set of simultaneously cleared markets for all commodities, including commodities for future and contingent delivery, there would be no macroeconomic problems, no need for money, and no room for fiscal and monetary policies of stabilization. Theorists who take full general equilibrium as their reference point naturally seek to explain alien phenomena as "market failures." Arrow discussed the inability of decentralized competitive markets to supply collective or public goods in optimal amounts. The public-good nature of common monetary units of account and universally acceptable media of exchange is, I believe, one reason why the general equilibrium paradigm has trouble incorporating money. But the departure from that paradigm that I would emphasize, the departure that sets the stage for macroeconomic theory and policy, is one emphasized by Keynes. It is the virtual absence of futures markets and of course contingent markets in any commodities other than money itself. As Keynes said [25, pp. 210–12],

An act of individual saving means—so to speak—a decision not to have dinner today. But it does *not* necessitate a decision to have dinner or to buy a pair of boots a week hence or a year hence or to consume any specified thing at any specified date. Thus it depresses the business of preparing today's dinner without stimulating the business of making ready for some future act of consumption. It is not a substitution of future consumption-demand for present consumption-demand,—it is a net diminution of such demand.... If saving consisted not merely in abstaining from present consumption but in placing simultaneously a specific order for future consumption, the effect might indeed be different. For in that case

Table 2.1
Flow-of-funds Matrix for Eleven Assets and Nine Sectors, 1979, Flows at Annual Rates. End-of-year Stocks in Parentheses (billions of dollars)

		Households	Commercial Banking	Savings Institutions	Insurance & Pension Funds	Miscellaneous Intermediaries	Businesses	Federal Government	State & Local Government	Rest of the World	Discrepancy
(1)	Currency and reserves	7.9 (107.1)	1.3 (46.8)					−9.2 (−153.9)			0 (0)
(2)	Demand deposits	15.1 (145.4)	−25.8 (−330.2)	−0.7 (0.6)	1.9 (11.4)	0.7 (6.9)	5.5 (87.4)	0.4 (14.3)	−1.5 (9.6)	4.4 (23.4)	0 (31.2)
(3)	Small time deposits	61.4 (1049.2)	−31.0 (−421.1)	−29.9 (−632.9)				0.1 (1.0)	−0.6 (3.8)		0 (0)
(4)	Shorts	85.1 (−295.6)	−30.7 (−276.4)	−13.5 (−4.4)	−0.7 (25.9)	−12.3 (−53.0)	2.8 (61.5)	−10.5 (−216.2)	2.0 (90.9)	−27.1 (35.1)	+4.9 (+41.0)
(5)	Longs	39.6 (246.3)	15.2 (226.8)	0.2 (76.9)	46.9 (492.4)	−2.6 (−39.0)	−26.3 (−353.2)	−68.4 (−464.5)	−6.4 (−232.7)	1.7 (47.0)	0.1 (0)
(6a)	Nonfinancial business equity: purchases	−20.6	0.1	−0.1	54.8	−3.4	−36.9			6.3	−0.2
(6b)	Nonfinancial equity: capital gains	151.8 (−748.2)	−0.1 (0.1)	... (4.2)	−28.0 (200.3)	6.3 (34.1)	−129.4 (−1029.5)			−0.8 (−42.7)	0.2 (−0.1)
(7)	Financial business equity	21.0 (−148.3)	−7.5 (−72.3)	... (0.5)	−7.4 (−41.4)	−6.8 (−40.7)				0.6 (5.5)	0.1 (−0.1)
(8)	Nonmarketables	79.2 (−889.5)			−71.8 (−732.9)			−7.4 (−156.6)			0 (0)

(9)	Mortgages	−104.9	31.1	48.5	14.2	0.1	−41.3	46.1	6.3	−0.1
		(−771.6)	(245.2)	(569.1)	(132.1)	(14.4)	(−428.1)	(215.7)	(23.2)	(0)
(10)	Loans	−54.8	66.3	3.9	8.0	27.6	−52.4	13.7	−1.6	−7.1
		(−486.1)	(610.0)	(60.1)	(60.1)	(134.7)	(−295.5)	(101.9)	(−22.7)	(−74.4)
(11)	Foreign assets	3.6	−0.8				23.8	1.2		−2.4
		(14.8)	(1.0)				(175.6)	(28.4)		(9.6)
									−3.6	−25.4
									(−88.1)	(−229.4)
(12)	Miscellaneous	7.2	−18.1	−4.0	−17.8	−9.4	−7.2	9.0	1.3	23.5
	(domestic)	(66.7)	(−29.9)	(−24.4)	(−147.9)	(−57.5)	(3.1)	(64.9)	(13.1)	(66.9)
										15.5
										(+45.0)
										11.0
(13)	Financial net	291.6	0.0	4.4	0.1	0.2	−261.4	−25.0	−0.5	−20.4
	worth	(2453.4)	(0.0)	(49.7)	(0.0)	(−0.1)	(−1778.7)	(−565.0)	(−114.8)	(−96.9)
										(52.4)
										11.0
										(52.4)
(6b)	− Capital gains	151.8	−0.1	...	−28.0	6.3	−129.4		−0.8	
(14)	= Net financial	139.8	0.1	4.4	28.1	−6.1	−132.0	−25.0	−0.5	−19.6
	saving									

Source: Flow-of-funds Accounts, Federal Reserve, 1981.

Notes and Definitions:
(1) Base money. Currency held by the nonbank public has been allocated entirely to households.
(2) Demand deposits include checkable deposits at both commercial banks and savings institutions.
(3) Small time deposits include all time and savings deposits of less than $100,000 at commercial banks and thrift institutions.
(4) "Shorts" include short-term government securities, federal funds and security repurchase agreements, time deposits in excess of $100,000, money market fund shares. Eurodollar deposits, commercial paper, and bankers' acceptances.
(5) "Longs" include longer-term government and agency securities, state and local government obligations, and corporate bonds.
(6) "Equity" includes only the equity liability of nonfinancial corporate business (NFC). Equity of financial business is shown separately in row (7).
(8) "Nonmarketables" include U.S. savings bonds and insurance and pension reserves.
(10) "Loans" consist mainly of consumer credit, trade credit, security credit, bank loans not elsewhere classified, and U.S. government and agency loans. The discrepancy in this row is due to trade credit.
(11) Foreign assets are claims held by the U.S. on foreigners, denominated in foreign currencies. Included are foreign deposits, foreign equity, direct investment abroad, and U.S. foreign exchange and net IMF position.

Table 2.1 (continued)

(6), (7) The following procedures and assumptions were used in order to separate out equity of nonfinancial corporations (NFCs) from equity of financial institutions (FI).

(i) Equity issued by rest of world (ROW) and Open-end investment companies (OEICs) (mutual funds) was allocated to households.

(ii) The division of remaining equity liability between NFC and FI was made by taking the equity liability of FIs to be equal to their reported net worth, the residual being allocated to business.

(iii) Business equity was then allocated to holders in proportion to their total holdings of equity (excluding equity issued by OEICs and ROW).

(iv) Purchases of equity were treated similarly (although in this case data on equity issue of business are directly available).

(v) In addition, retained earnings of business were treated as an issue of equity and allocated to holders in proportion to their holdings of business equity.

(vi) Capital gains are derived as the difference between the change in business equity holdings/liability and purchases (including retained earnings).

(14) "Net financial saving" as shown in the table will differ from National Income and Product Account figures for several reasons—conceptual differences between NIPA and the Flow-of-funds Accounts; unallocated discrepancies in the FFA; capital gains in assets other than business equity; and the treatment here by business retained earnings as an issue of equity of business and saving by other sectors.

the expectation of some future yield from investment would be improved, and the resources released from preparing for present consumption would be turned over to preparing for the future consumption....

The trouble arises, therefore, because the act of saving implies, not a substitution for present consumption of some specific additional consumption which requires for its preparation just as much immediate economic activity as would have been required by present consumption equal in value to the sum saved, but a desire for "wealth" as such, that is for a potentiality of consuming an unspecified article at an unspecified time.

In short, the financial and capital markets are at their best highly imperfect coordinators of saving and investment, an inadequacy which I suspect cannot be remedied by rational expectations. This failure of coordination is a fundamental source of macroeconomic instability and of the opportunity for macroeconomic policies of stabilization. Current macroeconomic theory perhaps pays too exclusive attention to labor markets, where Keynes also detected failures of competition to coordinate demand and supply.

D Statistics of Flows and Stocks of Funds

National income accounts, developed in the interwar period, provided the data for testing and estimating the models of Keynes and subsequent macroeconomists. Both theory and data dealt mainly with flows and their interrelations. Flow-of-funds accounts, notably those compiled by the United States Federal Reserve System since 1949, provide stock and flow data relevant to theoretical models of financial markets, the observations we seek to understand and explain.

In Tables 2.1 and 2.2 I show data for 1979, condensed into smaller numbers of sectors (columns) and asset categories (rows) than the Federal Reserve actually reports. In Table 2.1 there are nine sectors and eleven assets, the level of aggregation of a model that our group at Yale has been trying to estimate (Backus et al. [3]). In Table 2.2 the data are further aggregated, into four sectors and four assets, conforming as closely as possible to the theoretical model I shall be discussing here.

In the format of these tables, a column represents a sector's balance sheet (stocks) or sources and uses of funds (flows). A row distributes the stock or flow of an asset over the supplying and demanding sectors. The task of theory and estimation is to bring the columns to life by functions relating sectoral portfolio and saving decisions to relevant variables,

Table 2.2
Flow-of-funds Matrix for Four-asset Model, 1979, Flows at Annual Rates, End-of-year Stocks in Parentheses (billions of dollars)

	Households	Business	Government	Rest of the World	Discrepancy
Equity { Purchase	50.9	−58.1		7.3	−0.1
Equity { Capital gains	130.0	−129.4		−0.8	0.2
	(1314.0)	(−1369.0)		(54.9)	(0.1)
Bonds	103.1	−2.3	−83.3	−22.5	5.0
	(616.9)	(47.7)	(−822.4)	(116.9)	(40.9)
Foreign assets	6.7	23.8	1.2	−29.3	−2.4
	(62.8)	(175.6)	(28.4)	(−276.4)	(9.6)
Base money	9.2		−9.2		0
	(153.9)		(−153.9)		(0)
Miscellaneous	−3.8	−95.4	65.9	25.0	8.3
	(355.6)	(−633.0)	(268.2)	(7.8)	(1.4)
Financial net worth	296.1	−261.4	−25.4	−20.3	11.0 (52.0)
	(2503.2)	(−1778.7)	(−679.7)	(−96.8)	11.0 (52.0)
− Capital gains	130.0	−129.4		−0.8	
= Net financial saving	166.1	−132.0	−25.4	−19.5	

Source: Flow-of-funds Accounts, Federal Reserve, 1981.
(1) "Households" includes the household sector and the financial sector.
(2) Differences may arise between this and the previous table due to rounding.
(3) Corporate bonds are included in the equity row. Corporate bonds issued by financial institutions are assumed to be entirely held by households, that is, foreigners are assumed not to hold any. All foreign corporate bond issues are assumed to be held by "households" and are classified as foreign assets in this table.
(4) It is not possible to identify capital gains for corporate bonds from the Flow-of-Funds Accounts.
(5) "Miscellaneous" includes demand deposits, small time deposits, mortgages, loans, nonmarketables, equity liability of financial business, and other miscellaneous assets.

and to bring the rows to life as a set of simultaneous market-clearing equations.[2]

2 A Multiasset Model of the Determination of Output and Prices in the Short Run

A Sources of New Supplies of Private Wealth

There are three sources of supply of new financial wealth to private households in a modern capitalist economy: net accumulation of goods in inventories or productive capital I, government budget deficits D, and surpluses in current account transactions with other nations $\overline{CAS}$ (all symbols are listed in Appendix A). By financial wealth I refer to negotiable assets, whether real properties or paper claims (of which negative holdings are liabilities). I exclude illiquid assets such as future labor earnings (human capital) and entitlements to future government transfers, and prospective tax liabilities. During any period of time t household saving is the sum of the three items:

$$S = I + D + \overline{CAS} \quad \text{National income identity} \tag{1}$$

Since in any period of time, saving is also the excess of net national income Y over consumption C plus taxes T, and the deficit D is the difference between government purchases of goods and services G and taxes T, the accounting identity (1) can also be written as

$$Y = C + I + C + \overline{CAS} \quad \text{National income identity} \tag{2}$$

In either form the identity becomes an equation if any or all of its constituents are expressed as functions of economic variables. Then the equation will be satisfied only for certain sets of values of those variables. On this interpretation (1) or (2) is the familiar *IS* locus introduced by Hicks [23].

Let me be more precise about the three sources of asset supply on the right-hand side of (1). The illustrative model I wish to describe contains, I believe, the highest degree of asset aggregation compatible with analyzing the central issues of macroeconomics, in particular the workings of fiscal and monetary policies. Later in the paper I shall discuss several directions of disaggregation. I distinguish just four assets: *equities*, titles to physical capital and its earnings, generated by investment I; *government bonds* and *base money*, issued to finance deficits D; and *foreign currency assets*, earned by the current account surplus $\overline{CAS}$, consisting of the trade surplus X and earnings on the foreign assets themselves.

In reality of course, none of these categories is internally homogeneous. Physical capital takes many different forms, and so do the claims to them—direct titles, debts, and shares. Government securities vary in maturities and other terms. International claims and debts are even more heterogeneous. Moreover, banks and other financial intermediaries transform the liabilities of businesses, governments, and foreigners into a variety of obligations to suit the tastes and circumstances of household savers. Representing these complex realities by four assets is a great abstraction, comparable to many others in macroeconomics. In its defense, I remind you that the common textbook macromodel limits itself to two asset categories, money and everything else. That is, all nonmonetary assets and debts are, in the Hicksian *IS-LM* formalization of Keynes's *General Theory*, taken to be perfect substitutes at a common interest rate plus or minus exogenous interest differentials.

B Claims to Productive Capital

Private capital investment is the source of new claims to physical capital, modeled as equity shares, one share for each unit of capital. The aggregate stock of capital at any time consists of all surviving durable or storable goods, previously produced or imported but not consumed. These stocks are valued continuously in markets for the goods themselves (realistic examples are used vehicles and machinery, and existing residences and other buildings) and in markets for corporate securities or for entire businesses. These market valuations of old capital goods typically differ, up or down, from their replacement costs, that is, from the costs of producing and installing at a normal pace new capital goods of the same type. These deviations are, in turn, the incentives for rates of investment faster or slower than normal. When equity markets place high values on capital goods, the margin above replacement cost induces investors to speed up capital accumulation. This inducement is essentially what the great Swedish economist Knut Wicksell ascribed to a natural rate of interest higher than the market interest rate.

However, there is a limit to the acceleration of capital formation generated by arbitrage of such margins. Abnormally rapid accumulations of capital, exceptionally high rates of investment, impose extra costs on investing firms individually and on the economy collectively. These adjustment costs are a principal reason that positive differences of market valuations from normal replacement costs of capital can and do arise and persist, without triggering virtually instantaneous jumps in capital stock accomplished at virtually infinite rates of investment. Likewise low market valuations of existing capital slow down capital formation, but rarely shut gross investment off completely while stocks are consumed at maximum speed.

The account I have just sketched refers to replacement costs as current costs of production and installation at a normal rate of investment. By normal rate I mean investment that keeps the capital stock growing at the trend of the economy, in Harrod's terminology the "natural" growth rate of its exogenous resources as augmented by technological progress. The upshot, for purposes of a simple macroeconomic model, is an equation for net investment as follows:

$$I_t = q_t^K \Delta K_t = q_t^K K_{t-1} f(q_t^K) \quad \text{Investment function} \tag{3}$$

where

$$\Delta K_t + \delta K_{t-1} \geq 0$$

$$f(1) = g$$

$$f'(q_t^K) \geq 0$$

$$0 < f^{-1}(-\delta) < 1,$$

q_t^K is the ratio of market valuation of capital goods to normal replacement cost at time period t. Its normal value is 1, and the value that induces zero gross investment is $\bar{q} = f^{-1}(-\delta)$. K_{t-1} is the stock, valued at normal replacement cost, at the beginning of period t. The supply of productive services of capital available in period t is proportional to K_{t-1}. ΔK_t is the addition to K_{t-1} occurring in period t. δ is the rate of depreciation of capital. g is the natural rate of growth of the economy. (When no confusion can arise, I suppress the subscripts t and denote values of a variable in the preceding, current, and next periods as x_{-1}, x, x_{+1}.) Note that investment is valued at asset market prices rather than normal replacement costs both in (3) and in the national income accounting identities (1) and (2). The reason is that the deviations of q^K from 1 represent real costs of adjustment, including positive or negative rents, incurred by investing firms in changing the size of their installed capital.[3]

C The Financing of Government Deficits

Fiscal policy concerns the size of government expenditures and tax receipts, and the stocks and flows of assets issued by the government to finance budget deficits. Monetary policy concerns the composition of privately owned assets of government issue, in particular the relative amounts of monetary issue and nonmonetary public debt. Governmental monetary actions, whether taken by Treasury Departments or Finance Ministries or by central banks, determine the proportions in which a current deficit is financed by monetary and nonmonetary issues. Open market operations also change the composition of the existing debt.

Clearly it is not possible to model monetary policies, distinct from fiscal policies, without explicit allowance for at least one nonmonetary government obligation. (The theoretical literature contains many models in which government deficits can be met only by printing money. Though the consequences of greater or lesser budget deficits in these models are sometimes attributed to "monetary" policies and money growth rates, the primitive asset structure assumed confounds monetary and fiscal policy and excludes operations describable as "monetary" in the usual understanding of the word.) In the four-asset model I am now describing, I take the nonmonetary government debt to consist of perpetual bonds or "consols"—promises to pay one dollar each period forever. The government's aggregate obligation to pay these coupons in period t is the number of bonds outstanding at the end of the previous period B_{-1}. The market price of a consol in dollars is q^B.

The government's monetary issue corresponds to the usual concept of high-powered or base money, currency or its equivalent in central bank deposit liabilities. Base money bears a zero own-rate of interest. I have in mind a fiat issue, not one convertible on demand into gold or any other commodity. However, in a fixed-rate foreign exchange regime, the local currency is in effect convertible into foreign currency. The counterpart of the market price of bonds would be q^H, but it is identically equal to 1. The size and market value of the outstanding stock of high-powered money are both H_{-1}.

In reminding you at the outset of the national income accounting identity, I defined the deficit as G, government purchases, less tax revenues T. In this reckoning taxes are net of the government's transfer payments, which are negative taxes in the sense that the recipients have no contemporaneous reciprocal obligation to render goods and services to the government. Public debt interest might be regarded either as the purchase of a service or as a transfer payment. For my purpose, it is best to treat it as a transfer but to keep track of it separately.

A government may own marketable assets and earn income from them. I assume in this simplest model that the government does not buy or sell or own physical capital or privately issued equities or debts. But to model fiscal and monetary policy in an open economy it is necessary to allow for government transactions in foreign-currency assets and for its holdings of such assets as international reserves. These are represented as the fourth asset of the model. The government's holdings at the beginning of period t are $_G F_{-1}$ in units of foreign currency, valued in period t at $e \cdot _G F_{-1}$, where e is the domestic-currency price of a unit of foreign currency. Conceivably $_G F_{-1}$ is negative, that is, the government is a net debtor to foreigners. In any case, if ρ^F is the foreign-currency yield, the government's income on its reserves is $e\rho^F \cdot _G F_{-1}$.

Thus the budget deficit in dollars is, for commodity price level p,

$$pD = pG(\cdot) - pT(\cdot) + B_{-1} - e\rho^F \cdot _G F_{-1} \qquad \text{Government deficit} \qquad (4)$$

Here the parameters of fiscal policy are the relationships established by legislation defining purchases and taxes-less-transfers as functions $(\cdot)$ of economic variables. For example, $G(\cdot)$ may be each period an ad hoc constant G, while $T(\cdot)$ may be a function of contemporaneous real income, and of other current and past variables (including p for nominal tax and transfer systems neither indexed nor rapidly adjusted).

The deficit must be financed by transactions at current asset prices in the three assets high-powered money, consols, and foreign currency.

$$pD = \Delta H + q^B \Delta B - e\Delta_G F \qquad \text{Government deficit} \qquad (5)$$

$$\Delta H = \gamma^H pD + z^H \qquad \qquad \text{Supply of base money} \qquad (6)$$

$$q^B \Delta B = \gamma^B pD + z^B \qquad 0 \leq \gamma^H, \gamma^B \leq 1 \qquad \text{Supply of bonds} \qquad (7)$$

$$-e\Delta_G F = z^F \qquad \qquad \gamma^H + \gamma^B = 1$$

$$z^H + z^B + z^F = 0 \qquad \text{Supply of foreign currency assets by government} \qquad (8)$$

Here there are three independent parameters of monetary policy. One of them, say γ^H, which also fixes γ^B, determines the share of the current deficit financed by monetary issue. It is assumed that there is no systematic policy of financing budget deficits by selling foreign currency assets or borrowing in foreign currency. The other two policy parameters, say z^H and z^B, which together fix z^F, describe open market operations. A domestic open market purchase of government bonds is a positive z^H offset by a negative z^B of equal size. Intervention in the foreign exchange market to sell domestic currency for foreign currency assets is a positive z^H offset by a negative z^F of equal size. A "sterilized" acquisition of foreign currency assets is a positive z^B offset by a negative z^F of equal size.

D Supply of Foreign-Currency Assets to the Public

At this stage I assume that all capital transactions between the economy described by the model and the rest of the world occur in foreign-currency assets. The new supply of foreign currency to the economy as a whole, including both government and private agents, is its surplus on current account. This in turn consists of its surplus in commodity trade plus its earnings on existing foreign-currency holdings. Expressed in current domestic prices, the current account surplus is

$$e\Delta F + e\Delta_G F = pX(\cdot) + e\rho^F F_{-1} + e\rho^F \cdot {}_G F_{-1} \quad \text{Balance of payments} \tag{9}$$

Here F without the prefix subscript G refers to foreign-currency asset holdings of domestic private individuals. $X(\cdot)$ is the real trade surplus in domestic currency, a function of local economic activity, specifically of real national income Y, and of the real exchange rate eP^F/P (where P^F is the foreign-currency price of foreign tradable goods), as well as of other variables, lagged and contemporary, foreign and domestic. The sign of the relationship of X to the real exchange rate depends, as is well-known, on various elasticities; it is positive if excess-demand elasticities are high enough so that real devaluation improves the trade balance.

Using the relationships in the previous subsection, I derive from (8) and (9) the supply of foreign assets to the public:

$$eF = pX(\cdot) + e\rho^F(F_{-1} +_G F_{-1}) + z^F = p\overline{CAS} + z^F \quad \text{Supply of foreign currency assets to public} \tag{10}$$

E Total Saving

Equations (3), (6), (7), and (10) give the additional supplies in period t of the four assets, equities, base money, consol bonds, and foreign currency.

In constant dollars they add to $I_t + D_t + \overline{CAS}_t$, as in the national income identity (1).

F Demands for Asset Accumulations

The next step is to specify the demands for added holdings of the four assets, to match the added supplies described in 2.A–2.E. Since the sum of the four supply flows is total saving, specifying the four demands also implies a total saving function. Of course saving, specific or general, is not identical to increment in wealth. Asset holders also make capital gains or losses, some anticipated and others unexpected.

I assume that households seek for each asset $J (= K, B, F, H)$ a desired end-of-period holding $p_t A_t^J$, in market value at current-period asset prices in dollars. The A_t^J are functions; they jointly express fundamental portfolio management and wealth accumulation behavior. Households enter period t with certain holdings of the various assets J_{t-1}. These will turn out to be worth $q_t^J J_{t-1}$, where q_t^J is the dollar price of asset J determined in period t. Thus the net demand for new assets, $q_t^J \Delta J_t$ in dollar value, is $p_t A_t^J - q_t^J J_{t-1}$. It is this vector which must be equated to the supplies described in the previous section.

The four-equation system for a period t is given in detail below, now in real terms rather than in dollars.

$$A^K(\cdot) - q^K K_{-1} = q^K K_{-1} f(q^K) \qquad \begin{array}{l} Demand = \\ supply \\ equations: \\ \text{Equities market} \end{array} \qquad (11)$$

$$A^B(\cdot) - q^B B_{-1}/p = \gamma^B D + z^B/p \qquad \text{Bond market} \qquad (12)$$

$$\begin{aligned} A^F(\cdot) - eF_{-1}/p &= X(Y, ep^F/p) \\ &\quad + e\rho^F(F_{-1} +_G F_{-1})/p + z^F/p \end{aligned} \qquad \begin{array}{l} \text{Foreign-} \\ \text{currency} \\ \text{assets market} \end{array} \qquad (13)$$

$$A^H(\cdot) - H_{-1}/p = \gamma^H D + z^H/p \qquad \begin{array}{l} \text{Base money} \\ \text{market} \end{array} \qquad (14)$$

Their summation is the *IS* relation:

$$\begin{aligned} A^W(\cdot) - W_{-1}^* &= q^K K_{-1} f(q^K) + D + X(Y, ep^F/p) \\ &\quad + e\rho^F(F_{-1} +_G F_{-1})/p \quad \text{Total wealth} \end{aligned} \qquad (15)$$

Here W^*_{-1} is the sum of the second left-hand-side terms of the four preceding equations, that is, the value at period t prices of the assets inherited from the past.

Recall also the expression for the deficit D:

$$D = G - T(Y) + B_{-1}/p - e\rho^F \cdot {}_G F_{-1}/p \quad \text{Deficit defined} \tag{16}$$

G Gross Substitutability among Assets: Effects of Expected Returns

What are the arguments in the $A^J(\cdot)$ functions? In principle, the same vector appears in all the functions. The vector will include four kinds of variables: those that are within-period endogenous, that is, those whose values are determined by solving a set of simultaneous equations including the four equations (11) to (14); lagged values of within-period endogenous variables; expected future values of within-period endogenous variables; exogenous variables, past, contemporaneous, or future. The fact that A^W is the sum of the A^J means that (15) could be substituted for any of the previous four equations. It also means that the partial derivative of wealth demand with respect to any determining variable is the sum of the partial derivatives of specific asset demands with respect to the same variable. For example, the four specific marginal propensities to save from income sum to the overall marginal propensity to save.

Among the arguments in each asset demand function will be the several real yields expected from holding an asset one period, the vector (r^K, r^B, r^F, r^H). These involve expectations of commodity and asset prices in period $t+1$, as follows:

$$D = G - T(Y) + B_{-1}/p - e\rho^F \cdot {}_G F_{-1}/p \quad \text{Deficit defined} \tag{16}$$

$$q_t^K(1 + r_t^K) = R_t(Y_t, K_{t-1}) + Eq_{t+1}^K \quad \text{Equities, price and rate of return} \tag{17}$$

Holding of capital equity costing q^K from t to $t+1$ entitles the owner to receive the earnings R, which depend on the output Y produced in period t by use of the capital stock K_{-1}, and to sell the shares at a real price expected to be Eq_{t+1}^K.

$$q_t^B(1 + r_t^B) = (1 + Eq_{t+1}^B)/(p_t/Ep_{t+1}) \quad \text{Bonds, price and rate of return} \tag{18}$$

$$e_t(1 + r_t^F) = (1 + \rho_t^F)Ee_{t+1}(p_t/Ep_{t+1}) \quad \text{Foreign currency assets, price and rate of return} \quad (19)$$

$$1 + r_t^H = p_t/Ep_{t+1} \quad \text{Base money, rate of return} \quad (20)$$

With these relationships the asset prices (q^K, q^B, e) in (11)–(14) can be expressed in terms of the r^J vector, or vice versa. Clearly for given price expectations, there is an inverse relation between the current price and the real one-period expected yield on each asset. This remains true so long as the elasticity of expected asset price with respect to current price is less than 1. For equities and bonds it is true even if the elasticity equals or somewhat exceeds 1.

The assumption that the assets are gross substitutes means that the partial derivative of A^J is positive with respect to its own yield r^J but nonpositive with respect to other yields r^L $(L \neq J)$. In the present context this is a stronger assumption than it is for asset stock demands that are constrained to add to a constant independent of the vector of determining variables. Here the partial derivatives, own and cross, with respect to any expected yield sum to the total effect of that yield on desired end-of-period wealth. The gross substitutes assumption implies that the total effect is non-negative, and further that any effect of a single interest rate on wealth demand takes the form of demand for the asset whose interest yield has increased without spillover into the other assets, whose yields have not. These are plausible assumptions, and they are consistent with but not required by rational portfolio and saving behavior.

Portfolio theory provides a loose rationale for modeling distinct assets as imperfect substitutes, held jointly in positive amounts even though their expected yields differ (Markowitz [28, 29], Tobin [41]). It also provides a rationale for dependence of portfolio demands on the structure of expected yields. But it does not dictate that assets be gross substitutes. Assets with strong negative covariance of yields could be complements, with a rise in the expected return on one inducing an increase in a hedged package which includes both. Even in the absence of covariance complementarity, the income effects of an increase in the expected yield of one asset might cause the gross substitutes assumption to fail. For these reasons gross substitutability is, for asset demands as for consumption goods demands, a more restrictive assumption than utility maximization.

H Other Determinants of Asset Demands

The asset demand functions A^J are not necessarily the permanent portfolios households would choose at the prevailing values of expected yields and other determining variables. In any short period of time, they will adjust only partially to new information about the financial environment. Lags in response are rational in view of the costs of transactions and decisions. For example, when capital gains and losses alter portfolio shares, portfolio managers may be slow to make corrective transactions. For these reasons the A^J will be multivariate stock adjustment functions and involve the vector of initial holdings J_{-1}. One would generally expect the own effect of an initial stock to be negative and the cross-effects positive, with the own effects dominating in the summary wealth demand function A^W.

Current and recent real disposable incomes were major determinants of consumption in Keynesian models, but postwar theory has downplayed their role in favor of forward-looking calculations of long-run disposable resources.[4] The issue is the length of the household horizons within which earnings, taxes, and transfers are pooled and over which this pool of current and future resources is consumed at a fairly steady rate. The longer the horizon, the larger the share of an increase in current income that will be saved rather than consumed. No doubt households vary greatly in these horizons, from extremely liquidity-constrained consumers who live hand-to-mouth and spend quickly any cash receipts, to lords of dynasties who save all extra income for their descendants. Liquidity constraints, for example limitations on the intertemporal fungibility of future wages and pensions, are sufficiently binding for many households that current disposable income remains an important determinant of consumption.

Current income is also a measure of transactions volume, and as such affects particularly the demand for transactions money. In the four-asset model the transactions effect will show up in a relatively high income-elasticity of demand, direct or indirect, for base money.

As the previous discussion makes clear, "human capital," expected future wages, taxes, and transfers, is a determinant of current consumption and saving. Current disposable income may be an indicator of such wealth, but it is an incomplete and imperfect one. Good news about future disposable incomes within households' horizons will reduce current saving, bad news will increase it. Effects on the composition of saving are more difficult to analyze. The time and age profiles of disposable income no doubt influence portfolios, especially if assets differ in liquidity. But these effects average out for the economy as a whole. A more important consideration arises from the uncertainties of both asset returns and earnings from human capital. Their covariances are very relevant to portfolio choice. Risk-averse savers will favor assets with returns negatively correlated with their own wages. Wage earners who expect a highly cyclical macroeconomic future will be wary of equities, whose returns and values are likely to be low precisely when they are most likely to be unemployed. Those who expect stable employment, real wages, and profits will be skeptical of nominally denominated assets, bonds and money. Belief that inflationary periods will be stagflationary because of counterinflationary monetary policies would lead households seeking hedges against unemployment and lowered real wages to short-term dollar-denominated assets bearing market interest rates (not included in my illustrative model) rather than to equities or long-term bonds.

The lesson of the previous discussion is that asset demand functions cannot be expected to be stable in the face of significant variations in the economic environment. The variances and covariances of returns on the several assets reflect probability distributions of more fundamental shocks to the economy. These are exogenous shocks in technology, tastes, and foreign economies as well as in government policies. Their impacts depend, moreover, on the responses to them by both private agents and government policymakers. The perceived joint probability distributions of those impacts, as reflected in the estimated risks of various asset portfolios in combination with human capital, are undoubtedly different in the 1980s from the 1960s. Asset demand functions are different too. But the perceptions, conventions, and habits that underlie asset demand functions do not change suddenly. It is sufficient for our immediate purpose that the functions are stable over the medium-term horizons of economic fluctuations and stabilization policies.

Taxes and transfers have been mentioned as elements in current and future disposable incomes. Taxes on capital incomes also affect the after-tax returns to asset holdings. The obvious point that taxation lowers expected yields is not the whole story, because it changes the entire distribution of uncertain returns. If the government shares symmetrically in losses and gains, its tax reduces the risk as well as the average return on risky portfolios, while increasing the risk and return borne by payers of other taxes, for example, those on wages and consumption. The effect of a given tax system on saving, portfolio choice, and asset values is a large and complex topic, beyond the scope of this lecture.

I Macroeconomic Modeling Strategy: Stocks, Flows, and Specific Saving Functions

The innovation of the approach thus far described is the integration of saving and portfolio decisions. Functions for accumulation of particular assets are specified, and they add up to total wealth accumulation for the period. The markets which determine asset prices and interest rates coordinate these demand flows with the supply flows arising from real investment, the government deficit, and the external current account. The markets handle simultaneously flows arising from saving and accumulation and those arising from reshuffling of portfolios, both by private agents on the demand side and by the monetary authorities on the supply side. By the end of the period, simultaneously with the determination of the asset prices for the period, these market participants have the stocks of assets and of total wealth they desire at this time at the prevailing prices.

This is not the conventional strategy of short-run macroeconomic models. The conventional strategy is to model the determination of asset prices and interest rates as a temporary stock equilibrium independent of flows of new saving. This is done in the *LM* sector of the model, where wealth-owners, constrained by the net worth inherited from their past savings but revalued at current market prices of assets, choose the *stocks* of money and alternative assets they wish to hold at these prices. The stocks supplied to them are also predetermined by history, except for instantaneous discrete modifications engineered by the monetary authorities by open market operations at current asset prices. Although households are simultaneously saving to accumulate wealth, the *IS–LM* model contains no specific saving functions describing in what forms they wish to accumulate it. Their absence means that the composition of household portfolios at the end of the period is reshaped solely by the issues of new asset supplies to finance investment, government deficit, and current account surplus. This composition may not be what households want, but the correction is deferred until the asset-stock markets reopen at the beginning of the next period. The unwelcome implication is that wealth-owners and savers, in formulating their portfolio demands, ignore the fact that they are at the same time saving to augment their wealth. In contrast to the *LM* markets in stocks, the simultaneous *IS* equations are grinding out *flows* of goods and services.

In my 1969 article describing a multiasset framework for monetary analysis, I perpetuated the implausible bifurcation to which I now object.[5] I tried to generalize the stock equilibrium of asset prices and quantities to a larger collection of assets while winding up nonetheless with a single *LM* locus to be juxtaposed with an *IS* locus. This condensation, I now recognize, is not in general attainable. The major points of the 1969 paper did not depend on this feature, but the blending of stock adjustments and saving flows advocated in this lecture seems to me a preferable approach.

The interpretation of the solution to a Keynesian short-run macroeconomic system has always been ambiguous. This is especially true when the variables are not explicitly dated by points or periods of time. Is the solution an equilibrium in the sense of a position of rest? This can hardly be the case for a model whose very solution implies changes in stocks of capital, wealth, government debt, and other assets. Since the structural equations of the model depend on those stocks, they will not replicate the solution when the stocks are moving. Keynes himself recognized the problem but excused himself for ignoring the dynamics of accumulation by defining the horizon of analysis as short enough so that flows make insignificant difference to the size of stocks. The excuse makes tolerable sense for the stocks of physical capital and total wealth, but unbalanced government budgets, monetary operations, and external imbalances can alter the corresponding asset stocks quite rapidly. A model whose solution generates flows but completely ignores their consequences may be suspected of missing phenomena important even in a relatively short run, and therefore giving incomplete or even misleading analyses of the effects of fiscal and monetary policies.

A specific complaint in this spirit was the allegation that the standard macro model "ignored the government budget constraint," that is, the identity that requires the deficit to be financed by issue of one or another government liability.[6] This is true in the standard model unless it is dynamically extended by tracking over time the growth in asset stocks and its effects on asset prices and other variables. The formulation I presented above makes explicit the government's financing requirements and allows its issues of money and bonds to affect financial markets right away.

But neither the problem nor its solution is confined to government finance. Another example concerns international capital movements and the determination of the exchange rate (Branson [9a,b]). The recently popular aphorism "the exchange rate is an asset price" is a truth, but a half- or quarter-truth. It is a natural result of divorcing flows from stocks and of viewing asset markets simply as reconciling, wealth-constrained portfolio demands with existing stocks. The application of this model to international financial markets was, to be sure, an advance over older analyses of payments imbalances and exchange rates, which either neglected capital transactions altogether or assumed that flows induced by interest rate differentials or other factors would continue indefinitely regardless of their effects on composition of portfolios. But it is more natural to recognize that exchange rates are determined—or held at parities by official interventions—in markets in which demands and supplies for current and capital accounts are mingled (Tobin and de Macedo [53], Tobin [48]).

Here, as in other financial markets, practical participants and observers are acutely conscious of the flows of new issues and new demands, while economists focus on stocks. Each group is puzzled by the other's emphasis. The chances are that both are right.

J Macroeconomic Modeling Strategy: *Continuous or Discrete Time*

The issues just discussed are related to the modeling of time. The equations introduced above count time in discrete periods of equal finite length. Within any period, each variable assumes one and only one value. In particular, clearing of asset markets determines one set of asset prices per period. From one period to the next asset stocks jump by finite amounts. Therefore the demands and supplies for these jumps affect asset prices and other variables within the period, the more so the greater the length of the period. They will also, of course, influence the solutions in subsequent periods.

The same modeling strategy can be used with continuous time. The specific saving functions, as well as the total saving function, then tell the rate at which savers want to be increasing their stocks of particular assets and of total wealth. They will reflect both the continuous execution of long-run saving and portfolio plans and the speeds of adjustment of stocks to deviations from these plans that arise because of surprises, news, and altered circumstances or preferences.

Either representation of time in economic dynamics is an unrealistic abstraction. We know by common observation that some variables, notably prices in organized markets, move virtually continuously. Others remain fixed for periods of varying length. Some decisions by economic agents are reconsidered daily or hourly, while others are reviewed at intervals of a year or longer except when extraordinary events compel revisions. It would be desirable in principle to allow for differences among variables in frequencies of change and even to make those frequencies endogenous. But at present models of such realism seem beyond the power of our analytic tools. Moreover, many statistical data are available only for arbitrary finite periods.

Representation of economies as systems of simultaneous equations always strains credibility. But it takes extraordinary suspension of disbelief to imagine that the economy solves and re-solves such systems every microsecond. Even with modern computers the task of the Walrasian Auctioneer, and of the market participants who provide demand and supply schedules, would be impossible. Economic interdependence is *the* feature of economic life which we as professional economists seek to understand and explain. Simultaneous equations systems are a convenient representation of interdependence, but it is more persuasive to think of the economic processes that solve them as taking time than as working instantaneously.

In any event, a model of short-run determination of macroeconomic activity must be regarded as referring to a slice of time, whether thick or paper thin, and as embedded in a dynamic process in which flows alter stocks, which in turn condition subsequent flows.

K *Solution of the One-Period Model*

The four asset-market equations (11)–(14) are the core of the model, augmented by the definition (16) of the deficit D and by the relationships (17)–(20) between current and expected prices and the four one-period rates of return r^J. The solution and interpretation of this structure depend on which variables are regarded as within-period endogenous and which as exogenous or predetermined. If more than four variables are to be taken as endogenous, then one or more equations must be added.

Here I provide, both for illustration of method and for substantive interest, three variants: (1) a "Keynesian" version in which current real income Y is endogenous but commodity price p is predetermined; (2) a "classical" version in which price p is endogenous but Y is supply-determined by the capital stock K_{-1}, and an exogenous labor force; (3) a "mixed" version with both p and Y endogenous and connected by a within-period Phillips curve, a fifth equation. In all variants, the asset price expectations figuring in (17)–(19) are assumed to be less than unit-elastic with respect to the corresponding current prices, so that the current prices are inversely related to the rates of return r^J. However, in the "Keynesian" and "classical" variants, the commodity price expectation Ep_{+1} is assumed to be proportional to the current price p. This assumption fixes the expected inflation rate and thus r^H. In a variant of the "mixed" case, the expected inflation rate is taken to be the same as the current inflation rate, $Ep_{+1}/p = p/p_{-1}$, so that r^H is determined by the short-run Phillips curve.

The exogenous variables representing fiscal policy are government purchases G and a constant or shift parameter in the tax-transfer function T (to be interpreted, for simplicity, as not changing marginal tax rates on capital incomes). The parameters of monetary policy are γ^H, the share of the deficit financed by printing base money, and z^H and z^F, open market "sales" of money and foreign currency. In a regime of clean float of the exchange rate, z^F is zero; in a regime with discretionary intervention, sale of foreign exchange, either for money or for bonds, is a policy variable. In a regime of fixed exchange rates, which will not be analyzed here, z^F becomes an endogenous variable while e and r^F become exogenous.

The Keynesian variant

With p and r^H predetermined, the model can be solved for (r^K, r^B, r^F, Y). Equations (17)–(19), implicitly substituted to eliminate (q^K, q^B, e) from the core equations, can then be used to obtain these three asset prices.

Differentiation of the core equations (11)–(14) gives a set of equations in the differentials, with sign structures shown in (21). The fifth row, added for reference, refers to the IS equation (15).

$$\begin{bmatrix} + & - & - & +(?) \\ - & + & - & + \\ - & - & + & + \\ - & - & - & + \\ + & + & + & + \end{bmatrix} \begin{bmatrix} dr^K \\ dr^B \\ dr^F \\ dY \end{bmatrix}$$

$$= \begin{bmatrix} 0 & -A_T^K & 0 & 0 & 0 & + \\ +\gamma^B & -A_T^B - \gamma^B & +D & 1/p & 0 & + \\ 0 & -A_T^F & 0 & 0 & 1/p & + \\ +\gamma^H & -A_T^H - \gamma^H & -D & -1/p & -1/p & - \\ +1 & -A_T^W - 1 & 0 & 0 & 0 & ? \end{bmatrix} \begin{bmatrix} dG \\ dT \\ d\gamma^B \\ dz^B \\ dz^F \\ dr^H \end{bmatrix}$$

Comparative statics (21)

The sign structure of the Jacobian, except for the last column, follows from the gross substitutability assumption for the A^J functions, reinforced by the signs of partial derivatives of the other terms in the core equations, specifically the negative relations of asset prices to rates of return and the standard Marshall-Lerner elasticity conditions for the trade balance. The final column embodies the presumption that the marginal propensity to save from current income in every asset is positive. Given this presumption, the only ambiguity, indicated by (?), is the possibility that an increase in Y, by raising current earnings of capital R, raises q^K, investment, and the valuation of K_{-1} enough to exceed the new demand for equity wealth it induces. The marginal propensity to invest may exceed the marginal propensity to save in equities.

Assuming the sign structure shown, the determinant of the Jacobian is positive.[7] Even if the questionable sign is reversed, it may be positive and will definitely be so if the sum of the first and last entries in the column is positive. Given a positive Jacobian determinant, the structure of multipliers is shown in Table 2.3.

These are conventional macroeconomic results, qualitatively the same as comparable conclusions of *IS-LM* apparatus. Note, however, that—contrary to the classical Mundell [33] conclusion that monetary policies work and fiscal policies do not in a regime of floating exchange rates—expansionary policies of both kinds are here effective. In the Mundell model, fiscal expansion alone cannot increase aggregate demand because

Table 2.3
Multipliers for Keynesian and Classical Cases

		Endogenous Variables			
		dr^K $(-dq^K)$	dr^B $(-dq^B)$	dr^F $(-de)$	dY (Keynesian) dp (Classical)
Expansionary fiscal policy					
dG	Purchases ($\gamma^H = 1, \gamma^H < 1$)	$(-,?)$	$(-,?)$	$(-,?)$	$(+,+)$
$-dT$	Tax reduction, transfers	?	?	?	+
$dG + dT$	Balanced increase of budget	?	?	?	+
Expansionary monetary policy					
$-d\gamma^B$	More monetary finance of deficit	−	−	−	+
$-dz^B$	Open market purchases of bonds	−	−	−	+
$-dz^F$	Open market purchases of foreign-currency assets	−	−	−	+
$dz^B - dz^F$	Sterilized purchases of foreign-currency assets	?	+	−	?
$-dr^H$	Expectation of inflation	−	−	−	+

it appreciates the exchange rate and lowers the current account surplus; the foreign interest rate ties down domestic rates so that the velocity of money cannot be raised. In the present model, fiscal expansion does not completely "crowd out" net exports. Exchange appreciation lowers the demand for money both because the return on foreign assets is higher, given sticky exchange rate expectations, and because the value of foreign-currency wealth holdings is lower. This wealth effect requires, of course, that the holdings be positive. The asset substitution effects also imply that the floating rate does not insulate the economy from external demand shocks.

The ambiguities of sign of the multipliers for rates of return reflect the variety of possible substitution patterns in a multiasset model. For example, with bond financing of deficits, the equity return r^K may actually decline if bonds are a good substitute for money but a poor substitute for equities.

The classical variant

Formally, the classical model has qualitatively the same structure as (21), with the roles of p and Y interchanged. The multipliers for both are those in Table 2.3. The positive price effects on excess asset demands explicit in equations (11)–(14) may be reinforced by Pigou effects in the A^J functions themselves. Without them the top entry in the last column of the Jacobian, now the dp column, is zero. In any case the possible ambiguity of that sign is removed.

Monetary expansion is not neutral but lowers real interest rates and shifts the composition of output from consumption to investment. Fiscal expansion raises the price level, and if this does not induce enough saving and current account deficit to finance the increased budget deficit, it raises r^K and crowds out investment. Monetarist conclusions about fiscal policy require, as often argued in the past, that interest elasticities of money demand be zero (the first three items in the fourth row of the Jacobian).

The mixed model

Clearly an "aggregate supply" function, a positive within-period relation between p and Y can be appended to the model without changing its essential features. The effects of various policies and of other exogenous variables will then be split between price and real income, but will be in the same directions as shown in Table 2.3. These results depend on the assumption that expected inflation, and thus r^H, are independent of the current price p.

In the final column of (21) are given the signs of differentials for exogenous variation of r^H. In the middle two rows these reflect, in addition to the negative effects of r^H on A^B and A^F, its negative effects on q^B and e. The resulting multiplier signs appear in the final row of Table 2.3; not surprisingly, expectation of inflation is expansionary and inflationary.

Now suppose that r^H is endogenous, equal to r^H_{-1} plus an expectation revision related negatively to Y. This will add a fifth column to the Jacobian of (21), namely, the r^H column with signs reversed as it becomes the fourth column of the Jacobian. The relation of r^H to Y will add a row, $[000 + +]$, and possibly reverse the sign of the Jacobian determinant and of the multipliers for p and Y. In an *IS-LM* diagram in r-Y space the equivalent reversal would arise if the *LM* locus, after subtracting from it the inflation generated at each level of Y by a Phillips curve, crossed *IS* from above to below rather than in the normal way.

In models of this kind we are not free to dismiss such intuitively perverse solutions as unstable equilibria. There are no dynamics within the period or the slice of continuous time. The one-period model, simultaneous equations and all, is meant to say what actually happens. Dynamics and stability questions arise over a sequence of one-period solutions. In the example of the previous paragraph, the resolution probably lies elsewhere, for example in slowing down the translation of actual inflation into expected inflation.

3 Possible Extensions and Elaborations of the Model

A *Financial Intermediation, Loans, and Inside Money*

As Table 2.1 shows, banks and other financial institutions mediate between borrowers and lenders, making loans to businesses, governments, households, and others, and incurring liabilities to households and other creditors. The traditional business of commercial banks is to accept deposits and other obligations payable on demand or at specified times and to acquire assets of less liquidity and longer maturity. Almost all their assets and liabilities, except their owners' equity, are promises to pay currency. Other intermediaries likewise transform their assets into forms better tailored—in convenience of denomination, liquidity, maturity, and risk—to the preferences and circumstances of their creditors. Banks and other intermediaries, together with capital and credit markets, thus create "inside" assets, claims of agents on each other that wash out in aggregations of privately owned national wealth. In particular, banks create inside money, that is, deposits that serve on a par with government currency as generally acceptable transactions media or as close substitutes therefor, "backed" on the other side of their ledgers not by base money or government debt but by private loans and securities. In the United States the equivalence of bank deposits to currency is sustained by government deposit insurance, which in effect extends to deposits the government's fiat.

With banks and inside money, the nature of the demand for base ("outside") money is altered. In the United States, there are essentially two uses of base money: currency in public circulation and bank reserves. Banks are legally required to hold reserves, either in currency or on deposit in the central bank, in fractions of checkable deposits and certain other liquid liabilities. They may hold reserves in excess of requirements, or by borrowing from the central bank they can make their "net free reserve" positions negative. Thus the demand function for base money consists of three parts: the nonbank public's holdings of currency; required bank reserves, the required fraction of the public's demand for deposits; and net free reserves, a choice made by the banks in the light of the Federal Reserve discount rate and the rates available on loans and securities. The arguments in the three functions are the interest rates and other variables relevant for household or bank portfolio decisions.

The addition of bank deposits, of one or more varieties, to the asset list adds rows to matrices like Table 2.1. Whether it also adds to the list of endogenous interest rates depends on whether the nominal rate on deposits is, like the zero rate on currency, fixed by law or convention. Deposits with controlled interest rates are an example of an asset market not cleared by price. Banks are not on their deposit supply schedules. They would be ready to accept more deposits than the public wants at the controlled rate, but the smaller side of the market controls the quantity. Thus the banks' disposable deposits, that is, deposits net of required reserves, are available for allocation among free reserves, loans, and securities.

Banks and other intermediaries can bid for deposits and other liabilities carrying market-determined assets. These in principle add to the list of endogenous interest rates, although in practice certificates of time deposit may be nearly perfect substitutes for Treasury bills and other short open-market paper. Similarly, commercial loans, mortgages, and other assets characteristic of intermediaries may call for distinct rows and interest rates. Some loans may be rationed at administratively set interest rates, like the "prime," with excess supply from borrowers chronic or frequent. A way to model a privately administered non-competitive price is to imagine it to be reset for each period in relation to the excess supply observed in the preceding period. Then it is not a within-period endogenous price, and the endogenous variable corresponding to its row equation is a quantity.

The existence of monetary assets with fixed nominal interest rates—base money, deposits, and for short periods central bank loans—gives leverage to central bank monetary operations affecting their supplies. The reason is that other asset prices, interest rates, commodity prices, and real incomes must adjust to induce the public to absorb in their portfolios changes in these supplies. For the same reason and for good or ill, non-policy shocks to the supply of, or demand for, fixed-rate assets have leverage. In contrast, exogenous increases in the net supply of an asset bearing a flexible market-determined rate can in great part be accommodated by increases in the own-rate itself.

In an n-asset model, if there are less than n endogenous interest rates, the asset-market equations can determine, as shown above, at least one other variable, for example, Y or p or some combination of them. If all assets had market-determined rates, this degree of freedom would be lost. The trend of the financial system is to enlarge the range of assets that have variable market-determined rates, increasing the leverage of base money supplies and equivalent shocks on market interest rates. This trend makes the Hicksian LM curve more nearly vertical, rendering fiscal policies and other IS shocks less consequential. Whether it contributes to stability or instability of output and prices depends on the nature and strength of unpredictable and uncontrollable shocks to the demands for, and supplies of, the small remaining core of fixed-rate assets, and to the patterns of demands and supply among the variable-rate assets, especially between nominally denominated securities and equities. It is possible that q will be more rather than less variable in the new regime.

B Substitutability, Aggregation, and Estimation

In principle, the model should distinguish imperfectly substitutable asset categories and determine a separate rate of return for each. If two assets are perfect substitutes, their interest rates move together and can be represented as one variable. Then the two rows must be consolidated. In econometric practice this is also expedient for close though imperfect substitutes. The strong collinearities of time series of interest rates present difficult econometric problems. It is often not clear whether observed covariation is due to close substitutability or to pervasive common exogenous shocks. History has frequently not performed those experiments in variation of relative asset supplies that would test substitutability hypotheses and allow estimations of cross-elasticities. For this reason, estimations and simulations of models or partial models have relied heavily on priors about coefficients and their error distributions. In some cases these Bayesian methods, though inferior to standard procedures in fitting sample observations, have done better in out-of-sample forecasts (Smith and Brainard [36]).

C International Asset Transactions

In section 2 international capital movement was modeled in the most primitive fashion, by specifying a single foreign-currency asset in which domestic residents could borrow or lend at an exogenous foreign-currency interest rate. Foreigners were assumed not to demand domestic assets. Because of these simplifications, the supply-equals-demand equation for the foreign-currency asset was also the balance-of-payments equation. One step toward realism is to add foreign demands, with the same formats and properties *mutatis mutandis* as the domestic asset demand functions, to the equations for all local assets. Foreign portfolio managers are presumably concerned with returns in their own currencies. This amendment can be kept within the bounds of the "small country" assumption by continuing to assume that foreign interest rates, foreign incomes, and other relevant foreign variables are exogenous. The balance-of-payments equation is the previous foreign-currency asset balance equation, but with net demands now augmented by the sum of net foreign demands for domestic assets. This amendment leaves intact, with only minor qualifications, the conclusions of the simpler model.

The second step, however, introduces considerable complexity and ambiguity. This is to model two economies jointly and symmetrically, with residents of each country demanding asset holdings in both currencies and with macroeconomic variables endogenous in both countries. The "gross substitutes" assumption, the source of determinate qualitative results in section 2, no longer applies, because the same movement of the exchange rate has opposite meanings to investors in the two countries. Own-currency preferences arise from the facts that each country's residents expect to buy consumer goods in its currency and that the two countries' products are imperfectly substitutable. Obviously, succeeding steps, with n currencies and economies, would be still more difficult.[8]

4 Dynamics and Long-run Steady States

Each within-period solution generates new values of predetermined variables for the following period. These include of course stocks of portfolio assets and capital, which follow obvious transitional equations. Likewise, transitional equations could preset other variables by the solutions in the immediately preceding and other past periods. The inertia of commodity prices, and their relation to economic activity, could be modeled in this way, as could be adaptive expectations. Rational expectations dynamic solutions are also possible. However, dynamic solutions of a nonlinear system, even one of such small dimensionality as the one described in section 2, cannot be obtained analytically but require simulations.

With some special assumptions, the model has a steady-state solution like that of a monetary growth model (Tobin [39, 42, 43]). The most important assumptions, in addition to the familiar restrictions on production functions, technological progress, and exogenous resources, concern asset preferences and saving. The existence of steady states requires that at any constant set of rates of return all asset demands grow in proportion to the size of the economy. The same homogeneity is required of government purchases and tax revenues.

Which of the various feasible steady-state paths, all with the natural rate of growth of the economy g, is the long-run equilibrium depends on policy parameters. These are two parameters setting budget purchases and tax revenues as fractions s and τ of total output, and one parameter determining how deficits are financed, γ^B or γ^H. Open market operations have no place or purpose along an equilibrium path.

A steady-state solution determines the three rates of return (r^K, r^B, r^H). Capital accumulation occurs steadily at the natural rate of growth, and q is therefore equal to 1. Thus r^K is the net (after-tax) marginal product of capital, inversely related to the capital-labor and capital-output ratios, and to output and real wages per effective worker. The rate of return to base money, the negative of the inflation rate, is endogenous in the long run though not in the short-run one-period model. This is because rational expectations apply, as they always have, to steady-state solutions; expected and actual inflation must be the same.

I turn now to a brief discussion of the nature of a long-run equilibrium and of the accompanying issues of analysis, interpretation, and policy. Here I refer to a closed economy with three assets; the whole concept of steady long-run growth fails for open economies unless their several natural rates of growth happen to be identical. For convenience, I use continuous time. Let b and h be the stocks of bonds (consols) and high-powered (base) money at nominal market value, each as a fraction of nominal income. These will be constants over time in a steady state. The nominal interest rates on the two assets, also constant over time, are

$(r^B + \pi, 0)$ and the real rates (r^B, r^H), where $r^H = -\pi$. The nominal price of bonds q^B, again constant, is $1/(r^B + \pi)$. The nominal stock of each asset, in dollars, is growing at rate $g + \pi$, along with nominal income. The following two equations describe the financing of the deficit:

$$\gamma^B(s - \tau + (r^B + \pi)b) Yp = bYp(g + \pi)$$
$$\gamma^H(s - \tau + (r^B + \pi)b) Yp = hYp(g + \pi)$$
Steady-states supplies of bonds and base money (22)

Eliminating Yp from these equations and solving them for b and h gives:

$$b = \frac{\gamma^B(s - \tau)}{g - \gamma^B r^B - \gamma^H r^H}, \quad h = \frac{\gamma^H(s - \tau)}{g - \gamma^B r^B - \gamma^H r^H} \quad \text{Solution of (22)} \quad (23)$$

Note that the denominator could be written as $g - r^D$, where r^D is the appropriately weighted average real interest rate on the public debt, monetary and nonmonetary. I confine myself to nonnegative values of $s - \tau$, $g - r^D$, b, and h. Long-run asset demand functions are $a^K(\cdot)$, $a^B(\cdot)$, and $a^H(\cdot)$, each expressed as fractions of real income Y and containing as arguments the three r^J and the tax rate τ. As before, these add up to wealth demand a^W. Let k be the capital-output ratio, which with a normal constant-returns-to-scale production function in capital (endogenous) and effective labor (exogenous) will be inversely related to r^K.[9] The three equations determining the steady state are:

$$a^K(r^K, r^B, r^H, \tau) = k(r^K) = k \quad \begin{array}{l}\textit{Steady state}\\\textit{equations:}\\\textit{Capital, equities}\end{array} \quad (24)$$

$$a^B(r^K, r^B, r^H, \tau) = \frac{\gamma^B(s - \tau)}{g - \gamma^B r^B - \gamma^H r^H} = b \quad \text{Bonds} \quad (25)$$

$$a^H(r^K, r^B, r^H, \tau) = \frac{\gamma^H(s - \tau)}{g - \gamma^B r^B - \gamma^H r^H} = h \quad \text{Base money} \quad (26)$$

Their sum, a long-run *IS* relation, is

$$a^W(r^K, r^B, r^H, \tau) = k(r^K) + \frac{s - \tau}{g - \gamma^B r^B - \gamma^H r^H} \quad \text{Wealth} \quad (27)$$

Simple as system (24)–(26) looks, it leaves open a variety of possible relations between endogenous variables and policy parameters. Particular interest, of course, attaches to r^K because of its link to capital intensity, labor productivity, consumption per capita, and real wages. In the comparative statics of steady states, "expansionary" policies—high s, low τ, and high γ^H—may be associated with lower r^H (more inflation) and with lower r^K and higher capital intensity k. Or the steady-state association of policies and results may be quite the opposite.

The formal reason for these ambiguities is that the "gross substitutes" property, though assumed for the a^J functions, does not guarantee a dominant-diagonal Jacobian matrix. For example, in the H equation of (24) an increase of r^H raises the demand for base money on the left-hand side. But it also raises the supply, by diminishing the denominator on the right-hand side—and perhaps by more than the demand. For a similar reason the diagonal entry in the Jacobian might be negative in the B row.

The major possibilities can be illustrated graphically, though with some loss of generality, by aggregating $b + h$ and plotting their sum d against r^D, the weighted average defined above. This is done in Figures 2.1 and 2.2, where the rectangular hyperbola d_S is the "supply" of d, equal to $(s - \tau)/(g - r^D)$. Now imagine that r^B and r^H affect a^K only as they affect r^D; this special assumption is necessary for the graphical illustration. For any r^D, the K equation can then be solved for r^K, which will be positively associated with r^H. The corresponding k can be added to d_S to obtain w. Now r^K, together with the r^B and r^H that make up r^D, determines a^B and a^H in the second and third equations. Their sum is the demand for public debt a^D. In an equilibrium a^D and d_S must be equal, as at a point labeled E. In the bottom panels of the figures r^K is plotted against r^D. The r^K associated with k equal to $w - d_S$ is r^K_S, and the r^K associated with $w - a^D$ is r^K_a. They are equal in the equilibrium E. Expansionary policies raise r^K_S, but what that does to equilibrium r^K differs in the two cases.

Figure 2.1 is the analog of what I called in the short-run analysis the standard case, associated with a dominant-diagonal Jacobian. The demand effects of own-rates exceed the supply effects. Clearly an increase in $s - \tau$, raising the d_S hyperbola as indicated by the arrows raises r^D and r^K. Greater deficit spending "crowds out" capital, and part of the mechanism is *lowering* the inflation rate. It is quite possible that an increase in γ^H, greater monetization of deficits, works in the same directions; assuming r^H is less than r^D, one of its effects too is to shift d_S to the left.

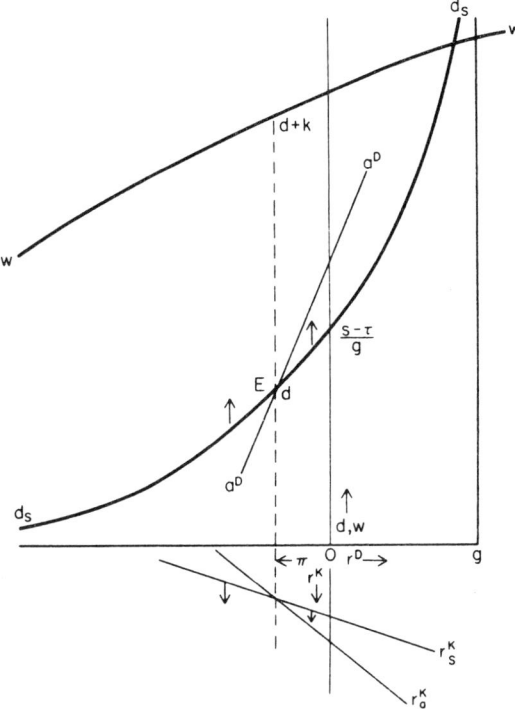

Figure 2.1
Steady state equilibrium of government debt and capital and their rates of return (standard case)

The stability of the equilibrium in Figure 2.1 is another question, which I must leave open. Skepticism of its stability arises not only from intuition but from the same model's short-run conclusion that the same policies are inflationary and may increase capital investment. Resolution of the apparent paradox would presumably require a rational expectations explanation of the price level, with economic agents foreseeing the steady state and internalizing the transversality conditions.

The alternative, Figure 2.2, shows a^D flatter than d_S. Here the same "expansionary" policies raise the inflation rate and "crowd in" capital, which replaces less attractive public debt. Here the demands for money and bonds are less responsive to rates of return; perhaps paradoxically, Figure 2.2 pictures the more monetarist world. Still another possibility,

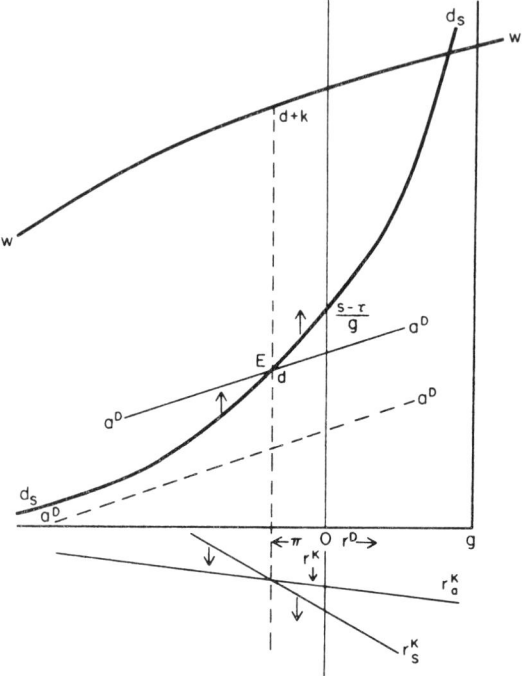

Figure 2.2
Steady state equilibrium of government debt and their rates of return (nonstandard case)

shown by the dashed a^D curve in Figure 2.2, is that there is no steady-state equilibrium at all. The deficit $s - \tau$ is so high that there is no r^D at which the supply of debt will be held in competition with capital. This is a recipe for hyperinflation.

In the United States total federal debt is about 24 percent of GNP, 6 percent base money plus 18 percent nonmonetary debt, implying $\gamma^H = 1/4$ and $\gamma^B = 3/4$. With inflation of 10 percent per year and nominal interest rates on debt instruments around 14 percent, r^D is 0.5 percent. Assuming a natural growth rate of 2.5 percent, $g - r^D$ is 2 percent. Implicit in these numbers is a steady-state budget deficit (exclusive of debt interest) of 0.48 percent of GNP. Thus d_S would double to 48 percent by a 100 basis point rise in r^D. Since it seems unlikely that demand a^D would rise as much, Figure 2.2 applies.

In any case, financial policies are not neutral in the long run any more than in the short run. The variation of r^K and capital intensity across steady states violates "super-neutrality," that is, invariance of real outcomes to the rate of inflation. Since inflation is the inverse of a real interest rate, this is scarcely surprising. In the background is the competition between capital and public debt for allocation of limited wealth. Such competition might not occur for consumers with infinite horizons, who would accumulate capital and every other asset until each of their yields equals a constant time preference rate. In contrast, savers with horizons of lifetimes or other finite periods will have finite demands for wealth and for every asset at any given rates of return (Tobin and Buiter [52, pp. 98–103]).

Paul Samuelson showed in his 1958 parable of overlapping generations that unassisted competitive markets do not necessarily attain socially optimal or even Pareto-optimal equilibria when mortal households cannot trade with each other across time. The insight reinforces Keynes's observation of the difficulties of market coordination without futures markets and helps to explain their absence.

Macroeconomic market failures make it possible that government financial interventions can improve welfare, but they by no means guarantee that actual policies will do so. The focus of my lecture has been on the ways fiscal and monetary policies alter macroeconomic outcomes in the short and the long run. I have not considered the optimal design of policies, or the optimal rules of government intervention in response to shocks that disturb the economy's path. Those are important items of unfinished business on the agenda of monetary theory and macroeconomics.

Appendix A

Y	Real net national product
S	Real private saving
I	Real net capital investment (including adjustment costs)
D	Real government deficit
C	Real private consumption
G	Real government purchases of goods and services
T	Tax revenues net of transfers, real
$\overline{CAS}$	Real current account surplus
K	Capital stock, real

B	Stock of bonds, nominal, measured by coupon payments per period
H	Stock of high-powered (base) money, nominal
F	Stock of foreign-currency assets privately owned, nominal in foreign currency
g^F	Stock of foreign-currency assets publicly owned, nominal in foreign currency
W	Private net worth, real
p	Commodity price
p^F	Foreign-commodity price, in foreign currency
e	Exchange rate: domestic-currency price of a unit of foreign currency
q^K	Ratio of market price of equities to standard replacement cost of a unit of capital
q^B	Nominal price of a bond paying $1 per period in perpetuity
γ^B	Fraction of deficit financed by selling bonds
γ^H	Fraction of deficit financed by issuing base money
z^J	$(J = B, F, H)$ additional government sale or issue of asset J, nominal
ρ^F	Interest rate on foreign-currency assets, in foreign currency
r^J	$(J = B, F, H)$ real one-period expected return on asset J
X	Trade surplus
g	Natural growth rate
δ	Capital depreciation rate
A^J	$(J = K, B, F, H)$ demand for asset J at end of period, real
R	Earnings per unit of capital, real
x or x_t	Value of a variable x in period t
x_{-1} or x_{t-1}	Value of x in period $t-1$
Ex_{+1} or Ex_{t+1}	Expected value of x in period $t+1$
Δx or Δx_t	$x_t - x_{t-1}$
S	Steady state C/Y
τ	Steady state T/Y
k	Steady state K/Y a^k steady-state demand for k
b	Steady state $q^B B/pY$ a^b steady-state demand for b
h	Steady state H/pY a^h steady-state demand for h
w	Steady state W/Y a^w steady-state demand for w
r^D	Average real interest rate on government debt, $\gamma^B r^B + \gamma^H r^H$
d	$b + h$
π	Inflation rate $\dfrac{dp}{dt} \cdot \dfrac{1}{p} = -r^H$

Notes

I am indebted to Kenneth Warwick for compiling Tables 2.1 and 2.2, and to Laura Harrison and Glena Ames for efficiently preparing the manuscript of the lecture under great pressure of time. Research reported here was supported by the National Science Foundation and the Cowles Foundation. Among my many intellectual debts, I mention here only my long partnership with William Brainard. Although his influence pervades the paper, he is not responsible for errors of commission and omission, except that there would be fewer if time had permitted him to read and comment.

1. Hahn [18, 19, 20, 21] has been an insightful contributor to the literature on this subject. The proceedings of a recent conference on it are reported in Kareken and Wallace [24].

2. See Backus et al. [3], Brainard and Smith [8], Smith and Brainard [35, 36], Backus and Purvis [4], and Friedman [14, 15].

3. The so-called q theory of investment was introduced as such in Tobin and Brainard [49] and has been further discussed and applied in Tobin [44]. Tobin and Brainard [50], Tobin [46], Ciccolo [12], Ciccolo and Fromm [13], Malkiel, von Furstenberg, and Watson [27], von Furstenberg [17], Summers [37], Abel [1], and by many other writers. Since it is a straightforward application of the neoclassical theory of the firm, it has many precursors.

4. Friedman [16] and Modigliani and Brumberg [31, 32] are seminal. My own work on consumption began with my doctoral thesis in 1947 and encompasses ten papers published over the years and reprinted in Tobin [45, chaps. 29–38].

5. However, my 1968 paper with William C. Brainard is not subject to this objection. Explicitly modeling time in discrete periods, we followed in that paper the procedure here recommended.

6. An early example of the complaint is Christ [10, 11]. The issue is discussed in Blinder and Solow [6, 7] and by Tobin and Buiter [51, 52], and Tobin [47].

7. A dominant-diagonal matrix has positive diagonal elements, nonpositive off-diagonal elements, and positive column sums. Its determinant is positive. It remains positive if any column is replaced by a nonnegative vector with no negative elements and at least one positive element.

8. On the topic of this subsection, see Tobin and de Macedo [53], which describes more fully the simple model and takes the first and second steps of amendment. In a subsequent paper, Tobin [48], I have discussed the internationalization of portfolios and its relation to the theory of exchange rates.

9. Pre-tax. I do not discuss here the taxation of capital income, but it could be analyzed by putting after-tax rates of return in the a^J functions and taking account also of the effects of taxation on risk, mentioned above.

References

1. Abel, Andrew B. "Empirical Investment Equations: An Integrative Framework." In *On the State of Macro-Economics*, edited by Karl Brunner and Allan H. Meltzer, Carnegie-Rochester Series on Public Policy 12, pp. 39–91. Amsterdam: North-Holland.

2. Arrow, Kenneth J. "General Economic Equilibrium: Purpose, Analytic Techniques, Collective Choice." *Les Prix Nobel en 1972*, Stockholm and *American Economic Review*, 64 (June 1975), 253–72.

3. Backus, David K., William C. Brainard, Gary Smith, and James Tobin. "A Model of U.S. Financial and Nonfinancial Economic Behavior." *Journal of Money, Credit, and Banking*, 12 (May 1980), 259–93.

4. Backus, David K., and Douglas D. Purvis. "An Integrated Model of Household Flow-of-Funds Allocations." *Journal of Money, Credit, and Banking*, 12 (May 1980, Special Issue), 400–21.

5. Baumol, William J. "The Transactions Demand for Cash: An Inventory Theoretic Approach." *Quarterly Journal of Economics*, 56 (November 1952), 545–56.

6. Blinder, Alan S., and Robert M. Solow. "Does Fiscal Policy Matter?" *Journal of Public Economics*, 2 (November 1973), 318–37.

7. ———. "Analytical Foundations of Fiscal Policy." In *The Economics of Public Finance*, by The Brookings Institution. Washington, D.C.: The Brookings Institution, 1974.

8. Brainard, William C., and Gary Smith. "The Systematic Specification of a Full Prior Covariance Matrix." Mimeographed, 1979.

9a. Branson, William H. "The Dual Roles of the Government Budget and the Balance of Payments in the Movement from Short-Run to Long-Run Equilibrium." *Quarterly Journal of Economics*, 90 (August 1976), 345–67.

9b. ———. "A 'Keynesian' Approach to Worldwide Inflation." In *Worldwide Inflation: Theory und Recent Experience*, edited by Lawrence B. Krause and Walter S. Salant, pp. 63–92. Washington, D.C.: The Brookings Institution, 1977.

10. Christ, Carl F. "A Short-Run Aggregate-Demand Model of the Interdependence and Effects of Monetary and Fiscal Policies with Keynesian and Classical Interest Elasticities." *American Economic Review*, 57 (May 1966), 434–43.

11. ———. "A Simple Macroeconomic Model with a Government Budget Restraint." *Journal of Political Economy*, 76 (January/February 1968), 53–67.

12. Ciccolo, John H. *Four Essays on Monetary Theory*. Ph.D. dissertation, Yale University, 1975.

13. Ciccolo, John H., and Gary Fromm. "'q' and the Theory of Investment." *Journal of Finance*, 34 (May 1979), 535–47.

14. Friedman, Benjamin M. "Financial Flow Variables and the Short-Run Determination of Long-Term Interest Rates." *Journal of Political Economy*, 85 (August 1977), 661–89.

15. ———. "The Determination of Long-Term Interest Rates: Implications for Fiscal and Monetary Policies." *Journal of Money, Credit, and Banking*, 12 (May 1980, Special Issue), 331–52.

16. Friedman, Milton. *A Theory of the Consumption Function.* Princeton: Princeton University Press, 1957.

17. von Furstenberg, George M. "Corporate Investment: Does Market Valuation Matter in the Aggregate?" *Brookings Papers on Economic Activity*, 2 (1977), 347–97.

18. Hahn, Frank H. "On Some Problems of Proving the Existence of Equilibrium in a Monetary Economy." In *The Theory of Interest Rates*, edited by Frank H. Hahn and Frank P. Brechling, pp. 126–35. London: Macmillan, 1965.

19. ———. "Equilibrium with Transactions Costs." *Econometrica*, 39 (May 1971), 417–39.

20. ———. "On the Foundations of Monetary Theory." In *Essays in Modern Economics*, edited by Michael Parkin and Avelino R. Nobay, pp. 230–42. New York: Harper and Row, 1973.

21. ———. "On Transactions Costs, Inessential Sequence Economies and Money." *Review of Economic Studies*, 40 (October 1973), 449–61.

22. Hicks, John R. "A Suggestion for Simplifying the Theory of Money." *Economica*, N.S. 2 (February 1935), 1–19.

23. ———. "Mr. Keynes and the 'Classics': A Suggested Interpretation." *Econometrica*, 5 (April 1937), 147–59.

24. Kareken, John H., and Neil Wallace (eds.). *Money of Monetary Economics.* Federal Reserve Bank of Minneapolis, 1980.

25. Keynes, John M. *The General Theory of Employment, Interest and Money.* New York: Harcourt, Brace, 1936.

26. Lucas, Robert E., Jr. "Econometric Policy Evaluation: A Critique." *Journal of Monetary Economics*, Supplement, Vol. 1. Carnegie-Rochester Conference Series on Public Policy, *The Phillips Curve and Labor Markets*, 1976.

27. Malkiel, Burton G., George M. von Furstenberg, and Harry S. Watson. "Expectations, Tobin's q, and Industry Investment." *Journal of Finance*, 34 (May 1979), 549–61.

28. Markowitz, Harry M. "Portfolio Selection." *Journal of Finance*, 7 (March 1952). 77–91.

29. ———. *Portfolio Selection: Efficient Diversification of Investments.* Cowles Foundation Monograph 16. New York: Wiley, 1959.

30. Miller, Merton H., and Daniel Orr. "A Model of the Demand for Money by Firms." *Quarterly Journal of Economics*, 80 (August 1966), 413–35.

31. Modigliani, Franco, and Richard Brumberg. "Utility Analysis and Aggregate Consumption Functions: An Attempt at Integration." Mimeographed, 1952. Published in *The Collected Papers of Franco Modigliani*, edited by Andrew B. Abel, Vol. 2, pp. 128–99. Cambridge: M.I.T. Press, 1980.

32. ———. "Utility Analysis and the Consumption Function: An Interpretation of Cross-Section Data." In *Post-Keynesian Economics*, edited by Kenneth K. Kurihara, pp. 388–436. London: Allen and Unwin, 1954.

33. Mundell, Robert A. "Capital Mobility and Stabilization Policy under Fixed and Flexible Exchange Rates." *Canadian Journal of Economics and Political Science*, 29 (November 1963), 475–85.

34. Samuelson, Paul A. "An Exact Consumption-Loan Model of Interest With or Without the Social Contrivance of Money." *Journal of Political Economy*, 66 (December 1958), 467–82.

35. Smith, Gary, and William C. Brainard. "Disequilibrium Models for Financial Institutions." Cowles Foundation Discussion Paper 535. New Haven, Conn.: Mimeographed, 1974.

36. ———. "The Value of A Priori Information in Estimating a Financial Model." *Journal of Finance*, 31 (December 1976), 1299–322.

37. Summers, Lawrence H. "Taxation and Corporate Investment: A q-Theory Approach." *Brookings Papers on Economic Activity*, 1 (1981), 67–140.

38. Tobin, James. *A Theoretical and Statistical Analysis of Consumer Saving.* Ph.D. dissertation Harvard University, 1947.

39. ———. "A Dynamic Aggregative Model." *Journal of Political Economy*, 63 (April 1955), 103–15.

40. ———. "The Interest-Elasticity of Transactions Demand for Cash." *Review of Economic and Statistics*, 38 (August 1956), 241–47.

41. ———. "Liquidity Preference as Behavior Towards Risk." *Review of Economic Studies*, 25 (February 1958), 65–86.

42. ———. "Money and Economic Growth." *Econometrica*, 33 (October 1965), 671–84.

43. ———. "Notes on Optimal Monetary Growth." *Journal of Political Economy*, 76 (August 1968), 833–59.

44. ———. "A General Equilibrium Approach to Monetary Theory." *Journal of Money, Credit, and Banking*, 1 (February 1969), 15–29.

45. ———. *Essays in Economics*, Vol. 2. Amsterdam: North-Holland, 1975.

46. ———. "Monetary Policies and the Economy: The Transmission Mechanism." *Southern Economic Journal*, 44 (January 1978), 421–31.

47. ———. "Deficit Spending and Crowding Out in Shorter and Longer Runs." In *Theory for Economic Efficiency: Essays in Honor of Abba P. Lerner*, edited by Harry I. Greenfield et al., pp. 217–36. Cambridge: M.I.T. Press, 1979.

48. ———. "The State of Exchange Rate Theory: Some Skeptical Observations." In *The International Monetary System under Flexible Exchange Rates: Global, Regional, and National. Essays in Honor of Robert Triffin*, edited by Richard N. Cooper et al. Cambridge: Ballinger, 1981.

49. Tobin, James, and William C. Brainard. "Pitfalls in Financial Model Building." *American Economic Review*, 58 (May 1968), 99–122.

50. ———. "Assets Markets and the Cost of Capital." In *Economic Progress: Private Values and Public Policy* (Essays in Honor of William Fellner), edited by Richard Nelson and Bela Balassa, pp. 235–62. Amsterdam: North-Holland, 1977.

51. Tobin, James, and Willem H. Buiter. "Long-Run Effects of Fiscal and Monetary Policy on Aggregate Demand." In *Monetarism*, edited by Jerome L. Stein, pp. 273–309. New York: North-Holland, 1976.

52. ———. "Fiscal and Monetary Policies, Capital Formation, and Economic Activity." In *The Government and Capital Formation*, edited by George M. von Furstenberg, pp. 73–151. Cambridge: Ballinger, 1980.

53. Tobin, James, and Jorge A. Braga de Macedo. "The Short-Run Macroeconomics of Floating Exchange Rates: An Exposition." In *Flexible Exchange Rates and the Balance of Payments*, edited by John S. Chipman and Charles P. Kindleberger, pp. 5–28. Amsterdam: North-Holland, 1980.

CHAPTER 3

A MODEL OF U.S. FINANCIAL AND NONFINANCIAL ECONOMIC BEHAVIOR

1 Introduction

At the beginning of this or any calendar quarter, economic agents in the United States—households, business firms, financial institutions, governments—held certain measurable quantities of a variety of assets, financial and real. The great bulk of financial assets were the debts of other resident agents; some were debts of foreigners. The bulk of real assets were land and reproducible consumers' or producers' durable goods located within the country. We also owned real properties abroad, just as foreigners owned some here. These asset and debt positions were the cumulative results of past saving and investment, past portfolio behavior, and past capital gains and losses, realized or unrealized.

During the current quarter, these balance sheets will change. Households will be deciding how much to add to their wealth and in what form. Businesses will be deciding how much real capital to accumulate and how to finance their investments. Governments will be running and financing budget surpluses or deficits; in this particular quarter no doubt they will be on balance in deficit and will have to issue new interest-bearing debts or new monetary liabilities. Probably they will issue some of each. The country's net position vis-à-vis the rest of the world will decline by the deficit in the external current account. This deficit too will have its financial counterparts. At the same time, all these agents, and foreigners as well, will be reshuffling their initial balance sheets. The transactions and revaluations resulting from portfolio shifts are indistinguishable from those connected with saving and accumulation. At the end of the quarter, there will be new balance sheets, to be adjusted again in the next quarter.

Reprinted by permission from the *Journal of Money, Credit, and Banking* 12(2) (May 1980): 259–293. Written with David Backus, William C. Brainard, and Gary Smith.

During each quarter the new asset stocks desired by some agents are somehow reconciled to new supplies offered by others. The process is closely linked to economic activity—production, consumption, employment, inflation—during the quarter. The links go in both directions. Current incomes help to determine household saving, business saving and investment, government deficits, and the current account deficit. Simultaneously, commodity prices, foreign exchange rates, interest rates, and asset revaluations influence consumer spending, domestic capital accumulation, and net foreign investment. Thus the mechanisms that maintain balance of asset demands and supplies are intertwined with those that balance flows of commodities and labor.

Several kinds of government policies affect the real and financial outcomes. Budget policies determine government purchases of goods and services, transfer payments, and taxes. In addition to their direct effects on commodity markets, these policies help to determine the government deficit and the new supplies of government liabilities. Financial and monetary policies determine how the deficit is financed, in particular by what combination of monetary issue and nonmonetary debt. In addition, the government may refinance its existing debt, and in particular the central bank may change the monetary issue by open market operations in outstanding government securities. Other relevant government policies are less aggregative and more structural; reserve requirements on banks and other financial institutions; regulation of interest rates on central bank or government assets or liabilities, and on intermediary liabilities to the public; specific taxes or tax credits, for example, with respect to investments, depreciation, capital gains and losses, property incomes.

Expectations about next quarter and many future quarters affect the current saving, investment, and portfolio behavior of economic agents. The relevant variables include commodity prices, asset prices, business profits, unemployment, government policies—any variables on which the outcomes of intertemporal decisions depend. Expectations, and the confidence with which they are held, vary among agents. In some degree, they are formed by previous experience; in some degree they depend on current economic performance.

The horizons relevant to current economic behavior differ markedly among households and among business firms. At one extreme are immortal institutions like Harvard and Yale, whose current expenditures are the outcome of calculations of indefinitely sustainable consumption, whose future receipts are so fungible forward and backward in time that it is only their present value that matters. At the other extreme are households, often poor or young or both, and businesses, often new or small or both, without cashable assets or lines of credit. Their current expenditures for goods and services, consumption or investment, are constrained by their cash receipts in the same quarter. There are many intermediate cases, including consumers whose horizons range from a few years to a lifetime. But the presence of both wealth-constrained and liquidity-constrained agents is a fact of considerable economic significance. Expectations, particularly those concerned with a long future, are more important for those for whom liquidity is not a binding constraint. Liquidity-bound consumers and businesses will spend all their disposable resources over a few quarters anyway. Thus we should not be surprised if both permanent income and current cash income are important for aggregate consumption, and for its response to temporary tax reductions and transfers. Likewise we should not be surprised if current cash flow, as well as long-run calculation of profitability, affects business investment.

Our objective is to model the process of asset accumulation and economic activity just sketched and to estimate models of this type for the United States. With such an empirical model, government policies, structural changes, institutional innovations, and demographic or technological trends can be simulated to estimate shorter- and longer-run consequences. Emphasis on financial markets and institutions permits systematic examination of financial policies and innovations, and of the financial consequences of other policies and developments. Consistent tracking of asset stocks is necessary to answer questions about the long-run impacts of short-run cyclical fluctuations and stabilization policies on capital accumulation.

Here is a sample of questions which the projected model is designed to address:

Effects of government budget deficits and debt. Do they crowd out or crowd in private capital formation? How does the answer to this question depend on the length of time allowed for the economy to adapt, on the degree of slack in resource utilization, and on the mixture of monetary and nonmonetary financing of the deficit? How do debt management and monetary policies, changing the relative supplies of government bonds of long maturity, government obligations of short maturity, and base money, affect the structure of interest rates and the paths of economic activity and prices? Has the historical decline, over the last three decades, in federal debt relative to private debt and equity raised or lowered the cost of capital for real investment? What would happen if this trend continued? How does social security affect private saving and capital formation?

Effects of regulations and innovations on financial intermediation. Structural innovation in financial institutions has proceeded rapidly in recent years, in part causing, and in part caused by, changes in government regulations. Their macroeconomic effects, as well as their consequences for financial variables, are the subject of considerable interest and conjecture. Further changes are in prospect. What are the effects of raising or lifting deposit rate ceilings? What happens when savings deposits, money market funds, overnight loans, and credit or overdraft lines become better and better substitutes for checking accounts?

A model suited to answer questions like these needs certain features that standard macroeconometric models usually do not have, including the following.

1. Disaggregation of assets and agents. Obviously it is difficult to investigate the effects of regulations of financial institutions and assets—interest rate ceilings, quantitative restrictions, reserve requirements, etc.—unless the specific institutions and assets are distinctly recognized in the model.

2. An explicit supply/demand modeling of asset markets and yield structures. As a rule, empirical models rely on historically estimated chains of relationships of yields—by maturity, risk class, and other differentiations—to determine yield structures. That procedure forecloses any possibility of altering rate relationships by changes in relative asset supplies.

2 Framework for Accounting and Analysis

The accounting framework is simple. Consider a matrix in which rows i represent assets or commodities (e.g., currency, government bonds, equities, consumption goods, labor services), and columns j represent

Table 3.1
Theoretical Model, Uses—Sources of Funds

		A Households	F Financial Intermediaries	J Nonfinancial Business	Government		Within-Period Endogenous Variable
1.	H base money	$PA^H(\cdot) - H^A_{-1}$	$+pD + (1-\rho)Df^H(\cdot) - H^F_{-1}$		$-\gamma_H(P(G-T) + bB_{-1}) - Z_H$	$= 0$	Y or P
2.	D deposits	$PA^D(\cdot) - D_{-1}$	$-(D - D_{-1})$				D
3.	B government bonds	$PA^B(\cdot) - P_B B^A_{-1}$	$+(1-\rho)Df^B(\cdot) - P_B B^F_{-1}$		$-\gamma_B(P(G-T) + bB_{-1}) - Z_B$	$= 0$	r_B
4.	E equity	$PA^E(\cdot) - P_E E^A_{-1}$	$-(PF^E(\cdot) - P^F_E E^F_{-1})$	$-(PJ^E(\cdot) - P^J_E E^J_{-1})$		$= 0$	r_E
5.	L loans	$PA^L(\cdot) - L^A_{-1}$	$+PF^L + (1-\rho)Df^L(\cdot) - L^F_{-1}$	$-(PJ^L(\cdot) - L^J_{-1})$		$= 0$	r_L
6.	IS equation	$-saving$	0	$+net\ investment$	$+government\ deficit$	$= 0$	
		$-P_{\Sigma}A^S + \Sigma P_S S^A_{-1}$	0	$+PI(q_K, K_{-1}) - Pq_K\delta K_{-1}$	$+P(G-T) + bB_{-1}$	$= 0$	
7.	Interest and dividends	$-R_{E_{-1}}PE^A_{-1} - r_{L_{-1}}PL^A_{-1} - bB^A_{-1}$	$-R_{E_{-1}}PE^F_{-1} - r_{L_{-1}}PL^F_{-1}$	$+RPK_{-1}$	$+bB_{-1}$	$= 0$	
		$(= -RPK_{-1} - bB^A_{-1})$	$+bB^F_{-1}$				
8.	Taxes and transfers	PT			$-PT$	$= 0$	
9.	Labor	$-Nw$		$+Nw$		$= 0$	
10.	Goods	PC		$P(-Y + I)$	$+PG$	$= 0$	
	Sum 1 to 6 =	0	0	0	0		
	Sum (1 to 5) + (7 to 10) =	0	0	0	0		

Table 3.2
Empirical Model, Uses—Sources of Funds; 1977 Flows at Annual Rates (End-of-year Stocks)

		Household	Commercial Banking	Savings Institutions	Insurance & Pension Funds	Miscellaneous Intermediaries	Businesses	Federal Government	State & Local Governments	Rest of the World	Discrepancies	Sum	Within-period Endogenous Variable
1.	Currency and reserves	8.3* (89.9)	3.3† (40.5)					−11.6 (−130.4)				= 0	Y or P
2.	Demand deposits	11.3 (114.6)	−23.2 (−276.4)	0.8 (4.7)	0.8 (7.7)	0.2 (5.9)	1.3 (74.5)	4.4 (7.0)	0.9 (14.1)	1.9 (18.4)	1.6 (29.6)	= 0	time deposits at commercial banks
3.	Time deposits at commercial banks	39.2 (428.8)	−42.6 (−473.3)					0.1 (0.9)	4.2 (41.6)	1.4 (11.4)	−2.4 (−9.4)	= 0	time deposits at commercial banks
4.	Time deposits at savings institutions	69.1 (563.0)		−69.1 (−563.0)								= 0	time deposits at savings institutions
5.	Shorts	13.1 (−52.9)	−28.7‡ (−40.6)	3.9 (29.0)	5.2 (20.3)	−7.2 (−32.5)	−3.3 (−45.2)	−18.0 (−193.1)	15.4 (51.9)	17.4 (57.9)	2.4 (9.4)	= 0	short rate
6.	Longs	5.9 (193.0)	13.1 (205.5)	5.0 (67.0)	52.8 (382.2)	−9.3 (−35.9)	−24.6 (−302.2)	−51.6 (−327.3)	−12.5 (−215.7)	21.2 (33.4)		= 0	long rate
7.	Equity§ Purchases	33.5	−0.6	0.4	−8.9	−2.5	−28.7			7.0		= 0	equity rate
	Capital Gains**	−82.8 (−777.0)	−4.8 (−57.5)	−0.0 (4.8)	−4.6 (−137.7)	−0.2 (−8.7)	102.3 (−893.0)			−10.2 (−39.7)			
8.	Nonmarketables	51.5 (726.7)			−40.1 (−588.7)			−11.4 (−138.1)				= 0	household nonmarketables
9.	Mortgages	−82.4 (−568.9)	27.7 (179.0)	62.0 (462.3)	6.1 (108.1)	−0.9 (15.1)	−37.0 (−349.6)	23.9 (139.5)	0.6 (14.7)			= 0	mortgage rate
10.	Loans	−49.8 (−368.1)	47.9 (426.1)	5.6 (44.4)	3.7 (46.8)	20.6 (78.4)	−26.8 (−208.4)	5.1 (76.2)	−1.2 (−21.2)	−1.8 (−38.7)	−3.4 (−35.4)	= 0	loans at commercial banks
11.	Miscellaneous	6.6 (−52.6)	7.9 (−3.3)	−3.9 (−9.4)	−14.9 (−114.0)	−0.7 (−22.2)	20.8 (158.8)	4.7 (67.6)	1.1 (10.6)	−25.3 (−121.4)	3.7 (−19.3)	= 0	[exogenous]
12.	Financial net worth	23.6 (2061.5)	0.0 (0.0)	4.6 (39.9)	0.0 (0.0)	0.0 (0.0)	4.1 (−1474.7)	54.3 (−497.7)	8.5 (−104.2)	11.7 (0.3)	1.8 (−25.1)	= 0	

13.	Capital gains	8.28	4.8	0.0	4.6	0.2	−102.3	0.1	0.0	10.2	0.4	= 0
14.	Net financial saving	106.4	4.8	4.6	4.6	0.2	−98.2	−54.2	8.5	21.9	1.4	= 0
15.	Discrepancy	−30.1		−8.8			30.4	2.8	7.9	−1.0	−1.4	= 0
16.	Investment less saving	−76.3		−5.4			67.8	51.4	−16.4	−20.9	0.0	= 0
17.	Interest, dividends and retained earnings	−194.0		0.0			176.9	29.1	−6.5	−5.5		= 0
	Interest and dividends	−156.2		0.0			139.1	29.1	−6.5	−5.5		= 0
	Retained earnings (net of depreciation)**	−37.8		0.0			37.8	—	—	—		= 0
18.	Taxes and transfers	79.1		12.9			313.1	−201.7	−199.1	−4.2		= 0
	Taxes	287.1		12.9			303.4	−374.5	−228.8	—		= 0
	Transfers	−207.9		—			9.6	172.7	29.7	−4.2		= 0
19.	Labor	−1196.3		—			988.4	66.4	141.5	—		= 0
20.	Goods and services	1288.6		6.2			−1679.2 +209.6[∥]	78.6	107.4	−11.1		= 0
21.	Miscellaneous	−53.7		−24.5			59.0	79.0	−59.8	—		= 0
Sum (1–11) +13 +15 + Sum (17–21) = 12 + 13 + 15 + 16 = 0		0	0	0	0	0	0	0	0	0	0	= 0

Sources: Flow-of-funds and National Income and Product Accounts.

* Currency held by the nonbank public has been allocated entirely to households.
† Bank reserves include required reserves of 3.8 (40.9) and net free reserves of −0.5 (−0.4).
‡ Bank holdings of shorts include assets of −4.5 (65.5) and liabilities of −24.3 (−106.1).
§ The equity liability of commercial banks, insurance and pension funds, and miscellaneous financial intermediaries are taken to be equal to the financial net worth reported by these institutions.
∥ Purchases of goods and services by business are that sector's gross physical investment. They are consequently included in business (−) and household (+) savings.
** Retained earnings of businesses (37.8) are treated as issues of equity to households.

economic sectors (e.g., households, commercial banks, nonfinancial businesses, governments, rest of the world). An entry x_{ij} then represents the net purchases—a negative entry means net sales—of the item during a particular quarter, or any time period. If the matrix is a complete closed system, each row and each column must sum to zero. A row accounts for all sectors' sales and purchases of a particular item, and they must balance. A column accounts for a single sector's purchases and sales of all items, and these also must balance. This format can accommodate any desired degree of disaggregation, varying the numbers of sectors and items. Tables 3.1 and 3.2 are illustrative.

The accounting framework comes to life as an economic model when the entries x_{ij}, at least some of them, become variables to be explained by the behavior of the sector. The rows, at least some of them, are then interpreted as markets, and the zero sums of these equations become conditions determining the values of some variables rather than merely ex post accounting identities. In general, a matrix of N rows will provide $N - 1$ independent equations and permit their simultaneous solution for $N - 1$ variables. These are the within-period endogenous variables of the model. If the period is a quarter, each of these variables is assumed to take on one and only one value each quarter, a value that is determined during that quarter.

The equation system describes these within-period endogenous variables as functions of (1) predetermined endogenous variables, state variables whose values for this period were fixed prior to the current period, whose values for next period will depend on this period's outcomes and (2) exogenous variables, whose values do not depend systematically on the outcomes of the system in either the current period or previous periods; these include (*a*) settings of policy instruments, (*b*) nonpolicy variables whose values, like those of policy instruments, must be known or assumed, and (*c*) random shocks drawn from probability distributions whose parameters must be assumed or estimated.

The most important predetermined endogenous variables, in our applications, are stocks of financial and real assets. The single-period model determines the increment to each stock, and thus fixes its new value for the next period. The stock-flow identities are auxiliary equations needed to track the economy from period to period. A long-run equilibrium is one in which stocks are in some sense stationary, i.e., their dollar values are all constant from period to period or are all growing by the same percentage.

Other variables might be treated as predetermined endogenous, if it were thought that their proximate determinants were all lagged by one period or more. For example, it might be convenient and reasonable to regard wages and prices as dependent on employment and output last period but not on contemporaneous measures of economic activity.

3 A Theoretical Model

Later in this paper we explain how we try to build an empirical model of the U.S. economy in the spirit of the previous section. But the architectural design may be clearer if we set it forth formally in a condensed and simplified theoretical model.

Imagine that there are (*a*) four sectors: households, financial intermediaries, businesses, and government; (*b*) five assets: high-powered money (currency and bank reserves), bank deposits, government bonds, business equity, and business loans; and (*c*) one commodity.

This model is summarized in Table 3.1. The four sectors define the columns. The first five rows refer to assets[1] available in this economy. The sixth row is the negative of the sum of the first five; thus over these six rows each column sums to zero. The sixth row is actually the well-known *IS* equation. It says:

−Household Saving + Business Investment + Government Deficit = 0.

The remaining rows are simply auxiliary accounts. They add nothing to the formal analysis. They also sum to the *IS* equation of row six. Indeed the final row, the tenth, is simply the national product equation, an alternative version of *IS*.

All the entries in Table 3.1 are purchases or sales during a discrete period of time, say a quarter or a year. The subscript −1 denotes variables predetermined at the end of the previous period, the subscript +1 the expected values of variables next period. Otherwise the variables are those of the current period. All the cell entries are in current dollars.

Households

The functions $A^S(\cdot)$ ($S = H, D, B, E, L$) tell the real amounts of asset S desired at the end of the period. The corresponding nominal quantity is

PA^S. From this is subtracted $P_S S^A_{-1}$, the dollar value of households' initial holdings of the asset at current period asset prices P_S. The difference is specific saving in the asset S, and the sum of the five items is total household saving in current dollars. The functions $A^S(\cdot)$ will all contain the same arguments. These will include (1) the vector of real yields r_S on the five assets, taking account of expectations of capital gain or loss, (2) the predetermined asset holdings, (3) some set or combination (like disposable income) of the items determining net receipts in rows 7–9 and the expectations of these items. As the sum of specific saving functions, total household saving will depend on the same list of variables.

In the bottom rows the income account is given. The convention is that business produces the entire real gross national product Y, retains I for replacement and net investment, and sells $C + G$ to other sectors. The real earnings RK_{-1}, net of depreciation, are distributed in dividends (R_E per equity share) and in loan interest, and Nw/P is paid to households for labor. Note that R_E includes only earnings on equity distributed as dividends or retained, whereas r_E—the yield relevant for portfolio and saving decisions—includes expected capital gains or losses as well.

Similarly, the income payment from government bonds in row 7 is simply the coupon, while the yield r_B relevant for portfolio and saving decisions depends also on expectations of bond prices and commodity prices.

$$\frac{P_B}{P}(1 + r_B) = \frac{b + P_{B+1}}{P_{+1}} = \frac{b + P_{B+1}}{P(1 + \pi_{+1})}. \tag{1}$$

If P_B is expected to remain unchanged, it will be equal to

$$\frac{b}{r_B \pi_{+1} + \pi_{+1} r_B} \approx \frac{b}{r_B + \pi_{+1}}.$$

Financial intermediaries

The financial intermediaries column in Table 3.1 exemplifies a number of the problems in modeling such institutions. In a practical model there would be several such columns. Here banks are taken to be representative financial intermediaries. They receive deposits and equity investments from the public, make loans to business, hold some government bonds, and hold some reserves in base money. The balance sheet in current dollars is:

Equity $P_E^F E^F$ + Deposits D = Loans L^F + Bonds $P_B B^F$ + Reserves H^F. Here it is assumed, in conformity with U.S. institutions, that the nominal interest rate on deposits is legally fixed; indeed it is taken to be zero, though it could be any other number. At this rate, banks would gladly accept more deposits but are not permitted to bid for them. Therefore the quantity of deposits D is simply PA^D, the quantity the public desires at existing rates. Required reserves are a prior claim of ρD and the disposable deposits $(1 - \rho)D$ are a (negative) prior claim, distributed among loans, government bonds, and net free reserves in the fractions f^L, f^B, and f^H, which identically sum to 1. These fractions are functions of the rates r_L and r_B, the reserve requirement ρ, and the central bank's discount rate. In Table 3.1 it is assumed that the loan interest rate r_L adjusts to clear the market. Another, and perhaps more realistic possibility in some past periods, is that banks regard business loans as a prior claim on their disposable funds and meet these demands at the prevailing rate, only later adjusting this rate in the direction that brings loan demand closer to the banks' desired supply.

Bank equity is taken in row 4 to be a perfect substitute for equity in nonfinancial business, a questionable simplification that could be avoided by further disaggregation of assets. The item in row 7 simply says that all real interest earnings are distributed as dividends to banks' shareowners.

Nonfinancial business

The balance sheet, in current dollars, is Equity $P_E^J E^J$ + Loans L^J = Capital $q_K PK$. Business holdings of financial assets, including money, are ignored. Loans are for one period, are denominated in dollars, and bear a nominal interest rate $r_L + \pi_{+1}$.

The business sector's desired increase in equity liability to shareowners during the period is $PJ^E - P_E^J E_{-1}^J$. Increases in equity occur either by issue of shares or by retention of earnings; retained earnings are considered as dividends paid matched by sales of shares. Businesses' desired increase in loan liability is $PJ^L - L_{-1}^J$. Loans are representative of several kinds of debt that would be distinguished in a more complete model for empirical application. Both are expressed in current prices. These two items must sum to $PJ^K - Pq_K K_{-1}$, which is equal to net investment $Pq_K \Delta K$. The necessary real gross investment I is $q_K(\Delta K + \delta K_{-1})$. The sector has two decisions, investment and financial structure. The latter could be further analyzed into two subchoices: how to finance its new investment, as between loans and equity, and whether and how to refinance its initial capital stock.

Because of the balance sheet identity, P_E and Pq_K are not independent:

$$P_E = \frac{Pq_K K_{-1} - L_{-1}}{E^J_{-1}}. \tag{2}$$

They are positively related by the leverage factor K_{-1}/E^J_{-1}. We can also use the balance sheet to show the relation of ΔE to ΔK and ΔL:

$$\left. \begin{array}{l} P_E \Delta E^J = Pq_K \Delta K - \Delta L \\ \Delta E^J = \dfrac{Pq_K \Delta K - \Delta L}{PE} = \dfrac{Pq_K \Delta K - \Delta L}{Pq^K_{K_{-1}} - L_{-1}} \cdot E^J_{-1} \end{array} \right\} \tag{3}$$

This equation tells how to track the quantity E^J, whether new shares are issued or earnings are retained, whether retained earnings are invested or used to repay debt, and so on.

Equity owners will receive in aggregate real dividends of R_{E+1} per share, equal to $R_{+1}K - r_L L/P$. But r_E, the real one-period return on equity at market price, also depends on what happens to equity prices relative to commodity prices:

$$\begin{aligned} 1 + r_E &= \frac{R_{+1}K - r_L L/P + (P_{E+1}/P_{+1})E}{(P_E/P)E} \\ &= \frac{R_{+1}K - r_L L/P}{q_K K + L/P} + \frac{P_{E+1}/P_{+1}}{P_E/P}. \end{aligned} \tag{4}$$

Thus

$$q_K = \frac{R_{+1}}{r_E + v} + \frac{L}{PK}\left(1 - \frac{r_L}{r_E + v}\right), \tag{5}$$

where $v = 1 - (P_{E+1}/P_{+1})/(P_E/P)$. Here v is less than zero if equity prices are expected to rise faster than commodity prices and is greater than zero if they are expected to rise more slowly. Normally v is negative, approximately equal to $-(l/1-l)\rho$, where l is the debt-to-capital ratio, and ρ is the rate of commodity inflation. Equation (5) connects q_K to r_E and r_L and to expected earnings of capital R. As shown in Table 3.1, q_K in turn is a major determinant of business investment, for reasons the authors have argued elsewhere [15, 16]. Given investment, the business sector will choose financing by reference to the real rates r_E and r_L.

Government

The government purchases goods in real amount G, collects taxes T in real terms, and pays interest on its bonds of bB_{-1}/P in real terms. The bonds are consols paying \$$b$ every period. The budget deficit in dollars $PG - PT + bB_{-1}$ is financed in fraction γ_B by selling bonds at their current market price P_B and in fraction γ_H, by printing high-powered money ($\gamma_H + \gamma_B = 1$). In addition, the government may engage in open market operations, selling bonds in amount \$$Z_B$ for money in amount $-\$Z_H$ ($Z_B + Z_H = 0$). Taxes are net of transfers and may be modeled as endogenous, dependent on incomes, production, consumption, and other current variables. Thus the policy instruments of government are G, the parameters of T, γ_H and Z_H. In addition, the central bank can change the reserve requirement ρ and its discount rate.

The model presented in Table 3.1 does not do justice to taxation. If taxes apply to rates of return, variation of tax rates will affect the portfolio, saving, and investment behavior central to the model. These substitutions effects are additional to the permanent or transitory disposable income effects of changes in taxes or transfers, which are essentially lump-sum changes so long as labor supply is not modeled as sensitive to after-tax wages.

The one-period model

The model of Table 3.1 has five independent equations, most conveniently and symmetrically the first five rows. Asset prices appearing in the five equations can be expressed in terms of real interest rates by using the auxiliary formulas (1) and (4). These equations will determine five within-period endogenous variables. Several choices are possible, among them:

1. A Keynesian model (r_E, r_L, r_B, D, Y)
2. A classical model (r_E, r_L, r_B, D, P)
3. A Phillips model (r_E, r_L, r_B, D, Y, P), adding a within-period relationship of P and Y.

In addition to parameters of government policy, variables exogenous for the one-period solution would include expectations of future commodity and asset prices or of their rates of change.

The comparative statics of solutions to models of this type are qualitatively quite robust. The standard IS/LM conclusions for fiscal and monetary effects on Y and/or P apply [14]. The one-period solutions change over time as asset stocks change. They can be tracked in principle, and in practice with numerical parameter values, but the dynamics are usually analytically intractable.

4 The Empirical Model: Balance Equations and Endogenous Variables

The model we are currently trying to estimate and simulate has the general structure of the theoretical model just reviewed, but is more disaggregated. Its coverage is shown in Table 3.2, which follows the same format as Table 3.1. We have aggregated the flow-of-funds data compiled by the Federal Reserve Board into the first fourteen rows of Table 3.2. The flows comprise the bulk of financial saving, lending, and borrowing, and they augment the stocks of financial assets and liabilities. Capital gains and losses—in practice estimated primarily for equity—are also shown in rows 7 and 13. They account for the difference between the increase of net worth (row 12) and the amount of "net financial saving" (row 14).

"Net financial investment" represents the algebraic sum of the previous rows. It is in principle the IS row, as in Table 3.1. As in that table, this row could also be reached by summing nonfinancial receipts and outlays. These entries are in rows 17 through 21, and their sum is in row 16 as "investment less saving." In principle, this is the same as row 14 with sign reversed. In fact there are statistical discrepancies, shown in row 15.

As in Table 3.1, business retained earnings, net of depreciation, are imputed to shareowners, mainly households, as if they were dividends. They are shown separately in row 17. This means that "investment less saving" of business is just net investment, as it should be in the IS equation. The retention of earnings also appears in other columns, mainly households, as saving. Correspondingly, above line 15, retention of earnings is an issue of equity by business and a purchase of equity by households and other shareowners.

In Table 3.2 we show only one commodity row and one labor row. Thus the "real" side of the economy is disaggregated less than the financial side, a reversal of the usual emphasis in macroeconometric models.

Work in process, however, is intended to disaggregate commodity and labor markets further. The commodity row of Table 3.2 attributes all gross production to the business sector. That sector keeps part of it, for gross fixed investment and inventory accumulation, and sells the rest to the other sectors. In the labor row, households supply worker-hours to the other sectors.

The first 10 rows of Table 3.2, plus the "*IS*" row 16, provide eleven equations of a model similar to the theoretical model described in the previous section. (Rows 12 and 13 are memoranda concerning the previous rows, but provide no independent information. Row 11—"miscellaneous"—can be taken as exogenous.)

There will be ten within-period endogenous variables. One choice of this list, not the only possible one, is given in the final column of the table. Each variable appears in the row with which it is most naturally associated—even though in principle all variables are involved simultaneously in the clearing of each market. Thus market-determined rates of return or asset prices are associated with the assets to which they refer. For some rows, quantities rather than prices are assumed to make the within-period adjustments. This occurs for financial assets on which interest rates are legally regulated (deposits) or are institutionally slow to adjust (bank loans).

The markets corresponding to the rows always "clear" ex post; actual transactions net to zero. But we distinguish between transactions realized ex post and transactions desired ex ante at the prevailing values of the within-period endogenous variables—prices, interest rates, incomes, etc. In some markets, those which we will label "cleared," these variables adjust so that realized and desired transactions coincide. In "noncleared" markets, some agents will be unable fully to execute desired transactions. (Smith and Brainard [10] discuss the modeling and estimation of rationed markets.) In Table 3.2 demand deposits are identified as a noncleared market. With the nominal interest rate on deposits restricted by law, banks generally stand willing to accept more deposits than are offered. Likewise the rates of returns on savings accounts are exogenously restricted by rate ceilings; in these markets too the institutions generally accept all deposits. However, there have been some periods of time when the ceilings were not effective and these markets were cleared by the deposit rates. Nonmarketable securities are similarly modeled. They are principally savings bonds available on tap from the federal Treasury. Thus in the short run the government's issues adjust to other sectors' demands.

Bank loans to business are also treated as an "uncleared" market. This is appropriate for most of the sample period to which a model may be fitted, although it seems less realistic today. Here the reason was not legal regulation but the behavior of the banking industry. In the short run, banks had explicit or implicit credit line commitments to their business customers, which they felt compelled to honor at going rates. Subsequently, if meeting these demands leads to more lending than the banks desire, the loan rate was increased. Or it was lowered if banks found themselves with too few loans. This adjustment of the loan rate, and administered price, we model as taking place between periods. The loan rate is another predetermined endogenous variable, and its adjustment is another transitional equation.

Going below row 16, we are implicitly treating the markets for labor and commodities as noncleared. Wages are determined by Phillips curve equations describing the sticky period-to-period adjustment for wages to labor market disequilibria. The labor market is "cleared" by workers' accepting what jobs are offered. Commodity transactions are also demand-determined within any period. Between periods prices move to keep up with normal unit labor costs, but with some sensitivity to demand pressures in the previous period.

An alternative formulation for any or all of these three noncleared markets would make both quantities and prices endogenous within a period. For example, the wage adjustment could depend in part on the contemporaneous excess supply, while the adjustment would not be sufficient to clear the market. The Phillips curve would then be another equation in the one-period model. In the extreme "classical" regime, markets would be cleared by flexible money wages and prices; therefore price P would replace output Y as an endogenous variable.

Rows 17, 18, and 21, which complete the accounts, are not really markets, and there are no prices that naturally correspond to the items. In the case of private transfers, households' receipts are taken to adjust passively to other sectors' outlays. In the case of taxes net of government transfers, transactions depend on the tax code and on existing laws defining entitlements to transfers. Given the legislation determining sectors' net tax liabilities, we can regard the row as determining the government's net receipts. Dividends and interest payments reflect predetermined asset positions and contractual obligations. Since these positions balance out, the payments and receipts based on them automatically sum to zero.

5 The Empirical Model: Sectors and Their Behavior

Columns refer to sectors. In this dimension, too, the model builder has discretion, within data limitations, about the degree of disaggregation. For each sector, the column entries sum to zero, as in Table 3.2.

In Table 3.2 four financial sectors are distinguished, in keeping with our emphasis on financial disaggregation. Indeed further disaggregation would be desirable. For example, for purposes of modeling monetary policy, the behavioral differences between money market banks and other commercial banks are important.

The key nonfinancial sectors are those for households, business, and federal government. With respect to households, there are several possible directions of useful disaggregation. One would be to segregate the entities like personal trusts and nonprofit organizations now lumped together with families and individual consumers. Another would be to make distinctions by age or other demographic characteristics. The split that we regard as most important, for reasons argued above, is between liquidity-constrained and wealth-constrained households. We are trying to implement this distinction empirically, in ways described elsewhere [12].

In the case of nonfinancial business, separate columns for corporate and noncorporate business would be desirable for some purposes. Corporations are the originators of equities and other financial claims for which market valuations are available. Another direction of disaggregation, columns for different industries, would be associated with addition of rows for different commodities.

For these sectors, financial institutions, households, and business, the column entries are to be explained by behavioral equations. The federal government column is partially exogenous, so far as purchases, transfer rules, tax functions, monetary policies, and debt issue are concerned. Budget outcomes are endogenous because realized outlays and revenues depend not only on policies but also on economic performance during the period. Other sectors—state and local governments and rest of world—

should be similarly modeled. At the current stage of the model under construction, these three sectors are lumped together as a completely exogenous column. For example, federal bonds, state and local bonds, and foreign bonds enter simply as exogenously supplied long-term marketable bonds.

Behavioral equations for financial institutions, households, and business follow general principles familiar from previous papers by the authors. For each sector we identify those "prior claims" that the sector takes as exogenous for the period. This quantity constrains its decisions about other entries in the column. It consists of items that are predetermined by earlier decisions or by inherited stocks—e.g., interest receipts or payments—or by the decisive side of noncleared markets—e.g., deposits as seen from banks' standpoint. Subject to the budget constraint imposed by these prior claims, a sector is imagined to formulate long-run target asset and wealth positions, based on current and expected interest rates, incomes, and other relevant variables. Actual positions are then adjusted towards these targets. Transitory factors, like windfall gains and losses, will also influence these adjustments.

In relating sectoral portfolio choices to asset yields, our general presumption is that our broad asset categories are gross substitutes. That is, an increase in an asset's yield increases the demand for the asset itself and decreases demand for others individually and collectively. In estimations, our priors conform to this presumption, but the final estimates are not constrained to do so.

In some cases it is convenient to imagine agents who make decisions sequentially or hierarchically. The substantive content of a hierarchical approach is that simplifying restrictions are placed on the explanatory variables. In principle, every entry in a column should depend on the same list of explanatory variables. In a hierarchical model, a sequence of simplified decisions are specified. For example, the consumption-saving decision might be assumed not to depend upon the fine detail of asset yields and inherited holdings that influence portfolio decisions, but on an average yield and on total initial wealth. The portfolio allocation might then be based upon asset yields, inherited holdings, and available saving, but not on some of the separate factors (such as income expectations, relative commodity prices, and demographic detail) which motivated that saving. Although theory tells us that separations of this type are legitimate only under rather strong assumptions, there is often a compelling need for plausible rough approximations in empirical work. In the current version of the model households have been depicted as first allocating income between consumption and savings and then making an independent allocation of the saving among the several assets. Similarly business firms have been described as making production and investment decisions separately from financing decisions. The Purvis-Smith discussion [7, 8] is concerned with the gains and costs of a hierarchical approach. The Backus-Purvis paper [1] espouses and implements an integrated model of household expenditure and financial decisions, which will be used in later versions of the empirical model.

6 Specification and Estimation of Asset Demand Equations

At the first stage in developing the empirical model described above, we have focused our attention on the financial markets corresponding to the first ten rows of Table 3.2. Understanding the behavior of these markets is crucial to understanding the response of the economy to policy actions and various shocks that impinge directly on financial sectors. A distinctive feature of the financial block of the model is that separate supply and demand equations are specified for a relatively large number of assets rather than relying on explicit aggregation or rate structure equations to reduce the dimensionality of the model. Such simplifying assumptions and restrictions are probably harmless for some purposes, but they beg many of the questions we would like to address. For example, with a term structure equation the ability of monetary and fiscal authorities permanently to alter the relative rates of return among financial and physical assets is ruled out a priori.

Similarly, debt accumulation for capital formation—crowding out or crowding in—and financial innovations or changes in regulations have consequences that depend crucially on the quantitative magnitudes of the substitution relationships among assets.

In this section we describe the specification and estimation of the asset demand and supply equations for households, commercial banks, savings institutions, and insurance and pension funds. These estimated equations will, in principle, allow us to simulate the response of financial variables —rates and quantities—to changes in exogenous supplies of and demands for assets of the other sectors—government, rest of the world, and business.

Asset Demand Specification

Although the various sectors demand and supply different assets, liabilities, and commodities, we have assumed that the equations that describe sectoral behavior have the same general form. Each sector's assets have been divided into two groups according to whether or not the items are directly controlled by the sector. This division differs from sector to sector, and in the short and long runs.

In the case of financial intermediaries—commercial banks, savings institutions, and insurance and pension funds—the controlled flows reflect portfolio decisions about the allocation of a predetermined aggregate of prior claims. In particular a typical intermediary is constrained by:

$$\sum_{i=1}^{n} a_i = W = NW - \sum_{i=1}^{n} R_i,$$

where the a_i are directly controlled financial items constrained to be equal to total disposable assets (W) equal to net worth minus prior claims R_i. (Predetermined liabilities, e.g., bank deposits, are a negative prior claim.)

We have separated the portfolio decision into two parts: determination of a long-run desired portfolio and short-run adjustment to that portfolio. Each sector's long-run portfolio allocation is assumed to depend upon such variables as rates of return, income, and the expected quantity of disposable assets:

$$\frac{a^*}{W^e} = Ax. \tag{6}$$

a^* is an n-dimensional vector of desired holdings; W^e is expected disposable assets; x is a k-dimensional vector of explanatory variables, with $x_1 = 1$; and A is the $n \times k$ matrix of long-run coefficients. If desired demands are required to satisfy the balance sheet identity, then

$$1 = \Sigma \, a_i^* / W^e = \sum_{i=1}^{n} A_{i1} + \sum_{j=2}^{k} \left(\sum_{i=1}^{n} A_{ij} \right) x_j$$

can hold for all values of x_j if and only if

$$\sum_{i=1}^{n} A_{i1} = 1$$

$$\sum_{i=1}^{n} A_{ij} = 0 \quad j = 2, \ldots, k.$$

That is, an increase in disposable assets must be held somewhere, and a change in any proportion must be at the expense of the remaining proportions.

It is assumed that the short-run asset demand functions take the familiar partial-adjustment form. However, our specification differs in two respects from the type frequently assumed. First, the adjustment of any particular asset depends, in principle, on a complete description of the short-run disequilibrium. For example, the speed with which a discrepancy between desired and actual holdings of bonds is eliminated depends upon whether the bond disequilibrium is the counterpart of a discrepancy between desired and actual holdings of cash, or desired and actual mortgages. Second, consistency requires that the variables that give rise to partial adjustment in the demand for one asset must give rise to offsetting adjustments in the demand for other assets, given the constraint on disposable assets. Thus the equations are of the form:

$$\Delta a = \underset{n \times n}{E} [a^* - a_{-1}] + \underset{n \times p}{F} (S - S^e) + \underset{n \times q}{G} z \;, \tag{7}$$

where the z are q explanatory variables that are thought to influence adjustment behavior directly and the $S_i - S_i^e$ are the sources of unanticipated changes in disposable assets (such as unplanned saving or unexpected capital gains) with $\Sigma(S_i - S_i^e) - W - W^e$.

The E_{ij} can be interpreted as the partial effects on holdings of the ith asset of a unit increase in $W^e - W_{-1}$ (and $W - W_{-1}$) which the sector desires to hold as the jth asset. The E_{ij} will sum across equations to one. E_{ij} is the partial effect on holdings of the ith asset of a unit increase in $S_j - S_j^e$ with $W^e - W_{-1}$ constant and $W - W^e$ increasing by one unit. The F_{ij} will therefore sum across equations to one. Finally, the G_{ij} will sum to zero since $W - W_{-1}$ is held constant.

Savings Institutions
Table 3.3 through 3.5 contain the structural equations and coefficient estimates for the three financial intermediaries. The specification of

Table 3.3
Savings Institutions

			Interest Rate Responses				
Dependence Variable	1	D66	$\ln(RSHORT)$	$\ln(RLONG)$	$\ln(RMORT)$	$\ln(RLOAN)$	$\ln\dfrac{RE}{RSHORT}$

A. Short-run Estimates

$\Delta DDC/W^e$
prior	none	0.0000	−0.0153	0.0090	−0.0150	−0.0017	0.0006
OLS	0.3298	0.0064	−0.0023	−0.0133	0.0060	−0.0003	−0.0091*
mixed	0.1897	0.0091	−0.0001	−0.0146	0.0096	0.0016	0.0013

$\Delta SHORT/W^e$
prior	none	0.0000	0.0195	−0.0030	−0.0450	−0.0127	0.0126
OLS	0.8347*	−0.0044	0.0018	0.0204*	−0.0244*	0.0005	0.0020
mixed	0.3190	−0.0068	0.0066	−0.0023	0.0176	−0.0016	0.0024

$\Delta LONG/W^e$
prior	none	0.0000	−0.0042	0.0840	−0.0900	−0.0010	−0.0068
OLS	0.5124*	−0.0086*	−0.0008	0.0089	−0.0017	−0.0004	−0.0007
mixed	0.2796	−0.0118	−0.0049	0.0175	−0.0168	−0.0016	−0.0046

$\Delta MORT/W^e$
prior	none	0.0000	0.0000	−0.0900	0.1500	−0.0025	−0.0065
OLS	−0.8077*	0.0037	−0.0003	−0.0120	0.0110	0.0003	0.0058
mixed	0.2056	0.0042	−0.0006	−0.0015	−0.0185	−0.0002	0.0002

$\Delta LOAN/W^e$
prior	none	0.0000	0.0000	0.0000	0.0000	0.0180	0.0000
OLS	0.1308	0.0029	0.0015	−0.0041	0.0091	−0.0002	0.0020
mixed	0.0060	0.0053	−0.0009	0.0010	0.0080	0.0019	0.0007

Adjustment Coefficients

	$\frac{\varphi DDC}{W^e}$	$\frac{\varphi SHORT}{W^e}$	$\frac{\varphi LONG}{W^e}$	$\frac{\varphi MORT}{W^e}$	$\frac{\varphi LOAN}{W^e}$	$\frac{\Delta FHLB}{W^e}$	$\frac{W - W^e - \Delta FHLB}{W^e}$
$\Delta DDC/W^e$							
prior	1.0000	0.1500	0.1500	0.1000	0.0500	0.1000	0.3000
OLS	0.8786*	0.4381*	0.2165	0.3157	0.3971	0.3122*	0.1338*
mixed	0.8555	0.2781	0.1342	0.1721	0.3449	0.1586	0.1484
$\Delta SHORT/W^e$							
prior	0.0000	0.8500	0.2500	0.2000	0.0500	0.1000	0.4000
OLS	0.7305*	1.3936*	0.6625*	0.8659*	0.5843*	−0.0669	0.3400*
mixed	0.1050	0.7493	0.3379	0.3606	0.3382	0.0350	0.4163
$\Delta LONG/W^e$							
prior	0.0000	0.0000	0.6000	0.2000	0.0000	0.0000	0.0000
OLS	0.3422	0.2800	0.7921*	0.5135*	0.5441*	−0.0447	0.3080*
mixed	0.0130	−0.0055	0.5356	0.2680	0.0464	−0.0029	0.0764
$\Delta MORT/W^e$							
prior	0.0000	0.0000	0.0000	0.5000	0.0000	0.8000	0.3000
OLS	−0.9826*	−1.1207*	−0.8119*	−0.8411*	−0.7805*	0.7401*	0.1905*
mixed	0.0137	−0.0061	−0.0018	0.1832	0.0465	0.8070	0.3445
$\Delta LOAN/W^e$							
prior	0.0000	0.0000	0.0000	0.0000	0.9000	0.0000	0.0000
OLS	0.0313	0.0089	0.1407	0.1459	0.2551*	0.0593*	0.0278
mixed	0.0128	−0.0158	−0.0059	0.0160	0.2240	0.0022	0.0144

Table 3.3 (continued)

Dependent Variable	1	D66	ln(RSHORT)	ln(RLONG)	ln(RMORT)	ln(RLOAN)	ln $\frac{RE}{RSHORT}$
B. Long-run Estimates							
DDC/W^e							
prior	none	none	−0.0180	0.0000	0.0000	0.0000	0.0000
OLS	0.1143	0.0071	−0.0087	−0.0298	0.0060	0.0002	−0.0125
$SHORT/W^e$							
prior	none	none	0.0250	−0.0200	−0.0500	−0.0150	0.0200
OLS	−0.2675	−0.0202	0.0083	0.0702	−0.0372	−0.0026	−0.0221
$LONG/W^e$							
prior	none	none	−0.0070	0.2000	−0.2500	0.0000	−0.0070
OLS	−0.1185	−0.0443	−0.0029	0.0701	−0.0383	−0.0028	−0.0260
$MORT/W^e$							
prior	none	none	0.0000	−0.1800	0.3000	−0.0050	−0.0130
OLS	1.6312	0.0512	−0.0122	−0.1332	0.0279	0.0098	0.0841
$LOAN/W^e$							
prior	none	none	0.0000	0.0000	0.0000	0.0200	0.0000
OLS	−0.3594	0.0063	0.0154	0.0227	0.0416	−0.0047	−0.0235

Notes: $\Delta X \equiv X - X_{-1}$, $\varphi X \equiv X^* - X_{-1}$ (the actual regressor is $-X_{-1}$). Sample period is 1954.I–1978.III excluding 1966.I (98 observations). D66 = 1 before 1966; 0 1966 and after. Data exclude mutual savings banks prior to 1966.
* t-statistic is greater than 2.0 in absolute value.

Table 3.4
Insurance and Pension Funds

Dependent Variable	1	Interest Rate Responses				
		$\ln(RSHORT)$	$\ln(RLONG)$	$\ln(REQUITY)$	$\ln(RMORT)$	$\ln \frac{RE}{RSHORT}$
A. Short-run Estimates						
$\Delta DDC/W^e$						
prior	none	−0.0135	0.1000	−0.0300	−0.0450	0.0000
OLS	0.0736	−0.0003	−0.0035	0.0005	0.0032	0.0001
mixed	0.0368	−0.0012	−0.0025	0.0000	0.0008	−0.0003
$\Delta SHORT/W^e$						
prior	none	0.0170	0.1000	−0.0300	−0.0450	−0.0140
OLS	0.1400	0.0018	0.0067	−0.0014	−0.0045	0.0034
mixed	0.2255	0.0038	−0.0083	−0.0020	0.0125	0.0029
$\Delta LONG/W^e$						
prior	none	−0.0035	0.4600	−0.1050	−0.2400	0.0140
OLS	0.5490*	−0.0023	0.0107	0.0001	−0.0095	−0.0022
mixed	0.6648	−0.0025	0.0114	0.0025	−0.0069	−0.0007
$\Delta(EQUITY$ $-CGEQ)/W^e$						
prior	none	0.0000	−0.2000	0.2250	−0.0750	0.0000
OLS	0.0866	−0.0039*	0.0012	0.0005	0.0055	−0.0014
mixed	0.0212	−0.0002	−0.0031	−0.0012	0.0032	−0.0004
$\Delta MORT/W^e$						
prior	none	0.0000	−0.4600	−0.0600	0.4050	0.0000
OLS	0.1508*	0.0048*	−0.0152*	0.0003	0.0054	0.0002
mixed	0.0516	0.0003	0.0025	0.0008	−0.0097	−0.0014

Table 3.4 (continued)

	Adjustment Coefficients						
	$\dfrac{\varphi DDC}{W^e}$	$\dfrac{\varphi SHORT}{W^e}$	$\dfrac{\varphi LONG}{W^e}$	$\dfrac{\varphi EQUITY}{W^e}$	$\dfrac{\varphi MORT}{W^e}$	$\dfrac{W - W^e - CGEQ}{W^e}$
$\Delta DDC/W^e$						
prior	1.0000	0.1000	0.1000	0.0000	0.0000	0.2000
OLS	0.2103*	0.0316	0.0792	0.0768	0.0611	0.0678
mixed	0.5130	0.1036	0.0124	0.0344	0.0425	0.0219
$\Delta SHORT/W^e$						
prior	0.0000	0.9000	0.2000	0.1000	0.1000	0.2000
OLS	0.1854*	0.4971*	0.1156	0.1483	0.1780*	0.1402
mixed	0.3001	0.7860	0.2079	0.2362	0.2816	0.2408
$\Delta LONG/W^e$						
prior	0.0000	0.0000	0.7000	0.3000	0.2000	0.4000
OLS	0.5463*	0.2797	0.5361*	0.5587*	0.5738*	0.5433*
mixed	0.0624	0.0335	0.7317	0.6512	0.6102	0.6741
$\Delta (EQUITY$ $-CGED)/W^e$						
prior	0.0000	0.0000	0.0000	0.5000	0.0000	0.1000
OLS	−0.1331	0.0851	0.1280	0.0692	0.0428	0.1069
mixed	0.0643	0.0371	0.0215	−0.0054	0.0148	0.0363
$\Delta MORT/W^e$						
prior	0.0000	0.0000	0.0000	0.1000	0.7000	0.1000
OLS	0.1912*	0.1066	0.1410*	0.1470*	0.1443*	0.1418*
mixed	0.0602	0.0398	0.0265	0.0436	0.0509	0.0269

Dependent Variable	1	ln(RSHORT)	ln(RLONG)	ln(REQUITY)	ln(RSHORT)	ln$\frac{RE}{RSHORT}$
B. Long-run Estimates						
DDC/W^e						
prior	none	−0.1050	0.0000	0.0000	0.0000	0.0000
OLS	−0.2987	−0.1906	0.5855	−0.0065	−0.2162	−0.0081
$SHORT/W^e$						
prior	none	0.0200	0.0000	0.0000	0.0000	0.0200
OLS	0.0592	0.0416	−0.1210	−0.0006	0.0540	0.0107
$LONG/W^e$						
prior	none	−0.0050	1.0000	−0.3000	−0.4500	−0.0200
OLS	−2.0151	−1.6227	4.9084	−0.0583	−1.7768	−0.1078
$EQUITY/W^e$						
prior	none	0.0000	−0.4000	0.4500	−0.1500	0.0000
OLS	6.0750	3.7498	−11.6946	0.1630	4.4129	0.2250
$MORT/W^e$						
prior	none	0.0000	−0.6000	−0.1500	0.6000	0.0000
OLS	−2.8204	−1.9781	6.3217	−0.0975	−2.4740	−0.1198

Notes: $\Delta X \equiv X - X_{-1}$, $\varphi X \equiv X^* - X_{-1}$ (the actual regressor is $-X_{-1}$). Sample period is 1954.I–1978.III (99 observations).
* *t*-statistic is greater than 2.0 in absolute value.

Table 3.5
Commercial Banking

					Interest Rate Responses				
Dependent Variable	1	$\ln(RDISC)$	$\ln(RSHORT)$	$\ln(RLONG)$	$\ln(RMORT)$	$\ln(RLOAN)$	$\ln\dfrac{RE}{RESHORT}$		$\dfrac{(1-k)DD_{-1}}{W^e}$

A. Short-run Estimates (Loan Disequilibrium)

Dependent Variable	1	$\ln(RDISC)$	$\ln(RSHORT)$	$\ln(RLONG)$	$\ln(RMORT)$	$\ln(RLOAN)$	$\ln\dfrac{RE}{RESHORT}$	$\dfrac{(1-k)DD_{-1}}{W^e}$
$\Delta EXRES/W^e$								
prior	none	0.0010	−0.0010	0.0000	0.0000	0.0000	0.0000	0.0000
OLS	0.0155	−0.0002	−0.0000	0.0002	−0.0018	0.0010	0.0003	0.0074*
$\Delta BORRES/W^e$								
prior	none	0.0050	−0.0050	0.0000	0.0000	0.0000	0.0000	0.0000
OLS	0.0291	0.0027	−0.0052*	0.0039	−0.0005	−0.0011	−0.0023	−0.0019
$\Delta ASHORT/W^e$								
prior	none	−0.0030	0.0257	−0.0915	−0.0442	0.1017	0.0600	0.0583
OLS	−0.1140	−0.0384*	0.0281*	0.0507	−0.0281	−0.0128	−0.0183	0.1925*
$\Delta LSHORT/W^e$								
prior	none	−0.0030	0.0624	−0.0625	−0.0157	0.0213	0.0288	0.0616
OLS	1.0949*	0.0263	−0.0208	0.0450	−0.0475	−0.0004	0.0083	−0.0306
$\Delta LONG/W^e$								
prior	none	0.0000	−0.0737	0.2230	−0.0525	−0.0535	−0.0756	−0.0965
OLS	−0.0084	0.0081	−0.0087	−0.0787*	0.0774*	0.0104	0.0007	−0.0895
$\Delta MORT/W^e$								
prior	none	0.0000	−0.0084	−0.0690	0.1125	−0.0695	−0.0132	−0.0235
OLS	−0.0171	0.0015	0.0067	−0.0211*	0.0005	0.0029	0.0113*	−0.0778*

Adjustment Coefficients

	$\dfrac{\varphi EXRES}{W^e}$	$\dfrac{\varphi BORRES}{W^e}$	$\dfrac{\varphi ASHORT}{W^e}$	$\dfrac{\varphi LSHORT}{W^e}$	$\dfrac{\varphi LONG}{W^e}$	$\dfrac{\varphi MORT}{W^e}$	$\dfrac{\Delta LOAN}{W^e}$	$\dfrac{W - W^e}{W^e}$	$\dfrac{-\Delta LOAN}{W^e}$
$\Delta EXRES/W^e$									
prior	1.0000	0.0000	0.0000	0.0000	0.0000	0.0000	0.0000	0.0000	0.0000
OLS	1.0052*	0.0245	0.0161	0.0155	0.0155	0.0074	0.0190*	0.0082*	0.0102*
$\Delta BORRES/W^e$									
prior	0.0000	1.0000	0.0000	0.0000	0.0000	0.0000	0.0000	0.0000	0.0000
OLS	−0.6252	0.8870*	0.0448*	0.0161	0.0293	−0.0108	0.0399	0.0232*	0.0441*
$\Delta ASHORT/W^e$									
prior	0.0000	0.0000	0.8500	0.1500	0.1750	0.1750	0.4700	0.4400	0.4500
OLS	−0.1926	1.0625	0.3355	−0.0623	−0.1119	−0.6726*	0.1480	0.5510*	0.4064*
$\Delta LSHORT/W^e$									
prior	0.0000	0.0000	0.1500	0.8500	0.0850	0.0850	0.1900	0.1800	0.1500
OLS	−1.1675	2.6691*	0.8511*	1.1047*	1.0899*	1.2343*	1.0865*	0.3538*	0.5818
$\Delta LONG/W^e$									
prior	0.0000	0.0000	0.0000	0.0000	0.7300	0.1300	0.2800	0.2600	0.3000
OLS	−0.3970	−3.5115*	−0.1707	−0.0095	0.1187	0.4714	−0.2416	0.0879	−0.0122
$\Delta MORT/W^e$									
prior	0.0000	0.0000	0.0000	0.0000	0.0100	0.6100	0.0600	0.1200	0.1000
OLS	2.8375*	−0.1318	−0.0769	−0.0645	−0.1415*	−0.0297	−0.0518	−0.0241	−0.0303

Table 3.5 (continued)

	1	$\ln(RDISC)$	$\ln(RSHORT)$	$\ln(RLONG)$	$\ln(RMORT)$	$\ln(RLOAN)$	$\ln\dfrac{RE}{RESHORT}$	$\dfrac{(1-k)DD_{-1}}{W^e}$
B. Long-run Estimates								
$EXRES/W^e$								
prior	none	0.0010	−0.0010	0.0000	0.0000	0.0000	0.0000	0.0000
OLS	0.0043	0.0004	−0.0012	−0.0020	−0.0005	0.0016	0.0008	−0.0002
$BORRES/W^e$								
prior	none	0.0050	−0.0050	0.0000	0.0000	0.0000	0.0000	0.0000
OLS	0.0465	0.0106	−0.0216	0.0007	−0.0086	0.0076	0.0052	−0.0569
$ASHORT/W^e$								
prior	none	−0.0030	0.0500	−0.0500	0.0000	−0.0250	0.0900	0.1200
OLS	0.4821	−0.0267	−0.0262	−0.2992	0.2519	0.0300	0.0076	−0.5986
$LSHORT/W^e$								
prior	none	−0.0030	0.0800	−0.0500	0.0000	−0.0250	0.0300	0.0800
OLS	2.0134	0.2738	−0.8218	0.3601	−0.8261	0.4352	0.3544	−1.8700
$LONG/W^e$								
prior	none	0.0000	−0.0900	0.4000	−0.0500	−0.2000	−0.1000	−0.1000
OLS	−0.6660	−0.0459	0.0622	0.1374	0.0983	−0.0726	−0.1581	1.2565
$MORT/W^e$								
prior	none	0.0000	−0.0100	−0.1000	0.2000	−0.1500	−0.0200	−0.0300
OLS	0.1743	−0.0033	0.1271	−0.2643	0.2629	−0.0584	−0.0113	−0.3534
$LOAN/W^e$								
prior	none	0.0000	−0.0240	−0.2000	−0.1500	0.4000	0.0000	−0.0700
OLS	−1.0546	−0.0289	0.6816	0.0673	0.2220	−0.3433	−0.1987	1.6227

Notes: $\Delta X \equiv X - X_{-1}$, $\varphi X \equiv X^* - X_{-1}$ (the actual regressor is $-X_{-1}$). Sample period is 1963.I to 1978.III (63 observations).
* t-statistic is greater than 2.0 in absolute value.

savings institutions in Table 3.3, essentially the same as Smith and Brainard [11], is typical. Disposable assets are the sum of time and saving deposits, FHLB borrowing, equity holdings (a small, exogenous number), and net worth. Long-run demands depend on the logs of various interest rates. The equity rate is the rate of discount on earnings implicit in observed market value of equity.[2]

In the spirit of the illustrative theoretical model of Table 3.1, the interest rates should be one-period yields. For long bonds, a one-period rate would allow for capital gains or losses due to expected changes in bond prices. In fact, we do not attempt to estimate directly short-term rates on long-maturity securities. Instead, our regressions include as *RLONG* the yield to maturity, and we try to capture interest rate expectations by an additional variable. The variable *ln (RE/RSHORT)*—*RE* is the 91-day treasury bill rate expected next quarter, from the Goldsmith-Nagan survey [4]—is intended to capture the effect of an expected change in the short rate. For given current short and long rates, an increase in the expected future short rate presumably implies a lower expected one-period return from holding longs. For investors with short horizons this would be associated with an increase in the demand for shorts, and a decrease in demand for longs (and other assets with distant maturities) as indicated by the prior means in the table. Nominal rates are used for all of the financial sectors on the grounds that these institutions are dealing entirely in nominally dominated claims and that real income effects of inflation are negligible.

Savings institutions, like all other sectors except commercial banks, are assumed always to be on their demand curves. Their effective demands are identical with short-run notional demands—however, because of costs of adjustment, short- and long-run notional demands differ. Discrepancies between actual and long-run desired asset holdings are eliminated by a general partial adjustment mechanism. Expected disposable assets for each sector is an adaptive process with an estimated geometric rate of growth appended:

$$WE = (1+g)(\delta W_{-1} + (1-\delta) WE_{-1}),$$

where g is the growth rate and δ is a weighting parameter set arbitrarily at 0.75. For savings institutions, unexpected funds have two components: changes in FHLB borrowing and unexpected inflows from other sources, primarily deposits. Each component is allocated separately in the short-run so that thrifts can react differently to changes in deposit liabilities and FHLB advances.

Insurance and Pension Funds

The specification of insurance and pension funds parallels that of savings institutions. Prior claims are life insurance and pension reserves, policy and other loans, and net worth and miscellaneous. Equity holdings are a major part of this sector's portfolio (approximately 30 percent in 1971) and (unrealized) capital gains are a substantial fraction of changes in the value of equity held. We have made the arbitrary decision that these gains do not lead (for one period) to revisions in the demands for other assets, but are kept in equity. Hence in the short-run tables, capital gains are netted out of disposable assets and the dependent variable for equity is net of (unrealized) capital gains.

Commercial Banks

The long-run demand equations for commercial banks are of the same general form as for the other financial intermediaries. However, in the short run banks can be off their notional demands. Banks are assumed to accommodate loan demand within the period, and to respond subsequently to an excess of loans in their portfolios by raising the loan rate. This accommodation implies that their effective demands for other assets will also differ from the notional demands. The specification in the short-run tables for banks is derived as shown in the following.

Partition the short-run *notional* flow demands as

$$\begin{pmatrix} \Delta a_1^n \\ \Delta a_2^n \end{pmatrix} = \begin{pmatrix} E_1 \\ E_2 \end{pmatrix}(a^* - a_{-1}) + \begin{pmatrix} F_1 \\ F_2 \end{pmatrix}(S - S^e).$$

The subscript 2 refers to loans. (Thus E_2, for example, is an n-dimensional *row* vector.) Let the *effective* demands be

$$\begin{pmatrix} \Delta a_1 \\ \Delta a_2 \end{pmatrix} = \begin{pmatrix} \Delta a_1^n \\ \Delta a_2^n \end{pmatrix} + \begin{pmatrix} \theta_1 \\ \theta_2 \end{pmatrix}(\Delta a_2 - \Delta a_2^n).$$

Δa_2 is the exogenous flow supply of loans; a fraction θ_2 of the difference between the supply and the notional demand is met by banks with spillovers, represented by the vector θ_1, into banks' demands for other assets. The θ_j sum to zero or, equivalently, the elements of θ_1 sum to $-\theta_2$. (To see this, note that $(\Delta \bar{a}_2 - \Delta a_2^n)$ is simply a z variable in equation (7).) Manipulation yields

$$\Delta a_1 = E_1(a^* - a_{-1}) + F_1(S - S^e) + \theta_1 \Delta \bar{a}_2$$
$$\quad - \theta_1[E_2(a^* - a_{-1}) + F_2(S - S^e)]$$
$$= [E_1 - \theta_1 E_2](a^* - a_{-1}) + [F_1 - \theta_1 F_2](S - S^e) + \theta_1 \Delta \bar{a}_2.$$

and

$$\Delta a_2 = (1 - \theta_2)E_2(a^* - a_{-1}) + (1 - \theta_2)F_2(S - S^e) + \Delta \bar{a}_2.$$

For estimation the model is underidentified without further restrictions on, or information about, θ_2:

$$\Delta a_1 = \left[E_1 - \frac{\theta_1}{\theta_2}E_2\right](a^* - a_{-1}) + \left[F_1 - \frac{\theta_1}{\theta_2}F_2\right](S - S^e) + \frac{\theta_1}{\theta_2}\Delta a_2.$$

It is easiest to interpret the disequilibrium short-run equations for commercial banks by assuming $\theta_2 = 1$. Then loans vary with other sector's demands for them, and the coefficients indicate how the remainder of the portfolio adjusts to accommodate loan demand. The interest rate responses and adjustment coefficients in a given row are now the sum of a variable's effect on the asset in question and a (negative) fraction $(-\theta_{ij})$ of the loan discrepancy.

Households

The household sector plays a central role in the model both because of the quantitative importance of its expenditures on current output and because of the magnitudes of its holdings of various assets and liabilities. The constraint on demands W is net worth. Households are the dominant demanders of equity, of the liabilities of intermediaries, and of the supply of mortgage credit. They are also important in the markets for short- and long-term securities and loans.

As discussed above, our intention in later versions of the model is to integrate consumption and portfolio behavior, but here we follow more conventional practice in separating the two decisions. Table 3.6 gives the short- and long-run assets and liability demand equations. They are similar to those of other sectors with the following exceptions. The equations include a transaction variable Y^α/W^e. (Y is personal income, inclusive of taxes, and α is a parameter to be estimated.) The likelihood function

Table 3.6
Households

A. Short-run Estimates

Dependent Variable		1	$\ln(RTDB)$	$\ln(RTDS)$	$\ln(RSHORT)$	$\ln(RLONG)$	$\ln(EQUITY)$	$\ln(RMORT)$	$\ln(RLOAN)$	$\ln\dfrac{RE}{RSHORT}$	$\dfrac{P^e}{P}$	$\dfrac{\sqrt{Y}}{W^e}$
$\Delta DDC/W^e$	prior	none	−0.0200	−0.0200	−0.0040	0.0000	0.0000	0.0000	0.0000	0.0000	0.0000	1.6000
	OLS	0.1659*	−0.0201*	0.0063	0.0043	−0.0095	−0.0003	0.0295*	−0.0053	0.0048	0.0002	5.8456*
	mixed	0.2947	−0.0224	0.0117	0.0022	−0.0086	−0.0008	0.0085	−0.0028	0.0007	0.0009	1.4387
$\Delta TDB/W^e$	prior	none	0.1767	0.1382	−0.0045	0.0020	−0.0900	−0.0115	0.0095	0.0150	0.0000	−0.7850
	OLS	0.0142	0.0141*	0.0092	−0.0007	0.0018	0.0018*	−0.0143	0.0011	−0.0004	0.0003	−1.3460*
	mixed	0.1229	0.0089	0.0364	−0.0007	−0.0086	0.0033	0.0024	−0.0026	0.0006	0.0007	−0.2757
$\Delta TDS/W^e$	prior	none	−0.1382	0.1767	−0.0078	0.0100	−0.1475	0.0105	−0.0105	0.0150	0.0000	−0.5000
	OLS	−0.0438	0.0027	0.0087	0.0020	−0.0026	−0.0005	−0.0004	−0.0136*	0.0012	−0.0001	−0.2972
	mixed	−0.0894	0.0015	0.0221	−0.0007	−0.0027	0.0014	0.0061	−0.0085	0.0017	−0.0004	0.2399
$\Delta SHORT/W^e$	prior	none	−0.0085	−0.0085	0.0200	−0.0100	−0.0200	−0.0040	−0.0040	0.0250	0.0000	−0.1600
	OLS	0.2582*	0.0019	−0.0021	0.0018	−0.0051	0.0004	0.0057	0.0109*	−0.0006	−0.0003	1.0537
	mixed	0.1168	0.0012	−0.0281	0.0076	−0.0038	−0.0025	−0.0017	0.0079	0.0047	−0.0007	−0.5397
$\Delta LONG/W^e$	prior	none	−0.0080	−0.0080	−0.0015	0.0830	−0.0525	−0.0145	−0.0145	−0.0475	0.0000	−0.0700
	OLS	0.0179	−0.0055	−0.0127	−0.0037	0.0138	−0.0001	−0.0054	0.0035	−0.0018	−0.0002	−1.2089
	mixed	0.1126	0.0062	−0.0181	−0.0043	0.0171	0.0017	−0.0062	0.0030	−0.0058	−0.0002	−0.2738
$\Delta EQUITY - CGEQ/W^e$	prior	none	0.0000	0.0000	−0.0025	−0.0800	0.2650	−0.0220	−0.0220	0.0000	0.0000	−0.0500
	OLS	0.0770*	0.0011	−0.0030	−0.0011	0.0076*	0.0002	−0.0071*	−0.0007	0.0003	0.0001	−0.3860
	mixed	0.0947	0.0022	−0.0033	0.0005	0.0038	−0.0002	−0.0093	−0.0011	0.0005	0.0001	−0.1231

Adjustment Coefficients

Dependent Variable		$\varphi DDC/W^e$	$\varphi TDB/W^e$	$\varphi TDS/W^e$	$\varphi SHORT/W^e$	$\varphi LONG/W^e$	$\varphi EQUITY/W^e$	$\varphi NONMKT/W^e$	$\varphi MORT/W^e$	$\varphi LOAN/W^e$	$\frac{W-W^e-CGEQ-CGNON}{W^e}$	constant
$\Delta NONMKT-CGNON/W^e$	prior	none	0.0000	0.0000	0.0000	0.0000	0.0750	−0.0100	−0.0100	0.0000	0.0000	0.0000
	OLS	−0.0230	−0.0039	−0.0024	0.0014	−0.0030	−0.0007	−0.0004	−0.0007	0.0014	0.0000	−0.4794
	mixed	0.0321	0.0029	−0.0017	−0.0007	−0.0047	0.0008	0.0068	−0.0018	0.0001	0.0002	−0.0867
$\Delta MORT/W^e$	prior	none	0.0000	0.0000	0.0000	0.0000	−0.0550	0.0690	−0.0150	0.0000	0.0000	0.0000
	OLS	0.0471*	−0.0007	0.0038	−0.0008	0.0033	−0.0004	−0.0091*	0.0028*	0.0001	0.0001	−0.9970*
	mixed	−0.0011	0.0024	−0.0039	−0.0022	0.0027	0.0000	−0.0005	0.0043	−0.0002	−0.0001	−0.1038
$\Delta LOAN/W^e$	prior	none	−0.0020	−0.0020	0.0003	−0.0050	0.0250	−0.0175	0.0665	−0.0075	0.0000	−0.0350
	OLS	0.4865*	0.0104*	−0.0078	−0.0033	−0.0063	−0.0005	0.0015	0.0019	−0.0050*	−0.0001	−2.1848*
	mixed	0.1380	−0.0030	−0.0152	−0.0017	0.0047	−0.0036	−0.0062	0.0013	−0.0022	−0.0004	−0.2758

B. Long-run Estimates

Dependent Variable		$\varphi DDC/W^e$	$\varphi TDB/W^e$	$\varphi TDS/W^e$	$\varphi SHORT/W^e$	$\varphi LONG/W^e$	$\varphi EQUITY/W^e$	$\varphi NONMKT/W^e$	$\varphi MORT/W^e$	$\varphi LOAN/W^e$	$\frac{W-W^e-CGEQ-CGNON}{W^e}$
$\Delta DDC/W^e$	prior	0.9000	0.1000	0.1000	0.1000	0.1000	0.1000	0.1000	0.1000	0.1000	0.2500
	OLS	1.1300*	0.0465	−0.0362	0.2831*	0.2440*	0.1909*	0.2342*	−0.1022	0.4735*	0.1962*
	mixed	0.9201	0.2329	0.3299	0.2308	0.2191	0.2860	0.1856	0.2856	0.2427	0.2888
$\Delta TDB/W^e$	prior	0.0500	0.8000	0.1000	0.0500	0.1000	0.0500	0.0500	0.0000	0.1000	0.1200
	OLS	−0.1580*	0.1060	0.0767	0.0122	−0.0274	0.0383	−0.0848	−0.0110	−0.0264	0.0276
	mixed	0.0316	0.3246	0.2379	0.1133	0.1485	0.1887	0.0922	0.1577	0.1335	0.1870
$\Delta TDS/W^e$	prior	0.0500	0.1000	0.8000	0.0500	0.1000	0.0000	0.1000	0.1000	0.0000	0.1700
	OLS	−0.1670*	−0.1074*	0.0174	−0.1133*	−0.1908*	−0.0532	0.0129	−0.0111	−0.0013	−0.0473
	mixed	0.0235	0.1120	0.1726	0.1005	0.1296	0.1191	0.1380	0.1593	0.1065	0.1232
$\Delta SHORT/W^e$	prior	0.0000	0.0000	0.0000	0.7000	0.1000	0.1000	0.0000	0.1000	0.1000	0.0800
	OLS	0.1861*	0.3349*	0.0497	0.4995*	0.3906*	0.2658*	0.3733*	0.1935	0.2195*	0.2828*
	mixed	0.0079	0.0593	0.0409	0.3982	0.1249	0.0891	0.1175	0.1539	0.1122	0.0865

Table 3.6 (continued)

						Adjustment Coefficients				
Dependent Variable	$\frac{\varphi DDC}{W^e}$	$\frac{\varphi TDB}{W^e}$	$\frac{\varphi TDS}{W^e}$	$\frac{\varphi SHORT}{W^e}$	$\frac{\varphi LONG}{W^e}$	$\frac{\varphi EQUITY}{W^e}$	$\frac{\varphi NONMKT}{W^e}$	$\frac{\varphi MORT}{W^e}$	$\frac{\varphi LOAN}{W^e}$	$\frac{W-W^e-CGEQ-CGNON}{W^e}$
$\Delta LONG/W^e$										
prior	0.0000	0.0000	0.0000	0.0500	0.5000	0.1000	0.0000	0.0000	0.0000	0.0300
OLS	−0.1248	−0.0077	0.0090	−0.0718	0.1184	−0.0018	−0.0053	0.0813	−0.0687	−0.0095
mixed	0.0040	0.0572	0.0403	0.0800	0.2404	0.1106	0.0738	0.0307	0.0199	0.0955
$\Delta EQUITY - CGEQ/W^e$										
prior	0.0000	0.0000	0.0000	0.0000	0.0000	0.5000	0.1000	0.0000	0.0000	0.1500
OLS	−0.0157	0.1820*	0.0411	0.0493	0.0860*	0.0720*	0.0752*	0.0636*	0.0963*	0.0666*
mixed	0.0028	0.0403	0.0297	0.0058	0.0039	0.0747	0.1201	0.0320	0.0162	0.0711
$\Delta NONMKT - CGNON/W^e$										
prior	0.0000	0.0000	0.0000	0.0000	0.0000	0.0000	0.5000	0.0000	0.0000	0.0500
OLS	−0.0040	−0.0913*	−0.0476	−0.0930*	−0.0986*	−0.0364	−0.0540	−0.0205	−0.0978*	−0.0362
mixed	0.0018	0.0389	0.0310	−0.0011	0.0053	0.0377	0.0385	0.0423	0.0288	0.0422
$\Delta MORT/W^e$										
prior	0.0000	0.0000	0.0000	0.0000	0.0000	0.0000	0.0000	0.5000	0.1000	0.0500
OLS	0.0303	−0.0115	0.3385*	0.0039	0.0268	0.0499*	−0.0571*	0.2801*	−0.1485*	0.0413*
mixed	0.0077	0.0623	0.0560	−0.0196	0.0151	0.0048	−0.0055	0.0233	0.0695	0.0052
$\Delta LOAN/W^e$										
prior	0.0000	0.0000	0.0000	0.0500	0.1000	0.1500	0.1500	0.2000	0.6000	0.1000
OLS	0.1231	0.5986*	0.5514*	0.4302*	0.4509*	0.4745*	0.5056*	0.5261*	0.5534*	0.4785*
mixed	0.0005	0.0725	0.0617	0.0921	0.1132	0.0893	0.2398	0.1150	0.2708	0.0975

Dependent Variable	1	$\ln(RTDB)$	$\ln(RTDS)$	$\ln(RSHORT)$	$\ln(RLONG)$	$\ln(EQUITY)$	$\ln(RMORT)$	$\ln(RLOAN)$	$\ln\frac{RE}{RSHORT}$	$\frac{P^e}{P}$	$\frac{\sqrt{Y}}{W^e}$
				−0.0050						0.0000	2.00
				0.0729						0.0088	98.32

B. Long-run Estimates

DDC/W^e											
prior	none										
OLS	−1.0630	−0.0250	−0.0312	1.0983	1.9618	0.1108	−1.6634	−0.9775	0.4169	0.0000	

TDB/W^e										
prior	none	0.2500	−0.2000	−0.0050	−0.0100	−0.1000	0.0000	0.0000	0.0250	0.0000	−1.00
OLS	−3.3552	0.0080	3.4397	0.2100	6.1785	0.3550	−5.2952	−3.0534	1.2850	0.0274	−293.40
TDS/W^e										
prior	none	−0.2000	0.2500	−0.0100	−0.0100	−0.1500	0.0000	0.0000	0.0250	0.0000	−0.60
OLS	−4.7424	0.0555	4.7771	0.2824	8.2979	0.4912	−7.0642	−4.1929	1.7137	0.0345	399.27
$SHORT/W^e$										
prior	none	−0.0100	−0.0100	0.0300	−0.0200	−0.0500	−0.0100	−0.0100	0.0500	0.0000	−0.20
OLS	2.8961	0.0330	−3.0621	−0.1795	−5.5802	−0.3186	4.7331	2.7907	−1.1490	−0.0232	−258.03
$LONG/W^e$										
prior	none	−0.0150	−0.0150	−0.0050	0.2000	−0.2000	−0.0200	−0.0200	−0.1000	0.0000	−0.10
OLS	−0.9319	−0.0130	0.8919	0.0338	1.7010	0.1005	−1.3866	−0.7982	0.3237	0.0060	78.67
$(EQUITY - CGEQ)/W^e$										
prior	none	0.0000	0.0000	−0.0050	−0.1600	0.5000	−0.0400	−0.0400	0.0000	0.0000	−0.10
OLS	3.4009	0.0398	−2.4356	−0.1381	−4.4074	−0.2436	3.6738	2.1716	−0.9005	−0.0175	−224.27
$(NONMKT - CGNON)/W^e$										
prior	none	0.0000	0.0000	0.0000	0.0000	0.1500	−0.0200	−0.0200	0.0000	0.0000	0.00
OLS	−6.8426	−0.0098	7.1121	0.4450	12.5590	0.7276	−0.10665	−6.3405	2.6126	0.0505	604.65
$MORT/W^e$										
prior	none	0.0000	0.0000	0.0000	0.0000	−0.1000	0.1500	−0.0600	0.0000	0.0000	0.00
OLS	6.5981	−0.0770	−6.6427	−0.4014	−11.5652	−0.6890	9.8517	5.8362	−2.3961	−0.0481	−556.43
$LOAN/W^e$										
prior	none	0.0000	0.0000	0.0000	0.0000	−0.0500	−0.0600	0.1500	0.0000	0.0000	0.00
OLS	5.0402	−0.0054	−5.1787	−0.3251	−9.1457	−0.5340	7.8178	4.5640	−1.9064	−0.0381	−435.60

Notes: $\Delta X \equiv X - X_{-1}$, $\varphi X \equiv X^* - X_{-1}$ (the actual regressor is X_{-1}). Sample period is 1954.I to 1973.III (99 observations).
* t-statistic is greater than 2.0 in absolute value.

for α for the complete system of equations, calculated at intervals of 0.2, had a sharply defined maximum at $\alpha = 0.5$—a square-root rule of sorts. Nominal interest rates are used in the regressions. But the equations also include the Juster/Survey Research Center [13, table 19B] price expectations variable. Our prior means were constructed by assuming that the effect of an increase in expected inflation accompanied by equal increases in market-determined nominal interest rates decreases the demand for demand deposits and currency, with the effect distributed across other assets.

Estimates

An important difference between this study and previous work is our explicit use of subjective prior information in the estimation. Most model-builders mine the data[3] in search of plausible estimates. We hope to profit from direct use of the same value information that leads investigators, ex post, to view some estimates as plausible and others unacceptable. In particular, we have used the Theil-Goldberger mixed estimation technique to combine our prior beliefs with the data. This involves specifying prior means and a variance-covariance structure for the structural coefficients.[4]

Our prior means, which are reported together with OLS estimates in Tables 3.3 through 3.6, are highly subjective, but we expect most economists will find them qualitatively plausible. The long-run coefficients reflect our belief that most pairs of assets are gross substitutes: stock demands depend positively on own rates and negatively on other rates. Own elasticities generally are in the range of 1 to 3 in absolute value. There is rough symmetry motivated by the idea that equal increases in all rates should not have large effects on demands. The adjustment matrix has diagonal elements between 0 and 1 with liquid assets adjusting more quickly than illiquid ones. Unexpected funds are allocated relatively more heavily into demand deposits and shorts than into other assets.

Unconstrained OLS results testify to the difficulty of obtaining significant and/or sensible coefficient estimates in models of this type. Fewer than half of the short-run rate responses and approximately half of the adjustment coefficients are significant, and there are a larger number of estimates quantitatively, if not significantly, far from the priors. Many are of the "wrong" sign, and some significantly so. Although these results are typical of what one gets from time series data, they do not provide a sensible basis for simulation. Many of the policy experiments that we anticipate simulating with the model depend critically on estimates of the supply and demand equations including their cross-elasticities, and it would be difficult to have much confidence in results that incorporate so many anomalies.

In previous work by Smith-Brainard [2] and Backus-Purvis [1], the use of prior information removed virtually all of the "peculiar" estimates in the adjustment matrix that occurred with OLS but was less successful in eliminating "wrong" signs on interest rates in the short- and long-run demand equations. Mixed estimation of the savings, insurance, and household sectors repeats this experience. As shown in Tables 3.3, 3.4, and 3.6, the use of prior information substantially "improved" the estimates of the adjustment coefficients. Perhaps the most dramatic change relates to savings institutions' short-run demand for mortages. According to the OLS estimates, an increase in the desired holdings of mortgages accompanied by an equal increase in disposable funds results in a *decrease* in mortgage demand, and increases in the desired holdings of other assets (accompanied by increases in disposable funds) lead to large sales of mortgages and purchases of assets not themselves desired. The mixed estimation virtually eliminates this anomaly. A number of other anomalous features of the OLS adjustment matrix are eliminated by using the mixed estimation procedure, and approximately three-fourths of the adjustment coefficients are substantially changed in the direction of the priors. The mixed estimates of the rate coefficients, taken as a group, do not appear qualitatively superior to the OLS estimates. For both estimation procedures, most of the own coefficients are of the "correct" sign, but from a third to a half of the cross-elasticities are of the "wrong" sign.

These results suggest that there are problems with our behavioral or statistical specifications. There are several possible statistical reasons for these problems. (1) We devoted little attention to the intertemporal structure of errors. The partial adjustment specification involves a large number of parameters which may compensate for the lack of a more flexible error structure. But to the extent that it does, the estimates of those parameters will conflict with our prior views of plausible speeds of adjustment and cross-effects. (2) We have not dealt with the estimation problems created by the simultaneity of the system. (3) In order to keep the prototype model simple, we have aggregated several sectors where we know (for example in the savings and insurance and pension sectors) that subsectors differ significantly in behavior. The simulations of the model below provide clues to a number of features of our behavioral specification that may be causing difficulty.

7 Simulation of the Financial Block

Simulation of the model and its subsectors using pure priors for the coefficients serves several purposes. First, simulation provides a direct test of the consistency of the system's specification. Although the qualitative nature of the equilibria of models like this can be derived analytically, the dynamics are intractable. Even if each individual sector behaves sensibly, the system as a whole may not. Second, simulation reveals unobvious qualitative implications of the coefficient priors and market specification for the response of the endogenous variables to policies or other shocks. In some cases there may be prior information about system-wide "multipliers." Discrepancies between such priors and the simulated multipliers would suggest reexamination of the specifications of individual sectors. Ideally, any prior information about reduced-form behavior would be used symmetrically with prior information about structural coefficients in the estimation itself. In any case, simulation provides a way of investigating the implications of the priors for the response of the system to various shocks and policy experiments for which there is no direct historical experience.

In this section we report results of simulating the financial block. The adjustment of financial variables required to satisfy asset demand and supply equations described in Table 3.2 is described, taking as predetermined the level of output, prices, and the capital stock, and taking the financial behavior of businesses, rest of the world, and government to be exogenous. Although simulations of the financial block alone do not test a number of the distinctive features of the model—those that relate to the endogeneity of capital stock and government debt,—understanding the behavior of the financial sector is a step toward understanding the complete model.

Simulation of the financial block did not reveal any outright inconsistencies of specification, but it did reveal a number of features of our specification with which we are not content. No doubt we will find others. The following are among the difficulties.

Table 3.7
Open Market Operation: $1 Billion Purchase of Short-term Securities

		Differences from Base Simulation			
Year	Qtr.	RSHORT	RLONG	REQUITY	RMORT
1971	1	−0.521	−0.210	−0.189	−0.276
1971	2	−0.379	−0.181	−0.069	−0.229
1971	3	−0.348	−0.184	0.022	−0.203
1971	4	−0.328	−0.287	−0.236	−0.359
1972	1	−0.304	−0.215	−0.085	−0.273
1972	2	−0.116	−0.144	0.067	−0.159
1972	3	−0.371	−0.342	−0.290	−0.435
1972	4	−0.315	−0.266	−0.097	−0.326
Average of last 3 Qtrs.		−0.267	−0.251	−0.107	−0.307
		Demand Deposits at Commercial Banks			
1971	1	3.024			
1971	2	4.271			
1971	3	5.057			
1971	4	1.965			
1972	1	3.883			
1972	2	5.505			
1972	3	1.118			
1972	4	3.847			
Average of last 3 Qtrs.		3.490			

Note: Rates are annual percentages. Stocks are in billions of dollars.

Capital gains are volatile and tend to induce large fluctuations in asset demands and rates. In the prototype model capital gains in equity are, in the first instance, held in equity, adjustment starting one period later. The intent was to implement the empirical evidence that capital gains and losses have relatively small effects on the demands for other assets in the short run. What the specification actually did, however, was simply postpone the strong effects of gains or losses for one quarter. We have now smoothed changes in q and therefore, capital gains in equity.

Another specification "error" that seems to be creating difficulties in the simulations is the assumption that banks fully accommodate loan demands. Perhaps because of the large variations in household loan demand resulting from the treatment of capital gains, loan demand is highly volatile and forces substantial and unrealistic reallocation of bank portfolios. One possible solution is to allow some adjustment of the loan rate

Table 3.8
Reserve Requirements: Increase of 0.01 in Required Reserve Ratio on Demand Deposits

		Differences from Base Simulation			
Year	Qtr.	RSHORT	RLONG	REQUITY	RMORT
1971	1	0.778	0.278	0.245	0.368
1971	2	0.574	0.266	0.113	0.342
1971	3	0.637	0.317	0.018	0.363
1971	4	0.479	0.413	0.304	0.516
1972	1	0.499	0.352	0.147	0.449
1972	2	0.297	0.288	−0.006	0.346
1972	3	0.526	0.499	0.359	0.633
1972	4	0.543	0.449	0.176	0.556
Average of last 3 Qtrs.		0.455	0.412	0.176	0.512
		Excess Reserves	Borrowed Reserves	Demand Deposits at Commercial Banks	Time Deposits at Commercial Banks
1971	1	−0.091	0.455	−3.733	−5.449
1971	2	−0.067	0.297	−5.411	−6.803
1971	3	−0.051	0.195	−6.802	−8.543
1971	4	−0.097	0.405	−2.997	−10.849
1972	1	−0.067	0.256	−5.394	−10.325
1972	2	−0.043	0.127	−7.163	−10.849
1972	3	−0.102	0.414	−2.307	−12.870
1972	4	−0.081	0.314	−5.614	−12.528
Average of last 3 Qtrs.		−0.075	0.285	−5.028	−12.082

Note: Rates are annual percentages. Stocks are in billions of dollars.

within the period, as may be anyway more realistic in recent years. Another is to assume some rationing of credit.

A third feature of the specification with which we are not completely happy is our assumption of partial adjustment. Slow adjustment of quantities forces large fluctuations in the endogenous interest rates to clear markets when there are exogenous shocks to quantities supplied. In the case of demand deposits and currency, which serve as buffers or "temporary abodes of purchasing power," the partial adjustment assumption seems particularly inappropriate.

Simulation Results
Tables 3.7 through 3.12 report a variety of simulations illustrating some of the experiments we wish to explore. The first two simulations illustrate

Table 3.9
Operation Twist: $1 Billion Purchase of Longs, Sale of Shorts

Year	Qtr.	Differences from Base Simulation			
		RSHORT	RLONG	REQUITY	RMORT
1971	1	0.004	−0.025	−0.020	−0.028
1971	2	0.025	−0.011	0.002	−0.009
1971	3	0.043	−0.013	0.002	−0.009
1971	4	0.001	−0.022	−0.019	−0.025
1972	1	0.024	−0.012	−0.001	−0.011
1972	2	0.035	−0.010	0.005	−0.007
1972	3	−0.001	−0.024	−0.021	−0.028
1972	4	0.019	−0.015	−0.002	−0.014
Average of last 3 Qtrs.		0.018	−0.016	−0.006	−0.016
		Demand Deposits at Commercial Banks			
1971	1	−0.015			
1971	2	0.128			
1971	3	0.136			
1971	4	−0.109			
1972	1	0.92			
1972	2	0.154			
1972	3	−0.134			
1972	4	0.077			
Average of last 3 Qtrs.		0.032			

Note: Rates are annual percentages. Stocks are in billions of dollars.

the response of the system to two standard tools of monetary policy: open market operations and changes in reserve requirements. Although there are fluctuations reflecting the aforementioned treatment of capital gains, the simulations are qualitatively in accord with usual presumptions. Increasing reserves or decreasing reserve requirements decreases all interest rates. Changes in the short and long rates are almost equal; the simulations assume that future expected short rates move with the current short rates. The mortgage rate moves more than these two rates, reflecting substantial responses by banks and other financial intermediaries. Moreover, the mortgage market is assumed to be cleared by the mortgage rate, with no rationing. Perhaps the mortgage market should be treated similarly to the loan market. The equity rate moves somewhat less than other rates, reflecting the less than perfect substitutes assumption of asset demands.

Table 3.10
Freddie Mac: $1 Billion Purchase of Mortgages, Sale of Longs

Year	Qtr.	Differences from Base Simulation			
		RSHORT	RLONG	REQUITY	RMORT
1971	1	0.005	0.012	0.007	−0.007
1971	2	−0.006	0.002	−0.004	−0.014
1971	3	−0.004	0.004	−0.001	−0.013
1971	4	0.003	0.006	0.004	−0.005
1972	1	−0.005	0.002	−0.003	−0.013
1972	2	−0.002	0.003	−0.000	−0.011
1972	3	0.002	0.005	0.003	−0.006
1972	4	−0.003	0.002	−0.003	−0.011
		Demand Deposits at Commercial Banks	Mortgage Liability of Households		
1971	1	0.056	0.151		
1971	2	−0.039	0.175		
1971	3	−0.014	0.199		
1971	4	0.043	0.228		
1972	1	−0.032	0.234		
1972	2	−0.008	0.237		
1972	3	0.033	0.249		
1972	4	−0.030	0.244		

Note: Rates are annual percentages. Stocks are in billions of dollars.

Simulations (not shown) of the effect of open market operations in long term securities and changes in reserve requirements on time deposits look very similar to those shown in Table 3.7 and 3.8. Together these results suggest that the (similar) effects of these actions on the excess demand for unborrowed reserves dominate their differences in other markets.

Tables 3.9, 3.10, and 3.11 report the consequences of changing the relative supplies of various assets. For these experiments, most individuals' "reduced-form" priors are probably less certain than for open market operations. As can be seen in Table 3.9, debt management is far from impotent, even though switching longs for shorts has a much smaller effect than switching either one for high-powered money. A one billion dollar shift from short to long debt (about one-third of one percent of government debt in 1971) decreases the long-short rate differential by about three and one-half basis points. The effect is remarkably close to previous estimates.[5]

Table 3.11
Stock Market Intervention: $1 Billion Purchase of Equity, Sale of Shorts

		Differences from Base Simulation			
Year	Qtr.	RSHORT	RLONG	REQUITY	RMORT
1971	1	0.017	−0.005	−0.023	−0.012
1971	2	0.029	−0.002	−0.001	−0.005
1971	3	0.055	−0.002	0.004	−0.001
1971	4	0.002	−0.016	−0.023	−0.022
1972	1	0.028	−0.005	−0.004	−0.007
1972	2	0.047	0.001	0.008	0.003
1972	3	−0.000	−0.019	−0.025	−0.025
1972	4	0.021	−0.008	−0.005	−0.010
Average of last 3 Qtrs.		0.003	−0.009	−0.007	−1.011
		Demand Deposits at Commercial Banks			
1971	1	0.065			
1971	2	0.125			
1971	3	0.160			
1971	4	−0.138			
1972	1	0.080			
1972	2	0.197			
1972	3	−0.172			
1972	4	0.054			
Average of last 3 Qtrs.		0.026			

Note: Rates are annual percentages. Stocks are in billions of dollars.

The effect of the recent meteoric rise of mortgage-backed bonds can be analyzed in a manner similar to debt management. In the model, the growth of such bonds appears as an increase in mortgage assets and long liabilities of federal agencies. In Table 3.10, a simulated issue of an additional one billion dollars of longs and purchases of mortgages results in a 0.2 billion dollar increase in mortgage credit granted to households; i.e., there is substantial slippage between the agency actions and households.[6] The rate differential created by such a transaction is small.

An important difference between this model and most other financial models is that capital is not perfectly substitutable for interest-paying financial assets. As a consequence, the magnitude of the effect of conventional monetary policy is only partially, and imperfectly, captured in the response of market rates on government securities. The substantial differences in the quantitative response of the required rate on capital and these rates can be seen in the simulations reported above.

Table 3.12
Regulation Q Ceilings on Deposit Rates: 25 Basis Point Increase at Both Commercial Banks and Savings Institutions

		Differences from Base Simulation			
Year	Qtr.	*RSHORT*	*RLONG*	*REQUITY*	*RMORT*
1971	1	−0.069	−0.018	−0.018	−0.036
1971	2	−0.077	−0.048	−0.035	−0.082
1971	3	−0.069	−0.060	−0.012	−0.094
1971	4	−0.030	−0.063	−0.039	−0.091
1972	1	−0.049	−0.069	−0.038	−0.108
1972	2	−0.002	−0.055	−0.006	−0.089
1972	3	−0.043	−0.087	−0.060	−0.126
1972	4	0.011	−0.061	−0.020	−0.095
Average of last 3 Qtrs.		−0.011	−0.068	−0.029	−0.103
		Demand Deposits at Commercial Banks	Time Deposits at Commercial Banks	Time Deposits at Savings Institutions	Mortgage Liability of Households
1971	1	−1.579	3.729	1.922	0.327
1971	2	−2.226	5.440	2.598	0.926
1971	3	−2.248	6.455	3.184	1.855
1971	4	−2.692	6.572	3.413	2.233
1972	1	−2.576	7.007	3.728	2.571
1972	2	−2.490	7.615	3.830	3.113
1972	3	−3.128	7.769	3.953	3.140
1972	4	−3.023	7.516	3.670	3.148
Average of last 3 Qtrs.		−2.880	7.633	3.818	3.134

Note: Rates are annual percentages. Stocks are in billions of dollars.

The imperfect substitutability of bonds and capital also means that increases in the quantity of government debt may decrease rather than increase the required rate of return on capital. There may be "crowding in" rather than "crowding out." In the complete model, the consequences of government deficits for supplies of government debt and crowding out will be reckoned automatically. The effect of such changes in relative supplies can be inferred from a simulation of the financial block by an "open market operation" involving government debt and equity. Indeed, such open market operations could conceivably be used as an instrument of monetary policy. Table 3.11 illustrates a one billion dollar shift from shorts to equity. The equity rate decreases but the impact is damped by the concurrent increase in q, which increases the supply of capital at market prices.

An important policy question for which there is no easy answer is the effect of changes in deposit ceiling rates on market interest rates, the cost of capital, and the degree of intermediation. Table 3.12 considers the effect of increase in the ceiling rates on deposits at both commercial banks and savings institutions. For such a change there is a substantial reduction in demand deposits and an increase in time and savings accounts. As can be seen from the table, such an increase is "expansionary" in that it lowers the rates on various assets, particularly mortgages.

The effects of increasing the ceiling rate at one or the other of the two types of intermediary separately can easily be simulated. Our priors imply a high degree of substitution between deposits, and either of these changes results in a substantial shift from one intermediary to the other. Increases in the ceiling rate on bank time deposits is contractionary, reflecting the absorption of reserves by reserve requirements on their deposits, whereas the increase in the rates at thrift institutions is expansionary.

8 Conclusion

It is our hope that with some improvement of the specification and the use of a somewhat more sensible error structure it will be possible to obtain estimates that are in rough accord with our priors and result in credible simulations. We also suspect, however, that it will be difficult to distinguish, on the basis of sample fits, our model from other models, those, for example, that assume perfect substitutes. Such discrimination may require the use of information about structural parameters from other sources: cross-section studies, other time series studies on different data, and studies of particular markets, like Friedman's on corporate bonds [3].

Notes

Partial support for the research reported herein was provided by the National Science Foundation.

1. Throughout, the term "assets" is used for both assets and liabilities. The latter are defined as negative assets.
2. Calculations are described in [8]. Our figures are based on more recent data.

3. We do not intend this as a derogatory term. As Leamer [5] points out, data-mining suggests purposeful search. Fishing, by contrast, has implications of unstructured activity.

4. Brainard and Smith [2] have developed a tractable procedure for computing the prior covariance matrix for a complete system of asset demands. The covariance matrices actually used in estimation are available on request.

5. Compare the results surveyed in [6, table 2].

6. One could reasonably argue that the major effect of these programs comes not from the shift in relative supplies, but rather from the increased liquidity of the secondary market for mortgages.

References

1. Backus, David, and Douglas Purvis. "An Integrated Model of Household Flow-of-Funds Allocations." *Journal of Money, Credit, and Banking* 12(2) (May 1980), 400–421.

2. Brainard, William, and Gary Smith. "The Systematic Specification of a Full Prior Covariance Matrix." 1979, mimeo.

3. Friedman, Benjamin. "Financial Flow Variables and the Short-Run Determination of Long-Term Interest Rates." *Journal of Political Economy*, 85 (1977), 661–89.

4. Goldsmith-Nagan. *Bond and Money Market Letter*, various issues, Washington, D. C.

5. Leamer, Edward. *Specification Searches*, New York: John Wiley, 1978.

6. Nordhaus, William, and Henry Wallich. "Alternatives for Debt Management," table 2. In *Issues in Federal Debt Management*. Federal Reserve Bank of Boston, 1973.

7. Purvis, Douglas. "Dynamic Models of Portfolio Behavior: More on Pitfalls in Financial Model Building." *American Economic Review*, (June 1978), 403–9.

8. Smith, Gary. "An Intrinsic Value Estimate of the Yield on Corporate Stock." 1978, mimeo.

9. ———. "Dynamic Models of Portfolio Behavior: Comment on Purvis." *American Economic Review*, 68 (June 1978), 410–16.

10. Smith, Gary, and William Brainard. "Disequilibrium Models for Financial Institutions." 1974, mimeo.

11. ———. "The Value of a Priori Information in Estimating a Financial Model." *Journal of Finance*, 31 (December 1976), 1299–1322.

12. Smith, Gary, and Kim Kowalewski. "The Spending Behavior of Wealth and Liquidity-constrained Consumers." Cowles Foundation Discussion Paper 536.

13. Survey Research Center. "Survey of Consumer Attitudes: Tables and Charts," table 19B, February 1979.

14. Tobin, James, and Willem Buiter. "Fiscal and Monetary Policies, Capital Formation, and Economic Activity." George von Furstenberg, ed., *The Government and Capital Formation*, Cambridge, MA: Ballinger, 1980, 73–151; *Essays*, Vol. 3, Chapter 11.

15. Tobin, James. "A General Equilibrium Approach to Monetary Theory." *Journal of Money, Credit, and Banking*, 1 (February 1969), 15–29; *Essays*, Vol. 1, Chapter 18.

16. Tobin, James, and William Brainard. "Pitfalls in Financial Model Building." *American Economic Review* (May 1968), 99–122; *Essays*, Vol. 1, Chapter 20.

CHAPTER 4

FINANCIAL INTERMEDIARIES

The tangible wealth of a nation consists of its natural resources, its stocks of goods, and its net claims against the rest of the world. The goods include structures, durable equipment of service to consumers or producers, and inventories of finished goods, raw materials and goods in process. A nation's wealth will help to meet its people's future needs and desires; tangible assets do so in a variety of ways, sometimes by yielding directly consumable goods and services, more often by enhancing the power of human effort and intelligence in producing consumable goods and services. There are many intangible forms of the wealth of a nation, notably the skill, knowledge and character of its population and the framework of law, convention and social interaction that sustains cooperation and community.

Some components of a nation's wealth are appropriable; they can be owned by governments, or privately by individuals or other legal entities. Some intangible assets are appropriable, notably by patents and copyrights. In a capitalist society most appropriable wealth is privately owned, more than 80 percent by value in the United States. Private properties are generally transferable from owner to owner. Markets in these properties, *capital markets*, are a prominent feature of capitalist societies. In the absence of slavery, markets in "human capital" are quite limited.

A person may be wealthy without owning any of the assets counted in appropriable *national wealth*. Instead, a personal wealth inventory would list paper currency and coin, bank deposits, bonds, stocks, mutual funds, cash values of insurance policies and pension rights. These are paper assets evidencing claims of various kinds against other individuals, companies,

Reprinted by permission from *The New Palgrave: A Dictionary of Economics*, Vol. 2, eds. John Eatwell et al., London: Macmillan Press Ltd., 1987, pp. 340–348.

institutions or governments. In reckoning personal *net worth*, each person would deduct from the value of his total assets the claims of others against him. In 1984 American households' gross holdings of financial assets amounted to about 75 percent of their net worth, and their net holdings to about 55 percent (Federal Reserve, 1984). If the net worths of all economic units of the nation are added up, paper claims and obligations cancel each other. All that remains, if valuations are consistent and the census is complete, is the value of the national wealth.

If the central government is excluded from this aggregation, *private net worth*—the aggregate net worth of individuals and institutions and subordinate governments (included in the 'private' sector because, lacking monetary powers, they have limited capacities to borrow)—will count not only the national-wealth assets they own but also their net claims against the central government. These include coin and currency, their equivalent in central bank deposit liabilities, and interest-bearing Treasury obligations. If these central government debts exceed the value of its real assets, *private net worth* will exceed national wealth. (However, in reckoning their net worth, private agents may subtract something for the future taxes they expect to pay to service the government's debts. Some economists argue that the subtraction is complete, so that public debt does not count in aggregate private wealth (Barro, 1974) while others give reasons the offset is incomplete (Tobin, 1980). The issue is not crucial for this essay.)

Outside Assets, Inside Assets and Financial Markets

Private net worth, then, consists of two parts: privately owned items of national wealth, mostly tangible assets, and government obligations. These *outside* assets are owned by private agents not directly but through the intermediation of a complex network of debts and claims, *inside* assets.

Empirical Magnitudes

For the United States at the end of 1984, the value of tangible assets, land and reproducible goods, is estimated at $13.5 trillion, nearly four times the Gross National Product for the year. Of this, $11.2 trillion were privately owned. Adding net claims against the rest of the world and privately owned claims against the federal government gives private net worth of $12.5 trillion, of which only $1.3 trillion represent outside financial assets. The degree of intermediation is indicated by the gross value of financial assets, nearly $14.8 trillion; even if equities in business are regarded as direct titles to real property and excluded from financial assets, the outstanding stock of inside assets is $9.6 trillion. Of these more than half, $5.6 trillion, are claims on financial institutions. The $9.6 trillion is an underestimate, because many inside financial transactions elude the statisticians. The relative magnitudes of these numbers have changed very little since 1953, when private net worth was $1.27 trillion, gross financial assets $1.35 trillion, $1.05 excluding equities, and GNP was $0.37 trillion (Federal Reserve, 1984).

Raymond Goldsmith, who has studied intermediation throughout a long and distinguished career and knows far more about it than anyone else, has estimated measures of intermediation for many countries over long periods of time (1969, 1985). Here is his own summary:

The creation of a modern financial superstructure, not in its details but in its essentials, was generally accomplished at a fairly early stage of a country's economic development, usually within five to seven decades from the start of modern economic growth. Thus it was essentially completed in most now-developed countries by the end of the 19th century or the eve of World War I, though somewhat earlier in Great Britain. During this period the financial interrelations ratio, the quotient of financial and tangible assets, increased fairly continuously and sharply. Since World War I or the Great Depression, however, the ratio in most of these countries has shown no upward trend, though considerable movements have occurred over shorter periods, such as sharp reductions during inflations; and though significant changes have taken place in the relative importance of the various types of financial institutions and of financial instruments. Among less developed countries, on the other hand, the financial interrelations ratio has increased substantially, particularly in the postwar period, though it generally is still well below the level reached by the now-developed countries early in the 20th century.

Goldsmith finds that a ratio of the order of unity is characteristic of financial maturity, as is illustrated by the figures for the United States given above (1985, pp. 2–3).

Goldsmith finds also that the relative importance of financial institutions, especially nonbanks, has trended upwards in most market economies but appears to taper off in mature systems. Institutions typically hold from a quarter to a half of all financial instruments. Ratios around 0.40 were typical in 1978, but there is considerably more variation among countries than in the financial interrelations ratio. The United States, at 0.27, is on the low side, probably because of its many well-organized financial markets (1985, Table 47, p. 136).

The volume of gross financial transactions is mind-boggling. The GNP velocity of the money stock in the United States is 6 or 7 per year; if intermediate as well as final transactions for goods and services are considered, the turnover may be 20 or 30 per year. But demand deposits turn over 500 times a year, 2500 times in New York City banks, indicating that most transactions are financial in nature. The value of stock market transactions alone in the United States is one third of the Gross National Product; an average share of stock changes hands every nineteen months. Gross foreign exchange transactions in United States dollars are estimated to be hundreds of billions of dollars every day. "Value added" in the financial services industries amounts to 9 percent of United States GNP (Tobin, 1984).

Outside and Inside Money

The outside/inside distinction is most frequently applied to money. *Outside money* is the monetary debt of the government and its central bank, currency and central bank deposits, sometimes referred to as "base" or "high-powered" money. *Inside money*, "low-powered," consists of private deposit obligations of other banks and depository institutions in excess of their holdings of outside money assets. Just which kinds of deposit obligations count as "money" depends on definitions, of which there are several, all somewhat arbitrary. Outside money in the United States amounted to $186 billion at the end of 1983, of which $36 billion was held as reserves by banks and other depository institutions; the remaining $150 billion was held by other private agents as currency. The total money stock M1, currency in public circulation plus checkable deposits, was $480 billion. Thus inside M1 was $294 billion, more than 60 percent of the total.

Financial Markets, Organized and Informal

Inside assets and debts wash out in aggregative accounting; one person's asset is another's debt. But for the functioning of the economy, the inside network is of great importance. *Financial markets* allow inside assets and debts to be originated and to be exchanged at will for each other and for outside financial assets. These markets deal in paper contracts and claims. They complement the markets for real properties. Private agents often borrow to buy real property and pledge the property as security; households mortgage new homes, businesses incur debt to acquire stocks of materials or goods-in-process or to purchase structures and equipment. The term *capital markets* covers both financial and property markets. *Money markets* are financial markets in which short-term debts are exchanged for outside money.

Many of the assets traded in financial markets are promises to pay currency in specified amounts at specified future dates, sometimes conditional on future events and circumstances. The currency is not always the local currency; obligations denominated in various national currencies are traded all over the world. Many traded assets are not denominated in any future monetary unit of account: equity shares in corporations, contracts for deliveries of commodities—gold, oil, soy beans, hog bellies. There are various hybrid assets: preferred stock gives holders priority in distributions of company profits up to specified pecuniary limits; convertible debentures combine promises to pay currency with rights to exchange the securities for shares.

Capital markets, including financial markets, take a variety of forms. Some are highly organized auction markets, the leading real-world approximations to the abstract perfect markets of economic theory, where all transactions occurring at any moment in a commodity or security are made at a single price and every agent who wants to buy or sell at that price is accommodated. Such markets exist in shares, bonds, overnight loans of outside money, standard commodities, and foreign currency deposits, and in futures contracts and options for most of the same items.

However, many financial and property transactions occur otherwise, in direct negotiations between the parties. Organized open markets require large tradable supplies of precisely defined homogeneous commodities or instruments. Many financial obligations are one of a kind, the promissory note of a local business proprietor, the mortgage on a specific farm or residence. The terms, conditions, and collateral are specific to the case. The habit of referring to classes of heterogeneous negotiated transactions as "markets" is metaphorical, like the use of the term "labour market" to refer to the decentralized processes by which wages are set and jobs are filled, or "computer market" to describe the pricing and selling of a host of differentiated products. In these cases the economists' faith is that the outcomes are "as if" the transaction occurred in perfect organized auction markets.

Financial Enterprises and Their Markets

Financial intermediaries are enterprises in the business of buying and selling financial assets. The accounting balance sheet of a financial intermediary is virtually 100 percent paper on both sides. The typical financial intermediary owns relatively little real property, just the structures, equipment, and materials necessary to its business. The equity of the owners, or the equivalent capital reserve account for mutual, cooperative, nonprofit, or public institutions, is small compared to the enterprises' financial obligations.

Financial intermediaries are major participants in organized financial markets. They take large asset positions in market instruments; their equities and some of their liabilities, certificates of deposit or debt securities, are traded in those markets. They are not just middlemen like dealers and brokers whose main business is to execute transactions for clients.

Financial intermediaries are the principal makers of the informal financial markets discussed above. Banks and savings institutions hold mortgages, commercial loans, and consumer credit; their liabilities are mainly checking accounts, savings deposits, and certificates of deposit. Insurance companies and pension funds negotiate private placements of corporate bonds and commercial mortgages; their liabilities are contracts with policy-holders and obligations to future retirees. Thus financial intermediaries do much more than participate in organized markets. If financial intermediaries confined themselves to repackaging open market securities for the convenience of their creditors, they would be much less significant actors on the economic scene.

Financial businesses seek customers, both lenders and borrowers, not only by interest rate competition but by differentiating and advertising their "products." Financial products are easy to differentiate, by variations in maturities, fees, auxiliary services, office locations and hours of business, and many other features. As might be expected, non-price competition is especially active when prices, in this case interest rates, are fixed by regulation or by tacit or explicit collusion. But the industry is by the heterogeneous nature of its products monopolistically competitive; non-price competition flourishes even when interest rates are free to move. The industry shows symptoms of "wastes of monopolistic competition." Retail offices of banks and savings institutions cluster like competing gasoline stations. Much claimed product differentiation is trivial and atmospheric, emphasized and exaggerated in advertising.

Financial intermediaries cultivate long-term relationships with customers. Even in the highly decentralized financial system of the United States, local financial intermediaries have some monopoly power, some clienteles who will stay with them even if their interest rates are somewhat less favourable than those elsewhere. Since much business is bilaterally negotiated, there are ample opportunities for price discrimination. The typical business customer of a bank is both a borrower and a depositor, often simultaneously. The customer "earns" the right for credit accommodation when he needs it by lending surplus funds to the same bank when he has them. The same reciprocity occurs between credit unions and mutual savings institutions and some of their members. Close ties frequently develop between a financial intermediary and non-financial businesses whose sales depend on availability of credit to their customers, for example between automobile dealers and banks. Likewise, builders and realtors have funded and controlled many savings and loan associations in order to facilitate mortgage lending to home buyers.

Financial intermediaries balance the credit demands they face with their available funds by adjusting not only interest rates but also the other terms of loans. They also engage in quantitative rationing, the degree of stringency varying with the availability and costs of funds to the intermediary. Rationing occurs naturally as a by-product of lending decisions made and negotiated case by case. Most such loans require collateral, and the amount and quality of the collateral can be adjusted both to individual circumstances and to overall market conditions. Borrowers are classified as to riskiness and charged rates that vary with their classification.

United States commercial banks follow the "prime rate convention." One or another of the large banks acts as price leader and sets a rate on six-month commercial loans for its prime quality borrowers. If other large banks agree, as is usually the case, they follow, and the rate becomes standard for the whole industry until one of the leading banks decides another change is needed to stay in line with open-market interest rates. Loan customers are rated by the number of half-points above prime at which they will be accommodated. Of course, some applications for credit are just turned away. One mechanism of short-term adjustment to credit market conditions is to stiffen or relax the risk classifications of customers, likewise to deny credit to more or fewer applicants. Similar mechanisms for rationing help to equate demands to supplies or home mortgage finance and consumer credit.

The Functions of Financial Markets and Intermediary Institutions

Intermediation, as defined and described above, converts the outside privately owned wealth of the economy into the quite different forms in which its ultimate owners hold their accumulated savings. Financial markets alone accomplish considerable intermediation, just by facilitating the origination and exchange of inside assets. Financial intermediaries greatly extend the process, adding "markets" that would not exist without them, and participating along with other agents in other markets, organized or informal.

What economic functions does intermediation in general perform? What do inside markets add to markets in the basic outside assets? What functions does institutional intermediation by financial intermediaries perform beyond those of open markets in financial instruments? Economists characteristically impose on themselves questions like these, which do not seem problematic to lay practitioners. Economists start from the presumption that financial activities are epiphenomena, that they create a veil obscuring to superficial observers an underlying reality which they do not affect. The celebrated Modigliani–Miller theorem (1958), generalized beyond the original intent of the authors, says so. With its help the sophisticated economist can pierce the veil and see that the values of financial assets are just those of the outside assets to which they are ultimately claims, no matter how circuitous the path from the one to the other.

However, economists also understand how the availability of certain markets alters, usually for the better, the outcomes prevailing in their absence. For a primitive illustration, consider the functions of inside loan markets as brilliantly described by Irving Fisher (1930). Each household has an inter-temporal utility function in consumptions today and at future times, a sequence of what we now would call dated "endowments" of consumption, and an individual "backyard" production function by which consumption less than endowment at any one date can be transformed into consumption above endowment at another date. Absent the possibility of intertemporal trades with others, each household has to do its best on its own; its best will be to equate its marginal rate of substitution in utility between any two dates with its marginal rate of transformation in production between the same dates, with the usual amendments for corner solutions. The gains from trade, i.e., in this case from auction markets in inter-household lending and borrowing, arise from differences among households in those autarkic rates of substitution and transformation. They are qualitatively the same as those from free contemporaneous trade in commodities between agents or nations.

The introduction of consumer loans in this Fisherian model will alter the individual and aggregate paths of consumption and saving. It is not possible to say whether it will raise or lower the aggregate amount of capital, here in the sense of labour endowments in process of producing future rather than current consumable output. In either case it is likely to be a Pareto-optimal improvement, although even this is not guaranteed *a priori*.

Similar argument suggests several reasons why ultimate savers, lenders, creditors prefer the liabilities of financial intermediaries not only to direct ownership of real property but also to the direct debt and equity issues of investors, borrowers and debtors:

Convenience of Denomination

Issuers of securities find it costly to cut their issues into the variety of small and large denominations savers find convenient and commensurate to their means. The financial intermediary can break up large-denomination bonds and loans into amounts convenient to small savers, or combine debtors' obligations into large amounts convenient to the wealthy. Economies of scale and specialization in financial transactions enable financial intermediaries to tailor assets and liabilities to the needs and preferences of both lenders and borrowers. This service is especially valuable for agents on both sides whose needs vary in amount continuously; they like deposit accounts and credit lines whose use they can vary at will on their own initiative.

Risk Pooling, Reduction and Allocation

The risks incident to economic activities take many forms. Some are nation-wide or world-wide—wars and revolutions, shifts in international comparative advantage, government fiscal and monetary policies, prices and supplies of oil and other basic materials. Some are specific to particular enterprises and technologies—the capacity and integrity of managers, the qualities of new products, the local weather. A financial intermediary can specialize in the appraisal of risks, especially specific risks, with expertise in the gathering and interpretation of information costly or unavailable to individual savers. By pooling the funds of its creditors, the financial intermediary can diversify away risks to an extent that the individual creditors cannot, because of the costs of transactions as well as the inconvenience of fixed lumpy denominations.

According to Joseph Schumpeter ([1911] 1934, pp. 72–4), bankers are the gatekeepers—Schumpeter's word is "ephor"—of capitalist economic development; their strategic function is to screen potential innovators and advance the necessary purchasing power to the most promising. They are the source of purchasing power for investment and innovation, beyond the savings accumulated from past economic development. In practice, the cachet of a banker often enables his customer also to obtain credit from other sources or to float paper in open markets.

Maturity Shifting

A financial intermediary typically reconciles differences among borrowers and lenders in the timing of payments. Bank depositors want to commit funds for shorter times than borrowers want to have them. Business borrowers need credit to bridge the time gap between the inputs to profitable production and their output and sales. This source of bank business is formally modeled by Diamond and Dybvig (1983). The bank's scale of operations enables it to stagger the due dates of, say, half-year loans so as to accommodate depositors who want their money back in three months or one month or on demand. The reverse maturity shift may occur in other financial intermediaries. An insurance company or pension fund might invest short-term the savings its policy-owners or future pensioners will not claim for many years.

Transforming Illiquid Assets into Liquid Liabilities

Liquidity is a matter of degree. A perfectly liquid asset may be defined as one whose full present value can be realized, i.e., turned into purchasing power over goods and services, immediately. Dollar bills are perfectly liquid, and so for practical purposes are demand deposits and other deposits transferable to third parties by check or wire. Liquidity in this sense does not necessarily mean predictability of value. Securities traded on well organized markets are liquid. Any person selling at a given time will get the same price whether he decided and prepared to sell a month before or on the spur of the moment. But the price itself can vary unpredictably from minute to minute. Contrast a house, neither fully liquid nor predictable in value. Its selling proceeds at this moment are likely to be greater the longer it has been on the market. Consider the six-month promissory note of a small business proprietor known only to his local banker. However sure the payment on the scheduled date, the note may not be marketable at all. If the lender wants to realize its value before maturity, he will have to find a buyer and negotiate. A financial intermediary holds illiquid assets while its liabilities are liquid, and holds assets unpredictable in value while it guarantees the value of its liabilities. This is the traditional business of commercial banks, and the reason for the strong and durable relations of banks and their customers.

Substitution of Inside for Outside Assets

What determines the aggregate liabilities and assets of financial intermediaries? What determines the gross aggregate of inside assets generated by financial markets in general, including open markets as well as financial intermediaries? How can the empirical regularities found by Goldsmith, cited above, be explained?

Economic theory offers no answers to these questions. The differences among agents that invite mutually beneficial transactions, like those discussed above, offer opportunities for inside markets. Theory can tell us little *a priori* about the size of such differences. Moreover, markets are costly to operate, whether they are organized auction markets in homogeneous instruments or the imperfect "markets" in heterogeneous contracts in which financial intermediaries are major participants. Society cannot afford all the markets that might exist in the absence of transactions costs and other frictions, and theory has little to say on which will arise and survive.

The macroeconomic consequence of inside markets and financial intermediaries is generally to provide substitutes for outside assets and thus to economize their supplies. That is, the same microeconomic outcomes are achievable with smaller supplies of one or more of the outside assets than in the absence of intermediation. The way in which intermediation mobilizes the surpluses of some agents to finance the deficits of others is the theme of the classic influential work of Gurley and Shaw (1960).

Consider, for example, how commercial banking diminishes the need of business firms for net worth invested in inventories, by channeling the seasonal cash surpluses of some firms to the contemporaneous seasonal deficits of others. Imagine two firms A and B with opposite and complementary seasonal zigzag patterns. A needs $2 in cash at time zero to buy inputs for production in period 1 sold for $2; the pattern repeats in 3, 4, ... B needs $2 in cash at time 1 to buy inputs for production in period 2 sold for $2 in period 3, and so on in 4, 5, ... In the absence of their commercial bank, A and B each need $2 of net worth to carry on business; from period to period each alternates holding it in cash and in goods-in-process between them the two firms always are holding $2 of currency and $2 of inventories. Enters the bank and lends A half the $2 he needs to carry his inventory in period 1; A repays the loan from sales proceeds the next period, 2; the bank now lends $1 to B, ... A and B now need only $1 of currency, each has on average net worth of $1.50 – $2 and $1 alternating; as before they are together always holding $2 of inventories. Moreover, with a steady deposit of $2 from a third party, the bank could finance both businesses completely; they would need no net worth of their own. The example is trivial, but commercial banking paper can be understood as circulation of deposits and loans among businesses and as a revolving fund assembled from other sources and lent to businesses.

As a second primitive example, consider the effects of introducing markets that enable risks to be borne by those households more prepared to take them. Suppose that of two primary outside assets, currency and tangible capital, the return on the latter has the greater variance. Individuals who are risk-neutral will hold all their wealth (possibly excepting minimal transactions balances of currency) in capital as long as its expected return exceeds the expected real return on currency. If these more adventurous households are not numerous and wealthy enough to absorb all the capital, the expected return on capital will have to exceed that on currency enough to induce risk-averse wealth-owners to hold the remainder. In this equilibrium the money price of capital and its mean real return are determined so as to allocate the two assets between the two kinds of households. Now suppose that the risk-neutral households can borrow from the risk-averse types, most realistically via financial intermediaries, and that the latter households regard those debts as close substitutes for currency, indeed as inside money if intermediation by financial intermediaries is involved. The inside assets do double duty, providing the services and security of money to those who value them while enabling the more adventurous to hold capital in excess of their own net worth. As a result, the private sector as a whole will want to hold a larger proportion of its wealth in capital at any given expected real return on capital. In equilibrium, the aggregate capital stock will be larger and its expected return, equal to its marginal productivity in a steady state, will be lower than in the absence of intermediation.

Intermediation can diminish the private sector's need not just for outside money but for net worth and tangible capital. These economies generally require financial markets in which financial intermediaries are major participants, because they involve heterogeneous credit instruments and risk pooling. In the absence of home mortgages, consumer credit, and personal loans for education, young households would not be able to spend their future wages and salaries until they receive them. Constraints on borrowing against future earnings make the age-weighted average net non-human wealth of the population greater, but the relaxation of such liquidity constraints increases household welfare. Financial intermediaries invest the savings of older and more affluent households in loans to their younger and less wealthy contemporaries; otherwise those savings would go into outside assets. Likewise insurance makes it unnecessary to accumulate savings as precaution against certain risks, for example the living and medical expenses of unusual longevity. It is an all too common fallacy to assume that arrangements that increase aggregate savings and tangible wealth always augment social welfare.

Deposit Creation and Reserve Requirements

The substitution of inside money for outside money is the familiar story of deposit creation, in which the banking system turns a dollar of base or "high-powered" money into several dollars of deposits. The extra dollars are inside or "low-powered" money. The banks need to hold only a fraction k, set by law or convention or prudence, of their deposit liabilities as reserves in base money. In an equilibrium in which they hold no excess reserves, their deposits will be a multiple $1/k$ of their reserves; they will have created $(1 - k)/k$ dollars of substitute money.

A key step in this process is that any bank with excess reserves makes a roughly equal amount of additional loans, crediting the borrowers with deposits. As the borrowers draw checks, these new deposits are transferred to other accounts, most likely in other banks. As deposits move to other banks, so do reserves, dollar for dollar. But now those banks have excess reserves and act in like manner. The process continues until all banks are "loaned up," i.e., deposits have increased enough so that the initial excess reserves have become reserves that the banks require or desire.

The textbook fable of deposit creation does not do justice to the full macroeconomics of the process. The story is incomplete without explaining how the public is induced to borrow more and to hold more deposits. The borrowers and the depositors are not the same public. No one borrows at interest in order to hold idle deposits. To attract additional borrowers, banks must lower interest rates or relax their collateral requirements or their risk standards. The new borrowers are likely to be businesses that need bank credit to build up inventories of materials or goods-in-process. The loans lead quickly to additional production and economic activity. Or banks buy securities in the open market, raising their prices and lowering market interest rates. The lower market rates may encourage businesses to float issues of commercial paper, bonds or stocks, but the effects of investment in inventories or plant and equipment are less immediate and less potent than the extension of bank credit to a business otherwise held back by illiquidity. In either case, lower interest rates induce other members of the public, those who indirectly receive the loan disbursements or those who sell securities to banks, to hold additional deposits. They will be acquiring other assets as well, some in banks, some in other financial intermediaries, some in open financial markets. Lower interest rates may also induce banks themselves to hold extra excess reserves.

Interest rates are not the only variables of adjustment. Nominal incomes are rising at the same time, in some mixture of real quantities and prices depending on macroeconomic circumstances. The rise in incomes and economic activities creates new needs for transactions balances of money. Thus the process by which excess reserves are absorbed entails changes in interest rates, real economic activity, and prices in some combination. It is possible to describe scenarios in which the entire ultimate adjustment is in one of these variables. Wicksell's cumulative credit expansion, which in the end just raises prices, is a classic example.

Do banks have a unique magic by which asset purchases generate their own financing? Is the magic due to the "moneyness" of the banks' liabilities? The preceding account indicates it is not magic but reserve requirements. Moreover, a qualitatively similar story could be told if reserve requirements were related to bank assets or non-monetary liabilities, and even if banks happened to have no monetary liabilities at all. In the absence of reserve requirements aggregate bank assets and liabilities, relative to the size of the economy, would be naturally limited by public supplies and demands at interest rates that cover banks' costs and normal profits. If, instead of banks, savings institutions specializing in mortgage lending were subject to reserve requirements, their incentives to minimize excess reserves would inspire a story telling how additional mortgage lending brings home savings deposits to match (Tobin, 1963).

Risks, Runs and Regulations

Some financial intermediaries confine themselves to activities that entail virtually no risk either to the institution itself or to its clients. An open-end mutual fund or unit trust holds only fully liquid assets traded continuously in organized markets. It promises the owners of its shares payment on demand at their pro rata net value calculated at the market prices of the underlying assets—no more, no less. The fund can always meet such demands by selling assets it holds. The shareowners pay in one way or another an agreed fee from the services of the fund—the convenience and flexibility of denomination, the bookkeeping, the transactions costs, the diversification, the expertise in choosing assets. The shareowners bear the market risks on the fund's portfolio—no less and, assuming the fund is honest, no more. Government regulations are largely confined to those governing all public security issues, designed to protect buyers from deceptions and insider manipulations. In the United States regulation of this kind is the province of the federal Securities and Exchange Commission.

Most financial intermediaries do take risks. The risks are intrinsic to the functions they serve and to the profit opportunities attracting financial entrepreneurs and investors in their enterprises. For banks and similar financial intermediaries, the principal risk is that depositors may at any time demand payments the institution can meet, if at all, only at extraordinary cost. Many of the assets are illiquid, unmarketable. Others can be liquidated at short notice only at substantial loss. In some cases, bad luck or imprudent management brings insolvency; the institution could never meet its obligations no matter how long its depositors and other creditors wait. In other cases, the problem is just illiquidity; the assets would suffice if they could be held until maturity, until buyers or lenders could be found, or until normal market conditions returned.

Banks and other financial intermediaries hold reserves, in currency or its equivalent, deposits in central banks, or in other liquid forms as precaution against withdrawals by their depositors. For a single bank, the withdrawal is usually a shift of deposits to other banks or financial intermediaries, arising from a negative balance in interbank clearings of checks or other transfers to third parties at the initiative of depositors. For the banking system, as a whole, withdrawal is a shift by the public from deposits to currency.

"Withdrawals" may in practice include the exercise of previously agreed borrowing rights. Automatic overdraft privileges are more common in other countries, notably the United Kingdom and British Commonwealth nations, than in the United States. They are becoming more frequent in the United States as an adjunct of bank credit cards. Banks' business loan customers often have explicit or implicit credit lines on which they can draw on demand.

Unless financial intermediaries hold safe liquid assets of predictable value matched in maturities to their liabilities—in particular, currency or equivalent against all their demand obligations—they and their creditors can never be completely protected from withdrawals. The same is true of the banking system as a whole, and of all intermediaries other than simple mutual funds. "Runs," sudden, massive, and contagious withdrawals, are always possible. They destroy prudent and imprudent institutions alike, along with their depositors and creditors. Of course, careful depositors inform themselves about the intermediaries to which they entrust their funds, about their asset portfolios, policies and skills. Their choices among competing depositories provide some discipline, but it can never be enough to rule out disasters. What the most careful depositor cannot foresee is the behaviour of other depositors, and it is rational for the well-informed depositor of a sound bank to withdraw funds if he believes that others are doing so or are about to do so.

Governments generally regulate the activities of banks and other financial intermediaries in greater detail than they do nonfinancial enterprises. The basic motivations for regulation appear to be the following:

It is costly, perhaps impossible, for individual depositors to appraise the soundness and liquidity of financial institutions and to estimate the probabilities of failures even if they could assume that other depositors would do likewise. It is impossible for them to estimate the probabilities of "runs." Without regulation, the liabilities of suspect institutions would be valued below par in check collections. Prior to 1866 banks in the United States were allowed to issue notes payable to bearers on demand, surrogates for government currency. The notes circulated at discounts varying with the current reputations of the issuers. A system in which transactions media other than government currency continuously vary in value depending on the issuer is clumsy and costly.

The government has obligation to provide at low social cost an efficient system of transactions media, and also a menu of secure and convenient assets for citizens who wish to save in the national monetary unit of account. Those transactions media and saving assets can be offered by banks and other financial intermediaries, in a way that retains most of the efficiencies of decentralization and competition, if and only if government imposes some regulations and assumes some residual responsibilities. The government's role takes several forms.

Reserve Requirements
An early and obvious intervention was to require banks to hold reserves in designated safe and liquid forms against their obligations, especially

their demand liabilities. Left to themselves, without such requirements, some banks might sacrifice prudence for short-term profit. Paradoxically, however, required reserves are not available for meeting withdrawals unless the required ratio is 100 percent. If the reserve requirement is 10 percent of deposits, then withdrawal of one dollar from a bank reduces its reserve holdings by one dollar but its reserve requirement by only ten cents. Only excess reserves or other liquid assets are precautions against withdrawals. The legal reserve requirement just shifts the bank's prudential calculation to the size of these secondary reserves. Reserve requirements serve functions quite different from their original motivation. In the systems that use them, notably the United States, they are the fulcrum for central bank control of economy-wide monetary conditions. (They are also an interest-free source of finance of government debt, but in the United States today this amounts to only $45 billion of a total debt to the public of $1700 billion.)

Last-resort Lending

Banks and other financial intermediaries facing temporary shortages of reserves and secondary reserves of liquid assets can borrow them from other institutions. In the United States, for example, the well organized market for "federal funds" allows banks short of reserves to borrow them overnight from other banks. Or banks can gain reserves by attracting more deposits, offering higher interest rates on them than depositors are getting elsewhere. These ways of correcting reserve positions are not available to troubled banks, suspected of deep-rooted problems of liquidity or solvency or both, for example bad loans. Nor will they meet a system-wide run from liabilities of banks and other financial intermediaries into currency.

Banks in need of reserves can also borrow from the central bank, and much of this borrowing is routine, temporary, and seasonal. Massive central bank credit is the last resort of troubled banks which cannot otherwise satisfy the demands of their depositors without forced liquidations of their assets. The government is the ultimate supplier of currency and reserves in aggregate. The primary *raison d'être* of the central bank is to protect the economy from runs into currency. System-wide shortages of currency and reserves can be relieved not only by central bank lending to individual banks but by central bank purchases of securities in the open market. The Federal Reserve's inability or unwillingness—which it was is still debated—to supply the currency bank depositors wanted in the early 1930s led to disastrous panic and epidemic bank failures. No legal or doctrinal obstacles would now stand in the way of such a rescue.

Deposit Insurance
Federal insurance of bank deposits in the United States has effectively prevented contagious runs and epidemic failures since its enactment in 1935. Similar insurance applies to deposits in savings institutions. In effect, the federal government assumes a contingent residual liability to pay the insured deposits in full, even if the assets of the financial intermediary are permanently inadequate to do so. The insured institutions are charged premiums for the service, but the fund in which they are accumulated is not and cannot be large enough to eliminate possible calls on the Treasury. Although the guarantees are legally limited to a certain amount, now $100,000, per account, in practice depositors have eventually recovered their full deposits in most cases. Indeed the guarantee seems now to have been extended *de facto* to all deposits, at least in major banks.

Deposit insurance impairs such discipline as surveillance by large depositors might impose on financial intermediaries; instead the task of surveillance falls on the governmental insurance agencies themselves (in the United States the Federal Deposit Insurance Corporation and the Federal Savings and Loan Insurance Corporation) and on other regulatory authorities (the United States Comptroller of the Currency, the Federal Reserve, and various state agencies). Insurance transfers some risks from financial intermediary depositors and owners to taxpayers at large, while virtually eliminating risks of runs. Those are risks we generate ourselves; they magnify the unavoidable natural risks of economic life. Insurance is a mutual compact to enable us to refrain from *sauve qui peut* behaviour that can inflict grave damage on us all. Formally, an uninsured system has two equilibria, a good one with mutual confidence and a bad one with runs. Deposit insurance eliminates the bad one (Diamond and Dybvig, 1983).

One hundred percent reserve deposits would, of course, be perfectly safe—that is, as safe as the national currency—and would not have to be insured. Those deposits would in effect *be* currency, but in a secure and conveniently checkable form. One can imagine a system in which banks and other financial intermediaries offered such accounts, with the reserves behind them segregated from those related to the other business of the institution. That other business would include receiving deposits which required fractional or zero reserves and were insured only partially, if at all. The costs of the 100 percent reserve deposit accounts would be met by service charges, or by government interest payments on the reserves, justified by the social benefits of a safe and efficient transactions medium. The burden of risk and supervision now placed on the insuring and regulating agencies would be greatly relieved. It is, after all, historical accident that supplies of transactions media in modern economies came to be byproducts of banking business and vulnerable to its risks.

Government may insure financial intermediaries' loans as well as deposits. Insurance of home mortgages in the United States not only has protected the institutions that hold them and their depositors but has converted the insured mortgages into marketable instruments.

Balance Sheet Supervision
Government surveillance of financial intermediaries limits their freedom of choice of assets and liabilities, in order to limit the risks to depositors and insurers. Standards of adequacy of capital—owners' equity at risk in the case of private corporations, net worth in the case of mutual and other nonprofit forms of organization—are enforced for the same reasons. Periodic examinations check the condition of the institution, the quality of its loans, and the accuracy of its accounting statements. The regulators may close an institution if further operation is judged to be damaging to the interests of the depositors and the insurer.

Legislation which regulates financial intermediaries has differentiated them by purpose and function. Commercial banks, savings institutions, home building societies, credit unions, and insurance companies are legally organized for different purposes. They are subject to different rules governing the nature of their assets. For example, home building societies—savings and loan associations in the United States—have been required to keep most of their asset portfolios in residential mortgages. Restrictions of this kind mean that when wealth-owners shift funds from one type of financial intermediary to another, they alter relative demands for assets of different kinds. Shifts of deposits from commercial banks to building societies would increase mortgage lending relative to commercial lending. Regulations have also restricted the kinds of liabilities allowed various types of financial intermediary. Until recently in the United States, only banks were permitted to have liabilities payable on demand to third parties by check or wire. Currently deregulation is relaxing specialized restrictions on financial intermediary assets and liabilities and blurring historical distinctions of purpose and function.

Interest Ceilings

Government regulations in many countries set ceilings on the interest rates that can be charged on loans and on the rates that can be paid on deposits, both at banks and at other financial intermediaries. In the United States the Banking Act of 1935 prohibited payment of interest on demand deposits. After the second world war effective ceilings on savings and time deposits in banks and savings institutions were administratively set, and on occasion changed, by federal agencies. Under legislation of 1980, these regulations are being phased out.

The operating characteristics of a system of financial intermediaries in which interest rates on deposits of various types, as well as on loans, are set by free competition are quite different from those of a system in which financial intermediary rates are subject to legal ceilings or central bank guidance, or set by agreement among a small number of institutions. For example, when rates on deposits are administratively set, funds flow out of financial intermediaries when open market rates rise and return to financial intermediaries when they fall. The processes of "disintermediation" and "re-intermediation" are diminished when financial intermediary rates are free to move parallel to open market rates. Likewise flows between different financial intermediaries due to administratively set rate differences among them are reduced when they are all free to compete for funds.

A regime with market-determined interest rates on moneys and near-moneys has significantly different macroeconomic characteristics from a regime constrained by ceilings on deposit interest rates. Since the opportunity cost of holding deposits is largely independent of the general level of interest rates, the "LM" curve is steeper in the unregulated regime. Both central bank operations and exogenous monetary shocks could be expected to have larger effects on nominal income, while fiscal measures and other shocks to aggregate demand for goods and services would have smaller effects (Tobin, 1983).

Entry, Branching, Merging

Entry into regulated financial businesses is generally controlled, as are establishing branches or subsidiaries and merging of existing institutions. In the United States, charters are issued either by the federal government or by state governments, and regulatory powers are also divided. Until recently banks and savings institutions, no matter by whom chartered, were not allowed to operate in more than one state. This rule, combined with various restrictions on branches within states, gave the United States a much larger number of distinct financial enterprises, many of them very small and very local, than is typical in other countries. The prohibition of interstate operations is now being eroded and may be effectively eliminated in the next few years.

Deregulation has been forced by innovations in financial technology that made old regulations either easy hurdles to circumvent or obsolete barriers to efficiency. New opportunities not only are breaking down the walls separating financial intermediaries of different types and specializations. They are also bringing other businesses, both financial and nonfinancial, into activities previously reserved to regulated financial institutions. Mutual funds and brokers offer accounts from which funds can be withdrawn on demand or transferred to third parties by check or wire. National retail chains are becoming financial supermarkets—offering credit cards, various mutual funds, instalment lending, and insurance along with their vast menus of consumer goods and services; in effect, they would like to become full-service financial intermediaries. At the same time, the traditional intermediaries are moving, as fast as they can obtain government permission, into lines of business from which they have been excluded. Only time will tell how these commercial and political conflicts are resolved and how the financial system will be reshaped (*Economic Report of the President*, 1985, ch. 5).

Portfolio Behaviour of Financial Intermediaries

A large literature has attempted to estimate econometrically the choices of assets and liabilities by financial intermediaries, their relationships to open market interest rates and to other variables exogenous to them. Models of the portfolio behaviour of the various species of financial intermediary also involve estimation of the supplies of funds to them, and the demands for credit, from other sectors of the economy, particularly households and nonfinancial businesses. Recent research is presented in Dewald and Friedman (1980).

Difficult econometric problems arise in using time series for these purposes because of regime changes. For example, when deposit interest rate ceilings are effective, financial intermediaries are quantity-takers in the deposit markets; when the ceilings are non-constraining or non-existent, both the interest rates and the quantities are determined jointly by the schedules of supplies of deposits by the public and of demands for them by the financial intermediary. Similar problems arise in credit markets where interest rates, even though unregulated, are administered by financial intermediaries themselves and move sluggishly. The prime commercial loan rate is one case; mortgage rates in various periods are another. In these cases and others, the markets are not cleared at the established rates. Either the financial intermediary or the borrowers are quantity-takers, or perhaps both in some proportions. Changes in the rates follow, dependent on the amount of excess demand or supply. These problems of modeling and econometric estimation are discussed in papers in the reference above. The seminal paper is Modigliani and Jaffee (1969).

Bibliography

Barro, R. 1974. Are government bonds net wealth? *Journal of Political Economy* 82(6), November–December, 1095–117.

Dewald W. G. and Friedman. B. M. 1980. Financial market behavior, capital formation, and economic performance. (A conference supported by the National Science Foundation.) *Journal of Money, Credit and Banking*, Special Issue 12(2), May.

Diamond, D. W. and Dybvig, P. H. 1983. Bank runs, deposit insurance, and liquidity. *Journal of Political Economy* 91(3), June, 401–19.

Economic Report of the President. 1985. Washington, DC: Government Printing Office, February.

Federal Reserve System, Board of Governors. 1984. *Balance Sheets for the US Economy 1945–83*. November, Washington, DC.

Fisher, I. 1930. *The Theory of Interest.* New York: Macmillan.

Goldsmith, R. W. 1969. *Financial Structure and Development.* New Haven: Yale University Press.

Goldsmith, R. W. 1985. *Comparative National Balance Sheets: A Study of Twenty Countries, 1688–1978.* Chicago: University of Chicago Press.

Gurley, J. G. and Shaw, E. S. 1960. *Money in a Theory of Finance.* Washington, DC: Brookings Institution.

Modigliani, F. and Miller, M. H. 1958. The cost of capital, corporation finance and the theory of investment. *American Economic Review* 48(3), June, 261–97.

Modigliani, F. and Jaffee, D. M. 1969. A theory and test of credit rationing. *American Economic Review* 59(5), December, 850–72.

Schumpeter, J. A. 1911. *The Theory of Economic Development.* Trans. from the German by R. Opie, Cambridge, Mass.: Harvard University Press, 1934.

Tobin, J. 1963. Commercial banks as creators of "money". In *Banking and Monetary Studies,* ed. D. Carson, Homewood, Ill.: Richard D. Irwin.

Tobin, J. 1980. *Asset Accumulation and Economic Activity.* Oxford: Blackwell.

Tobin, J. 1983. Financial structure and monetary rules. *Kredit und Kapital* 16(2), 155–71; *Essays,* Vol. 1, Chapter 16.

Tobin, J. 1984. On the efficiency of the financial system. *Lloyds Bank Review* 153, July, 1–15; *Policies for Prosperity,* Chapter 26.

CHAPTER 5

MONEY

Money as a Social Institution and Public Good

Among the conventions of almost every human society of historical record has been the use of *money*, that is, particular commodities or tokens as measures of value and media of exchange in economic transactions. Somehow the members of a society agree on what will be acceptable tender in making payments and settling debts among themselves. General agreement to the convention, not the particular media agreed upon, is the source of money's immense value to the society. In this respect money is similar to language, standard time, or the convention designating the side of the road for passing.

The reason for the universality of money as a social institution is that it facilitates trade. Trade among individuals enables them to achieve much higher standards of living than if each person or family were restricted to autarchic subsistence. Because of economies of scale, division of labour among specialists yields enormous gains. Of course, trades have always taken place by barter, and even in modern economies many exchanges occur without money. Barter is usually bilateral, thus in Jevons's famous phrase it requires "a double coincidence [of wants], which will rarely happen" (1875:3). Multilateral trade is much more efficient, permitting each trader bilateral imbalances provided her trade in aggregate is balanced. Imagine, for example, that for lack of double coincidences no bilateral trades are possible among A, B and C because A wants C's goods, B wants A's and C wants B's. Obviously three-way exchange would benefit everyone.

Reprinted by permission from *The New Palgrave Dictionary of Money and Finance*, Vol. 2, eds. John Eatwell et al., London: Macmillan Press Ltd., 1992, pp. 770–779.

Multilateral barter is conceivable. It could be arranged by putting participants in simultaneous communication with each other—in person as at a village market or a commodity or stock exchange, or by modern telecommunications. But any multi-participant multi-commodity market would need a clearing mechanism. A trader would not have to be balanced with every other trader. But in the absence of a money each trader would have to be balanced in every commodity. This would be awkward and inefficient. Participants would need to come to market with inventories of many goods. A natural conclusion of any one market session would be intertemporal deals, commodities acquired today in exchange for promised future deliveries of the same or other commodities. Without money, this too would be awkward: a typical trader would end up with debts to or claims on other traders in many specific commodities.

One could imagine using intrinsically valueless tokens during a market session to lubricate barter—like poker chips for scorekeeping in a stakeless poker game. The tokens would make it possible to price each commodity in a common *numéraire* rather than in each of numerous other commodities. But if the tokens became worthless at the end of the session, each participant would have to be required to return as many tokens as he or she started with. Otherwise no one would sell useful goods for tokens, for fear of leaving the market with them rather than with commodities of value. If instead the tokens will be acceptable tenders in this and other markets in future—well, then they are money (on these issues see Hawtrey 1927, ch. 1; Starr 1972; Shubik 1984; Kareken and Wallace 1980).

The social convention makes a society's money generally acceptable within it, and the practice of general acceptability reinforces the convention. Y accepts money from X in exchange for goods and services and other things of value because Y is confident that Z, A, B, ..., and indeed X will in turn accept that same money. Moreover, money is accepted from the bearer immediately and impersonally—without delay, without identification. Since an economic agent's purchases and sales, outlays and receipts, are not perfectly synchronous, each agent's inventory of money fluctuates in size as money circulates throughout the economy. These fluctuations in individual money holdings enable essential intertemporal exchanges to take place. Workers are paid for their labour today, and next week they buy the food and clothing that are the truly desired proceeds of their work. The farmer and the tailor accumulate money from those sales; on payday they pay it out to their hired hands.

The moneys chosen by societies have varied tremendously over human history. So have their languages. In each case, what is universal and important is that something is chosen, not what is chosen. The variety of choice defies generalizations about the intrinsic properties of moneys. Livestock, salt, glass beads and seashells have served as money. Major grain crops were natural media for payments of wages and rents, and therefore in other transactions and accounts. Cigarettes were money in prisoner-of-war camps. On the island of Yap debts were settled by changing the ownership of large immovable stone wheels. The practice continued after the sea flooded their site and the stones were invisible at the bottom of a lagoon. (Similarly when gold was international money in the twentieth-century, title to it often changed while the gold itself, safe in underground vaults, never moved.)

Some moneys have been commodities valued independently of their monetary role, intrinsically useful in production or consumption. Others have been tokens of no intrinsic utility and negligible cost of production, coins or pieces of paper. Commodity moneys derive their value partly, and token moneys wholly, from the social convention that designates them as money.

In modern nation-states the sovereign government can generally determine the society's money. For example, the United States constitution assigns to the federal government (thus, not to the states) the power "to coin money, regulate the value thereof, and of foreign coin." The central government defines the monetary unit, decides in what media taxes and other debts to the government itself may be paid, and defines what media are legal tender in the settlement of other debts and contracts (Starr 1974).

Precious Metals as Money

Gold and silver have histories going back many centuries as the moneys of choice of many societies and as international media of exchange. Copper coinage antedates them, but copper became too abundant and was relegated to subsidiary coins. The precious metals are durable. They are divisible into convenient denominations. They can be made into ingots, bars and coins of standard weights. When used as moneys, they have been sufficiently scarce—relative to the non-monetary demands for them—as to pack considerable value into convenient portable forms. They glitter. They have long been prized for ornament and display. Gold and silver, one or the other or both, were the basic moneys of Europe and of European dominions and settlements throughout the world from the 17th century, or before, until recently. In modern times gold, in particular, acquired awesome mystique (Keynes 1930).

Sovereigns minted these precious metals on demand into coins of their own realms, with their own names. In addition to minting *full-bodied* coins for public circulation, sovereigns commonly provided *token* coins made of metals, convenient for retail transactions, negligible in intrinsic value but convertible into the basic money of the realm. Many full-bodied coins circulated across national boundaries with values equivalent to their weight. For example, the original monetary unit of the United States was the silver dollar of Spanish America.

Until the late nineteenth century silver was more prevalent than gold as a monetary commodity. From medieval times silver was the English money of account; the pound sterling was initially a weight of silver. England and many other countries coined both silver and gold, but there were frequent periods when bimetallism degenerated *de facto* into one standard or the other. This happened when their prices at the mint diverged enough from their relative values in other countries or in commerce to offset the costs of arbitrage. Then "Gresham's law" would take over, and the metal undervalued at the mint, the "good money," would disappear from monetary circulation, "driven out" by the "bad money" overpriced at the mint (Hawtrey 1927: 202–4, 283).

In England in 1717 Isaac Newton, Master of the Mint, unintentionally overvalued gold, pushing silver out of circulation and in effect putting England on a gold standard. The switch was formalized in 1816. During the nineteenth century other European countries and the United States likewise gravitated from bimetallism to gold. Alexander Hamilton, America's first Secretary of the Treasury, complemented the silver dollar with gold coins. But it was not until the late nineteenth century that gold overtook silver as the basic money of the United States. The values of sterling and dollars in gold set by Newton and Hamilton, implying an exchange rate of $4.86 per pound, lasted until 1931, with several wartime interruptions.

The heyday of the international gold standard was 1880–1914, when all major national currencies were convertible into gold at fixed rates. Silver, like copper before it, was eventually demoted to token coin status (Hawtrey 1927, chs. 16–20).

Functions of Money

A triad long familiar to students of introductory economics lists the functions of money: (1) unit of account, or *numéraire*, (2) means of payment, or medium of exchange, and (3) store of value.

The U.S. dollar, for example, is the unit of account in the United States. Prices of everything are quoted in dollars, and accounts are kept in dollars. The various media that change hands in transactions—coins, paper currency, deposits—are denominated in dollars. That does not prevent anyone who cares to do so from quoting prices in a foreign currency or in bushels of wheat, or from finding sellers who will accept them in payment for other things. It just would not be very efficient as a general practice.

To be sure, some societies have used, and kept accounts in, more than one money—in both gold and silver or, for example, in Japan two centuries ago, both in coins and in standard weights of rice. Today some national currencies may be acceptable means of payment in other jurisdictions—dollars in Russia, Israel and Canada, yen in Hawaii, Deutschemarks in Eastern Europe. The reason may be the frequency of cross-border tourism and trade. Or it may be that as a consequence of hyperinflation people turn to a "hard" foreign currency as unit of account. For still a different reason, a new European currency, the ecu, may become a *numéraire* parallel to national currencies like pounds, francs and Deutschemarks during the period of transition to a common currency.

A society's money is necessarily a store of value. Otherwise it could not be an acceptable means of payment. (New York subway tokens cannot be generally acceptable money; they can become valueless any day, even for use as subway fare. U.S. food stamps, intended to be in-kind welfare benefits, are exchanged with cash at par, while grocery brands' discount coupons are disqualified by their expiration dates.)

Money is the principal means of payment of a society, but it is only one of many stores of value—and quantitatively a minor one at that. Through most of human history land has been the major form of wealth, increasingly augmented by livestock and reproducible capital—buildings, tools, machines and durable goods of all kinds. Claims to much of this wealth today take the form of bonds and shares and other securities. In the United States, basic money is only 6 percent of total privately owned wealth.

Even though a particular commodity or token is established as the generally acceptable medium for discharging debts denominated in the unit of account, it need not be and generally is not the sole means of payment in use. *Derivative* media, often termed *representative* money, arise and circulate as media of exchange. They are promises to pay the *basic*, sometimes called *definitive*, money on demand. In the commercial city states of northern Italy, merchants left gold with goldsmiths for safekeeping. They then found it convenient to circulate the "warehouse" receipts in place of the gold. Those payable to bearers were precursors of paper currency and banknotes. Those payable to named persons, and on their order to third parties, were precursors of cheques. Indeed, once the goldsmiths realized that they need not keep 100 percent gold reserves against the outstanding claims upon them, and that they could lend their certificates to merchants promising to deliver gold later, they became banks.

Besides providing token coins, states issued paper currency redeemable in gold or silver, or delegated the privilege to a private bank chartered to serve the state, like the Bank of England, founded in 1694. In addition, ordinary private banks issued their own notes, backed only by their own promises to pay basic money, gold or silver. In the nineteenth and twentieth centuries, governments and their central banks came to monopolize the issue of paper currency. This was not a catastrophe for banks. In modern economies, demand deposits in banks, transferable to third parties by cheque or wire or other order, have become the most important derivative media of exchange.

Whether derivative moneys were officially or privately issued, the ability of the issuers to carry out their promises to redeem them in basic money, gold or silver, was a recurrent problem. In wars and other emergencies governments often suspended these promises and issued irredeemable paper money. The trend in the twentieth century was to dispense with commodity money and to replace it with *fiat* money of no intrinsic value. Within each nation, the official derivative money, government currency, became the basic money. In 1933 United States paper dollars became inconvertible into gold except by foreign governments or central banks.

Internationally, gold was dethroned in 1971 as the medium for settlement of imbalances of payments between countries. Governments are no longer prepared to buy or sell gold at prices fixed in their own currencies. Gold is traded freely in private markets all over the world. Its price fluctuates as people speculate about its future. In the United States there is still an official weight of gold that theoretically corresponds to the dollar—0.0231 oz, that is a gold price of $43.22, about one eighth of the free market price. But the U.S. government is not prepared to sell any gold for dollars at the official price—or at the free market price, for that matter.

The U.S. monetary base (M0) is the amount of fiat currency the government, mainly its central bank, the Federal Reserve System, has issued. It is a "debt" to the public on which the government pays no interest and against which the government holds virtually no assets (other than its remaining gold stock, $11 billion at the official price, and its drawing rights at the International Monetary Fund, $19 billion). Derivative promises to pay dollars are now, directly or indirectly, commitments to pay this fiat money. Those promises include bank deposits and all other debts, private and public, denominated in dollars and payable at specified future times, tomorrow or 30 years hence.

In the United States in the fourth quarter of 1991 the stock of *transactions money* (M1) held by economic agents other than the federal government and banks averaged $890 billion, $265 of currency (paper and coin) and $617 of chequable deposits available on demand. The banks held reserves of $53 billion in currency in their vaults or on deposit in the 12 Federal Reserve Banks, collectively the American central bank. The sum of currency in public circulation and the currency or equivalent held as bank reserves is the *monetary base* (M0), $318 billion. It is often called *high-powered* money: every dollar of M0 was supporting $2.80 of M1, and GNP transactions of $18.20 a year.

Sovereigns have long profited from their money monopolies. Their mints charged "seigniorage" fees—and sometimes they cheated. Likewise, issue of currency bearing zero interest is a way for a government to pay its bills, easier than taxation and cheaper than interest-bearing debt. By regularly issuing base money to keep up with economic growth and inflation, the sovereign collects seigniorage year after year. In the United

States today seigniorage is a minor source of revenue. Since base money is only 6 percent of GNP, growth of dollar GNP at 7 percent a year means new issue of base money of only 0.42 percent of GNP, 1.68 percent of the federal budget. But for many less developed countries printing money is a major way of financing public expenditures; seigniorage is a major source of revenue, because implicit taxation by inflation is politically easier than explicit taxation.

Commodity Money vs. Fiat Money

The age of fiat money, first in one nation after another and finally internationally as well, has been more inflationary than the century of silver and gold standards between the Napoleonic wars and World War I. During and following the 1914–18 war the gold standard broke down, and attempts to re-establish it during the Great Depression did not succeed. The Bretton Woods regime established in 1945 linked the world's currencies to gold via their fixed parities with the U.S. dollar, because foreign governments could convert dollars into gold at a fixed price. But this system differed radically from the pre-1914 gold standard in that currency exchange rates could be and were frequently changed. The discipline imposed on a government and economy by an exchange parity fixed for a long time was diluted. In 1971, when this discipline became too much for the U.S. itself, the gold–dollar parity gave way, and the international monetary system was wholly a regime of fiat money.

Discontent with inflation since World War II, and with the volatility of currency exchange rates since 1971, has led to agitation for return to the gold standard or some other commodity money. A commodity standard, if adhered to, provides a real anchor for nominal prices; its discipline prevents hyperinflation.

However, although the long-run trend of prices during the gold standard period was flat, there were violent inflationary and deflationary fluctuations around it. More important, real economic activity was highly volatile, to a degree that would be politically unacceptable nowadays (Cooper 1982, 1991).

Irving Fisher, writing during the gold standard era, was greatly concerned by the instability of prices. He was complaining, in effect, about the volatility of the relative price of gold. Ideally, he would define the dollar in terms of a representative package of goods and services, the bundle priced in a comprehensive index number. Thus he revived the idea of a "tabular standard," proposed by several early-nineteenth-century writers, and described with approval by Jevons (1875, ch. 25). But exchange between paper currency and such bundles is impractical. Fisher proposed instead to make periodic adjustments of the gold content of the dollar, raising or lowering it in proportion to the rise or fall in the price index since the previous adjustment. In effect, the Treasury would be selling gold for dollars to fight inflation and buying gold for dollars to fight deflation (Fisher 1920).

A recent proposal by Robert Hall (1982) would tie the dollar to a composite commodity "ANCAP" of ammonium nitrate, copper, aluminium and plywood. Because ANCAP's prices have historically mirrored general indices, it is meant to be a feasible proxy for the economy's aggregate market basket (other proposals for commodity standards are described in Cooper 1991).

The Fisher strategy could be followed, even imposed as a nondiscretionary rule on the central bank, in a regime of fiat money. The market operations to implement it would be carried out in securities rather than in gold. The fundamental issue is not the monetary standard but whether stabilizing a price index should be the exclusive objective of monetary policy, to the exclusion of stabilization of real output growth and employment.

Free Market Money?

Would it be possible to privatize money? Certainly it is possible to privatize derivative issues of money, promises to pay fixed amounts of base money on demand. But United States experience suggests that the supply of money, even derivative "low-powered" money, cannot safely be left to free market competition.

Before the establishment of the national banking system in 1864, private banknotes were the only paper currency of the United States. The several states freely chartered banks, and those banks freely issued their own banknotes. These were promises to pay silver dollars, but so-called "wildcat" banks contrived to make it tough for noteholders to find them. There was no central bank to control the aggregate issue of banknotes.

The notes circulated at varying discounts from par and often became worthless, stranding innocent holders.

As a result, Congress established a system of nationally chartered banks in 1864, and taxed state banknotes out of existence. Only nationally chartered banks could issue notes, and these had to be fully backed by U.S. Treasury debt securities. In effect, they were Treasury currency, supplementing various direct issues of Treasury currency (including the inconvertible "greenbacks" the union government issued during the 1861–5 Civil War, which were made convertible into specie in 1879). Central banking did not begin in the United States until the Federal Reserve Act of 1914, which confined the issue of banknotes to Federal Reserve Banks.

Although private banks, state and national, were out of the business of issuing demand notes, they were still in the business of accepting demand deposits, the increasingly prevalent form of derivative money. Banks' balance sheets were regulated, but depositors were at risk. Their banks might not be able to pay in gold or equivalent on demand. After the epidemic bank failures of the 1920s and 1930s, Congress initiated a system of federal deposit insurance. Deposits in banks and other financial institutions became governmentally guaranteed, like banknotes after 1864. In the 1980s, these deposit guarantees became an expensive burden on federal taxpayers.

Could government get out of the money business altogether? It seems barely possible with commodity money and not possible with fiat money. If the government defined the *dollar* as a certain weight of gold or ANCAP or some other commodity or bundle, then private entrepreneurs could issue "dollars," either chequable deposits or paper notes. They would be promises to pay the bearer the equivalent in the chosen commodities. The commodities themselves would not necessarily circulate on their own; indeed ANCAP and other composites could not.

The money entrepreneurs would have to keep inventories of the commodity as reserves. If one hundred percent reserves were required, the currency would be like goldsmiths' warehouse receipts, and the private issuers would earn just a small fee for "minting" the commodity into paper. Left to themselves, they would become banks, acquiring risky and illiquid assets while incurring demand liabilities. *Caveat emptor* would reign. The rates various banks would have to pay to attract funds would reflect depositors' appraisals of the risks. Notes and cheques of risky banks would not be honoured at par. In short, the very problems that resulted in consensus that issue of money cannot safely be left to unregulated free markets would recur.

Could the government's role be confined to defining the unit of account, the commodity equivalent of a dollar, in the same way that the government—through the Bureau of Standards in the United States—defines weights and measures? Could the system operate without any government-owned or government-issued base money? In its absence, clearings among private banks would require awkward transfers of ownership of the commodities kept as reserves against their liabilities. Very probably some one bank or consortium would arise as an unofficial central bank, and its liabilities would play the role of base money, the medium in which clearing imbalances among other banks are settled. The central bank, official or unofficial, would have to hold inventories of the standard commodity, gold or ANCAP or whatever, and be prepared to convert currency into the commodity and *vice versa*. That institution, history also suggests, would eventually be nationalized.

A fortiori, if there is neither an official definition of the "dollar" nor any issue of dollars by the government or a quasi-governmental institution, there would be no standard commodity for private banks to compete in supplying to the public. Barter trading would be the rule, and the public-good advantages of social agreement on money would be lost. Since the institution of money is a public good, it is not surprising that its advantages cannot be realized by private market competition unassisted and uncontrolled.

How Can Money Have Positive Value in Exchange?

Economists have long regarded the theory of value as the central question of their discipline. What determines the prices at which goods and services are traded for each other? The prices in question include the wages of labour in terms of consumer goods, the rent of land in terms of its produce, and many other relative prices. They encompass interest rates and asset prices, thus the terms of trade of commodities to be delivered in future for commodities available today. They cover interregional and international trade, where the prices of concern are the terms on which imports can be obtained by exports.

Money, however, is an embarrassment to value theory. According to standard theory, something can have positive value only if it generates positive marginal utility in individuals' consumption or positive marginal productivity in the making of goods and services that do generate marginal utility. The embarrassing puzzle is sharpest for fiat money. All of its value comes from the fiat that makes it money. Fiat money has no intrinsic non-monetary source of value. It cannot be eaten or worn or be used in any other way that generates utility for consumers, except a few numismatists. Nor can it contribute to the production of things that consumers do value. It can be produced at zero social cost. Yet it is a scarce commodity for any individual agent. Why is it worth anything at all? That the institution of money is of value to the society as a whole as a public good does not automatically give it value to individuals in market exchanges.

The uphill struggle of modern economic theorists to cope with these challenges is exhibited in the proceedings of a recent conference (Kareken and Wallace 1980). Their solutions relied principally on the overlapping generations model, which unrealistically assigns to money the function of being the sole or the principal store of value that links one generation to the next. The most careful, thoughtful and perceptive formal models of the roles of credit and money in transactions and strategies, in partial equilibrium and general equilibrium systems, are those of the game theorist Martin Shubik (1984).

It was argued at the beginning that a condition for fiat money to be held and valued today is that it will be acceptable in exchange for intrinsically useful commodities tomorrow. But this bootstrap story may not work. Suppose the world itself is known to be finite; its end will come at a definite future time. In the last period, one minute before midnight so to speak, you may need money to buy whatever consumer goods might generate utility, at least solace. Otherwise you will be confined to your own resources. But who will sell you anything, knowing that the money will be worthless while the goods might be a source of some utility? Thus money is worthless one minute before midnight, and by iterations of the same argument, it is worthless today. Even if the institution of money had public-good value between now and the end of the world, the money itself would have no market value to individuals.

The escape from this logical impasse is that we do not all and will not all expect with certainty the end of the world at any definite time. We always do, always will, assign some probability to its continuation. Since there are many other paradoxes involved in thinking about human behaviour in a world with no chance of a future beyond a definite time, it is best not to take that prospect seriously in economic modelling.

Formal general equilibrium theory, which describes the imaginary world of frictionless barter, does of course express the prices of goods and services in a *numéraire*. It is tempting to identify *numéraire* prices as money prices. But the *numéraire* is just a mathematical normalization convenient for handling the fact that the supply-equals-demand equations for N commodities determine only the $N - 1$ relative prices. Those relative prices are, by construction, independent of the scalar arbitrarily attached to the *numéraire*.

Standard value theory does, of course, have something to say about the value of commodity money in terms of other goods and services. In a gold standard regime, the relative prices of gold in other commodities have to be the same at the mint and in the market; they cannot depend on whether the gold is circulating in coins or being used in jewellery, dentistry or rocketry. That is simply a condition of the absence of arbitrage profits. It definitely does not say that under the gold standard the relative price of gold is the same as it would be if gold were not money. As argued above, gold's role as money must increase the demand for it, and that must affect its price unless it is supplied perfectly elastically. The same will be true of any other commodity or bundle of commodities chosen as the monetary standard. A substantial part of the value of any commodity used as money arises from the convention or the fiat that makes it money. The distinction between commodity money and fiat money is not absolute.

The Neutrality of Money

Although business managers, financiers, politicians and workers worry a great deal about monetary institutions and policies and their consequences for economic activity and well-being, pure economic theory minimizes these consequences. Theory puts the burden of proof on anyone who contends that money and monetary inflations or deflations do much good or much ill.

Classical economists liked to insist that money is a veil, obscuring but not altering the real economic scenario (Robertson [1922] 1959: 7). Their modern descendants expound "real business cycle theory," premised on the view that economic developments that matter to societies and individuals are independent of monetary events and policies (Prescott 1986). It is true that economic fluctuations and trends are frequently misinterpreted by stressing superficial monetary phenomena to the neglect of resources, technologies and tastes. But money does matter, really.

Does an economy arrive at the same *real* outcomes (in variables like volumes of production, consumption and employment, and in relative prices such as the purchasing power of wages and the price of oil relative to that of bread) as it would without the institution of money? Clearly not. Without money, confined to barter, the economy would produce a different menu of products, less of most things. People would spend more time searching for trades and less in actual production, consumption and leisure.

That is not the comparison the classical economists, old and new, intend by the "veil" metaphor. Their fantasy is a frictionless, costless system of multilateral barter, in which relative prices and the allocations of labour and capital among various productive activities are determined in competitive markets. Their proposition is that the outcomes of an economy with money are the same as those that would arise from their ideal barter model. The corollary is that real economic outcomes are independent of the particular nature of the monetary institutions (Dillard 1988).

These propositions cannot be true of commodity money. Real economic outcomes with commodity money will differ from those with fiat money, and will also depend on what commodity is selected as money. Inventories of the chosen commodity have to be held for exchange purposes and for governmental and bank reserves, beyond the stocks held in connection with the commodity's non-monetary uses in production and consumption. In growing economies demands for monetary inventories will be steadily increasing. The relative demands for monetary and non-monetary inventories are bound to change with economic and technological developments that alter the incentives to produce the commodity and change its prices in terms of other goods and services. Examples are discoveries or exhaustions of gold and silver deposits and innovations in mining and processing technologies. Since the monetary commodity's price is fixed in money, its output will decline when there is general inflation and rise when there is deflation. Intertemporal choices involving the monetary commodity, as well as contemporaneous choices, will be significantly affected by its monetary use.

The availability of moneys, whether commodity or fiat, whether basic or derivative, as stores of value necessarily brings about significant deviations in real outcomes from the hypothetical regime of frictionless barter. This is true even though that regime is postulated to include markets in state-contingent commodity futures, "Arrow–Debreu" contracts (Arrow and Debreu 1954). Holding monetary assets gives agents more flexibility: they can convert them into consumption of any kind at any time in any "state of nature," though not at predictable prices. The flexibility is a convenience to individual agents. But, as Keynes saw, it opens the door to "coordination failures" which are the essence of macroeconomics— demand for goods and services may at times diverge seriously from supplies (Keynes 1936, chs. 16, 17).

The Classical Dichotomy

It is possible to recognize that an economy with monetary institutions is different in real outcomes from a barter economy, even from an ideal frictionless barter economy, and still to argue that its real outcomes are independent of the purely nominal parameters of those institutions. It would be terribly convenient if the determination of the absolute price level, the reciprocal of the value of the monetary unit in a representative bundle of consumer goods, could be split off from the determination of relative prices and the associated real quantities.

Don Patinkin (1956) called this separation the *classical dichotomy*. Only monetary shocks would affect the general price level, and those shocks would raise or lower the nominal prices of all commodities in the same proportions. Only real shocks—to tastes, technologies and resource supplies—would affect relative prices and real quantities. This proposition would not exclude the fact that the monetary institutions themselves matter. The choice between commodity money and fiat money, the choice among possible commodity standards, and the arrangements for derivative moneys might well affect the social efficiency of markets and trade.

What are the nominal parameters whose settings, according to the classical dichotomy, would make no real difference? For a commodity money, such a parameter is the definition of the monetary unit in terms of the standard commodity, for example the weight in gold of a dollar. For fiat money, the key nominal parameter is the quantity of money—base money, all transactions money, or some even more inclusive aggregate.

Why should cutting the gold content of the dollar from 0.0484 ounces to 0.0286 ounces, raising the dollar price of gold from $20.67 to $35.00 (as Franklin Roosevelt did in 1933), make any real difference? The dollar values of existing public and private stocks of gold, and of monetary claims to gold would rise in the same proportion. Will not all other commodity prices do likewise? Then all relative prices and real quantities, including those of gold, will be the same as before.

For fiat money systems, and for commodity standards where issues of derivative moneys have become essentially independent of the commodity, the *quantity theory of money* achieved similar dichotomization. According to the theory, which might more accurately be called the quantity-of-money theory of prices, an increase in the nominal quantity of money would raise all nominal commodity prices in the same proportion, leaving relative prices and real quantities unchanged. Quantity theorists argue that an increase in the quantity of money is equivalent to a change in the monetary unit. A hundred-fold increase in the stock of French francs would be—would it not?—the same as De Gaulle's decree changing the unit of account to a new franc equivalent to 100 old francs. Since the units change could make no real difference, the other way of multiplying the money stock could not either.

These analogies fail, for several related reasons. In most economies money is by no means the only asset denominated in the monetary unit. There are many promises to pay base money on demand or at specified dates. If there is a thorough units change, like De Gaulle's, all these assets are automatically converted to the new unit of account. Roosevelt's devaluation of the dollar relative to gold was not a pure units change. He did not scale up the dollar values of outstanding currency or even of Treasury bonds with provisions for such revaluation. Naturally private assets and debts expressed in dollars were not scaled up either. Likewise, when the quantity of money is changed by normal operations of governments or central banks or by other events, the outstanding amounts of other nominally denominated assets are not scaled up or down in the same proportion. They may remain constant, as when money is printed to finance government expenditures. They may move in the opposite direction, as when central banks engage in open-market operations, which typically increase the amount of base money outstanding by buying bills or bonds, thus reducing the quantities of them in the hands of the public.

The Quantity Theory

The quantity theory goes back to David Hume, probably farther, but its major and most effective protagonists have been Irving Fisher (1911) and Milton Friedman (1956).

In its crudest form, the quantity theory is a mechanistic proposition strangely alien to the assumptions of rational maximizing behaviour on which classical and neoclassical economic theories generally rely, as J. R. Hicks eloquently pointed out in a famous article (1935). Specifically, it ignores the effects of the returns to holding money on the amounts economic agents choose to hold. The technology of monetary circulation fixes the annual turnover of a unit of money. Suppose that every dollar "sitting" supports just V dollars per year "on the wing," to use D. H. Robertson's famous terms ([1922] 1959: 30). Suppose, further, that the economy is assumed to be in real equilibrium and the supply of money is doubled. The public will not wish to hold the additional money until the dollar value of transactions is doubled, and this requires prices to double.

Surely the demand for money to hold is not so mechanical. The velocity of money can be speeded up if people put up with more inconvenience and risk more illiquidity in managing their transactions. Money holdings depend, therefore, on the opportunity costs, the expected changes in the value of money and the real yields of other assets into which the same funds could be placed. Fisher and Friedman would agree.

The quantity theory can still be rationalized, as a proposition in comparative statics. Compare, for example, two stationary situations of a given economy, in each of which the money supply and price level are constant over time. Let the money supply in the second situation be twice that in the first. Then an equilibrium in the second situation will be the equilibrium of the first with a nominal price level twice as high. This will be true even if the demand for money is modelled as behavioural, not mechanical, and is allowed to depend on interest rates, expected inflation and other variables.

However, it is not sufficient to double solely the quantity of money, narrowly defined. All exogenous nominal quantities, including outstanding stocks of debts and assets, must also be doubled. Or the second equilibrium must be interpreted as a stationary state that will be reached only when all these other nominal stocks have had time to adjust endogenously to the new quantity of money. This quantity theory does not apply to short-run changes in monetary quantities engineered by central banks, for the same reasons that render the "units change" metaphor inapplicable.

In its interpretation as a proposition in long-run comparative statics, the quantity theory supports "neutrality" as asserted in the classical dichotomy. Neutrality has come to have two meanings in monetary economics. Simple *neutrality* means that real economic outcomes are independent of the levels of nominal prices. *Superneutrality* means that those outcomes are also independent of the rates of change of nominal prices.

The case for superneutrality appeals to, and depends upon, the "Fisher equation." Early on, Fisher (1896) saw the importance of distinguishing between nominal and real rates of interest on assets and debts denominated in monetary units. *Ex post*, the algebraic difference between them is by definition the rate of inflation or deflation. This is a tautology. But Fisher (1911) is also credited with a meaningful proposition: anticipation of inflation (deflation) raises (lowers) nominal rates of interest but does not alter real rates of interest. The corollary is that whatever is the time path of money stocks that determines the path of prices, the paths of real economic variables are the same. Fisher himself was enough of a classical economist to believe this as a long-run theoretical truth, but enough of a pragmatic empiricist to find that nominal rates were very slow to incorporate adjustments for ongoing inflations and deflations.

The Price of Money

A 1975 conference on monetarism at Brown University is remembered for a pithy observation by Milton Friedman, offered only half in jest:

For the monetarist/non-monetarist dichotomy, I suspect that the simplest litmus test would be the conditioned reflex to the question, 'What is the price of money?' The monetarist will answer, 'The inverse of the price level'; the non-monetarist (Keynesian or central banker) will answer, 'the interest rate'. The key difference is whether the stress is on money viewed as an asset with special characteristics, or on credit and credit markets, which leads to the analysis of monetary policy and monetary change operating through organized "money," i.e. "credit," markets, rather than through actual and desired cash balances. Though not so obvious, the answer given also affects attitudes toward prices: whether their adjustment is regarded as an integral part of the economic process analyzed, or as an institutional datum to which the rest of the system will adjust (Stein 1976: 316).

"What am I," asked the chairman of the session, George Borts, "if I answer 'one'?"

Any durable good has at least two "prices," the price at which it can be bought or sold, and the price of the services it renders per unit time. The price of the good itself is the present value of the expected, though uncertain, values of the services it will render in future. For money, the first price is its purchasing power. Its services come in two forms: as a store of value, the capital gain or loss from changes in its purchasing power, and, as a medium of exchange, the benefits it yields in convenience, effort-saving and risk reduction. Without cash on hand, an economic agent may find it costly to make desirable transactions, or to forgo them. The marginal productivity of holding money is the value of an additional dollar in reducing those costs.

What is the marginal opportunity cost to which agents will equate the marginal productivity of holding money? It depends on what alternatives are available. If money proper were the only store of value in the economy, the opportunity cost of holding money would be the marginal utility of immediate consumption relative to future consumption. Although this set-up is all too common in the literature, it confuses theories of money and of saving. Acknowledging the availability of other stores of value makes the cost of holding money the difference between the real capital gain or loss on money and the real rate of return on the non-money assets in which a marginal dollar could be invested.

If money proper were the only store of value in the monetary unit of account, though not the only one in the economy at large, the relevant opportunity cost would be the return on real capital—that is, storable or durable commodities. In modern economies, however, the immediate substitutes for money are promises to pay money in future. Since money and these substitutes are affected equally by price level changes, the opportunity cost is simply the nominal interest rate on those non-money substitutes. (This assumes zero nominal interest on money itself.)

Friedman's Keynesian is careless if he calls any of these opportunity cost concepts the price of money. These are prices of the services of money. Friedman's monetarist is right, therefore, to say that the price of money is the reciprocal of the commodity price level—the real price, that is, for Borts was right about money's nominal price. Of course, there are as many relative prices as there are non-monetary commodities, and any average value of money requires using an arbitrary commodity price index.

To implement Friedman's asset valuation approach to the price of money, suppose that the nominal supply of money per capita, real per capita output and the real interest rate all follow arbitrary variable paths, anticipated in advance. Assume, at least for illustrative purposes, the Allais–Baumol–Tobin model of the demand for money (Baumol and Tobin 1989). The marginal productivity of nominal cash holdings for a representative agent is the reduction in the frequency and cost of exchanges back and forth between money and dollar-denominated interest-bearing substitutes. It is, by the usual approximation equal to $a(t)y(t)/(2m(t)^2 v(t))$, where a is the real cost of one of those exchanges, y is the agent's real income per period, m is the agent's average nominal cash holding, and v is the value of money, the reciprocal of the price level. Of these, a, y and m are arbitrary exogenous functions of time, while the valuation v is a function of time to be determined. Let $r(t)$ be the exogenous path of the real interest rate. The value of money at any time T is the discounted value of its future marginal productivities:

$$v(T) = a(T) \int_T^\infty \exp\left(-\int_T^t r(s)\,ds\right) y(t)/(2m(t)^2 v(t))\,dt, \qquad (1)$$

$$v'(T) = r(T)v(T) - a(T)y(T)/(2m(T)^2 v(T)), \qquad (2)$$

$$r(T) - v'(T)/v(T) = a(T)y(T)/(2m(T)^2 v(T)^2). \qquad (3)$$

Equation (3), with the nominal interest rate on the left, is the familiar equation for optimal *real* cash holdings. It involves the stronger Fisher equation, because the real rate has been taken as exogenous.

Interpreted as the price dynamics of the economy, these equations describe the time path of the "price of money." The level of prices at each time converts the autonomous nominal money supply into the real quantity on which its marginal productivity depends. The price path itself generates the rates of price change which, added to the autonomous real interest rates, give the nominal rates. The marginal productivity of money at each point in time is equated to the nominal interest rate. Future as well as current values of money supplies, as well as other variables, affect current prices. An expected increase in future money supply raises prices today, and so does an expected future increase in real rates of interest. The Fisher equation is essential to maintain the assumed dichotomy between the paths of real and nominal variables (for a calculation in this same spirit, see Sargent and Wallace 1981).

Money and Macroeconomics

In the above scenario, a key institutional fact is that the nominal interest rate on money proper is fixed, at zero. Expected inflation makes money's real interest rate negative and reduces the attraction of holding money compared to assets bearing the economy's real interest rate. For the same reason, an increase in that real interest rate is a disincentive to hold money.

However, the same institution—the fixed nominal interest rate on money—threatens the classical dichotomy. It calls into question the Fisher equation, which is central to the independence from monetary influence of the real rate of interest and related real variables. It calls it into question in principle, in long runs and short, in equilibrium and in disequilibrium. If expected inflation diminishes demand for money, it by the same token increases demands for other assets, both interest-bearing promises to pay money and real capital. These substitutions will reduce the real interest rates on those assets; their nominal interest rates will rise less than the full inflation premium. This effect—associated in the literature with the names of Mundell (1963) and Tobin (1965, 1969)—refutes superneutrality, which is essential to neutrality in any general dynamic meaning. That is to say, it is not possible to determine the real interest rate and related real variables independently of the money equation, or to determine the value of money from the demand = supply equation for money by itself.

This is true whether the economy is assumed to be classical, with full employment assured by flexibility of nominal interest rates and prices, or Keynesian, with aggregate demand short of full employment. However, the real effects of expected price inflation and deflation are a reason for doubting the efficacy of price flexibility in sustaining or restoring full employment equilibrium in the face of aggregate demand shocks (Fisher 1933; Keynes 1936, ch. 19; Tobin 1975).

Irving Fisher, Alfred Marshall and other monetary economists of the early twentieth century regarded neutrality in any sense as properties of long-run static equilibrium, not of the dynamic transitions that dominate empirical observations of monetary and real variables. According to them, people are slow in translating experience of inflation into their expectations of the future. This is how Fisher interpreted the strong positive correlations he found between inflation rates and real output (Fisher 1911). However, the Mundell–Tobin effect suggests a still stronger conclusion, since it calls into question the Fisher equation even when inflation expectations are correct and people are not victims of "money illusion."

In Friedman's litmus test there is much more at stake than meets the eye. The issue is how the price level, whose reciprocal is the "price of money," is determined. The monetarist's trained instinct is to think of it as determined by the demand = supply equation for money "as an asset with special characteristics." With the absolute price level thus determined, the function of markets for goods and services is to generate real, relative prices, just as in Walrasian general equilibrium theory. Those real variables, in turn, are exogenous to the path of the "price of money."

The Keynesian's trained instinct, on the other hand, is to think of the price level as an index of nominal prices of goods and services. As Keynes (1936, Book I) emphasized—for labor markets especially—markets in our monetary economies determine in the first instance nominal prices, not real prices. The price "level" is a synthetic aggregate of multitudes of individual prices determined in diverse imperfect markets, often decided by administrative decisions or by negotiations. For price determination the most relevant equations of a macroeconomic model are price and wage equations, often members of the Phillips curve family. These specify inertia of varying degrees in nominal prices and relate their changes to measures of real excess demand or supply. As a result, price indices move smoothly and sluggishly over time, not "jumping" like the price of a financial asset sensitive to market views of the future.

With the price level determined in goods markets, the function of the money demand = supply equation is to generate interest rates. That explains the Keynesian's instinctive response to the test question. Of course, the Keynesian recognizes that the endogenous variables of a simultaneous equations system are determined jointly, not equation by equation. That real variables are among those endogenous variables can be attributed to the fact that there is usually a non-zero discrepancy between the price path determined by the full system and the path that would be generated by the monetarist's asset price of money. The non-monetarist view does not take price "as an institutional datum to which the rest of the system will adjust," but it does rely on variables besides prices to equate "actual and desired cash balances."

The equation of money demand and supply is just one of many relations in a theoretical or econometric macroeconomic model. The small tail cannot wag the big dog. That was too much to expect. The price level is a factor common to the valuation of many assets denominated in the monetary unit, many of them close substitutes for transactions money. Their quantities now and in future must make a difference. Of course monetary policies and supplies, current and prospective, are important determinants of the price level, and so are credit markets. But the channels of these influences run through demands and supplies in markets for goods and services. Understanding the process belongs to the messy subject of macroeconomics. Finance theory, however elegant, cannot provide a shortcut.

Monetary events and policies are not a sideshow to the main performance. The real variables of a monetary economy are hopelessly entangled with monetary phenomena. They do not behave as if an economy enjoying the societal advantages of money were a frictionless multilateral barter economy seen through a veil. That barter economy would never have business cycles characterized by economy-wide excess demands and supplies of labour and other goods and services. The public-good advantages of the institution of money do not come so cheap. Among their costs are fluctuations in business activity and in the value of money itself. Pragmatic monetary economics is a central part of macroeconomics in general.

Bibliography

Arrow, K. J. and Debreu, G. 1954. Existence of equilibrium for a competitive economy. *Econometrica* 22(3), July: 265–90.

Baumol, W. J. and Tobin, J. 1989. The optimal cash balance proposition: Maurice Allais's priority. *Journal of Economic Literature* 27(3), September: 1160–62.

Cooper, R. N. 1982. The gold standard: historical facts and future prospects. *Brookings Papers on Economic Activity* 1: 1–45.

Cooper, R. N. 1991. Toward an international commodity standard? In *Money, Macroeconomics, and Economic Policy*, ed, W. C. Brainard, W. D. Nordhaus, and H. W. Watts, Cambridge, Mass.: MIT Press.

Dillard, D. 1988. The barter illusion in classical and neoclassical economics. *Eastern Economic Journal* 14(4), October–December: 299–318.

Fisher, I. 1896. *Appreciation and Interest.* Publications of the American Economic Association, 3rd series 11(4); reprinted, Fairfield, NJ: A. M. Kelley, 1991.

Fisher, I. 1906. *The Nature of Capital and Income.* New York: Macmillan.

Fisher, I. 1911. *The Purchasing Power of Money.* New York: Macmillan.

Fisher, I. 1920. *Stabilizing the Dollar.* New York: Macmillan.

Fisher, I. 1933. The debt-deflation theory of great depressions. *Econometrica* 1, October: 337–57.

Friedman, M. 1956. *Studies in the Quantity Theory of Money.* Chicago: University of Chicago Press.

Hall, R. E. 1982. Explorations in the gold standard and related policies for stabilizing the dollar. In *Inflation: Causes and Effects*, ed. R. E. Hall, Chicago: University of Chicago Press.

Hawtrey, R. G. 1927. *Currency and Credit.* London: Longmans, Green & Co., 3rd edn.

Hicks, J. R. 1935. A suggestion for simplifying the theory of money. *Economica*, NS 2(1), February: 1–19.

Jevons, W. S. 1875. *Money and the Mechanism of Exchange.* London: King.

Kareken, J. H. and Wallace, N. (eds) 1980. *Models of Monetary Economics.* Minneapolis: Federal Reserve Bank.

Keynes, J. M. 1930. Auri sacra fames. In *Essays in Persuasion*, reprinted in *The Collected Writings of John Maynard Keynes*, vol. 9, London: Macmillan, 1972; New York: Harcourt Brace.

Keynes, J. M. 1936. *The General Theory of Employment, Interest, and Money.* Reprinted in *The Collected Writings of John Maynard Keynes*, vol. 7, London: Macmillan, 1973; New York: Harcourt Brace.

Mundell, R. A. 1963. Inflation and real interest. *Journal of Political Economy* 71(2), June: 280–83.

Patinkin, D. 1956. *Money, Interest, and Prices.* New York: Harper and Row; 2nd edn, 1965.

Prescott, E. 1986. Theory ahead of business cycle measurement. *Federal Reserve Bank of Minneapolis Quarterly Review*, Fall: 9–22.

Robertson, D. H. 1922. *Money.* Cambridge Economic Handbook, 4th edn, Chicago: University of Chicago Press, 1959.

Sargent, T. J. and Wallace, N. 1981. Some unpleasant monetarist arithmetic. *Federal Reserve Bank of Minneapolis Quarterly Review* 5(3), Fall: 1–17.

Shubik, M. 1984. *A Game-Theoretic Approach to Political Economy*. Cambridge, Mass.: MIT Press.

Starr, R. M. 1972. The structure of exchange in barter and monetary economies. *Quarterly Journal of Economics* 86(2), May: 290–302.

Starr, R. M. 1974. The price of money in a pure exchange economy with taxation. *Econometrica* 42(1), January: 45–54.

Stein, J. L. (ed.) 1976. *Monetarism*. Amsterdam: North-Holland.

Tobin, J. 1965. Money and economic growth. *Econometrica* 33(4), October: 671–84; *Essays*, Vol. 1, Chapter 9.

Tobin, J. 1969. A general equilibrium approach to monetary theory. *Journal of Money, Credit, and Banking* 1(1), February: 15–29; *Essays*, Vol. 1, Chapter 18.

Tobin, J. 1975. Keynesian models of recession and depression. *American Economic Review* 65(2): 195–202; *Essays*, Vol. 3, Chapter 5.

CHAPTER 6

LIQUIDITY PREFERENCE, SEPARATION, AND ASSET PRICING

My 1958 paper, "Liquidity Preference as Behavior Towards Risk" was intended primarily as a contribution to positive macroeconomics rather than to management science. One problem was to explain why people would hold moneys and near-moneys bearing lower rates of return than the yields on other marketable assets, in particular promises to pay money in future. The second problem was to explain how the demand for moneys and near-moneys could be inversely related to those yields. Keynes had postulated such a relationship and I had found it well substantiated empirically for the United States.[1]

Though I was strongly influenced by Keynes and sympathetic to his General Theory, I was not entirely satisfied by his resolution of these two related problems. The paper was designed to provide a firmer foundation for "liquidity preference" and the liquidity preference function.

The reason for my dissatisfaction was that Keynes's "speculative motive" for money demand seemed, in modern parlance, to violate the canons of rational expectations. As I interpreted Keynes, he was sticking to the classical view: an agent's expectations of short-term returns must be identical for all the assets he chooses to hold; otherwise he will hold as much of those assets with highest expected returns as his wealth and market institutions permit, and as little as possible—zero or negative amounts—of the rest. On this view, holders of money and low-yield short securities were agents who expected long-term bonds to decline in value so much in the period immediately ahead that their net short-term yields would be no larger than those on money and near-money. This was Keynes's solution to the first problem.

Reprinted by permission from *Zeitschrift für Betriebswirtschaft* 3 (March 1983): 53.

For his solution to the second one, his derivation of the downward-sloping liquidity preference curve, he required two assumptions: agents' expectations of future interest rates are less than unit-elastic with respect to variation of the current interest rate, and agents have diverse interest expectations. From these it follows, as I showed in the paper, that the lower the current interest rate the more agents there are who regard money and short assets as preferable.

This theory was realistic enough for the 1930s, when Keynes perceived that many financiers regarded the higher interest rates of the 1920s as normal levels to which markets would sooner or later return. Meanwhile portfolio managers stayed liquid and short in order to avoid capital losses on bonds. The theoretical difficulty was that the persistence of unrealized expectations of interest rates seemed a transient, fragile, and theoretically inconsistent building block for a "general" theory. Eventually expectations must accord with experience; an equilibrium theory should not be built on the assumption that the interest rate the model generates differs systematically from the expectations that determine the behavior the model describes. This point had been made by Wassily Leontief and William Fellner,[2] and it seemed valid to me.

But clearly if Keynes's speculators had, individually or in aggregate, unbiased expectations, there would be no justification for a liquidity preference function with negative sensitivity to the current rate of interest. This is why I sought an explanation for "liquidity preference" that did not depend on biased expectations.

Of course, transactions requirements for media of exchange and the costs of transactions between cash and interest-bearing assets could provide an explanation for negative elasticity of demand for cash with respect to interest rates. Keynes had ignored this effect, but Baumol in 1952[3] and I in 1956[4] had both derived it from inventory-theoretic considerations. I did not regard this as the whole story, and that is why I took up the "speculative motive" in the 1958 paper. Keynes's theory of liquidity preference did not concern simply the demand for money in the narrow sense of transactions media. He was referring to the broader portfolio choice between assets of negligible or small capital-value risk and long-term securities with prices quite sensitive to variations in interest rates. I had been working on portfolio theory for several years, and the pioneering work of Harry Markowitz,[5] a colleague at the Cowles Foundation at

Yale in 1955–56, had been a fruitful stimulus. Differentials in yields were clearly not confined to transactions money versus all other assets but a general phenomenon. That is why I thought it important to embed "speculative" liquidity preference in a broad theory of portfolio choice.

And that is why I thought it necessary to show that my results were not restricted to a two-asset choice, between "money", a safe asset with a zero or fixed nominal interest rate, and an asset with capital-value risk arising from interest rate variation. This was the motivation for the "separation theorem," showing that the choice could be described as one between the safe asset and an optimal portfolio of numerous risky assets.

This separation was ingeniously and fruitfully exploited by Lintner[6] and Sharpe[7] to develop their capital asset pricing model. I have always had reservations about this inversion, primarily concerns about aggregation. Although I was for reasons given above dissatisfied with Keynes's exclusive reliance on divers and sticky expectations, I would certainly wish to recognize, now as then, that agents differ greatly in their wealth, liquidity and borrowing constraints, in their transactions costs and tax liabilities, in their views of the future, and in their attitudes toward risks. My 1958 formal model of expected utility maximization described the behavior of an individual portfolio manager, and I imagined market-wide demand functions for "money" and other assets to be aggregations of such behavior across individuals of different circumstances and tastes. For example, I allowed for risk-loving and risk-neutral as well as risk-averse investors. In this Marshallian approach, the structure is analogous to the aggregation of individually optimized demands for consumption goods and services. In neither case would I, now or then, regard as realistic the view that market outcomes can be modeled as if they result from choices of a single optimizing agent.

A striking deficiency of that assumption is its inability to explain either the immense volume of financial transactions we observe daily or the extreme differences among agents in portfolios and investment strategies. It is most improbable that the marginal buyers and sellers who make prices are the same from day to day or from market to market. There are other problems too. Transactions costs limit the number of assets in many portfolios and make assets' independent risks less reducible by diversification than CAPM assumes. Empirical application of CAPM usually infers the joint probability distribution of asset returns from historical variations of the very market prices the model seeks to explain. This "bootstrap" approach is subject to the objection that the price movements reflect portfolio adjustments themselves as well as fundamental exogenous shocks. The capital losses on a security whose price declined during the period of observation because of an increase in its supply or an event that diminished investors' appraisals of its prospects are misleading indicators of the security's place in future portfolios.

Students of macroeconomics and finance are discovering more and more common interests and mutually instructive communication and collaboration. Some of us are principally interested in how economies work and how government policies may make them work better or worse. Others are mainly interested in guiding individuals and businesses to rational choices in their own interests. Positive economics relies, as always, heavily on the assumption that agents do behave rationally. Management science, in finance as in other applications, has to place its putative or actual clients in a realistic macroeconomic environment. Their interdependence, evident as it was in 1958, is even more clearly recognized today. The two groups of scholars can contribute together to the formidable theoretical and empirical work that remains to be done. I feel deeply honored by this issue of the *Zeitschrift für Betriebswirtschaft*, and I wish my German colleagues well in their future research.

Notes

1. In Liquidity Preference and Monetary Policy, Review of Economics and Statistics 29, May 1947, 124–131; *Essays*, Vol. 1, Chapter 3.

2. W. Leontief, Postulates: Keynes' General Theory and the Classicists, in S. E. Harris, ed., The New Economics (New York: Knopf, 1947), 232–42, especially 238–39.
W. Fellner, Monetary Policies and Full Employment (Berkeley, Calif.: University of California Press, 1946), 149.

3. W. J. Baumol: The Transactions Demand for Cash: An Inventory Theoretic Approach, Quarterly Journal of Economics 56, November 1952, 545–56.

4. J. Tobin: The Interest Elasticity of Transactions Demand for Cash, Review of Economics and Statistics 38, August 1956, 241–47; *Essays*, Vol. 1, Chapter 14.

5. H. Markowitz: Portfolio Selection, Journal of Finance 7, March 1952, 77–91, and Portfolio Selection (New York: Wiley, 1959).

6. J. H. Lintner: The Evaluation of Risk Assets and the Selection of Risky Investments in Stock Portfolios and Capital Budgets, Review of Economics and Statistics 47, February 1965, 13–37.

7. W. F. Sharpe: Capital Asset Prices: A Series of Market Equilibrium Under Conditions of Risk, Journal of Finance 19, September 1964, 425–442.

PART II

MACROECONOMIC THEORY

CHAPTER 7

PRICE FLEXIBILITY AND OUTPUT STABILITY:
AN OLD KEYNESIAN VIEW

In this symposium I shall play the role in which I was cast, the unreconstructed old Keynesian. Time was when I resisted labels and schools, naively hoping that our fledgling science was outgrowing them. I had, to be sure, been drawn into economics when *The General Theory* was an exciting revelation for students hungry for explanation and remedy of the Great Depression. At the same time, I was uncomfortable with several aspects of Keynes's theory, and I sought to improve what would now be called the microfoundations of his macroeconomic relations.

The synthesis of neoclassical and Keynesian analysis achieved in the 1950s and 1960s promised a reconciliation of the two traditions, or at least an understanding of the different contexts to which each applies. The hope and the promise were premature, to say the least. In the last 20 years, the dominant trend in macroeconomics has dismissed Keynesian theory. Nevertheless, Keynesian models continue to prove useful in empirical applications, forecasting and policy analysis. Macro-econometric models are mostly built on Keynesian frameworks. The gulfs between doctrine and observation, between theory and practice, are chronic sources of malaise in our discipline.

I have benefited from Gregory Mankiw's "refresher course" in modern macroeconomics (1990). He writes that recent developments—methodological, new classical, and new Keynesian—are to old macroeconomics as Copernicus was to Ptolemy. It just takes time before Copernican truths can outdo Ptolemaic approximations in practical applications.

Considering the alternatives, I do not mind being billed as a Keynesian, an old Keynesian at that. But old Keynesians come in several varieties, and I speak for no one but myself. Nor do I defend the literal text of *The General Theory*. Several generations of economists have criticized, amended, and elaborated that seminal work. I shall argue for the validity of the major propositions that distinguish Keynesian macroeconomics from old or new classical macroeconomics.

Summary of the Keynesian Case

The central proposition of Keynesian economics is commonly described as follows: "According to the Keynesian view, fluctuations in output arise largely from fluctuations in nominal aggregate demand. These fluctuations have real effects because nominal wages and prices are rigid" (Ball, Mankiw, and Romer, 1988, p. 1). On the contrary, I shall argue that Keynesian macroeconomics neither asserts nor requires nominal wage and/or price rigidity. It does assert and require that markets not be instantaneously and continuously cleared by prices. That is a much less restrictive assumption, and much less controversial. It leaves plenty of room for flexibility in any commonsense meaning of the word.

Keynesian models were said to be vulnerable to the charge that "the crucial nominal rigidities were assumed rather than explained," although "it was clearly in the interests of agents to eliminate the rigidities they were assumed to create.... Thus the 1970s and 1980s saw many economists turn away from Keynesian theories and toward new classical models with flexible wages and prices" (Ball, Mankiw, and Romer, 1988, p. 2). Those market-clearing models have not just flexible prices but *perfectly* and *instantaneously* flexible prices, an assumption that is surely more extreme, more arbitrary, and more devoid of foundations in individual rational behavior than the imperfect flexibility of Keynesian models.

The central Keynesian proposition is not nominal price rigidity but the principle of effective demand (Keynes, 1936, ch. 3). In the absence of instantaneous and complete market clearing, output and employment are frequently constrained by aggregate demand. In these excess-supply regimes, agents' demands are limited by their inability to sell as much as they would like at prevailing prices. Any failure of price adjustments to keep markets cleared opens the door for quantities to determine quantities, for example real national income to determine consumption demand, as described in Keynes's multiplier calculus.

For this reason, Keynesian macroeconomics alleges that capitalist societies are vulnerable to very costly economy-wide market failures. Individuals would be willing to supply more labor and other resources in return for the goods and services the employment of those resources would enable them to consume now or in the future, but they cannot implement this willingness in market transactions. As the quotation from Ball, Mankiw, and Romer suggests, many contemporary theorists cannot believe any theory that implies socially irrational market failures. They suspect that individual irrationalities are lurking somewhere in the theory. In continuously price-cleared competitive markets, they know, individually rational behavior implies collectively rational outcomes. But this theorem does not apply if markets and price-setting institutions do not produce perfectly flexible competitive prices. Individual rationality does not necessarily create the institutions that would guarantee "invisible hand" results. Keynes was not questioning the rationality of individual economic agents; he was arguing that their behavior would yield optimal results if and only if they as citizens organized the necessary collective institutions and government policies. In the same spirit though in different contexts, some modern theoretical research has shown that welfare-improving policies may be designed even when asymmetries of information and incompleteness of markets prevent the achievement of global optima.

Ball, Mankiw, Romer and others style themselves as New Keynesians. Their program is to develop improved microeconomic foundations for imperfectly flexible prices. In the process, they hope to illuminate the paradox that individually rational or near-rational behavior can result in significant collective market failures. These are certainly laudable objectives. In the end, I suspect, the program will not change the essential substance of Keynesian macroeconomics. But it will make Keynes more palatable to theorists.

In Keynesian business cycle theory, the shocks generating fluctuations are generally shifts in *real* aggregate demand for goods and services, notably in capital investment. Keynes would be appalled to see his cycle model described as one in which "fluctuations in output arise largely from fluctuations in nominal aggregate demand" (Ball, Mankiw, and Romer 1988, p. 2). The difference is important. The impact on real purchases of a one-time one percent shock to aggregate nominal spending will be eroded if and as nominal prices increase in response, and eliminated once prices have risen by the same one percent as nominal spending did. But suppose it is real demand that initially rises one percent. At the prevailing prices nominal spending will rise one percent too. But if and as prices rise in response, the one percent real demand shock becomes an ever larger amount of nominal spending. Its impact is not mechanically eroded by the price response; if it is absorbed, the process is subtle and indirect.

The big issue between Keynes and his "old classical" opponents was the efficacy of the economy's natural market adjustment mechanisms in restoring full employment equilibrium, once a negative real demand shock had pushed the economy off that equilibrium. Keynes and Keynesians said those mechanisms were weak, possibly nonexistent or perverse, and needed help from government policy. That is still the major question of macroeconomic theory and policy, even though new classical economists finesse it by assuming that the economy can never be pushed out of equilibrium even for a moment. Keynes's classical contemporaries and predecessors would never have drawn real-world lessons from theories based on such an assumption. Their successors strain credulity when their models imply that markets are cleared and joblessness is voluntary when measured unemployment is 10 percent as truly as when it is 5 percent.

Keynesian theory of nominal wage stickiness does not deserve the disdain with which it is commonly regarded. It is not dependent on "money illusion." But Keynes certainly would have done better to assume imperfect or monopolistic competition throughout the economy, in both product and labor markets. In markets of these kinds, nominal prices are decision variables for sellers or buyers or are determined by negotiations between them. They therefore move only at discrete intervals. Despite considerable effort over the years to give macroeconomics improved microfoundations along these lines, there is plenty of scope for the "New Keynesian" program of theoretical and empirical research on this topic.

In the absence of perfect flexibility, does greater flexibility of nominal prices strengthen the equilibrating mechanisms, or does it weaken them? Keynes doubted that the problems of involuntary unemployment and underutilized capacity would be mitigated by greater flexibility of nominal wages and prices. On the whole, he favored stable nominal wages. Critics of Keynesian macroeconomics forget this strand of the argument when they assume that without absolute "rigidity" aggregate demand could never be deficient. Fortunately, this issue has been receiving greater attention in the last few years, with considerable support for Keynes's position.

Macroeconomics with Effective Demand Constrained

The empirical relevance of Keynesian economics is based on its assertion that situations of pervasive excess supply often occur. An advanced capitalist industrial economy is frequently in a state in which most labor and product markets are not clearing at prevailing prices. As a result, workers are involuntarily unemployed and capital capacity is underutilized. The effective constraint on output is the aggregate demand for goods and services; likewise the effective constraint on employment is the amount of labor required to produce that output.

Keynesian unemployment must be differentiated from both frictional and classical unemployment. Frictional unemployment occurs because of microeconomic flux. Demands and supplies are continually shifting, bringing unemployment and excess capacity in some sectors and contemporaneous labor shortages and capacity bottlenecks elsewhere. The gross aggregates of these frictional excess supplies and excess demands vary together positively over time. In contrast, cyclical excess supplies and demands are negatively correlated; in economy-wide recessions and depressions, excess-supply markets and sectors predominate, while the reverse is true in inflationary booms. The amount of frictional unemployment depends on the strength of intersectoral shocks and on the mobility of factors of production in responding to them. Large and protracted shocks, for example in technology or in supplies and prices of key commodities like energy, convert frictional unemployment to *structural* unemployment. Neither is remediable by demand expansion alone.

A common species of classical unemployment occurs when jobs are limited because of excessive real wage rates imposed by governmental or trade union regulations. For individuals who would like to work at or below the wage floor, such unemployment is involuntary. For the workers collectively whose bargaining strength or political clout established the regulations, the unemployment could be regarded as the voluntary consequence of their exercise of monopoly power.

Identification of observed unemployment as classical or Keynesian is sometimes difficult. In either case unemployment might be observed to be associated with real wages above their full employment equilibrium values. In the Keynesian case, this could result from perfect competition among producing firms; they would be paying workers the high marginal products associated with low employment. The big difference between the two cases is that in the Keynesian case, but not in the classical case, real wages would decline on their own and output and employment would increase, in response to expanded demand. In the classical case removal of the regulations would be essential.

There are several variations on the classical unemployment theme. One case is queuing for a high-wage job. An artificially high wage in a particular sector could draw workers from employment elsewhere to wait and hope. This model was originally designed to explain the heavy unemployment in the urban centers of developing countries, where the queuing requires living near the scarce jobs, far from alternative means of subsistence in traditional agriculture. It fits less well in advanced economies, where workers can search and apply for better jobs while employed. Another source of voluntary unemployment may be unemployment insurance benefits and other transfers that increase the reservation prices of persons without jobs. However, in the United States, where unemployment is measured by large household surveys conducted monthly by the Census, persons without jobs will be counted not as unemployed but as "not in labor force" unless they report they have been actively searching. Although some misreporting doubtless occurs, it is small, not always in the same direction, and cannot begin to account for the cyclical variability of unemployment rates.

Agents who are unable to sell as much as they would like at prevailing prices restrict demands in other markets. Unemployed workers cut their consumption. Demand-constrained firms restrict their hiring of labor and their purchases of other inputs. Keynes's insight that quantities actually sold, if smaller than sales desired at existing prices, will keep demands in other markets below equilibrium values, was rediscovered and elaborated by self-styled "disequilibrium theorists" 30 years later (Barro and Grossman, 1971). In old Keynesian economics, multiplier theory formalized the determination of quantities by quantities. It did not and does not, however, preclude the relevance of other determinants of demand, notably prices and interest rates. In this respect it is more general than most of its latter-day extensions in "disequilibrium theory." In demand-constrained regimes, any agent's increase in demand—for example, more investment spending by a business firm—has positive externalities. It will increase the attainable consumption of third parties. In some modern literature, this idea of Keynes is revived and elaborated under the label "strategic complementarity" (Cooper and John, 1988).

Liquidity constraints are an important but extreme form of effective demand constraint. Some wage earners, no doubt, depend on each week's wages to buy the goods for that week's consumption. But Keynes's principle does not depend on such short horizons for consumption-smoothing. Expectations of future spells of unemployment, enhanced by present and recent experience, can limit the current consumption and durables purchases even of long-horizon households. Liquidity constraints and prospective effective demand constraints can also limit business investment. Common observation suggests that households and businesses, and governments too, differ widely in their horizons, i.e. the length of the future period over which expected resources are regarded as potentially available for spending today. These horizons, moreover, doubtless change over time with circumstances and behavior.

The multipliers relating change in aggregate demand to demand shocks, from policies or other events, are not as large as they were thought to be when the concept was first introduced and estimated in the 1930s. One reason is a substantial structural change in democratic capitalist economies. Governments are much larger relative to private sectors than before World War II, and their fiscal institutions are "built-in stabilizers." Their expenditures are quite unresponsive to current business conditions, while their revenues (net of transfers to the private sector) are cyclically sensitive and thus moderate swings in private incomes. A second reason is that economists have come to recognize that, thanks to accommodating capital markets as well as to their own foresight, most economic agents have horizons longer than one year.

While this consideration implies that multipliers of transient shocks are lower than for permanent changes, it by no means implies that they are zero. Both consumption and investment appear to be sensitive to contemporaneous and recent incomes. For most agents capital markets are far from perfect; in particular future and current labor incomes are not fungible. Moreover, expectations of economic futures, individual, national, and global, are influenced by current events, perhaps to an irrational extent.

As Keynes explicitly observed, his theory refers to economies with incomplete markets. In his day futures markets were rare, and contingent futures markets even rarer. They are still scarce. As Keynes explained, decisions not to spend now are not coupled with any definite orders for future or contingent deliveries. Typically they result in accumulations of assets that can be spent on anything at any future time. The multiplier effects of lower current spending propensities are not offset by specific and firm expectations of higher future demands.

Business Cycles as Demand Fluctuations

According to Keynesian macroeconomics, business cycles are fluctuations in aggregate effective demand, carrying output and employment in their wake. They do not reflect movements in market-clearing supply–equals–demand equilibria.

Supplies of labor and other factors of production move fairly smoothly from year to year and from cycle to cycle. So does economy-wide factor productivity, largely reflecting technological progress. Equilibrium output and employment cannot be as variable as actual cyclical observations. In the neoclassical neo-Keynesian synthesis, trend growth is supply-determined; markets are cleared; supply truly creates its own demand. In cyclical departures from trend, demand evokes its own supply. Keynesian short-run macroeconomics does not pretend to apply to problems of long-run growth and development.

Equilibrium cycle theories (Plosser, 1989) are unconvincing. They rely on incredible volatility in technology, retrogressive as well as progressive. They rely on extreme intertemporal substitutions among work, leisure, and consumption. Or they contrive informational asymmetries and misperceptions that seem easy to correct. For example, a few years ago a popular theory attributed business cycles to confusions by suppliers of products and labor between increases in their own real prices, on the one hand, and economy-wide inflation, on the other. Evidently businesses and households were assumed to ignore the flood of current statistics on prices and money supplies.

I am using the word equilibrium to mean Walrasian market-clearing by prices, as is the current usage of both new classical macroeconomists and disequilibrium theorists. Keynes used it otherwise, to refer to a position of rest. That is why he referred to outcomes with involuntary unemployment as equilibria on a par with full employment, and why he termed his theory "general" in the title of his book. The basic issue is not semantic. It is whether situations of general excess supply can and do exist for significant periods of time, whether or not they are called equilibria.

Some passages of *The General Theory* can be read to assert that involuntary unemployment is much more than a temporary cyclical phenomenon, that it is in the absence of remedial policies a chronic defect of capitalism. This was a natural enough view in the 1930s. In Alvin Hansen's American Keynesianism (e.g., Hansen, 1938) secular stagnation was a central proposition. Formally, however, the analysis of *The General Theory* is limited to a time period short enough that the changes in capital stock resulting from non-zero investment can be ignored.

Postwar Keynesians, for the most part, have not regarded protracted depression as a likely outcome.[1] Chronic inflationary gaps could also occur, and alternations between excess-supply and excess-demand regimes were highly probable. Keynesian macroeconomics is two-sided. Deviations on both sides of Walrasian market-clearing can occur, though not necessarily with symmetrical symptoms. Excess demand in aggregate is mainly an "inflationary gap," generating unfilled orders and repressed or open inflation, rather than significant extra output and employment. Macroeconomic stabilization requires two-sided countercyclical demand management.

In any case, habitual application of Keynesian remedies reinforces whatever natural mechanisms tend to return the economy to its full employment growth path. Expectations that those remedies will be used contribute to the stability of that equilibrium path.

The Efficacy of Classical Adjustment Mechanisms: Interest Rates

Suppose that shocks to current real demands for goods and services create, at existing prices and wages, excess supplies of labor and capital services. What are the variables whose changes would avert or eliminate macroeconomic disequilibrium? The leading candidates are current prices, which include both wages of labor as well as prices of products, and interest rates, which involve future as well as current prices. In what follows, I shall set forth Keynesian skepticism regarding the efficacy of these classical adjustment mechanisms.

If these mechanisms respond instantaneously to shocks, no actual discrepancy between demand and supply will occur or be observed. The shocks will be wholly absorbed in the market-clearing variables. This is the assumption of equilibrium business cycle theory and of the "real business cycles" approach. It is this assumption that, among other things, enables new classical macroeconomists to dismiss out of hand real aggregate demand shocks and to react with incredulity when Keynesians mention them. However, if these adjustments do not occur instantaneously but take real time, then Keynesian situations of excess supply do occur. They occur even if prices and interest rates are falling at the same time. The consequence is that the quantity adjustments of the multiplier process start working counter to the possible equilibrating effects of interest rate and price reductions.

In standard Walrasian/Arrow-Debreu theory, perfect flexibility of all wages and prices, present and future, would maintain full employment equilibrium. Short of that, an old question of macroeconomic theory is whether, given current nominal wages and prices, changes in future money wages and prices—that is, in nominal interest rates—could do the job.

In old classical macroeconomics, interest rates are the equilibrators of both capital markets and goods markets. Their adjustment is crucial to the Say's Law story, which dismisses as vulgar superficiality notions that an economy could suffer from shortfalls in demand for commodities in aggregate. Market interest rates keep investment equal to saving at their full-employment levels—and therefore keep aggregate demand equal to full employment output—even if nominal product prices and wages stay put. Indeed classical doctrine is that the real equilibrium of the economy is independent of nominal prices, as if it were the outcome of moneyless frictionless multilateral Walrasian barter.[2]

Can interest rates do the job? The Keynesian insight is that the institutionally fixed nominal interest rate on currency, generally zero, limits the adjustment of nominal interest rates on non-money assets and imparts to them some stickiness even when they are above zero. As a result, after an aggregate demand shock they may not fall automatically to levels low enough to induce sufficient investment to absorb full employment saving. As a result, aggregate demand—consumption plus investment—will fall short of full employment supply.

The case for significant non-zero interest elasticity of money demand is simply that the opportunity costs of holding money fall as the interest rates available on non-money substitutes decline. As those rates approach the interest paid on money itself, zero at the lowest, the opportunity costs vanish. The interest rate on money sets the floor for other nominal market interest rates. The familiar specific money demand models—transactions costs, risk aversion, regressive interest rate expectations—all depend on the fixed nominal interest floor.

The interest-elasticity of money demand is a key parameter in macroeconomic theory. Three cases can be distinguished. One is a classical extreme, often associated with the quantity theory of money: the elasticity is zero. At the other extreme is the Keynesian liquidity trap: market interest rates are so close to the floor that people are on the margin indifferent between money and other assets. In between is the vast middle ground, where the interest-elasticity of money demand is somewhere between zero and negative infinity. Undergraduate students of macroeconomics know, or used to know, that in standard models monetary policy can effectively alter spending in the classical and intermediate cases but not at the liquidity trap extreme. They also know, or used to know, that fiscal policy is effective in the liquidity trap and intermediate cases but not at the classical, monetarist extreme.

My focus here is somewhat different. The question is the efficacy of market interest rates as automatic stabilizers in the face of real demand shocks, when monetary quantities, fiscal parameters, and other policy instruments are fixed. The answer is not in dispute for the two extremes: they work in the classical case and not in the liquidity trap. Who owns the middle ground? Quantity theorists used to contend that classical propositions obtain everywhere outside the liquidity trap. But the middle ground belongs to the Keynesians. Real demand shocks will move aggregate income despite their effects on interest rates, for the same reason that fiscal policies will do so. Unless the real supply of money is increased by monetary policy or by price reduction, the interest rate will not fall enough after a negative aggregate demand shock (the same thing as a negative investment-minus-saving shock) to maintain investment–equals–saving equality at full employment. The interest rate that would do that job would also require additional money supply—unless money demand is perfectly inelastic with respect to market interest rates.

Recent structural changes have made the monetary system more monetarist, more like what the quantity theorists said it always was. Bank deposit interest rates, even on the checkable deposits used for most transactions, now are market-determined and move up and down along with rates on non-money assets. The differential between them, the opportunity cost important in cash management, is less systematically related to the general level of interest rates than it used to be. This development has undoubtedly made the demand for deposits less elastic with respect to the interest rates that matter for demands for goods and services. (On these developments see Tobin, 1983).

However, the zero floor on nominal interest rates is still there. The monetary base, currency held outside banks plus bank reserves, remains interest-free. The money market in which the demand for and supply of bank reserves are equated is the fulcrum of the banking system and of the entire structure of interest rates. States of nature in which equilibrium would require negative real interest rates still have positive probability. Since nominal rates cannot be negative, full employment would not be possible in those contingencies unless expected inflation made real rates negative. The possibility of these states will influence the portfolio and investment decisions of rational agents.

Money demand is not the whole story. Keynes also stressed liquidity preference in a different form, sticky long-term interest rates. Because traditional expectations of future long rates persist in slumps, current long rates do not automatically follow short rates down far enough to induce the spurts in investment needed for recovery.

Classical and new classical theories assert that capital markets generate equilibrium real rates independently of what is happening to nominal interest rates and commodity prices. But the evidence is that nominal interest rates do matter. Changes in them are usually changes in real rates. Likewise changes in inflation expectations are not fully offset by changes in nominal rates. The "Fisher equation" asserts that real interest rates are independent of nominal rates and inflation expectations, but Irving Fisher himself concluded from his empirical investigations that the proposition held if at all only in very long runs. Modern research has confirmed his findings.

The Efficacy of Classical Adjustment Mechanisms: Nominal Wages and Prices

If interest rate adjustments cannot suffice, no matter how rapidly asset markets clear, the job falls to nominal prices. If it is a crime not to accept the instantaneous clearing by prices of product and labor markets as the foundation of macroeconomics, then Keynes and Keynesians are certainly guilty. But it is a caricature of Keynesian economics, no less false because it is widely believed, to attribute to Keynesians the assumption that nominal prices are perfectly rigid, for the entire time period over which the analysis is intended to apply. In fact Keynes himself did not contend that nominal prices and product prices are fixed independently of amounts of excess supply or demand, and neither do most Keynesians today.

The "fixprice" method used in many textbooks was a convenient device for expounding the Keynesian calculus of adjustments of quantities to quantities and to interest rates. It was carried to extreme in modern formal "disequilibrium theory." The method is misleading when it conveys the impression that Keynesian economics assumes price rigidities and indeed is defined by that assumption. It is especially misleading if it gives the idea that such an assumption is necessary. This impression of Keynesian theory, whether the result of caricatures by its enemies or careless expositions by its friends, appears to be the source of the defection of many economists.

Consider a spectrum of the degree of nominal price flexibility from complete flexibility at one extreme to complete rigidity at the other. Complete flexibility means instantaneous adjustment, so that prices are always clearing markets, jumping sufficiently to absorb all demand or supply shocks. Complete rigidity means that nominal prices do not change at all during the period of analysis. In between are various speeds of price adjustment, various lengths of time during which markets are not clearing. Here again, as in the case of interest rate effects and despite common beliefs to the contrary, Keynesians own the middle ground. It is not true that only the arbitrary and gratuitous assumption of complete rigidity converts nominal demand shocks into real demand shocks and brings multipliers and IS/LM processes into play. Any degree of stickiness that prevents complete price adjustment at once has the same qualitative implications, and can even be treated by the fixprice method on an "as if" basis.

Keynes argued that nominal wage would not fall rapidly in response to excess supplies of labor. At the same time, he asserted that real wages could fall if product prices rose as necessary to induce firms to expand employment. This asymmetry led many critics to suppose that Keynes was attributing "money illusion" to workers and to dismiss Keynesian theory out of hand. Why would workers accept a cut in *real* wages achieved by an increase in the price of wage goods but resist cuts in money wages? Keynes's reason for this asymmetry is both empirically realistic and theoretically impeccable. Workers are concerned primarily with relative wages, with how their pay compares with the pay of those to whom they regard themselves at least equal in merit. Those concerns do not depend on money illusion, they are certainly not irrational, and there is a great deal of empirical evidence of their importance.

Labor markets are disaggregated and desynchronized. To any single worker or local group, a nominal wage cut appears to be a loss in relative wages; there is no assurance that others will also take cuts. On the other hand, an increase in the cost of living is the same for everybody. Workers may be perfectly prepared to receive lower real wages with unchanged relative wages, but labor market institutions give them no way to communicate this willingness.

The hole in this story is that it does not explain how the relative-wage concerns of employed workers prevail when there are unemployed workers willing to work for less pay—real, nominal, and relative. The power of insiders vis-à-vis employers and outsiders evidently derives from the costs of turnover among members of an interdependent working team. Insider power has lately been the subject of considerable theoretical and empirical inquiry, notably by Assar Lindbeck and his colleagues (Lindbeck and Snower, 1990). Labor economists have long observed that queues of jobseekers outside the factory gate have little effect on the wages paid to employees inside. Hard times do bring wage cuts, but usually by so damaging the financial and competitive positions of employers that they can credibly threaten layoffs of senior workers and even plant closings and bankruptcies.

All Keynesian macroeconomics really requires is that product prices and money wages are not perfectly flexible, whatever may be the rationale for their behavior. After all, the Walrasian auctioneer of classical macroeconomics is itself not an implication of optimizing behavior. It is a fictitious institution with no presumptive priority over alternative institutional assumptions.

Seeking to win the game on his opponents' home field, Keynes pretended to be assuming pure competition in all markets. But his insights regarding labor markets implicitly recognized that wages are administered or negotiated prices, and for that reason alone are not perfectly flexible, not prices set in impersonal auction markets. His product markets, however, remained Marshallian. Given money wages and given the overall aggregate demand constraint, competition equated product prices to marginal cost. Thus real wages were equal to marginal productivity. But, as the existence of excess supply would imply, those wages exceeded the wages necessary to induce workers to supply the actual volume of employment.

Marginal productivity theory implies that real wages and employment or output would be negatively correlated in business cycles. But this implication has been repeatedly refuted by empirical observations. This is not a blow to Keynesian policy recommendations, quite the contrary. If it is possible to expand demand and increase output and employment without lowering real wages, so much the better—there is less reason to worry that observed unemployment may be classical.

Clearly product markets, as well as labor markets, should be modeled as imperfectly competitive. There too prices are decision variables, a fact that at the very least suggests that they don't change every hour. When the economy is in a Keynesian excess-supply regime, dynamics of adjustment determine the paths of wages, markups, and product prices. The path of real wages lies between the classical labor demand the supply curves, and could be either pro-cyclical or counter-cyclical. Likewise, the paths of output and employment typically diverge from production functions. In the past 50 years a great deal of empirical work has been done on these relationships. Phillips curves and Okun's law are among the best known examples.

In addition, more formal models of nominal price inertia have been developed. Arthur Okun (1981) provided a theory of "invisible handshakes," in which price adjustments are moderated in the interest of maintaining long-run customer-supplier relationships. Stanley Fischer (1977) and John Taylor (1980) formalized wage stickiness in models of overlapping staggered contracts. These models can apply even to nonunion shops where wages are administered rather than negotiated; employers with large work forces change announced wage scales periodically. In a monograph that has attracted too little attention, Katsuhito Iwai (1981) gave Keynesian macroeconomics rigorous microfoundations in a model of monopolistic competition. A microeconomic world of imperfect competition is a Keynesian macroeconomic world, where nominal prices are imperfectly flexible.

Keynes's explanation of money-wage stickiness is the usual focus of discussion and criticism. It is to the second strand of his argument, commonly ignored, that I wish to direct major attention. Even if money wages and prices were more flexible, even if excess supplies of labor were to lead more rapidly to cuts in money wages, this greater flexibility would not prevent or cure unemployment. Given a contractionary shock in aggregate demand, deflation of money wages and prices would not restore real demand to its full employment value. This classical market-clearing adjustment mechanism was, in Keynes's view, much too frail to bear the weight of macroeconomic stabilization. In fact, Keynes recommended stability rather than flexibility in money wages.

Keynes did not challenge the efficacy of price adjustment mechanisms in clearing particular markets in the Marshallian partial equilibrium theory on which he had been reared. He did challenge the mindless application of those mechanisms to economy-wide markets. Founding what came to be known as macroeconomics, he was modeling a whole economy as a closed system. He knew he could not use the Marshallian assumption that the clearing of one market could be safely described on the assumption that the rest of the economy was unaffected.

Consider the difference between a local market for a particular kind of worker and the national market for all labor. Excess supply in the local printing trades, for example, would in a competitive market cause printers' wages to fall. Declining nominal wages would be declining real wages; both would be falling relative to the rest of the economy. The adjustments themselves would not have any noticeable effects on local printing firms' schedules of demand for printers or on workers' supply schedules. But suppose there is an economy-wide excess supply of labor. How is the conventional adjustment apparatus to be deployed?

The orthodox instinct is to think of the price in this market as the real wage. It is in terms of the real wage that the employers' downward sloping demand schedule, following the law of diminishing marginal productivity, is expressed. In the same terms are expressed workers' marginal choices between the consumption rewards of paid employment and the utilities of other uses of time. The orthodox expectation and prescription is that real wages fall to eliminate unemployment.

But, Keynes asks, how do workers and employers engineer an economy-wide reduction in real wages? The unemployment is nation-wide, but the markets where wages are set are decentralized. In every local market it is the money wage, not the real wage, that is determined. If money wage rates fall in all these excess-supply local labor markets, will real wages in fact fall?

It is certainly far from obvious. The relevant labor demand curves are the nominal values of marginal products. These values will fall, the demand curves shift down, if and as product prices fall. Product prices will fall because nominal labor incomes decline along with wage rates; as a result, workers' money demands for the products they produce will decline too. Here, then, is a case in which demand and supply schedules do not stay put while the price adjustment to excess supply takes place. It is illegitimate to appeal to the intuition that seems so credible for single markets. Instead, the question is whether proportionate deflation of all nominal prices will or will not increase aggregate effective real demand.[3]

Two issues in this debate need to be distinguished. The first concerns the relation of real aggregate demand to the *price level*. The second concerns its relation to the expected *rate of change* of prices. In discussing them, I shall not distinguish between money wages and nominal product prices or between their rates of change, but rather follow the assumption, conventional in this debate, that they move together. I remind you that the theoretical argument refers to a closed economy—maybe the United States in years gone by, or post-1992 Europe, or the whole OECD area.

Keynes in Book I of *The General Theory* denied that real aggregate demand was related at all to the price and money wage level. In effect, he turned the classical neutrality proposition against the classicals. If all money wages and prices are lowered in the same proportion, how can real quantities demanded be any different? Thus, if a real shock makes real demand deficient, how can a purely nominal price adjustment undo the damage?

Actually Keynes himself provided an answer in Chapter 19. If the nominal quantity of money remains the same, its real quantity increases, interest rates fall, and real demand increases. This scenario is often called the "Keynes effect." This mechanism would fail if demand for money became perfectly elastic with respect to interest rates—as in the liquidity trap discussed above—or if demand for goods for consumption and investment were perfectly inelastic.

Pigou (1943, 1947), Patinkin (1948, 1956 [1965]), and other authors provided another scenario, the "Pigou effect" or "real balance effect," which alleges a direct effect of increased wealth, in the case at hand taking the form of the increased real value of base money, on real consumption demand (possibly also on investment demand as wealth-owners seek to maintain portfolio balance between real and nominal assets). This effect does not depend on reduction of interest rates.

To an astonishing degree, the theoretical fraternity has taken the real balance effect to be a conclusive refutation of Keynes. Perhaps it does refute his claim to have found underemployment *equilibria*. If involuntary unemployment and excess capacity are pushing nominal wages and prices down, the economy is not in equilibrium in any sense. It is not in a position of rest, markets are not clearing, and expectations are not being realized. Equilibrium requires wages and prices so low that the purchasing power of net monetary wealth is so great that aggregate real demand creates jobs for all willing workers. In principle, as Leontief observed, prices could be low enough to enable you to buy the whole GNP for one thin dime.

Nevertheless the real balance effect is of dubious strength, and even of uncertain sign. Most nominal assets in a modern economy are "inside" assets, that is the debts of private agents to other private agents. They wash out in accounting aggregation, leaving only the government's nominal debt to the private sector as net wealth. Some, though probably not all, of that debt is internalized by taxpayers. The base of the real balance effect is therefore quite small relative to the economy—in the United

States the monetary base is currently only 6 percent of GNP. A 10 percent increase in the value of money would increase net wealth by 0.6 percent of GNP and, if the marginal propensity to spend from wealth were generously estimated at 0.10, would increase spending by 0.06 percent of GNP.

While Don Patinkin (1948) stressed the theoretical importance of the real balance effect, he disclaimed belief in its practical significance. In the Great Depression, he pointed out, the real value of net private balances rose 46 percent from 1929 to 1932, but real national income *fell* 40 percent.

That inside assets and debts wash out in accounting aggregation does not mean that the consequences of price changes on their real values wash out. Price declines make creditors better off and debtors poorer. Their marginal propensities to spend from wealth need not be the same. Common sense suggests that debtors have the higher spending propensities— that is why they are in debt! Even a small differential could easily swamp the Pigou effect—gross inside dollar-denominated assets are 200 percent of United States GNP.

Irving Fisher (1933) emphasized the increased burden of debt resulting from unanticipated deflation as a major factor in depressions in general and in the Great Depression in particular. Therefore, I like to call the reverse Pigou-Patinkin effect the Fisher wealth redistribution effect (not to be confused with other Fisher effects). It is quite possible that this Fisher effect is stronger than the Pigou and Keynes effects combined, particularly when output and employment are low relative to capacity.[4]

Aggregate Demand and the Rate of Change of Prices

The previous argument refers to *levels* of nominal wages and prices. An even more important argument refers to *rates of change*. The Keynes and Pigou effects compare high prices and low as if they were timeless alternatives, without worrying about the process of change from high to low in real time. Economists of their day argued in this way quite consciously, as dictated by the rules of the comparative statics games they were playing.

The process of change works on aggregate demand in just the wrong direction. Greater expected deflation, or expected disinflation, is an increase in the real rate of interest, necessarily so when nominal interest

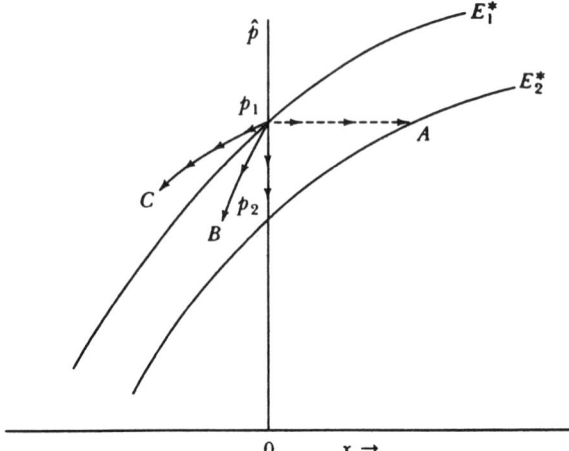

Figure 7.1
The problematic stability of price adjustment

rates are constrained by the zero floor of the interest on money. Here is another Fisher effect, another factor Fisher stressed in his explanation of the Great Depression. Keynes stressed it too, as a pragmatic dynamic reinforcement of the lesson of his static general theory.

The problematic stability of price adjustment is evident in Figure 7.1. Here the horizontal axis represents expected price deflation or inflation, x. The vertical axis represents p the log of the price level. An upward sloping curve like E_1^* plots combinations (x,p) of expected price change and price level that generate the same aggregate real demand E. The slope reflects the assumptions that demand is related negatively to the price level and positively to its expected rate of change. In given circumstances, a higher curve refers to a lower demand E and a lower curve to higher demand. The curvature of the E^* loci reflects the assumption that the "Keynes effect" of increases in real money balances in lowering interest rates declines as those balances increase and interest rates fall.

Suppose that initially the "isoquant" E_1^* makes demand equal to full employment equilibrium output Y^*, here taken to be constant. Points above or left of that isoquant are positions where E is lower than Y^*, characterized by Keynesian unemployment. Points below or right of E_1^* are positions of macroeconomic excess demand. In Figure 7.1, the equilibrium inflation rate (expected and actual) and price are $(0, p_1)$. Suppose now that a discrete one-time negative shock to real demand shifts the isoquant for $E = Y^*$ down to E_2^* so that the new equilibrium inflation rate and price are $(0, p_2)$. The old isoquant E_1^* now implies an E lower than Y^*. To restore equilibrium the price level must fall from p_1 to p_2. How is the price decline to be accomplished? One scenario is the Walrasian miracle, an instantaneous precipitous vertical descent, so that there is no time interval during which actual or expected price changes are other than zero. If jumps of that kind in p are excluded, there is no path of actual price changes and rationally expected prices that avoids departure from $E = Y^*$ during the transition. It would take a burst of positive inflation, actual and expected, to offset the negative demand shock, as at point A. But this would move the price level in the wrong direction.

The likely scenario is a path like B or C in Figure 7.1: The excess supply that now characterizes the initial equilibrium point $(0, p_1)$ and the first isoquant starts prices declining, and the anticipation of their decline is bad for aggregate demand. Along B the real balance effect is strong enough to overcome the negative effects of the deflation; aggregate demand E is increasing as the path hits lower isoquants. The new equilibrium may be attained, though probably by a damped cyclical process. Along C, however, the price level effect is too weak to win out, and the gap of E and Y below Y^* is increasing.

Fisher and Keynes were right. In Tobin (1975), I exhibited a simple formal macroeconomic system, classical in the sense that it has only one equilibrium, which is characterized by full employment, indeed by a "natural" rate of unemployment. Given a zero natural real growth rate and a constant nominal monetary base, the price level is constant in that equilibrium.

Several specifications of the short-run dynamics of this model are possible. One is a Keynesian specification, as follows: (1) Production increases when desired purchases exceed actual current output, but not by the full amount of the gap. This adjustment can be thought of as response to undesired changes in inventories or unfilled orders. (2) Nominal prices follow expectations plus or minus a "Phillips curve" adjustment to the difference between actual and full employment output. (3) Price change expectations adapt to the difference between actual and expected inflation or deflation.

Alternatively, the price change expectations could be regarded as rational expectations of the Phillips curve price adjustment mechanisms. That is, the impossibility of instantaneous jumps to the new equilibrium would be as intrinsic to the structure of the system as the system's static equations themselves.

The stability of this system requires, first, that the dynamics of output at constant prices, involving marginal propensities to spend and adjustments to excess or deficient inventories and other manifestations of demand/output gaps, is stable. Assuming this condition is met, stability depends on the relative strengths of the price level effects on demand—both "Keynes" and "Pigou" as modified by "Fisher wealth redistribution"—and the real interest effect—another "Fisher"—of expected deflation (or disinflation). The latter is the product of two coefficients, the response of price change expectations to actual change (equal to one if expectations are rational) and the response of real demand to expected price change. The real interest effect may well dominate if the real balance effect is weak, especially if the Fisher wealth redistribution effect overshadows it, and if the demand for money is highly sensitive to interest rates. The equilibrium is then unstable. Moreover, because of the curvature of the E^* loci, the system could be stable locally but unstable for large displacements.

I have experimented with simulations of a discrete-time approximation to this model, subjecting it to stochastic shocks to real aggregate demand. One extreme case is "Walrasian": prices vary from period to period as necessary to keep goods markets always cleared, prices are always anticipated to equal their expected value corresponding to zero shock, and both output and aggregate demand always equal equilibrium full employment output. An opposite extreme is "rigid-price Keynesian": prices are constant at their expected equilibrium value and expectations of price change are constant at zero. In between the extremes, nominal prices adjust with some inertia to excess real demand or supply, and expectations of price change adapt, more or less speedily, to observed changes.

In these simulations the underlying "fixprice" dynamics are stable, and its parameters are the same in all cases. "Greater price flexibility" can mean two things: (1) a larger Phillips curve coefficient relating price change to excess real demand or supply; (2) if expectations are taken to be adaptive, a larger coefficient of adaptation of price change expectations to actual price changes.

The issue is whether greater price flexibility increases or decreases the ratio between the standard deviation of the actual output gap and the standard deviation of the stochastic real demand shock. That ratio is zero in the Walrasian case, where the shock is always wholly absorbed in prices. It is of course positive for the rigid-price case. What happens in the intermediate cases? Not surprisingly, the results depend mainly on the same condition that determines stability or instability with respect to a single unrepeated shock. Greater flexibility in sense (1), a faster "Phillips" adjustment, diminishes the test ratio when the stability condition is met—that is, the price level effect on demand is negative and bigger than the price change effect—and raises it otherwise. Greater flexibility in sense (2), faster adjustment of price expectations, always raises the test ratio.[5]

Policies, Expectations, and Stability

Keynes stressed the central role of long-term expectations. He had in mind in particular expectations of real variables—effective demands and real returns on investments. They might be either stabilizing or destabilizing. If business managers believe that recessions will be quickly reversed, their actions will help to bring about recoveries. If they expect business activity to continue to be subnormal or to fall further, their pessimism may turn recession into depression. That is why policies and policy expectations are very important. After World War II, widespread perception that government fiscal and monetary policies would keep recessions short and shallow helped to keep them short and shallow. In these circumstances, the economy would work well if, as Keynes advocated, employers and workers keep average money wage rates stable, so that actual and expected price and wage changes are not a source of instability.

In the 1930s both Fisher and Keynes saw deflation as a cause of depression in production and employment, and advocated monetary and gold policies of reflation for recovery. Today, however, unexpectedly high prices are regarded as bearish economic news, and unexpectedly low prices as bullish. Is this a paradox? Does it mean that price flexibility is stabilizing after all? Again, policies and policy expectations are crucial. Today the public understands the high priorities central banks attach to inflation control. If prices are above the path to which the central bank is committed, it will take measures to contract demand. The faster private agents respond by lowering prices and wages, the sooner the monetary authorities will reflate. In this sense, price flexibility is stabilizing.

In contrast, extrapolative expectations are destabilizing. Policies—policy rules if you like—that create and sustain regressive expectations of output and price departures from equilibrium are stabilizing. Those facts are wholly consistent with the contentions of Fisher and Keynes, and of this paper, that in the absence of activist "feedback" policies, monetary and fiscal, flexibility may well be destabilizing, both to prices and to real macro variables. Governments and central banks should not expect disinflation or deflation alone to maintain or restore full employment.

Appendix

Here I give further information regarding the simulations mentioned in the text. The variables in the model are the following:

Y	Real aggregate output, constant dollars per year.
Yf	Real aggregate output at full employment capacity, constant dollars per year. Assumed constant and equal to 1 in all simulations.
E	Real aggregate demand for goods and services, constant dollars per year.
p	Log of the price level, current dollars per constant dollar.
$p$dot	Rate of change per period in the price level: $p(t) - p(t-1)$
x	Expectation of $p(t+1) - p(t)$, the rate of change per period in the price level.
uE	Stochastic shock to E, constant dollars per year.
v	Random variable i.i.d, constant dollars per year.
pf	Value of p that would equate E and Yf, generally hypothetical.

The equations of the model are first set out on the assumption that discrete time t is measured in periods equal to a year. That is, the variables take on just one value each year. Later in this Appendix the model will be modified to allow periodicity different from one year. For periodicity of a year, the equations follow:

- Aggregate Demand is a function of Capacity Output (+), Actual Output (+), Price (−), and Expected Price Change (+):

$$E(t) = Eyf^* Yf(t) + (1 - Sy)^* Y(t) + Ep^* p(t) + Ex^* x(t) + uE(t). \tag{A1}$$

- Output Change is a function of the Lagged Difference between Aggregate Demand and Output (+):

$$Y(t) = Ay^*(E(t-1) - Y(t-1)) + Y(t-1). \tag{A2}$$

How come E and Y are not equal to each other, as the national income/expenditures identity suggests they must be? The closest numerical national income accounting approximation to E is Final Sales, which excludes inventory accumulation. Conceptually E should exclude

PRICE FLEXIBILITY AND OUTPUT STABILITY

only unintended, undesired inventory accumulation (or depletion), and likewise should include unintended and undesired saving, taking the form of additional unfilled orders or other forms of demand rationing.

- Expectations-augmented Phillips Curve: Price Change is equal to Lagged Expected Price Change minus a function of the Output Gap (+):

$$p(t) = p(t-1) + x(t-1) - Ap^*(Yf - Y(t-1)). \tag{A3}$$

- Adaptive Price Change Expectations: Change in Expected Price Change is equal to Difference between Actual and Lagged Expected Price Change (+):

$$x(t) = x(t-1) + AX^*(p(t) - p(t-1) - x(t-1)). \tag{A4}$$

- First Order Autoregressive Shock to Aggregate Demand:

$$uE(t) = h^*uE(t-1) + (1-h)v(t). \tag{A5}$$

- Some obvious substitutions reduce the basic model to three linear first-order difference equations in Y, p, and x:

$$Y(t)/Ay = Eyf^*Yf - Sy^*Y(t-1) + Ep^*p(t-1) + Ex^*x(t-1), \tag{A6}$$

$$p(t) = p(t-1) + x(t-1) - Ap^*(Yf(t-1) - Y(t-1)), \tag{A7} = (A3)$$

$$x(t) = x(t-1) - Ax^*Ap^*(Yf(t-1) - Y(t-1)). \tag{A8}$$

Here is a list of the parameters of the model:

Aggregate demand coefficients:

Eyf Marginal propensity to consume from capacity real income, representing permanent income. Assumed positive, less than 1.

Sy Marginal propensity to save from actual real income, short for $1 - Ey$. Assumed positive, less than 1.

Ep Effect of price level on real aggregate demand. This is a combination of the so-called Keynes effect (with nominal money supply constant an increase in p lowers real money supply and raises real interest rates, with negative effect on E) and the so-called Pigou or real balance effect (with privately owned nominal net assets constant an increase in p lowers net aggregate real wealth and affects E negatively, independently of any effects on interest rates.) Thus Ep is generally assumed to be negative, although the text expresses some skepticism of this convention, based on doubts about the sign of the Pigou effect.

Ex Effect of expected price inflation on E, assumed to be positive for reasons given in text.

Adjustment speed coefficients (non-negative):

Ay Speed at which Output catches up with Demand.
Ap Effect of Output Gap on inflation.
Ax Speed at which Expected Price Change adapts to actual Price Change.
h Relative weight of past Demand shock in current Demand shock. Non-negative, not greater than 1.

This model, equations A6, A7, A8, is a discrete-time linear stochastic version of the model in (Tobin, 1975) described in the text. One convenient difference is that here the log of price is taken as the relevant price variable; this makes the difference equations linear if the coefficients above listed are constants. Note, however, that price is the only variable that appears in logarithmic form in the model. I resist transforming income variables in an aggregate demand equation into logarithms. It violates the national expenditure identity, and anyway marginal propensities, not elasticities, seem the intuitively sensible coefficients.

The three equations A6, A7, and A8 reduce to a third-order difference equation whose properties in the absence of stochastic shocks can be calculated from the values of the coefficients. One of the stability conditions is that Sy be non-negative, a condition assumed to prevail throughout the simulations here reported. The crucial necessary and sufficient condition is the one discussed in the text, that $Ep + Ax^*Ex$ is less than zero. For any setup, that is for any set of assumed parameter values, whether or not this condition is satisfied can be calculated and reported. Of course, if Ep is positive, as it can be if Fisher debt effects overcome Pigou asset effects and interest rates are either insensitive to real money supplies or fairly irrelevant to aggregate demand, then the stability condition fails. It can fail anyway. Besides testing a setup for stability, it is possible to ascertain whether or not the dynamics of the model are cyclic or geometric.

Simulations are run for several setups. Table 7.A1 shows the values assumed for the parameters in each one. The two extremes are Setup W for "Walrasian" and Setup K for "Keynesian." In Setup W, equation (A7w) is substituted for (A7), guaranteeing that $E = Y = Yf$. This is just an assumption, not the consequence of any specified dynamic mechanism of adjustment to actual failures of markets to clear. Somehow prices are flexible enough within any period to absorb completely any shock $uE(t)$. Nevertheless expected inflation x is always zero. Independent of any fluctuations in actual price and actual price change, agents always act on the expectation that no inflation will occur, as would be true on average over many periods.

$$p(t) = pf(t) \qquad \text{(A7w)}$$

$$x(t) = 0 \qquad \text{(A8w)}$$

Just as Setup W implements perfect flexibility, Setup K embodies the opposite extreme, perfect rigidity of nominal price. Price is taken to be constant at its equilibrium value pf^*, the pf which makes $E = Yf$ for a zero demand shock. Inflation is always zero, so x is likewise constant at zero.

$$p(t) = pf^* \qquad \text{(A7k)}$$

$$x(t) = 0 \qquad \text{(A8k)}$$

Setup Kb is a minor variation of K, with much faster adjustment of Y to E. (Ay is 0.8 instead of 0.2).

There is one other special case, Setup MPF (Myopic Perfect Foresight). Here expected price change x is always equal to actual price change:

$$x(t) = p(t) - p(t-1). \qquad \text{(A8mpf)}$$

This speed-up of adaptation of expectation to realization is a recipe for radical instability.

Four other setups, with various intermediate parameter values, are also simulated. Table 7.A1 summarizes seven setups. Ia differs from I only in the value of h, zero instead of 0.5. II and III differ from I by assuming somewhat faster "Phillips curve" price adjustment and much slower adaptation of x to experience. Slow adaptation is a source of stability.

Each simulation starts at equilibrium values with uE equal to zero. These values are: $Y^* = 1 = Yf = E^*$, and $pf^* = (Sy - Eyf)/Ep$. (This latter is a negative number, but recall that p is a logarithm. In the simulations to be reported, pf^* is always the same, -0.833, because the coefficients in (A6) on which it depends are the same in all setups.) From the

Table 7.A1
Simulations with Various Setups and Common Realizations

Setup	W	K	MPF	I	II	III	Ia
Parameters							
Eyf	0.4	0.4	0.4	0.4	0.4	0.4	0.4
Sy	0.65	0.65	0.65	0.65	0.65	0.65	0.65
Ep	−0.3	−0.3	−0.3	−0.3	−0.3	−0.3	−0.3
Ex	0.3	0.3	0.3	0.3	0.3	0.3	0.3
Ay	0.2	0.2	0.2	0.2	0.2	0.2	0.2
Ap	$p = pf$	$p = pf$	0.5	0.5	0.65	0.65	0.5
Ax	$x = 0$	$x = 0$	$x = $ pdot	0.4	0.1	0.05	0.4
h	0.5	0.5	0.5	0.5	0.5	0.5	0
Stable Y?	Assumed	Yes	No	No	Yes	Yes	No
Stable p	No	Assumed	No	No	Yes	Yes	No
Cyclical?	Yes	No	Yes	Yes	No	No	Yes
Realization 91-1, 50 Periods							
std(uE)	0.007	0.007	0.007	0.007	0.007	0.007	0.013
std(Y)/std(uE)	0	0.55	43.78	5.67	1.08	0.79	3.57
std(p)/std(uE)	3.35	0	162.81	33.19	4.86	2.99	35.60
Realization 91-2, 50 Periods							
std(uE)	0.016	0.016			0.016	0.016	
std(Y)/std(uE)	0	0.68			1.86	1.39	
std(p)/std(uE)	3.33	0.00			7.32	4.83	
Realization 93-1, 50 Periods							
std(uE)	0.016	0.016	0.016		0.016		
std(Y)/std(uE)	0	0.77	37.91		2.1		
std(p)/std(uE)	3.33	0	203.44		11.82		

initial conditions the dynamic model is run for 50 periods or "years," driven by a realization of the random series v. This is drawn from a uniform distribution within the interval $(-.05, .05)$. The same realization is used for several setups, to facilitate comparison of the results. The statistics compared are the ratios of the standard deviations of Y and p to the standard deviation of the random demand shock uE for the realization. Table 7.A1 gives these statistics, for three realizations.

Table 7.A2 reports averages of these statistics over ten 50-period realizations, but for only two setups, I and II. These two make a contrast, because I is stable and II is unstable and cyclic. The point is to show that the differences apparent in single realizations as shown in Table 7.A1 are not eccentric.

The main conclusion from these simulations is that the stability condition is the best indicator of whether and to what extent stochastic fluctuations of aggregate demand will generate output fluctuations of greater amplitude. Setups that generate high output variability are also likely to produce high price variability. The best recipe for stability is insensitivity of price expectations to actual price movements. That is why Setups W, K, II, and III do so much better than MPF and I. It's hard to improve on the Keynesian performance. The trick is to maintain a long-run view of price trends that keeps inflation expectations constant in

Table 7.A2
Output and Price Variability in Selected Setups (Averages of ten realizations of 50 periods each)

Setup	Kb Stable Noncylic	I Unstable Cyclic	II Stable Cyclic
Average std(Y)/std(uE)	1.16	113.55	2.14
Std dev of std(Y)/std(uE)	0.07	67.75	0.76
Average std(p)/std(uE)	0.00	375.80	11.39
Std dev of std(p)/std(uE)	0.00	245.03	4.20

Table 7.A3
Simulations with Common Setups, Various Periodicities

Realization 91-1	std(Y) std(uE)	std(p)/ std(uE)	std(Y) std(uE)	std(p)/ std(uE)	std(Y) std(uE)	std(p)/ std(uE)
Setup Periods per year	I	I	II	II	W	W
8	10.72	51.96	1.99	7.76	0.00	3.36
4	10.95	43.15	1.55	6.75	0.00	3.32
2	10.58	41.31	1.38	5.93	0.00	3.32
1	5.67	33.19	1.08	4.86	0.00	3.39
Setup Periods per year	III	III	IV	IV	K	K
8	1.99	3.97	2.11	68.48	0.55	0.00
4	1.66	3.25	2.93	13.39	0.54	0.00
2	0.93	2.96	4.42	16.48	0.56	0.00
1	0.79	2.99	3.56	19.13	0.55	0.00

spite of price fluctuations that are equilibrating in the short run. The Walrasian simulations assume this ideal combination, without specifying any mechanism that would do the trick.

The only shocks simulated here are aggregate real demand shocks. Shocks to Yf and other shocks to equations (A2), (A3), and (A4) could and should be modeled. Purely monetary shocks could be modeled as changes in Ep. Possibly setups that perform relatively well with respect to real demand shocks would not rank so high against other kinds of shocks.

Table 7.A3 reports a much more complicated and laborious series of simulations. Their rationale requires some explanation. One way to study the effects of increased price flexibility is to change the coefficients of the model, moving from one setup to another. For example, raising the absolute values of coefficients Ep, Ap, and Ax might be thought to be increasing price flexibility—although results in Table 7.A1 suggest that these changes destabilize both output and price. Since several coefficients are relevant, there is no unique way of altering "the" degree of price flexibility in the model. Another possibility, mentioned in the text in reference to (Delong and Summers 1986), is to speed up the whole model uniformly by increasing the number of model periods corresponding to a year of real time.

In the 50-period simulations so far reported, the assumption was that each variable took on a new value once a period, only once. The sizes of the coefficients in the setups were motivated by the assumption that the one period corresponded to one year. If the number of periods per year is to be changed, it is necessary to maintain the same real-time behavioral assumptions.

When, for example, the periodicity is doubled from 1 to 2 times per year, some of the coefficients for dynamic simulations for any given setup must be altered. Let z be the value for periodicity 1 and $z2$ for periodicity 2. Here are the required alterations:

$Ex2 = 2Ex$

$Ay2 = 1 - (1 - Ay)^{1/2}$

$Ap2 = Ap/2$ \hfill (A9)

$Ax2 = 1 - (1 - Ax)^{1/2}$

$h2 = h^{1/2}$

The meaning of actual inflation $p(t) - p(t-1)$ and expected inflation x depend on periodicity, becoming price change per half-year instead of per year. That is why the coefficient Ex has to be doubled to keep behavior the same. The other coefficients in (A1) remain the same, because E, Y, and Yf are all defined as annual rates, and the meaning of p is also independent of periodicity. Adjustment coefficients are changed so as to keep speeds of adjustment at annual rate comparable.

Equations like (A9) also relate coefficients z4 to z2 and z8 to z4.

The experiments reported in Table 7.A3 assume various periodicities, periods per year of 1, 2, 4, and 8. The procedure was as follows for the one realization here reported: A series of 400 random numbers, v8, was drawn, uniformly distributed with limits plus and minus $0.05/2^{3/2}$. From the series v8 was computed a series of 400 values of uE. For each setup the dynamic simulation was run, and the average of successive groups of 8 "observations" of the several variables constituted an "annual" series of 50 "years." From these annual series were calculated the test statistics std(Y)/std(uE) and std(p)/std(uE), for periodicity 8. Next the series v4 was obtained from the sums of the 200 successive pairs of v8, and the same procedures for obtaining new values of uE and the economic variables were repeated. The average of successive groups of 4 again constituted series of 50 "years," assuming periodicity 4. Analogous calculations provided simulations for periodicities 2 and 1.

The results shown in Table 7.A3 do not suggest any approach to Walrasian results as periodicity is increased. This is not surprising, since Ep and Ax^*Ex, the key determinants of stability, are virtually independent of periodicity. Ep remains the same, and although Ax and Ex both vary with periodicity, their variations are offsetting. Nevertheless further calculations, including still higher numbers of periods per year, are desirable.

Notes

I would like to express my gratitude for the faithful and valuable research assistance of Mitchell Tobin, Yale College 1992 (no relation).

1. In Tobin (1955), stagnation is one possibility, the stable solution of a non-linear model whose unstable solution is a repetitive cycle.

2. Dudley Dillard (1988) calls this the "barter illusion" of classical economics.

3. In formal general equilibrium theory the stability of markets determining relative prices cannot be guaranteed without special assumptions. This is *a fortiori* true if money is introduced and markets determine nominal prices. See the survey by Franklin Fisher (1987).

4. I have exhibited a dominant Fisher effect and examined its macroeconomic consequences in an IS/LM model that also has a Keynes effect, in Tobin (1980, Chapter 1). See also Caskey and Fazzari (1987).

5. At long last the question whether price flexibility (in any sense short of the Walrasian auctioneer fairy tale) is stabilizing has begun to receive considerable attention. Delong and Summers (1986) have investigated this question using the Fischer–Taylor staggered-contract model (Fischer, 1977; Taylor, 1980), amended to allow both price-level and price-change effects on demand. Their most interesting simulation has the intuitively desirable property that close to the limit of perfect price flexibility greater price flexibility means greater real stability, while farther away from it the reverse is true. Similar results are obtained by Caskey and Fazzari (1988) and Chadha (1989).

References

Ball, Lawrence, N. Gregory Mankiw, and David Romer, "The New Keynesian Economics and the Output-Inflation Tradeoff," *Brookings Papers on Economic Activity*, 1988 *1*, 1–65.

Barro, Robert, and Herschel Grossman, "A General Disequilibrium Model of Income and Employment," *American Economic Review*, March 1971, *61*, 82–93.

Caskey, John, and Steve Fazzari, "Aggregate Demand Contractions with Nominal Debt Commitments," *Economic Inquiry*, October 1987, *25*, 583–97.

Caskey, John, and Steven Fazzari, "Price Flexibility and Macroeconomic Stability: An Empirical Simulation Analysis," Washington University Department of Economics, Working Paper 118, January 1988.

Chadha, Binky, "Is Increased Price Inflexibility Stabilizing?" *Journal of Money Credit and Banking*, November 1989, *21*, 481–97.

Cooper, Russell, and Andrew John, "Coordinating Coordination Failures in Keynesian Models, *Quarterly Journal of Economics*, August 1988, *100*, 441–63.

De Long, J. Bradford, and Lawrence H. Summers, "Is Increasing Price Flexibility Stabilizing?" *American Economic Review*, December 1986, 76 1031–44.

Dillard, Dudley, "The Barter Illusion in Classical and Neoclassical Economics," *Eastern Economic Journal*, October–December 1988, *14*, 299–318.

Fischer, Stanley, "Long-term Contracts, Rational Expectations, and the Optimal Money Supply Rule," *Journal of Political Economy*, February 1977, *85*:1, 191–205.

Fisher, Franklin, M., "Adjustment Processes and Stability." In Eatwell, John, Murray Milgate, and Peter Newman eds., *The New Palgrave: A Dictionary of Economics.* London: Macmillan, 1987, 26–29.

Fisher, Irving, "The Debt-Deflation Theory of Great Depressions," *Econometrica*, October 1933, *1*, 337–57.

Hansen, Alvin H., *Full Recovery or Stagnation.* New York: W. W. Norton, 1938.

Iwai, Katsuhito, *Disequilibrium Dynamics*, (Cowles Foundation Monograph 27). New Haven: Yale University Press, 1981.

Keynes, John Maynard, *The General Theory of Employment, Interest, and Money.* New York: Harcourt Brace, 1936.

Lindbeck, Assar, and Dennis J. Snower, *The Insider-Outsider Theory of Employment and Unemployment.* Cambridge: MIT Press, 1990.

Mankiw, N. Gregory, "A Quick Refresher Course in Macroeconomics," *Journal of Economic Literature*, December 1990, *28*, 1645–60.

Okun, Arthur M., *Prices and Quantities: A Macroeconomic Analysis.* Washington, D.C.: The Brookings Institution, 1981.

Patinkin, Don, "Price Flexibility and Full Employment," *American Economic Review*, September 1948, *38*, 543–64.

Patinkin, Don, *Money, Interest, and Prices.* New York: Harper and Row, 1956, 2nd ed., 1965.

Pigou, Arthur Cecil, "The Classical Stationary State," *Economic Journal*, December 1943, *53*, 313–51.

Pigou, Arthur Cecil, "Economic Progress in a Stable Environment," *Economica*, August 1947, *14*, 180–90.

Plosser, Charles I., "Understanding Real Business Cycles," *Journal of Economic Perspectives*, Summer 1989, *3*:3, 51–77.

Taylor, John, "Aggregate Dynamics and Staggered Contracts," *Journal of Political Economy*, February 1980, *88*, 1–23.

Tobin, James, "A Dynamic Aggregative Model," *Journal of Political Economy*, April 1955, *63*, 103–15; *Essays*, Vol. 1, Chapter 8.

Tobin, James, "Keynesian Models of Recession and Depression," *American Economic Review (Papers and Proceedings)*, May 1975, *55*, 195–202; *Essays*, Vol. 3, Chapter 5.

Tobin, James, *Asset Accumulation and Economic Activity.* Oxford: Basil Blackwell, 1980.

Tobin, James, "Financial Structure and Monetary Rules," *Kredit und Kapital*, 1983, *16*, 155–71; Chapter 14 below.

CHAPTER 8

MACROECONOMICS UNDER DEBATE

Economics has always derived inspiration and energy from the burning issues of the day. Economists have shared the concerns of their fellow citizens and have addressed them as analysts, teachers, and advocates. Their own controversies have mirrored the ideological and political debates of their societies and epochs. From these encounters have developed principles and methods that outlasted their practical origins and gave our subject the cumulative continuity and internal dynamics of a discipline. Adam Smith's challenge to mercantilism, Ricardo's attack on the Corn Laws, and the Austrian School's response to Marxism are examples.

Reaganomics is a political counter-revolution against the economic ideas alleged to have motivated policies over the past half century. Thatcherism is a similar reaction in the United Kingdom. Throughout the noncommunist developed world the spirit of the times reflects disillusionment with past policies; their intellectual foundations are rejected in favor of opposing theories old and new. Within our profession, the same counter-revolutionary war is waged—in journals, classrooms, and conferences rather than in popular media, political debate, and elections. The parallelism is not accidental. The great inflation and stagflation of the 1970s were the common inspiration. Economists' ideas spill easily and rapidly into wider currency, frequently propagated by economists themselves. In a memorable passage Keynes observed that men of affairs and crusading zealots unconsciously echo the theories of bygone academics [1936, pp. 383–384]. Today the lags are short, the academics are not even bygone, and the debts are not always unconscious.

This chapter was presented as a Mitsui Lecture, University of Birmingham, England, March 1983.

In Reaganomics we economists have no trouble discerning the presence, albeit in distorted and exaggerated forms, of several fashionable strands of professional opinion. Their common thread is one of the Great Ideas of intellectual history: the miraculous efficiency and optimality of decentralized market processes free of government intervention. The overriding goal is to reduce the economic size, burden, and activity of government.

Monetarism, especially in its more recent form, the *new classical macroeconomics*, extends to macroeconomic policy the grasp of these central principles. The new vogue is to forswear counter-cyclical measures, scornfully called "fine-tuning," in favor of firm steadiness in the policy instruments themselves. Market processes will then, it is argued, take the economy to its best equilibrium.

Supply-side economics has been identified with some ludicrous claims and forecasts. Qualitatively, however, it is new emphasis on an old theme: the importance of incentives and rewards for thrift, work, enterprise, and risk-taking. The corollaries are de-emphasis of redistribution via taxes and transfers and devaluation of public consumption and investment.

Finally, *traditional financial and fiscal orthodoxy*, always opposed to manipulation of fiscal and monetary powers for macroeconomic objectives, has gained renewed respect and influence in the counter-revolutionary climate.

However, the several branches of conservative economics are not fully consistent with each other. Though they are all represented in government, their ideological messages and policy counsels are frequently not harmonious.

The common target of the counter-revolutions in macroeconomic theory and policy is Keynesian economics, the ideas of the *General Theory* as elaborated, modified, and applied since World War II. The Keynesian revolution itself was inspired by real world events, the Great Depression, and by the patent incapacity of the existing economic orthodoxy to provide either explanation or remedy. Four decades later the Great Inflation evoked the monetarist and classical revivals and discredited Keynesian orthodoxy. In both cases intellectual history was obviously shaped by events external to our discipline and by the political, ideological, and analytical vacuums and opportunities they created.

But that is by no means the whole story. The discipline itself imposes an internal logic on its developments, as the revolution and counter-revolutions in macroeconomics also exemplify. In discussing "macroeconomics under debate" today, I shall emphasize the internal debate and describe the theoretical issues among the contestants, revolutionary and counter-revolutionary. A good place to begin, a good frame of reference, I think, is Walrasian general equilibrium theory—the basic paradigm of our discipline, and as it happens, the scientific counterpart of the common central theme of the conservative counter-revolutions, the Invisible Hand. Within the profession the vulnerability of Keynesian economics, even as modified in the "neoclassical synthesis" of the two postwar decades, to recent challenges is its long-standing failure to come to terms with this powerful theoretical tradition. In discussing the debate in this framework, I shall also be led to comment on contemporary attempts to reformulate Keynesian economics to overcome this failure.

I The Invisible Hand and the Neoclassical Paradigm

The "invisible hand" *is* one of the Great Ideas of intellectual history. According to Adam Smith, market competition transmutes selfish and myopic individual actions into the wealth of nations [1776, p. 400]. Central direction is not necessary. The system demands of its participants neither altruism nor omniscience. Natural self-interest is enough motivation; every-day local observation is enough information. All that is required of the participants is respect for property rights and contractual obligations. All that is required of government is to establish and enforce those laws and to defend the society against internal and external enemies. Government interferences in markets are generally inefficient because they prevent individuals from making mutually and socially beneficial trades and contracts.

This momentous idea has flourished for two centuries. As political ideology it provided the economic content of nineteenth-century liberalism and of twentieth-century conservatism. In both phases it has been the weapon of bourgeois business and capital against rival interests and movements—landed aristocracies, labor unions, bureaucrats, populists, socialists. Simultaneously, economic theory developed and refined Smith's insight. The task of giving rigor and precision to the relation of individual actions and aggregate outcomes has engaged the best minds of our profession, including Walras, Pareto, Hicks, Samuelson, Debreu, and Arrow.

The propositions that survived this process are more sophisticated and more limited than the conjectures of earlier writers and the extravagant claims of the ideology.

Modern general equilibrium theory describes an economy with two principal features, individual optimization and price-cleared competitive markets. Each individual agent, given her endowments of productive resources and other commodities and given their market prices, buys and sells and produces so as to maximize her utility, a function of the quantities she consumes of the several commodities. Firms maximize the wealth of the agents who own them. These choices imply aggregate schedules relating demands for and supplies of all commodities to all their prices. Market prices, equating demands and supplies and governing quantities produced, bought, and sold by all agents, are determined simultaneously for all commodities and resources. Under certain assumptions the system of simultaneous equations has at least one solution, a "competitive equilibrium" of the economy, and may have many solutions. Each competitive equilibrium is "Pareto-optimal," i.e. no re-allocations of goods among agents could fail to make at least one agent worse off. Moreover, any feasible allocation which is Pareto-optimal corresponds to some competitive equilibrium based on some initial distribution of endowments. The model encompasses intertemporal choices, time-consuming production technologies, and uncertainties about the future by a simple ingenious expedient, extending the list of commodities, prices, and markets by distinguishing the dates and contingencies in which commodities are to be delivered.

Where does the modern version of the theory leave the Invisible Hand? Two quite opposite responses are conceivable. On one hand there is the good news: the intuitions of Adam Smith and many later writers can indeed be rigorously formulated and proved. The bad news is that the theorems depend on a host of conditions, many of dubious realism. Restrictions on preferences and technologies are stringent. The concept of social optimality, the Pareto criterion, is weak. The theory does not describe a process in real time by which the economy reaches an equilibrium solution. When commodities are multiplied to cover future and contingent deliveries, the possibility that competitive markets do or could exist for all of them is remote. The modern version might be taken to refute, not to support, the applicability of invisible hand propositions to real-world economies.

Wiser economic theorists have always been cautious. Joseph Schumpeter called the Walrasian system the *magna charta* of economics because it showed that the central problem of allocation of resources and final goods was in principle solvable. (In fact the formal proof came not from Walras [1874], who only showed that there were as many equations as unknowns, but three quarters of a century later from Arrow [1953] and Debreu [1959].) Schumpeter's own description of economic progress under capitalism, however, relied on wholly different mechanisms. A common view—shared for example by Walras, Wicksell, Fisher, Marshall, and Pigou—was that neoclassical analysis disclosed important and ultimately decisive tendencies but did not literally describe how observed prices and quantities were determined. Anglo-Saxon economics in the nineteenth and early twentieth centuries, less mathematical and more pragmatic than on the continent, was especially characterized by loose adherence to the *magna charta*.

Neoclassical theory itself developed an "anatomy of market failure," a catalog of ways in which departures from the conditions under which markets theoretically deliver optimal outcomes might occur and conceivably call for government interventions. These include: monopolies and other deviations from pure competition; public goods and bads and other externalities, i.e. extra-market ways in which one individual's actions give utility or disutility to others; absence of markets, in particular for future and contingent deliveries; inadequacies of information. The categories overlap. A standard mode of argument and analysis regarding any actual or proposed government intervention developed. The first question is why the market does not solve the problem, if it is solvable at all. The answer must be to identify one or more of the recognized market failures and to show that the intervention remedies it. The presumption is that the market works. The burden of proof is on the advocate of intervention.

Of course interventions can be advocated on grounds of distributional equity, whether or not there is a market failure. Long ago neoclassical economics washed its hands of such messy questions by saying there is no way to compare the utility of one person with that of another. Pareto-optimality is no help. Redistributions always make someone worse off. Interventions that make everyone better off are virtually impossible to find. The best the neoclassical paradigm can do is to point out that if a given redistribution is to be made there are more and less efficient ways of accomplishing it. The more efficient ways, not surprisingly, generally rely on market processes, and so far as possible on redistributions of initial endowments rather than of final outputs.

Many of the ablest minds attracted into professional economics find their exposure to general equilibrium theory the most exciting intellectual experience of their lives. Elegant, rigorous, mathematically powerful, the theory reaches far from obvious results. It gives economics a theoretical core that "softer" social sciences lack and often envy. It "is the only game in town." It especially enchants those who were drawn into the profession more because it challenges their mathematical and logical skills than because it might help to solve real-world puzzles and problems. They are particularly disposed to regard general equilibrium propositions as reference points, and to assign burdens of proof to anyone who consciously or unconsciously alleges otherwise. Supporting this attitude is the "methodology of positive economics." [Friedman 1953, pp. 3–43] The patent and admitted unrealism of assumptions does not matter. The question is whether the outcomes of the system as a whole are *as if* they were solutions of the postulated system. Since the system in its full generality generates precious little in the way of propositions refutable by observations, it is not very vulnerable to tests of "as if" methodology [Sonnenschein 1973].

II Money and General Equilibrium

Money has always been an awkward puzzle for neoclassical general equilibrium theory [Kareken and Wallace 1980]. The use of a conventional unit of account, Walras's *numeraire*, is no problem; any arbitrary commodity or package of commodities will serve this purpose, and the results do not depend on the choice. But the holdings of intrinsically useless paper as stores of value is a puzzle. How can fiat moneys command any value in terms of the goods and services that enter utility and production functions? Even commodity moneys raise the question, because they acquire more value from their monetary status than they would otherwise have.

The question is not answerable in the standard general equilibrium framework. With frictionless, costless, simultaneously cleared auction markets for all commodities, there is no need for money holdings to bridge gaps between sales and purchases or to mitigate costly searches for advantageous barters. Common sense tells us that money is held and has value because, absent the super-computer of the Walrasian multi-market auctioneer, the use of money facilitates exchanges.

It is not easy to incorporate this common-sense observation in the standard paradigm, for two main reasons. First, transactions technologies do not fit the formulations of input-output relations needed to solve the system. Second, money has attributes of a public good; the standard paradigm has well-known difficulties handling externalities occurring when the utility or productivity of a commodity to any one agent depends on how many others use it.

The makeshift compromise in neoclassical theory has been the alleged *neutrality* of fiat money. The idea is simple: Whatever functions money may perform, whatever holdings agents may therefore desire, the *real* equilibrium must be independent of the stock of money as measured in its own nominal units. After all, it cannot matter whether the unit of account is a dollar or a dime. If a units change multiplies the nominal quantity by ten, the system will remain in equilibrium with all prices multiplied by ten, future and contingent prices as well as spot. All relative prices, including real interest rates, and all quantities will be the same as before.

Buttressed by this reasoning, older neoclassical economists and their reincarnations in new classical macroeconomics assert that money is just a veil. Anyone who looks through it can see that the real economy is the same as if the veil were not there. In extreme form the proposition is clearly false. If money performs real functions for individuals and for society, the equilibrium of a monetary economy cannot be the same as that of a barter economy. Indeed that of a barter economy, given the costs of search and barter, could not be the Walrasian solution [Hahn 1982]. But the extreme proposition is not needed. Monetary exchange can yield a solution different from barter, presumably a superior one because money compensates at least in part for the absence of the Walrasian auctioneer. But the altered and improved solution could be independent of the size of the stock of nominal money.

Money neutrality in this sense is the basis for the "classical dichotomy" [Patinkin 1955] separating the determination of real variables and relative prices from the determination of the absolute price level, the reciprocal of the value of money. The dichotomy is the fundamental rationale of the quantity theory of money, the proposition that absolute prices are proportional to the stock.

However, the analogy of money stock variations to units changes requires extreme caution in application. A thorough change of units would re-scale proportionately the nominal quantities of all individual holdings of all existing assets and debts denominated in the monetary unit of account, and of all expectations of future quantities of money and of promises to pay money in every future contingency. The operations by which governments and central banks alter stocks of money involve issuing currency or its equivalent to make transfer payments or to buy goods and services or to buy outstanding promises to pay currency in future. These operations obviously do not alter all nominal stocks, present and future, individual and aggregate, proportionately. They leave unchanged the aggregates and the distributions of most pre-existing assets and debts. The application of the neutrality proposition to actual real-world monetary policies is a prime example of the fallacy of misplaced concreteness. Those who attribute real consequences to monetary policies and events are not *per se* guilty of attributing irrational "money illusion" to households and business managers.

As previously observed, wise neoclassical economists have been circumspect in application of general equilibrium results. This caution has embraced the implications of neutrality and dichotomy. Quantity theorists from David Hume to Irving Fisher to Milton Friedman expected to see plenty of important real consequences of monetary policies and events for long short runs. It is only recently that neutrality has been more sweepingly and indiscriminately applied.

In logic non-neutralities are not confined to any short run. For example, a permanent change in the growth rates of government-issued currency and promises to pay currency in future is not an operation that can be assimilated to a units change, because it would not alter all present and future nominal stocks in the same proportion. Variations of money growth and inflation rates alter the *real* rate of return on monetary assets which carry a nominal interest rate fixed at zero or any other number, and therefore have further real consequences [Tobin 1965]. More generally, if an economy approaches a steady state, its constellation of real variables is bound to be influenced by the monetary events occurring along the path [Hahn 1982].

III Keynes and the Neoclassical Paradigm

In the *General Theory*, John Maynard Keynes had the audacity to claim discovery of massive, endemic, possibly chronic market failure, not just one of the minor exceptions to market performance in the usual canonical list. Keynes was quite explicit in this contention, opposing his "general" theory to what he called "classical" theory, which he relegated to the status of a special case. (He clearly meant theory that would now be called "neoclassical" to distinguish it from the classical economics of Britain prior to the advent of marginalism and subjective utility circa 1870.) The market failure is the unemployment of labor and other productive resources whose owners would gladly accept employment for remuneration no greater than their prevailing marginal productivities and would gladly purchase the output the employment would produce.

Ever since 1936, today more than ever, this claim has been received with incredulity by theorists whose trained instincts lead them to use general competitive equilibrium as presumptive point of reference. Keynes did not help them understand his point. In keeping with the ethnocentrism of English economics, especially in Cambridge, he paid little attention to continental writers. His main "classical" target was another Cambridge economist, Professor A. C. Pigou. He attacked F. A. von Hayek, who had moved from Austria to London, and he briefly cited Walras as an exemplar of "classical" interest theory [Keynes 1936, pp. 19, 32, 56, 59–60, 176–177]. Keynes used only simple mathematics, and that sparingly. His language, terminology, and style of argument were pragmatic and worldly like Alfred Marshall's rather than rigorous and abstract like Walras's. Although he did in fact set forth a system of simultaneous equations, he did not present it with formal clarity. Most students owe their understanding of it to elucidations by Hicks and others. Anyway his structural and behavior equations differ from those of full-blown neoclassical general equilibrium models by their heroic aggregation. The consumption function, for example, represents the economy as a whole;

its derivation from the consumption choices of individual agents is loose and informal.

For years general equilibrium theorists have said they "simply don't understand" Keynes, or for that matter any macroeconomics, which owes its identification as a distinguishable branch of economics to the Keynesian revolution. Frequently, not always, this is a polite way of saying they believe or suspect it is wrong. That in turn means that Keynesian theory must assume somewhere, implicitly or explicitly, irrational, non-optimizing behavior by individual agents. "Money illusion" is the most frequent example, i.e. imputing to individuals as workers or consumers behavior motivated by the monetary outcomes rather than those real outcomes which can be the only ultimate source of utility. Or Keynes must assume that for some unexplained reasons markets do not clear, for example that nominal wages and prices are rigid or sticky.

Keynes contributed to the sources of these disbeliefs by insisting that his conclusions applied to the *equilibrium* of a *competitive* system. He attacked the classicals on their own ground. He appeared to charge that though the classicals had the right pieces of the puzzle they had not assembled them correctly. He was not content to regard the Great Depression as an especially slow and painful example of the time it takes neoclassical equilibrium tendencies to win out. Nor did he attribute the difficulties of the system to imperfections and monopolistic elements ignored in the competitive model, even though at the very time he was writing, microeconomic theories stressing these phenomena were flourishing in his Cambridge as well as in Cambridge, Massachusetts [Chamberlin 1933, Robinson 1933, Shove 1930, Sraffa 1926, Young 1930].

Despite these obstacles to communication, the *General Theory* is clear enough about the sources of macroeconomic market failure to enable careful and open-minded readers to grasp the points. Ultimately the basic reason for incredulity is the presumption against so enormous a market failure: surely rational individuals would find ways to conclude bargains that make all parties better off and thus to escape the Keynesian impasse. This viewpoint leaves the skeptics with the uncomfortable task of reconciling observed unemployment, both in the Great Depression and in other business cycles, with the presumptions of neoclassical faith. This task was pretty much finessed until the recent ambitious attempts at reconciliation by the new classical macroeconomics, discussed below.

In Keynesian theory there are several interrelated sources of the macroeconomic market failure. First, Keynes was explicit about the incompleteness of markets, particularly the absence of future and contingent markets. He observed that savers abstaining from present consumption do not simultaneously place specific orders either for future consumption or for capital goods. Instead they acquire generalized stores of value, which they can spend when they please on what they please. Savers and investors, lenders and borrowers, are not the same individuals. Convenient and efficient as it is, the divorce of saving from specific future consumption and from contemporaneous investment imposes on capital and commodity markets an immense burden of coordination. The spot market signals from reduced consumption do not guide producers to make inventory and fixed investments to prepare for future consumption demands; the signals may even elicit perverse behavior [Keynes 1936, pp. 210–12]. Intrinsically unreliable expectations and information have to fill the market gaps. The tests that investment projects must pass can easily be the wrong hurdles, especially when capital-building projects have to compete with returns expected on monetary assets [Keynes 1936, pp. 210–244].

Second, Keynes emphasized the essential unpredictability, even in a probabilistic sense, of the returns to real and monetary assets. They depend on what future buyers will be prepared to pay for them, and that in turn depends on what those buyers' expectations will be about what future buyers.... The indeterminacy is both cause and effect of the absence of markets for future and contingent deliveries. For this reason, Keynes regarded the "state of long-term expectations" as an autonomous determinant of investment and aggregate demand, not as an endogenous variable [Keynes 1936, pp. 147–164].

Third, Keynes observed that prices, including wages, are quoted and set in the monetary unit of account. The practice is socially and individually convenient, but it does have real consequences. It is difficult for agents, especially workers, to make effective their true demands and supplies at real, relative prices [Keynes 1936, pp. 4–22]. He did not note, perhaps because he regarded it as self-evident, that the use of a nominal numeraire would make no difference if a Walrasian auctioneer continuously cleared and re-cleared all markets simultaneously, knowing at each moment everyone's demands and supplies as functions of all prices. Keynes was probably thinking implicitly of more realistic wage- and price-setting mechanisms, in which specific prices are set locally and subsequently adjusted only with delay and cost. Consequently his point was misunderstood and seemed vulnerable to the "money illusion" accusation. Now in the context of contract theory and other models of non-Walrasian price-setting, his intuitions—including the importance of wage comparisons in local wage bargains—are being formally modeled.

Fourth, Keynes's principle of effective demand is a clear statement of the role of quantity variation, as well as price variation, in clearing markets. Individuals' demands are constrained by what they actually sell at prevailing prices, and this may be less than what they would like to sell at those prices given their endowments. Unemployed workers consume less than they would like because they sell less labor than they would like [Keynes 1936, pp. 23–36]. That, not failure to understand that supply of labor can be an endogenous decision, is the reason income is a principal argument in a Keynesian consumption function. Quantity equilibration becomes a key process whenever relative prices, including interest rates, are slow to move. This can happen even when nominal prices are quite flexible, as Keynes observed in his story wherein goods prices follow money wages down and workers are unable to lower their real wages [Keynes 1936, pp. 257–279]. In this story the price stickiness is elsewhere in the economy, in the determination of interest rates. One interpretation of the "general" in General Theory is allowance for quantity as well as price variation in clearing markets.

Fifth, Keynes rejected neutrality of money. Money competes with other assets, including real capital, as a vehicle for holding wealth. The yield on money, its implicit advantages in liquidity and safety included, influences the returns savers and investors require of other assets. Consequently real interest rates are not independent of monetary phenomena. Keynes was particularly concerned, writing in the Great Depression, that the advantages of holding moneys and near-moneys would prevent interest rates from falling low enough to induce real investment sufficient to match the economy's potential saving [Keynes 1936, pp. 222–244]. Curiously, unlike Irving Fisher, Keynes did not note that price inflation was a way to lower the real return on money, probably because he saw that actual events were bringing deflation, moving the real return on money in the wrong direction.

IV Syntheses of Neoclassical and Keynesian Economics

Two developments in macroeconomics subsequent to Keynes derived their impetus in large measure to the gap in understanding, language, and credibility between Keynesian theory and general equilibrium theory. These are first, the neoclassical synthesis, the mainstream macroeconomics of the quarter century after World War II, and second, more recently, formal disequilibrium theory.

The first might better be called the neoclassical neo-Keynesian synthesis. Several of its architects, notably Hicks [1946] and Samuelson [1948], were in the 1930s and 1940s active participants in the development and refinement of pure neoclassical theory. They were among the writers who were bringing at long last Walras, Pareto, and the continental tradition into English-speaking economics. At the same time, living through the Great Depression, they were impressed by the realism and relevance of Keynes. In the cautious vein of older neoclassicals, they found the neoclassical paradigm useful for long-run trends but saw nothing problematic in departures from those trends for a variety of reasons, e.g., market imperfections, adjustment costs, information lags. These departures need not imply any irrationality or any permanent failure of markets to clear; the properties of full general equilibrium should not be expected to hold every day or every year.

Keynes's analysis looked like a good model of lapses from full employment equilibrium. Its long-run stagnationist pessimism could be dropped. It was empirically and theoretically unsound, the more so if Keynesian stabilization policies themselves reinforced the mechanisms that return the economy to its long-run growth track. The debate over Keynes's pretension to a permanent equilibrium with involuntary unemployment could be declared a draw; it was largely semantic and anyway operationally irrelevant. Keynes's comparative statics methodology worked well enough in the short run. Dynamics could be added. The structural equations could be both improved theoretically and tested and estimated empirically. Principles of neoclassical welfare economics could be applied to macroeconomic policy choices, correcting Keynes's intimations that wasteful make-work projects have zero opportunity cost when resources are idle and providing criteria for choices among the several instruments of macroeconomic stabilization available.

This "synthesis," however, did not still the complaints that macroeconomics could not be understood or believed because it had no firm "microfoundations." Its authors and practitioners were too busy with pragmatic macroeconomics to develop formally the several sources of market failure described by Keynes.

The second development, formal disequilibrium macroeconomics, presented Keynes's ideas in a manner designed to communicate them to general equilibrium theorists, though not necessarily to make them more acceptable.[1]

In these models the vector of prices is, for reasons not explained, stuck at values other than the Walrasian general equilibrium solution. Agents—consumers, workers, employers—are constrained in their demands and supplies by the actual transactions they are able to consummate at these wrong prices. They cannot effectuate their "notional" demands and supplies—the transactions they would choose to make at these prices if constrained only by their endowments—because those will not clear the markets except at the "right" prices of the Walrasian solution. But the markets may nonetheless clear at some vector of quantities, which replace prices as the equilibrating variables. Finding this disequilibrium equilibrium, with agents solving their constrained optimization problems, is a task engaging the same mathematical techniques and analytical talents as standard general equilibrium theory. That is one reason why it seems to enable some theorists to understand what Keynes meant. The approach holds considerable promise. Perhaps some day it will fulfill Keynes's vision of a "general" theory, of which both his own and Walrasian equilibrium will be special cases.

As a contribution to macroeconomics, however, these models have so far added little new. Recall the "principle of effective demand" in Keynes, his stress on output variation as equilibrator of saving and investment, his concern that prices, specifically real wages and interest rates, are wrong. Why these points, clear enough in Keynes and in many subsequent expositions, suddenly become revelations when repeated in somewhat different language is a mystery. Nor have the repetitions altered or improved the substance of standard macroeconomic analyses of underemployment. Indeed they are in many ways more primitive, neglecting monetary and financial markets, fiscal institutions and policies, intertemporal phenomena, and the dynamics of prices and wages. They also miss a basic point of Keynesian logic: there could be an underemployment equilibrium or disequilibrium even if prices happened to be the "right" ones for full Walrasian equilibrium.

The new models are, it is true, in some ways more general. They call attention to the possibilities and properties of outcomes neither Keynesian nor Walrasian, e.g. classical unemployment and over-full employment. They apply the fixed-price variable-quantity calculus to larger numbers of markets simultaneously.

In contrast to these two developments, a school of self-styled post-Keynesians regard any synthesis or reconciliation, in substance or in language, of Keynes and neoclassical economics as a betrayal of the revolution. They reject equilibrium analysis altogether, stress the historical, institutional, and evolutionary aspects of economic development, and emphasize the macroeconomic implications of the non-competitive structures of modern economies. Their valid points do not add up to a coherent theory, but many of them will have to be tackled in eclectic work in macroeconomics in future. Many mainstream Keynesian economists have long agreed that Keynesians macroeconomics cannot be grounded on pure or perfect competition in product and labor markets. As increasing numbers of them have come to the conclusion that wage and price controls or other incomes policies are at least occasionally necessary to prevent inflation at full employment, the practical gap between them and post-Keynesians has narrowed.

V The Monetarist Counter-revolution

The quantity theory of money, the central proposition of monetarism, has two guises. One is the fundamental neutrality proposition discussed above. As there noted, the axiom that paper money is not held or valued for its own sake is unexceptionable but offers limited mileage in application to real-world monetary operations. The other quantity theory is a brand of pragmatic macroeconomics, methodologically similar to Keynesian theory and no less a specialized deviation from full-blown neoclassical general equilibrium. It too has a long history. For example, Irving Fisher breathed life into his famous identity, the Equation of Exchange $MV = PQ$ by analyzing and studying empirically the behaviors and institutions that determine the velocity V of the supply of transactions media M, and the properties of the economy that determine the division of MV impulses between price level P and quantity Q in short and long runs [Fisher 1911]. The influential monetarist resurgence under Milton Friedman this past quarter century follows the same tradition, though emphasizing subjective factors in money demand as well as transactions mechanics [Friedman 1956]. This movement I call Monetarism I to distinguish it from the later and theoretically purer Monetarism II, a.k.a. the new classical macroeconomics. Though Monetarism I borrows credence from the neutrality proposition, that proposition neither implies Monetarism I nor limits its applicability.

The debates of the last quarter century between Keynesians and Monetarists I concerned matters of substantial importance in macroeconomic policy, but from a theoretical standpoint they were internal to standard macroeconomics. They concerned: the theoretical plausibility and empirical validity of alternative specifications of aggregative equations and models; the relative usefulness of alternative languages, one based on the national income = expenditure identity, the other on the Equation of Exchange; the plausibility of differing estimates of parameters, notably the interest-elasticity of money demand and the speeds of price and output adjustments in response to variations in aggregate nominal demand, MV; the reliability and stability of crucial behavioral equations, money demand and aggregate expenditure; the relative importance of money supply shocks and real demand and supply shocks in generating business cycle fluctuations; the role of expectations of monetary policies in generating inflation expectations affecting interest rates; and the empirical constancy of real interest rates. These are all important questions, with decisive implications for policy. Monetarists' answers to them led them to assign minor macroeconomic importance to fiscal policy, to oppose activist "stabilization" policies of any kind, and to advocate central bank policies focussed on steady growth of money supplies unmodified by concern for interest rates or any other variables. But they do not raise fundamental issues of theory and method. They are in principle, if not in practice, resolvable by established techniques of theoretical and econometric research in macroeconomics.

Inflation in the late 1960s and 1970s brought widespread support to Monetarism I, both inside and outside the economics profession. Keynesian theory was perceived to be incapable of explaining or foreseeing the inflation, and Keynesian policies to be incapable of arresting it. More and more people agreed with the monetarists that Keynesian economics actually promoted inflation.

The *General Theory* provides no theory of persisting inflation except in cases when real aggregate demand chronically exceeds the full employment output potential of the economy. For the usual case of underemployment, the theory explains why prices will be positively related to employment but not why they might continue to rise with employment stable or even falling. Postwar periods of inflation at times when the economy did not appear to be at full employment underscored the gap. As a practical matter, it was filled by the Phillips curve, interpreted to offer a policy tradeoff between unemployment and inflation. Statistical findings that rates of wage and price inflation varied inversely to the unemployment rate were elevated into a structural equation of the model. As the economy approached full employment, the curve became very steep, approaching the vertical. While thoughtful devotees of the Phillips curve were aware that longer-run inflationary consequences of increases in employment would be greater than short-run impacts because of feedbacks from actual inflation on to expectations and patterns of wage settlement and price-settings, they were encouraged by initial empirical indications that such feedbacks were slow and incomplete. At the same time, they never believed that unemployment could be pushed indefinitely low without running into classic excess-demand inflation, as Keynesian theory itself envisaged when aggregate real demand exceeded full employment output. Indeed there was a long-standing belief among Keynesian economists that price stability could not be maintained at full employment without some form of wage and price controls or incomes policies. The empirical question, important for policy, was to identify the unemployment rate that indicated "full employment."

Milton Friedman's 1967 Presidential Address [1968] argued, as Phelps had independently argued shortly before [1967], that there could be no permanent trade-off of unemployment and inflation. Full employment, renamed the natural rate of unemployment, was the point of inflation stability, at whatever rate was consistent with the growth of money stocks. At higher unemployment rates, prices would be decelerating, and at lower rates accelerating. The moral for policy was not to aim at any unemployment rate, or at any other real variable. Follow a stable monetary growth policy, preferably one consistent with price stability, and unemployment will gravitate to its natural rate, i.e. whatever it gravitates to will be the natural rate. Though not denying that monetary policies have real consequences in short runs, Friedman was now stressing more fundamental neoclassical propositions, the neutrality of money, than in the earlier monetarist-Keynesian debates. He had already moved in this direction when he tried to conclude the controversy over the relevance of the interest-elasticity of money demand to the efficacies of fiscal and monetary policies by saying in effect that it was irrelevant if prices were flexible and the economy was in full employment equilibrium [Friedman 1966]. In any case his Presidential Address was the bridge from old monetarism to new.

Robert Lucas followed up and went further. He offered an interpretation of Phillips-curve statistical correlations that deprived them of indicating any tradeoff possibility exploitable by policy even in the short run [Lucas 1972]. That price increases are associated with gains in employment and production indicates only that workers and business managers were temporarily confused between relative prices and absolute prices. They mistook a general price increase due to a monetary shock for a favorable improvement in their real terms of trade. But the monetary authority cannot fool them for long. Markets clear at prices reflecting the best information, including anticipations and perceptions of policy, that agents have. This was the beginning of the most fundamental counterrevolution.

VI Stagflation as a Test of Macroeconomic Theories

Was the stagflation of the 1970s a *prima facie* refutation of Keynesian macroeconomics? Economic theories and the policies based upon them stand or fall in professional esteem by their perceived congruence with large and long-lasting events. Gross and simple historical tests are much more persuasive than sophisticated econometrics. What Keynes called classical orthodoxy, exemplified by Pigou's theory of unemployment and by the famous or notorious "Treasury View," was discredited by the Great Depression, for which it appeared to have neither explanation nor remedy. Mainstream Keynesian macroeconomics itself gained credibility and converts over the first two decades after World War II from the prosperity and growth to which its policies were perceived to have contributed. But the Great Inflation and Stagflation of the 1970s, it is commonly asserted and believed, refuted this brand of macroeconomics as decisively as the Great Depression undermined the classical target of the Keynesian revolution forty years earlier. Monetarism and the new classical macroeconomics were the counter-revolutions that benefited from the turn of events. They in turn are in danger of flunking the latest test, the disinflation and depression of the early 1980s, though it is too early to be sure or to identify the intellectual beneficiaries of the latest economic disappointments.

Is a verdict against Keynesian macroeconomics justified by the evidence of the 1970s? In two well read polemics, New Classical macroeconomics argue that the verdict is self evident.[2] NeoKeynesian theory of the 1950s and 1960s was just incapable of envisaging the combination of high and rising unemployment with high and rising inflation observed in the 1970s. The Phillips curve, embraced by Keynesians in the preceding decades, predicted not positive but negative correlation of inflation and unemployment. Nor was the 180-degree mistake, in their indictment, a harmless academic error. Keynesian policies, recommended and adopted in order to lower unemployment by riding up the Phillips curve, generated much more inflation than bargained for, while *raising* unemployment at the same time. In the review of my book cited above, Lucas expressed astonishment that an accomplice to such monumental error still speaks or writes about such matters in public.

What did Keynesian economists think in the 1960s about the relation of unemployment and inflation and about the dependence of both outcomes on macroeconomic policies? How and why did a curve through A. W. Phillips's scatter diagram [Phillips 1958] become a structural equation in theoretical and textbook models and in large macro-econometric models? Such a structural equation was needed to "explain" the inflation of the mid-1950s; that inflation, which peaked below 5%, may seem trivial in today's retrospect, but it caused considerable alarm at the time. It occurred at rates of unemployment, 4% plus, then regarded as too high to correspond to "full employment." Standard macroeconomic theory of that day did not envisage continuing, persistent inflation in an underemployed economy. Wage and price *levels* were supposed to be positively associated with employment, for reasons given in Chapter 21 of the *General Theory*.

This relation implied that prices would be rising in cyclical upswings but would settle down if output and employment were stabilized. Continuing inflation, a wage-price spiral, would occur in response to an "inflationary gap," an excess of aggregate real demand over full employment output.

The disturbing observation of the 1950s was a wage-price spiral in the apparent absence of excess demand. This species of inflation was dubbed "cost-push" in distinction to the classic variety "demand-pull." Just naming the phenomenon and treating it as an unexplained exogenous event was intellectually unsatisfying. The Phillips curve came along to fill the gap, attributing inflation to both cost and demand pressures simultaneously and avoiding the dubious knife-edge discontinuity of the "inflationary gap" model.

However, incorporation of the Phillips curve into the standard macroeconomic model did *not* imply that demand expansion could increase employment and production without limit, and always with definite and limited inflationary cost. There remained the notion of full employment, beyond which demand expansion would unleash wage-spiral inflation qualitatively different from Phillips curve inflation, engendered by excess demand not removed by price rises. There had long been a Keynesian theory of this kind of inflation, of its mechanics and its speed, provided by Keynes himself and subsequent contributions [Keynes 1940, Holtzman 1950, Koopmans 1942, Smithies 1942].

Indeed Keynes himself and others had for a long time recognized that prices and their rates of increase were essentially indeterminate at levels of demand greater than or equal to full employment output. A common formula around Harvard in the late 1940s when I was a graduate student was that a modern mixed economy could not enjoy more than two of three desiderata: full employment, price stability, and freedom from wage and price controls.

The Samuelson–Solow article "Analytical Aspects of Anti-Inflation Policy" [1960] is frequently cited as a notorious example of the naiveté with which Keynesians embraced the notion of a Phillips tradeoff exploitable in both long and short run by demand management policies. In truth, the authors were quite agnostic about the long run, and canvassed various possible ways that policy-induced movements along the short-run curve might shift the curve itself.

[It] might be that ... low-pressure demand would so act upon wage and other expectations as to shift the curve downward in the longer run—so that over a decade, the economy might enjoy higher employment with price stability that our present-day estimate would indicate. But also the opposite is conceivable. A low-pressure economy might build up within itself over the years larger and larger amounts of structural unemployment.... The result would be an upward shift of our menu of choice, with more and more unemployment being needed just to keep prices stable.

Subsequent history suggests that these were both reasonable concerns.

Even before the "natural rate" articles of Phelps and Friedman, some Keynesians were quite aware of the feedbacks from actually realized price and wage inflation via expectations and emulative or catch-up patterns on to subsequent inflation, of the implication that the Phillips curve is steeper and the tradeoff less favorable in the long run than in the short, and of the possibility that the long-run Phillips curve is vertical and allows no trade off at all. Let me quote Tobin writing in 1966 [Tobin 1967]:

Nor do we know the answer to the even more basic question whether continuation of 4 percent unemployment would, so long as it generates any inflation, generate an accelerating inflation. This would be the orthodox prediction: Wages and other incomes rise because people want real gains, and the bargaining power of individuals and groups depends on the real situation. If they find that they are cheated by price increases they will simply escalate their money claims accordingly. On this view the Phillips curve would blow up if growth at a steady utilization rate were maintained. Only cyclical interruptions in the learning process have saved us from accelerating inflation. On this interpretation, the only true equilibrium full employment is the degree of unemployment that corresponds to zero inflation— any higher rate of utilization can be called excess demand. This is a dismal conclusion if true, because it appears to take a socially explosive rate of unemployment—more than 6 percent in the U.S.A.—to keep the price level stable.

What Keynesians of that day were not prepared to do was to identify as full employment equilibrium the point of price or inflation stability on the Phillips curve, or to believe that inflation or acceleration and deflation or deceleration are symmetrical consequences of deviations up or down from that point, or to accept the "natural rate" as Walrasian equilibrium. We regarded a Phillips curve as an empirical aggregate summary of imperfectly competitive wage- and price-setting institutions and of disequilibrium adjustments.

Was the combination of higher inflation with higher unemployment something that could never have been foreseen by the macroeconomic theories and models of the 1960s? The world-wide "wage explosion" of 1970–71 occurred during a recession. It could not be explained either by unemployment, which was rising, or by contemporaneous or recent price increases, which the wage gains overshot. But it was no surprise to Samuelson, Solow, and others who thought "cost-push" shocks could occur at any time. A "cost-push" shock, it was well understood, causes simultaneously more inflation and more unemployment, in proportions depending on the degree of policy accommodation. Thus a positive correlation of the two outcomes was not a complete novelty either in theory or in practice. No one in the 1960s foresaw the commodity price and oil shocks later in the 1970s or thought about the macroeconomic consequences of such shocks. The failure of foresight and imagination does no one credit, but it does make it difficult to speculate how an economist in the 1960s would have analyzed the case had it been presented to him.

The relevant question is not the one Lucas would hypothetically present. His question would be as follows: Observe as of 1969 the prospective true paths of money supplies during the succeeding ten years and say on this information alone what outcomes in inflation and unemployment you would anticipate. This formulation conceals the reasons for the monetary expansions. They did not come out of the blue. They did not occur because central bankers wanted to ride up Phillips curves and to lower unemployment at some inflationary cost. They were accommodations, grudging and partial, of commodity price increases external in origin. These were prototypical stagflationary shocks, reducing aggregate demand and raising costs and prices simultaneously. They increased unemployment as well, the more so because they were incompletely accommodated. Had the monetary authorities not accommodated them at all, unemployment would have risen even more, at the same time that prices were rising faster. Nothing in this story is inconsistent with Keynesian analysis or warrants filing for intellectual bankruptcy.

As I understand Lucas and Sargent, they should not have expected a rise in unemployment in the 1970s had they been told in advance only the rates of money growth. Their best guess of the equilibrium unemployment rate in the 1970s would have been the average actual unemployment rate of the 1960s. They would logically have guessed that all the extra money creation would go into prices. Had they been told in advance of the supply shocks, they—unlike Keynesians—would have or should have expected shifts in terms of trade between oil and other goods to have no more than very transient effects on overall price indexes.

The 1970s caught us all, Keynesians and monetarists and new classicals, unprepared. But the decade is no decisive evidence for or against any school of macroeconomics.

VII The New Classical Macroeconomics

Monetarism II *aka* the New Classical Macroeconomics *aka* Equilibrium Business Cycle Theory is not just a revival of pre-Keynesian neoclassical or "classical" macroeconomics. It is a more literal and sweeping affirmation of its assumptions. What theorists of those older times were content to regard as long-run tendencies their contemporary successors take to apply every day. Agents optimize continuously. Flexible prices clear all markets. The mythical Walrasian auctioneer functions perfectly. In the latter two respects the new classicals are at the opposite pole from the new disequilibrium school discussed above.

However, their models differ from those of full general equilibrium theory in two important and related ways, which I suppose qualify them as macroeconomic models. Like Keynes they assume a monetary economy; money would have no place in an Arrow–Debreu world. Like Keynes, they assume the absence of most of the futures and contingent futures markets which complete the Arrow-Debreu version of general equilibrium.

Also as in Keynes, expectations play an important role in an economy where markets do not provide contractual insurance against all contingencies. Here the resemblance stops. Keynes thought for reasons recounted above that savers and investors could not have fully rational expectations of the future variables that would determine the outcomes of their decisions, because those outcomes will depend on the behavior and thus the expectations of others. In contrast, the new classicals take expectations to be unbiased forecasts, not themselves sources of shocks. In their models, expectations of the variables, both their mean values and other moments of probability distributions, are those which the models themselves would generate. The actors all calculate them from the same model, the one known to the author. Disturbances to the system come chiefly from surprises in government policies. Rational expectations take the place of the missing Arrow-Debreu markets and enable the full general equilibrium to be realized.

New classical macroeconomic models rely heavily, even more uncritically than Monetarism I, on the neutrality of money. Though explicitly justified by the "units change" analogy [Lucas 1981, pp. 558–567], the proposition is applied to real world money supply operations and to short runs as well as long. Indeed in models designed to illuminate effects of policies, or rather their lack of real effects, M's are altered exogenously without specification of the transactions by which governments and central banks bring the changes about. The primitive way in which monetary and financial markets are modeled could be remedied, but not without peril to the more striking policy conclusions of the school.

An implication of money neutrality is a purely monetary theory of inflation. Friedman has told the world that inflation is everywhere and at all times a monetary phenomenon. Both brands of monetarism have ridiculed attributions of inflation to trade unions, OPEC shocks, taxes, and other non-monetary institutions and events. Paradoxically the "classical dichotomy" they thus embrace as explanation of inflation also implies that inflation is costless and painless. Yet the main appeal of monetarism is that, in contrast to Keynesian economics, it provides an explanation and remedy for inflation.

The methodology of new classical macroeconomics, like that of neoclassical general equilibrium theory, stresses the requirement that the behavior assumed of economic agents be rooted explicitly in individual optimizations. This is an especially rigorous requirement, because the new classicals regard the entire path of the economy as one of continuous, continuously changing, equilibrium. What less ambitious theorists might regard as lagged adjustment behavior, which economic theory neither can nor need explain, the new classicals propose to bring within the tent of optimization. That is not easy, to say the least. Moreover, as I mentioned above, neoclassical general equilibrium theory is too general to yield conclusions, even as to the direction of effects, in macroeconomics or elsewhere. How can the new classicals, seeking even greater generality, do better? There are no free lunches for them either. When new classical models give definite conclusions about the effects of policies or other variations, they obtain them by simplifications. One short cut is to assume all agents are alike in preferences, endowments, or both; in advanced analyses two or three types of agents are assumed, with emphasis on their differences in age. Another short cut is to attribute to the agents special preference or utility functions of mathematical form tractable in carrying out the obligatory optimizations. These expedients enable the theorists to claim that their behavior equations have the microfoundations that are fatally missing from Keynesian and Monetarist I models. But what you gain on the swings you lose on the roundabouts.

Empirically the main challenge to new classical macroeconomics is how to explain as moving *equilibrium* the fluctuations in general economic activity we actually observe. The theory implies that labor "markets," for example, are in the same equilibrium, cleared by wages and prices, at 11% or 25% unemployment as at 3% or 5% unemployment, with the same balance of supply and demand. On the surface this seems to be refuted by all kinds of evidence, on vacancies, quits, layoffs, hours of work, and wage movements. Moreover, the theory has trouble accounting for the persistence of slumps and booms, rather than serially uncorrelated noisy wobbles around smooth trends [Okun 1980, Tobin 1980]. The two types of business cycle theory offered by the school seem equally implausible. One is a completely real model, explaining fluctuations in employment and production as swings in tastes and technologies, evoking decisions to shift the timing of work and leisure. The other, building on Lucas's interpretation of Phillips curve statistics recounted above, finds the origins of fluctuations in unanticipated money supply policies. But these have real consequences only because of inadequacies and asymmetries of information arbitrarily assigned to market participants, and they have cyclical consequences only with the help of further arbitrary assumptions. Whether these are more or less objectionable, more or less "ad hoc," than the much-criticized Keynesian assumptions of wage and price inertia seems a question more of taste than of principle.

The emphasis of new classical theories on expectations, especially expectations of policy, rather than on inertia, made many economists and policy makers optimistic about "credible threat" policies for disinflation [Fellner 1980]. The idea was that government should make clear its determination relentlessly to diminish monetary growth to non-inflationary rates, whatever the consequences for employment and production. If this was understood, it was argued, wage and price inflation would decline much more quickly than in the past, when workers and business managers expected counter-cyclical monetary and fiscal policies to restore their markets. Both Prime Minister Thatcher in Britain and Federal Reserve Chairman Volcker in the United States recently followed this policy. Disinflation occurred all right, but it was no less fraught with painful real consequences than in recessions under prior policy regimes. The 1980s may be as difficult for monetarism as the 1970s were for Keynesianism and the 1930s for old style neoclassical orthodoxy.

VIII Supply-side Economics and Fiscal Orthodoxy

I turn finally to two other trends in current macroeconomic debate, important both within the profession and without, so-called "supply-side" economics and old-fashioned fiscal and financial orthodoxy. These are less novel in methodology and more diffuse in content than the identifiable counter-revolutions discussed above. They are renewed emphases of long-standing neoclassical themes, allegedly ignored or underrated in Keynesian and neo-Keynesian macroeconomics.

"Supply-side" economics is not a coherent theory. It has no great book or prophet, no Walras or Keynes or Friedman or Lucas. Its identification as a distinct counter-revolution comes from media enthusiasm for its simplistic label, which suggests that Keynesian macroeconomics went wrong in theory and practice by exclusive attention to the "demand side." In the policy debates of the late 1970s and early 1980s, the supply-siders' diagnosis was that government spending, taxes, and regulations were retarding economic growth. Their prescription was to reduce drastically government presence in the economy in all these dimensions. In these conclusions supply-siders agreed with other conservative counter-revolutionaries. However, they disagreed sharply on tactics. While traditional orthodoxy argued for lowering public expenditures and receipts in step, supply-siders proposed to lower taxes first, recognizing that lowering expenditures is more difficult politically and administratively. Sometimes this tactic was rationalized by the judgment that politicians will spend less if they have smaller tax receipts and face large deficits. But more typically supply-siders argued that deficits do not matter very much—a point of view that ironically allied them with Keynesians—and would in any case be removed by the economic growth the tax reductions would stimulate [Ture 1980, Wanniski 1975 and 1978].

This claim took the form of the famous Laffer curve, employed to assert that in our over-taxed society lowering tax rates will actually raise revenues. A slightly more modest claim was that the lower rates would evoke enough extra saving to make up for any net loss of tax receipts, so that public sector borrowing requirements would not be greater. These propositions are reminiscent of the more extravagant claims of demand-side pump-primers, not generally accepted in Keynesian analyses of fiscal policy. The supply-siders were, however, relying not on the re-employment of idle resources, but rather on additional economic activity and productivity in full employment equilibrium. The distinction has become blurred in fiscal policy debates in 1982 and 1983, when the economy has been depressed.

Although monetarists generally share supply-siders' aversion to government, supply-siders perceived that monetarist anti-inflation policies could hamper their scenario for economic growth. Specifically, recession and high real interest rates could nullify the incentives of "supply-side" tax cuts for investment, enterprise, risk taking, and work. As this actually happened in 1981–83, supply-siders found further affinity to their Keynesian enemies.

As for disinflation, however, the supply-side alternative to unadulterated monetarism clearly could not be the incomes policies favored by some Keynesians. Instead, some supply-siders offered the hope that productivity growth stimulated by their tax cuts would do the job, a prospect even less likely than Laffer curve miracles. Their monetary solution was to return to the gold standard, a discipline which was supposed to have the same salutary self-fulfilling effect on expectations as the "credible threats" of relentless monetary restriction advocated by new classical rational expectations theorists [Mundell 1981].

Stripped of its more ludicrous cocktail-napkin extravagances, supply-side economics simply emphasizes the familiar incentive and substitution effects dear to standard neoclassical economics and attacks the distortions or dilutions of these effects by taxes, transfer payments, and regulations. Its more sober protagonists describe it as simply "good microeconomics" [Penner 1981]. Since theorists of all persuasions acknowledge incentive and substitution effects, the main issues are quantitative: Are these effects empirically as large as the supply-siders' estimates?

The more sophisticated practitioners of supply-side economics regard it as the application of neoclassical public finance theory. Given the government's programmatic requirements, there is no way to avoid some distortions of price signals. There is no way to collect taxes or make transfers in "lump sums," i.e. in ways which would not give households and businesses some inducements to inefficient tax-avoiding or transfer-increasing behavior. The problem is to find the "second-best" welfare economic solution. Some ways of collecting revenues and making transfers and other outlays create fewer distortions than others.

Of course a final judgment cannot be reached without considering distributional effects too. Supply-siders, sometimes explicitly but often implicitly, feel that in the past redistribution has been overemphasized with blind disregard of allocational distortions. Furthermore, they call specific attention to the possibly inadvertent extra distortions caused in the 1970s by the interaction of inflation with tax codes written in nominal dollar terms [Feldstein 1983].

It is fair to say that Keynesian and neo-Keynesian macroeconomics, in its focus on the massive market failure it attributed to inadequate aggregate demand and to involuntary unemployment of labor and existing capital, underplayed the allocational effects of relative prices, as distorted by taxes and transfers, on labor supply, unemployment, saving, investment, and portfolio choice. But these matters were certainly not entirely ignored [Hall and Tobin 1955]. In the neo-Keynesian neo-classical synthesis, they arose in the context of long-run growth and therefore in the choice of instruments for short-run demand stabilization. It was after all the Kennedy administration, in the heyday of neo-Keynesian influence on policy, which introduced the investment tax credit and lowered top-bracket marginal income tax rates. Likewise neo-Keynesian theorists advocated a mix of fiscal and monetary policies combining tax disincentives to consume with monetary low-interest incentives to invest, as a means of allocating more resources to capital formation in order to promote long-run growth.

Prior to the coining of the "supply-side" slogan, revisionist thinking in the same spirit had substantial influence in macroeconomic policy debate. A central issue throughout the 1970s was the upward drift of actual unemployment rates and of the rates apparently consistent with stable inflation. How much unemployment was involuntary and "Keynesian," how much was voluntary or frictional? A new view arose, which attributed increasing amounts of unemployment to voluntary search or personal choice, influenced by unemployment compensation and other transfer programs, and by minimum wages and other regulations. In its strongest form, this new view alleged that most unemployment was of short duration, caused little discomfort to the unemployed, and was neither a social problem nor a condition remediable by macroeconomic demand management [Feldstein 1978, pp. 155–158].

Another revisionist argument challenged the policy-mix recommendation of the mainstream Synthesis, and this too stressed the importance of tax distortions magnified by inflation. Residential investment, it was argued, was heavily subsidized by the deductibility of nominal mortgage interest and the freedom from taxation of implicit rental incomes on owner-occupied homes. On the other hand, non-residential investment, much more strategic for economic growth, was penalized by the inadequacy of depreciation allowances and the taxation of purely nominal capital gains on inventories and other assets. Consequently the recommendation was for a tight money policy to control inflation and to deter over-investment in housing via high real interest rates, accompanied by tax concessions to stimulate saving and fixed business investment [Feldstein 1980, pp. 182–186].

This recipe was consistent with another proposal, advanced under the supply-side banner. The idea was to pursue a high-interest-rate tight monetary policy in order to appreciate the exchange rate, gaining counter-inflationary headway by lowering the domestic prices of internationally traded goods. This would reduce the country's trade surplus or increase its trade deficit. The compensating increase in demand would be obtained by an "easy" fiscal policy, achieved by supply-side tax cuts [Mundell 1975]. The troubles with this recipe are several: It is not a game that every country can play; one country's lower prices of traded goods are another country's higher prices. Anyway, the price advantage occurs only once; continuing counter-inflationary help requires continuing appreciation of the currency resulting from an ever wider interest differential above the rest of the world. Finally, since this policy mix crowds out foreign investment in favor of domestic uses of resources, its effect on the growth of future consumption opportunities is not necessarily favorable.

Fiscal and financial orthodoxy has been a durable opponent of Keynesian theory and policy. It has received a new lease on life in the contemporary climate of disillusionment with government. The focus is on two major points, limiting the size and growth of government and balancing the government budget. Government, it is alleged, tends to become too big because of a bias in the politics of representative democracy. The gains from specific public expenditures, purchases of goods and services or transfers, are concentrated on minorities with intense special interests. The costs are widely diffused, and therefore have inadequate weight in the budgetary process. In legislatures the organized interest groups prevail over the unorganized taxpayers. The costs may be further diffused and disguised by deficit financing, postponing the taxes to future years and future generations or substituting inflation for taxes honestly and explicitly enacted. For these reasons, the orthodox view condemns Keynesian economics for attempting, with considerable success, to eliminate the discipline of the norm of balancing the budget [Buchanan and Wagner 1977]. To restore and solidify the balanced budget norm and to overcome the alleged political bias toward large and growing government are the purposes of constitutional amendments recently proposed, favored by more than thirty state legislatures and by the U.S. Senate.

A macro-economic argument against deficit financing is that it "crowds out" private investment in favor of public and private consumption. This is also an argument against pay-as-you-go social retirement insurance—it replaces private saving without substituting any public saving [Feldstein 1976]. The Synthesis agrees that crowding out can be a problem at full employment. Indeed this is the basis for its recommendation of an easy-money-tight-budget policy mix. The orthodox view, however, does not discriminate as between situations of underemployment and full employment. Keynesians would not worry about "crowding out" in situations where idle resources are available both for government and private use, and where their re-employment would generate the saving to finance both government deficits and private investment. This is an ancient controversy. During the Great Depression the orthodox economists of the U.K. Treasury opposed Keynes's public works proposals on the grounds that they would simply substitute public employment for more productive private employment [H. M. Treasury 1928–29]. The famous "Treasury View" was echoed in the U.S. at the time, and it has recurred in every recession, including that of 1981–82.

In this respect fiscal orthodoxy differs from some other strands of contemporary conservative economics. Supply-siders, as already noted, are not so worried about deficits and advocate a bold tax-cutting strategy for stimulating investment. For a different reason, some new classical rational expectations theorists are not at all worried about crowding out. They argue that rational taxpayers will save enough to pay postponed taxes, so that the macroeconomic effect of government expenditures is the same whether they are financed by contemporaneous taxes or by borrowing [Barro 1974].

IX Optimistic Conclusion: A New Synthesis?

The present disarray of world economies, macroeconomic policies, and macroeconomics itself is certainly disheartening. But I am an optimist at heart, and I feel that the worst is over. The unprecedented shocks that generated economic turmoil from 1966 to 1980 are not likely to be a recurrent feature of the economic environment. In a more benign climate public opinion will not support ideological extremes and simplistic nostrums. Policies will be more pragmatic and more respectful of hard-learned lessons of the past. Within professional macroeconomics, the slow but trustworthy internal discipline of our science will prevail over our methodological and doctrinal conflicts. The developments I have reviewed here, revolutionary and counter-revolutionary as many of them are, have already inspired serious theoretical and empirical research transcending those divisions. The objectives, common to scholars across the whole spectrum, are to understand and model more satisfactorily the roles of expectations and inertia; the reasons for explicit and implicit contracts and for their absence, and for the inclusion of some contingencies and the neglect of others; the setting of prices and the processes of search in the absence of Walrasian auction markets, and the role of quantity variations in balancing demands and supplies. Eventually, I should think in the 1990s, a new synthesis will replace the present disarray of macroeconomics.

Notes

1. The seminal article is by Clower [1965]; Leijonhufvud [1968], Grossman [1971], Barro and Grossman [1971] developed the theme. It has been the focus of a group of French theorists, whose prolific work is well summarized in Malinvaud [1978].
2. Notably in two well read polemics, one by Lucas and Sargent [1978], the other Lucas's review of a book of my own [Lucas 1981, pp. 558–567].

Bibliography

Arrow, K. J. 1953. "Le rôle des valeurs boursières pour la répartition la meilleure des risques." *Econométrie* Paris, Centre National de la Recherche Scientifique, 41–48.

Barro, R. J. 1974. "Are Government Bonds Net Wealth?" *Journal of Political Economy* 82 (November/December): 1095–1117.

Barro, R. J., and H. I. Grossman. 1971. "A General Disequilibrium Model of Income and Employment." *American Economic Review* 61 (March): 82–93.

Buchanan, J. M., and R. E. Wagner. 1977. *Democracy in Deficit*. New York: Academic Press.

Chamberlin, E. M. 1933. *The Theory of Monopolistic Competition*. London: Oxford University Press.

Clower, R. 1965. "The Keynesian Counter-Revolution: A Theoretical Appraisal." in F. H. Hahn and F. P. R. Brechling, eds., *The Theory of Interest Rates*. London: MacMillan and Co.

Debreu, G. 1959. *The Theory of Value*. New York: John Wiley and Sons, Inc.

Feldstein, M. 1983. *Inflation, Tax Rules, and Capital Formation*. Chicago: University of Chicago Press.

Feldstein, M. 1980. "Tax Rules and the Mismanagement of Monetary Policy." *American Economic Review* 70 (May): 182–186.

Feldstein, M. 1978. "The Private and Social Costs of Unemployment." *American Economic Review* 68 (May): 155–158.

Feldstein, M. 1976. "Social Security and Savings in the Extended Life-Cycle Theory." *American Economic Review* 66 (May): 77–86.

Fellner, W. 1980. "The Valid Core of Rationality Hypothesis in the Theory of Expectations." *Journal of Money, Credit, and Banking* 12, no. 4, part 2 (November): 763–787.

Fisher, I. 1911. *The Purchasing Power of Money*. New York: MacMillan and Co.

Friedman, M. 1968. "The Role of Monetary Policy." *American Economic Review* 59 (March): 1–17.

Friedman, M. 1966. "Interest Rates and the Demand for Money." *Journal of Law and Economics* 9 (October): 71–86.

Friedman, M. 1956. "The Quantity Theory of Money—A Restatement," *Studies in the Quantity Theory of Money*, pp. 3–24. Chicago: University of Chicago Press.

Friedman, M. 1953. "The Methodology of Positive Economics," *Essays in Positive Economics*, pp. 3–42. Chicago: University of Chicago Press.

Grossman, H. I. 1971. "Money, Interest, and Prices in Market Disequilibrium." *Journal of Political Economy* 79 (September–October): 269–273.

Hahn, F. 1982. *Money and Inflation.* St. Louis: Blackwell.

Hall, C. A., and J. Tobin. 1955. "Income Taxation, Output, and Prices." *Economia Internazionale* 8 (August): 522–538.

Hicks, J. R. 1946. *Value and Capital.* 2nd ed. Oxford: Oxford University Press.

Holzman, F. D. 1950. "Income Determination in Open Inflation." *Review of Economics and Statistics* 32 (May): 150–158.

Kareken, J. H., and N. Wallace (eds.). 1980. *Money of Monetary Economics.* Federal Reserve Bank of Minneapolis.

Keynes, J. M. 1940. *How to Pay for the War.* New York: Harcourt, Brace.

Keynes, J. M. 1936. *The General Theory of Employment, Interest, and Money.* London: Macmillan and Co.

Koopmans, T. 1942. "The Dynamics of Inflation." *Review of Economics and Statistics* 24 (May): 53–65.

Leijonhufvud, A. 1968. *On Keynesian Economics and the Economics of Keynes: A Study in Monetary Theory.* Oxford: Oxford University Press.

Lucas, R. E. 1981. "Tobin and Monetarism: A Review Article," *Journal of Economic Literature* 19 (June): 558–567.

Lucas, R. E. 1972. "Econometric Testing of the Natural Rate Hypothesis." In O. Eckstein, ed., *The Econometrics of Price Determination: Conference, October 30–31, 1970.* Washington: Board of Governors of the Federal Revenue System, pp. 50–59.

Lucas, R. E., and T. Sargent. 1973. "After Keynesian Macroeconomics." In *After the Phillips Curve: The Persistence of High Unemployment and High Inflation.* Boston: Federal Reserve Bank of Boston.

Malinvaud, E. 1978. *The Theory of Unemployment Reconsidered.* Oxford: Oxford University Press.

Mundell, R. A. 1981. "Gold Would Serve into the 21st Century." *Wall Street Journal* 198 (September 30): 28.

Mundell, R. A. 1975. "Inflation from an International Viewpoint." in D. I. Meiselman and A. B. Laffer, eds., *The Phenomenon of Worldwide Inflation.* Washington: American Enterprise Institute, pp. 141–152.

Patinkin, D. 1955. *Money, Interest, and Prices: An Integration of Monetary and Value Theory.* Evanston: Ill.: Row, Peterson.

Penner, R. 1981. "Policies Affecting Savings and Investment." In *Proceedings of the Colloquium on Alternatives for Economic Policy.* New York: Conference Board.

Okun, A. 1980. "Rational-Expectations-with-Misperceptions as a Theory of the Business Cycle." *Journal of Money, Credit, and Banking* 12, no. 4, part 2 (November): 817–825.

Phelps, E. 1967. "Phillips Curves, Expectations of Inflation, and Optimal Unemployment over Time." *Economica* 34 (August): 254–281.

Phillips, A. W. 1958. "The Relations between Unemployment and the Rate of Change of Money Wage Rates in the United Kingdom, 1861–1957." *Economica* 25 (November): 283–299.

Robinson, J. 1933. *The Economics of Imperfect Competition.* London: Macmillan and Co.

Samuelson, P. A. 1947. *Foundations of Economic Analysis.* Cambridge, Mass.: Harvard University Press.

Samuelson, P. A. and R. M. Solow. 1960. "Analytical Aspects of Anti-Inflation Policy." *American Economic Review* 50 (May): 177–194.

Shove, G. F. 1930. "The Representative Firm and Increasing Returns." *Economic Journal* 40 (March): 94–116.

Smith, A. 1776. *The Wealth of Nations.* New York: E. P. Dutton and Co.

Smithies, A. 1942. "The Behavior of Money National Income under Inflationary Conditions." *Quarterly Journal of Economics* 57 (November): 113–128.

Sonnenschein, H. 1973. "The Utility Hypothesis and Market Demand Theory." *Western Economic Journal* 11 (December): 404–410.

Sraffa, P. 1926. "The Laws of Returns under Competitive Conditions." *Economic Journal* 36 (December): 535–550.

Tobin, J. 1980. "Are New Classical Models Plausible Enough to Guide Policy?" *Journal of Money, Credit, and Banking* 12, no. 4, part 2 (November): 788–799.

Tobin, J. 1967. "The Cruel Dilemma." In A. Phillips, ed., *Price Issues in Theory, Practice, and Policy.* Phildelphia: University of Pennsylvania Press; *Essays*, Vol. 2, Chapter 25.

Tobin, J. 1965. "Money and Economic Growth." *Econometrica* 33 (October): 671–684; *Essays*, Vol. 2, Chapter 9.

H. M. Treasury. 1928–29. *Memoranda on Certain Proposals Relating to Unemployment*, reports of the Minister of Labor and of the Treasury, Command Paper No. 3331, Parliamentary Accounts and Papers, 1928–29, Volume XVI, pp. 1–15 and 43–54.

Ture, N. 1980. Testimony before the U.S. Congress, Joint Economic Committee, May 21, 1980.

Walras, L. 1874. *Eléments d'économie politique pure.* Lausanne: Corbaz.

Wanniski, J. 1978. *The Way the World Works: How Economies Fail and Succeed.* New York: Basic.

Wanniski, J. 1975. "The Mundell-Laffer Hypothesis." *The Public Interest* 39 (Spring): 31–52.

Young, A. A. 1930. In R. T. Ely, ed. *Outlines of Economics*, pp. 562–563. New York: Macmillan and Co.

CHAPTER 9

ON THE WELFARE MACROECONOMICS OF GOVERNMENT FINANCIAL POLICY

I Capital Saturation versus Monetary Saturation

The optimal quantity of money, or more precisely the optimal time path of money supply, is a time-honored issue of the macroeconomics of the long run. Individual agents use scarce resources, or lose utility, when they try to economize their holdings of money. Costs due to scarcity of real balances of money can be avoided if the real return just from holding balances is equivalent to the returns on alternative stores of value. Any yield differential disadvantages to money will induce agents to restrict their holdings until the implicit service yield of their balances—marginal productivity or marginal utility—fills the gap in explicit returns. Since fiat money is costless to the society, such restrictions and the associated costs appear to be wasteful.

This is the case for monetary saturation, argued for example by Friedman (1969). Assuming the nominal explicit interest on money to be zero, Friedman's optimal supply path requires, in a long-run steady state, deflation at a rate equal to the real rate of return on alternative assets, in particular capital. The deflation would be accomplished by holding the growth of nominal money supply below the economy's real growth trend. Slow or negative *nominal* money growth is the way to saturate the public with *real* money balances.

Optimal accumulation of money, however, may conflict with optimal accumulation of capital. In nonmonetary neoclassical growth models, the optimum steady-state capital stock is determined by the generalized "golden rule," requiring the net marginal productivity of capital to equal the growth rate plus the time preference rate (plus a term allowing for the diminishing marginal utility of consumption when technological progress is steadily raising per capita productivity). If the accumulation of wealth in the form of money displaces accumulation of wealth in the form of capital, and vice versa, it is possible that these two alleged optima are not compatible.

I raised this question in Tobin (1965), showing that secular inflation, making money a less attractive store of value, had the advantage of diverting saving to capital investment and wealth to capital stock. I assumed that the amounts of saving and wealth were limited, so that the two stores of value could not simultaneously be optimal. I did not introduce explicitly the real costs of keeping money scarce but simply emphasized the gains from capital accumulation. One purpose of this paper is to remedy the imbalance of the old paper.

In subsequent discussion in the literature, some theorists presented models in which both optima can be achieved at the same time. The classic article is by Sidrauski (1967). The key assumption is that agents have infinite horizons and will accumulate any or both, or all, assets to the point that the marginal productivity or marginal utility of holding each asset equals the rate of time preference. Asset accumulations displace consumption; they do not displace each other.

Some models of this kind are "super-neutral" in the sense that the capital stock and its path are independent of the rate of inflation, the scarcity of money, and the path of the nominal money stock. The capital optimum will be attained by private saving and investment whether or not the government provides the optimal amount of money. This is true in Sidrauski (1967). Others are not super-neutral but assume such complementary interdependence of capital and money in utility or production functions that the capital optimum cannot be achieved without the monetary optimum. In these models general deflation, not inflation, augments the capital stock; cf. Fischer (1983).

Clearly the infinite horizons attributed to savers are a crucial element in models which deny that money and capital are substitutes in wealth holdings. Savers with shorter horizons, for example, mortal life-cycle savers, will have finite capacities for accumulating wealth. They will not be willing to hold whatever amounts of every asset provide returns that meet some constant threshold of time preference. The limitation is clear in overlapping generation models, where it has been shown too that Friedman's candidate for optimal money supply is not optimal; cf. Weiss (1981) and Woodford (1983). In my paper here, wealth demand is modeled as life-cycle saving theory.

In a series of important papers beginning in 1965, Phelps (1972, 1979) saw the capital/money conflict as a problem in the "second-best" welfare economics of public finance. Public expenditures must be financed. Explicit taxation is one way. Printing money is another way. Selling promises to pay money in future, whether raised by taxation, printing money, or still further borrowing, is a third way. Printing money exacts an implicit tax, the reduction in the purchasing power of money and promises to pay future money. The ability of the government to finance expenditures by issuing money is the "seignorage" associated with its soverign monetary monopoly. Both explicit and implicit taxes are distortionary. The distortion of the inflation tax is the diversion of resources or loss of utility associated with the scarcity of money, already mentioned. But there are also distortions in explicit taxes; lump-sum taxes are not available. The problem is to optimize the choice of taxes, given the necessity of government expenditure. This formulation correctly connects the money-supply process to the government budget, and I shall do likewise in this paper.

An important advantage of this approach is to show how an efficient, though "second-best," steady-state growth may be consistent with a permanent government budget deficit. Superficially at least, growth theory seems to suggest some inconsistency. On the one hand, the Phelps (1961) "golden rule" says that the marginal productivity of capital should not be less than the natural growth rate, lest the economy be inefficiently overcapitalized. On the other hand, the elementary dynamics of deficits and debt says that stability in the size of the debt relative to the economy requires that the real interest rate on the debt be no higher than the real growth rate of the economy. Indeed if the primary deficit, i.e., excluding debt service from expenditure, is positive, the debt interest rate must be lower than the economy's growth rate. Of course, there is a zero-debt balanced-budget equilibrium position, whatever the interest rate, but it is not very interesting realistically, especially if the economy's basic money supply has to be generated by deficits.

How can it be that the real interest rate is no less than the growth rate, as required for efficiency in capital accumulation, and at the same time less than the growth rate, as required for fiscal stability? One possibility is that money, in purchasing power terms, is sufficiently scarce so that its service yield makes up the difference between the marginal productivity of capital and the explicit return on money. An additional possibility is that the pre-tax real interest rate, which is relevant for capital efficiency, exceeds or equals the growth rate while the after-tax rate, which is relevant for the government budget and for the holders of debt, is below the growth rate.

II Optimal Inflation and Short-run Inflation/Unemployment Tradeoffs

The social costs and benefits of disinflation have been a practical policy issue of great moment in recent years, and likewise a question of theoretical debate among economists. The period of unemployment above the natural rate necessary to decelerate prices entails heavy social costs in lost output. The benefits in reduction in the permanent inflation rate seem, at first glance anyway, small in comparison. The identifiable benefits are reductions in what are sometimes called the "shoe-leather" costs of anticipated inflation, I once allowed myself to say, "It takes a heap of Harberger triangles to fill an Okun gap"; cf. Tobin (1976).

In a celebrated paper, Feldstein (1979) challenged this view. He argued that the benefit of permanent disinflation lasts forever, and its size grows with the economy. In principle, if the present value of such a stream of benefits is calculated by a social discount rate lower than the growth rate, its present value is infinite. It therefore dominates any finite cost of the investment in unemployment and recession necessary to bring about the disinflation. Feldstein concludes:

> In the important case in which the growth of aggregate income exceeds the social discount rate..., if the inflation rate is above its optimal level, the economy should then be deflated to reduce the inflation rate regardless of the temporary consequences for unemployment.

Feldstein recognizes that the determination of optimal inflation is a problem of "second-best" calculus, of optimal taxation. He *assumes* that the current inflation rate is above the optimum. This enables him to enter in the integrand of his calculation of the present value of inflation reduction a positive social gain for every future date, a gain moreover that grows secularly with the economy. The assumption is essential to his argument, and it is quite gratuitous. If it happened that the prevailing inflation rate were less than optimal, the integrands would be negative and the investment in transitional unemployment Feldstein recommends would not be justified at any social discount rate.

The social discount rate is also, of course, a crucial element in Feldstein's cost/benefit calculation. He uses the after-tax real rate on long-term corporate bonds as a revealed indicator of society's discount of future consumption. The claim that this rate is lower than the economy's natural sustainable growth rate is responsible for the large—in the limit, infinite—present value of the benefits of the assumed positive growing gains from inflation reduction, however miniscule they may be year by year.

Feldstein's discount rate raises several issues. First, the after-tax real bond rate may not be a representative indicator of effective intertemporal consumption discounts for individuals and households. Many private agents have portfolios that include assets and debts bearing much higher rates; many are at liquidity-constrained or credit-rationed corners, where no quoted market rate is indicative of the operational discount.

Second, these market rates are not the proper guide for choice of optimum steady-state paths for the indefinite future unless the horizons of living savers and consumers are infinite, so that they internalize the preferences and constraints of future generations. If individuals' horizons are their own lifetimes, observed interest rates reflect age as well as time preferences in consumption. More important, their demands for wealth are finite, and have to be described as a function of the market interest rates they face. When demand for total wealth is limited, one asset (e.g. money) cannot be absorbed in greater quantity unless holdings of another (e.g. capital) are reduced. To put the point somewhat differently, there is no single rate that can be used to evaluate all future steady-state consumption paths regardless of level and shape. In other well-known papers Feldstein relies heavily on life-cycle models of consumption and saving and indeed draws from them striking policy conclusions, notably the crowding out of capital investment by unfunded social security. It is surprising that in analyzing the costs of inflation he uses a model that would be appropriate only for a population of infinite-horizon consumers.

The third point is especially relevant for the analysis that will follow in the next section. As I shall show, the fact that the after-tax real interest rate is lower than the growth rate is not a *prima facie* reason to believe the inflation rate is too high. This fact could, or could not, characterize a steady state with an optimal combination of inflation and explicit income taxation. However, it will in general be true of such an optimum that the pre-tax productivity of capital exceeds the growth rate. Since another of Feldstein's favorite themes is the deterrent effect of taxation of capital income on capital accumulation, he should not be surprised by the possibility that it might not be efficient to substitute more general income taxation for the inflation tax.

III A Model of the Long-run Inflation/Capital Tradeoff

The model to be presented in this section concerns the long-run tradeoff between "taxation" of money balances by inflation and explicit taxation of the earnings of capital and labor. Lower explicit taxation of income stimulates capital formation in two ways: one, by diminishing the wedge between before-tax returns to investment and after-tax returns to saving; two, by raising the inflation rate and making money less attractive relative to capital as a store of value. Increasing the capital/output ratio, within limits, raises per capita consumption. On the other hand, the higher inflation rate diverts resources from production of consumption goods to transactions designed to economize money holdings. In the absence of lump-sum taxes, the economy cannot be saturated with money without suffering losses from heavy distortionary taxation. Given the dependence of the economy on a base of outside money, the economy cannot be saturated with capital without incurring losses from impairing the attractiveness of money as a vehicle of saving.

I illustrate the tradeoff between these two forms of taxation in a simple steady-state growth model, in which there are only two assets for wealth-owners, money and capital. Even in a simple model, the conditions for an optimum are quite complex.

Money is base or "high-powered" money, and it comes into existence to pay for government purchases in excess of the revenues generated by a proportional tax on both wages and capital incomes. Suppose the economy is growing at a natural rate g, composed of labor force and population growth at rate μ plus labor-augmenting technological progress at rate λ. The government is purchasing for collective consumption the fraction $1 - \gamma$ of production, leaving γ for private use; it is taxing $1 - u$ of the income earned in production, leaving u for private disposition. Let m be real money balances and y real output and income per effective (augmented) worker, and let π be the inflation rate, so that $g + \pi$ is the rate of growth of the nominal money stock. Then the government budget equation is:

$$(g + \pi)m = (u - \gamma)y. \tag{1}$$

Here $u - \gamma \ (= (1 - \gamma) - (1 - u))$ must be positive, as deficits are the only source of money stock. Rearranging gives an expression for the inflation rate:

$$\pi = \frac{(u - \gamma)y}{m} - g. \tag{2}$$

This relationship is shown in Figure 9.1. As m becomes indefinitely large π approaches $-g$. As m goes to zero, π becomes indefinitely large. In the model u and γ are policy parameters, of which only u will be varied for our present purpose, while π, m and y are endogenous in the sense that they differ across steady states.

Money is both a store of wealth and a transactions medium. The demand for money is modeled as in the Baumol cash inventory analysis. There are N payment cycles per time period, say per year. Households receive their incomes in lump-sums at the beginning (end) of each cycle and then dispose of their incomes at a steady rate of outlay. Businesses and government receive payments at a steady rate and at the end (beginning) of each cycle (e.g. month) make lump-sum income payments to households for labor and capital services received during the previous cycle. Within each cycle, an agent can make in-and-out transactions between money, which bears zero nominal interest, and claims to capital bearing market nominal interest at annual rate i. Money alone is used for factor and commodity payments.

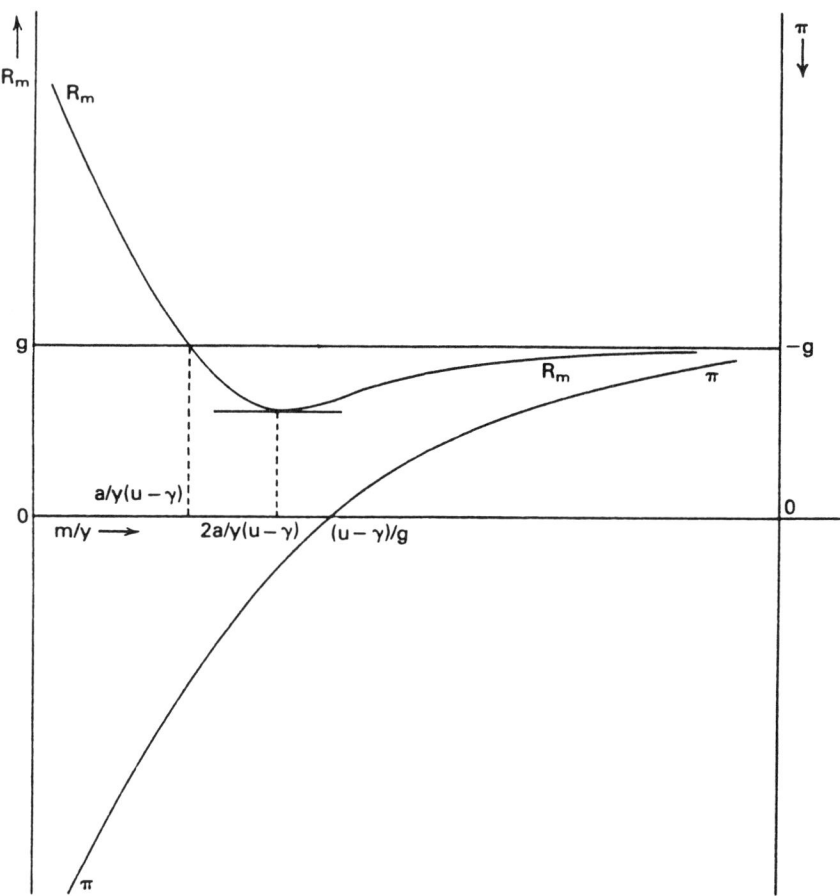

Figure 9.1

Every asset transaction between money and interest-bearing claims involves a real cost, which is divided equally between the two parties to the transaction. The social cost per transaction is independent of its size. It is a constant a, expressed in terms of commodities per augmented worker. Note the implication: Transactions technology does not benefit from the technological progress occurring at rate λ in production. Otherwise steady-state paths with labor-augmenting progress would not exist; growth of income over time would yield economies of scale in cash management and limit growth in demand for real balances. Here I confine such scale economies to those associated with differences among steady-state paths in the ratio a/y of transaction cost to output.

Each household receives periodically a lump-sum payment of y/N. If n is the number of cash-economizing transactions the household makes per cycle, its costs are $na/2$ and its interest earnings are $(1 - 1/n)(y/2N \cdot i/N)$. When no in-and-out transactions are induced, its average money balances m_h are $y/2N$. Otherwise the number of transactions n is approximated by $y/2Nm_h$, and the cash management strategy that maximizes interest earnings net of transactions costs is $m_h = (y/2N)^{1/2}(a/2)^{1/2}(i/N)^{-1/2}$. This is, however, only half the economy-wide m, average real cash holdings per (augmented) worker. The holdings of the payors of income, business and government, make up the other half. Thus:

$$m = 2m_h = y^{1/2}a^{1/2}i^{-1/2}. \tag{3}$$

Likewise the resource cost, equal to na or $ya/2Nm_h$ per cycle amounts to Nna or ya/m per year. It is easily seen from (3) that this is equal to im. The marginal saving in transaction cost from increasing cash holdings is ya/m^2, which may be regarded as the marginal productivity of money, its implicit service yield. The total return to holding money R_m is this service yield less the rate of inflation. R_m, I assume, must be equated to the after-tax real return on capital uR.

$$R_m = \frac{ay}{m^2} - \pi \quad (m < y/N)$$

$$R_m = -\pi \quad (m \geq y/N). \tag{4}$$

As m goes to zero, R_m becomes indefinitely large. Beyond the point of full liquidity, $m = y/N$, the service yield of money vanishes and R_m is simply the negative of the inflation rate. In Figure 9.1, R_m is plotted against m, taking into account the relationship of π to m from (2):

$$R_m = \frac{ay}{m^2} - (u - \lambda)\frac{y}{m} + g \quad (m < y/N)$$

$$R_m = -(u - \gamma)\frac{y}{m} + g \quad (m \geq y/N). \tag{5}$$

As m becomes indefinitely large, R_m approaches g.

However, there is also a finite value of m, namely $a/(u-\gamma)$ at which R_m is equal to g. The slope $\partial R_m/\partial m$ is given by

$$\frac{\partial R_m}{\partial m} = -\frac{2ay}{m^3} + \frac{(u-\gamma)y}{m^2}. \tag{6}$$

When m is equal to $a/(u-\gamma)$, the slope is $-(u-\gamma)y/m^2$, indicating that for larger values of m, R_m is smaller than g. In fact the minimum R_m is reached when $m = 2a/(u-\gamma)$. From that point R_m rises to approach g from below.

The inflation rate is zero when $m = (u-\gamma)y/g$. What is the corresponding value of R_m? It will be greater than, equal to, or smaller than g as $y/a \lesseqgtr g/(u-\gamma)^2$. In Figure 9.1, R_m is smaller than g at a zero inflation rate. While this is not necessarily the case, it is certainly a possibility that cannot be excluded.

I take y to be a Cobb-Douglas function of k, the stock of capital per augmented worker,

$$y = k^\alpha. \tag{7}$$

Assuming for simplicity that there is no physical depreciation, the before-tax return to capital R is $\alpha k^{\alpha-1}$ or $\alpha y/k$.

The final building block needed is the steady-state demand for total wealth per augmented worker, $m+k$. The life cycle model implies that this is proportional to after-tax wage income $u(1-\alpha)y$ by a factor that depends on the after-tax return to saving (uR or R_m), as well as on the growth constants μ and λ. Whether an increase in this rate of return has a positive or negative effect on demand for wealth turns on the degree of curvature in the curves of indifference between consumptions at different ages and on the shape of the age profile of labor earnings. I assume that wealth demand is positively related to uR.

$$m + k = \hat{w}(uR)^\beta u(1-\alpha)y. \tag{8}$$

In summary, a steady-state is characterized by its monetary intensity m and its capital intensity k, both measured as real quantities per effective worker. Consumption per effective worker is:

$$c(m,k) = \gamma y - \frac{a}{m}y - gk. \tag{9}$$

If steady states are evaluated by the sum of private and collective consumption, the objective is to maximize $\hat{c} = c + (1 - \gamma)y$:

$$\hat{c}(m,k) = y\left(1 - \frac{a}{m}\right) - gk = k^\alpha\left(1 - \frac{a}{m}\right) - gk. \tag{10}$$

Bliss requires full liquidity ($m \geq y/N$) and golden rule capital intensity ($R = g$). Although it might be possible to imagine institutional arrangements that could always achieve this grand optimum, those of our model economy cannot necessarily do so. The reasons are that capital income is taxed and that money can be provided only by running budget deficits that divert saving from capital formation. The objective $\hat{c}$ can be maximized only subject to those institutional constraints. If $R = g$, then $R_m = ug$. The quantity of money associated with deflation at rate ug is, applying (2), $(u - g)y/g(1 - u)$. This is $1/(1 - u)$ times the quantity of money associated with zero inflation. Presuming that money of this amount provides full liquidity, equaling or exceeding y/N, its accumulation may not leave room in the public's wealth holdings for the golden-rule capital stock.

The intensities m and k are both functions of the income tax rate $1 - u$; the problem is to maximize $\hat{c}(m(u), k(u))$ with respect to u.

It is instructive to consider the locus (m, k) consistent with any arbitrary $\hat{c}$. From (10),

$$\left(\frac{\partial k}{\partial m}\right)_{\hat{c}} = \frac{ay/m^2}{R(1 - a/m) - g}. \tag{11}$$

This is negative for $R(1 - a/m) > g$. Within the pairs (m, k) capable of generating a given $\hat{c}$, it is never efficient to accumulate capital beyond the k at which $R(1 - a/m) = g$. If this were done, there would be a lower k, and a lower investment requirement gk, at which the same consumption $\hat{c}$ could be provided with the same money stock m. Thus the condition $R(1 - a/m) = g$ sets maxima k for all $\hat{c}$. Likewise there is a minimum necessary capital intensity for each $\hat{c}$, namely the one that assumes money saturation, determined by $k^\alpha - gk = \hat{c}$ and $m = k^\alpha/N$. These points are illustrated in Figure 9.2. The family of isoconsumption loci is shown in Figure 9.3.

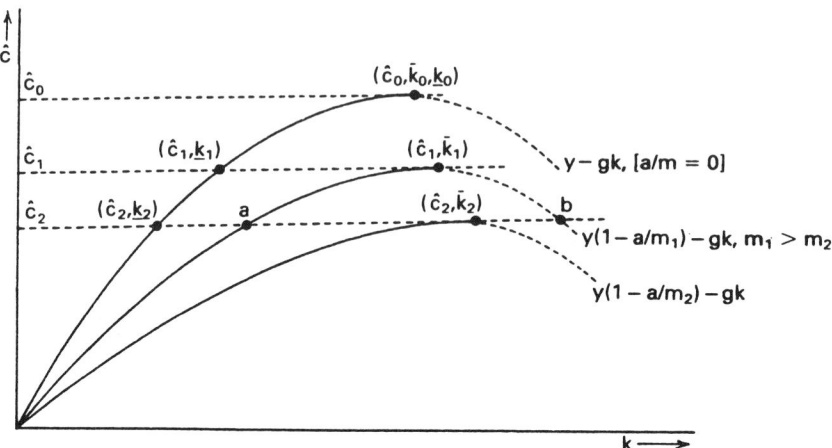

Figure 9.2
Three levels of $\hat{c}$ are shown, together with their maximum efficient capital stocks $\bar{k}$, and minimum feasible capital stocks $\underline{k}$. $\hat{c}_0$ is the maximum technologically (but not institutionally) possible $\hat{c}$. Although $\hat{c}_2$, for example, could be achieved with k's above $\bar{k}_2$, this would not be efficient: point b has the same monetary intensity as point a but requires more capital.

The change in the objective $\hat{c}$ from variation of u—increases in u result from tax *reductions*—are as follows:

$$\frac{\partial \hat{c}}{\partial u} = (R(1 - a/m) - g)\frac{\partial k}{\partial u} + \frac{ay}{m^2}\frac{\partial m}{\partial u}. \tag{12}$$

(Recall that ay/m^2 is also the nominal after-tax interest rate i, equal to $uR + \pi$.)

The two intensities m and k are tied to each other and to u by the following pair of equations:

$$m + k - \hat{w}(u\alpha k^{\alpha-1})^\beta(1 - \alpha)uk^\alpha = 0 \quad \text{Wealth} \tag{13}$$

$$m^2 u\alpha k^{-1} - m^2 gk^{-\alpha} + m(u - \gamma) = a \quad \text{Money} \tag{14}$$

Equation (13) is derived from (8), the demand for wealth, using the production function (7) to convert R and y into functions of k. Equation (14) is the demand for money function (3), with similar conversions of R and y into functions of k and with inflation expressed in terms of the government budget equation (1). Indeed (14) is the equation for R_m previously discussed and plotted in Figure 9.1:

WELFARE MACROECONOMICS OF GOVERNMENT FINANCIAL POLICY 249

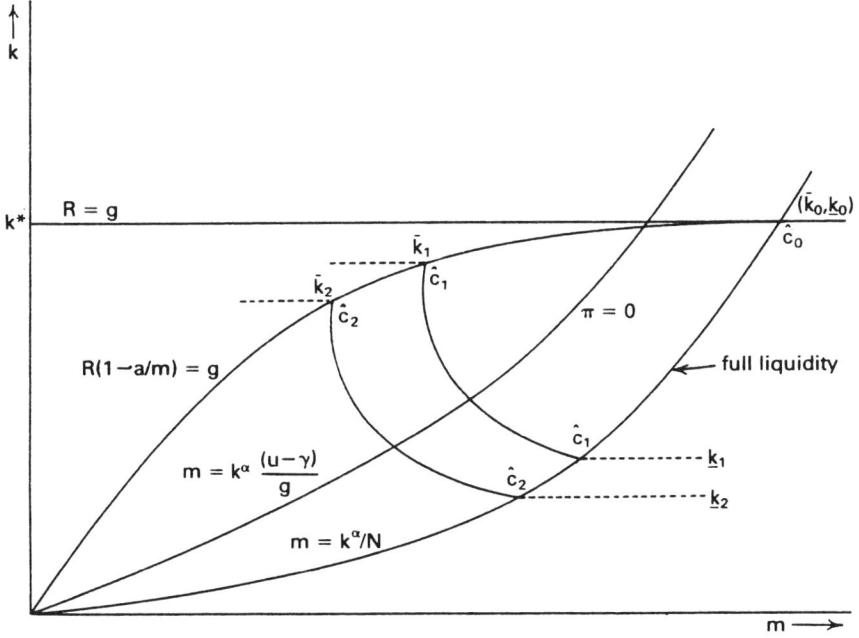

Figure 9.3
Iso-consumption loci are illustrated in (m, k) for two levels of consumption $(\hat{c}_1 > \hat{c}_2)$, and the corresponding minimal and maximal values of k are indicated (see figure 9.2). The horizontal line for $R = g$ corresponds to the golden rule capital stock, which will produce $\hat{c}_0$ of figure 9.2. The intermediate locus is for zero inflation.

$$R_m = uR = \frac{ay}{m^2} - \frac{(u-\gamma)y}{m} + g.$$

The effects of varying u are given by:

$$\begin{bmatrix} 1 & 1 - v\frac{(m+k)}{k} \\ \frac{m}{y}(uR - g) + \frac{a}{m} & -\frac{m^2}{ky}(uR - \alpha g) \end{bmatrix} \begin{bmatrix} \frac{\partial m}{\partial u} \\ \frac{\partial k}{\partial u} \end{bmatrix} = \begin{bmatrix} (1+\beta)\frac{(m+k)}{u} \\ -m\left(1 + \frac{Rm}{y}\right) \end{bmatrix} \quad (15)$$

Here the partial derivatives have been transformed into terms that are easier to understand and to sign. The constant v in the first row of the Jacobian is $\alpha - \beta(1 - \alpha)$. It will be positive for $\alpha > \beta/(1+\beta)$ (or $\alpha/(1-\alpha) > \beta$), but it is likely to be a small number relative to $k/(m+k)$.

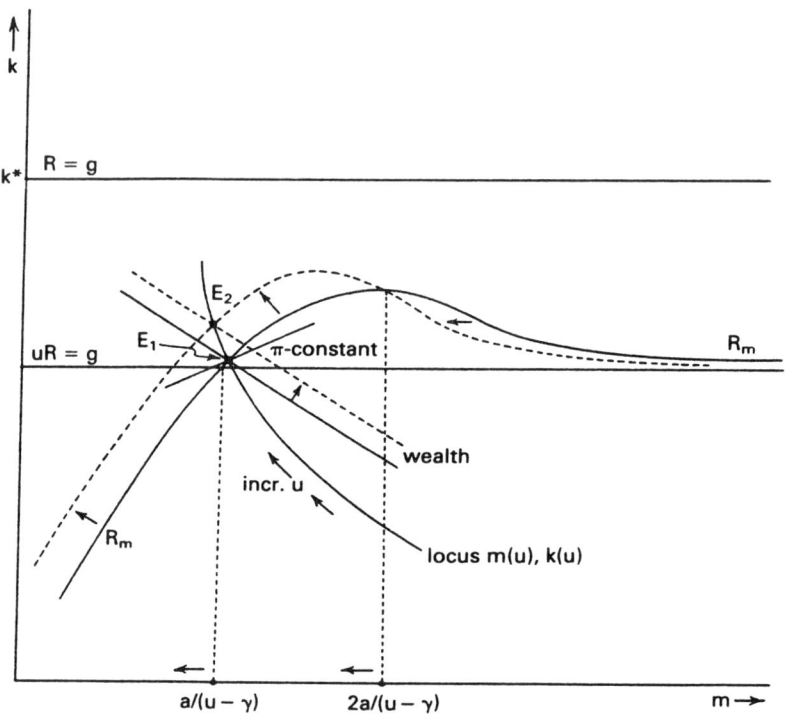

Figure 9.4
Points E_1 and E_2 are intersections of two relations between m and k, one (R_m) derived from money demand and the other (wealth) from wealth demand. The solid curves intersecting at E_1 are drawn for a constant u, and the dashed curves intersecting at E_2 for a higher constant u. E_1 and E_2 are points on a locus of such intersections also pictured. Both E_1 and E_2 are inside the "football" of figure 9.3. If E_2 is above the iso-consumption locus through E_1 (not shown) the tax reduction illustrated is a gain in steady-state consumption. If E_2 is a point of tangency to a $\hat{c}$ locus, it is an optimal point.

It is instructive to plot the two relationships (13) and (14) in the (m,k) space of Figure 9.3, for given u. This is done in Figure 9.4. The first equation, the wealth demand function, implies a negatively sloped relationship,

$$\left(\frac{\partial k}{\partial m}\right)_u = \frac{1}{v(m+k)/k - 1},$$

except for extremely high values of m/k.

This locus shifts to the right as u increases. The second equation has essentially the same form as R_m in Figure 9.1. When k is such that $uR = g$, m is $a/(u - \gamma)$. For higher k, uR falls below g. Its minimum and thus the maximum k, is reached when m is $2a/(u - \gamma)$, and R_m is $g - (u - \gamma)y/2m$. From this point R_m rises asymptotically to g, and k falls correspondingly to the level whose marginal product is g/u. Assuming that uR always exceeds αg—we know that $R \geq g$ in the absence of gross over-capitalization, and tax revenues are presumably less than aggregate wages—an increase in u shifts this locus upwards.

The directions of shift of the two curves are indicated in Figure 9.4. In the region of interest, the wealth demand curve is negatively sloped and the money demand curve positively sloped. With increases in u, their intersection may move either northwest or northeast. The locus of such intersections represents the constraint on the choices (m, k) and thus on the attainable values of $\hat{c}$. Clearly there are a number of possibilities. The optimal choice may lie on either of the two envelopes of Figure 9.3, or in their interior.

Whether an increase in u decreases or increases m, it raises the rate of inflation. The new intersection is on an R_m curve that involves higher k and y at every level of m. Equation (1) defines a family of constant inflation curves like that for zero inflation depicted in Figure 9.3. Consider the member of the family that passes through the original intersection E_1; it is shifted down by increase in u. If its slope at E_1 (y/mR or $k/m\alpha$) is smaller than that of the R_m locus, then we can be sure that the new intersection E_2 is above it, i.e., on the locus for a higher inflation rate π. It can be shown that this is so for any positive π. The reason that m may nevertheless be larger at E_2 is as follows: y is greater, and its positive effect on demand for money may exceed the negative effect of the increase in i ($= uR + \pi$), which is moderated by the fall in R.

The main point is that the position of the economy may be, as in Figure 9.4, one characterized simultaneously by: positive inflation, after-tax real interest rate less than the growth rate, and steady-state consumption less than it would be with a lower tax rate and higher inflation. Such a configuration is shown in Figure 9.4. It cannot be excluded *a priori* as Feldstein has done.

References

Feldstein, Martin S.: The Welfare Cost of Permanent Inflation and Optimal Short-run Economic Policy, *Journal of Political Economy 87*, No. 4 (August), 749–68, 1979.

Fischer, Stanley: Inflation and Growth, National Bureau of Economic Research Working Paper No. 1235, 1983.

Friedman, Milton: *The Optimum Quantity of Money*, Chicago: Aldine, Ch. 1, 1–50, 1969.

Phelps, Edmund S.: The Golden Rule of Accumulation: A Fable for Growthmen, *American Economic Review 51*, No. 4 (September), pp. 638–43, 1961.

Phelps, Edmund S.: *Inflation Policy and Unemployment Theory*, New York: Norton, especially Ch. 6, 170–228, 1972.

Phelps, Edmund S.: *Studies in Macroeconomic Theory, Vol. 1: Employment and Inflation*, New York: Academic Press, Chs. 6–8, 1979, reprinting papers published in 1965, 1973 and 1971.

Sidrauski, Miguel: Rational Choice and Patterns of Growth in a Monetary Economy, *American Economic Review 57*, No. 2 (May), 534–44, 1967.

Tobin, James: Money and Economic Growth, *Econometrica 33*, No. 4, (October), 671–84, 1965; reprinted in *Essays*, Vol. 1, Chapter 9.

Tobin, James: Inflation Control as Social Priority, unpublished, 1976; published in Hebrew translation in *The Economic Quarterly 24*, No. 92–3 (April) 1977.

Weiss, Laurence: The Effects of Money Supply on Economic Welfare in the Steady State, *Econometrica 48*, No. 3 (April), 565–76, 1980.

Woodford, Michael: Transactions Costs, Liquidity and Optimal Inflation, unpublished, 1983.

CHAPTER 10

THE MACROECONOMICS OF GOVERNMENT FINANCE

Summary

This chapter is a critical survey of literature on the implications of government financial policy for economic activity. The central question is whether the mode of financing of a given path of real government purchases—by taxes, non-monetary debt issue, or money creation—has real effects, in particular real effects of macroeconomic consequence.

In Section 1, the Introduction, we define the issues with greater detail and precision. We briefly review economists' views, over the past fifty years, of the burden of public debt and the neutrality of money. Section 2 is a review of the 1960s vintage mainstream macroeconomics of fiscal and monetary policies, often called the "neoclassical synthesis." We review its implications for both short-run fluctuations and long-run trends. We include this review because the earlier tradition covers some problems and issues now neglected, because its analyses and results may still have some validity, and because they did set the stage for—one might say they provoked or inspired—the recent literature surveyed in Sections 4–6. The earlier tradition and the recent literature differ in methodology, and in Section 3 we discuss the "microfoundations" methodology that dominates contemporary macroeconomics.

Sections 4–6 are a selective critical survey of recent contributions, theoretical and empirical, designed to summarize the current state of play on the central issues: Section 4, the debt neutrality hypothesis of Robert Barro; Section 5, the effects of financing government expenditures by

Reprinted by permission from the *Handbook of Monetary Economics*, Vol. 2, eds. Benjamin Friedman and Frank Hahn, Amsterdam: North-Holland, 1990, pp. 889–959. Written with Michael Haliassos.

printing money rather than taxing, monetary superneutrality, and the "Fisher effect" of inflation on interest rates; Section 6, open market operations, and shifts between bond- and money-financing of government expenditures induced by the adoption of financial policies which are unsustainable over the longer run. In each section we first set forth the neutrality theorems purporting to show the irrelevance of the financing choice. Then we discuss articles elaborating or criticizing the theorems. In each case we conclude with a review and evaluation of some empirical tests. We conclude in Section 7 with short summary remarks.

1 Introduction

In the years 1945–1970 fiscal and monetary policies were widely regarded, both by economists and by policy-makers, as important instruments of macroeconomic stabilization. Counter-cyclical variation of budget deficits (counting surpluses as negative deficits) was accepted as stabilizing, whether it arose as the passive result of built-in responses of revenues and outlays to economic activity or as the result of active tax and expenditure adjustments. Likewise, reactive counter-cyclical monetary policy was regarded, both by economists and by central bankers, as a useful, even an essential, stabilizer.

Subsequently, considerable disillusionment with "discretionary" policies, scornfully labeled "fine-tuning," swept professional and lay opinion. Government's ability and willingness to offset destabilizing non-policy shocks were questioned, and variability of policy instruments themselves became the favorite culprit for cyclical fluctuations. This shift of sentiment persuaded leading central banks to heed the advice of monetarists to adopt and adhere to money stock targets independent of the state of the economy, although never and nowhere to the degree the monetarist theorists prescribed.

In fiscal policy, the same shift revived the popularity of the norm of annual budget balance. In the United States in 1986 thirty-two state legislatures, the President, and majorities of both Houses of Congress supported a Constitutional Amendment mandating a balanced budget. Many economists now favor binding the central government to a fiscal rule limiting deficits. Others, however, advocate rules limiting the size and growth of government expenditures. Whether public claims on national resources are financed by taxes, by borrowing, or even by printing money is, in their view, of secondary importance.

The neoclassical counter-revolution in macroeconomic theory has lent powerful support to these intellectual trends. The two crucial strands in the New Classical Macroeconomics are *rational expectations* and continuous competitive *market clearing*. They reinforce the trained instincts of economists that unfettered markets yield optimal outcomes, that in particular there are no macroeconomic market failures which government need or can correct. They emphasize expectations of future policies as determinants of private behavior, a point especially important for macroeconomics. The famous "Lucas critique" of macroeconometrics [Lucas (1976)] says that the structures of behavior allegedly detected in econometric models will collapse if governments change policies to try to exploit them. Moreover, rational expectations models limit or obliterate the scope of monetary and other financial policies: if they are systematic, private agents will understand them and, by altering their behavior, undermine them; if they are random, the confusion of the public will make the outcomes inefficiently volatile.

1.1 The Central Questions

The expenditures of a sovereign central government can be financed by tax receipts, printing money, or borrowing. Does it matter in what proportions these three sources of finance are used to finance a given program of expenditures? Do deficits (excesses of expenditures over tax revenues) affect important macroeconomic variables: real output and its growth, unemployment, prices and inflation rates, nominal and real interest rates? Given the size of a deficit, does it make a difference whether it is covered by money or borrowing? These are the central questions to which this chapter is addressed.

Those questions are most significantly posed on several assumptions: the money is fiat money, inconvertible paper; it is not commodity money; it is not even convertible into gold or foreign currency at a guaranteed rate of exchange. Public borrowing usually takes the form of the government's promises to pay amounts of its money at future dates. Most models assume that the government does not promise to deliver commodities or foreign currencies; its debt is not indexed to money prices of commodities.

In practice, of course, many governments do borrow foreign currencies or index their debts to prices of commodities or foreign currencies in their own moneys. Those means of financing raise quite different issues, easier to analyze if not easier for the borrowing governments to manage.

A closed economy is a convenient assumption for most of the issues and literature of concern in this paper. Financial policies in open economies are specifically treated elsewhere (Dornbusch and Giovannini, 1990).

Not all governments have the tripartite financing choice described above. In some countries there is no internal way to finance deficits other than printing money. Essentially fiscal and monetary policy are the same thing. Deficits create money, and there is no other way to create government (as opposed to bank) money. The literature of economic theory contains many models in which deficits are 100 percent monetized and fiscal and monetary policy are indistinguishable. It also contains models in which government money is the only store of value for the whole society. Land and capital are assumed away. These models not only exclude analysis of non-monetized deficits but also evade the issue of "crowding out," the alleged displacement of capital formation by the absorption of saving in government debt.

Our survey will cover some models of all these varieties. But the most relevant, in our view, allow governments both monetary and non-monetary alternatives to taxes in financing current outlays and allow private savers stores of value other than government obligations.

1.2 Some Doctrinal History
The burden of public debt. The major question has long been whether borrowing, rather than taxing, to finance a given program of public expenditures can shift the burden of those expenditures to future generations. Laymen instinctively answer "Yes." For example, President Eisenhower solemnly preached against deficit spending, on behalf of the grandchildren and later descendants of his contemporaries. Among economists, however, the long-standing orthodox view was that internal debt could not shift the burden. "We owe it to ourselves." The resources used for government expenditures, for example war, are in a closed economy with full employment necessarily drawn from other *current* uses of resources. The reduction in resources available for current non-government use is

the same regardless of the method of financing. Subsequent payments from taxpayers to contemporaneous bondholders redistribute income between members of future generations. But these transfers involve no draft on resources in aggregate, other than the deadweight loss of non-lump-sum taxes. That may have been deferred, but not the full real burden of the expenditures themselves.

This view was stated forcefully by Lerner (1943, 1944) in his theory of *functional finance.* He attacks as myths the balanced-budget norm and the fear that deficits burden future generations. As a Keynesian, he does not take full employment for granted. Given the government's expenditure program, the function of taxation is to control private spending; taxes should be set and varied as necessary to equate spending to full employment output. The debt should be monetized to the degree that will bring about the real interest rate needed to sustain the optimal rate of capital investment. Given the government's expenditure program and the desired rate of capital accumulation, adjustment of taxes will make sure that consumption demand equals the remainder of full employment output.

Lerner saw clearly that fiscal and monetary stimuli are substitutes in demand management. Various mixes of the two policies can achieve full employment. Which mix to choose depends on other objectives, specifically the desired division of output between consumption and investment. Lerner did not see that this degree of freedom in macroeconomic policy undermined his assertion that the burden of government could not be shifted to future generations.

After World War II the theory of the burden of public debt excited lively controversy among economists. See the symposium edited by Ferguson (1964), reviewed by Tobin (1965b). In the symposium and elsewhere, James Buchanan attacked the orthodox "no-shift" view on the ground that deficit spending clearly defers what he regarded as the true burden, compulsory payment of taxes. He argued that lending to the government, in contrast, is voluntary and therefore burdenless.

However, the more successful revision of doctrine was what may be called the *capital stock criterion.* This was the prevailing view of public debt burden among American Keynesian architects of the "neoclassical synthesis" and "neoclassical" growth models in the period 1946–65. Franco Modigliani was a forceful advocate of this criterion, also in the Ferguson volume. Government financial policies can, after all, affect the consumption opportunities of future generations. An important test is whether we would endow our descendants with a smaller or larger stock of capital, public and private, human and non-human, foreign and domestic. The neoclassical synthesis placed great emphasis on the monetary–fiscal policy mix, which Lerner had recognized as important. The criterion is quite consistent with Lerner's strictures on the policy mix. The same short-run path of real output can be achieved with tight money and high deficits or with tight budgets and easy money. The former combination will have higher real interest rates and lower capital accumulation and growth. On a flow basis, the deficit "crowds out" productive investment; on a stock basis, the debt displaces capital in the wealth portfolios of private savers.

The next move in this contest revived the older "no-shift" orthodoxy. Robert Barro's extraordinarily influential article, "Are Government Bonds Net Wealth?" (1974), rejected the theory of consumption and saving behavior underlying the arguments of Modigliani and other mainstream neoclassical Keynesians. According to Barro, private citizens will rationally anticipate the future taxes that any current deficit will impose on themselves or their descendants. The present value of these tax liabilities will be exactly the same as those of the debt instruments issued to finance the deficit. Internalizing the circumstances and utilities of their dynasties, current citizens will regard their net wealth as independent of current taxes and deficits. If their taxes are cut, they will not consume more; they will save the full amount of the tax cuts to enable themselves or their heirs to pay the postponed taxes. Buying the debt instruments themselves would be the perfect hedge. Much of this chapter, especially Section 4, will be devoted to discussion of this doctrine, which Barro called the Ricardian Equivalence Theorem [Ricardo (1817; 1951)].[1]

Debt neutrality, as asserted by the Equivalence Theorem, is to be distinguished from monetary neutrality. The debt burden controversy concerns *real* variations in tax revenues, current and anticipated, balanced by equal and opposite variations in real amounts of net public borrowing (or repayment and lending) at market interest rates. Debt neutrality means that these variations have no real effects. Monetary neutrality, on the other hand, means that variations in *nominal* quantities of government-issued fiat money have no real effects.

Patinkin (1956) called this ancient orthodoxy the *classical dichotomy*. Nominal variables have nominal effects. They do not alter real quantities. They may change the general price level but they do not affect relative prices. They may alter nominal interest rates but not real rates. The quantity theory of money asserts that variations of money stocks are wholly absorbed in nominal prices. This is what happens when government expenditures are financed by issuing money rather than by taxes. The nominal interest rate on base money is fixed, usually at zero. The public is induced to hold the new money by the price increases that raise the nominal values of income, wealth, and transactions. The conclusion is that only the real size, nature, and distributional impacts of government activities affect the behaviors of economic agents and real outcomes. Debt neutrality takes this conclusion further, excluding the timing of taxes from policies of real consequence.

A quantity-theory proposition stressed by Friedman (1970), for example, is that the consequences of increasing the money stock are the same no matter how it is increased. Printing money to finance deficits has the same effect as printing money to buy back government debt obligations. Critics objected that deficit financing increases private wealth, and therefore private demand for goods and services, more than open market operations of equivalent size. The reason is that in the latter case wealth-owners sell assets to acquire money. But if government bonds are not net wealth, the two ways of increasing money stock are identical in effect, as Friedman asserted.

Wealth effects on real consumption and other demands for goods and services have played an important role in macroeconomic theory. They are the source of the real balance effect, resulting from deviations of price levels from expectations [Pigou (1943, 1947), Patinkin (1948)]. These deviations alter the real values of nominal assets—and debts. Private assets exceed private debts to the extent that government debts do not give rise in private calculations to future tax obligations. Ricardian equivalence confines the real balance effect to monetized government debt. Perhaps it obliterates the effect altogether. Wealth-owners may not regard an increase in their holdings of government money as net wealth if they expect it to be eroded by future inflation. Seignorage in modern times is not literally the sovereign's take from coinage. The government can finance part of its budget by meeting the growth in public demands for its fiat money. These demands grow faster the higher the inflation rate, and the higher the economy's real growth. Seignorage is a kind of tax, alternative to explicit taxation.

The real balance effect came into macroeconomics as an answer to Keynes's contention that the market economy lacked an effective mechanism for restoring full employment, once a demand shock had jarred it out of equilibrium. Keynes challenged neoclassical economists' reliance on nominal price adjustments, on the neoclassical ground that real demand should be independent of nominal prices. In particular, Keynes said workers were incapable of lowering real wages by lowering nominal wages, although lower real wages were essential to remedy unemployment. Latter-day skepticism of the real balance effect strengthens Keynes's challenge. Today's new classical macroeconomists finesse the problem of equilibrating adjustment by assuming continuous equilibrium, to which nominal price developments are irrelevant.

The co-existence of monetary and non-monetary government debt continues to be a source of problems and puzzles in macroeconomic theory. Price changes affect the values of both the same way. Currency always bears zero interest; obligations to pay currency in future pay a variable market-determined rate. How come they differ in yields? The answer is that money provides implicit yields, services in kind, that make up for its lack of explicit return. These non-pecuniary yields, and therefore the explicit yield advantages of debt instruments, depend inversely on the real quantity of money. Recognition of this relationship and of its macroeconomic importance is one of Keynes's major contributions to monetary theory.

The fixed nominal interest on money has another major implication. Neutrality with respect to nominal price levels does not imply neutrality with respect to temporal changes in prices. Those changes—inflations and deflations—alter the real rate of return on money, and possibly on other nominal assets and debts as well. Variations in real interest rates are real events and are likely to have real effects. Since money and other assets are substitutes, albeit imperfect, variations in real rates on money will be transmitted to other assets, nominal and real, at least in the short run. This effect, often bearing the name of Mundell (1963b) or Tobin (1965a), will be discussed in Section 5 below. Models that somehow deny these effects are termed "superneutral."

2 Government Finance in Traditional Macroeconomics

2.1 The IS/LM Framework

Although Keynes eloquently stressed the heretical implications of his *General Theory* (1936) for fiscal and monetary policies, he did not actually model them explicitly. Hicks' (1937) algebraic formulation of the Keynesian model proved to be a fruitful and durable framework for macroeconomic policy analysis. Generations of students learned the "IS/LM" calculus of aggregate demand, and it is still the tool of instinctive first recourse of many macroeconomists. Indeed, it is still the basic framework of macroeconometric models, large and elaborate as they have become because of disaggregations and lags.

Fiscal policy shifts the IS curve, monetary policy the LM curve. What could be simpler? The behavioral and structural parameters on which the effects of the policies on aggregate demand depend are easily discerned: the impotence of monetary policy in the liquidity trap (flat LM) or in the event both investment I and saving S are insensitive to interest rates (vertical IS); the impotence of fiscal policy if money demand is insensitive to interest rates (vertical LM) or if investment or saving or both are perfectly interest-elastic (flat IS); and all the cases in between. The analysis can be extended to derive aggregate real demand as a function of price level, allowing for the effects of prices on real supplies of money and wealth, and this "AD" function can confront an aggregate supply "AS" relation between the same variables.

As was Hicks' original intention, the same apparatus can show the effects of financial policies in the "classical" world of market-sustained full employment. Indeed, IS/LM graphs generally look qualitatively the same when the horizontal axis denotes price level, p, rather than real output, Y. The effects of inflation expectations—Mundell–Tobin effects—can be shown very simply, given the approximation that IS involves the real interest rate but LM the nominal rate.

Early in its life the Hicksian model was extended to open economies [Fleming (1962), Mundell (1963a)] and to the analysis of macro policies with and without international capital mobility and under fixed and floating exchange regimes.

Policy analysis with the framework was not confined to shifts in policy-determined variables; the policy-makers could be modeled as following rules, and the rules built in to IS and LM relations themselves. Welfare judgments among alternative rules would depend on the stochastic environment, for example, as in Poole's classic paper (1970) on the variances and covariances of real demand shocks and financial shocks.

2.2 Fiscal Multiplier Theory

Keynesian analysis of fiscal policy began with the "multiplier," invented by Kahn (1931) to formalize and quantify the instinctive beliefs of Keynes and others that deficit spending for public works during the Depression would create not only direct jobs but also indirect jobs, probably much more numerous. At the same time, the analysis showed why the chain of spending and job creation was not endless, why the multiplier was finite. Kahn's discovery paved the way for the *General Theory* itself, which could not have been written without the consumption function. Although the original idea of the multiplier referred to increases in government purchases, it was later realized that the same logic applies to private expenditures induced by tax reductions or transfer payments.

The explicit implications of multiplier theory for fiscal policy were developed in the late 1930s and the 1940s, largely by Alvin Hansen and his followers, mainly young colleagues and students at Harvard [Hansen (1941)]. Hansen (1953) was also an exponent of the IS/LM framework. As he realized, the multiplier tells the amount of horizontal shift of the IS curve resulting from a fiscal stimulus or other real demand shock, but this is not the end of the story. In any case, fiscal multiplier theory yielded some important elaborations and clarifications:

(1) Government budgets are partly endogenous. Congresses or parliaments enact tax codes, but the revenues they realize depend on their tax bases, and these vary with the state of the economy. The same is true of some budget outlays, notably entitlements to transfers like unemployment compensation, welfare, and farm subsidies. Legislation specifies rules for determining eligibilities and amounts, but the outlays then are open-ended and depend on the economy.

(2) In consequence, budget deficits are partly endogenous. In practice, they are, for given tax and entitlement codes and given expenditure programs, inversely related to economic activity, i.e. to national product. It is important to distinguish these endogenous variations in deficits (or sur-

pluses) from those arising from exogenous policy changes in the codes and programs. The former have no multiplier consequences; they are already built into the multiplier and into the IS curve. The latter are multiplicands; they do have the consequences described by the multiplier and by shifts of IS. The distinction is the reason for calculating cyclically corrected budget deficits from year to year, eliminating endogenous cyclical variations and isolating programmatic changes. Deficit measures calculated for this purpose have, over a history that goes back to the late 1940s, been dubbed "full employment," or "high employment," or "structural."

(3) Taxes and transfers, as well as earned factor incomes, affect consumption spending. A common assumption has been that consumption and saving both depend positively on after-tax, "disposable" incomes. This implies, given the procyclicality of taxes minus transfers, that the multiplier is smaller the larger are the parameters that link tax liabilities positively, and transfer entitlements negatively, to income. A small multiplier limits fluctuations caused by non-policy shocks, and for that reason the elements of fiscal structure that lead to a small multiplier are called "built-in stabilizers." The same stabilizing structure makes deficits *more* sensitive to macroeconomic conditions.

(4) Not all structural budget changes of equivalent dollar amount have the same effects on aggregate demand. One reason is that they differ as to "multiplicand." For example, part of a lump-sum tax cut or transfer increase will be saved, so that the multiplicand per dollar will be less than a dollar; in contrast, a dollar government purchase of goods and services increases aggregate demand for national product by a dollar even if no indirect multiplier effects occur. This distinction is the source of the celebrated "balanced-budget multiplier theorem," which says that a fully tax-financed one-dollar increase in government *purchases* raises aggregate demand by one dollar.

2.3 Cumulative Effects of Deficits

Keynes stated explicitly that his model applied to a short run in which the flow of investment determined by its solution alters negligibly the stock of capital. Indeed, that is his definition of "short run." The IS/LM version has this same limitation. It is necessary because changes in the stock of capital would alter the investment function, perhaps also the saving function and other behavioral relationships, and therefore alter also the equilibrium solution. The same is true of other stocks and flows. Saving accumulates wealth. Government budget deficits add to the stock of public debt. Current deficits on international accounts diminish the nation's net foreign claims.

IS/LM analysis usually ignores these stock-flow identities. Strictly speaking, fiscal multipliers apply to the effects of larger or smaller values of policy instruments, expenditures or tax rates, at an instant of time. No matter how large the deficit, a flow, it cannot change the stock of debt in zero time. Thus, the IS/LM snapshot cannot answer questions about alternative means of financing continuing deficits.

Of course, the LM relation, unlike IS, is equality of demand and supply of a stock, the stock of money. The snapshot model allows this stock to vary, presumably by open market exchanges for other assets, notably government securities. These exchanges, however, take no time and involve no saving or dissaving, although they may alter the value of those assets and of total wealth. Note that the IS/LM model contains a consumption/saving function describing the rate at which the public desires to accumulate wealth. But it contains no function telling in what forms, monetary and non-monetary, the public wishes to accumulate it. The money-demand function tells how, given pre-existing asset stocks as altered by instantaneous open market operations, the public chooses to divide its wealth between money and other assets.

These properties of the short-run Keynesian model were well understood by its architects. But in the 1960s and 1970s a number of critics "discovered" what they called the government budget "restraint" (surely a misnomer) or "constraint," and accused standard short-run macroeconomics of erroneously ignoring it or even violating it [Christ (1968), Currie (1978)]. What they meant but mislabeled is simply the budget flow identity: outlays equal tax revenues plus security issues plus new money creation. No error is involved in confining the analysis to a short enough time period so that the resulting stock changes do not matter. The question is, however, whether the comparative-static solutions of such a snapshot model with respect to policy variations are misleading. In particular, the standard model says that, except for extreme shapes of IS and/or LM, pure fiscal stimulus, i.e. 100 percent bond-financed increases of expenditures or reductions of taxes, raises aggregate demand. The critics said that this conclusion might be reversed as the time period is extended and the deficits raise the stocks of securities relative to those of money. Some econometric equations showed fiscal multipliers dying out and even reversing sign with the passage of time [Anderson and Carlson (1970), Modigliani and Ando (1976)].

It is hard to see how this reversal would occur in an under-employed economy with constant real money supply if the two-asset framework of the IS/LM model is maintained. In that framework, government debt securities and capital are perfect substitutes in portfolios, each bearing "the" real rate of interest, and the portfolio choice between that composite asset and money depends on income, wealth, and the nominal interest rate, as in the money-demand function. Could upward shifts of LM due to the rising stock of government securities, i.e. to rising private wealth, more than offset the upward IS shift and consign the economy to a higher interest rate at lower income? Both of those outcomes would diminish the demand for money. Only an increase in wealth could do the reverse. A decline in income would diminish the demand for wealth; only the rise in real interest could do the reverse. It could achieve the reversal only if it induced portfolio managers to hold more wealth not only in the assets whose yields had increased but also in the other one, money. So the story apparently depends on an unlikely combination of effects.

This technical issue—the permanence or transience of positive effects of pure fiscal stimulus on aggregate demand—inspired formal dynamic analysis. Blinder and Solow (1974) showed how the economy would gravitate to an equilibrium of budget balance: incomes would rise until they generated enough revenue flow to offset the continuing fiscal stimulus, inclusive of the rising debt interest outlays. Tobin and Buiter (1976) obtained essentially the same result, with more elaborate modeling of the effects of wealth and capital stock on saving and investment and of the dynamics and stability conditions of the model.

The upshot of these papers is to maintain over the longer run the conclusion of short-run analysis: pure fiscal policy is expansionary unless the interest elasticity of money demand is zero. However, the endogeneity of interest rates makes budget outlays for debt service endogenous also. Just as in short-run IS/LM analysis there can be perverse comparative statics—expansionary policies cannot balance the budget except at lower output and interest rates. Just as in short-run analysis, these equilibria are unstable. A surprising conclusion is that the long-run multiplier for fiscal stimulus may well be higher if deficits are not monetized than if they are. The equilibrium interest rate is lower if they are monetized, and it takes less income to raise enough revenues to balance the budget.

These scenarios are meant to extend the calculus of aggregate demand to situations in which stocks are allowed to vary endogenously with the passage of time. To focus on the direction and magnitude of stock effects, the authors assume that output is demand-determined. The scenarios cannot be taken as realistic simulations, because supply limitations and price movements will intervene.

Tobin and Buiter also analyze the full employment case where prices are flexible. Output is supply-determined but varies with the capital stock. The comparative statics of balanced-budget equilibrium says that fiscal stimulus is expansionary and *lowers* interest rates, because it takes more income and thus more capital to generate the necessary revenues. The stability of the equilibrium requires that price expectations adapt fairly quickly to price experience. As the authors noted at the time, the long-run comparative statics of models of this type do not depend on counting government debt as net wealth. The budget-balance condition does the trick. Although these papers assume stationary labor force and productivity, they could be formulated as growth models, where the natural counterpart of budget balance is growth of debt (in real terms) at the economy's natural growth rate. Possibly more serious matters are the assumptions that all non-monetary assets are perfect substitutes, that saving and wealth demand are interest-inelastic, and that stochastic disturbances are absent.

2.4 Dynamics of Deficits and Debt

Some fifty years ago Roy Harrod in England and Evsey Domar in the United States independently originated modern macroeconomic growth dynamics. Domar (1944) applied his model to the growth of public debt. He saw the importance of comparing the debt interest rate (net of taxes paid on such interest) and the growth rate of output and income. Specifically, assume that enough taxes are levied to pay debt interest but not to pay for all other expenditures. The debt will grow. Will tax rates have to be raised without limit? Yes, if and only if the after-tax interest rate on the government's debt obligations exceeds the growth rate. The insight is important in interpreting the Ricardian Equivalence Theorem. In a growing economy, the "government budget constraint" that rational taxpayers will internalize is not that the public debt cannot grow, not even that it cannot grow indefinitely, but that it cannot grow forever faster than the economy itself.

Thus, interest on the outstanding debt differs significantly from other items in the budget. Interest outlays depend on the size of the debt accumulated in the past, on interest rates, on the degree of monetization, and on the composition of the interest-bearing debt by maturities and other characteristics of securities. Like taxes and transfers, interest expenses are, given prior fiscal history, largely endogenous. However, they do not depend directly on economic activity, but on interest rates as determined by the interactions of the economy, the financial markets, and monetary policy. Legislators have even less control over interest outlays in the short run than over tax revenues and entitlement transfers.

The *nominal* deficit, in dollars per year, is at any moment the rate $\dot{D}$ at which the nominal debt D is growing. Let X be the nominal *primary* deficit, the excess at that moment of the rate per year of expenditures, i.e. purchases and transfers, over the rate of accrual of tax revenues, excluding interest outlays from transfers and excluding tax liabilities on such interest from revenues. The primary deficit is what the deficit would be, other things equal, if there were no outstanding debt. Let i be the average nominal interest rate, after taxes, on non-monetary debt, and let H be the nominal amount of monetary debt, the monetary base. Then the deficit is:

$$\dot{D} = X + i(D - H). \tag{2.1}$$

This is the deficit as conventionally calculated and debated.

However, there are good economic reasons to prefer other measures. A *real* deficit would convert D, H, and X to real quantities, "deflating" them by a price index, p.

Still another measure would charge as the cost of debt service the real interest rate rather than the nominal rate. Let the real after-tax interest on the non-monetary debt be r, equal to $i - \pi$, where π is the rate of inflation. The real inflation-corrected deficit is:

$$\frac{\partial}{\partial t}(D/p) = \dot{D}/p - \pi D/p = X/p + rD/p - (r + \pi)H/p. \tag{2.2}$$

The logic of this concept is "inflation accounting." The government's primary budget is geared to real programs, which cost more dollars when prices are higher; if the tax law is indexed, either formally or by periodic legislative adjustment, real tax revenues are neutral with respect to prices. The deficit is government dissaving, its claim on the nation's private saving in this sense: the amount of investment and other non-governmental claims on private saving that the government either crowds out (when aggregate supply limits output) or makes unnecessary for the maintenance of aggregate demand (when supply is not a constraint).

Private savers are presumably interested in real wealth and real streams of present and future consumption. If so, they will save extra in dollars to offset depreciation by inflation of their net real holdings of nominal assets, including government debt. They will understand that part of their nominal interest receipts is return of principal rather than income. Eisner (1985) has shown how conventional accounting overstated deficits in inflationary years of the 1970s; inflation accounting converts those deficits into real surpluses. However, saving behavior may not be inflation-neutral in the short run, even if savers eventually adapt.

The logic of inflation accounting can be pushed a step further to allow for real growth of output and income as well as inflation. Suppose that savers are interested in maintaining the ratio of their wealth to their income. Let d, h, and x be the ratios of D, H, and X, respectively, to nominal income pY. Let the growth rate of real income Y be g. Then the growth in the debt/income ratio d is:

$$\frac{\partial}{\partial t}(D/pY) = \dot{d} = \dot{D}/pY - (D/pY)(\pi + g) = x + (r - g)d - (r + \pi)h.$$

(2.3)

The first two terms by themselves say that unless the primary deficit is negative, the debt will grow faster than national income if the net real interest rate on the debt exceeds the growth rate of the economy. The last term is equivalent to a reduction of the primary deficit. It is the seignorage "income" of the government, the interest savings due to its power to print interest-free money. To the extent that this term is augmented by inflation, it represents the "inflation tax." In the United States h is small relative to d, of the order of 10–12 percent. Seignorage on base money is small at low or moderate rates of inflation, but there may be other ways in which inflation collects real tax revenue.

According to equation (2.3), the steady-state value of the ratio is:

$$d^* = (x - (r + \pi)h)/(g - r). \tag{2.4}$$

Equation (2.3) itself says that the ratio d will be increasing if the primary deficit x less the seignorage term $(r + \pi)h$ is non-negative and the real interest rate r exceeds the growth rate g. Indeed,

$$\dot{d} = (d - d^*)(r - g). \tag{2.5}$$

The steady-state debt/GNP ratio will be unstable, ceteris paribus, if and only if the interest rate on government debt exceeds the growth rate of the economy. A positive d^*, implying positive steady-state deficits, is compatible with $r - g > 0$ provided the primary deficit less seignorage is negative, but any initial deviation from d^* will be magnified.

Crowding out of capital accumulation (in open economies of net claims on the rest of the world as well as domestic capital) is the social cost of deficit finance that does not create its own saving. Suppose that the central bank's monetary policy keeps the economy at full employment with a constant inflation rate. Having no reason to expect future tax increases, consumers buy government debt issues with funds that otherwise would have financed domestic (and foreign) investment. The deficits finance private and public consumption. In a stable scenario $(r < g)$ the shift from one steady state to another produces a slow and undramatic reduction in capital and consumption per capita. In an unstable scenario, developments are more spectacular and frightening. To the dynamic of equation (2.5) is added another destabilizing feedback—as capital becomes more and more scarce and its marginal productivity rises, the debt interest rate rises too. Eventually the deficit absorbs all private saving, investment ceases, the capital stock gradually wears out, and equity values plummet. The story [Tobin (1986a)] is meant not as a forecast but as a cautionary tale.

2.5 *Multi-asset Models*

Macroeconomic models, both theoretical and empirical, are aggregative in several dimensions: over agents, time periods, commodities, markets, and assets. Index number problems, essentially insoluble, abound. Mostly we ignore them and try to muddle through. In monetary and financial economics, aggregation of assets is especially problematical. Some theoretical monetary models actually contain only one store of value, "money," thus managing to confuse the theory of money with the theory of saving. Consider the "islands" parables supporting the "Lucas supply curve," in which intertemporal consumption and leisure choices also determine demands for money. Some other models allow only two assets, base money and capital. As observed above, these models can illuminate some points, but their asset menu allows no distinction between fiscal and monetary policies.

The standard IS/LM model distinguishes two assets, money and everything else. The constituents of the second category, capital and nonmonetary government obligations, are taken to be perfect substitutes, all bearing essentially the same market interest rate. Because of money's use in transactions and its other characteristics, the other assets are not perfect substitutes for money, whose fixed (usually zero) nominal yield is generally smaller than the yield of alternative holdings. As noted above, this model does allow for distinct treatment of monetary and fiscal policies and shocks.

Nevertheless, it has several shortcomings. Equities in real capital and obligations to pay fixed amounts of money are affected differently by various shocks to inflation, productivity, taxes, and other variables. They are portfolio substitutes, but by no means perfect. Their sources of supply are quite different. A three-asset menu—capital, base money, and government non-monetary debt—allows both monetary and fiscal policies to be more faithfully modeled. Open market operations between money and Treasury obligations, which may be bills maturing tomorrow or next week, are not the same as operations in equity or capital goods markets.

The three-asset model sheds light on the problem of Subsection 2.3. What happens when the stock of non-monetary debt is increased relative to the stocks of base money and capital, as the result of a period of bond-financed deficit spending? In particular, what happens to the rate of return wealth-owners require in order to hold the existing capital stock? If this rate goes down—that is, the prices of equities go up—the increase in stock of government debt is favorable to capital investment and to aggregate demand. If the rate goes up, the growth in debt is contractionary. The answer depends, speaking loosely, on whether money and debt are better substitutes than capital and debt. If so, the outcome is expansionary; if not, contractionary [Tobin (1961, 1963)].

Since government debts are futures contracts in government currency, they might be expected to be close substitutes for currency. This is especially true of Treasury bills maturing tomorrow, next week, or next month. By bank reserve requirements and other legal differentiae, governments seek to reduce the substitutability of money and short bills. Long-term government bonds, while connected to short-term obligations by a chain of maturity substitutions, also share many of the sources of risk of ownership of capital or private equities and bonds. It takes more than a three-asset model to handle the complexities of the situation. Tobin (1963) distinguishes long and short debts and considers the effects of debt management, i.e. variations in the maturity structure of non-monetary government debt.

B. Friedman (1977, 1978) has investigated both theoretically and empirically the basic issue: whether, as he puts it, debt accumulation "crowds in" or "crowds out" private capital formation. His conclusion is that the substitution elasticities are such that debt crowds *in*. This must be understood as a demand-side effect, which will prevail only if unemployed resources are available and the central bank does not contract the money stock.

Multi-asset models can be extended to "inside" assets and debts (deposits and other intermediary liabilities, and private loans and securities). In the process, the money markets and reserve requirements through which central bank operations affect banks, financial markets, and the economy can be explicitly shown.

Banks and other financial intermediaries hold, involuntarily and voluntarily, a considerable amount of public debt, monetary and nonmonetary. This enables their depositors, the indirect owners of that debt, to hold more convenient and more liquid assets than the debt itself. A much more important macroeconomic function of financial intermediaries is to monetize or to make more liquid the ownership of private debts, the obligations of businesses, entrepreneurs, home-owners, and consumers. Their investments are financed at lower rates and on easier terms than if they had to be financed directly by conservative savers, who accept intermediary liabilities as close substitutes for government money and securities.

A short-run macro model should be regarded as referring to a slice of time or a finite period, with inputs from the past, modified by the solutions of the model in the present, passed on as data for the immediate future. At each time demands for additional amounts of all the assets are equated to the new supplies. New supplies of equities come from capital investment; new supplies of government bonds and base money, in proportions determined by monetary policy, come from the government deficit; new supplies of foreign-currency assets come from net exports. Rates of return, and output and/or prices as well, adjust to induce wealth-owners to absorb these additional supplies in their portfolios. The sums, both of demands and of supplies, equal the additions to wealth. Equations for inside assets and debts can be added; their net new supplies are zero. The non-government sector can be disaggregated, for example into households, non-financial businesses, various financial intermediaries, and the rest of the world. The model is the natural framework for giving life to the Flow of Funds statistics (published in the United States by the Federal Reserve).

The standard short-run comparative statics experiments can be run. For the most part, the qualitative conclusions of IS/LM stand up, but other questions can be asked and answered. Likewise the model's long-run, steady-state properties can be investigated. For details see Tobin (1982) and B. Friedman (1980).

3 "Microfoundations" and Parables

In the last twenty years the traditional macroeconomics of government finance has come under heavy theoretical and empirical fire, especially within the profession. The attackers begin with the strong prior belief that strictly financial policies and institutions cannot have real consequences. Some entertain the hypothesis that even the government's real purchases and activities make no difference, because they simply displace private purchases and activities for which they are perfect substitutes. Otherwise, the government can alter real outcomes by doing real things, including the incentives and disincentives of its taxes, subsidies, and transfers. Given these characteristics, the real economy will be the same whether government outlays are financed by taxing or by borrowing or by printing money.

The philosophy underlying this approach is that government financial policy can do nothing that individuals could not have done on their own. There is no role for government as an intermediary between parties who could not have interacted otherwise; or as a creator of missing markets; or as a risk-pooler across agents subject to different sources of uncertainty; or as an agent with superior information utilizing this advantage to influence the economy in beneficial ways or simply conveying this information to others. Indeed, in most models aspects such as these are regarded as unnecessary complications or as arbitrary frictions. In subsequent sections we review this literature and its critics, both theoretical contributions and empirical findings.

Many contemporary theorists adhere to classical propositions more loyally than their original proponents: money is a veil, which may confuse unwary and myopic observers but does not affect the reality behind. Competitive markets work for the best, allocating resources among alternative uses, among different households and agents, among present and future times, and among possible contingent states of nature. Financial variables, nominal magnitudes, do not enter anyone's utility functions, resource constraints, or production technologies. Government financial interventions in markets can be undone by private agents, and optimizing agents surely will undo any real consequences. The neutrality of real outcomes with respect to nominal and financial disturbances and policies is the central message. The burden of proof, in the contemporary intellectual climate, is on those who would question these renascent classical propositions.

This trend is one facet of the New Classical Macroeconomics, which assumes continuous market-clearing and rational expectations; denies the existence of Keynesian unemployment; denies both the efficacy of and the need for policies of demand stabilization; and explains business fluctuations as optimal intertemporal substitutions in production and consumption.

Much recent literature expounds, tests, and criticizes the newly popular neutrality propositions. By and large, the exponents and the critics share the same methodologies. These involve models with explicit "microfoundations"; that is, they base economy-wide general equilibrium results on the optimizing behaviors of agents interacting in specified markets. However, critics also incorporate institutional constraints, missing markets, market imperfections, informational asymmetries, and externalities. The neutrality of money, the irrelevance of government finance, the ineffectiveness of macro policies, and the optimality of market outcomes are propositions that flow easily from and only from models that approximate or mimic Arrow–Debreu general equilibrium specifications. In these models, commodities are defined not just by their physical characteristics but by the times and contingencies of their deliveries. The microfoundations, the deep parameters, are the preferences of individuals, their endowments of commodities, and the technologies that transform commodity inputs into outputs. When government activities and policies are introduced, the question is whether any of these "deep" parameters are altered. If not, if, in particular, agents' opportunity sets remain the same, the conclusion is that the interventions under study make no real difference. Otherwise, the interventions matter. Many papers, some of which we review below, are variations on this theme.

The common methodology makes this literature, even more than most economic theory, a collection, indeed a battle, of parables. These fables are quite abstract and economically primitive. Each is designed to fit some "stylized" facts, particularly qualitative generalizations from macroeconomic time series. Each is intended to have a *moral* relevant to some realistic institutional observation of the world. The methodology limits the scope and realism of the parables; it is very difficult to draw any "big picture" inferences from this literature.

Walrasian and Arrow–Debreu models, in their full generality, yield important theorems concerning the existence and optimality of competitive market-clearing equilibria. They are silent on the comparative-static effects of exogenous shocks and interventions on individual and aggregate outcomes, even on the signs of those effects. The permissible scope of tastes, endowments, and technologies, especially of their heterogeneity among agents, is too great. Yet those effects are the central agenda of macroeconomics, which has always relied on simplifications and specializations of general equilibrium theory.

How can short cuts be made while adhering to microfoundations methodology? One way is to model the whole economy as a single "representative agent," a Robinson Crusoe. Then society's economic choices are those of a single optimizer, whose tastes and opportunity sets are just microcosmic versions of those of the whole society. It is easy to derive the basic propositions of the "Modigliani–Miller" theorem for government—neutrality, irrelevance, ineffectiveness—from models of this kind. It is hard to see why Robinson Crusoe has a government, or why that projection of himself has different objectives from those of private citizen Crusoe.

The "representative agent" model has other implausible implications: there are plenty of markets and market prices, but no transactions take place. There are, in particular, zero "inside" assets and debts. The problems of coordination emphasized by Keynes and other macroeconomists—between investors and savers, borrowers and lenders, capitalists and workers—are finessed. However, recent literature begins to recognize the shortcomings of this approach and to introduce two or more kinds of agents: rich and poor, liquidity-constrained and liquidity-unconstrained, even-period and odd-period bank customers.

The most usual differentiation among agents in current models is by birth date. The overlapping generations model with two-period lifetimes is heavily used, itself a parable with many instructive morals. Everyone is essentially the same, but in each period old and young coexist and trade. Government has a potential role as an immortal institution somehow embodying a compact among the generations. In contrast, a single representative agent model must make Crusoe himself ageless and immortal if it is to handle the intertemporal allocations—saving and capital accumulation—now properly regarded as central to macroeconomics.

On these allocations there is in principle a big difference between agents with finite horizons (because of mortality, generational selfishness, illiquidity, and/or myopia) and agents with infinite horizons (because of immortality, generational altruism, liquidity, and/or foresight). For the issues of theory and policy at stake, this difference is crucial. Infinite-horizon agents in steady states will typically accumulate wealth to the point at which assets yield returns equal to the agents' constant marginal rates of intertemporal substitution in consumption. Their demand for wealth will be infinitely elastic with respect to asset yields. Finite-horizon agents, on the other hand, will have finite demands for wealth at any rate of return; their savings may or may not respond positively to asset returns, but they will not respond infinitely. The rate of interest is determined by "thrift" *and* (marginal) "productivity" in the finite-horizon case, but by thrift alone in the infinite-horizon case.

One important issue to which the distinction is relevant is that of "superneutrality" in an economy with fiat money. Fiat currency has no intrinsic utility in consumption or production. And—this is crucial—its own yield is exogenously constant, usually zero. A dollar greenback today is a dollar tomorrow and tomorrow. Imagine that the stocks of fiat money and of promises to pay fiat money in future, and indeed the values of all predetermined and exogenous present and future nominal variables, are known. Suppose that all those values are scaled up or down in a common proportion. *Neutrality* means that no real variables—quantities or relative prices or interest rates—are different, while all nominal prices are scaled up or down in that same proportion. The common sense of this conclusion is that no one cares whether the unit of account is a dollar or a dime, and the contrived mental experiment is equivalent to a units change. The theoretical sense is simply that quantities of fiat money and other nominal variables do not enter anyone's utility or production functions.

Superneutrality, on the other hand, relates to a different experiment. All the nominal quantities are scaled up or down, not by a common factor but in proportion to their distance in time from the present, i.e. by $\exp(\pi t)$. It is not obvious that the paths of real variables are invariant to π, which can be identified with the rate of inflation. Such invariance is necessary and sufficient for *superneutrality*. But it certainly cannot be deduced simply from the absence of money illusion, the common sense of *neutrality*. Clearly, at least one real, relative price is immediately altered by the experiment; the real rate of interest on fiat money depends inversely on π. This alteration is bound to have repercussions throughout the system.

Superneutrality is usually defined, most precisely in relation to Solow-type aggregate growth models, as invariance of paths of capital stock and consumption with respect to monetary growth and price inflation. This invariance can arise from infinite elasticities of desired wealth with respect to yields on saving, as described above [Sidrauski (1967)]. Independently of how much capital they accumulate, these consumers will hold quantities of money, in real purchasing power, such that its real return too equals their constant supply-price of saving. The real return on money has two parts, the negative of the inflation rate and the implicit service return of money as means of payment; the latter depends inversely on the size of average real balances held. In Tobin (1965a, 1968, 1982), however, consumer-savers have finite horizons and finite demands for wealth, money and capital compete for room in their portfolios, and higher inflation increases the relative attractiveness of capital. This "Tobin effect" tends to raise capital stock and consumption. Against it is the resource cost (sometimes called "shoeleather cost") of handling transactions with smaller real cash balances, which tends to reduce real incomes, consumption, and desired wealth [see Tobin (1986b)].

4 Financing Deficits with Non-monetary Debt

This section addresses the question of whether a shift from tax finance to bond[2] finance of given real government expenditures on goods and services with unchanged monetary policy absorbs any private saving. If it does not, "debt neutrality" prevails, i.e. investment, aggregate demand, realized income, employment, real interest rates, inflation, and the long-run capital intensity of the economy are not influenced by the choice between tax- and debt-financing. After a brief discussion of crowding out and of the interest sensitivity of saving, we investigate the theoretical conditions for debt neutrality. Then we present the implications of relaxing each of these conditions. We conclude with a review of available empirical tests of the debt neutrality proposition.

4.1 Crowding Out and the Interest Elasticity of Saving

A bond-financed decrease in taxation may lead to "crowding out" of two kinds: lower investment expenditure *flows*; and a lower desired ratio of the capital *stock* to real GNP in a long-run steady state. There are two main sources of stock and flow crowding out: supply constraints and monetary constraints. In standard discussions, these cause interest rates to rise, thus lowering both investment expenditure and the desired capital stock. For a given tax cut, the extent of crowding out would be smaller, the larger the interest-sensitivity of desired private saving and of the desired wealth-to-income ratio.[3] These are, of course, standard results in traditional IS/LM and growth models.

A recently popular framework for exhibiting interest sensitivity is the two-period life-cycle model in which a representative agent chooses consumption in each period so as to maximize his utility $U(C_1, C_2)$ subject to the constraint that the present discounted value of lifetime consumption is equal to the labor income received in the first period.[4] In this model, saving responds positively (negatively) to the interest rate if the elasticity of substitution between present and future consumption is greater than (less than) one. For a "Cobb–Douglas" utility function, the elasticity of substitution is unity and saving is interest insensitive. The convenience of the Cobb–Douglas specification, the dependence of the sign of response on the choice of utility function, and the failure of a significant number of empirical studies to identify interest-rate effects on desired saving, have created a presumption in favor of postulating interest insensitivity.

The validity of this postulate has been challenged by Boskin (1978) and Summers (1981, 1982). Summers argues that the choice of a Cobb–Douglas utility function does not allow the marginal propensity to consume to depend on after-tax interest rates, and that the use of a two-period model in which all income is received in the first period obscures the negative effects of increases in interest rates on the present discounted value of lifetime labor income, human wealth. He incorporates both effects by considering a multi-period life-cycle model with an additively separable, constant-elasticity-of-substitution utility function and the constraint that the present value of lifetime consumption equal the sum of assets and of human wealth. Summers reports simulations showing that consumption responds more negatively to the rate of return when the elasticity of substitution is greater. Permanent changes in the after-tax interest rate reduce consumption by more or increase it by less than do transitory changes.

Among empirical studies, Boskin's estimate of an interest elasticity of U.S. saving of 0.4 is widely regarded as too high, and has been criticized by Howrey and Hymans (1978) as being sensitive to the choice of sample period and to arbitrary details of data construction. Summers criticizes statistical estimates of consumption functions for using current disposable income as a proxy for human wealth, for errors in measuring interest rates and expected inflation, and for simultaneity bias. His own estimates, based on first-order conditions of an agent's intertemporal optimization problem, also suggest that the elasticity is quite high. These estimates are derived from an optimization model, and the overidentifying restrictions imposed by the first-order condition are often rejected by the data. Whether the interest elasticity of saving is positive is still an open question, especially in view of the stylized fact of a trendless U.S. wealth-to-GNP ratio over long periods of time despite the upward trend in real rates.

Whether desired saving and wealth-to-income ratios are interest sensitive or not, life-cycle models do not imply infinite interest elasticities. When they are amended to incorporate people's concern for their descendants by allowing the size of bequests to enter the utility function, they still do not imply infinite planning horizons, in contrast to the alternative assumption that the utilities of descendants are what matters. The importance of bequests [as documented, for example, by Kotlikoff and Summers (1981), and Mirer (1979)], is not necessarily inconsistent with crowding out. The choice of how to incorporate the bequest motive is a matter of empirical plausibility.

4.2 The Theory of Debt Neutrality and the Optimum Debt Level

4.2.1 Debt Neutrality

In 1974 Robert Barro presented the case for debt neutrality. According to this doctrine, also known as the "Ricardian neutrality" or "Ricardian equivalence" or "tax discounting" hypothesis, a bond-financed tax decrease does not affect agents' consumption demand, despite its effect on contemporaneous disposable income. When the economy is in a short-run, full-employment equilibrium, debt finance affects neither the path of prices nor that of interest rates. Finally, capital intensity in a long-run steady state is similarly unaffected. Clearly, one of the strongest implications of this doctrine is that bond-financed tax decreases and the associated deficits do not lead to any crowding out of private capital formation. Similar conclusions apply to variations of social security taxes, which transfer income between the young and the old.

A striking insight of the theory is that finite lives do not necessarily imply finite planning horizons: if the utility of every generation enters that of its predecessor, every agent incorporates the utility and budget constraints of the whole dynasty of successors into the decision concerning consumption and bequest levels.

A second key element in standard formulations of the theory is the assumption that government will not be able to service the debt by issuing more bonds forever, and that it will, therefore, eventually have to raise taxes. When this is so, it is inappropriate to analyze the effects of the bond-financed tax cuts without considering the implications of the associated future tax liabilities.[5] According to Barro, taxpayers will not alter consumption in response to changes in tax law because they regard them merely as changes in the timing of present and future tax liabilities of unaltered total present value.

While both issues will be dealt with extensively below, it is instructive to include a few comments on the latter one here. Practical macroeconomists and macroeconometricians have long factored into their policy analyses and forecasts consumers' and investors' anticipations of tax changes actually scheduled or under serious political and legislative consideration. An implication of life-cycle or permanent income theories of consumption is that current consumption will respond less to tax changes consumers regard as temporary than to those they regard as permanent. Financial market variables also have been used as indicators of expectations. If crowding out is expected to occur through higher interest rates in future, long-term rates should stand above short rates in the present. If deficits are expected to lead to inflation in future, this too should increase nominal longer-term interest rates.

"Ricardian equivalence" raises two interrelated questions. One is what constraint the government actually is under, or will behave as if it is under. The second is what private taxpayers and other agents believe to be the constraints and policies of the government. What degree of rationality must individuals possess in order to know not only how the economy works under given government policies, but also how policy decisions of the entire sequence of future governments are arrived at? In the absence of any schedule for increasing taxes and in a political and ideological climate against taxation, would a citizen of the United States in the 1980s rationally expect future fiscal corrections?

The first question is easier to tackle analytically. Suppose that the interest rate exceeds the economy's growth rate. Then, if a limitless increase in the public debt relative to national product is to be ruled out, the present value of future tax revenues—discounting by the difference between interest and growth rates—must exceed the similarly discounted present value of expenditures by the amount of the current debt. This can be shown through recursive substitutions into the single-period government budget identity, and it is usually termed the "intertemporal government budget constraint." Although this constraint is incorporated in all standard discussions of debt neutrality, it is also possible for the real after-tax interest rate on bonds to be lower than the rate of growth of real GNP. In this case, the debt-to-GNP ratio is stable and the government can continuously issue new bonds to finance interest payments without ever having to increase taxes.

The argument usually employed in support of debt neutrality is that the condition for a stable steady-state debt-to-GNP ratio conflicts with the Phelps "golden rule" condition for dynamic efficiency. According to that condition, an economy with $g > R$ is overcapitalized in the sense that disinvestment could make consumption per capita higher in at least one year without lowering it in any year.

However, the efficiency condition refers to the net marginal productivity of capital, R. There are two respects in which R is not the same as r, the net interest rate on government debt. One is that the relevant marginal contribution of capital to social product is pre-tax, while the cost of debt service is after-tax. Since the Treasury cannot in fact rely on lump-sum taxes, the after-tax rate is lower. The second is that the marginal product of capital exceeds the interest rate on government debt by a risk premium. In the United States safe debt interest rates have generally been below the economy's growth rate, while mean returns on capital have been above. This is indicated by the fact that gross profits, RK, chronically exceed gross investment, gK [Abel et al. (1986)]. It is, therefore, possible to meet the debt stability condition without violating the dynamic efficiency condition for the economy. However, Ricardian Equivalence depends on the debt interest rate's exceeding the growth rate, and on the public's believing correctly that the government will not allow the ratio of its debt to the economy's output and income to increase without limit.

We now turn to the debt neutrality theorem. Tobin (1980) listed the restrictive conditions necessary for it to hold. A complete set of such conditions is the following:

First, agents are either immortal or, if finitely lived, linked by an unbroken infinite dynastic chain of intergenerational gifts and bequests. This condition is needed for agents to have infinite planning horizons and to be able and willing to undo any government financial policy that would redistribute real income intertemporally.

Second, capital markets are perfect, without liquidity constraints or credit rationing. Thus, private agents can lend and borrow on the same terms as the government, which has no role to play as a financial intermediary.

Third, all taxes, transfers, and subsidies are lump sum. This ensures that their effects on present and future agents are independent of agents' behavior. Hence agents can neutralize them only by compensating changes in their own intergenerational transfers.

Fourth, debt servicing through issuing more debt forever, is infeasible. Future tax increases, equal in present value to today's tax cuts, are required. Therefore, given rational expectations, these increases are foreseen by all living agents. This condition has been discussed above.

Formal proofs of the debt neutrality proposition usually employ an overlapping generations model where the utility of each generation is a function of its own consumptions in the two periods of its life, as well as of the maximum attainable utility level of the subsequent generation (and possibly of the immediately preceding one). It is shown that the effect of a bond-financed tax cut on the budget constraints of each generation can be offset by an appropriate change in voluntary intergenerational transfers. Thus, the maximum attainable utility levels of all generations are unaffected by the deficit, and optimal consumption levels do not change.

The intuitive reason for bond neutrality is that under the set of conditions presented above, the introduction of government bonds does not provide agents with opportunities they did not have under tax financing of government spending. Government bonds are simply a means whereby the current generation can undertake expenditure for which future generations will have to pay through increased taxes. If the optimal sizes of bequests both prior to and after the deficit are interior, then the current generation already had the option of transferring wealth from subsequent generations to itself by reducing the size of its bequest, but did not choose to do so. A similar logic applies to intergenerational gifts, and to retirement of outstanding debt by new taxes.

4.2.2 Tax Smoothing and Optimal Debt
Suppose now that all the conditions necessary for debt neutrality do hold. If the choice between bond- and tax-financing does not entail any

of the usually assumed costs (such as shifting the burden of the debt on to future generations and crowding out capital), then what determines the optimal path of government debt for a given path of government expenditures?

In his 1979 paper, Barro considers an economy in which debt neutrality holds, the paths of government spending and of real GNP are given, and (consistent with debt neutrality) the real rate of return on bonds relative to that on private debt is not affected by the amount of government debt outstanding. He assumes that perpetual bond finance is not possible. For a given initial bond stock and present value of government spending, the intertemporal government budget constraint determines the present value of tax revenues. The optimal type and timing of taxation remain to be determined with reference to their social costs.

Having ruled out most of the traditionally assumed costs through the postulate of debt neutrality, Barro postulates costs associated with the collection of government revenues. These costs are assumed to be a function of contemporaneous tax revenue and tax base. Abstracting from the choice of tax composition, the optimal timing of taxes is that which minimizes the present value of the tax collection costs for the present value of taxes dictated by the intertemporal government budget constraint. The solution can be shown to imply a constant (planned) average tax rate. This constancy, along with the given present value of taxes, determines the optimal level of tax revenues at each point in time, and accordingly the path of the government's bonded debt.

Barro shows that if the perceived duration of transitory changes in government spending and in income is constant, a temporary increase in government expenditure should have a positive (but less than one-for-one) effect on the current rate of growth of debt; whereas a temporary increase in the rate of growth of real income should have a negative effect. The debt-to-income ratio would be expected to remain constant on average, but would rise in periods of abnormally low income or high government spending. Expected inflation raises the growth rate of nominal debt by an amount equal to the inflation rate, because the optimal level of taxes is the same as under zero expected inflation, the real rate on bonds is assumed to be unaffected by changes in expected inflation, and the increase in nominal interest payments has to be financed through bonds.

4.3 The Conditions for Debt Neutrality

We now investigate how dependent debt neutrality is on its assumptions by relaxing them one by one.

4.3.1 Infinite Horizons and Intergenerational Transfers

Blanchard (1985) relaxes the assumption of infinitely-lived dynasties. He assumes that each agent is faced with a probability p of dying, constant through the agent's life. Here an agent can be interpreted either as an individual or as a dynasty with probability p of dying out.[6] Insurance markets costlessly eliminate the risk of leaving unanticipated bequests. Agents contract to pay their whole wealth, w, to the insurance company when they die in exchange for receiving pw in every period of life. Negative bequests are prohibited.

Agents are assumed to maximize expected utility of consumption over an infinite horizon with uncertainty only as to the time of death. When the instantaneous utility function is isoelastic,[7] aggregate consumption is a linear function of the sum of aggregate human and non-human wealth. Human wealth is defined as the present value of future after-tax labor income accruing to those currently alive. Under the simplest distributional assumption, that after-tax labor income is equal for all agents at all times, and given the constant probability of death, all agents have the same human wealth. Assume that the number of people who die at each instant is equal to the size of the new cohort born at that instant, so that population is constant. Then[8] aggregate human wealth accumulates at a rate equal to $(r+p)$. The intuitive reason for this key result is that agents discount income available tomorrow relative to income available today not only by the rate of return they could earn on it if it were available today, but also by the probability that they will not be alive so as to receive it.

Now consider a decrease in lump-sum taxes today, accompanied by an increase in taxes of equal present value T periods from now. This present value is calculated using interest rates r faced by the immortal government. Thus, the reallocation of taxes raises human wealth, as calculated by private agents, by an amount equal to the current tax cut times the probability that someone currently alive will have died by the time the future tax increase takes place. The longer taxes are deferred, the larger the effect on human wealth. Given that aggregate consumption is a function of human plus non-human wealth, this reallocation of taxes raises consumption. Debt neutrality fails.

One interpretation of this paper is that debt neutrality fails when agents have finite horizons, since the expected lifetime of an agent at each point in time is $1/p$. As p goes to zero, neutrality is approached as a limiting case. An alternative interpretation is that agents represent dynasties with infinite horizons but with a probability that they end because of exogenous events. It is also possible, however, that the chain of intergenerational transfers is broken because some members decide against further transfers.[9]

Drazen (1978) shows that a key element in determining whether dynasty members decide to break the chain or not is the weight their utility functions attach to the utility of other generations. Consider a utility function for generation i, $U_i = U_i(c_i^1, c_i^2, U_{i+1}^*)$, where c_i^1 and c_i^2 are real consumption levels of generation i in each of its periods of life and U_{i+1}^* is the maximum attainable utility of the next generation. Assume that utility functions do not differ between generations and that real wage income is constant. If bequests are invested at the time they are put aside by the parent, the extra utility that a parent receives from one dollar of consumption when old is exceeded by the utility of his descendant from consumption of $1 + r$ dollars of bequest. If the father weighs the descendant's utility equally to his (i.e. if $\partial U_i / \partial U_{i+1}^* = 1$), then bequests will be positive. If he discounts his descendant's utility by a rate equal to (larger than) the market rate of interest, optimal bequests will be zero (negative). If negative bequests (i.e. indebting your children for your own current consumption) are not allowed, agents will be at a corner solution of zero bequests, and the issue of government bonds will have real effects by allowing agents to shift the burden of their current spending to future generations.[10]

Finally, concern about both parents and descendants can be formalized by postulating that $U_i = U_i(U_{i-1}^*, c_i^1, c_i^2, U_{i+1}^*)$. Then a bequest that raises the descendant's utility also raises the utility of the father. But in doing so, it raises the utility of the descendant further. For bequests not to lead to infinite utility, at least one generation must discount the utility of the other. If a generation weighs the utility of both adjacent generations sufficiently less than its own, then neither the gift nor the bequest motives will be operative and the introduction of government bonds will have real effects.[11]

Inoperative intergenerational links may exist for other reasons, for example that neither all members of a given generation nor all members of the same dynasty across generations are equal in natural endowments. Laitner (1979) postulates that there is an entire distribution of labor incomes in each generation. He assumes, somewhat artificially, that there is no correlation between the labor income of a family at a point in time and the incomes of its descendants. He then shows that a bond-financed tax cut that is repaid through tax increases T periods from now can affect consumption. This is because the government can always pick a finite T so large that some descendants within $0 < t < T$ have zero bequests with positive probability. Similarly, if the government makes transfers to and later levies taxes on all families (or a random cross-section of them), consumption will rise in a positive percentage of cases even with one-period bonds. This is because some families in each generation (or some generations of the same dynasty) cannot afford to leave bequests.

Not only is the ability of all future dynasty members to leave bequests uncertain, but also one's own ability to do so may not be foreseen at the beginning of one's career. Feldstein (1988) introduces uncertainty as to income in the second half of a parent's working life. Despite the presence of lump-sum taxes and the assumption that bequests are solely motivated by intergenerational altruism, current consumption rises as a result of debt finance (including the introduction of an unfunded social security system). The logic is that if the parent were sure that he would not leave a bequest, any increase in current disposable income arising from a tax cut would be divided between the two periods of his life. Since zero-bequest circumstances have positive probability, the parent will raise his current consumption to some extent. Even when the parent, blessed with good luck late in life, actually makes a bequest, the consumption of the second generation is reduced as a result of the tax cut the parent earlier enjoyed.

Although many of the papers on debt neutrality emphasize intergenerational transfers, most of them do not do full justice to human reproductive biology. Notable exceptions are two papers by Bernheim and Bagwell (1988) and Abel and Bernheim (1986). Bernheim and Bagwell (1988) demonstrate that in a properly specified dynastic framework, where everybody is "altruistic" towards members of the same dynasty and where the size of bequests per se is not a source of utility, redistributions of wealth leave everybody's consumption and resource allocation unaffected, prices play no role in resource allocation, and apparently distortionary taxes do not induce any change in individual behavior. Since these implications of the dynastic framework seem completely unrealistic, Bernheim and Bagwell argue that this framework should not be trusted for policy analyses. Debt neutrality is attacked through a *reductio ad absurdum*.

Specifically, Bernheim and Bagwell point out that when two individuals belonging to different families marry and have children, concern for common grandchildren links their two original families. The fact that these grandchildren also get married and have children means that more families of the current generation are linked by their common concern for those distant descendants, etc. Once it is established that two families of the same generation are linked, we can extend the chain further by moving up or down the family tree. Moreover, dynasties will typically be linked through multiple channels. Everybody is a part of every dynasty.

The authors assume that in each period t there is a chain of operative linkages connecting any two living individuals, where each link consists of a transfer made sometime between periods t and $t + T$, with T an integer. They show that for each sufficiently small perturbation of deficit and tax policies, there exists an equilibrium in which factor prices, labor supplies, consumption, and purchases of physical capital are unaffected by the perturbation. The perturbation simply leads to offsetting private transfers and bond purchases. This is true not only for government financial perturbations, but for *all* exogenous shocks, for example in the natural endowments of different agents. These results survive the introduction of various types of uncertainty and informational asymmetries.

Can a dynastic framework with frictions generate plausible conclusions? Abel and Bernheim (1986) introduce frictions such as (a) the derivation of pleasure directly from the act of giving; (b) the existence of both selfish and altruistic parents combined with incomplete information about others' preferences; and (c) social norms dictating that parents should divide transfers equally among all their children. Their overall conclusion is that frictions tend to make redistributional policies non-neutral, but they lead to paradoxes of other kinds.

As an example, consider case (c). Suppose that no parent is selfish; that the size of transfers is not a direct source of utility; and that parent i receives a transfer. In response to it, he raises his transfers to both his children by the same amount. Now consider the two sets of parents of the spouses of those children. They observe that one of their children is better off and, as a result, increase their consumption and lower their transfer. Because of the social norm, however, this reduction of transfers applies to their other children as well. In turn, the families of the spouses of those other children raise their transfers, etc.

Thus, although exact Ricardian equivalence with respect to policies that affect children equally is maintained here, redistributional policies that affect children differentially are not neutralized by the parents due to egalitarian constraints. It would seem that the Berhneim–Bagwell paradox has been resolved and the Barro theorem rescued from the reductio ad absurdum. The disturbing feature of this setup, however, is that an exogenous increase in the wealth of any given individual is never Pareto improving, i.e. always makes some people worse off. In view of this paradoxical implication, and of similar implications for other frictions, Abel and Bernheim conclude that such frictions cannot provide Ricardian equivalence with a plausible theoretical foundation.

Gifts and bequests can be viewed not only as manifestations of altruism but also as assets transferring consumption from one period of life to the other. Buiter (1979, 1980) and Carmichael (1982) suggest that, under certain conditions, government bonds are perfect substitutes for gifts and bequests in this role. For example, when gifts to parents are reduced, agents can increase their first-period consumption since they offer less to their parents, and lower their second-period consumption since they receive less from their children. Thus, a bond-financed tax cut that substitutes second- for first-period consumption may be neutralized through an appropriate general adjustment of gift and bequest levels for all generations. This result does not require that taxes be eventually raised to service the debt.[12]

4.3.2 Perfect Capital Markets?

A second condition for debt neutrality is that there are no capital market imperfections leading to credit rationing. There is now a substantial volume of research on the sources and implications of credit rationing, starting with the seminal paper of Weiss and Stiglitz (1981). As an example, suppose that because certain individuals have relatively bad collateral, they can only borrow at a rate r_H which is higher than that for others, r_L. As recognized by Barro (1974), when a government bond is bought by a low-discount-rate individual and the proceeds and taxes associated with it are both distributed in the same way among the two classes of individuals, the bond is in effect a loan from the low-discount-rate to the high-discount-rate individuals. The net wealth of the low-discount group is unaffected, but that of the other group rises since the rate r_H by which they discount the future tax liabilities is higher than the rate r_L by which those who hold the bonds discount the stream of coupon payments. Thus, one would expect the consumption of the high-discount group to go up in response to the increase in their net wealth.

This idea is imbedded in a formal model of credit rationing by Webb (1981). Webb argues that the government's ability to enforce tax repayments is superior to that of private lenders. There may be a higher default penalty for taxes than for private debts, and tax withholding ensures that the government receives payment before any other payments are made. The rate at which the government borrows and lends is therefore below that offered to individual borrowers in the private capital market. A substitution of government for private debt raises agents' net wealth due to this difference in interest rates. It may even be sufficiently large to bring the total volume of private debt below the critical level required to eliminate the occurrence of default in the private market. Debt neutrality fails.

The relative quantitative importance of finite horizons and of capital market imperfections is addressed in two recent papers. Poterba and Summers (1986) employ a life-cycle simulation model to consider the effects of debt-financed transfers of one dollar to each living person for K years. It is assumed that the debt is never repaid, but beginning in period $K + 1$, the government levies lump-sum taxes on working individuals to meet its interest payments and maintain a target real debt stock, aggregate or per capita. Simulations for a range of parameter values suggest that although deficit policies may transfer substantial tax burdens to future generations, they have only trivial short-run effects on consumption and saving. The intuitive reason is that for all but the oldest consumers, marginal propensities to consume out of wealth are quite small. This conclusion is only strengthened by considering realistic debt repayment periods. When the effects of current deficits are simulated on the basis of alternative scenarios for future deficits, even dramatic changes in deficit paths have only minor effects on consumption and saving.

These results suggest that in the absence of liquidity constraints and myopia, the distinction between overlapping generations and infinite-horizon models may be of little practical importance in evaluating short-run (but not necessarily long-run) effects of deficit policies.

Hubbard and Judd (1986a, 1986b) provide additional support for emphasizing liquidity constraints rather than finite horizons. In one illustration they consider agents with logarithmic utility functions and constant probabilities of death and of experiencing a wage increase from w_1, to w_2. With no capital market imperfections and for plausible parameter values, numerical simulations indicate that the marginal propensity to consume (MPC) out of a five-year tax cut financed with a twenty-year delay, during which time people die at a rate of 2 percent per year, would only be about 0.05. Finite horizons per se are not sufficient to generate sizeable effects on consumption. By contrast, the MPC is more than quadrupled when 20 percent of the work force are liquidity constrained and consume all their wages.[13]

4.3.3 Lump-Sum Taxation?

The third condition for debt neutrality is that taxes and transfers are lump-sum. It is well known that governments cannot typically rely on such taxes for the bulk of their revenues. It is thus appropriate to check the robustness of the theorem under distortionary taxation. When taxes are not lump-sum, the behavior of descendants can be adjusted so as to reduce the impact of tax increases, and this will be taken into account by the current generation experiencing the tax cut. Specifically, there is no reason for the parents to raise their bequest by the entire present value of future taxes implied by the current budget deficit. They will raise their consumption, knowing that their children will manage to reduce their future tax liabilities.

There has been some research on non-lump-sum taxes when the tax base is uncertain. When the increase in expected future taxes is combined with a current tax cut equal to its present value, the present value of total expected tax payments is unaffected. However, an increase in future income taxation reduces uncertainty surrounding disposable income.

When income taxes are levied on descendants of the current generation, this logic implies that there will be downward pressure on bequests and upward pressure on current consumption, to the extent that the size of bequests is influenced by the parents' internalization of risk faced by their descendants. In fact, simulations by Barsky, Mankiw and Zeldes (1986) show that for plausible parameter values, the marginal propensity to consume out of a current tax cut associated with uncertain future tax liabilities is in the neighborhood of values implied by neo-Keynesian models that ignore the future tax liabilities.

4.3.4 Limitless Debt?
All of the above conditions deal with whether a substitution of lower taxes and more bonds today for higher taxes in the future affects agents' opportunity sets. The question addressed in our introductory discussion of debt neutrality above was whether bond-financed tax cuts do in fact necessitate future tax increases. This was the subject of the early debate between Barro (1976) and Feldstein (1976), who focused on whether the real after-tax interest rate on bonds is higher or lower than the rate of growth of real GNP.

Some recent research on whether real consumption is affected by tax cuts which are never paid for through higher future taxes has been conducted in a game-theoretic framework. An example is the paper by O'Connell and Zeldes (1987) who take up a suggestion by Gale (1983). Gale interprets Barro's dynastic framework as a game played among successive generations. He shows that this game has a vast multiplicity of equilibria, leaving individual behavior indeterminate. O'Connell and Zeldes look at a refinement of this equilibrium set. They start with an overlapping generations model in which debt neutrality cannot be ruled out with respect to debt that is repaid through higher future taxes. They then ask whether current tax cuts would affect consumption if the government never increases taxes in the future. They find that the set of quasi-steady-state Nash equilibria (i.e. those involving unchanged consumption) is unaffected by this experiment. However, there also exist pairs of equilibria across which government financing produces real effects. The authors present an economy with bequests where debt neutrality fails. This is because under certain conditions dynasties behave as though they value terminal wealth, which in turn depends on the size of government debt. Per capita consumption rises, despite the fact that the set of equilibria is unaffected by financial policy.

4.4 Empirical Tests of Debt Neutrality

There are two main approaches to empirical testing of debt neutrality. One consists of structural estimates of consumption or savings functions or of financial sector behavior, and of tests for the statistical significance of taxes, transfers, government debt, and (sometimes) social security wealth. The other is to utilize the assumption of rational expectations to derive cross-equation restrictions and jointly test debt neutrality along with rational expectations and the assumed model of behavior.

4.4.1 Structural Estimation

The older approach is structural estimation. The main implications of the debt neutrality hypothesis for the consumption function are that: (i) for a given path of government purchases, variation of taxes has no effect, i.e. the coefficient on taxes in a consumption or saving function should be zero; (ii) since transfer payments are analogous to tax reductions, the same holds for the coefficient on transfers; (iii) since a change in the stock of bonds does not generate a wealth effect on consumption, its coefficient should also be zero;[14] and (iv) if a proxy for social security wealth is included, its coefficient should also be zero, since according to Barro, households will save enough to compensate future generations for the extra tax burdens required to pay higher social security benefits.

There are two main issues that differentiate papers in this strand. The first is the extent to which they test and correct for simultaneity bias resulting from possibly endogenous right-hand-side regressors, such as income, wealth, taxes, transfers, and social security wealth. The second concerns the proxies used for permanent income and the permanent (as opposed to transitory) levels of policy variables.

Early papers estimating consumption or savings functions without allowing for simultaneity bias include Barro (1978), Kochin (1974), and Tanner (1979), who all find support for debt neutrality. On the other hand, Buiter and Tobin (1978) reach the opposite conclusion.

Feldstein (1982) allows for endogeneity of tax revenues and of income by using the lagged value of taxes and of income as instruments. He uses current GNP and then current personal disposable income as proxies for the corresponding permanent levels of these variables. Results do not favor debt neutrality. Feldstein looks at U.S. data for 1930–77 with the war years 1941–46 omitted. When real per capita GNP is used in a regression with real per capita consumer expenditure as the dependent variable, the hypothesis that the coefficient on taxes is not negative can be rejected at approximately the 20 percent significance level, the coefficient on the debt variable does not support the irrelevance of debt, and that on transfers is significant and positive. However, the coefficient on social security wealth is smaller than its standard error. Results are more strongly against debt neutrality when personal disposable income per capita is used as a proxy for permanent income. Feldstein also finds an insignificant coefficient on the government purchases variable suggesting that government spending does not directly crowd out private consumption by providing a substitute for it.

In a recent paper, Seater and Mariano (1985) estimate specifications similar to those of Barro (1978) and Feldstein (1982) by two-stage least squares with first-order serial correlation correction, in an attempt to remove simultaneity bias. They argue that Feldstein's use of only lagged taxes and income as instruments may not be sufficient, as these instruments may still be correlated with the error due to the high degree of serial correlation in the series for income and taxes. They use a variety of instrument sets and for each one they apply Hausman tests to determine which right-hand-side variables are endogenous. They then perform the second-stage regressions using fitted values for these variables which did not pass the Hausman test. Although the endogeneity of regressors is sensitive to the choice of instrument set, the conclusions from the second-stage regressions are fairly robust. For Barro's specification, they find support for tax discounting. When using Feldstein's specification, both taxes and transfers become significant for the periods 1931–40/1947–74, questioning tax discounting. However, in a specification which includes unemployment, taxes become insignificant while transfers remain significant.

In the main body of their paper, Seater and Mariano follow Barro (1983) in specifying consumption as a function of: (i) permanent income; (ii) the cost of government represented by its "permanent" real expenditure on goods and services G^p; (iii) current real government expenditure on goods and services G to capture the possibility that increases in G for given G^p partially substitute for private consumption; and (iv) real after-tax interest rates since they induce intertemporal substitution. They estimate permanent income and permanent government expenditure only from these series' own histories. The regressions they run include separately four "financing" variables, namely real tax collections, real transfers, the real market value of outstanding government debt, and social security wealth. The estimation technique is instrumental variables and the sample is 1929–75. The government financing variables, including transfers, are jointly and individually insignificant, in regressions both for total consumption and for consumption of non-durables.

Kormendi (1983) examines roughly the same period (1930–76) under the assumption that government consumption (defined as the portion of government spending that yields utility to the private sector in the current period) is substitutable for private consumption, in the limit perfectly. This is yet another equivalence, challenging the effectiveness even of variations in government expenditure on goods and services. He derives a private consumption function based on this "consolidated approach." The counterpart of integrating private and government consumption is a "total disposable income" that includes the resource flow both from net private incomes and from taxes, since the latter effectively represent claims to government-provided goods and services. "Government" here means federal, state, and local government. Private consumption is a function of total real NNP, government consumption, wealth, and any discrepancy between the values of foregone private goods or services and those provided by government (which Kormendi calls "government dissipation"). By contrast, the standard permanent-income approach would make consumption a function of personal disposable income (defined as income net of taxes, corporate retained earnings, transfers, and government interest payments on its debt), but not of government consumption. Moreover, the market value of government bonds should not affect consumption under debt neutrality. Thus, Kormendi obtains a set of testable restrictions, similar to Feldstein's, to differentiate the two approaches.

In his estimation, Kormendi uses current and lagged NNP as proxies for permanent NNP. Looking at differenced U.S. data between 1930 and 1976, he finds support for the "consolidated approach," with a fairly high implied substitutability between government and private consumption. With regard to government bonds, Kormendi's results show that there is less than 5 percent probability that future taxes implied by government debt are less than 90 percent discounted. However, the coefficient on transfers is significantly positive, a result which Kormendi attributes to redistribution of income among classes with different spending propensities.

Kormendi's strong results have been challenged by Barth, Iden and Russek (1986), by Modigliani and Sterling (1986), and recently by Feldstein and Elmendorf (1987). The first paper updates Kormendi's sample through 1983, distinguishes between federal and state–local government debt, and also looks at more recent postwar periods. The results raise some doubts about the robustness of Kormendi's findings. Modigliani and Sterling show that when Kormendi's separate tax, transfer, and government interest variables are combined into a single "net tax" variable, the sum of its distributed lag coefficients is significantly negative in the consumer expenditure equations and is not significantly different from the sum of the lag coefficients on NNP. The government purchases coefficient is statistically insignificant. They also point out that Kormendi's specification does not allow for the relatively long lags required to approximate permanent income, and that his practice of running regressions in first differences is inconsistent with his own estimated auto-regressive coefficient, which is below unity.

Feldstein and Elmendorf argue that Kormendi's results are mainly due to the inclusion of the Second World War years. In that period, deficits were run to finance a massive increase in defense spending while rationing, patriotic appeals, and shortages were producing abnormally high saving rates. When they exclude these years, they obtain insignificant effects on private consumption of government purchases, along with significant negative effects of tax receipts.

No clear conclusions on debt neutrality emerge from the articles reporting structural estimations. Results seem quite sensitive to the choice of data, of variables to be included, and to estimation procedures. Kormendi's hypothesis that government purchases replace private consumption to significant degree remains a conjecture which requires further testing.

4.4.2 An Alternative to Structural Estimation
A second set of tests seeks to avoid structural estimation that is subject to misspecification bias. Aschauer (1985) defines effective consumption as

the sum of private consumption plus θ times government purchases of goods and services, where θ represents the number of units of private consumption required to yield the same utility as one unit of government goods and services. He shows that the first-order conditions for utility maximization[15] are (i) the intertemporal budget constraint and (ii) a condition involving consumption similar to the one estimated by Feldstein, but with the discounted values of future labor income and government purchases also entering the regression.

The procedure then is to combine this relationship with an assumed process for forecasting current government purchases and derive the cross-equation restrictions implied by the joint hypotheses of rational expectations, debt neutrality, the specific optimization model, and the postulated process for government spending. Aschauer estimates the system by FIML both with and without parameter constraints and carries out a likelihood-ratio test for the restrictions implied by the hypotheses. He finds that the restrictions cannot be rejected at the 10 percent significance level (or lower).

Plosser (1982) considers a model combining the efficient market hypothesis, a simple version of the expectations theory of the term structure,[16] and an assumed moving-average representation of policy variables to derive and test cross-equation restrictions. The first two assumptions ensure that the surprise in the holding return of an n-period bond bought at time t and sold at time $t+1$ as an $(n-1)$-period bond is negatively related to the unexpected movement in the current one-period rate, $(R_{1,t+1} - E_t R_{1,t+1})$, and to the revisions in the forecasts of future one-period rates, $(E_{t+1} R_{1,t+j} - E_t R_{1,t+j})$, $j = 2, \ldots, (n-1)$. He also assumes that the reduced form for the one-period interest rate includes government spending, government debt held by the public, and government debt held by the monetary authority. The vector of exogenous[17] variables, augmented by the error in R_1 which is orthogonal to the policy variable, is assumed to have a moving-average representation. Under those assumptions, the current surprise in holding period returns is a function of the contemporaneous innovations in the exogenous variables (including policy variables) which are orthogonal to the innovations in the other exogenous variables.

Plosser jointly estimates an assumed autoregressive scheme for policy variables with one form of the equation for the innovations in holding returns. The technique is to stack the two equations to form a single regression and estimate it using a non-linear GLS procedure. He uses 1954–78 quarterly U.S. data and finds that the effects of surprises in government financing on nominal rates of return are statistically insignificant, with point estimates of the "wrong" sign. Innovations in government spending, on the other hand, do have significant effects on interest rates. Plosser tentatively attributes those to intertemporal substitutions.[18]

Although this strand of literature provides an interesting alternative to structural estimation, it is also subject to the criticism that the processes assumed to be used by the public in forecasting may contaminate expectational variables with measurement error. This would bias the tests towards finding no impact of policy surprises, thus favoring debt neutrality.

4.4.3 Potential for Future Research
There is no clear conclusion emerging from the empirical research on debt neutrality. This is disturbing, though not very surprising. Bernheim (1987) points to some of the difficulties: picking the proper measure of debt or deficit; purging regressors of endogeneity by the choice of appropriate instruments; not allowing the limited significance of short-run effects to obscure the potentially considerable significance of long-run effects. Another problem is the distinction between the anticipated and unanticipated components of fiscal variables. Anticipated policy changes in a world without frictions would have little contemporaneous effect when actually implemented, but this does not mean the policies are irrelevant for individual behavior. To make things worse, current private behavior may be mainly a response to what current policy settings imply about future settings, specifically to the debt repayment horizon that taxpayers perceive as likely.

Econometric difficulties notwithstanding, one cannot ignore what must be the best "controlled experiment" for the hypothesis, namely the U.S. tax cuts of the early 1980s. Poterba and Summers (1986), among others, have drawn attention to the fact that private saving has declined while taxes have been cut and enormous chronic deficits have arisen. Their regressions show that when tax collections were reduced by legislation, consumption did increase, despite the fact that tax changes were anticipated.

These events have to be explained away before it can be claimed that there is strong empirical support for debt neutrality.

5 Financing Deficits with Money

This section deals with substitutions of money for tax financing. Every dollar of deficit is a dollar increase in the stock of high-powered money. If changes in the rate of monetary growth have no real effects, then money is said to be "superneutral," as in Section 3.

Usually, superneutrality refers to the invariance of the capital stock (or the capital–labor ratio), and of real per capita aggregate consumption with respect to changes in monetary growth. Effects on real (per capita) money holdings are not regarded as violating superneutrality. We present both models focusing on invariance of steady-state equilibrium values of real variables, and those investigating the transition path.

5.1 Superneutrality in the Steady State

Tobin (1965a) made a case against monetary superneutrality based on portfolio effects of changes in the rate of monetary growth. A higher rate of nominal money growth is associated with a higher rate of steady-state inflation. Since the nominal interest rate on money is constant, usually at zero, this higher inflation lowers the real rate of return on money and makes it less attractive to hold. When the asset demand for capital depends not only on its own real rate of return, but also on how this rate compares with that on the alternative available assets, higher inflation encourages a portfolio shift away from money and into capital. Thus, money is not superneutral. This is known as the "Tobin effect" or the "Mundell effect."[19]

Increases in inflation may favor capital accumulation, at the expense of real money balances. But they also increase the resources needed to effect any given volume of transactions. These "shoeleather costs," which were not explicitly recognized in Tobin (1965a), should be set against the gains from the portfolio effects in assessing consumption and welfare. Tobin (1986b) shows that there are cases in which it is optimal for the government to raise inflation so as to reap the benefits from increased capital and output, despite the resulting increase in "shoeleather costs".

The Tobin effect is what exponents of superneutrality question. They consider variations in deficits and in monetary growth arising from changes in the size of transfers or taxes for given government purchases of goods and services. Superneutrality is proved by showing that the equilibrium condition for the size of the capital stock in the steady state is unaffected by the changes in inflation associated with changes in money-financed deficits.

The classic defense of superneutrality is Sidrauski (1967). He considers a representative individual who maximizes the discounted sum of time-separable utility over an infinite horizon. Instantaneous utility is a function of real consumption and of the flow of services of money, assumed proportional to the real money stock. The agent chooses real consumption, as well as how to divide his saving between the two available assets, money and capital. Saving is the difference between income plus government transfers and consumption. Transfers are in money, in amounts unrelated to individuals' previous holdings. The government does not purchase goods and services, and it finances transfers through money creation at a constant rate. The population grows at a constant rate.

Sidrauski's main result is that the sizes of the long-run capital stock and of real consumption are independent of the rate of monetary growth. The reason is that an infinitely-lived agent will accumulate each asset up to the point where its net yield just compensates for the postponement of consumption. This point is where its marginal product equals the sum of the rate of time preference, the rate of population growth, and the rate of depreciation. The equilibrium condition is not affected by changes in the rate of inflation.

Of course, the opportunity cost of holding cash balances (in terms of foregone consumption) rises with inflation. Since the level of consumption remains unchanged, the increase in the marginal yield of cash balances necessary to re-establish equilibrium is brought about through a reduction in real money holdings. Thus, superneutrality does not extend to the per capita real money stock. Since utility is a positive function of both consumption and real money balances, monetary expansions that raise inflation lead to welfare losses.[20]

In view of the source of Sidrauski's superneutrality result, it is not surprising that superneutrality fails when real money balances affect the net marginal product of capital in terms of consumption. A simple setup is presented in Dornbusch and Frenkel (1973), where it is assumed that output available for consumption is a fraction of production (net of output used to meet capital needs arising from population growth). This fraction is in turn assumed to be increasing with real per capita money holdings. Instantaneous utility is a function only of consumption, and the agent maximizes the discounted sum of utilities over an infinite horizon. Although steady-state equilibrium again requires equality of the net marginal product of capital with the rate of time preference, the former now depends on the size of per capita money balances. The new steady state with higher inflation will generally involve both lower per capita money holdings and lower capital stock. This is the opposite of the Tobin effect.

In the same class of models, an earlier paper by Levhari and Patinkin (1968) explicitly incorporates the real money stock in the production function and shows that superneutrality fails. It also shows that when the Golden Rule holds, i.e. the net marginal product of capital equals the natural rate of population growth, it is in general possible to raise per capita output and hence welfare by lowering inflation (or increasing deflation) so as to induce greater real money holdings, even though the real rate of interest and net marginal product of capital are above the natural growth rate. It will generally not be optimal to increase the real money stock to the point where money holders are satiated, i.e. where the rate of deflation equals the net marginal product of capital. The welfare optimum will involve neither Phelps' Golden Rule capital stock nor Friedman's optimal quantity of money.

An alternative mechanism negating superneutrality in steady states is suggested by Brock (1974), who introduces a labor-leisure choice into Sidrauski's model. Since the additional first-order condition involves the marginal utilities of consumption and of leisure, it now becomes necessary for those two marginal utilities to be independent of money if the steady-state levels of capital, labor, and consumption are to be unaffected by changes in the rate of monetary growth. Brock shows that when money affects the marginal utility of leisure, money growth affects the labor supply curve and thus the steady-state stock of capital.[21]

A key feature of the Sidrauski model that allows it to exhibit superneutrality is the infinity of agents' horizons. Drazen (1981) shows that for a given individual who lives for two periods, both the substitution and the income effects on capital holdings of an increase in the return to money (lower inflation or higher deflation) are negative when consumption and money balances are normal goods. The negativity of the income effect can be explained as follows. An increase in the return to money arising from a reduction in inflation implies ceteris paribus higher income in the second period of life. Given the usual concavity conditions on utility, the agent will want to spread this increase over both periods. When consumption and real balances are "normal goods," this implies higher consumption and money balances in the first period. Since the usefulness of capital to the agent as an asset is only in transferring income from the first to the second period, a redistribution of income in the opposite direction can be accomplished by lowering capital holdings. This negative income effect, combined with the unambiguously negative substitution effect, produces a negative total effect of an increase in the return to money.

Now, in view of the government budget identity, a reduction in monetary growth and inflation is associated with a reduction in transfer income, a lower deficit. The overall effect on the demand for capital of a reduction in the rate of monetary expansion is the sum of the effect (just described) of the increase in the return to money and the effect of the reduction of transfers. If transfers are distributed in proportion to first-period money holdings, then this overall effect is zero. (The transfers amount to nominal interest on money and exactly offset the effect of inflation on the real return to holding money.) If transfers are heavily weighted towards the old, it is possible that deflationary policy would increase demand for capital. This is because the reduction in the transfer income of the old would more than offset the effect described in the previous paragraph, inducing people to hold more capital in order to shift income and consumption to the second period of their lives.

Thus, the Tobin effect is observed if this does not occur (e.g. when transfers are sufficiently weighted towards the young).[22] Under this condition, Drazen shows that the result generally extends to the economy-wide capital–labor ratio.

Haliassos (1987) shows that superneutrality is not an inescapable feature of infinite-horizon setups, but is due to the commonly used but unrealistic assumption that portfolio adjustments are simultaneous across different agents. When portfolio holding periods are staggered, each portfolio is held over a period of time during which real rates of return change. Even when these changes are deterministic, staggering can generate a determinate optimal composition of portfolios: assets become imperfect substitutes under perfect foresight. Holding period returns are still tied to the rate of time preference as in the Sidrauski model. But the variability of rates of return and of return differentials within each holding period can be influenced through policy. Changes in the rate of growth of nominally denominated assets affect inflation and the real rate of return of money. Since relative asset supplies are unchanged, the optimal composition of private portfolios is also invariant to the policy change. But interest income on the optimal portfolio is affected. If the same level of consumption out of portfolio income is to be maintained, real rates on non-monetary assets have to adjust. It is also shown that real wealth and real taxes net of transfers are affected by the policy change.

Siegel (1983) shows that superneutrality will also fail in general when labor-augmenting (Harrod-neutral) technological change is incorporated into the model.[23] This creates an asymmetry between the production function and, therefore, the budget constraint, which are stationary in efficiency units, and the utility function, which is stationary in per capita values. The first-order equilibrium condition for the marginal product of capital involves the rate of growth of real per capita consumption and money holdings. In the absence of technical progress, these terms are zero. However, when technological change is present, these rates of growth are positive: real consumption and money holdings are constant only per efficiency unit of labor, i.e. the scale of each economic unit increases at the rate of technical progress. The coefficients on those rates of growth are functions of the marginal utility of consumption and of its derivatives with respect to per capita consumption and money holdings. Superneutrality now requires that these coefficients be unaffected by changes in monetary growth. This will be true for utility functions which are separable in consumption and money holdings; and for non-separable functions which are isoelastic in an index of real per capita consumption and real money holdings, $c^\gamma m^\beta$, where the sum of the constants satisfies $\gamma + \beta < 1$.

5.2 *Superneutrality along the Transition Path*

We now turn to the issue of whether changes in the rate of nominal money growth are superneutral when the economy is outside its steady state, but moving towards it.

Fischer (1979) considers a model similar to Sidrauski's with perfect foresight. He examines the class of utility functions displaying constant relative risk aversion, of which logarithmic utility is a special case. The result is that although in such a model the steady-state value of the capital stock is invariant to changes in the rate of monetary expansion, such superneutrality does not prevail on the transition path to the steady state, except in the case of logarithmic utility.[24] Fischer shows that higher rates of nominal monetary growth are associated with higher rates of capital accumulation on the transition path. Moreover, as the capital stock approaches its steady-state value from below, a larger rate of monetary expansion implies lower consumption. Fischer does not provide an estimate of the quantitative significance of these effects.

Cohen (1985) suggests a rationale for Fischer's results, using a model that emphasizes the distinction between consumers and producers. Nominal rates of interest vary along the transition path due to two conflicting factors: the increase in inflation pushes them upwards, while the decrease in real rates pushes them downwards. When the intertemporal elasticity of substitution is unity, the two effects cancel each other out and monetary policy cannot affect nominal interest rates. However, when the intertemporal elasticity of substitution is below (above) unity, the nominal rates on the transition path are above (below) their steady-state values. In those cases, monetary policy affects capital accumulation by influencing the rate of growth (or decline) of nominal rates towards their steady-state value.

This effect on accumulation comes about because the specification of the instantaneous utility function[25] allows consumption and real money holding to be treated as a composite commodity, the "price" of which is an increasing function of the nominal interest rate. Now when monetary policy raises all nominal rates, it also affects the equilibrium sequence of the relative price of the composite good from one period to another (which is a function of nominal interest rates). Cohen shows that the effect on interest rates has no consequence for the amount of consumption in his model. However, the effect on intertemporal relative prices of the composite good is such that an increased rate of monetary growth lowers the demand for the consumption good (unless elasticity is unity), while leaving the supply unaffected. The resulting decrease in consumption allows faster capital accumulation to take place all along the transition path.

Asako (1983) shows that it is possible for a utility function with constant relative risk aversion (CRRA) other than the logarithmic to violate superneutrality on the transition path in a direction opposite from that suggested by Fischer. In particular, this is true of the CRRA utility functions with relative risk aversion exceeding unity when consumption and real money holdings are perfect complements, i.e. their desired ratio does not depend on economic conditions. In this case, the rate of capital accumulation is slower, the higher the rate of monetary expansion. Moreover, neither consumption nor the real money stock is affected by changes in money growth in the steady state. This superneutrality is even stronger than Sidrauski's, and it is due to the perfect complementarity of c and m.

5.3 Empirical Tests of Superneutrality

Superneutrality asserts invariance of capital stock and consumption with respect to inflation rates and monetary growth. These are propositions about long-run paths. Invariance of capital implies, even derives from, invariance in the real interest rates to which marginal productivity of capital is equal in equilibrium. These invariances are all very difficult to test. Consequently, empirical research on superneutrality has focused primarily on tests for the existence and stability over time of the famous hypothesis about interest rates put forward by Fisher (1930) [and modified by Darby (1975)]. The Fisher hypothesis is that a change in inflation will be fully reflected in an equal change in nominal interest rates, without affecting the real rate of interest. Darby's modification restates the hypothesis in terms of after-tax real and nominal interest rates. One strand of the modern literature focuses on tests for the presence of a Fisher effect, sometimes allowing for taxation. The other strand focuses on the stability of the response of nominal rates to inflationary expectations over time. Here we illustrate both.

5.3.1 The Presence of the Fisher Effect

Tests of the Fisher hypothesis up to the early 1970s typically involved regressing the nominal interest rate on a distributed lag of past inflation rates as a proxy for expected inflation, a constant intended to represent the invariant real rate, and an error assumed to be distributed independently of past, present, and future price levels. The extraordinarily long lags typically implied by the estimates were taken as evidence against the Fisher hypothesis (even by Fisher himself).[26]

Sargent (1973) was the first to utilize rational expectations in testing the Fisher hypothesis. Sargent argues that even when Fisher's theory is correct, the estimated lag functions do not necessarily represent optimal forecasts of inflation. He combines rational expectations with the natural rate hypothesis (NRH) embodied in the Lucas aggregate supply curve to construct a model in which the real rate of interest is independent of the expected part of the money supply. His test of the Fisherian hypothesis is simply to test this model. He does so indirectly by testing NRH, defined as the idea that unemployment is independent of the systematic part of the money supply.

Sargent proposes two tests of NRH. In the first, the unemployment rate is regressed on lagged unemployment rates and on other variables included in the information set in period $t - n - 1$, where n is the order of the autoregressive process followed by the unemployment disturbance. NRH implies that all those other variables are statistically insignificant, i.e. that the innovation in unemployment is not affected by past values of any variables, including policy variables. The alternative test proposed by Sargent involves estimating an equation for unemployment which incorporates not only lagged unemployment and the unexpected part of inflation, but also the expected part of inflation. The null (Fisherian) hypothesis is that the coefficient on expected inflation is zero, and it is tested against the alternative that it is not.

Although Sargent finds that the evidence on NRH (and hence on Fisher) is mixed, he points to the lack of an alternative model that would outperform NRH in tracking unemployment. Sargent feels that if an investigator has priors in favor of NRH, the evidence is not sufficient to reject them.

Fama (1975) suggests using a joint test of the hypotheses (i) that the expected real rate of return on Treasury bills is constant and (ii) that agents make optimal use of their information concerning inflation over the next month when setting the nominal interest rate today. The latter is a version of the efficient markets hypothesis (EMH).[27] If the hypotheses jointly hold, then it should not be possible to use any subset of information available as of $t - 1$ (e.g. the history of real rates) to come up with a better prediction of r than the constant $E(r)$. This in turn means that the autocorrelations for r are zero for all lags, and this can be tested by checking the sample autocorrelations for r.

A further set of tests can be obtained by generalizing the model of bill market equilibrium so that constancy of $E(r)$ becomes a special case. Specifically, if estimating the regression

$$\pi_t = \alpha_0 + \alpha_1 R_t + \varepsilon_t \tag{5.1}$$

yields coefficient estimates that are inconsistent with the hypothesis that $\alpha_0 = -E(r)$ and $\alpha_1 = 1$, the model of a constant $E(r)$ is rejected. Market efficiency can then be tested by checking whether ε_t is autocorrelated. If EMH holds, R_t summarizes all available information about $E(\pi_t|I_{t-1})$, including past values of the disturbance. These past values should be of no use in predicting π_t, which implies that ε_t should be serially uncorrelated. This logic can be generalized to any piece of information in $t-1$. An example is:

$$\pi_t = \alpha_0 + \alpha_1 R_t + \alpha_2 \pi_{t-1} + \varepsilon_t, \tag{5.2}$$

where EMH implies that α_2 is zero and ε_t is serially uncorrelated.

Although Fama's empirical results[28] did not reject his joint hypothesis, subsequent research has challenged their robustness. Nelson and Schwert (1977) argue that looking at the ex post real rate may generate an "errors in variables" problem, since it is possible for the autocorrelation function of the ex post real rate to be close to zero at all lags even if the ex ante real rate fluctuates considerably and is highly autocorrelated.[29] As for the test of whether $\alpha_2 = 0$ in (5.2), when the authors replace π_{t-1} with optimal predictors of inflation, which make use of more observations on past inflation and of the time series properties of the inflation rate, the coefficient on the optimal predictor is large and significant, putting EMH into question.

Garbade and Wachtel (1978) focus on equation (5.1), where the null hypothesis is that α_0 and α_1 are the same over three subperiods. They argue that the alternative specified by Fama, namely that the coefficients changed by a discrete amount from one subperiod to the next but remained constant within each subperiod, makes it quite unlikely that the null will be rejected in its favor. Instead they allow each coefficient to follow a random walk without drift. Fama's finding that α_1 is stable and equal to 1 cannot be rejected by their tests, either. The conclusion survives even when α_0 is assumed to depend linearly on time within each of six specified subintervals and the nature of this dependence is different for each one. However, when such piecewise-linear time-variation of α_0 is regarded as the alternative hypothesis, the null hypothesis of a constant real rate $-\alpha_0$ is rejected, irrespective of whether the constraint $\alpha_1 = 1$ is imposed or not.

The question whether nominal interest rates have adjusted sufficiently to compensate investors both for changes in (expected) inflation and for the effects of interest taxation is addressed by Tanzi (1980). Using data on six- and twelve-month Treasury bills, he ran the following regression over the 1952–75 period:

$$R_t = r_t + \beta E(\pi_t)/(1 - T_t), \tag{5.3}$$

where R is the lender's required rate, r is the after-tax rate he would have received if expected inflation were zero, $E(\pi_t)$ is expected inflation, and T is the tax rate on interest income. Tanzi rejects the hypothesis that $\beta = 1$. Since the estimate of β is below 1, he concludes that agents are not free of "fiscal illusion," and are not sufficiently compensated for the effects of changes in taxes on their nominal interest income.

While the Fisher hypothesis postulates constancy of the net marginal productivity of capital, most empirical papers use data on CPI-corrected returns on financial assets (i.e. nominally denominated interest-bearing claims such as Treasury bills). Carmichael and Stebbing (1983) point out that the poor results of existing tests may be partly due to a higher degree of substitutability at the margin between money and such financial assets than between financial assets and capital. One crucial fact about money is that its nominal rate of return is "regulated" (usually set equal to zero) and consequently changes in inflation change its real after-tax rate of return by the same amount. If nominally denominated assets are close substitutes for money, this one-to-one sensitivity to inflation should also be (approximately) true for their real after-tax rate, even if the marginal productivity of capital is fully governed by the rate of time preference and other parameters independent of inflation. This inverted Fisher hypothesis for financial assets is not rejected by data on three-month U.S. Treasury bills and by two Australian interest-rate series (short- and long-term).[30]

5.3.2 The Fisher Effect over Time

Tests of how the magnitude of the Fisher effect has behaved over time have mainly focused on two partitions of the available data sample. One is into the pre World War II and post World War II, while the other partitions the post World War II era into various subsamples. We briefly illustrate both.

Friedman and Schwartz (1976, 1982) and Summers (1983) have found essentially no evidence of the Fisher effect in the pre World War II period in either Britain or the United States. They have found much stronger correlations between short-term nominal interest rates and either ex post inflation or other proxies for expected inflation rates in the post World War II period (especially post-1960). This led Friedman and Schwartz to suggest that perhaps financial markets "learned their Fisher" only gradually.

The findings concerning the United States were recently challenged by Barsky (1987). He argues that the observed difference in the magnitude of the Fisher effect is not due to a shift in any structural relationship but to differences in the stochastic process generating inflation. While inflation was essentially a white-noise process before World War I, it became a non-stationary ARIMA process in the post-1960 period. Barsky shows that an underlying Fisher effect is consistent with any observed correlation between current nominal interest rates and actual inflation rates in the current (or next) time period. The reason is that the latter simply reflect the persistence of inflation.

In addition, Barsky raises doubts as to whether regressions of nominal interest rates on inflation are reliable in assessing whether real rates are affected by changes in expected inflation. A case in point is that of the gold standard years prior to 1913, which look the least Fisherian in regressions involving nominal interest rates [e.g. Summers (1983)], but do not exhibit negative correlation between ex ante real rates and past inflation.[31]

Barsky attempts to reconcile this discrepancy by the fact that inflation in those years was virtually white noise. As a result, the variance of anticipated inflation was substantially lower than the variance of actual inflation, and OLS regression would lead to the incorrect conclusion that nominal interest rates failed to respond to inflation. Summers tries to allow for this by "band filtering" the data, i.e. considering only low-frequency components which can be thought of as easily forecastable. The hope is that then expected inflation can be proxied by actual inflation. McCallum (1984b) accepts the substantive conclusions of the Summers study but points out that low-frequency estimation is affected by misspecification of the distinction between anticipated and unanticipated movements in the regressors.[32] Barsky shows that the covariance between anticipated and ex post inflation does not increase relative to the variance of inflation as the frequency is lowered. This suggests that band filtering in this case may not have resulted in a better proxy for expected inflation.[33]

Cargill and Meyer (1980) focus on the post World War II period and ask whether length of maturity is relevant for the existence and magnitude of the Fisher effect over time.[34] They run regressions of the form

$$R_t = \beta_0 + \beta_1 r_t + \beta_2 E(\pi_t) + u_t \tag{5.4}$$

over subperiods between 1954 and 1975. Coefficients on expected inflation, $E(\pi_t)$, are almost always positive and significant; they decline with increases in maturity. Many of the coefficients are close to or significantly above unity. However, estimates of β_2 vary significantly between subperiods. Estimates for some maturities decline quite substantially for the period 1970-75 relative to 1960-75.

6 Monetary Policies

The previous section discussed substitutions of money for tax financing of a given path of government expenditures and the effects of the corresponding changes in the rate of nominal money growth. In this section we discuss shifts between alternative modes of non-tax financing of government expenditure. In most setups, fiscal policy is taken as given. In a few, taxes are also varied so as to eliminate effects of asset market exchanges on agents' opportunity sets.

Some of the models reviewed focus on the common type of open market operations, namely exchanges of money for nominal bonds. Others, however, discuss exchanges of money for real capital or for indexed bonds. Even when the term "capital" simply refers to stored amounts of the consumption good, money-capital exchanges should be distinguished from temporary increases in government expenditure G financed through money creation. The asset swaps considered are associated with a *given G*. We first investigate the relevance or irrelevance of various asset exchanges for the real allocation of resources. We then discuss shifts between bond and money financing which are necessary when certain financing policies are unsustainable over the longer run.

6.1 Asset Exchanges
We start with models exhibiting neutrality of asset exchanges and then consider setups in which open market operations have been shown to be non-neutral.

6.1.1 Neutral Asset Exchanges
Wallace (1981) investigates whether there is a class of open-market exchanges between fiat money and "capital" (in the form of a stored consumption good) that would leave the equilibrium sequences for real consumption allocations and for the price level unaffected. He considers a two-period, pure-exchange, overlapping generations model with a single consumption good that is storable via a constant returns to scale, stochastic technology. Complete markets in contingent claims on second-period consumption are assumed. Open-market operations consist of purchases and costless storage by the government of the consumption good in exchange for fiat money.[35] Money is not dominated in return. The government sets the (possibly contingent) paths of government consumption, $G(t)$; of the endowment vector for each generation t, $w(t)$; of the path of government storage, $K^g(t)$; and of the nominal money supply path, $M(t)$. An equilibrium is described by a sequence of real consumption levels, prices of consumption claims, aggregate storage, prices of the good, and nominal money.

Wallace starts with an equilibrium for a policy $\{G(t), w(t), K^g(t) = 0\}$. He then identifies policies $\{G(t), \hat{w}(t), \hat{K}(t)\}$ which support the same equilibrium configuration (with the exception of the money sequence). The choice among them is irrelevant for the equilibrium outcome. While such policies leave the price path unaffected, they combine open market operations with changes in taxes net of transfers which "pay out" to agents any additional net interest income the government receives as a result of the change in its portfolio. This is necessary if private opportunity sets are to remain unaffected.[36] Wallace does point out that this analysis is probably most useful as a benchmark case for assessing the real effects of asset exchanges.

While Wallace's policies involve auxiliary fiscal changes, Chamley and Polemarchakis (1984) consider "pure" open market operations but alter the price process so as to pay out to private agents the altered returns on the government's portfolio. In addition, they do not assume the existence of a complete set of contingent markets. Suppose that the economy is in equilibrium when the quantity of money is fixed for all time periods and government holdings of capital are zero (along with government expenditures and taxes for simplicity). Then suppose that the government announces a new contingent sequence for its capital holdings. The authors show that this policy change has no effect on the time paths of the allocation of goods and of the aggregate capital stock, as long as money maintains a non-zero value in terms of the capital good.[37] Individuals reduce their capital and increase their money holdings in a way that maintains both the value of each agent's portfolio and the real return on it. Thus, any intertemporal program that was feasible for a private agent before the policy change is also feasible after it. Moreover, the portfolio response of agents is consistent with equilibrium in the markets for capital and for money.[38]

The result extends to economies with many assets, in which case only the prices of the assets involved in the exchange are affected by it. It fails when short sales are bounded below or not feasible, and when open market exchanges involve money and assets denominated in nominal terms. The reason for the latter is the effect on the returns of a nominally denominated asset induced by the change in the path of the price of money. This effect is such that the conditions which the prices of money and of bonds have to satisfy for neutrality are not satisfied for a general distribution of total nominal returns on the nominal asset.

Peled (1985) focuses on neutrality of open market exchanges of fiat money for indexed government bonds in the context of a single-good, pure-exchange, overlapping generations model. Random endowments generate stochastic bond price and aggregate price levels and inflation. However, indexed bonds promise a given amount of the perishable consumption good. Peled considers a given path of taxation. He shows that if one starts with a financing scheme that results in money being willingly held, then one can change the path of bond issues almost arbitrarily and still be able to find offsetting changes in the path of money creation that would leave the paths of real consumption, taxes, and the price of bonds unaffected.[39] These exchanges do not affect the value of the government portfolio. The assumed existence of intragenerational markets for money and bonds is crucial for the result.[40]

Until recently it was thought that irrelevance results could be obtained only in models where money is not dominated in return. Sargent and Smith (1987) show that such results can also be obtained in a class of models where money is dominated in real rate of return. In those models, money is dominated because some fraction of the population (the "poor") are assumed to be prevented by law from holding assets other than money. The "rich" can trade in all markets.[41] Specific assumptions about the distribution of income ensure that the poor cannot afford to hold any asset other than money. A byproduct of these assumptions is that the rich, who are not excluded from any market, will not hold money, but only stored goods and state-contingent claims to future consumption. In other respects, the overlapping generations setup is similar to that of Wallace (1981).

When open market exchanges of currency for "capital" (i.e. goods for storage) are undertaken, irrelevance with respect both to consumption and to the price system is ensured—as in Wallace—through lump-sum transfers or taxes which distribute the change in earnings on the government portfolio.[42] Sargent, Smith, and Wallace interpret the offsetting changes in taxes net of transfers, which are necessary for irrelevance in their models, as defining a "constant" fiscal policy. The difference here is that the rich are treated differently from the poor. Specifically, the poor must be induced to raise their saving to absorb the higher real stock of currency, while the rich must reduce their saving by the amount of capital purchased by the government. Irrelevance theorems when money is dominated due to legal restrictions seem to require that such restrictions be different across agents. For instance, if the original Wallace (1981) setup is augmented to include identical "reserve requirements" across all agents, money is dominated in return but irrelevance is not obtained.

Finally, Benninga and Protopapadakis (1984) adopt a specification for utility similar to that in Sidrauski (1967) in a two-period, Arrow–Debreu, state-preference economy with complete markets, heterogeneous consumers and firms, one good, and fixed labor supply. They ask whether shifts from one financing mode to another, holding the revenue raised through the third mode constant, would be "neutral". They are considered "strongly neutral" when both consumption and money holdings are unaffected.

A shift between bonds and taxes will be strongly neutral if it leaves the present value of taxes (including "inflation taxes") for each consumer unchanged, and if the interest rate is unchanged. The first condition ensures that each agent's budget constraint remains unaltered by the policy shift; the second guarantees that real money holdings will also be unaffected. This result is a direct extension of those on debt neutrality to models incorporating money and uncertainty. In order for an open market purchase to be weakly neutral, a decline in the inflation rate must occur, lowering nominal interest rates, inducing agents to hold a larger real stock of money, while keeping the cost of holding money constant and allowing the government to receive more revenue from issuing money. This holds for a restricted class of utility functions: separability of utility in consumption and money is a sufficient condition for weak neutrality.[43] Finally, a shift in financing between money and taxes is weakly neutral only if the government undertakes an elaborate scheme of adjusting each individual's taxes in a way that offsets the changes in the cost to each individual of holding money.

Interestingly, Benninga and Protopapadakis show that in their model, no economy can be invariant under both policy shifts between money and taxes and policy shifts between money and debt. The reason is that if the present value of taxes is changed, then the cost of holding money and the revenue from money creation must also change for neutrality to hold. However, under debt-money neutrality government revenue from money creation is fixed.

6.1.2 Non-neutral Asset Exchanges

We now turn to models exhibiting non-neutrality of open market asset exchanges. Grossman and Weiss (1983) consider a pure exchange, Clower-constraint model with two types of infinitely-lived consumers, firms, and banks. Consumers of each type visit the bank once every two periods to withdraw money directly deposited into their accounts, in order to finance their perfectly foreseen consumption over the two periods.[44] Consumers are assumed to be the only ones who hold money.

When there is an open market purchase, the addition to the money stock flows into the banks and has to be absorbed wholly by a subset of the population. This subset consists of the people who have exhausted previous money holdings and are there to make a withdrawal. Since money is only held for consumption purposes, agents are going to withdraw more only if they decide to consume more. Real and nominal interest rates have to drop in order to induce that group to decide to consume more. Moreover, price effects will only be gradual, since the members of this group will spend their increased holdings gradually until their next trip to the bank. Consumers of the other type cannot increase their nominal spending before their predetermined time comes to visit the bank. Thus, they respond to higher prices by reducing real consumption.[45]

A similar staggered-withdrawals setup is presented in Rotemberg (1984), except that his model incorporates capital, does not assume that output is constant, and postulates that money is withdrawn at the beginning of the period and is available for spending in the current and in the next period. The model is consistent with rate-of-return dominance of capital over money in the steady state. Rotemberg shows that there is no Tobin effect in his model, in the sense that the unique steady-state equilibrium size of the capital stock that involves positive consumption is independent of the rate of growth of the money stock. However, an increase in the rate of monetary growth, and hence in inflation, leads people to consume more right after they withdraw money; and less in the period in which they do not go to the bank and have to finance consumption with money withdrawn in the previous period. The extent of this distortion in the consumption path is partly determined by the assumption that the frequency of an agent's bank visits does not change with inflation.

Now consider an open market purchase of capital. If this had no effect on prices, consumption and hence withdrawals would also be unaffected: people at the bank would not want to hold the extra money made available to them. In fact, the price level has to rise. Rotemberg's numerical simulations of the unique non-explosive path show that the price increase results in a fall in consumption of those who do not visit the bank in that period, which raises capital, and hence output, in the following period, albeit by a small amount. How the magnitude of output response would be affected by allowing people to visit the bank more frequently in response to inflation is an open question.

Open market operations have also been shown to have real effects when portfolio adjustments are staggered, even when we abstract from the transactions role of money. Haliassos (1987) presents such a setup in which even under infinite horizons and perfect foresight, an open market operation affects the level and variability of the real rates of return on non-monetary assets as well as the level of real wealth. The reason is that the open market operation affects the optimal composition of private portfolios. If a given level of consumption out of portfolio income is to be maintained, real rates of return have to adjust. New rates of return on non-monetary assets absorb the brunt of adjustment, since the real rate on money is tied to the rate of growth of nominal government debt.

So far the models in this section postulate infinite horizons. Waldo (1985) constructs an overlapping generations, pure-exchange model in which the nominal and real interest rates fall and the price level rises less than proportionately to the money supply increase associated with an open market purchase. The measures of fiscal policy that are held constant are government spending and the total budget deficit, taking account of interest payments and inflation tax revenues. Thus, the effects on the total deficit of any variations in inflation and interest rates are offset through changes in lump-sum taxes.[46]

In Waldo's model the reason agents hold currency is to finance small transactions. Interest-bearing demand deposits, which are claims to government bonds, can only be transferred at a lump-sum cost, and are consequently used to effect large transactions. When an open market purchase takes place, the nominal interest rate falls to induce agents to substitute currency holdings for demand deposits. The excess demand for goods that results from the drop in nominal interest rates is then offset by an increase in the price level that reduces the real stock of wealth.

A different experiment, namely an increase in the rate of monetary growth (and of inflation), leads to a fall in currency demand and to an increase in goods demand. The price level rises, both to reduce the real currency supply and to lower goods demand. The effect on the nominal interest rate depends on the relative inflation elasticities of savings and currency. Even if the nominal interest rate rises, it does not do so by as much as inflation: the real interest rate definitely falls.[47]

6.2 Consequences of Persistent Deficits

We turn now to the question of whether persistent budget deficits are inflationary. There are two sets of issues here. One is whether such deficits are financed by issuing bonds for a given money path, or vice versa. The other is whether it is the primary or the total budget deficit which is kept constant over time.

Smith (1982) considers a constant total budget deficit. He compares a "monetarist" policy of maintaining a target path for money while financing deficits through bonds to a "bondist" policy of maintaining a target path for the bond stock while issuing money to finance the deficit. He shows that in a dynamic IS/LM model, a zero-inflation steady state may not be stable under the monetarist strategy, whereas it is more likely to be stable under the bondist strategy. The rationale is that fixed tax rates and government spending (including debt service) make government saving procyclical. Under a bond target, the change in money supply dictated by the government budget identity is countercyclical. By contrast, under a monetary target, the government must sell bonds to the public when a drop in output causes an increase in the budget deficit. Although the dynamic behavior of the model is complicated, Smith suggests that crowding out effects play a crucial role in generating the instability associated with the monetarist policy.

Of course, such crowding out effects are absent in a Ricardian world. The issue of whether persistent bond-financed deficits are inflationary in such a setup was addressed by Barro (1976) and by McCallum (1984a). Barro suggests that they would be inflationary if the rate of growth of the bond stock exceeded the rate of growth of output, the simplest example being that of an economy without population growth. The reason is that in this case the present value of the government's future taxing capacity is bounded. McCallum agrees that persistent primary budget deficits are inflationary, but shows that the result does not carry over to total budget deficits. He points out that a positive growth rate of bonds can be permanently maintained in a stationary Ricardian economy, provided that this growth rate is smaller than the rate of time preference. This is because a household's disposable income also includes interest payments from the government. As a result, taxes can exceed household output and yet be smaller than disposable income. (Presumably the assumption of lump-sum taxation plays a crucial role here. Otherwise the distortionary consequences of such high taxes would be considerable.) It remains true that debt cannot grow forever faster than disposable income.[48]

One of the most controversial recent papers investigating the inflationary implications of persistent primary budget deficits is that by Sargent and Wallace (1981). They assume that persistent bond-financed deficits will eventually have to be monetized. The reason they invoke is an upper bound on the public's demand for bonds, but McCallum's analysis is also pertinent here. The strategy they consider is "monetarist" up to a point and from then on it becomes "bondist."

The fiscal authority is assumed to behave in its design of policy as a Stackelberg leader, whereas the monetary authority takes the role of a Stackelberg follower. All variations in the deficit considered are due to changes in G, since the size of after-tax per capita endowments is assumed constant and the economy is on its full-employment path with a real income growth equal to the constant rate of population growth, n. Monetary policy is determined by the choice of the rate of growth of the nominal stock of high-powered money, H. This rate of growth is assumed to be equal to θ up to time t^*, when the assumed arbitrary upper limit to private sector demand for bonds is attained. Thus, for $t < t^*$, the amount of bond financing is residually determined by the size of the primary deficit, the government budget constraint, and θ. From then on the amount of bond financing is determined by the requirement that the per capita bond stock be kept constant at that maximum level, while it is the rate of growth of H that is now residually determined.

The private sector in their model consists of the "rich" and the "poor," while the government consists of a fiscal and of a monetary authority. A transactions motive for holding money is not incorporated, nor is there any element of uncertainty. Bonds and claims to capital are assumed to be of sufficiently large denominations for the poor not to be able to afford them, and legal restrictions are assumed (somewhat artificially) to prevent the poor from pooling funds and the rich from acting as financial intermediaries for the poor. Thus, money is held only by the poor, while the rich hold their wealth in the form of bonds and of capital which bear the same real rate of return, R. It is assumed that R is fixed and that it exceeds the rate of population growth and the rate of return on money (equal to minus the inflation rate).

Buiter (1982) doubts whether this setup is appropriate for discussing issues of inflation and of government debt. First, in Sargent and Wallace's formulation, government spending, $G(t)$, is wasteful, since it does not enter in private utility functions and reduces the amount of resources available for consumption or investment. Second, the presence of the postulated constraints on the portfolio behavior of the poor imply that Pareto-optimal policies should involve a deflation rate of $-R$, thus making available to all agents intertemporal market terms of trade equal to the technological intertemporal terms of trade for the economy as a whole. Third, to the extent that the constraints imposed on the poor imply underaccumulation of capital, the government should act as a net lender to the private sector and/or give subsidies to the rich.

These objections notwithstanding, two interesting questions have been asked in the context of this model. First, what are the effects on the time path of inflation of adopting a more restrictive monetary policy today? Second, what are the effects on inflation of fiscal actions that result in larger real per capita total deficits? This second question includes cases of "fiscal irresponsibility," where fiscal authorities allow the deficit to exceed the maximum seignorage obtainable in steady state. We discuss both questions here.

6.2.1 Effects of Monetary Restriction

The effects of tighter money today are the focus of the Sargent–Wallace paper. On the basis of the setup described above, the authors derive two results. The first is that when money demand is independent of the inflation rate, a lower value of θ (and thus a lower rate of inflation) for $t < t^*$ always necessitates a higher rate of growth of money and higher inflation after t^*. This is because the lower θ for $t < t^*$ causes a higher level of the real per capita bond stock to be attained at $t = t^*$ and maintained thereafter. Since R is assumed to exceed n, this means that the size of the real per capita debt service (corrected for inflation and growth) for $t \geq t^*$ is larger. As a result, the rate of monetary growth (and consequently inflation) is also larger beyond t^* in order to finance the higher real per capita total (as opposed to primary) deficit.

The second result concerns the case where money demand decreases with expected inflation. Current inflation depends on the entire anticipated future path of the money supply. When a lower θ for $t < t^*$ implies higher rates of monetary growth after t^*, it becomes possible to construct examples in which these higher later rates dominate the lower earlier rates and produce higher inflation even before t^*. It should be noted, however, that this occurs only for specific parameter configurations.

Darby (1984) has noted that the Sargent–Wallace result in which monetary policy is fully dictated by the stance of fiscal policy requires that the real after-tax rate on bonds exceed the natural rate of growth of the economy. When the sign of this inequality is reversed, a given budget deficit can be dynamically consistent with a range of values for θ. As long as θ remains within this range, changes in monetary policy can take place today without having to be reversed over the longer run. Darby points to evidence showing that even long-term, before-tax yields on government bonds have not approached corresponding growth rates of real output in the United States. This is *a fortiori* true of after-tax yields.[49] Thus, there may be more flexibility in the choice of monetary policy than implied by the Sargent–Wallace analysis.

Buiter (1983b) suggests that even when the real rate on bonds exceeds the natural rate of growth and when money demand depends on expected inflation, a lower value of θ for $t < t^*$ need not imply a higher rate of growth of the nominal money stock and higher inflation after t^*. While it is still true that the inflation rate for $t \geq t^*$ is higher the higher the real per capita bond stock, it is not clear that a lower value of θ for $t < t^*$ always implies a higher real per capita bond stock from t^* onwards. Specifically, a lower value of θ implies a higher real per capita bond stock for $t \geq t^*$ if it lowers the real discounted present value of the government's new money creation between $t = 0$ and $t = t^*$.

6.2.2 *Effects of Larger Deficits*

Buiter (1985) explores the consequences for the time path of inflation of fiscal policies that result in large real per capita total deficits, including the case where they exceed the "maximum seignorage" obtainable in a steady state. Real seignorage is defined as the amount of real resources that a government acquires in a period simply by virtue of the fact that private agents will hold the currency it prints. The per capita measure of this is equal in the steady state to the product of the real money stock times the sum of the inflation rate and the natural rate of growth of output. By raising inflation, the government also lowers real money demand. The two effects go against each other and there generally exists a maximum amount of real per capita seignorage that the government can extract.

Buiter examines the properties of the differential equation derived from the government budget constraint, assuming that the real per capita bond stock is kept constant at b and that nominal money demand per capita, m, depends inversely on the inflation rate, π:

$$\dot{m} = d + (R - n)b - (\pi + n)m, \tag{6.1}$$

$$m = c_1 - c_2\pi, \quad c_1, c_2 > 0, \tag{6.2}$$

where d is the real primary deficit per capita, n is the natural rate of growth of output, and R is the real rate of return on bonds. The expression on the right-hand side of equation (6.1) is the per capita measure of the real, inflation and growth-corrected budget deficit. Excessively high values of this measure are regarded as instances of "fiscal irresponsibility."

The point Buiter makes is that in the Sargent–Wallace model, the effect of fiscal irresponsibility can never be hyperinflation. In other words, fiscal policy in this model cannot generate unbounded increases in the inflation rate.

Specifically, in the case considered by Sargent and Wallace, where $d + (R - n)b$ is below the maximum amount of seignorage (or inflation tax) that could be attained in a steady state of the system, the above equation of motion has two equilibria (m, π), and there seems to be no economic criterion for choosing between them. If we consider the locally unstable equilibrium (as Sargent and Wallace do), an increase in the deficit will indeed raise the long-run rate of inflation, but by a finite amount. Alternatively, if the locally stable equilibrium is chosen, a finite reduction in the long-run inflation rate will result. This difference in signs mirrors the opposite effects on the amount of steady-state seignorage generated by a reduction in monetary growth.

However, it is also conceivable that the real total per capita deficit (adjusted for inflation and growth) will be set by the fiscal authority so irresponsibly as to exceed the maximum seignorage obtainable in the steady state. Buiter shows that in this case enough seignorage revenue could be generated so as to cover this difference through a process involving continuously increasing m, and continuously falling rates of inflation and monetary growth outside the steady state. This process is one of "hyperdisinflation," and it is unsustainable in the Sargent–Wallace model, since m in that model is bounded from above and cannot grow forever. The reason for this boundedness of m is that money is held by the poor to finance second-period consumption and both income and the supply of consumer goods are bounded. Indeed, some have argued (not entirely convincingly) that an unsustainable process would not even get started in a rational expectations world. The conclusion is that the case against fiscal irresponsibility provided by the Sargent–Wallace model emphasizing inflation, cannot rest on fears of hyperinflation, but only (at worst) on fears of finite increases in inflation rates.

7 Concluding Remarks

There are two ways to evaluate a theoretical hypothesis. One is to ask how well it survives relaxations of assumptions, especially to see how dependent it is on patently unrealistic premises. An alternative criterion is the consistency of the theory's implications with empirical observations, the validity of its predictions. This test ignores the plausibility of assumptions. According to Milton Friedman's "methodology of positive economics," the crucial question is whether the economy behaves *as if* the theory were valid.

Our pragmatic view, following Tjalling Koopmans, is that all opportunities for testing should be seized, from the plausibility of primitive assumptions to the congruence of ultimate implications with observations. Empirical testing is too difficult, and too often ambiguous, to permit us to rely exclusively on the "as if" criterion in choosing among hypotheses.

Let us try to evaluate the three strong neutrality propositions reviewed in Sections 4, 5, and 6 by both kinds of criteria.

Debt neutrality fails the first criterion by a wide margin. In Section 4 we reviewed a series of papers showing how sensitive the Barro–Ricardo Equivalence theorem is to relaxing any one of numerous assumptions. Few economists can believe that all those assumptions hold in practice. But the profession, including even some of the harshest critics of debt neutrality, seems willing to overlook such unrealism and focus on the "as if" criterion instead.

We discussed the empirical literature but found the results inconclusive. More empirical research is needed and should be possible. Recent data on saving rates and deficits, especially in the United States, seem *prima facie* difficult to reconcile with debt neutrality. However, the inability of researchers to agree, even for identical sample periods and similar sets of variables, is not encouraging. We seem to need new tests as well as new data.

To reject debt neutrality is not to dismiss the sensible idea that expectations of future taxes, as of other future policies, affect current consumption and saving decisions, especially when there are credible signals of political and legislative intent.

We are reluctant to recommend more research on deficits, given the already huge volume of literature on the subject. However, there seems to be room for analysis of the effects of persistent budget deficits in a greater variety of circumstances. For example, what are the consequences of unsustainable policies not reversed before the situation gets "out of hand"? Both the profession and the lay public need a plausible "doomsday scenario" in debating the needs for and merits of fiscal austerity programs.

Superneutrality is the subject of a considerable literature examining critically its necessary assumptions. One necessary assumption for superneutrality, as well as for debt neutrality, is that consumer-savers' horizons are infinite. But this is not sufficient; a number of interesting papers identify departures from superneutrality even with infinite horizons. Although the literature provides a fairly good understanding of cases in which superneutrality fails, it is more difficult to dismiss this proposition as dependent on patently unrealistic assumptions than to dismiss debt neutrality. There is room for more research both on identifying conditions implying departures from superneutrality and on evaluating the realism of such conditions.

The most obvious gap, however, is in the empirical literature on superneutrality. The Fisher hypothesis has received much attention, but few papers test superneutrality directly. Perhaps more could be done following the methodology of Sargent's (1973) paper, specifying a model where superneutrality holds and carrying out joint tests of superneutrality and the underlying model. Sargent focused on the Fisher hypothesis, but the same methods could be used to test invariance of real per capita consumption or of the capital stock.

Testing superneutrality should not be the sole aim of research on the effects of inflation on capital accumulation. If there are such effects, it is important to identify their direction and importance, whether positive because of Mundell or Tobin effects or negative because of the real costs of economizing money balances.

Monetary policies, distinguished from fiscal policies, involve exchanges of assets between the government or its central bank and private agents. Models exhibiting irrelevance of asset exchanges show entire classes of policies that support the same equilibrium allocations. If this is correct, it does simplify the policy-maker's problem! Within this literature, there is still room for models exploring the precise conditions under which such policy classes exist. It is also interesting to examine whether the equilibrium in question is the only one supported by each policy in a given class. If there are multiple equilibria associated with each policy, irrelevance classes may be difficult to define.

Whether open market operations as typically implemented in practice are irrelevant is a different question. A reader of this literature must keep in mind exactly what assets are being exchanged in each model. Some papers redefine the terms "open market operations" and "constant fiscal policy" and then try to justify their model-based redefinitions. It does not then follow that *all* feasible asset exchanges are irrelevant.

There is little empirical research related to this species of irrelevance literature. One reason may be that the asset swaps in the models do not resemble actually observed central bank operations. However, it should be possible to find historical approximations to at least some of the modeled asset exchanges and to test directly the hypothesis of neutrality. Indeed, if there are no such incidents, one may be tempted to ask whether it is the literature that is irrelevant, i.e. irrelevant to the monetary institutions and practices of real-world economies.

The foregoing remarks were stimulated by our surveys of neutrality literature in Sections 4–6. As they indicate, contemporary theory of fiscal and monetary policy is far removed from the practical concerns of policymakers. In Section 3 we explained how current "microfoundations" methodology inevitably creates a wide gulf between theory and application. There was not always such a gulf. As our review in Section 2 of older traditions in macroeconomics indicates, fiscal theory and fiscal policy were once closely linked, each contributing to the other. The same was true of monetary theory and monetary policy. The major challenge to theorists today is to model enough of the heterogeneities, institutional idiosyncracies, and market imperfections of actual economies to make their theories useful to empirical researchers and interesting to policy practitioners.

Notes

Haliassos' research was partially supported by the Graduate Research Board of the University of Maryland, College Park.

1. The point was not wholly absent from the previous discussion. For example, in Tobin's review (1965b) of the Ferguson book, he offers a comment which "questions the consumption-saving behavior assumed in the Modigliani notion of the burden. Is it not based on some asymmetrical illusion? Society fools itself into consuming more, thinking that possession of government paper provides for its future. Why don't those who will have to pay taxes to service the debt ... consider themselves poorer and save more accordingly? This observation threatens not only Modigliani's concept of debt burden but equally the belief that the government can influence investment and growth by varying the fiscal-monetary mix. Indeed it comes dangerously close to denying that any internal financial and monetary arrangements are of any real consequence." Nevertheless, the author goes on to suggest that the government as a financial intermediary can "diminish some of the needs which generate saving," and to claim that the weight of empirical evidence is that "the private income and wealth corresponding to government deficit and debt stimulate consumption."

2. For simplicity, we use the term "bond" to refer to all non-monetary government debt of whatever maturity and form. We are not distinguishing bonds from bills or notes.

3. In an open economy, international capital mobility causes foreign capital to flow into the country experiencing the tax cut, resulting in an appreciation of its currency, a fall in net exports, and hence a total or partial displacement of foreign investment by the bond-financed budget deficit.

4. The life-cycle model is due to Fisher (1930) and to Modigliani and Brumberg (1954). An extensive discussion of the two-period consumption decision can be found in Feldstein and Tsiang (1968).

5. This sensible idea had been noted by Ricardo and by others before Barro, but it is not sufficient by itself to establish the equivalence of taxation and of bond financing. Indeed, Ricardo in 1817 argued against the practice of not repaying government debt accumulated during wars. His reasons were that either people would be fooled into thinking that they are richer or they would try to shift the burden onto others, possibly by emigrating. In either of these two cases, their current real consumption would go up [see Ricardo (1951, esp. pp. 244–249)].

6. The assumed invariance of the probability of death with age ensures that the propensity to consume out of wealth is the same for people of all ages, despite the fact that their wealth levels may differ. This allows the derivation of an aggregate consumption function for general population structures. One drawback is that it does not capture the varying behavior of agents throughout their lives.

7. An isoclastic utility function in consumption c is of the form:

$u(c) = (c^{1-\sigma})/(1-\sigma), \quad \sigma \neq 1; \quad u(c) = \log c, \quad \sigma = 1.$

The (constant) elasticity of substitution is equal to $1/\sigma$.

8. If aggregate human wealth is denoted by H, income by Y, and non-human wealth by W, then in the logarithmic utility case,

$C = (p+\theta)(H+W), \quad \dot{H} = (r+p)(H-Y), \quad \dot{W} = rW + Y - C.$

9. Blanchard also shows that for a logarithmic utility function, the steady state r is between θ and $\theta + p$, and is an increasing function of θ. The finiteness of horizons discourages capital accumulation, since $r = \theta$ for infinite horizons. If labor income declines through life, this tends to raise the steady-state capital stock, with an ambiguous net effect and the possibility that the steady-state r will be negative (i.e. below the zero natural rate of growth of real GNP). In this case the level of the capital stock exceeds the "golden rule" level and the economy is dynamically inefficient, as in Diamond (1965). Finally, for the class of isoelastic utility functions the lower the elasticity of substitution, $1/\sigma$, the lower the steady-state capital stock.

10. Considerations such as wage growth, taxation of interest, and population growth (in certain cases) further reduce the likelihood of positive bequests.

11. The discussion above assumes that bequests are in the form of non-human capital. Drazen argues that a significant share of bequests is in the form of investment in human capital, namely expenditure on the education of descendants. At least up to a certain level of education, such investment yields a higher rate of return than that on non-human wealth and could be used to enhance the father's own second-period consumption. When the father cannot enforce this liability on his descendant, the introduction of government bonds facilitates the transfer and thus has real effects. The enforceability of loans between parents and offspring would mitigate the importance of such considerations.

12. An exchange with Burbidge [Burbidge (1983, 1984) and Buiter and Carmichael (1984)] shows that in order for this stronger neutrality proposition to hold, the same type of intergenerational transfer has to be operative both before and after the tax cut, a condition which is difficult to meet for large increases in the amount of debt introduced, since these are likely to induce movement to corners with respect to transfers. When this happens, bonds are not neutral, as argued above. By contrast, Burbidge's formulation yields neutrality even for large additions to the stock of bonds, provided that gifts or bequests exist before the tax cut and that future tax increases are necessary.

13. A liquidity constraint may be regarded as a very short horizon, much shorter than a lifetime. Hubbard and Judd also point to the relevance of the distribution of the tax cut for the effect on the aggregate MPC. In particular, if the tax cut is not uniform but results in greater relative relief for the high-income group, the effect of borrowing constraints on the aggregate MPC out of a temporary tax cut is dampened. This questions the practice of regarding the measured MPC as a good indicator of the proportion of liquidity-constrained individuals in economies with proportional or progressive tax systems.

14. If both the stock of bonds and that of total wealth (including bonds) are entered, then the coefficient on the bond stock should be the negative of that on wealth, so that the total effect of bonds is zero.

15. Aschauer assumes that a representative agent maximizes a quadratic utility function with a positive discount rate over an infinite horizon, subject to the constraint that the present value of "effective consumption" is equal to net wealth (excluding government bonds) plus the present discounted value of labor earnings plus (a multiple of) the present value of government expenditure.

16. See Shiller and McCulloch (1990) for a discussion of empirical tests of the expectations theory of the term structure.

17. The assumption that these variables are exogenous can be relaxed with minor changes in the interpretation, as shown by Plosser.

18. The results are unchanged when the assumed information set of agents is augmented to include current and lagged short- and long-term interest rates as predictors of future values of policy variables; and when the processes for policy variables are differenced to eliminate non-stationarity.

19. Note that when private saving is interest-sensitive, as discussed in Subsection 4.2, the magnitude of the Tobin effect is smaller, because desired saving and the desired wealth-to-income ratio are also lowered.

20. Sidrauski is careful to distinguish these steady-state results from short-run effects. He notes that in his model, increases in monetary growth imply increased disposable income and consumption in the short run.

21. It is still possible to obtain invariance of the capital–labor ratio, provided that the production function exhibits constant returns to scale. Except in this limited sense, however, superneutrality is lost when the choice between labor and leisure is explicitly incorporated into the model.

22. Tobin, and other contributors to this debate, were always assuming that transfers were independent of money holdings. If they were random or equal per capita, they would in Drazen's terms be weighted to the young.

23. In similar vein, Tobin (1968) had shown that steady states with transactions requirements for money exist only if Harrod-neutral technological progress occurs at the same steady rate in both goods production and in transactions.

24. Asako (1983) notes that for more general utility functions, a sufficient condition for super-neutrality on the transition path is that the function be separable in consumption and real money balances, i.e. $u_{cm} = 0$. Deriving necessary conditions for general utility functions is more difficult.

25. $U(c,m) = (1/(1-s))(c^\alpha m^{1-\alpha})^{1-s}$, if $s \geq 0$ and $s \neq 1$,

$U(c,m) = \log c^\alpha m^{1-\alpha}$, if $s = 1$.

26. The first researcher to test the Fisher hypothesis was Fisher himself. In 1930 he concluded that "when prices are rising, the (nominal) rate of interest tends to be high, but not so high as it should be to compensate for the rise" (1930, p. 43). In addition, Fisher observed a relationship between interest rates and past inflation rates. He interpreted this as supporting a modified version that allows for less than perfect foresight and consequently effects that are smaller and slower than price changes.

27. The nominal one-month rate of return on a one-month Treasury bill paying $1 at time t is $R_t = (1 - v_{t-1})/v_{t-1}$, where v_{t-1} is the price of the bill determined in period $t - 1$. Fama postulates that the market sets v so that it perceives the expected real return on the bill to be the constant $E(r)$. This model of market equilibrium is combined with the assumption that the market makes optimal use of all available information concerning the stochastic rate of change of purchasing power π_t, over the next month.

28. Fama uses data on U.S. Treasury bills with one month to maturity over the period from January 1953 through July 1971, and for various subsamples. He also performs similar tests for bills of up to six months of maturity. In all cases, he assumes that the behavior of the Consumer Price Index is the relevant measure of inflation. The results of both autocorrelation and regression coefficient tests support EMH with respect to the history of inflation rates, and do not reject the model of constant expected real rates. Combining these two

findings, Fama concludes that we cannot reject the hypothesis that all variation through time in R reflects variation in correctly-assessed expected rates of change in purchasing power.

29. This happens when the variance of errors in inflationary expectations is large relative to the variance of the ex ante real rate.

30. The U.S. sample is 1953 I–1978 IV; the Australian is early or mid-sixties to end of 1981. To test their hypothesis, Carmichael and Stebbing make use of portfolio arbitrage conditions on real after-tax rates of return among the three assets, and of the assumptions that expectations are unbiased and that individuals know their marginal tax rates.

31. Another case is that of the postwar period, which looks Fisherian on the basis of nominal rate regressions, but exhibits a strong negative relationship between inflation and expected real returns on short-term instruments.

32. See also their exchange in Summers (1986) and McCallum (1986).

33. At any rate, given that expected inflation probably fluctuated very little in the pre-1913 period, that part of the sample is probably not very informative as to the validity of the Fisher hypothesis.

34. They consider a wide range of maturities of government and commercial financial instruments, and look at the "term structure" of inflationary expectations, so as to match each instrument with the (geometric) average of one-period expected inflation rates over its time to maturity.

35. The supply of fiat money is costlessly manipulated by the government. In period t, consumers demand claims on consumption in period $t+1$, while firms (which are owned by members of generation t) supply those claims, storing the good and money in the process. In their roles as consumers, agents maximize their expected utility of consumption in the two periods of their life. As producers, they choose to undertake one or both of the two risky projects of storing money and of storing the good.

36. Wallace shows that $\{\hat{K}^g(t)\}$ is any non-negative sequence bounded by $\{K(t)\}$, and $\{\hat{w}(t)\}$ is any endowment sequence that meets a particular set of restrictions. The point of the restrictions is to ensure (a) that the distribution of income among agents is unchanged, and (b) that the differences in net interest received by the government as a result of the change in its "portfolio" of the stored good and of money are offset by changes in taxes net of transfers. In this framework, the boundedness of $K^g(t)$ from above is necessary, because otherwise no feasible value of private storage exists that is consistent with unchanged total accumulation.

37. A sufficient condition for a positive price of money in period t is that both the contemporaneous government capital holdings and the total return on capital be positive.

38. Wallace's neutral policies can be seen as combinations of (1) an open market operation (given taxes net of transfers), which does affect the price of money, with (2) changes in the supply of money via taxes net of transfers that offset the first price effect without affecting the real quantity of money. Chamley and Polemarchakis show that monetary policies of this type do exist even in their more generalized framework. Sargent (1987, esp. p. 322) states a general neutrality theorem which encompasses those of Wallace, and Chamley and Polemarchakis as special cases.

39. Note that not all financing policies which involve the same path of taxes and lead to the same government revenue leave the real allocation of resources unaffected. The added condition is that they also generate identical "deficit" paths for all periods $t > 1$ over which they are in effect. "Deficit" here refers to the change in the real value of government monetary plus non-monetary debt. When this is true, unchanged aggregate consumption is guaranteed to old agents and aggregate private saving is also unchanged.

40. If such markets were absent prior to the government intervention, then the government could facilitate risk-sharing asset exchanges among diverse individuals through its open market

operations. Then, government intervention would have real effects. On the other hand, neutrality is no contingent on the lump-sum nature of taxes.

41. The empirical rationalization usually offered is that laws can exist (such as Peel's Bank Act of 1844) which impose a restriction on the minimum size of privately issued securities.

42. The authors show that invariance can also be accomplished without variation in lump-sum taxes when the menu of assets is sufficiently enriched to allow the government to borrow from (and lend to) private agents. Again, the condition for irrelevance is that the open market operations in capital be accompanied by government exchanges in debt markets so as to leave private agents' budget sets unaltered.

43. This is more restrictive than the conditions imposed by Sidrauski, due to the inclusion of uncertainty into the model.

44. Deposits are not checkable. Firms deposit into consumers' accounts, since consumers own shares to firms' profits. In addition to shares, the asset menu includes both interest-bearing deposits and government bonds which are perfect substitutes for deposits.

45. In fact, it is possible to show that when utility is logarithmic (or when it is homothetic and demand for second-period consumption rises with inflation), the model generates damped oscillatory price behavior with overshooting after two periods and a fall in the current nominal and real rates. Two-period nominal interest rates also fluctuate, rising above their steady-state value on even dates and falling below it on odd dates, until the price path converges to its steady state. The oscillations are produced by the fact that in odd periods the types who exhaust their money holdings, and consequently have a propensity to spend out of them equal to one, are also the ones whose money holdings are larger than in the steady state. With output assumed fixed, such fluctuation in nominal spending generates fluctuations in the price level.

46. This allows inflation and the debt mix to be determined independently of each other and eliminates any income effects of inflation, so that results only depend on substitution effects. It is different from Sargent and Wallace (1981) where government spending and the narrowly defined deficit are held constant. In that model, open market purchases that lower interest rates imply lower inflation rates through the government budget identity.

47. If one uses Waldo's setup but assumes that government spending and the primary budget deficit are held constant [i.e. the notion of constant policy in Sargent and Wallace (1981)], an open market purchase does put downward pressure on interest rates and (via the budget identity) on inflation rates, but the effects on savings and the price level are ambiguous. If inflation effects dominate, savings rise and the price level falls to clear the goods market. The opposite happens when interest rate effects dominate.

48. These conclusions hold in per capita terms when the size of each household grows at a rate n and utility is a function of per capita consumption and money holdings.

49. This evidence is consistent with the analysis of Tobin (1986).

References

Abel, A. B. and B. D. Bernheim (1986) "Fiscal policy with impure intergenerational altruism," mimeo.

Abel, A. B., N. G. Mankiw, L. H. Summers and R. J. Zeckhauser (1986) "Assessing dynamic efficiency: Theory and evidence," NBER Working Paper 2097.

Anderson, L. C. and K. M. Carlson (1970) "A monetarist model of economic stabilization," *Federal Reserve Bank of St. Louis Review*, 54: 7–25.

Asako, K. (1983) "The utility function and the superneutrality of money on the transition path," *Econometrica*, 51: 1593–1596.

Aschauer, D. A. (1985) "Fiscal policy and aggregate demand," *American Economic Review*, 75: 117–127.

Barro, R. J (1974) "Are government bonds net wealth?," *Journal of Political Economy*, 82: 1095–1117.

Barro, R. J. (1976) "Reply to Feldstein and Buchanan," *Journal of Political Economy*, 84: 343–350.

Barro, R. J. (1978) *The impact of social security on private saving: Evidence from the U.S. time series.* Washington: American Enterprise Institute.

Barro, R. J. (1979) "On the determination of the public debt," *Journal of Political Economy*, 87: 940–971.

Barro, R. J. (1983) *Macroeconomics.* New York: Wiley.

Barsky, R. B. (1987) "The Fisher hypothesis and the forecastability and persistence of inflation," *Journal of Monetary Economics*, 19: 3–24.

Barsky, R. B., N. G. Mankiw and S. P. Zeldes (1986) "Ricardian consumers with Keynesian propensities," *American Economic Review*, 76: 676–691.

Barth, J. R., G. Iden and F. S. Russek (1986) "Government debt, government spending, and private sector behavior," *American Economic Review*, 76: 1158–1167.

Benninga, S. and A. Protopapadakis (1984) "The neutrality of the real equilibrium under alternative financing of government expenditures," *Journal of Monetary Economics*, 14: 183–208.

Bernheim D. B. (1987) "Ricardian equivalence: An evaluation of theory and evidence," *NBER Macroeconomics Annual*, 2: 263–304.

Bernheim, D. B. and K. Bagwell (1988) "Is everything neutral?," *Journal of Political Economy*, 96: 308–338.

Blanchard, O. J. (1985) "Debt, deficits, and finite horizons," *Journal of Political Economy*, 93: 223–247.

Blinder, A. S. and R. Solow (1974): "Analytical foundations of fiscal policy," in: *The economics of public finance.* Washington: Brookings Institution.

Boskin, M. J. (1978) "Taxation, saving, and the rate of interest," *Journal of Political Economy*, 86: S3–S27.

Brock, W. A. (1974) "Money and growth: The use of long run perfect foresight," *International Economic Review*, 15: 750–777.

Buchanan, J. M. (1964) "Concerning future generations," in: J. M. Ferguson. ed., *Public debt and future generations.* Chapel Hill: The University of North Carolina Press.

Buiter, W. H. (1979) "Government finance in an overlapping-generations model with gifts and bequests," in: G. M. von Furstenberg, ed., *Sociál security versus private saving.* Cambridge, Mass.: Ballinger.

Buiter, W. H. (1980) "'Crowding out' of private capital formation by government borrowing in the presence of intergenerational gifts and bequests," *Greek Economic Review*, 2: 111–142.

Buiter, W. H. (1982) "Comment on T. J. Sargent and N. Wallace 'Some unpleasant monetarist arithmetic'," NBER Working Paper 867.

Buiter, W. H. (1983a) "The theory of optimum deficits and debt," NBER Working Paper 1232.

Buiter, W. H. (1983b) "Deficits, crowding out, and inflation: The simple analytics," NBER Working Paper 1078.

Buiter, W. H. (1985) "A fiscal theory of hyperdeflations? Some surprising monetarist arithmetic," NBER Technical Working Paper 52.

Buiter, W. H. and J. Carmichael (1984) "Government debt: Comment," *American Economic Review*, 74: 762–765.

Buiter, W. H. and J. Tobin (1978) "Debt neutrality: A brief review of doctrine and evidence," Cowles Foundation Paper 497.

Burbidge, J. B. (1983) "Government debt in an overlapping-generations model with bequests and gifts," *American Economic Review*, 73: 222–227.

Burbidge. J. B. (1984) "Government debt: Reply," *American Economic Review*, 74: 766–767.

Cargill, T. F. and R. A. Meyer (1980) "The term structure of inflationary expectations and market efficiency," *Journal of Finance*, 35: 57–70.

Carmichael, J. (1982) "On Barro's theorem of debt neutrality: The irrelevance of net wealth," *American Economic Review*, 72: 202–213.

Carmichael. J. and P. W. Stebbing (1983) "Fisher's paradox and the theory of interest," *American Economic Review*, 73: 619–630.

Chamley, C. and H. Polemarchakis (1984) "Assets, general equilibrium, and the neutrality of money," *Review of Economic Studies*, 51: 129–138.

Christ, C. F. (1968) "A simple macroeconomic model with a government budget restraint," *Journal of Political Economy*, 76: 53–67.

Cohen, D. (1985) "Inflation, wealth, and interest rates in an intertemporal optimizing model," *Journal of Monetary Economics*, 16: 73–85.

Currie, D. (1978) "Macroeconomic policy and the government financing requirement: A survey of recent views," in: M. Artis and R. Nobay, eds., *Studies in contemporary economic analysis*, Vol. 1. London: Croom-Helm. (1978).

Darby, M. R. (1975) "The financial and tax effects of monetary policy on interest rates," *Economic Inquiry*, 13: 266–276.

Darby, M. R. (1984) "Some pleasant monetarist arithmetic," *Federal Reserve Bank of Minneapolis Quarterly Review*, 1984: 32–37.

Diamond, P. A. (1965) "National debt in a neoclassical growth model," *American Economic Review*, 55: 1126–1150.

Domar, E. (1944) "The 'burden of the debt' and the national income," *American Economic Review*, 34: 798–827; also in his *Essays in the theory of economic growth.* New York: Oxford University Press (1957).

Dornbusch, R. and J. A. Frenkel (1973) "Inflation and growth: Alternative approaches," *Journal of Money, Credit and Banking*, 5: 141–156.

Dornbusch, R. and A. Giovannini, Chapter 23 in Benjamin Friedman and Frank Hahn, eds., *Handbook of Monetary Economics*, Amsterdam: North-Holland (1990), pp. 889–959.

Drazen, A. (1978) "Government debt, human capital, and bequests in a life-cycle model," *Journal of Political Economy*, 86: 505–516.

Drazen, A. (1981) "Inflation and capital accumulation under a finite horizon," *Journal of Monetary Economics*, 8: 247–260.

Eisner, R. (1985) *How real is the deficit?* New York: Free Press.

Fama, E. F. (1975) "Short-term interest rates as predictors of inflation," *American Economic Review*, 65: 269–282.

Feldstein, M. (1976) "Perceived wealth in bonds and social security: A comment," *Journal of Political Economy*, 84: 331-336.

Feldstein, M. (1982) "Government deficits and aggregate demand," *Journal of Monetary Economics*, 9: 1-20.

Feldstein, M. (1988) "The effects of fiscal policies when incomes are uncertain: A contradiction to Ricardian equivalence," *American Economic Review*, 78: 14-23.

Feldstein, M. and D. W. Elmendorf (1987) "Taxes, budget deficits, and consumer spending: Some new evidence," *American Economic Review*, forthcoming.

Feldstein, M. and S. C. Tsiang (1968) "The interest rate taxation, and the personal savings incentive," *Quarterly Journal of Economics*, 82: 419-434.

Ferguson, J. M., ed. (1964) *Public debt and future generations.* Chapel Hill: The University of North Carolina Press.

Fischer, S. (1979) "Capital accumulation on the transition path in a monetary optimizing model," *Econometrica*, 47: 1433-1439.

Fisher, I. (1930) *The theory of interest.* New York: Macmillan.

Fleming, J. M. (1962) "Domestic financial policies under fixed and under floating exchange rates," *IMF Staff Papers*, 9: 363-379.

Friedman, B. M. (1977) "Financial flow variables and the short-run determination of long-term interest rates," *Journal of Political Economy*, 85: 661-689.

Friedman, B. M. (1978) "Crowding out or crowding in? Economic consequences of financing government deficits," *Brookings Papers on Economic Activity*, 9: 593-641.

Friedman, B. M. (1980) "The determination of long-term interest rates: Implications for fiscal and monetary policies," *Journal of Money, Credit and Banking*, 12: 331-352.

Friedman, M. (1970) "A theoretical framework for monetary analysis," *Journal of Political Economy*, 78: 193-238; Reprinted in R. J. Gordon, ed., *Milton Friedman's monetary framework.* Chicago: University of Chicago Press (1974), pp. 1-62.

Friedman, M. and A. Schwartz (1976) "From Gibson to Fisher," *Explorations in Economic Research*, 3: 288-289.

Friedman, M. and A. Schwartz (1982) *Monetary trends in the United States and the United Kingdom.* Chicago: University of Chicago Press for the NBER.

Gale, D. (1983) *Money: In disequilibrium.* Cambridge: Cambridge University Press/Nisbet.

Garbade, K. and P. Wachtel (1978) "Time variation in the relationship between inflation and interest rates," *Journal of Monetary Economics*, 4: 755-765.

Grossman, S. and L. Weiss (1983) "A transactions-based model of the monetary transmission mechanism," *American Economic Review*, 73: 871-880.

Haliassos, M. (1987) "Multi-asset economies with staggered portfolio adjustments," University of Maryland Working Paper 88-14.

Hansen, A. H. (1941) *Business cycles and national income.* New York: Norton.

Hansen, A. H. (1953) *A guide to Keynes.* New York: McGraw-Hill.

Hansson, I. and C. Stuart (1986) "The Fisher hypothesis and international capital markets," *Journal of Political Economy*, 94: 1330-1337.

Hicks, J. R. (1937) "Mr. Keynes and the 'Classics'; A suggested interpretation," *Econometrica*, 5: 147-159.

Howrey, E. P. and S. Hymans (1978) "The measurement and determination of loanable funds saving," *Brookings Papers on Economic Activity*, 3: 655-685.

Hubbard, R. G. and K. L. Judd (1986a) "Finite lifetimes, borrowing constraints, and short-run fiscal policy," mimeo.

Hubbard, R. G. and K. L. Judd (1986b) "Liquidity constraints, fiscal policy, and consumption," *Brookings Papers on Economic Activity*, 1986-1: 1–50.

Kahn, R. F. (1931) "The relation of home investment to unemployment," *Economic Journal*, 41: 173–198.

Keynes, J. M. (1936) *The general theory of employment, interest, and money.* London: The Macmillan Press for The Royal Economic Society. (1973).

Kochin, L. A. (1974) "Are future taxes anticipated by consumers?," *Journal of Money, Credit and Banking*, 6: 385–394.

Kormendi, R. C. (1983) "Government debt, government spending, and private sector behavior," *American Economic Review*, 73: 994–1010.

Kotlikoff, L. and L. H. Summers (1981) "The importance of intergenerational transfers in aggregate capital accumulation," *Journal of Political Economy*, 89: 706–732.

Laitner, J. P. (1979) "Bequests, golden-age capital accumulation, and government debt," *Economica*, 46: 403–414.

Lerner, A. P. (1943) "Functional finance and the federal debt," *Social Research*, 10: 38–51.

Lerner, A. P. (1944) *The economics of control.* New York: Macmillan.

Levhari, D. and D. Patinkin (1968) "The role of money in a simple growth model," *American Economic Review*, 58: 713–753.

Lucas, R. E. (1976) "Economic policy evaluation: A critique," in: K. Brunner and A. Meltzer, eds., *The Phillips curve and labor markets.* Carnegie-Rochester Conference Series on Public Policy, 1: 19–46.

McCallum, B. T. (1984a) "Are bond-financed deficits inflationary? A Ricardian analysis," *Journal of Political Economy*, 92: 123–135.

McCallum, B. T. (1984b) "On low-frequency estimates of long-run relationships in macroeconomics," *Journal of Monetary Economics*, 14: 3–14.

McCallum, B. T. (1986) "Estimating the long-run relationship between interest rates and inflation: A reply," *Journal of Monetary Economics*, 18: 87–90.

Miller, M. H. and F. Modigliani (1961) "Dividend policy, growth and the valuation of shares," *Journal of Business*, 34: 235–264.

Mirer, T. W. (1979) "The wealth–age relation among the aged," *American Economic Review*, 69: 435–443.

Modigliani, F. (1964) "Long-run implications of alternative fiscal policies and the burden of the national debt," in: J. M. Ferguson, ed., *Public debt and future generations.* Chapel Hill: The University of North Carolina Press.

Modigliani, F. and A. Ando (1976) "Impacts of fiscal actions on aggregate income and the monetarist controversy: Theory and evidence," in: J. L. Stein, ed., *Monetarism.* Amsterdam: North-Holland, pp. 17–42.

Modigliani, F. and R. Brumberg (1954) "Utility analysis and the consumption function: An interpretation of cross-section data," in: K. K. Kurihara, ed., *Post-Keynesian economics.* New Brunswick.

Modigliani, F. and A. Sterling (1986) "Government debt, government spending, and private sector: Comment," *American Economic Review*, 76: 1168–1179.

Mundell, R. A. (1963a) "Capital mobility and stabilization policies under fixed and floating exchange rates," *Canadian Journal of Economics and Political Science*, 29: 475–485.

Mundell, R. A. (1963b) "Inflation and real interest," *Journal of Political Economy*, 71: 280–283.

Nelson, C. R. and G. W. Schwert (1977) "Short-term interest rates as predictors of inflation: On testing the hypothesis that the real rate of interest is constant," *American Economic Review*, 67: 478–488.

O'Connell, S. A. and S. P. Zeldes (1987) "Ponzi games and Ricardian equivalence," mimeo.

Patinkin, D. (1948) "Price flexibility and full employment," *American Economic Review*, 38: 543–564.

Patinkin, D. (1956) *Money, interest, and prices.* Evanston: Row Peterson.

Peled, D. (1985) "Stochastic inflation and government provision of indexed bonds," *Journal of Monetary Economics*, 15: 291–308.

Pigou, A. C. (1943) "The classical stationary state," *Economic Journal*, 53: 343–351.

Pigou, A. C. (1947) "Economic progress in a stable environment," *Economica*, 14: 180–190.

Plosser, C. I. (1982) "Government financing decisions and asset returns," *Journal of Monetary Economics*, 9: 325–352.

Poole, W. (1970) "Optimal choice of monetary policy instruments in a simple stochastic model," *Quarterly Journal of Economics*, 84: 197–216.

Porterba, J. M. and L. H. Summers (1986) "Finite lifetimes and the effects of budget deficits on national savings," M.I.T. Working Paper 434.

Ricardo, D. (1817) *On the principles of political economy and taxation*, edited by Piero Sraffa with the collaboration of M. H. Dobb. Cambridge: Cambridge University Press for the Royal Economic Society (1951).

Rotemberg, J. J. (1984) "A monetary equilibrium model with transactions costs," *Journal of Political Economy*, 92: 40–58.

Sargent, T. J. (1973) "Rational expectations, the real rate of interest, and the natural rate of unemployment," *Brookings Papers on Economic Activity*, 1973-2: 429–472.

Sargent, T. J. (1987) *Dynamic macroeconomic theory.* Cambridge, Mass.: Harvard University Press.

Sargent, T. J. and B. D. Smith (1987) "Irrelevance of open market operations in some economies with government currency being dominated in rate of return," *American Economic Review*, 77: 78–92.

Sargent, T. J. and N. Wallace (1981) "Some unpleasant monetarist arithmetic," *Federal Reserve Bank of Minneapolis Quarterly Review*, 5: 1–17.

Seater, J. J. and R. S. Mariano (1985) "New tests of the life cycle and tax discounting hypothesis," *Journal of Monetary Economics*, 15: 195–215.

Shiller, R. and J. H. McCulloch (1990) "The term structure of interest rates," *Handbook of Monetary Economics*, Vol. 2, eds. B. Friedman and F. Hahn. Amsterdam: North-Holland, ch. 13, 627–722.

Sidrauski, M. (1967) "Rational choice and patterns of growth in a monetary economy," *American Economic Review*, 57: 534–544.

Siegel, J. J. (1983) "Technological change and the superneutrality of money," *Journal of Money*, Credit and Banking, 15: 363–367.

Smith, G. (1982) "Monetarism, bondism, and inflation," *Journal of Money, Credit and Banking*, 14: 278–286.

Summers, L. H. (1981) "Capital taxation and accumulation in a life cycle growth model," *American Economic Review*, 71: 533–544.

Summers, L. H. (1982) "Tax policy, the rate of return, and savings," NBER Working Paper 995.

Summers, L. H. (1983) "The nonadjustment of nominal interest rates: A study of the Fisher effect," in: J. Tobin, ed., *Macroeconomic prices and quantities: Essays in memory of Arthur Okun*. Washington: Brookings Institution.

Summers, L. H. (1984) "The after tax rate of return affects private savings," Harvard Institute of Economic Research Discussion Paper 1042.

Summers, L. H. (1986) "Estimating the long-run relationship between interest rates and inflation: A response to McCallum," *Journal of Monetary Economics*, 18: 77–86.

Tanner, E. J. (1979) "An empirical investigation of tax discounting," *Journal of Money, Credit and Banking*, 11: 214–218.

Tanzi, V. (1980) "Inflationary expectations, economic activity, taxes, and interest rates," *American Economic Review*, 70: 12–21.

Tobin, J. (1961) "Money, capital, and other stores of value," *American Economic Review*, 51: 26–37.

Tobin, J. (1963) "An essay on the principles of debt management," in: *Fiscal and debt management policies*, prepared for the Commission on Money and Credit. Englewood Cliffs: Prentice-Hall. Reprinted as *Cowles Foundation*, Paper No. 195, New Haven (1963).

Tobin, J. (1965a) "Money and economic growth," *Econometrica*, 33: 671–684.

Tobin, J. (1965b) "The burden of the public debt: A review article," *Journal of Finance*, 20: 679–682.

Tobin, J. (1968) "Notes on optimal monetary growth," *Journal of Political Economy*, 76: 833–859.

Tobin, J. (1978) "Comment from an academic scribbler" (on *Democracy in deficit*, by J. M. Buchanan and Richard E. Wagner), *Journal of Monetary Economics*, 4: 617–625.

Tobin, J. (1980) *Asset accumulation and economic activity*. Chicago: The University of Chicago Press.

Tobin, J. (1982) "Money and finance in the macroeconomic process," *Journal of Money, Credit and Banking*, 14: 171–204.

Tobin, J. (1986a) "The monetary–fiscal mix: Long-run implications," *American Economic Review*, 76: 213–218.

Tobin, J. (1986b) "On the welfare macroeconomics of government financial policy," *Scandinavian Journal of Economics*, 88: 9–24.

Tobin, J. and W. H. Buiter (1976) "Long run effects of fiscal and monetary policy on aggregate demand," in J. L. Stein, ed., *Monetarism*. Amsterdam: North Holland.

Tobin, J., W. C. Brainard, D. Backus and G. Smith (1980) "A model of U.S. financial and nonfinancial economic behavior," *Journal of Money, Credit and Banking*, 12: 259–293.

Waldo, D. G. (1985) "Open market operations in an overlapping generations model," *Journal of Political Economy*, 93: 1242–1257.

Wallace, N. (1981) "A Modigliani–Miller theorem for open-market operations," *American Economic Review*, 71: 267–274.

Webb, D. C. (1981) "The net wealth effect of government bonds when credit markets are imperfect," *Economic Journal*, 91: 405–414.

Weiss, A. and J. E. Stiglitz (1981) "Credit rationing in markets with imperfect information," *American Economic Review*, 71: 393–410.

CHAPTER 11

MANDATORY RETIREMENT SAVING AND CAPITAL FORMATION

1 Introduction: The Contesting Views

Recent debate on the macroeconomic effects of mandatory retirement saving has run the gamut from B to F.[1] The B position is that pension institutions, public and private, make no difference. National saving and capital formation are the same with them or without them. The F position is that these institutions, because they have incompletely funded their future obligations, increase consumption at the expense of capital formation.

Suppose that more generous pensions are announced for present and future annuitants and that sufficient new taxes or payroll deductions are levied on currently employed workers to pay the increase to contemporaneous beneficiaries. The F position is that the workers will not reduce their consumption; they will pay the new levies from the voluntary saving that would otherwise have bought them the consumption in old age now assured them by their pensions. At the same time, the current beneficiaries will consume their gains. The result is an increase in consumption, at the expense of investment.

The B position is that neither active workers nor their retired contemporaries will alter consumption. These beneficiaries will, directly or indirectly, transfer their gains to the generations that will have to pay more taxes or wage deductions. They will take less support from their children, or plan to bequeath more to their descendants.

Reprinted by permission from *The Determinants of National Saving and Wealth*, eds. Franco Modigliani and Richard Hemming, London: Macmillan Press, Ltd., 1983. Written with Walter Dolde.

These two views have sharply different policy implications, and they are based on quite different models of individual consumption and saving. The F view relies on the life cycle model, according to which individuals consume their lifetime resources within their lifetimes. They do not internalise, i.e. adapt their consumption, to the expectation that their descendants will have to pay higher premiums for retirement benefits. Therefore, inauguration or liberalisation of pensions financed from contemporaneous mandatory savings does result in a once-for-all-time increase in the national propensity to consume. This would not happen if the pensions, or pension improvements, were deferred so that each cohort of beneficiaries received no more than its prior contributions had earned.

The B model attributes to consumer-savers a dynastic cross-generational view; horizons are essentially infinite. So long as the dynasty's intertemporal budget constraint, involving the present values of taxes, pensions, and other endowments, is the same, the consumption of each generation will be the same.

The evidence of household budget surveys does not support the implication of the strict life cycle model that retired consumers are dissavers, living off their pensions and previously accumulated assets. In 1972–73, for example, families (including single individuals) with head aged 65 or more (average age 73) were net savers, on average 9.2 percent of disposable income. They owned financial assets worth 2.3 times annual income and a home valued 2.1 times income. Half their income came from social insurance and other pensions and annuities. These aged families are making gifts and contributions totalling about 10 percent of their income. These observations suggest that at least part of the mandatory retirement saving done by these households is being channeled into bequests and gifts.[2] There is surely some truth in the Barro effect, especially for the more affluent.

The two approaches have in common the view that the institutions—mandatory social and private retirement plans—matter very little. They are to a good first approximation a transparent veil through which the basic intertemporal preferences of individuals may be seen to prevail. In the B model, this is true however and whenever the pensions are financed. In the F model it is true if the pensions are funded.

There are other, old-fashioned, approaches. One we could call the L (for liquidity) view. This would attribute to households much shorter horizons than either the life cycle or the dynastic model. If workers had no voluntary saving to reduce and no liquid assets to consume, their consumption would have to fall by the full amount of their mandatory saving. Likewise if pensioners were liquidity-constrained they would consume all their annuities. In aggregate the L model agrees with the B model: nothing happens. But the L model differs by predicting a shift of consumption from the younger to the older generation. A more realistic and pragmatic version would expect less than 100 percent adjustments by both generations, and entertain the empirical possibility that the marginal propensity to consume of the old, who might be saving for bequests, would be smaller than that of the young. In this case the assumed transfer would reduce aggregate consumption.

In earlier post-war years, when the U.S. social insurance system was younger and its coverage of the population less complete, George Katona (1965) reported surveys indicating that covered workers actually saved more from their disposable incomes (*after* social security and other taxes) than similar uncovered workers. Even though they could look forward to social insurance benefits, they were doing more voluntary saving for old age than their uninsured brethren. This finding can be rationalised by the hypothesis that social insurance enabled workers to cross a critical threshold previously beyond their reach, namely to make economic independence in old age a feasible aspiration. Now that the great social transition from dependence on children, usually including residence with them, has been so generally made, the Katona effect is probably no longer relevant. But it does suggest that institutions are not as vacuous as economic analysts frequently assume.

Philip Cagan (1965) came to conclusions similar to Katona's in studying private pension plans.

2 Has Anything Really Happened?

In Figure 11.1 we have plotted, for several household budget surveys from 1935–36 to 1972–73, the ratio of saving to income against the ratio of income to mean income in the survey.[3] (Income is disposable income, after payroll and other direct taxes, and after receipt of pensions, social security benefits, and other transfers. Saving does not include payroll taxes for social insurance but does include employees' contributions to

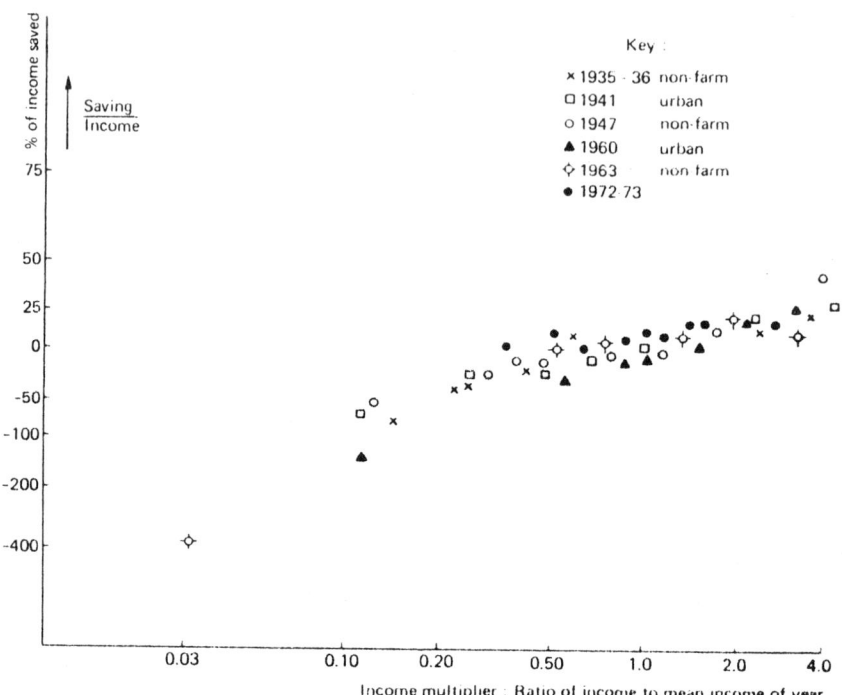

Figure 11.1
Income multiplier

private pension funds as well as other life insurance and annuity premiums. In each survey the basic data are from income brackets, but the average income in each bracket has been adjusted for family size to a standard size of 3.5.) As Dorothy Brady and Rose Friedman pointed out long ago (1947) this simple transformation of budget data makes the points of different surveys, widely separated in time, fall into a common track. The result is consistent with either or both permanent income and relative income models of saving. The point of Figure 11.1 is that the Brady–Friedman conclusions encompass post-war surveys increasingly vulnerable to the impacts of social security wealth and in some degree of private pension wealth. One might have expected those impacts to show up in a downward drift of the scatters for the more recent surveys.

Figure 11.1 underscores the point that Feldstein, as he recognises, is suggesting that total saving ratios, individual and aggregate, would have risen sharply in the post-war period had they not been compressed by social security. This is, of course, a difficult proposition to evaluate. According to the life cycle model, there is no permanent absolute-income effect on saving ratios. Aggregate saving *might* rise as a share of income from changes in age distribution, interest rates, wage income profiles, rates of growth of productivity, normal retirement spans, etc. Assessing the direction and magnitude of these effects would require simulation models of the sort we present below. But aggregation effects would not necessarily show up in cross-section scatters like those in Figure 11.1, whereas the social security effect should. A possible source of an absolute-income effect is that the propensity to bequeath rises with lifetime income, but we do not have evidence on this point.

The foregoing discussion ignores the Keynesian question, and the body of our paper will likewise assume it away. But it is certainly relevant to any operational policy discussion—for example, the capital formation lost because retirement obligations were not funded, or the increases in investment and future production that would result if they were funded. On the F view, unfunded increases in contributions and benefits increase the national propensity to consume. The assumption that capital formation is correspondingly crowded out assumes that the path of real GNP is constrained by resources or by macro policy judgements of the authorities, in the United States the President, Congress, and Federal Reserve System. This has not been continuously the case in the 1970s and previous post-war decades. When it was not, the additional consumption need not, given accommodative monetary policies, have crowded out private investment. The other side of the coin is that funding will not automatically be translated into higher investment. It would require actively stimulative monetary policies to induce the investment corresponding to the funding.[4]

Even without Keynesian problems, it may not be accurate to treat social insurance funding in isolation from other government finance. Under the unified federal budget accounting practices in force in the U.S. since 1967 social insurance receipts and outlays are included in the budget totals and affect the deficits or surpluses that are the foci of fiscal politics. It is not safe to assume that a surplus or deficit in the social security accounts translates dollar for dollar into surplus or deficit for the federal government as a whole. The vanishing of the social insurance trust fund may have been offset at least partially by an increase in other taxes or a reduction in other outlays in order to keep the overall deficit down. Likewise funding might be offset by greater deficit spending in the rest of the budget. Thus the impact of the social security system on the saving available for capital formation depends intermediately on its impact on other fiscal behaviour.

3 Relevant Differences between Mandatory Saving and Voluntary Saving

We turn now to some features of public and private pension plans in the United States which render the mandatory and contractual saving for these pensions less than perfect substitutes for voluntary individual saving. The argument is that voluntary saving will be reduced significantly less than a dollar for every dollar of mandated saving. Thus the rise in the national propensity to consume is smaller than the F model says, and indeed would be negative for fully funded plans.

The underlying motivation for mandatory retirement saving, under public and private plans, has been the popular aspiration for higher standards of living, leisure time, and economic independence in old age. Longer expectancies of life and health have made these objectives more salient. General economic progress has brought them within reach. But why are they not pursued solely by individual voluntary saving? Why do they involve collective saving programmes, in which individuals are required to participate as a condition of their employment? These collective vehicles for mandatory retirement saving have arisen and multiplied in number and size at the insistence of the participants. They have not been imposed from above without consent. The presumption is that they are not trivial but bring about behaviour different from what would happen if they did not exist.

National retirement and survivors' insurance has been adopted and expanded because people really do want to shift consumption to old age. Workers, through collective bargaining and less formal competitive pressures, have chosen to defer compensation for their work for the same reason. The government has fostered this process by deferring taxes on part or all of the deferred compensation, enabling the individual to gain not only the interest on the taxes but the benefit of a lower marginal tax rate.

Retirement saving plans have a significant insurance dimension. Compulsory membership is efficient in avoiding adverse selection, or the costs of controlling for adverse selection. Risk-averse participants might otherwise save for improbably long survival and for improbably high medical costs. Private insurance against these risks must incur the costs of adverse selection or of controlling for it, as well as the administrative costs of smaller and more variable pools. In this respect the compulsory plans could reduce the total saving of these participants, while increasing their lifetime expected consumption and welfare—an example that warns us against the facile identification of capital formation effects as welfare effects. On the other hand, risk-loving or uninformed individuals may not on their own provide even actuarially for these contingencies of old age. A civilised society will not let anyone go without subsistence or medical care, even if the inability to pay for them is the result of personal improvidence. This fact, which may in some cases contribute to such improvidence, is a justification for compulsory participation, which increases the total saving of those individuals.

Mandatory retirement saving is in a sense a collective manifestation of the "Christmas Club" syndrome. The phenomenon is that individuals deliberately discipline themselves to save for a future goal, whether Christmas shopping or retirement, by making it costly or impossible to stop doing so. Other examples are the use of mortgage or instalment credit to make purchases which some consumers could finance in whole or part by drawing on liquid assets. The rationale is that they fear they will not in fact restore their assets, while the debt repayment contract forces them to do the equivalent saving. In these cases the household seeks to protect its true long-run utility maximisation against less valid short-run temptations, self-disciplinary behaviour that is no less real for being ruled out of standard economic models.

The assets acquired by mandatory retirement saving are illiquid pension rights, death or disability benefits, and claims to medical care in case of need. They cannot be cashed in advance, or pledged as loan collateral. Their full value is often realisable only by continued participation contribution. These features impose the intended self-discipline, and they make the mandatory savings considerably less than perfect substitutes for other savings.

Substitution is possible only for households who would otherwise own or acquire more liquid, intertemporally fungible, assets than the pension rights they are forced to accumulate. Many households are in this position, but many are not. The major accumulation of a typical household, other than pensions and retirement annuities, is equity in a residence. This too has limited liquidity. For many households the discipline that illiquidity imposes is that economic reverses, losses of income or extraordinary consumption needs, will be met by squeezing normal consumption outlays rather than by dissaving.

Survey data leave little doubt that liquidity constraints are important determinants of consumption. Otherwise it is difficult to understand why there is not more lifetime spreading of consumption. In 1972–73 families under 25 years of age had on average less than $900 in financial assets. Their discretionary dissaving was only $400, and they were paying a similar amount in insurance and retirement premiums. In an arbitrary common sense attempt to classify households as liquidity-constrained or simply wealth-constrained. Kowalewski and Smith (1979) found that 65 percent of the households in the 1963 Survey of Changes in Family Finances (Federal Reserve Board), owning 14 per cent of net household wealth, failed to meet any of the following four tests: (i) ratio of liquid assets to annual consumption plus contractual saving at least 1/4; (ii) ratio of non-contractual saving to consumption plus contractual saving at least 1/12; (iii) positive net purchases of financial securities; (iv) net wealth excluding family home at least twice consumption plus contractual saving. They then estimated a classification function involving only demographic, stock, and state variables. Households classified by this function not only in the 1963 Survey but in other cross-sections showed substantial and significant differences in consumption behaviour.

Another reason that mandatory and contractual saving for old age is an imperfect substitute for other saving is that the plans are redistributive. For an individual participant, the connection between contributions and the actuarial value of the benefits to be received is quite loose. In federal old age and survivors' insurance, the relationship of an individual's anuities and other benefits to payroll taxes paid on his or her behalf is a complicated non-linear formula. For example, in 1979 the gross return on the taxes paid on the first $2,160 of annual earnings was six times as high as on the taxes paid on taxed earnings above $13,020. The progressivity of this schedule means that those workers who are most likely to have long horizons and liquidity receive a relatively bad deal and have both motivation and capacity for voluntary saving. Those who receive a relatively good deal lack the liquidity to maintain their consumption while paying the payroll taxes. There are similar redistributive effects in many private plans. However, the tendency to reward employees of long tenure at the expense of those of short tenure—who may be receiving nothing, or anyway much less than the value of the contributions incident to their employment—tends to bias the outcome in the other direction.

4 Social Security and Induced Retirement

One effect of social retirement insurance seems quite clear. It has led to earlier retirements and longer retirement spans. Although the labour force participation of men aged 65 and over has trended downward in the United States since 1890, the decline accelerated after the introduction of social security. The rate was 54.0 percent in 1930, 41.8 percent in 1940, 41.4 percent in 1950, and fell to 19.3 percent in 1977. Probably the effect is due less to the pensions *per se* than to heavy tax on earnings implicit in the calculation of retirement benefits for persons between the ages of 62 and 72.[5]

Martin Feldstein (1974) points out that the early retirement effect mitigates the displacement of saving by unfunded social insurance.[6] Working fewer years, the family must save more to support a longer retirement. The result is lower lifetime consumption of goods, but greater consumption of leisure. Alternatively and more realistically, in view of the concomitant upward trend in labour force participation of women younger than 65, the net result is substitution of male retired leisure for female housework.

5 Effects of the Low Return to Unfunded Retirement Insurance

The return yielded by a pay-as-you-go retirement plan in a steady state is the natural rate of growth of the economy. This rate of return is generally less than the after-tax real return to private saving in the capital markets. If it is so perceived, participants will wish to save voluntarily to make up the loss.

In Feldstein's seminal article (1974) calling attention to the displacement of capital formation by "social security wealth" (SSW), he estimated a time series of such wealth and found that it carries a significant positive coefficient in regression explaining personal consumption.[7] He calculated SSW both gross, GSSW, an estimate of the present value of future benefits, and net, NSSW, which subtracted from GSSW the present value of future payroll taxes. These are aggregate figures at each date, for all taxpayers and beneficiaries.

The regressions also included current and lagged disposable income, from which payroll taxes had already been subtracted. Feldstein suggested that this subtraction roughly justified the use of GSSW in several of the regressions, including the one from which he concluded that social security had halved personal saving. It is, however, surprising that the coefficient of disposable income was the same in the NSSW regressions as in the GSSW regressions. In principle one would have expected the negative effects of payroll taxes to show up in higher coefficients of disposable income when payroll taxes were not removed from social security wealth. Instead the substitution of NSSW for GSSW merely increased the SSW coefficient; the two series share an upward trend, along with many other time series. These results cast doubt on whether the SSW series really represent the conceptually intended variables.

There is a more serious problem. The computations of SSW did not impose the "pay-as-you-go" constraint on the system. It was precisely this feature of the system that Feldstein was, with considerable justice, complaining about. For it is this feature, compared to funding, that results in the alleged crowding-out of capital formation. In Feldstein's calculations, however, consumers expect certain benefits without expecting the taxes to pay for them year by year. He froze benefit expectations at the historical average of the ratio of single-retiree annual annuity to disposable income per capita. (His figure was 0.41, approximately the level of 1965–70, although the actual figure was 0.46 in 1960 and has been 0.48 in recent years.) At the same time, he froze the ratio of payroll taxes to disposable income at the 1971 level. The two freezes are not consistent. As everybody knows, payroll tax rates have been steadily rising and are scheduled to rise further. Otherwise the system cannot stay out of deficit with the present menu of benefits. Feldstein attributed to participants an exaggerated view of their social security wealth.

The unfunded social insurance system cannot sustain a rate of return on contribution in excess of the rate of growth of the system. In its youth the system was growing very fast, as it was expanded to cover more and more of the labour force. Consequently the early beneficiaries were able to enjoy very high rates of return. Now that the system is mature, its real return is limited to the growth of real payrolls, essentially labour force and productivity. Mistaken extrapolation of the past ratios of benefits to contributions could lead participants to under-save, and this is what Feldstein's regressions predict.

Feldstein assumes, quite properly, that the real interest rate available to individuals on market saving, and presumably also on funded private pension contributions, exceeds the real growth rate of the economy.[8] If the market rate is used to discount future taxes and benefits, then in a steady state the net social security wealth of a young worker beginning his career is negative. The present value of his lifetime consumption will be reduced by this amount. Capital formation will reflect this reduction as well as the substitution of future social security benefits for other saving. The wealth effect can be substantial. Suppose the real interest rate is 0.04 and the growth rate of the population is 0.01. Assume that all active workers at any time receive the same wage, which is growing over time at a rate of 0.02, and that workers retire for 10 years after working 45 years. Then an unfunded retirement insurance scheme, which each year collects 10 percent of wages and disburses them in benefits, diminishes the initial human capital of a worker by 2.6 percent. If workers spread discounted consumption evenly over their lifetimes, aggregate consumption will be diminished by the same percentage. Aggregating this behaviour over workers of all ages in a steady state results in a reduction in capital stock from 50 percent of human wealth to 35 percent of human wealth. The aggregate "social security wealth" of the population in percentage of its human wealth is 22 percent gross and 12 percent net.

This point of the example is that in principle social security wealth is negatively, not positively, related to consumption and at the same time negatively related to the capital stock. Direct regression of the capital stock on SSW would be a more relevant test of the extended life cycle hypothesis than regressions of consumption.

6 The Purpose of Simulations

Regressions of aggregate time series do not seem a fruitful way to investigate the complex stock-flow relationships involved in lifetime saving behaviour. If the economy were in a steady state in which households are simply realising their plans, aggregate wealth and income would be perfectly correlated. It would not be possible, or even conceptually meaningful, to distinguish income effects from wealth effects. Actual observations do not come from steady states, but they certainly contain pervasive trend growth effects. Deviations of measured wealth and income from collinear tracks reflect a mélange of cyclical fluctuations, disequilibrium adjustments, adaptations to new demographic, economic, and policy parameters, errors of observation, and miscellaneous noise. It is hard to imagine how to interpret the resulting coefficients, and especially hard to see how they can be used for thought experiments that try to make comparisons across steady states differing in parameters.

The Ando–Modigliani[9] equation used by Feldstein (1974) does not distinguish planned wealth from unplanned wealth. The life cycle model does not suggest that consumption behaviour will be changed simply because planned saving increases wealth over time by the expected amount, but the coefficient of wealth probably includes some of the common trend of consumption, income, and wealth. To the unknown extent that the coefficient tells the impact of unplanned accretions of wealth, it does not convey information about planned saving behaviour—which is the principal matter at issue in discussions of social security, for example. Finally, aggregate time series say nothing about the important differential impacts of parameter and policy changes on households of different circumstances (even ages!) and tastes.

For these reasons, we think it is fruitful to investigate the issues by simulations, in particular by simulations that allow comparisons of steady states. These also make it possible to consider households differing not only in age but in other relevant characteristics: liquidity, bequest motivation, income level. Such simulations, however "realistic" we try to make their assumptions, cannot tell us about the real world. Their advantage is that they enable us to trace consistently and fully the effects of various changes of parameters and policies. Here we have considered only steady states. The technique could be applied also to disequilibrium adjustments and cyclical fluctuations. The ultimate test would be the congruence of the outcomes of the analogue economy of the simulations, with both time series and cross-section data.

7 The Research Strategy

We have on previous occasions employed simulation analysis similar in spirit to that presented here; Tobin (1967), Tobin and Dolde (1971), Dolde (1973). Simulation analysis, like the more frequently encountered theoretical and statistical research methods, has both advantages and disadvantages.

The principal advantage of simulation analysis over pure theory is that it permits investigation of behaviour far too rich to be tractable for theoretical analysis. Pure theory further suffers the difficulty that even when feasible, it may yield indeterminate results. The signs of important relationships may depend on quantitative restrictions on parameters rather than just qualitative assumptions. Simulations may at least give guidance on whether interesting relationships are "large and positive," "near zero," "large and negative," or somewhere in between. Finally, we would observe that pure theory gains its simplicity by assuming a large number of zero restrictions on parameters relating to variables which might be included in the analysis but must be excluded to obtain the simplicity. Thus it is not obvious that theoretical models are uniformly "more general" than simulation models.

The proof of the pudding is in the eating, and statistical investigation thus has an obvious attraction. In too many cases, however, we find it difficult or impossible to discern statistically the behaviour of interest. The data often have disappointingly little information content, even in large samples. Likelihood functions often appear to be long, wide and gently rolling in parameter space rather than sharply peaked. Even where parameter estimates appear to possess statistical significance, extreme caution is called for in their interpretation, especially in inferring causality. In time series, for example, timing of changes in social security taxes and benefits often is influenced by other macroeconomic events which affect spending and saving as well. Thus part of the correlation of consumer behaviour with social security changes may not be causal, but rather reflect the dependence of both on other events. In cross-section data, saving, spending and wealthholding are all correlated with age, as is the immediate impact of changes in the social security system. Finally there is the difficult problem of households' expectations about the social security system. A very large part of the growth of benefits and taxes has occurred within the last decade or so. Could this sort of growth of benefits have been reasonably anticipated during their working life by the currently retired? To the extent that the current generosity of the system is a "surprise," it should not provide an explanation of saving and wealthholding of the aged.

In contrast with statistical work, of course, simulation analysis makes no formal test of the conformity of a model with some set of data. As with pure theory, the importance of simulation results depends on the plausibility of the assumptions of the model.

A clear advantage of simulation over statistical analysis is the ability to investigate counterfactual events whose effects are not reflected in any data base. This ability is shared with pure theory, but again simulation analysis possesses much greater facility for experiments involving changes in policy variables and key parameters.

The simulations reported here are for a dynamic steady state economy in which all households possess perfect foresight. There is no uncertainty. Naturally we regard the analysis of steady states as a first rather than a final step in determining the effects of mandatory retirement saving on capital formation. In future research we plan to relax the steady-state assumptions and investigate the implications of mandatory retirement saving for the actual U.S. population and economy over the next several decades. In the meantime the current results can give some guidance to the equilibrium to which we might converge if alternative scenarios persist.

8 Overview of the Model

Households, firms, and the national government comprise the units whose behaviour is modelled. Much of the behaviour of households and firms is represented as explicit maximising behaviour. The design of private pension plans, however, is simply treated parametrically. Similarly all aspects of government behaviour are taken as exogenous, while effects to be inferred as policy instruments are set at different levels.

Households differ in two respects: by age and by "economic group." The three economic groups in the current model differ in labour productivity and in propensity to grant bequests. Since this is a steady-state model, those with higher bequest propensities inherit greater bequests from their ancestors. Labour productivity and inheritances/bequests are correlated across economic groups: those with the greatest inherited wealth also have the highest labour productivity. Ability and willingness to invest in human capital could well account for this, although such a process is not made explicit in the model. There is no mobility among economic groups.

Households begin their economic life at age 18. We ignore any age difference between male and female adults. All households exhibit identical fertility and mortality behaviour. Because the utility function described below has as its arguments variables expressed "per equivalent adult," the behaviour of a cohort of households of a given age and economic group is the same whether viewed as the outcome of a single decision made by the entire cohort or as the aggregation of individual decisions.

The arguments of the lifetime utility function are housing and non-housing consumption for each period. Bequests should appear as arguments of the utility function as well. Computational difficulties, however, necessitated a parametric treatment of bequests and inheritances. Households maximise lifetime utility subject to an exogenous non-property income stream and an interest rate earnable or payable on net worth at each point in time. The non-property income stream consists of labour earnings—labour is supplied inelastically and there is no unemployment—social security benefits, private pension benefits, and other government transfer payments. All of these are net of any taxes, as is the interest rate. Non-property income also is augmented by gifts *inter vivos* and inheritances and later reduced, by committed bequests. A second set of constraints limits the set of feasible life cycles in housing and other consumption. Unsecured borrowing cannot exceed some fraction of a year's non-property income.

Because of the dynamic steady-state assumptions, only the life cycle plan of the household currently at the formation stage need be analysed. Consumption, earnings, and wealth holding of other age groups will differ by a factor reflecting only the growth rates of population and labour productivity. Similarly national aggregates can be derived readily from the base household's life cycle.

Firms produce all output except that of owner-occupied housing. There are no costs to adjusting factor inputs, so static profit maximisation suffices to describe firm behaviour. Firms decide on how much labour and capital to employ and how much output to produce. Full wage and capital rental flexibility guarantee full employment. In a perfectly anticipated steady state, of course, the wage-per-effective-worker/rental ratio is constant.

There is only one production process. Its output can be used as the non-housing consumption good, as government purchases, or as investment in plant and equipment or in housing. The composite good is the numeraire.

Firms pay out the entirety of their sales proceeds. In addition to factor payments for labour and capital rental, they pay taxes and make contributions to private pension plans. There is no depreciation. Firms behave as if none of these taxes or transfers is lump-sum. Rather they view them all as being proportional to gross factor payments. Thus there is a payroll tax on employers for social security which is proportionate to the wage bill. The corporate profits tax is included here as a proportional tax on capital rental.

Private pension plans are non-contributory defined benefit plans proportional to earnings in the period from age 55 to 64. Current contributions to pension reserves are viewed as proportional to wage and/or capital rental payments.

The government purchases output, makes general transfer payments and social security benefit payments, and collects taxes. Households pay proportional taxes, not necessarily all at the same rate, on property income, private pension benefits, on inheritances, and on labour income. The latter bears both a personal income tax and a payroll tax for social security. Firms pay proportional taxes on capital rental payments and a payroll tax for social security.

Non-uniform tax rates drive wedges between before- and after-tax rates of return on the various assets in which the public can hold its wealth. Wealth can be held as capital "rented out" to corporations, as owner-occupied housing, and as government debt. Both the social security and private pension systems have cumulative surpluses, which they hold either as government or corporate debt. In this model with uncertainty and transaction costs, all debt and corporate capital are perfect substitutes as stores of wealth and must therefore have equal yields to wealth holders. Only corporate capital is subject to a tax before its return is distributed. Thus the social return to capital, its marginal productivity, will exceed the social return on other forms of wealth-holding in equilibrium. Households pay the same proportionate tax rate on all forms of property income save one. The exception is the use value of owner-occupied housing, which is completely untaxed. Households' desires to arbitrage this tax subsidy to homeowning are less than infinite, however, since housing yields no return other than its consumption value.

9 Numerical Results

In this section we summarise solutions for the model for eight cases. Appendix A presents the equations and variables of the model. Appendix B indicates the parameter values and exogenous variables for the base case and the changes which generated the other seven cases. Complete solutions for the base case and for the case of fully funded retirement systems appear in Appendix C.

Table 11.1 provides a key to the eight cases we examined. Both population and labour input remain unchanged across all eight cases. Thus a

Table 11.1
Definition of Cases Examined

Case 1	Base Case
Case 2	Retirement Systems Fully Funded—both social security and private retirement systems fully funded
Case 3	Social Security Benefits Increased—social security benefits are doubled as a percentage of labour earnings
Case 4	Private Retirement Benefits Increased—private retirement benefits are doubled as a percentage of labour earnings
Case 5	Bequest Motive Increased—inheritances and bequests are increased by 10 percent as a proportion of labour earnings
Case 6	Unsecured Borrowing Prohibited
Case 7	Borrowing Limits Increased—maximum permitted unsecured borrowing increased by 10 percent as a proportion of labour earnings
Case 8	Capital Taxes Reduced—rates of taxation on corporate capital, personal property income, private pension benefits, and inheritances all reduced by 10 percent relative to the rate of taxation of labour earnings

comparison of absolute levels of variables across cases also indicates proportionate changes in per capita and per worker experience.

Table 11.2 indicates the levels of six aggregate variables for the eight cases. The final column of Table 11.2 presents an approximate utility-based comparison of the base case with each of the other cases. The entries in this column indicate for each case the amount by which non-housing consumption of middle level (group 2) households would have to be changed during ages 18–24 to leave them indifferent between the case in question and the base case. A minus sign (−) indicates a preferred case in which consumption could be reduced during the first seven years. The units are percentages of non-housing consumption levels during those seven years. Thus, for example, households in group 2 prefer the base case to case 3, but would be indifferent between the two if non-housing consumption during ages 18–24 were augmented in case 3 by 36 percent of its level in the base case.

From Table 11.2 we observe a high correlation between the ranking of cases on the utility measure and on aggregate consumption. The quantitative differences between aggregate consumption and the utility measures across cases are more complex, most importantly because of aggregation.

Case 2, with fully funded retirement systems, exhibits the greatest difference from the base case. Household net worth is 40 percent higher than in the base case, but the capital stock is higher by 130 percent. The difference is the increase in the social security trust fund from 18 to 1195 (Appendix C) and in private pension reserves from 146 to 280 (Appendix C). Cash flow profiles are uniformly higher, as are non-housing consumption profiles for groups 1 and 2. Group 3 rotates its non-housing consumption profile, consuming more before age 35 and less thereafter. Housing profiles are also higher for all economic groups, with group 3 rotating its profile to augment initial housing by a greater proportion. Wealth profiles are also higher for each group for each age. The profile for group 3 is changed greatly, with much more accumulation between ages 35 and 55.

Clearly a society given the choice between cases 1 and 2—including as initial endowments the smaller capital stock of case 1 or the larger capital stock of case 2—would select case 2, including the obligation to maintain full funding of retirement benefits. Our current model does not permit

Table 11.2
Results of Steady-state Simulations

Case	Non-housing Consumption C	Housing Stock H	Capital Stock K	Household Net Worth W	Net National Product Y	Non-housing Output YNH	Utility Comparison[a] %
1 Base	596	822	1465	2582	913	852	—
2 Retirement Systems Fully Funded	678	1085	3386	3529	1049	1008	−20
3 Social Security Benefits Increased	546	709	962	1939	843	773	36
4 Private Retirement Benefits Increased	582	789	1299	2394	892	829	2
5 Bequest Motive Increased	629	892	1828	3032	960	904	−7
6 Unsecured Borrowing Prohibited	606	844	1612	2756	926	868	0
7 Borrowing Limits Increased	595	820	1450	2564	911	850	−0
8 Capital Taxes Reduced	591	798	1417	2506	906	844	4

[a] Measure of consumption change required to equate utility to base case. Thus a negative entry is an improvement over the base case. See text for explanation.

assessments of the feasibility or desirability of the transitions between alternative steady states.

Case 3, in which the ratio of social security benefits to labour earnings is doubled, also reflects major differences from the base case. Here, all of the aggregate and individual measures of economic activity are lower. The basic change to which households respond is a rotation of the cash flow profile—higher after age 65 but lower before. Cash flow during the working years is lower because the doubling of social security benefits requires a doubling of social security contribution rates with the trust fund a fixed proportion of net national product. Thus the increase in social security benefits is essentially unfunded. Further, the counter-clockwise rotation of the cash flow portfolio reduces both the desire and the ability of households to accumulate wealth.

By comparison to cases 2 and 3, the differences of the remaining cases from the base case are more moderate. Because they are smaller to begin with, doubling private retirement benefits relative to labour earnings (case 4) causes smaller changes than a relative doubling of social security benefits (case 3). In the base case, aggregate social security benefits are four times as large as aggregate private retirement benefits ($Q = 42.2$, $P = 9.9$ in Appendix C).

Increasing bequests and inheritances relative to labour earnings by 10 per cent (case 5) raises all of the aggregate economic indicators. Cohorts receiving larger inheritances can grant larger bequests and enjoy higher consumption along the way. Again our steady state model is an inadequate vehicle for addressing issues concerning transitions between steady states.

Elimination of unsecured borrowing (case 6) and a modest increase in unsecured borrowing (case 7) cause appropriately scaled changes in the economic aggregates. Clearly the borrowing constraints are binding, or no differences would be observed. Preventing or permitting households to raise early consumption at the expense of later consumption or accumulation of down payment for a house raises or lowers aggregate wealth and capital. In terms of utility comparisons, the disutility associated with tighter borrowing constraints apparently completely offsets the increased utility from higher average consumption.

Reducing capital tax rates by 10 percent relative to other tax rates (case 8) yields surprising results indeed. Wealth and capital stock are both lower, as are the other economic aggregates. Since government outlays are fixed as a proportion of net national product, other tax rates must rise to offset the decrease in capital tax rates. The resulting lower labour earnings profile reduces corresponding economic activity, including wealth accumulation, and more than offsets the increase in real returns from cutting capital taxes.

Appendix A: Specification of the Model

A1 Equations of the Model

Households

Maximise $\sum_i \frac{\alpha_{ij}}{\rho} c_{ij}^\rho + \sum_i \frac{\zeta_{ij}}{\rho} h_{ij}^\rho$ utility function

subject to

$\dot{w}_{ij} + c_{ij} \leq r(w_{ij} - h_{ij}) + e_{ij}$ instantaneous budget constraint

$w_{ij} - h_{ij}(1-m) \geq \bar{w}_{ij}$ limit on unsecured debt

$e_{ij} = (1 - t_v - t_s)\beta_{ij}v_n n_{ij} + q_{ij} + (1 - t_b)p_{ij} + z_{ij} - b_{ij}$ non-property earnings = labour + social security + private pensions + other government transfers − net bequests granted

$r = u_h(1 - t_u)$ yield on household wealth except housing

α_{ij}, ζ_{ij} reflect survival probabilities, fertility, equivalent adult weights, time preference, housing, bequest utilities

Production

$Y_{NH} = \Theta K^\Phi (JL)^{1-\Phi}$ production, except housing services

$v = (1 - \Phi) Y_{NH}/L$ marginal product of labour

$u = \Phi Y_{NH}/K$ marginal product of capital

$L = \sum_i \sum_j \beta_{ij} n_{ij}$ natural labour force, in terms of fully employed males 25 and over

$\dot{J} = \gamma J$ Harrod-neutral technical progress

Identities and equilibrium

$K = W - D_s - D_g - D_p - H$ capital is wealth not absorbed as debt for social security, other government, private pensions or housing (D_s, D_p currently negative in actual U.S.)

$W = \sum_i \sum_j w_{ij}$ aggregate wealth

$C = \sum_i \sum_j c_{ij}$ aggregate consumption

$H = \sum_i \sum_j h_{ij}$ aggregate housing

$Y_{NH} = C + \dot{K} + \dot{H} + G$	output, except housing services
$Y_{NI} = Y_{NH} + u_h H$	national income
$\dot{D}_g = G + Z_g - T_g + u_h D_g$	general government deficit
$D_g = \dot{D}_j/(\gamma + n)$	general government debt outstanding
$T_g = t_v v_h L + t_u u_h (W - H) + t_c u K + t_b P$	general government taxes
$\dot{D}_s = Q - T_s + u_h D_s$	social security deficit
$D_s = \dot{D}_s/(\gamma + n)$	social security debt outstanding (possibly negative)
$Q = \sum_i \sum_j q_{ij}$	aggregate social security benefits
$T_s = t_s v_h L + t_p v_h L$	social security revenues
$\dot{D}_p = P - X + u_h D_p$	private pension deficit
$D_p = \dot{D}_p/(\gamma + n)$	private pension debt outstanding (possibly negative)
$P = \sum_i \sum_j p_{ij}$	private pension benefits
$X = x_v v L$	private pension revenues
$v_h = v(1 - x_v)(1 - t_p)$	household wage
$u_h = u(1 - t_c - x_u)$	household returns
$0 = \sum_i b_{ij}$	current inheritances = current bequests

A2 Variables of the Model

b_{ij}	net bequests granted by economic group j of age i (negative for net inheritance)
C	aggregate consumption
c_{ij}	consumption of economic group j of age i
D_g	cumulative deficit, general government
D_s	cumulative deficit, social security system
D_p	cumulative deficit, private pension system
e_{ij}	non-property earnings of economic group j of age i
G	government purchases of goods and services
H	aggregate housing stock
h_{ij}	housing stock of economic group j of age i
i	age group
j	economic group
J	state of Harrod-neutral technical progress
K	physical capital stock
L	natural labour force
n_{ij}	labour force of economic group j of age i
Q	aggregate social security benefits
q_{ij}	social security benefits of economic group j of age i
P	aggregate private pension benefits

p_{ij} private pension benefits of economic group j of age i
r after tax real return realised by households on lending/borrowing
T_g general government taxes
T_s social security taxes
t_b tax rate on private pension benefits
t_c tax rate on corporate capital
t_i tax rate on intergenerational transfers
t_p tax rate on corporate payroll, on corporations, for social security
t_s tax rate on corporate payroll, on households, for social security
t_u personal income tax rate on property income
t_v personal income tax rate on labour income
u rental rate on capital gross of all taxes and pension contributions
u_h rental rate on capital realised by households gross of personal income taxes
v wage cost, gross of all taxes and pension contributions
v_h wage rate, gross of personal income and personal social security tax
W aggregate wealth
w_{ij} wealth of economic group j of age i
$\bar{w}_{ij}$ lower limit on wealth (possibly negative) of economic group j of age i
X aggregate private pension contributions
x_v private pension contribution rate for defined benefit plans, from labour earnings
Y_{NH} output except housing services
Y_{NI} national income
Z_g general government transfers
z_{ij} general government transfers to economic group j of age i

Appendix B: Parameter Values for Cases

Table 11B.1 indicates parameter values for the base case. Table 11B.2 presents those parameters which were changed in each case. Unless indicated in Table 11B.2, other parameters maintain the same value as in the base case.

Table 11.B1
Parameter Values for Base Case (Case 1)

MPDS	NINCS	ITER	ITERW	NYVAR	NYAVAR	NYBVAR	ITPRNT	ITWPRT
6	3	910	499	39	60	60	100	0
	EPS		EPSW		ADJ		ADJW	
	0.0010		0.0001		0.5000		0.5000	

AGE VECTOR

18.0000	25.0000	35.000	45.0000	55.0000	65.0000
85.0000					
THETAP	PHI	H	GAMMA	GPOP	DGRAT
11.3000	0.2000	1.000	0.0200	0.0000	0.0100
GRAT	TVR	TUR	TCR	DSRAT	TSR
0.2300	0.2500	0.5000	0.4000	−0.0004	0.0700
TPR	DPRAT	XVR	XCR	XUR	RHO
0.0700	−0.0032	1.000	0.0000	0.0000	−4.0000
DNPMT1	DNPMT2	DNPMT3	TBR	TIR	
0.2000	0.2000	0.2000	0.1400	0.1000	
HEIGHT1	HEIGHT2	HEIGHT3			
0.0250	0.1250	5.0000			

NB

0.1000	0.2400	0.2800	0.2600	0.2100	0.0600
2.3400	5.7000	6.5800	6.0500	4.8500	1.2900
0.4400	1.0800	1.2500	1.1600	0.9200	0.2400

BORRAT

−0.2000	−0.2000	−0.2000	−0.2000	−0.2000	0.0000
−0.2000	−0.2000	−0.2000	−0.2000	−0.2000	0.0000
−0.2000	−0.2000	−0.2000	−0.2000	−0.2000	0.0000

ALPHA

5.5800	19.8000	21.0000	4.4900	0.9630	0.6310
16.40000	58.0000	61.8000	13.2000	2.8300	1.8600
1.6600	5.8900	6.2700	1.3400	0.2870	0.1890

KSI	2.1700	7.7200	8.1900	1.7500	0.3670	0.2460
	6.4000	22.6000	24.1000	5.1500	1.1000	0.7250
	0.6470	2.3000	2.4500	0.5230	0.1120	0.0737
ZRAT	0.0010	0.0017	0.0018	0.0014	0.0011	0.0019
	0.0051	0.0086	0.0090	0.0071	0.0057	0.0095
	0.0003	0.0005	0.0006	0.0004	0.0004	0.0006
QRAT	0.0000	0.0000	0.0000	0.0000	0.0420	0.4640
	0.0000	0.0000	0.0000	0.0000	0.0420	0.4640
	0.0000	0.0000	0.0000	0.0000	0.0140	0.1550
PRAT	0.0000	0.0000	0.0000	0.0000	0.0088	0.0976
	0.0000	0.0000	0.0000	0.0000	0.0088	0.0976
	0.0000	0.0000	0.0000	0.0000	0.0088	0.0976
SHAPE	0.4700	0.4700	0.5300	0.7100	1.0000	
	0.4700	0.4700	0.5300	0.7100	1.0000	
	0.1400	0.1400	0.4300	0.5700	1.0000	

Table 11.B2
Changed Parameter Values for Other Cases

Case 2	Retirement Systems Fully Funded—DSRAT and DPRAT, respectively the ratios of the negative of the social security and private retirement reserves to Y, become endogenous, taking on whatever values are necessary so that both retirement systems are fully funded
Case 3	Social Security Benefits Increased—QRAT, the ratio of social security benefits to final average labour earnings, is doubled for each age and income group
Case 4	Private Retirement Benefits Increased—PRAT, the ratio of private retirement benefits to final average labour earnings, is doubled for each age and income group
Case 5	Bequest Motive Increased—HEIGHT, the ratio of inheritances to labour earnings during ages 45–54, is increased by 10 percent for each economic group
Case 6	Unsecured Borrowing Prohibited—BORRAT, the ratio of permitted unsecured borrowing to labour earnings, is set to zero
Case 7	Borrowing Limits Increased—BORRAT raised by 10 percent
Case 8	Capital Taxes Reduced—TUR, TCR, TBR, TIR, tax relatives for TU, TC, TB, TI, are reduced by 10 percent relative to other tax rates

Appendix C: Solutions for Cases 1 and 2

Table 11C.1 presents the solution for the base case. Aggregate variables appear first, followed by those for age-economic groups. The first row under each heading indicates the profile expected or planned by a household of economic group 1 currently aged 18. The six columns correspond to the intervals 18–24, 25–34, 35–44, 45–54, 55–64, and 65–84.

The second and third rows correspond similarly to profiles for groups 2 and 3. (Units here are not commensurate with the aggregates, but might represent, say, thousands of dollars per household.) For example, group 3 households currently aged 8 expect to have non-housing consumption of 131.2 on average during ages 45–54.

Rows 4 through 6 show current values aggregated for all households in an age-income cell. Economy-wide aggregates are the sum of these 18 numbers. For example, aggregate non-housing consumption of group a households aged 25 to 34 is 80.1.

Table 11C.1
Solution for Base Case

C	DG	DS	DP	G	K
596.4686	456.3534	−18.2541	−146.0331	209.9299	1464.7970
L	Q	P	R	TG	TS
33.0500	42.1827	9.8830	0.0401	286.5138	41.1979
TB	TC	TP	TS	TU	TV
0.1279	0.3655	0.0335	0.0335	0.4568	0.2284
U	UH	V	VH	W	X
0.1163	0.0738	19.2962	18.5894	2581.8764	2.0198
XC	XU	XV	Y	ZG	KDOT
0.0000	0.0000	0.0032	912.7680	52.0261	29.2901
DGDOT	DSDOT	DPDOT	WDOT/W	H	HDOT
9.1274	−0.3651	−2.9208	0.0200	822.2757	16.4444
YNH	B	TI			
852.1001	255.1343	0.0914			

Consumption Profiles, for Base Cohort, Then by Age

1.8979	3.3954	4.6928	5.0909	4.3139	3.8479
6.5083	12.8716	18.1580	19.3070	15.0331	12.6081
31.1222	63.9005	172.6691	131.2058	104.4568	73.1197
1.9835	4.2806	4.8438	4.3022	2.9848	3.9644
33.5850	80.1219	92.5397	80.5596	51.3562	64.1360
10.1646	25.1748	55.6953	34.6496	22.5851	23.5413

Cash Flow Profiles

2.0838	3.5531	4.9003	5.3273	5.5343	3.2269
7.1075	13.4395	18.9611	21.6109	23.2319	5.2209
34.4390	67.5701	190.0169	266.9299	414.3115	−485.5955
2.3339	4.9423	5.5806	4.9671	4.2248	4.0337
39.3044	92.3018	106.6182	99.4904	87.5657	32.2230
12.0536	29.3713	67.6242	77.7765	98.9369	−189.6871

Social Security Benefits Profiles

0.0000	0.0000	0.0000	0.0000	0.2177	1.1863
0.0000	0.0000	0.0000	0.0000	1.0260	5.5492
0.0000	0.0000	0.0000	0.0000	1.0361	5.5558
0.0000	0.0000	0.0000	0.0000	0.1662	1.4829
0.0000	0.0000	0.0000	0.0000	3.8672	34.2490
0.0000	0.0000	0.0000	0.0000	0.2472	2.1702

Private Pension Benefits Profiles

0.0000	0.0000	0.0000	0.0000	0.0456	0.2495
0.0000	0.0000	0.0000	0.0000	0.2150	1.1672
0.0000	0.0000	0.0000	0.0000	0.6512	3.4983
0.0000	0.0000	0.0000	0.0000	0.0348	0.3119
0.0000	0.0000	0.0000	0.0000	0.8103	7.2041
0.0000	0.0000	0.0000	0.0000	0.1554	1.3666

Table 11C.1 (continued)

Wealth Profiles

0.5337	0.4788	0.1538	0.0043	11.8862	0.0000
1.5176	1.0461	−0.4340	15.6581	1112.5661	0.0000
10.9094	21.2634	164.8885	1813.9324	6439.5942	0.0000
0.2594	0.6417	0.3432	0.0731	3.7031	7.3334
3.6416	8.1258	1.9364	28.4098	202.4935	342.9101
1.6568	6.1339	27.7095	239.5500	842.3428	864.6121

Borrowing Limits

−0.3818	−0.7835	−1.1164	−1.2662	−1.2491	0.0000
−1.8095	−3.7686	−5.3137	−5.9674	−5.8429	0.0000
−5.3760	−11.2821	−15.9491	−18.0777	−17.5118	0.0000
−0.3718	−0.8923	−1.0410	−0.9666	−0.7807	0.0000
−8.6995	−21.1910	−24.4626	−22.4922	−18.0309	0.0000
−1.6358	−4.0151	−4.6472	−4.3126	−3.4203	0.0000

Other Transfer Profiles

0.8394	1.1483	1.4667	1.4096	1.3750	1.4020
0.8401	1.1469	1.4658	1.4136	1.3755	1.4005
0.8345	1.1549	1.4619	1.4096	1.3774	1.4020
0.9401	1.5973	1.6703	1.3143	1.0496	1.7525
4.6458	7.8769	8.2420	6.5078	5.1844	8.6436
0.2921	0.5020	0.5203	0.4107	0.3286	0.5476

Housing Profiles

2.9895	4.5776	6.3113	6.3513	6.3525	6.0642
10.2588	16.6358	24.0739	24.3985	23.6775	19.8688
49.0448	81.2472	162.7276	206.8215	164.6500	115.2550
3.1244	5.7710	6.5144	5.3673	4.3952	6.2476
52.9392	103.5535	122.6894	101.8040	80.8871	101.0705
16.0182	32.0798	52.4886	54.6186	35.5998	37.1070

Labor Income Profiles

1.6597	3.2073	4.5703	5.1835	5.1136	0.8922
7.8657	15.4275	21.7523	24.4283	23.9188	3.8852
23.3685	46.1851	65.2900	74.0038	71.6874	11.4208
1.8589	4.4613	5.2048	4.8330	3.9036	1.1153
43.4973	105.9550	122.3130	112.4611	90.1547	23.9793
8.1790	20.0757	23.2358	21.5628	17.1015	4.4613

Inheritance/Bequest Profiles

0.0195	0.0377	0.0606	0.0920	0.1278	−0.2613
0.4621	0.9063	1.4410	2.1679	2.9897	−6.1783
16.3573	32.3282	140.3675	210.9015	358.4211	−554.7152
0.0218	0.0524	0.0690	0.0858	0.0976	−0.3266
2.5554	6.2246	8.1029	9.9805	11.2689	−38.1322
5.7250	14.0524	49.9547	61.4512	85.5039	−216.6872

Table 11C.2
Solution for Base Case 2

C	DG	DS	DP	G	K
677.9218	524.4157	−1195.1433	−280.0370	241.2955	3386.4757
L	Q	P	R	TG	TS
33.0500	50.2844	11.7812	0.0207	310.3952	28.8394
TB	TC	TP	TS	TU	TV
0.1270	0.3630	0.0197	0.0197	0.4537	0.2269
U	UH	V	VH	W	X
0.0595	0.0379	22.8153	22.1622	3529.0917	6.7563
XC	XU	XV	Y	ZG	KDOT
0.0000	0.0000	0.0090	1049.3566	59.7993	67.6845
DGDOT	DSDOT	DPDOT	WDOT/W	H	HDOT
10.4911	−23.8976	−5.5995	0.0199	1085.3979	21.7025
YNH	B	TI			
1008.4096	304.0471	0.0907			

Consumption Profiles, for Base Cohort, Then by Age

2.2836	4.1290	5.7300	6.2285	5.2767	4.4519
7.9398	15.8384	22.4391	23.4472	17.7364	13.9898
37.7997	78.2882	160.3792	120.3543	92.1699	64.5189
2.3867	5.2054	5.9143	5.2635	3.6509	4.5866
40.9722	98.5896	114.3578	97.8348	60.5909	71.1645
12.3455	30.8432	51.7311	31.7839	19.9285	20.7722

Cash Flow Profiles

2.4785	4.2452	5.8626	6.3852	6.6323	3.8028
8.5810	16.2550	22.9396	26.1496	28.0741	6.2314
41.4446	81.3421	227.6271	319.4634	495.0872	−579.0459
2.7759	5.9050	6.6765	5.9535	5.0630	4.7536
47.4532	111.6383	128.9891	120.3853	105.8169	38.4596
14.5056	35.3577	81.0091	93.0834	118.1065	−226.1914

Social Security Benefits Profiles

0.0000	0.0000	0.0000	0.0000	0.2595	1.4142
0.0000	0.0000	0.0000	0.0000	1.2230	6.6149
0.0000	0.0000	0.0000	0.0000	1.2350	6.6228
0.0000	0.0000	0.0000	0.0000	0.1981	1.7678
0.0000	0.0000	0.0000	0.0000	4.6099	40.8269
0.0000	0.0000	0.0000	0.0000	0.2946	2.5871

Private Pension Benefits Profiles

0.0000	0.0000	0.0000	0.0000	0.0544	0.2975
0.0000	0.0000	0.0000	0.0000	0.2563	1.3914
0.0000	0.0000	0.0000	0.0000	0.7763	4.1702
0.0000	0.0000	0.0000	0.0000	0.0415	0.3718
0.0000	0.0000	0.0000	0.0000	0.9659	8.5877
0.0000	0.0000	0.0000	0.0000	0.1852	1.6290

Table 11C.2 (contd.)

Wealth Profiles

0.8272	0.8322	0.4626	0.2449	13.3438	0.0000
2.6001	2.3486	0.5712	22.7777	135.5567	0.0000
16.8425	27.8741	733.9648	3065.7251	8211.1379	0.0000
0.4117	1.8458	0.6811	0.3052	4.3937	7.8020
6.3902	15.4554	7.7474	45.5716	257.3913	391.3376
2.6198	8.6612	115.1473	480.8484	1181.4033	1001.8788

Borrowing Limits

−0.4552	−0.9340	−1.3309	−1.5094	−1.4891	0.0000
−2.1571	−4.4925	−6.3342	−7.1135	−6.9651	0.0000
−6.4086	−13.4490	−19.0123	−21.5497	−20.8752	0.0000
−0.4432	−1.0636	−1.2409	−1.1523	−0.9307	0.0000
−10.3703	−25.2618	−29.1618	−26.8121	−21.4940	0.0000
−1.9500	−4.7863	−5.5397	−5.1408	−4.0772	0.0000

Other Transfer Profiles

0.9648	1.3199	1.6858	1.6203	1.5804	1.6114
0.9656	1.3183	1.6848	1.6248	1.5810	1.6097
0.9592	1.3274	1.6803	1.6203	1.5832	1.6114
1.0806	1.8359	1.9199	1.5107	1.2065	2.0143
5.3400	9.0538	9.4735	7.4802	5.9589	9.9351
0.3357	0.5770	0.5980	0.4721	0.3777	0.6295

Housing Profiles

4.1045	6.4118	8.8307	8.9672	8.7716	8.0056
14.2805	23.7861	34.2054	34.5274	31.8750	25.1559
67.9695	116.2554	206.6152	216.4753	165.7670	116.0369
4.2897	8.0834	9.1148	7.5780	6.0690	8.2478
73.6926	148.0620	174.3233	144.0675	108.8915	127.9652
22.1991	45.8011	66.6448	57.1681	35.8413	37.3587

Labor Income Profiles

1.9785	3.8233	5.4481	6.1790	6.0957	1.0636
9.3764	18.3906	25.9301	29.1201	28.5127	4.6314
27.8568	55.0555	77.8298	88.2171	85.4558	13.6143
2.2159	5.3181	6.2045	5.7613	4.6533	1.3295
51.8516	126.3051	145.8048	134.0607	107.4701	28.5848
9.7499	23.9315	27.6985	25.7042	20.3861	5.3181

Inheritance/Bequest Profiles

0.0232	0.0449	0.0722	0.1097	0.1524	−0.3114
0.5508	1.0803	1.7176	2.5840	3.5635	−7.3640
19.4963	38.5320	167.3044	251.3741	427.2032	−661.1667
0.0260	0.0625	0.0822	0.1022	0.1163	−0.3893
3.0457	7.4191	9.6579	11.8958	13.4314	−45.4498
6.8237	16.7491	59.5411	73.2439	101.9123	−258.2701

Notes

The views expressed are those of the authors and do not necessarily represent those of the General Electric Company. Walter Dolde's research was supported in part by the Graduate School of Industrial Administration, Carnegie-Mellon University, where he was formerly a faculty member.

1. Barro, Robert J. (1974, 1976, 1978); Feldstein, Martin (1974, 1976, 1977).
2. U.S. Department of Labor, Bureau of Labor Statistics (1978).
3. For the earlier five surveys, the data are tabulated in Projector (1968), Table 4, p. 9. The 1972–73 data were calculated by the authors from U.S. Department of Labor, BLS (1978), Table 1.
4. This has been eloquently argued in Eisner (1979). See also Tobin (1976).
5. However, as Blinder and Gordon (1979) have pointed out, the U.S. system does include incentives for deferring retirement.
6. The nature of this effect can be illustrated in the simple Modigliani–Brumberg model. Let the life span be 1, of which the final fraction r is spent in retirement, while income is earned at rate y during the previous interval $(0, 1 - r)$. The even rate of consumption is $(1 - r)y$. Assume a stationary population, evenly distributed over all ages. Wealth per capita is

$$\frac{r}{2} y(1 - r).$$

That is, the wealth/income ratio is half the retirement span. Now suppose an unfunded social insurance system collects taxes of ty from workers to pay benefits of

$$\frac{1 - r}{r} ty$$

to the retired. This system does not change the lifetime consumption opportunity of any participant; hence consumption will still be $(1 - r)y$ throughout life. It does, however, change per capita wealth excluding 'social security wealth,' i.e. productive capital. This becomes

$$\frac{(r - t)}{2} y(1 - r).$$

Its derivative with respect to t is

$$\frac{y}{2}\left[(1 + t - 2r)\frac{\partial r}{\partial t} - 1 + r\right],$$

where $\frac{\partial r}{\partial t}$, presumably positive, is the early retirement effect. Assuming $t < r < 1/2$, this derivative is negative if $\frac{\partial r}{\partial t} = 1$ and becomes positive only if $\frac{\partial r}{\partial t}$ exceeds

$$\frac{1}{1 + \frac{t - r}{1 - r}}.$$

Further repercussions arise from the effects of reducing capital and labour inputs.

7. Since the conference at which we presented this paper in preliminary form, it has turned out that there were computational errors in Feldstein's 1974 calculations; the empirical findings did not survive their correction. See Leimer and Lesnoy (1981). Our following remarks may nonetheless be a relevant comment on the concepts and methods of the study.

8. This is not the assumption he always makes. He asserts the opposite in assessing the benefit/cost balance of measures to reduce anticipated inflation. See Feldstein (1979).

9. Ando and Modigliani (1963).

References

Ando, Albert and Modigliani, Franco (1963), "The 'Life Cycle' Hypothesis of Saving: Aggregate Implications and Tests," *American Economic Review*, 53 (March), 55–84.

Barro, Robert J. (1974), "Are Government Bonds Net Wealth?," *Journal of Political Economy*, 82 (November/December), 1095–117.

——— (1976), "Reply to Feldstein and Buchanan," *Journal of Political Economy*, 84 (April), 343–9.

——— (1978), *The Impact of Social Security on Private Saving: Evidence from the U.S. Time Series* Washington, DC: (American Enterprise Institute).

Blinder, Alan S., Gordon, Roger H. and Wise, Donald E. (1979), "Reconsidering the Working Disincentive Effects of Social Security," mimeo, National Bureau of Economic Research.

Brady, Dorothy S. and Friedman, Rose D. (1974). "Savings and the Income Distribution." *Studies in Income and Wealth*, 10 (New York: National Bureau of Economic Research) 247–65.

Cagan, Phillip (1965), "The Effect of Pension Plans on Aggregate Saving," *NBER Occasional Paper*, No. 95.

Dolde, Walter (1973), "Capital Markets and the Relevant Horizon for Consumption Planning," unpublished Ph.D dissertation, Yale University.

Eisner, Robert (1979), "Social Security and Capital Accumulation," mimeo, September 14.

Feldstein, Martin (1974), "Social Security, Induced Retirement and Aggregate Capital Accumulation," *Journal of Political Economy*, 82 (September/October), 905–26.

——— (1976a), "Perceived Wealth in Bonds and Social Security: A Comment," *Journal of Political Economy*, 84 (April), 331–6.

——— (1976b), "Social Security and Saving: The Extended Life Cycle Theory," *American Economic Review*, 66 (May), 77–86.

——— (1977), "The Social Security Fund and National Capital Accumulation," in Federal Reserve Bank of Boston, *Funding Pensions: The Issues and Implications, for Financial Markets*, 32–4.

——— (1979), "The Welfare Cost of Permanent Inflation and Optimal Short-Run Economic Policy," *Journal of Political Economy*, 87, 749–68.

Katona, George (1965), *Private Pensions and Individual Saving*, University of Michigan Survey Research Center, Monograph 40.

Kowalewski, Kim and Smith, Gary (1979), "The Spending Behavior of Wealth- and Liquidity-Constrained Consumers," Cowles Foundation Discussion Paper 536, September.

Leimer, Dean R. and Lesnoy, Selig D. (1981), "Social Security and Private Saving: A Reexamination of the Time Series Evidence Using Alternative Social Security Wealth Variables," *American Economic Review* (May).

Projector, Dorothy S. (1968), *Survey of Changes in Family Finances* (Washington, DC: Board of Governors of Federal Reserve System).

Tobin, James (1967), "Life Cycle Saving and Balanced Growth," in Wm. Fellner (ed.), *Ten Economic Studies in the Tradition of Irving Fisher* (New York: Wiley), 231–56.

―――― and Dolde, W. (1971), "Wealth, Liquidity, Consumption," in *Consumer Spending and Monetary Policy: The Linkages*, Federal Reserve Bank of Boston, Conference Series No. 5.

―――― (1976), DISCUSSION: of "Public Pension Funding and U.S. Capital Formation: A Medium-Run View," in *Funding Pensions: Issues and Implications for Financial Markets*, Federal Reserve Bank of Boston, *Proceedings*, 206–12.

US Dept. of Labor (1978), Bulletin 1992, *Consumer Expenditure Survey: Integrated Diary and Interview Data, 1972–73*, Table 1 and Table 3.

CHAPTER 12

INVENTORIES, INVESTMENT, INFLATION, AND TAXES

This paper, exhumed for this conference,* is a relic of an earlier period in the United States, the stagflation of the 1970s. In those times, business managers and economists complained loudly about over-taxation of profits by a tax code that was not indexed to inflation. According to Martin Feldstein, who with his colleagues at Harvard produced an impressive volume of research on the effects of taxes on capital formation, the burdens and disincentives of personal and corporate income taxes during inflationary times were a major cause of the "stag" linked to the "flation." He and his associates were concerned with over-taxation both of inventory profits and of returns to fixed capital. [Feldstein, 1983]

Diagnoses with this message were influential in the political arena. The Economic Recovery Tax Act of 1981 (ERTA), a Reagan Administration initiative supported in the Congress by legislators of both parties, made generous concessions in the taxation of business and property income. A major ostensible purpose was to offset the alleged punitive and deterrent effects of the deadly combination of the previous tax code with high inflation rates. Despite this rationale, the legislation did not provide the obvious direct and specific remedy, namely indexation of past costs in reckoning taxable income. Instead, it offered other remedies, notably Accelerated Cost Recovery, which only three years later, when inflation had abated, appeared extravagant and inefficient to the same Administration and legislators who had enacted ERTA. They hailed the repeal of those concessions as a major reason why the Tax Reform of 1986 was the greatest fiscal legislation in history. Such is American politics.

---

*International Society for Inventory Research Conference, Wesleyan University, Connecticut, June 17, 1987; CFDP 849; published in A. Chikán and M. Lovell, eds., *Economics of Inventory Management*, Elsevier Science Publishers, 1988, pp. 285–304; CFP #712, 1989. Reprinted by permission.

The 1986 Act did not index costs either, although the initial Treasury proposal of 1984 would have done so. Consequently the concerns of the 1970s may recur if and when serious inflation returns, making my paper relevant once again in this country. And it may be relevant elsewhere too.

There are two Parts of the paper. The first directly concerns inventories. The second concerns fixed investment. I include the second, even in this conference, for two reasons. First, fixed capital can be conceived as an inventory of a kind, its depreciation being analogous to the storage costs of inventories. Like purchases of capital goods, purchases or production of inventories prepare for production of goods for final sale over many future dates. Second, the economic and mathematical arguments in the second part are isomorphic to those of the first part. Indeed, the second part could be applied to inventories if, as many theories would have it, inventories have a gross marginal productivity analogous to that attributed to fixed capital.

In both Parts I consider two non-neutralities arising from the interaction of income taxation and inflation. One arises from the use of historical cost in reckoning profits; inflation raises the tax liability on given real income. The second arises from the deductibility of nominal interest; during inflation this means that some repayments of principal in real terms are deductible. Interest deductibility lowers the effective tax. The first effect deters, while the second effect encourages, investment in inventories and fixed capital.

Let me summarize in advance the main point of the algebraic calculations that follow: The historical cost effect, negative for after-tax profits, is a monotonically increasing but bounded function of the inflation rate. Its slope declines with inflation and is asymptotically zero. The reason is obvious. No matter how high inflation is, the most the taxpayer can lose is the full value of the deduction for replacement cost. On the other hand, the value of the interest deduction, positive for after-tax profits, is linear in inflation and unbounded. In Figures 12.1 and 12.3, the two effects are superimposed. At inflation rates below π^* the negative first effect is the larger; at higher rates the positive second effect dominates. Thus the net result depends on the magnitude of the inflation, and on other parameters.

In the debate about the importance of tax-cum-inflation effects in raising effective taxes and handicapping investment, the complainants generally ignored or dismissed the interest effects. They rationalized this neglect by pointing out that interest deducted by businesses is taxable income to individuals, so that the same distortion increases the real borrowing cost facing firms. However, there is no evidence that during the stagflation of the 1970s the real cost of capital to firms increased at all, certainly not to the extent necessary to nullify the advantages to borrowers of full deduction of nominal interest. This point is further discussed at the end.

1 Inventories, FIFO and LIFO

The exaggeration of taxable inventory gains attributed to inflation is, to begin with, mysterious and paradoxical. U.S. tax law allows firms to choose between first-in-first-out (FIFO) and last-in-first-out (LIFO) accounting conventions. Obviously LIFO is virtually equivalant to indexation—not quite, because current sales may exceed current purchases, requiring some inputs to be priced at earlier and lower prices. Nevertheless, most U.S. companies use FIFO. Many did shift to LIFO during the era of inflation, but an amazingly large number did not.

In 1980, the Commerce Department's Inventory Valuation Adjustment reduced the stated profits of nonfinancial corporations by 15 percent. Taxes on those phantom profits lowered after-tax economic income by 13 percent. These were bigger adjustments than the Department's Capital Consumption Adjustment for understatement of depreciation. Lawrence Summers [1981] estimated the effects of FIFO as approximately equivalent to an increase in the corporate tax rate of 1 1/3 points for every point of inflation.

It is not clear why firms voluntarily choose, and persist in choosing, an accounting convention that appears to be so avoidable and expensive. It is true that switching to LIFO would reduce reported earnings during inflations, while also entailing revaluations of stocks of materials, products, and work-in-process in nominal balance sheets. There are also a number of technical legal and accounting complications in tax administration and other governmental regulations. It would be a virtually irreversible decision. On balance, nevertheless, the use of FIFO seems to be based on misconception and inertia. [Foss, 1981, especially Chapter 6].

To count the tax-cum-inflation FIFO distortion as a reason for macroeconomic anti-inflationary policies or for lightening the burdens of taxes on capital income seems very dubious.

It is time to set forth the model.

The firm has sales volume of $S(t)$ at time t. For these sales goods inputs were purchased at various times $t - \theta$, in amounts $c(\theta)$ per unit of sales volume. The total commodity-input cost of sales at time t is

$$C(t) = S(t) \int_0^\infty c(\theta) d\theta = S(t)c \tag{1}$$

where $c = \int_0^\infty c(\theta) d\theta$ is less than or equal to 1. Purchases of goods at time t preparatory for sales at time $t + \theta$ are $S(t + \theta)c(\theta)$. Thus total purchases are

$$P(t) = \int_0^\infty S(t + \theta)c(\theta) d\theta \tag{2}$$

The inventory stock at time t consists of all the goods previously purchased for sales at times after t. For any particular future time $t + \tau$, this consists of $\int_\tau^\infty S(t + \tau)c(\theta) d\theta$. Thus the stock,

$$H(t) = \int_0^\infty S(t + \tau) \int_\tau^\infty c(\theta) d\theta d\tau = \int_t^\infty S(x) \int_{x-t}^\infty c(\theta) d\theta dx \tag{3}$$

From (3) may be derived the change in stock,

$$H'(t) = -S(t)c + \int_t^\infty S(x)c(x - t) dx = -S(t)c + \int_0^\infty S(t + \theta)c(\theta) d\theta$$

$$H'(t) = -S(t)c + P(t) \tag{4}$$

A special case of interest, on which I shall concentrate, is that sales are growing at a steady rate g: $S(t) = S(0)e^{gt}$. Then

$$H(t)/S(t) = \int_0^\infty e^{g\tau} \int_\tau^\infty c(\theta) d\theta d\tau \tag{5}$$

The inventory/sales ratio is a constant, denoted h, larger for higher g. (If $g = 0$, sales, purchases, and stocks are constant; $P = cS$.) With steady growth, there is some f such that $P(t - f) = cS(t)$. Since $P(t) - cS(t) = gH(t)$, this implies that $P(t - f) = P(t) - gH(t)$.

INVENTORIES, INVESTMENT, INFLATION AND TAXES

Consider now steady growth at g and steady inflation at π. Suppose that all inventory is financed by short-term debt costing interest at rate $r + \pi$. The cash flow at time t in dollars is Sales − Purchases + Net Borrowing − Interest − Taxes:

$$S(t)e^{\pi t} - P(t)e^{\pi t} + (g+\pi)H(t)e^{\pi t} - (r+\pi)H(t)e^{\pi t} - \text{Taxes} = \text{Cash Flow} \tag{6}$$

There are two ways of identifying the tax base:

A. The deductible "cost of goods sold" is specific to the sales at each time t. In this case the constant-dollar cost is $C(t)$, and the only question is whether the price of the goods covered by $C(t)$ is the current price at t—purest LIFO—or the actual price paid at various times $t - \theta$ —FIFO.

B. Goods purchased are not identified with sales. All purchases $P(t)$ are deductible at the current price (LIFO). Or only goods equal in quantity to $C(t)$ are deductible and are assumed to have been purchased at earlier time $t - f$ such that $P(t-f) = C(t)$ (FIFO).

In all cases nominal interest is deductible. The tax rate is T.

A. LIFO. The cash flow is

$$e^{\pi t}\{[S(t) - P(t) + (g-r)H(t)] + T(r+\pi)H(t) - TS(t)(1-c)\}$$
$$= e^{\pi t}\{[S(t)(1-c) - rH(t)](1-T) + T\pi H(t)\} \tag{7}$$

A. FIFO. The cash flow is

$$e^{\pi t}\left\{[S(t) - P(t) + (g-r)H(t)] + T(r+\pi)H(t) \right.$$
$$\left. - T\left[S(t)\left(1 - \int_0^\infty c(\theta)e^{-\pi\theta}d\theta\right)\right]\right\}$$
$$= e^{\pi t}\left\{[S(t)(1-c) - rH(t)](1-T) + T\pi H(t) \right.$$
$$\left. - TS(t)\left(c - \int_0^\infty c(\theta)e^{-\pi\theta}d\theta\right)\right\} \tag{8}$$

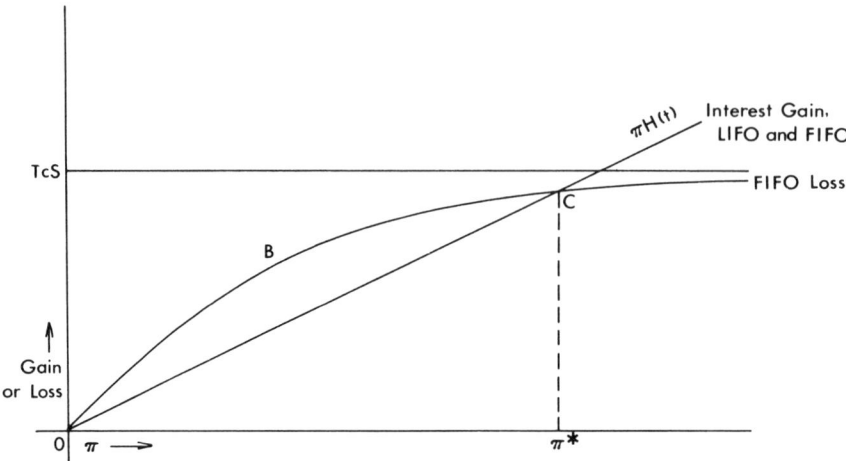

Figure 12.1
Inflation effects on taxation of inventory profits: loss from use of FIFO and gain from nominal interest deductibility (model A)

According to (7) each point of inflation increases LIFO cash flow by TH. Comparing (8) and (7) gives the loss due to FIFO accounting. It is

$$\text{A. LIFO} - \text{A. FIFO} = TS(t) \int_0^\infty c(\theta)(1 - e^{-\pi\theta}) d\theta \tag{9}$$

This loss goes from zero at $\pi = 0$ to TcS asymptotically as π goes to infinity. Its derivative with respect to π is $TS(t) \int_0^\infty \theta c(\theta) e^{-\pi\theta} d\theta$, which is positive but declining with π. However, the real gain due to interest deductibility πH is positive and proportional to π. This gain prevails over the FIFO loss for inflation rates π above π^*, where

$$\pi^* h = c - \int_0^\infty c(\theta) e^{-\pi^*\theta} d\theta \qquad (h = H/S, \text{a constant}) \tag{10}$$

These results are shown in Figure 12.1.

An example may be instructive. Suppose $c(\theta)$ is quadratic, as follows:

$$c(\theta) = a\theta - b\theta^2 \quad \text{if } \theta < a/b, \; c(\theta) = 0 \text{ otherwise.} \tag{11}$$

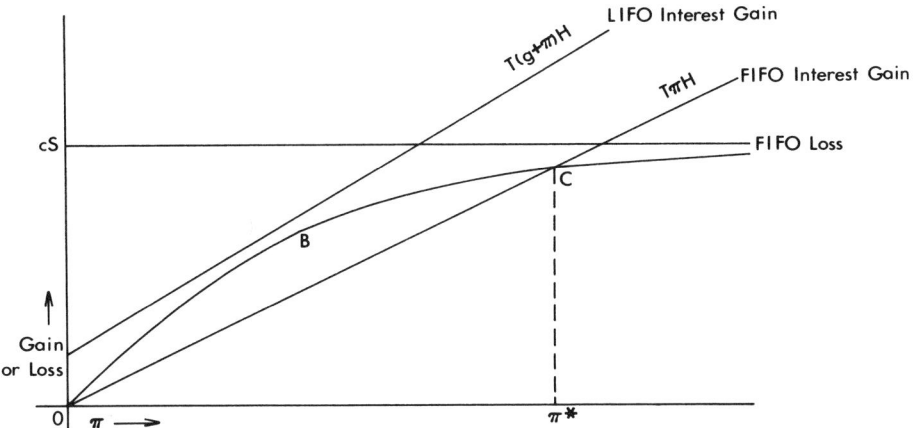

Figure 12.2
Inflation effects on taxation of inventory profits: loss from use of FIFO and gain from nominal interest deductibility (model B)

Choose a, b so that $c = \int_0^{a/b} c(\theta)d\theta = 1$, and so that $h = H/S = 1/12$. Then $a = 6^3$, $b = 6^4$, and $a/b = 1/6$. It turns out that in Figure 12.1 points A and B coincide at the origin—$\pi^* = 0$; the interest gain is never smaller than the FIFO accounting loss for positive π.

B. LIFO Cash flow is

$$e^{\pi t}\{[S(t) - P(t) - (r+\pi)H(t)](1-T) + (g+\pi)H(t)\}$$
$$= e^{\pi t}\{[S(t) - P(t) + (g-r)H(t)](1-T) + T(g+\pi)H(t)\} \quad (12)$$

B. FIFO Cash flow is (recall $P(t-f) = P(t) - gH(t) = cS(t)$)

$$e^{\pi t}\{[S(t) - P(t) + (g+\pi)H(t) - (r+\pi)H(t)]\} - T\{S(t)e^{\pi t}$$
$$- P(t-f)e^{\pi(t-f)} - (r+\pi)H(t)e^{\pi t}\}$$
$$= e^{\pi t}\{[S(t) - P(t) + (g-r)H(t)](1-T) + T\pi H(t)$$
$$- T(1 - e^{-\pi f})P(t-f))\} \quad (13)$$

In case B, the real loss due to FIFO is

$$\text{B. LIFO} - \text{B. FIFO} = TgH(t) + TcS(t)(1 - e^{-\pi f}) \quad (14)$$

The first term is an advantage of B. LIFO independent of inflation. The total real non-neutral tax term for B. FIFO subtracts the second term from the interest gain $T\pi H$: $T\pi H - T(1 - e^{-\pi f})cS$, with derivative $TH - fe^{-\pi f}cS$. The critical inflation rate π^* is given by

$$e^{-\pi^* f} = Th/fc \tag{15}$$

Note that in case B the interest gain for LIFO is $T(g + \pi)H$ and always exceeds that for FIFO.

Figure 12.2 shows these results for case B.

2 Investment Incentives with Taxes Distorted by Inflation

Here I consider essentially the same two non-neutralities as in Part I. However, the distortion due to historical cost accounting, FIFO above, appears as inadequate allowance for depreciation in reckoning taxable profits. The strength of this distortion relative to the gain from deductibility of nominal interest depends on a number of parameters: the inflation rate, the tax rate, the true economic depreciation rate, the tax allowance for depreciation, the growth rate of the firm, and the debt-equity ratio.

Once again, the method is to compare steady states defined by inflation rates and other parameters. The calculations do not concern transitions from one steady state to another. In particular, the model assumes steady inflation, with actual and expected inflation rates identical. The same inflation rate applies to the firm's outputs and inputs, including purchases of capital goods.

For each steady state, I seek the rate of discount of the future stream of dollar net receipts that will make their present value equal to the current commodity-price value of the firm's capital stock (q, the ratio of the former to the latter, equal to one.) That discount rate is what the nominal cost of capital to the firm must be to sustain that steady state. The impact of inflation, or of more rather than less inflation, is measured by what happens to that nominal rate. That rate will in equilibrium be the after-tax rate of return required by those who buy or hold, via the stocks and bonds issued by the firm, claims to the earnings of the firm's capital. I am particularly interested in whether the cost of capital has to rise by the same amount as inflation in order to keep the firm's q equal to one, or by more or less.

Consider a corporate firm in a steady state with a real capital stock of 1 at time 0, which is and has been growing at rate g. The real gross yield of capital is R at every point in time. The dollar price of output and of capital goods is 1 at time 0 and is increasing at rate π. Capital evaporates at rate δ. Earnings net of depreciation are taxed at the corporate income tax rate T. Debt is a fraction γ of the nominal value of the capital stock, and bears a nominal interest rate i. The nominal interest outlay is deductible in calculating taxable income. I look for the nominal discount rate ρ that makes the value at time 0 of the stream of dollar cash flow equal to the \$1 value of the capital at this date. Presumably the corporate bond rate i is lower than ρ but is related positively to ρ by a coefficient that depends positively on the debt/equity ratio, here assumed constant over time. The relationship assumed is: $i - \pi = \beta(\rho - \pi)$ with $\beta < 1$. Thus $i = \beta(\rho - \pi) + \pi$.

The basic identity for cash flow in dollars is:

Cash Flow = Gross Earnings − Taxes on Gross Earnings

− Gross Investment + Tax Savings on Depreciation

+ Tax Savings on Debt Interest.

Gross Earnings at time t are $Re^{(g+\pi)t}$, and the corresponding tax liability is simply T times that quantity. The tax savings on debt interest are $T\gamma i e^{(g+\pi)t}$. (Note that if tax deduction were allowed only on the nominal value of real interest, the saving would be $T\gamma(i - \pi)e^{(g+\pi)t}$.) Gross investment is $(g + \delta)e^{(g+\pi)t}$.

Calculation of tax savings on depreciation is somewhat more complicated. Dollar gross investment at time $u \leq t$ was $(g + \delta)e^{(g+\delta)u}$. The undepreciated amount remaining at time t is $(g + \delta)e^{(g+\delta)u - \delta(t-u)}$. The total tax saving for depreciation is therefore:

$$T\delta(g+\delta)e^{-\delta t}\int_{-\infty}^{t} e^{(g+\pi+\delta)u} du = [T\delta(g+\delta)e^{(g+\delta)t}]/(g+\delta+\pi) \qquad (16)$$

Note that if replacement cost depreciation were allowed the tax saving would simply be $T\delta e^{(g+\pi)t}$. The fraction of this lost is $\pi/(g + \delta + \pi)$.

I now seek the discount rate ρ that makes q, the present value of the cash flow, equal to 1:

$$1 = \{R(1-T) - (g+\delta) + T\delta(g+\delta)/(g+\delta+\pi) + T\gamma\beta(\rho-\pi) + T\gamma\beta\pi\}$$
$$\times \int_0^\infty e^{(g+\pi-\rho)t} dt \qquad (17)$$

With the assumption that ρ exceeds $g + \pi$—otherwise present value is not finite—and with some tedious algebra, an explicit expression for ρ can be found:

$$(\rho - \pi)(1 - T\gamma\beta) = (R - \delta)(1 - T) - T\delta\pi/(g+\delta+\pi) + T\gamma\beta\pi \qquad (18)$$

Some special cases will help to elucidate (16). If the two non-neutral features of the tax code were removed, the second and third terms on the right hand side would vanish. If, further, $\gamma\beta = 1$, then the real rate of interest, before and after corporate tax, would simply be the internal return net of depreciation: $\rho - \pi = R - \delta$. This limiting case would apply to a 100 percent debt-financed firm. (Full debt financing was assumed for inventories in Part I.) Inflation would be neutral, and the required nominal discount rate ρ would vary point for point with inflation π. For a pure equity firm $(\gamma\beta = 0)$, $\rho - \pi = (R - \delta)(1 - T)$, again independent of inflation. In both these polar cases, the depreciation non-neutrality will make a difference, but debt interest deductibility will not matter for a pure equity firm. Failure to use debt finance, given a tax code that treats it more favorably than equity, is a puzzle of the same nature as FIFO accounting.

From (18) can be calculated the derivative of the required real rate $r \ (= (\rho - \pi)(1 - T\gamma\beta)$ with respect to π:

$$\partial r/\partial \pi = -T\delta(g+\delta)/(g+\delta+\pi)^2 + T\gamma\beta \qquad (19)$$

This derivative is equal to $T\gamma\beta - T\delta/(g+\delta)$ at $\pi = 0$ and increases with π. Consequently, if $\gamma\beta$ exceeds $\delta/(g+\delta)$, the share of depreciation in gross investment, inflation is always expansionary, i.e. the required real discount rate must rise to keep q from exceeding 1. If $\delta\beta$ is smaller than $\delta/(g+\delta)$, there is a positive finite value of π at which increases in π become expansionary. For example, take $\delta = .075$, $g = .025$, and $\gamma\delta = .04$. These are realistic values; the last one is the ratio of U.S. nonfinancial

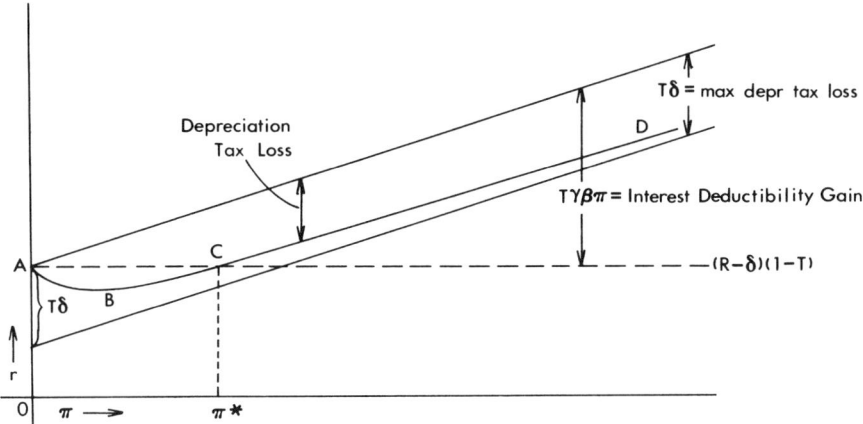

Figure 12.3
Inflation effects on after-tax return to business capital: decrease due to historical cost depreciation and increase due to deductibility of nominal interest

corporations' net interest payments to the sum of such payments and after-tax profits in 1978. They imply that inflation becomes expansionary beyond a rate of 3.7 percent and that above 8.75 percent inflation the real discount rate r must be at least as high as when inflation is zero. The latter value corresponds to the π^* of Part I. Figure 12.3 depicts the relationship. Point B represents the 3.7 of the example and point C the 8.75 percent. If the example is realistic, the complaints of the 1970s had some merit for the inflation rates prevailing most of the decade.

The reason the interest deduction comes to dominate as the inflation rate rises is that the historical depreciation tax loss is limited to $T\delta$, i.e. to the loss that would occur if no tax saving for depreciation were ever allowed. (A similar limit played the same role in Part I.) In the example, if the corporate tax rate is 40 percent, the maximum possible fall in the real internal rate of return is .03. This non-linearity is shown in Figures 12.3 and 12.4. In contrast, the interest deductibility gain is proportional to the inflation rate, as shown in Figure 12.3, which is analogous to Figure 12.1 for inventories.

The tax code allowed accelerated depreciation, even before 1981 and ERTA. Assuming the permitted accelerations were more than realistic approximations to true depreciation, they contributed to the after-tax

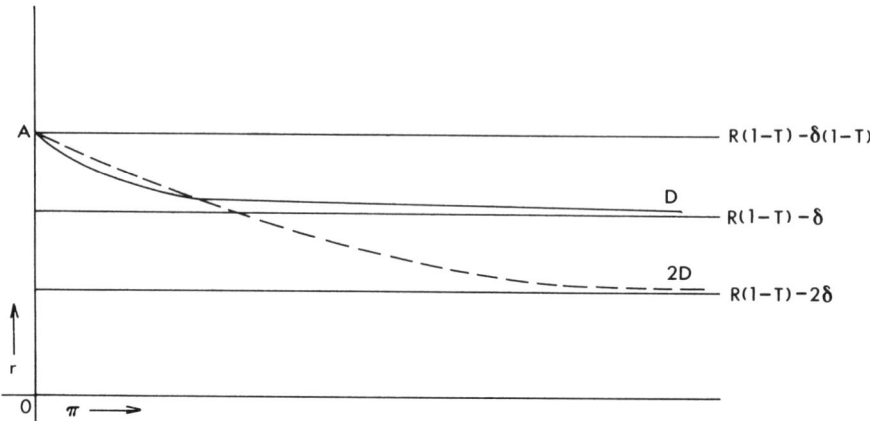

Figure 12.4
Inflation effects on after-tax return to business capital: decrease due to historical cost depreciation with and without acceleration

internal rate of return in a way not covered in equation (18). Consequently firms had more to lose during inflation from historical cost accounting.

For illustration, suppose that corporations are allowed to depreciate capital for tax purposes at twice the true rate δ. Then a replication of the calculations above yields, in place of (18),

$$(\rho - \pi)(1 - T\gamma\beta) = (R - \delta)(1 - T) + T\delta(g - \pi)/(g + 2\delta + \pi) + T\gamma\beta\pi \tag{20}$$

It is the second term on the right hand side that is changed from (18). Note that in the absence of inflation the gain from acceleration would be $Tg\delta/(g + 2\delta)$; acceleration is of no advantage to a non-growing firm, for whom deferment of taxes does not alter their present value. Inflation erodes the advantage of acceleration. But in the limit the loss to the internal rate of return cannot exceed $2T\delta(g + \delta)/(g + 2\delta)$. With the numbers assumed in the previous illustration, this limit is .0343, higher than the .03 without acceleration. The value of π above which $\partial r/\partial \pi$ is positive becomes 1.86 percent, and the value of π at which the real internal rate of return is higher than for zero inflation becomes 3.93 percent. These numbers are lower than without acceleration.

From 1962 to 1986 the tax code allowed an Investment Tax Credit (ITC). Depreciation was allowed on the full historical cost of capital goods, even though part of the cost had been claimed as tax credit. Taking this fact into account and assuming that the debt/equity ratio was not changed by the ITC, the ITC's contribution to the real internal rate of return was not affected by inflation. An ITC of α raises the real internal rate of return by $\alpha(g + \delta)$; for example, an α of 10 percent raises it by 1 percent with $g + \delta$ equal to .10, as assumed in the example above.

In the context of the debate about the alleged stagflationary effects of tax-cum-inflation distortions in the 1970s, my calculations ignore any changes in the tax code made as rough compensation for the inadequacy of historical cost accounting. In fact, the outcry was at least partly responsible for a reduction of 3.2 points in the corporate income tax rate in the ten years prior to 1981. If $R - \delta$ is taken to be 12.5 percent, the rate reduction alone raised the after tax internal rate of return by 0.4 percent. In addition, the ITC was liberalized and supposedly made permanent.

Another question of policy relevance concerns ρ, the pre-tax nominal discount rate applied by the holders of corporate securities to the future yields of corporate capital. As noted at the beginning, this question is also relevant to the possible importance of FIFO accounting in raising effective tax rates and discouraging business activity, inventory demand, and overall investment. The question considered above was how ρ must change in order to sustain the same steady state, i.e. one with the same path of the capital stock. Must it rise more or less than the inflation rate? The assumption was that if ρ must rise more than π, an increase in π is expansionary, while if it must rise less, an increase in π is contractionary.

However, holding $\rho - \pi$ constant is not neutral for individual owners of corporate securities. Personal income and wealth taxation also contains some non-neutral features. In particular, both interest income and capital gains are taxed on a nominal basis. To a taxpayer with an unchanged marginal tax rate of μ, applied to nominal returns, the after-tax real return is $(1 - \mu)\rho - \pi$. If this is to be invariant to inflation, ρ must rise by $1/(1 - \mu)$ points for every point of inflation. An increase of this order of magnitude could easily be more than the corporate or business sector could absorb, because $1/(1 - \mu)$ surely exceeds $\gamma\beta$.

During the unhappy 1970s a number of steps were taken to reduce μ. These included: reduction by about one-third in the maximum effective tax on capital gains; generous provisions for deferment of taxes on saving for retirement; reduction in maximum marginal personal income tax rates; adjustment of rate brackets in partial compensation for inflation.

There were and still are many ways in which personal income taxpayers escape, reduce, or defer taxes on interest incomes and other asset returns. Eugene Steuerle [1981] estimated that less than one third of property incomes shows up as taxable personal income. The above theoretical greater-than-one elasticity of pre-tax interest rates to inflation certainly is not supported by evidence.

An estimate of the μ's relevant in securities markets can be obtained by comparing high grade tax-exempt bond rates with *Aaa* corporate bond rates. The implicit marginal tax rate was 0.27 in 1964, 0.27 in 1972, and 0.34 in 1979. These are if anything over-estimates of μ, since highly taxed investors are naturally concentrated in the tax-exempt market. The sharp acceleration of inflation increased the tax-exempt nominal rate only by 3.2 points between 1964 and 1979, and only by 1.2 points after 1972. The course of taxable *Aaa* rates is consistent either with constancy of the *pre*-tax real rate or with a model in which the after-tax nominal *Aaa* rate followed the tax-exempt rate and the marginal tax rate effective in the bond market was about 1/2. What the experience seems to contradict very strongly is constancy of the *after*-tax real rate on corporate securities. That rate declined. Interest rates do not appear to be governed by a constant inter-temporal substitution rate for consumer-savers.

For these reasons, I believe that interest deductibility was a source of gain to business debtors during inflation, not offset by any significant increase in their real cost of borrowing from personal income taxpayers. The allegation that tax-cum-inflation distortions were crippling the economy in the 1970s were, therefore, exaggerations.

There were plenty of other factors to explain the stagflation. The prices of business inputs rose faster than those of outputs, thanks to oil and energy prices. The risks of cyclical fluctuations in real demand and real earnings increased, thanks to the proclivity of the authorities to counter inflation periodically with restrictive monetary policies, as in 1970, 1974, and 1980, and by price controls in 1971. Excess capacity inhibits investment. A slowdown in growth of total factor productivity, the sources of which are still not understood, occurred in the mid-1970s. These changes in the environment were reflected in the stock market, where real rates as measured by earnings/price ratios shot up. But it is hard to explain the unhappiness of corporate investors simply by inflationary tax distortions.

A final remark of a theoretical nature: In the article cited above, Lawrence Summers counted the full decline he estimated in the real after-tax internal rate of return to nonfinancial businesses as deterrent to accumulation of fixed capital. Nearly half of the decline was over-taxation of inventory gains due to use of FIFO. This did not seem appropriate to me, because inventory gains cannot be regarded as returns to fixed capital. Goods stocked and work-in-process are the product of all factor inputs, labor and natural resources as well as capital services. Thus over-taxation of inventory gains should reduce the demand for all inputs, not just capital. We need an "Austrian" production function to model inventories, recognizing the time lags, more likely distributed than point-to-point, between inputs and outputs and sales. When I studied introductory economics from Taussig's textbook at Harvard fifty years ago, we learned that labor, for example, is paid its *discounted* marginal product, discounted over the period of production. A major question of technology is what flexibility and choice, if any, exist in lag structures like the $c(\theta)$ function taken as fixed in Part I, and how they are related to other features of production technology, like capital/labor intensities. Perhaps these are matters on which an amateur like myself will be instructed during this conference.

CHAPTER 13

THE NATURAL RATE AS NEW CLASSICAL MACROECONOMICS

Friedman, Lucas, and Market Clearing

In retrospect, Friedman's 1967 Presidential Address to the American Economic Association (Friedman, 1968) was the opening shot of the new classical macroeconomics, the precursor of Lucas's "misperceptions" explanation of Phillips curve observations and of the "policy ineffectiveness proposition." Like Lucas (1973) and other new classicals, Friedman deploys ancient classical money-is-a-veil doctrine to argue that only real prices and real wages can determine real quantities of production and employment. Apparent relations between money prices and real quantities, like the Phillips curve, are bound to be ephemeral, especially if policymakers try to exploit them. The Friedman–Lucas doctrine is that the economy behaves as if markets were determining real prices all the time. Those prices are the arguments in supply and demand functions, and equalities of demand and supply shape the path of the economy.

The natural rate, according to Friedman, is "the level that would be ground out by the Walrasian system of general equilibrium equations" (1968, p. 8). The sentence continues with the proviso that "imbedded" in these equations are "market imperfections, stochastic variability in demands and supplies, the cost of gathering information about job vacancies and labour availabilities, the cost of mobility, and so on," phenomena that no one knows how to imbed in them. After this gesture Friedman forgets about these awkward non-Walrasian phenomena and applies classical doctrine unconditionally.

Reprinted from *The Natural Rate Hypothesis Twenty-Five Years On*, ed. Rod Cross, Cambridge: Cambridge University Press, 1995, ch. 3, with permission from the publisher.

How do deviations from the natural rate occur? There are two possible answers, not necessarily exclusive, new classical and Keynesian. In new classical theory, departures from the natural rate result from distortions of demand and supply schedules because of misperception, misinformation, or incorrect expectations regarding the real wages and prices relevant to those schedules. Markets still clear, supply still equals demand, just as in natural rate equilibrium, but the prices, wages, and quantities determined in those markets differ from natural rate outcomes. Friedman describes graphically the dynamics of the expectational adjustments that lead to accelerations of prices up or down when employment and output are higher or lower than their natural rate values. Lucas introduces here the powerful tools of rational expectations, but that does not make his story essentially different from Friedman's. Both of them say that unanticipated monetary policy and inflation can raise employment temporarily, but only temporarily and only by fooling workers and employers.

Keynes and Uncleared Markets

Keynesian "full employment" is the counterpart of the natural rate. It too is a real classical equilibrium, in which equality of the marginal productivity of labour and the marginal disutility of work determines real wages and the volumes of employment and output. But the Keynesian explanation of departures from full employment is quite different from the Friedman–Lucas description. It is that markets are not clearing. Lapses from full employment occur when there is excess supply of labour, involuntary unemployment. Some workers are unemployed even though they are willing to work at prevailing real wages, or less, and are no less efficient and productive than employed workers. This involuntary unemployment arises not because of the usual classical culprits, interferences with competition by trade unions and government regulations, but because market prices adjust slowly, certainly not instantaneously, to aggregate demand shocks (Keynes, 1936, Book I).

The idea that adjustments to shifts of supply and demand curves are not immediate would not have troubled the classical economists of Keynes' generation. It is only their latter-day successors, Friedman,[1]

Lucas, and other new classicals who assume that observed prices and quantities are continuously the outcomes of price-cleared markets. "Real business cycle" theorists represent the ultimate in this intellectual tradition; they do not even recognise the distortions of supply and demand schedules that explain departures from the natural rate in Friedman and Lucas. For them, the natural rate is just the actual rate, whatever it is today.

Frictional and Involuntary Unemployment

A simplistic aggregative interpretation of either Keynes's full employment or Friedman's natural rate would imply that in those equilibria unemployment would be zero—involuntary unemployment, that is. Voluntary choice to be out of the labour force is not at issue. The US Census Current Population Survey measure of unemployment is a close empirical approximation to the relevant concept of involuntary unemployment; it counts as unemployed any persons who were not employed any time during the survey week but report that they have been looking for work during the past four weeks.

Keynes is almost as cavalier as Friedman on this point. He allows "frictional" unemployment to coexist with full employment, and he gives several reasons that "there will always exist in a non-static society a proportion of resources unemployed 'between jobs'" (Keynes, 1936, p. 6). However, a better theory of the relation of unemployment and inflation would provide a more complete account of frictional unemployment, and of Friedman's various addenda to Walrasian equations.

A more crucial question for each of the two theories is whether they ever imply involuntary unemployment. The Keynesian model obviously does. In natural rate theory, however, labour markets are always clearing. Although workers may misperceive and underestimate the real wages they face, they are getting as much employment as they desire in present circumstances as they understand them. The Census would not count them as unemployed. Of course, new classical macroeconomists have never regarded involuntary unemployment as reported in surveys as meaning anything they need to explain. Critics may regard that omission as a serious defect.

Keynes' Monetary Economy

Both Keynes' full employment and Friedman's natural rate relate nominal wage or nominal price change to discrepancies from those equilibria. In Friedman and Lucas, these movements are the market-clearing results of adjustments of demand and supply to revised estimates of current and future real wages and prices. In Keynes, they are the natural competitive responses to excess supply or excess demand. While classicals, new or old, viewed markets as generating real prices and wages, Keynes stressed that we live in a monetary economy, in which the wages and prices determined in markets, both in equilibrium and during disequilibrium adjustments, are wages and prices expressed in the monetary unit of account. Because these adjustments take real time, real wages and prices will deviate from their equilibrium values for finite periods of time, perhaps even for extended periods of time. But this does not reflect money illusion in agents' behaviour, nor irrational expectations, nor imperfect or asymmetrical information.

The Phillips curve is the natural extension to economy-wide labour markets of the conventional dynamics of supply and demand both in Marshallian sectoral markets and in Walrasian general equilibrium. Until the last 20 or 30 years economists of all persuasions recognised that supply and demand do not clear continuously, that it takes real time for prices and quantities to adjust to shifts in the curves. The common scenario, long used by teachers and texts of introductory economics, was and is that prices move down when there is excess supply, roughly proportionately to the amount, and likewise move up in response to excess demand. This informal but intuitive dynamics convinces students that supply/demand analysis makes sense. For a single market, small relative to the whole economy, it is reasonable to interpret these movements as adjustments in both real and nominal prices at the same time.

Keynes' important insight was that this story does not carry over to economy-wide adjustments of money wages to excess demands or supplies. Clearly the economy-wide nominal prices of commodities, which translate money wages into real wages, are not independent of nominal labour costs. The dynamics are much more complex and chancy than uncritical analogy to the textbook story for single small markets suggests. Indeed, as Keynes pointed out, downward adjustments of money wages may not reduce the real wage at all, and may not eliminate or reduce the unemployment that triggered them. Yet new classicals ignore Keynes (1936) chapter 2. They finesse all the anomalies raised by the fact that their models make behaviour depend only on real prices while actual markets generate nominal prices.[2]

In labour markets unemployment and vacancies are consequences and indicators of failures of markets to clear at prevailing prices. To describe the failure another way, prices are not flexible enough, instantaneously flexible enough, to equate demand and supply at every moment of time. As older generations of economists took for granted, excess supplies and demands—unemployment and vacancies respectively in particular labour markets—commonly occur and trigger movements of prices and quantities—specifically money wages and employment.

Keynes argued, of course, that nominal wages are sticky. His argument exploited the truth that money wages are determined in a host of disaggregated markets, not in a single economy-wide market or national negotiation. In every particular market workers and employers might well believe that a money wage cut would be a cut in their wages relative to those of workers elsewhere, and resist it on those grounds. Although Keynes purported to be adopting the classical assumption that both product and labour markets are purely competitive in the absence of monopolistic combinations or government regulations, his discussion of the realities of labour markets seems to recognise monopolistic competition and bilateral bargaining as normal features or wage determination.

The Phillips Curve

Phillips (1958) was well within Marshallian and Keynesian traditions when he plotted nominal, not real, wage changes against unemployment rates. Friedman missed the point when he called this choice a "basic defect." This is not to deny that changes in money wages in labour markets will reflect expected nominal wage and price movements throughout the economy, as well as pressures from excess supply, unemployment, and excess demand, job vacancies. If the real economy and monetary quantities are growing at different rates, equilibrium nominal prices will be moving too. In a full and continuing equilibrium, expectations will be confirmed by future events. If equilibrium prices are moving, consumers, workers, and business managers will anticipate those trends.[3]

The Phillips curve came to prominence on the American macroeconomic scene in the 1950s, when money wages and prices appeared to accelerate while employment was less than what was regarded as "full." A new category of inflation had been discovered and a new term invented, "cost-push" as distinguished from "demand-pull." But a name is not an explanation, and there was no theory of the sources of cost-push. A different approach, consistent with Phillips curve observations, was to regard "full employment" as a zone rather than a point, and inflation not as an either–or discontinuity but as a matter of degree, depending on the prevalence of excess demand markets in the economy.

Essential to this rationale is recognition of three characteristics of the sources of Phillips curve observations. Two of them I have already discussed: that, as Keynes stressed, the wages and prices determined in markets are expressed in the monetary unit of account, and that *disequilibrium* in a market—excess supply or demand at prevailing prices—is a crucial source of changes in wages or prices. The third is the multiplicity of labour and product markets and the diversity of the demand/supply circumstances of the several markets.

The Beveridge Curve

We know from common observation that excess supplies and excess demands exist simultaneously in the economy. Specifically, in some labour markets unemployed workers outnumber job vacancies, while in others at the same time vacancies exceed unemployment. One might, as I suggested (Tobin, 1972), define a single labour market narrowly enough so that vacancies and unemployment do not coexist within it.

At any moment there are both vacancies markets, those with excess demand, and unemployment markets, those with excess supply. Of course, the identities of markets within the two classes are always changing, as supply/demand balances shift. Yet over the economy as a whole there is considerable stability in the relation between aggregate vacancy and unemployment rates, as they vary in business fluctuations. This is a negative relationship: high vacancies go with low unemployment, and vice versa. Moreover, the marginal decrease in vacancies per unit increase in unemployment declines with the unemployment rate. This relation is often called the Beveridge curve. William Beveridge (1945) defined employment as full if unemployment is no more numerous than vacancies. In this context it is easy to define frictional unemployment, namely the maximum amount or unemployment consistent with Beveridge's criterion of full employment.

In practice it is difficult to implement this conceptual framework literally, because vacancies and idle workers cannot be measured so that one vacancy is really comparable to one unemployed worker. But the framework is useful. For example, consider the frequently recurring controversy whether observed increases in unemployment are frictional or structural, on the one hand, or cyclical and "Keynesian," on the other. In the former case, there would be in effect an increase in the natural rate or, to use a more appropriately neutral term, the non-accelerating inflation rate of unemployment (NAIRU), and demand stimulus would not be the appropriate remedy. In the latter case, there would be an increased shortfall from full employment, and Keynesian demand policy would be called for. In the former case, the Beveridge curve would have shifted outward, in a way that increased both vacancies and unemployment. In the latter case, there would have been movement along an unchanged Beveridge curve, not an outward shift.

"Stochastic Macroequilibrium" and the NAIRU

In my own Presidential Address in 1971 (Tobin, 1972), I described a Phillips curve theory based on what I called stochastic macroequilibrium: "stochastic because random intersectoral shocks keep individual labor markets in diverse states of disequilibrium; macroequilibrium, because the perpetual flux of particular markets produces fairly definite aggregate outcomes of unemployment and wages." In this model I was following contributions by Lipsey (1960), and by Archibald and Holt (in Phelps, *et al.* 1970). Here it is again.

The microeconomics of the Phillips curve is that money wages rise in excess demand labour markets and fall in excess supply markets, in approximate proportions to the amounts of excess demand or supply. These are movements relative to market-clearing wages, which may themselves be moving. Economy-wide average wage change depends on both vacancies and unemployment. The macro Phillips and Beveridge curves arise as joint outcomes of the events in individual markets and of the distribution of excess demands and supplies among them. As the aggregate number of jobs increases relative to the labour force, more markets will experience vacancies and fewer will exhibit excess supplies of workers. The rate of wage inflation will be greater, and as the norms of wage settlements rise in response, Friedman's unbounded acceleration may occur.

Individual markets are subject to stochastic shocks in supply and demand. If these shocks were to cease, adjustments of prices and of quantities—e.g. movements of workers towards markets with higher wages and greater excess demands—could bring equilibrium with markets cleared. The only aggregate quantity of jobs compatible with such an equilibrium is a quantity equal to the labour force. This equilibrium would carry with it a "natural rate" of unemployment, namely zero, at stable wages and prices.

Suppose, however, the macroeconomic environment is stable, as measured by the aggregate number of jobs, while the distribution of these jobs among individual markets is constantly changing. Even if the distribution of excess demand and supply across markets remains constant, the positions of individual markets in the distribution are in continuous flux.

What is happening to money wages depends on the dynamics of adjustment to excess demands and supplies. Since these adjustments take time, there are bound to be some vacancies and some unemployment. The balance between them will vary with the macro environment, the aggregate of jobs. Beveridge full employment will not necessarily result in average wage change of zero (relative to the equilibrium trend). The NAIRU can well involve unemployment in excess of vacancies, jobs fewer in aggregate than the labour force. This would happen if downward adjustments of wages in excess supply markets are slower than upward adjustments in excess demand markets. Non-linearity of response of this kind introduces an inflationary bias to the system. The same non-linearity of response would imply that the NAIRU is higher the greater the dispersion of excess demands and supplies across markets.

The model also allows for mobility of workers towards markets with higher wages and more vacancies. Within limits, the greater is such endogenous mobility the fewer will be the mismatches reflected in frictional unemployment and the lower will be the NAIRU.

My 1971 model assumed—with one exception—that, for any given aggregate quantity of jobs relative to labour force, increases in average money wages over time would ultimately feed fully into wage determination in every sector. This is a recipe for a vertical long-run Phillips curve à la Friedman. But I did point out a possible exception, a way in which a long-run trade-off might be preserved. Suppose that in any market money wages will not actually decline unless and until a high rate of unemployment has persisted for several periods. This barrier might temporarily prevent the wage change in the sector from falling as far below the general norm as would be appropriate to prevailing excess supply in the sector. If the wage change norm were high, that rate of unemployment would without delay generate a wage increase appropriately below the norm but still non-negative. But if the wage increase norm were so low that it would take a money wage decline to bring about that same differential, the decline would be postponed and for a while there would be no change. Eventually, however, this barrier would give way.

This phenomenon is realistic, whether or not it is irrational. Even if it could be said to show money illusion, it is not a permanent non-homogeneity in any market. However, the positions of markets are always shifting. So there may always be some markets at the nominal barrier, their identities always changing. If so, increasing the aggregate number of jobs will at the same time reduce the unemployment rate and increase the average rate of wage inflation. The effects of actual wage change on the wage norm are diluted by the fact that money wages remain unchanged in those sectors at the money wage floor. There is a permanent trade-off in aggregate, though not in any one market. But the long-run Phillips curve will still become vertical when the average wage increase and the general wage increase norm are high enough so that no adjustments in any market would require nominal wage cuts. I am afraid that critics did not understand this subtle and ingenious argument; they just thought I was committing a vulgar error.

In Conclusion

The symmetry between accelerating inflation and accelerating deflation in Friedman's model has always been hard to believe. Unemployment lower than the natural rate spells exploding inflation, he says, and unemployment higher spells galloping disinflation and deflation. In contrast, in Keynes open-ended inflation results from an "inflationary gap" in aggregate demand, while a "deflationary gap" leads to comparative stability of prices or price trends. The asymmetry stems from Keynes' observation of the downward stickiness of money wages.

I am inclined to believe in an S-shaped short-run Phillips curve for both individual markets and the economy at large (as I suggested in Tobin, 1955). At low unemployment rates and high vacancy rates, the curve would become quite steep. At high unemployment rates and low vacancy rates, as for example in 1982 in the U.S., the marginal response of wage inflation to additional unemployment would be increasing. For intermediate unemployment and vacancy rates the curve would be fairly flat, making it hard to locate any precise NAIRU. In this central flat range, transient microeconomic ups and downs in prices and wages would be more important than macro events and policies. After all, it is difficult to believe in a knife-edge natural rate or full employment, implying that small changes in the tightness of labour markets have immense qualitative and quantitative consequences. *Natura non facit saltum*, so it says on Marshall's title page.

The NAIRU is not a Walrasian solution. It has no particular claim to be called "natural" or "optimal." Its dynamic and distributional determinants come from institutional features of markets and from stochastic intermarket flux rather than from rational utility maximising determinants of real supply and demand relations. We economists do not, not yet anyway, have a general theory of optimisation applicable to dynamic adjustment mechanisms, because neither the objectives of such behaviour nor the constraints upon it can be, except in simple specific cases, formulated in terms of the utility and production functions which make us feel comfortable and on which we base ordinary supply and demand functions. Our models should of course be consistent with rational behaviour, including the absence of money illusion, in equilibrium. But in a monetary economy, in which markets, imperfect or perfect, grind out money wages and prices along with real quantities, we have no right to rule out *a priori* money effects on real variables during disequilibrium adjustments. This was Keynes' message, and both friends and foes in the profession were quite obtuse and wrong in attributing to him gratuitous assumptions of irrational money illusion.

In the end, the most destructive feature of natural rate theory is not its sensible warning against overdoing policies to expand aggregate demand in order to reduce unemployment below an inflation-safe rate. It is its inhibition against expansionary demand policies in any circumstances. This comes from new classical macroeconomics and real business cycle theory, and they are next-of-kin heirs of Milton Friedman's 1967 Presidential Address, very likely the most influential article ever published in an economics journal. Its influence reached way beyond the profession— for example, to European and Japanese governments and central banks and to *The Economist* and other opinion leaders. Europe has never really recovered from the recessions of 1974–5 and 1979–82, and now the entire advanced democratic capitalist world is stagnating.

Notes

1. Until I re-read Friedman's Presidential Address in order to write this chapter, I had the impression that Friedman accepted a Keynesian non-market-clearing explanation of unemployment in excess of the natural rate. Now, however, I think the wage and price adjustments in his paper are better interpreted as corrections of expectations than as responses to excess demand or supply. The spirit of Lucas is also evident in Friedman's stress that the monetary authority "cannot use its control over nominal quantities to peg a real quantity." The word "peg" does leave some ambiguity about the length of time for which a particular value of a target variable is the policy objective. But the spirit of his paper, reinforced by the critical dismissal of "fine tuning," suggests that the monetary authority should eschew any real target at any time.

The Presidential Address is not the only evidence of Friedman's drift towards a new classical or "real business cycle" position. In his ultimate defence of his position that fiscal policy has no macroeconomic consequence he embraced the classical view that price flexibility keeps the economy at full employment (natural rate) anyway. He said, "It is important that we try to determine as accurately as possible the characteristics of the demand function for money, including the elasticity of demand with respect to interest rates. But in my opinion no 'fundamental issues' in either monetary theory or monetary policy hinge on whether the estimated elasticity can for most purposes be approximated by zero or is better approximated by -0.1 or -0.5 or -2.0, provided it is seldom capable of being approximated by $-\infty$" (Friedman, 1966, p. 85). This cannot be true unless real aggregate output is independent of interest rates and that cannot be true unless perfect or near-perfect price flexibility keeps the economy at full employment independent of fiscal and monetary policies and events.

2. Dillard (1988) called this contradiction the "Barter illusion in classical and neoclassical economics." I have discussed these issues at length elsewhere (Tobin, 1993).

3. That norms for wage increases would reflect actual experience and expectation of economy-wide wage and price inflation was widely appreciated before 1967 by economists who found the Phillips curve a useful macroeconomic tool. The famous or infamous Samuelson–Solow article (1960) recognises this explicitly.

Consider also the following part of a paper presented in October 1966:

> [We do not] know the answer to the ... basic question whether continuation of 4 percent unemployment would, so long as it generates any inflation, generate an accelerating inflation. This would be the orthodox prediction: Wages and other incomes rise because people want real gains, and the bargaining power of the

individuals and groups depends on the real situation. If they find that they are cheated by price increases they will simply escalate their money claims accordingly. On this view the Phillips curve would blow up if growth at a steady utilization rate were maintained ... On this interpretation, the only true equilibrium full employment is the degree of unemployment that corresponds to zero inflation—any higher rate of utilization can be called excess demand. This is a dismal conclusion if true, because it appears to take a socially explosive rate of unemployment—more than 6 percent in the USA—to keep the price level stable (Tobin, 1967).

I would add that when President Kennedy's Council of Economic Advisers in 1961 set 4% unemployment as the goal of macro policy, we were not proposing to take a ride up a Phillips curve to purchase lower unemployment than the 7% then prevailing at the expense of more inflation. We believed, maybe wrongly but not obviously so then or now, that 4% was at that time consistent with stable low inflation. We proposed also to take out insurance by incomes policy, "wage price guideposts." Inflation accelerated in the late 1960s when Vietnam war fiscal and monetary policy carried unemployment down to 3%.

References

Beveridge, W. H., 1945. *Full Employment in a Free Society*, New York: W. W. Norton.

Dillard, D., 1988. "The Barter Illusion in Classical and Neoclassical Economics," *Eastern Economic Journal*, 14 (October–December), 299–318.

Friedman, M., 1966. "Interest Rates and the Demand for Money," *Journal of Law and Economics*, 9, (October), 71–85.

———. 1968. "The Role of Monetary Policy," *American Economic Review*, 58(1) (March), 1–17.

Keynes, J. M., 1936. *The General Theory of Employment, Interest and Money*, New York: Harcourt Brace and London: Macmillan.

Lipsey, R. G., 1960. "The Relation between Unemployment and the Rate of Change of Money Wage Rates in the United Kingdom, 1862–1957: A Further Analysis," *Economica*, 27 (February), 1–31; reprinted in AEA Series (1966), *Reading in Business Cycles*, 456–87.

Lucas, R. E., Jr., 1973. "Some International Evidence on Output–Inflation Tradeoffs," *American Economic Review*, 63(3) (June), 326–34.

Phelps, E. S. *et al.*, 1970. *Microeconomic Foundations of Employment and Inflation Theory*, New York: W. W. Norton and London: Macmillan.

Phillips, A. W., 1958. "The Relation between Unemployment and the Rate of Change of Money Wage Rates in the United Kingdom, 1861–1957," *Economica*, 25 November, 283–99.

Samuelson, P. A. and Solow, R. M., 1960. "Analytical Aspects of Anti-Inflation Policy," *American Economic Review*, 50 (May), 177–94.

Tobin, J., 1955. "A Dynamic Aggregative Model," *Journal of Political Economy*, 63(1) (April), 103–15.

———, 1967. "Unemployment and Inflation: The Cruel Dilemma," in A. Phillips (ed.), *Price Issues in Theory, Practice and Policy*, Philadelphia: University of Pennsylvania Press.

———, 1972. "Inflation and Unemployment," *American Economic Review*, 62(1) (March), 1–18.

———, 1993. "Price Flexibility and Output Stability: An Old Keynesian View," *Journal of Economic Perspectives*, 7 (Winter), 45–65.

PART III

MACROECONOMIC POLICY

CHAPTER 14

ON THE THEORY OF MACROECONOMIC POLICY

1 Jan Tinbergen and the Theory of Policy

A great privilege and honor it is for me to speak here today to all of you who are joining me in homage to Jan Tinbergen. I have long regarded Jan Tinbergen as the model economist, the personal example I most hope young economists will follow. He was and is of course a scientist, full of curiosity about how the world works. But his motivation has always been more than curiosity. He wants to know how the world works so that he can make it work better. Knowledge is the foundation of policy. It was natural for Tinbergen to set forth a formal theory of policy nearly fifty years ago (Tinbergen 1952 and 1956), and it was equally natural for him to relate the theory to practical problems of policy in The Netherlands and elsewhere and to implement it and illustrate it with the help of theoretical and econometric models. Thus Tinbergen was the originator of the subject on which I propose to speak to you today.

For many social scientists public policies are phenomena to be described, analyzed, and understood, just like other aspects of individual and social behavior. Those scholars seek to tell how politics and government work, not to try to make them work better. This is certainly a legitimate standpoint, in economics most prominently represented by James Buchanan and other public choice theorists. They regard do-gooders like Tinbergen and me as naïve. We think we have an audience, the general public or legislators or government administrators. We assume that to some degree they identify their personal interest with the public interest, wish to

---

This chapter, presented as the Tinbergen Lecture, Royal Netherlands Economic Association, Utrecht, 1989, is reprinted from *De Economist* 138(1) (1990): 1–14.

promote social welfare, and respect reason and fact. Certainly that is the spirit in which Tinbergen conceived his theory of policy.

Tinbergen embedded policy in a mathematical economic model. Some variables in the model are identified as policy instruments, some as objectives of policy-makers. Policy instruments are "exogenous" in the sense that policy-makers are free to set their values. There are other exogenous variables, whose values are set by nature or foreigners or other forces external to the model. The model also contains "endogenous" variables; their values depend on the exogenous variables, policy or non-policy. Target values for some endogenous variables are the objectives of policy. Those objective variables are not the only endogenous variables, but they are the ones that matter.

You can imagine solving such a model so that the solution, or what econometricians call the "reduced form," tells directly how the objectives depend on the policy variables. It is easiest to think of this solution for a set of linear equations. The first truth, simple but illuminating, is that the policy-maker cannot hope to hit targets for more objective variables than the number of instrument variables. The second truth is that the availability of N instruments does not guarantee that as many as N objective targets can be hit. There must be N *independent* instruments, in the sense that the effects of any one instrument on the objectives are not proportional to those of any other, or of any combination of others. The third truth is that a redundancy of instruments is conceivable, more instruments than needed to hit all the attainable targets, whether or not some other targets are unattainable.

Very frequently some tradeoffs are ineradicable. For example, we probably don't know how to get more equity from the economy without losing efficiency. The array of policy instruments does not include tools that could overcome this familiar tradeoff. For this reason, instruments are insufficient. Yet at the same time, for a given standard of efficiency we might be able to identify numerous combinations of instruments that would yield the same degree of equity. In that sense, instruments are redundant.

2 Applications in Macroeconomics

Rather than pursuing that example, let me turn to my topic of macroeconomics. Tinbergen's framework may seem simple common sense, but it was not obvious beforehand. In the early days of the Keynesian revolution, the idea was to throw everything available at the problem of the moment, depression, unemployment or war-generated inflation. Against unemployment, for example, spend more on public works, cut taxes, print more money, and lower interest rates—all. So undiscriminating and single-minded an attack was perhaps justified during the Great Depression because the target was so remote and so central, and because the constraints on the instruments were so tight that over-shooting was not a worry.

After the Second World War, Keynesian economists learned to regard fiscal policy and monetary policy as distinct macroeconomic instruments, substitutes for one another. (It is true that they are not always independent. If printing money is the only way to finance government deficits, then there is no monetary policy independent of fiscal policy. Likewise a small open economy with a fixed foreign exchange rate may not be able to have its own monetary policy.) Fiscal and monetary policies are both instruments of demand management, of short-run or counter-cyclical economic stabilization.

The two standard objectives of demand management are full employment and price stability, one a numerical target for an unemployment rate variable, the other a numerical target for a price inflation variable. Well, we have two objectives and two instruments. Can't we achieve macroeconomic bliss? At least one popular American macro textbook misread Tinbergen and said so, and some economists who should know better have slipped into the same mistake. The fallacy is an example of the second truth. With respect to the two targets, fiscal policy and monetary policy are collinear instruments.

That unfortunate fact of life is a consequence of what I call the "common funnel theorem." The theorem says that the consequences of a given volume of aggregate demand, on the one hand, for output and employment and, on the other, for money prices and wages are independent of the sources and composition of that volume of demand. Neither fiscal nor monetary instruments affect the target values directly. Both affect them through the same medium, aggregate demand. The demands generated by fiscal policies and those generated by monetary policies are poured, along with demands from all other sources, into a common funnel. How much goes into prices and how much into output depends on the outflow from the funnel. The output/price or unemployment/inflation tradeoff is inexorable; that is to say, it can't be eliminated or mitigated by altering the fiscal/monetary policy mix.

Another way to put the point is this: A certain volume of aggregate demand will place the economy at a certain point on the aggregate supply (AS) curve relating output to price level or on the short-run Phillips curve relating unemployment to inflation. Whether that volume is supported by an easy fiscal policy combined with a tight monetary policy or by a tight fiscal policy combined with an easy monetary policy will not shift the AS curve or the Phillips curve and, therefore, will not alter the points reached on those curves.

I guess that many of you are busy thinking of exceptions to my common funnel theorem. I recognize that deviations are easy to imagine, but they are generally unsystematic. For example, the composition of aggregate demand will usually depend on the mix of the two policies. An easy fiscal/tight money mix will be expected to result in relatively more private and public consumption and less investment than the opposite mix. Quite possibly this difference in composition, in any given economy at any particular time, carries with it some difference in price behavior. I just don't see that there is any way for a macro theorist to generalize about that difference or for a macro policy-maker to count on it.

However, there is one systematic exception I will acknowledge. It applies to an open economy in a regime of floating exchange rates with free movement of funds across currencies. An easy fiscal/tight money policy mix means higher interest rates are associated with any given real GNP. They attract internationally mobile funds and appreciate the local currency. The appreciation makes prices of internationally tradable goods lower in local currency. The improvement in overall price indexes and their inflation is probably only temporary, because the price declines are borrowed from other countries and are accompanied by deterioration in the home economy's trade balance and current account. This is not a game every country can play at once. It is a "beggar-thy-neighbor" tactic against inflation in one country, just as policies that lead to exchange depreciation are "beggar-thy-neighbor" tactics against unemployment.

Most economists nowadays think there is no permanent unemployment-inflation tradeoff. That proposition contains both good and bad news. The good news is that the conquest of inflation entails no cost in unemployment. The bad news is that the amount of irreducible—"natural"—unemployment may be very high. Anyway the short-run tradeoff is a practical problem in anti-recession or anti-inflation policy-making, and the inability of the two instruments, fiscal and monetary, to overcome the tradeoff is a serious handicap.

Frustrated by the high unemployment rates seemingly necessary for disinflation or for price stability, many macroeconomists have, at various times, stressed the need for additional independent policy tools. The tie between prices and output or wages and employment due to the common funnel might be broken by price and wage controls or incomes policies. It is interesting that both Keynes and Tinbergen viewed money wage rates as a possible policy instrument. Perhaps direct wage/price instruments could lower the natural or inflation-safe rate of unemployment. Perhaps structural reforms—which Tinbergen termed "qualitative" policies to distinguish them from quantitative instruments—could make the short-run tradeoff less painful or even lower the natural unemployment rate.

The two instruments, fiscal and monetary, should be together capable of hitting some pair of targets. One member of the pair would be a real GNP and employment target, with whatever price outcome is conjoined to it. That would be a target for aggregate demand, most likely the natural or inflation-safe unemployment rate. What would be the second target? It might be a variable connected with external balance, the exchange rate or international reserves or the current account.

More fundamentally, the fiscal/monetary policy mix affects the composition of national output as between investment and consumption. As noted above, a tight-fiscal/easy-money policy mix would favor investment, both domestic and foreign. Those who are concerned for the future standard of living of the society relative to the present would naturally favor that policy mix. The opposite combination of policies in the United States in the 1980s has led to a binge in current consumption at the expense of future Americans.

Although we commonly speak of monetary and fiscal policies each as univariate, as I have been doing here, we know that under each heading fall numerous specific instruments. The monetary authority can set reserve requirements and impose other restrictions on bank portfolios, can set its own discount and lending policies and rates, and can engage in open market operations in a variety of assets, foreign and domestic, short and long. From a macroeconomic viewpoint, most of these monetary instruments are different ways of doing the same thing, and the central bank chooses among them on quite subsidiary considerations. However there might be some gain in the scope of macroeconomic control from using a variety of open market interventions, in foreign exchange and in long-run securities or even equities, not just in the usual very short-term markets.

The variety of fiscal instruments is even greater. In macroeconomics we look mainly at direct impacts on aggregate spending on goods and services. For government purchases, the impacts are obvious. For taxes and transfers, we emphasize the income effects on spending. Traditional fiscal theory, therefore, treats the items in government budgets as collinear instruments. But attention to incentive and substitution effects enriches the policy menu. Although income tax cuts encourage almost exclusively consumption, an investment tax credit, such as was in effect in the United States from 1962 to 1986, mainly stimulates investment. In that respect, the investment tax credit was a substitute for easy monetary policy as an instrument for moving the composition of current GNP in favor of future growth. With respect to that objective, public investment outlays should of course be differentiated from collective consumption.

3 Uncertainty about the Effects of Instruments

The theory of policy so far discussed assumes that the effects of policy instruments on endogenous variables, including policy objectives, are known with certainty, or assumes that expected values are all that matter. Things are quite different when considerations of risk are added in an essential way. My Yale colleague and collaborator William Brainard amended Tinbergen's theory in a classic article (Brainard 1967). The essential point is to recognize the errors in the regression coefficients in the macroeconomic model, as well as the additive errors in equations.

In the theory so amended, policy instruments are much less likely to be redundant. For hitting the same targets with smaller variance, more instruments are always helpful, provided their coefficient errors have some statistical independence. The argument is just an application of portfolio theory. The policy-maker is the portfolio manager, and the instruments are the assets. But the objectives of the policy-maker are more complex than those of a wealth-owner. The wealth-owner is trying to maximize expected return for a given amount of risk and then to choose her most desirable efficient combination of return and risk. The policy-maker has a number of incommensurable policy-objective variables, not just one, and has to weigh the expected values and risks of all of them.

Risk aversion imparts some conservatism to policy. In this respect the Brainard theory is probably realistic. With coefficient uncertainty, big doses of policy medicine enlarge the variance of the outcomes, however much they may improve the expected values. A cautious central banker will not, for example, aim for low unemployment even if the expected value of the associated inflation were acceptable if he thought that the probability of a large inflationary deviation from the mean outcome was also high.

What is important, more precisely, is the standard error of the regression (or reduced-form) forecast of a policy-objective variable. That error, we know, is positively related to the distances of the regressors from their mean values in the sample data on which the model was estimated. Policy-makers do not like to move into *terra incognita*. They do not like to move in big steps. They like to gain observations close to the territory where they are going to operate.

We should, however, not exaggerate the "take-it-easy" moral of this theory. The warning is against big departures from experience, not against big doses of policy instruments *per se*. Policy instruments often have the same effects on endogenous objectives as some non-policy exogenous variables, and their coefficient errors are likewise highly correlated. Consider, for example, a central bank's increase in the supply of base money and an exogenous decline in the demand for base money, say public's demand for currency or the banking system's demand for excess reserves. Both the policy move and the non-policy events have the same macroeconomic effects. Thus it would not be conservative to withhold a large increase in base money supply if the authorities knew that it would offset a large autonomous increase in demand for base money. Indeed a compensatory injection of base money, even if large, is the conservative thing to do. The same might apply to fiscal policy, where government outlays and taxes have effects equivalent to some exogenous private demands for goods and services. In the Great Depression it was not conservative of governments to try to keep their budgets balanced.

4 Pitfalls in Policy Exploitations of Empirical Regularities

The estimation of policy effects is of course very tricky. Years ago we thought of policy instruments as completely autonomous, exogenous to the economy we were modeling, uninfluenced by the endogenous variables of that economy, insulated from the random disturbances in their values. But if policy-makers themselves were following some rules, even roughly, then their settings of instruments were not exogenous. Observed correlations of instrumental and objective variables may reflect the behavior of the makers of policy, not the behavior of the economy. Those correlations are misleading if they are interpreted as telling how the economy would respond if policy-makers acted differently from the rules they followed in the sample period of observation. "Goodhart's law" says that in economics any observed regularity will vanish if policy-makers attempt to exploit it.

There are numerous examples in macroeconomics. Before central bankers fell under the sway of monetarism, they followed accommodative, at least partially accommodative, policies. When expansion of the economy increased the demand for bank credit and for deposits and currency, the central bank allowed the supplies to expand as well. In recessions, they allowed money and credit aggregates to shrink along with the economy. Milton Friedman and other monetarists cited the time series correlations of money stocks and nominal national incomes as evidence of the sovereign power of monetary policy, and alleged that stabilizing money supply would stabilize the economy. But when central bankers took the criticisms of the monetarists seriously and ceased to be so accommodative, the correlations became much weaker.

Fiscal policy provides another example of how misleading a guide to policy simple correlations can be. Government deficits have generally been negatively correlated with economic activity, seemingly contradicting the Keynesian view that deficit spending would be expansionary. Of course, the paradox is only superficial. There are two explanations for it. One is the endogenous variation of government finances in response to fluctuations in economic activity. Tax codes and expenditure laws are such that revenues automatically—that is, without new policy decisions or legislation—move procyclically and expenditures countercyclically. Because of this endogeneity, it is a mistake to regard the deficit as an instrument. Tax and expenditure laws and formulas are instruments; given them, budget outcomes are endogenous. The "full employment budget" and numerous variants of it are an attempt to eliminate these endogenous cyclical effects and to provide a rational quantitative measure of fiscal policy.

A variant of this confusion occurred in the 1980s in the United States. Standard macroeconomic models, both theoretical and econometric, say that deficit spending policies will raise real interest rates. Apologists for the Reagan deficits appealed to the absence of positive simple correlations between deficits and interest rates. The absence of such correlations reflects the fact that the same fluctuations of economic activity that move deficits countercyclically move interest rates procyclically. They don't tell what happens when deficits are massively increased by policy rather than moved endogenously. We found out in the 1980s, when both real interest rates and federal deficits were much higher than in any previous post-1945 recovery.

The second explanation of negative correlations between deficits and economic activity is that governments often reinforce the "built-in stabilizers" with endogenous changes in fiscal policy: tax cuts, generous transfers, and public works to combat recession, tax increases and expenditure economies and postponements to fight inflation.

Of course the whole purpose of econometrics, as Tinbergen and the other giants of the 1930s, 1940s, and 1950s developed it, was to solve exactly this problem of sorting out causes and effects. The idea was to specify equations that would stand up in the face of changes in policies and policy rules—and in the face of non-policy shocks as well. Yet if observed data record little variation in policies or policy rules, or in non-policy variables equivalent to them, the most sophisticated techniques will be unable to forecast the effects of policy innovations.

The celebrated "Lucas critique" (Lucas 1976) goes still further, asserting that the structural or behavioral equations of macroeconometric models would not be stable under changes in policy rules, or policy regimes, because private economic agents adapt their own behavior to that of the government. Applied to monetary policy, the argument is that since changes in purely nominal magnitudes cannot make any real difference to rational agents, changed settings of monetary instruments are effective only when they are unexpected or misperceived. Applied to fiscal policy by Robert Barro (1974), the argument is that changes in taxes and transfers can have no macroeconomic effects, specifically no effects on economy-wide spending and saving, because rational agents will know that reverse changes of equivalent present value will occur in the future.

Lucas, Barro, and other exponents of the New Classical Macroeconomics are guilty of the fallacy of misplaced concreteness. They apply to the hurly-burly of short-run adjustments and fluctuations theorems that might under ideal conditions apply to long runs and long horizons. The logical consequence is the "real business cycle theory" of Kydland and Prescott (1982) and others. This approach is premised on the idea that both individuals and society at large adapt rationally and optimally to all unavoidable natural, technological, and external shocks to which the economy is subject. The observed fluctuations in business activity which we call cycles are, in this view, simply the history of those adaptations. Money matters not at all, and Barro-type intertemporal substitutions nullify fiscal policies—although of course public claims on real resources do make a difference. There is no business cycle problem, in the sense of Keynes, Tinbergen, and the builders and estimators of macro models.

Recent history has not been kind to these approaches. Relative to them, the old-fashioned macroeconometric models have been doing well. Jan Tinbergen is a modest man, and he never thought that econometric equations, his or others', would last forever. I am sure he is now, and was fifty years ago, prepared to believe that clear changes of policy regime, like other changes in the environment of economic activity, alter structural equations and their coefficients. Lucas and company have made us more sensitive to such possibilities, properly so.

5 Relations between Qualitative and Quantitative Policies

Tinbergen distinguished quantitative policies—setting and changing the values of instrument variables—from qualitative policies—alterations in structure by regulation, deregulation, and institutional innovation. In important respects these are substitutes for each other. The more numerous are effective built-in fiscal stabilizers, the less necessary are discretionary changes of fiscal instruments. If one thinks of policy rules as equations of the system, then if other structural equations are altered, whether by deliberate qualitative policies or spontaneously, the policy equations will need to be changed too.

One way to look at policy rules and other structural equations is to regard the model as a whole as a mechanism converting exogenous shocks into fluctuations of endogenous variables, including those which are policy objectives. For example, in a classic article William Poole (1970) showed that, although the same expected value of real national product could in principle be obtained either by setting the money stock or by setting interest rates, the variance of that policy objective around its target mean would depend on the instrument used. This insight can be generalized to policy rules and to the variance-covariance matrix of several objective variables.

In the Poole model, the policy rule in question is the central bank's supply of money in response to a short-term interest rate. The central bank does not know whether an observed increase in the interest rate is the result of strength in the goods market (upward IS shift) or of an increased demand for money (inward LM shift). Accommodation is desirable in the latter case but not in the former. The coefficient of the interest rate in the central bank's supply curve can be chosen so as to minimize the variance of national output. To pursue and generalize the Poole example, now suppose that, as actually has been happening, the government relaxes legal ceilings on the rates banks can pay depositors. This deregulation sharply reduces the built-in accommodation of the monetary system, because a general rise in interest rates no longer induces private agents to economize money holdings. As a result, a more accommodative optimal money-supply rule is now optimal (Tobin 1983).

6 What Can Economists Say about Policy Objectives?

In his classic 1953 book Tinbergen begins with a brief mention of "a collective ophelimity function" as the object to be maximized. This function—sometimes called social utility or social welfare—would make commensurable the numerous economic outcomes that matter. It would be something like a weighted average of their values. But after the first page

Tinbergen deals only with vectors of quantitative objective outcomes, without trying to rank the vectors, much less summarize them in scalar scores. I have taken the same standpoint throughout this lecture so far.

Yet the pervasiveness of intractable tradeoffs, the lack of sufficient independent instruments to hit several important goals simultaneously, makes ranking and scoring of vectors of policy goals very important. We can wash our hands of the task by assigning both the burden and the privilege to the political process, to public opinion and government policy-makers. After all, we economists have no business imposing our own social values. But economics cannot and should not, I think, dodge these issues completely. Our discipline can at least contribute to clarity and sophistication of thought about social choices. Many practical objectives of policy are not ultimate values but measurable variables somewhere between those values and actual tools of policy. In this sense they are intermediate instruments.

For example, in macroeconomics the two traditional short-run objectives, low unemployment and price stability, are not ends in themselves. Even real national product is not a goal *per se*. We economists are disposed to consider consumption (including leisure, public goods, and other non-market commodities) as the activity that generates utility or ophelimity. We usually score outcomes for individual consumers by the utility attaching to their prospective streams of consumption over time, and over contingent "states of nature" as well.

Our standard paradigm says that tastes, together with technologies and resource endowments, are the deep fundamental data of an economy, from which all economic behaviors and outcomes are derived. The paradigm is vulnerable to several difficulties, which we occasionally acknowledge but commonly sweep under the rug. Even at an individual level, utility is not clearly and unambiguously formulated; people are often ambivalent or schizophrenic. Tastes are not wholly exogenous and stable. They are transient and inchoate. They are much influenced by changing social and cultural trends, by information and disinformation, by habits and traditions, by advertising and other sales promotion efforts. Utility is a weak reed on which to hang intertemporal choices, especially those involving uncertainty. Although contemporary theory places heavier and heavier weight on utility, it is hard to believe the concept can bear the burden.

Moreover, we know there is no way to aggregate individual preferences into social rankings, let alone to combine individual utilities into a collective ophelimity index. As if this were not obvious, Kenneth Arrow proved it rigorously years ago. The impossibility applies to aggregations across contemporaneous cohorts, *a fortiori* across generations living and unborn. No wonder so many of today's macro theorists purchase mathematical rigor by assuming that society can be represented by a single consumer, if not immortal at least identical in endowments and tastes generation after generation.

A common diagnosis of the current United States economic problem is that my country, in both private and public sectors, is saving too little. The implicit value judgment is that currently living generations are mistreating future generations; we are consuming at their expense. One symptom and vehicle of this misbehavior is the United States current account deficit. (Its counterpart in Japanese and European, mainly German, surpluses might similarly represent excessive saving.) The policy moral is to tighten fiscal policy in the United States (and ease it in the surplus countries).

The contrasting *laissez faire* view is that these payments imbalances, and the differences in saving behavior underlying them, reflect rational personal and national choices. They require and invite no policy moves. Americans want to consume more now and less later; Japanese and Germans want to do the reverse. International and intertemporal markets permit both sides to do what they want. There is no problem.

The *laissez faire* view is mistaken, I think. The current U.S. generation does not realize what it is doing, what the future consequences and costs will be. As voters and consumers, they have been deliberately misinformed—by politicians whose priority was to cripple the civilian public sector of the nation by demagogically exploiting the public's natural distaste for taxes. In this situation, I think Jan Tinbergen would agree in principle, it is the duty of the economist to help the public make informed and rational choices, not to acquiesce in the mindless faith that everything is always for the best.

The big issues of stabilization policy in the last thirty years have, as I already noted, frequently involved the unemployment–inflation nexus. Macroeconomists have not helped the public understand and assess the costs of inflation. Are there indeed costs of inflation *per se*? Or are they costs of any price changes, whether up or down, or of deviations either way of prices from previous expectations? At a more primitive level, the general public and politicians confuse absolute price levels and relative prices, or general across-the-board inflation and changes in specific prices. They also confuse continuing inflationary trends with one-shot changes in prices.

Even economists often charge to inflation the inevitable social costs of phenomena of which inflation is a symptom (like wars and OPECs). The true policy issue presented by an unavoidable adverse shock requires comparing its costs under alternative policy responses, some of which might entail more inflation than others. Policy responses in Europe, North America, and Japan to the oil price shocks of 1973–74 and 1978–79 aimed at disinflation and generated severe recessions in the process. Were these the least-cost responses to those shocks? I do not answer the question. I just say that it is the correct question.

"Time inconsistency" is a popular recent topic in the theory of policy. Typically the government is assumed to have, for some unexplained reason, social objectives different from those of the society it is governing. (This sounds like Buchanan's public choice theory, but here it is not a question of elected officials and bureaucrats who are manipulating the political system in their own interests.) The government deceives the public in order to make the economy come out the government's preferred way. The usual application is to the inflation-unemployment tradeoff, assumed to be absent in the long run. The government makes private agents think that prices will be stable and behave accordingly. Then the government exploits those expectations and behaviors by an inflationary policy, which produces a bulge of employment and output. The people don't really want so much employment and output, so the bulge recedes after they catch on to the government's true strategy. Does this make sense? If the government is rational it knows that the strategy cannot work repeatedly. If the government is benign it doesn't wish a non-optimal outcome anyway.

A common analogy is to the classroom teacher who wants the students to study but does not care to inflict a test on them and on herself. The teacher announces the test but then cancels it at the last minute. But maybe the students really want both the study and the test, and anyway a teacher cannot credibly threaten tests that never take place.

The time inconsistency story is another example of the treatment of the economy as a whole as a single individual. Likewise in the 1970s several macro theorists held forth the prospect of painless disinflation accomplished by credible threat of resolutely restrictive monetary policy. The threat would be that, regardless how severe the recession, how great the unemployment, how widespread the bankruptcies, the government and central bank would persevere until inflation dropped to zero. Workers and unions could not count on macro-policies to save their jobs; they would have to lower their money wage rates. Business managers could not count on macro-policies to save their markets and their solvencies; they would have to lower their prices. According to the theory, under this threat the inflation would melt so fast that the threatened hardships would not occur.

Events under Mrs. Thatcher and Paul Volcker did not confirm the theory. Was Volcker guilty of "time inconsistency" in declaring premature victory?

The trouble is, I think, that the actual game does not involve just the two players government and private economy. It is an $n+1$-person game, one government (maybe more actually) and n private sectors, who are playing against each other as well as against the government. Here is a manifestation of the problem of coordination, the central problem of macroeconomics. The typical private player has no incentive to act constructively in response to the government's threat unless he thinks many other players will do likewise. No one can see the spectacle in the theater or stadium if everyone stands, but who has the incentive to obey a general admonition to sit down? When the teacher tells her grade school class there will be no picnic unless all gum-chewing ceases, would any rational child who shares the general liking of gum stop? Threats against everybody in general addressed to nobody in particular rarely work.

In the theory of policy under uncertainty, one objective is a low variance of outcomes. If we had scalar ophelimity, it would be a low variance of that index. What we actually mean by "low variance" deserves thought. Is fluctuation over time bad in itself? We don't care much about diurnal, weekly, seasonal, or in some cases even year-to-year fluctuations.

Policy plans involve re-settings of the various instruments in order to achieve desirable future paths of the objective variables. The re-settings would not in general be decided in advance, only the rules that relate them to experience. The variances of concern are *ex ante* estimates of measures of deviations of actual realizations from expected paths. Those measures are related to the variances over time of the processes determining the objective variables, but they are not the same thing.

7 Concluding Remarks

I have spoken of policy "rules," but I close by warning against taking the concept too literally. In monetary policy in particular there has been a long debate on rules *versus* discretion. This debate overlaps the argument about blind *versus* feedback rules. "Discretion" means "feedback" in practice because policy-makers take account of information, rather than setting instruments independently of observations. "Leaning against the wind" was a Federal Reserve rule throughout the 1950s and much of the 1960s. It means partial but not complete accommodation, but it allows lots of room for discretion, *i.e.* for consideration of circumstances not foreseen or even foreseeable in any formula.

Rules are bound to be pretty simple. It's not possible to formulate rules for policy-makers that cover all contingencies, any more than it is possible to write Arrow-Debreu contracts. In the United States we are fortunate that the Federal Reserve abandoned monetarist rules in 1982. Thanks to some skillful pragmatic fine-tuning by Paul Volcker and now Alan Greenspan, America, unlike Europe, has enjoyed a long and successful recovery. For one thing, the recovery has reduced unemployment by at least one more percentage point than anyone would have thought inflation-safe ten years ago. The Federal Reserve has been willing to learn by experience how far it was possible to go.

Even in the 1950s Jan Tinbergen was acutely aware of the problem of international coordination of national macroeconomic policies. That is a much bigger problem today, because of the massive size, fluidity, and extraordinary technical efficiency of global financial markets. We used to say that it is not possible for every sovereign nation to achieve its goals regardless of events elsewhere. Now, clearly, it is not possible for any nation to do so. By the same token, the policies of each country spill over into outcomes elsewhere. For example, although every government and central bank may aim for price stability within its jurisdiction, it is not feasible to accomplish adjustments to international imbalances in payments without changes in national price levels relative to each other. This is true whether the international monetary regime involves fixed or floating exchange rates.

The Group of Seven creates the shadow of coordination but not the substance. True international coordination is the biggest challenge to the theory and practice of macroeconomic policy for the next decade. It is a political challenge, of course, but also an intellectual one worthy of a Jan Tinbergen.

References

Barro, Robert, 1974, "Are Government Bonds Net Wealth?," *Journal of Political Economy*, 82, pp. 1095–1117.

Brainard, William C., 1967, "Uncertainty and the Effectiveness of Policy," *American Economic Review*, 57, pp. 411–425.

Kydland, F. E. and E. C. Prescott, 1982, "Time to Build and Aggregate Fluctuations," *Econometrica*, 50, pp. 1345–1370.

Lucas, Robert E., 1976, "Econometric Policy Evaluation: A Critique," in: K. Brunner and A. Meltzer (eds.), *The Phillips Curve and Labor Markets*, Amsterdam.

Poole, William, 1970, "Optimal Choice of Monetary Policy Instruments in a Simple Stochastic Macro Model," *Quarterly Journal of Economics*, 84, pp. 197–216.

Tinbergen, Jan, 1952, *On the Theory of Economic Policy*, Amsterdam.

Tinbergen, Jan, 1956, *Economic Policy: Principles and Design*, Amsterdam.

Tobin, James, 1983, "Financial Structure and Monetary Rules," *Kredit und Kapital*, 16, pp. 155–171. Chapter 19 below.

CHAPTER 15

STABILIZATION POLICY TEN YEARS AFTER

When the Brookings panel first met ten years ago, the U.S. government's managers of aggregate demand were cooling an economy suffering from an inflation 4 points higher than ten years before. The unemployment rate was 4.5 percent. Four years later, at the time of the panel's thirteenth meeting, the demand managers were cooling an economy suffering from an inflation 6 points higher still. The unemployment rate was 5 percent. As the panel meets today, the government's managers of aggregate demand are cooling an economy suffering from an inflation 7 points higher than ten years before. The unemployment rate is 7 percent and rising.

Higher inflation, higher unemployment—the relentless combination frustrated policymakers, forecasters, and theorists throughout the decade. The disarray in diagnosing stagflation and prescribing a cure makes any appraisal of the theory and practice of macroeconomic stabilization as of 1980 a foolhardy venture. The patent breakdown of consensus spares me the task of seeking and describing collective views. I will just give my own observations and confess my own puzzlements.

In one respect demand-management policies worked as intended in the 1970s. On each of the occasions I described at the beginning, the managers succeeded in cooling the economy. Thus the decade is distinguished by its three recessions, all deliberately induced by policy. Likewise the expansionary policies adopted to reverse the first two recessions, beginning in 1971 and 1975 respectively, promoted recoveries, and in 1977 the new Carter administration succeeded in sustaining and reinforcing the expansion. Figure 15.1 shows the changes of nominal and real GNP during

Reprinted by permission from *Brookings Papers on Economic Activity*, Washington, D.C.: Brookings Institution, 1980, pp. 19–72.

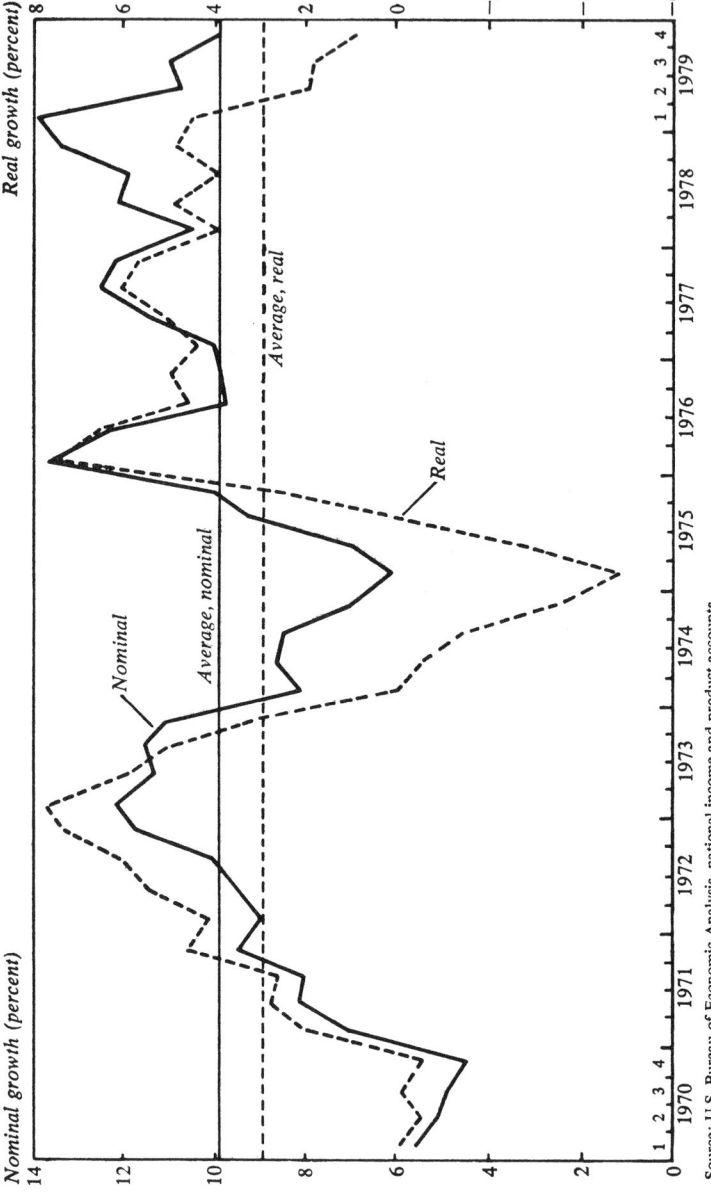

Figure 15.1
Rates of growth of GNP, nominal and real, 1970:1–1979:4[a]

Source: U.S. Bureau of Economic Analysis, national income and product accounts.
a. Data are percent changes from a year earlier.

the decade. The major turns in direction conformed to the desires and intentions of the managers of aggregate demand.

However, the expansions of 1973 and 1978–79 and the recessions of 1974–75 and 1980 were doubtless more than the managers bargained for. One reason was that when the patient did not respond promptly to moderate medication the impatient physicians multiplied the dosage. In June 1974 and again in March 1980 the Federal Reserve, frustrated in waiting for evidence of a downturn responding to previous restrictive measures and alarmed by continued bad news of inflation, sharply boosted nominal interest rates. On both occasions the cycle was already beyond its peak, and the final blows were overkill.

The conformity of real to nominal GNP movements depicted in figure 15.1 and the greater amplitude of the nominal series make a striking prima facie case that nominal demand fluctuations were calling the tune. The exceptions occurred during the autonomous commodity price shocks of 1974 and 1979.

Whatever difficulties there were in the management of nominal demand, the major disappointments came at the next stage. The inflationary components of the expansions, 1971–73 and 1975–79, were unexpectedly and distressingly large. The disinflationary consequence of the first contraction, 1969–71, was discouragingly small. Indeed, money wages "exploded" while unemployment was rising. Price inflation fell sharply at and after the trough of the second contraction. OPEC-1, decontrol, and food shortages had produced the double-digit inflationary bulge, and once the resulting price increases were absorbed or reversed overall inflation rates subsided quickly. But wage inflation stayed on a somewhat higher plateau, spelling price trouble especially when productivity growth later slowed to a halt. The disinflationary rewards of the 1980 recession remain to be seen.

U.S. stabilization policy in the 1970s was complicated by important new developments in the world economy.

International constraints became even more compelling than they had been in the 1960s. Foreign trade was greater relative to GNP, and the growing size and efficiency of Eurocurrency institutions linked U.S. financial markets more tightly to those in other jurisdictions. In August 1971 the United States abrogated the Bretton Woods agreement, made the dollar inconvertible into gold, and forced other major countries to appreciate their currencies against the dollar. These steps led in 1973 to abandonment of pegged exchange rates in favor of "dirty" floating. But the new regime did not in the end fulfill the hope, long nurtured by economists, that floating would relax the international constraints on domestic policies.

The major economic events of the decade were the extraordinary changes in world supplies and prices of specific commodities. Their interaction with macroeconomic indicators and events confronted both policymakers and analysts with problems for which they were unprepared. In the United States in particular, analyses of inflation had habitually focused on the wage-price patterns of the "fixprice" sector. In the 1970s the "flexprice" sector, instead of being a passive and innocuous appendage, was a major source of macroeconomic shocks. Shortages and price increases in foodstuffs, metals, and other primary materials were the salient feature of the worldwide 1973 inflationary boom. Then, of course, OPEC and the energy crisis dominated the world economic scene for the rest of the decade, as they will likely continue to do for the foreseeable future. The cartel's price and supply are obviously not "flex" in the sense of being determined in competitive markets, but they are certainly detached from the familiar wage-price-production milieu of domestic industry.

These events have complicated the game and escalated the stakes, but the tormenting issues of strategy have remained essentially the same throughout the period since the Second World War. Can the instruments of demand management achieve both monetary stability and satisfactory real economic performance? If so, how? If not, what are the terms of feasible choices, and what criteria should guide them? If the macroeconomic instruments are inadequate for the goals, is it useful to supplement them with incomes policies temporarily or permanently?

I begin by describing what I call the consensus macroeconomic model, vintage 1970, of which the core was the augmented Phillips curve. A loose consensus on the framework for thinking about demand management left ample scope for differences about structural details and values of parameters and for practical disagreements of diagnosis and prescription. I then review the failures of the consensus framework to prepare economists and our audiences for the macroeconomic surprises of the 1970s; I discuss both the damage to the framework and its repair. Some of the new problems arise from the revelation that the supply and demand blades of the macroeconomic scissors are not as disjointed as the earlier consensus framework found it convenient to assume. Consequently, this topic leads me naturally into a discussion of supply-side economics and policy recommendations.

As I implied at the beginning, an analysis of demand management can be approached in two stages. The first concerns the connections from policy instruments to dollar spending on goods and services. The second concerns the impact of nominal spending on prices and real output. I am not arguing for any separation theorem, only for some convenience of exposition. In 1980 the issues concerning the first stage seem secondary to those of the second stage. Nevertheless, I then take another look at the old monetarist debate, the conduct of monetary and fiscal policy, and the monetary-fiscal mix.

Finally, I return to the big analytical and policy issues of the second stage, concluding with some thoughts on where to go from here.

The Consensus Macroeconomic Framework, Vintage 1970

Ten years ago there was a broad consensus on the structure of the system that the managers of aggregate demand were trying to stabilize. The consensus pervaded the Brookings panel and was gradually becoming embodied in most macroeconometric models used for forecasting and policy analysis. It left plenty of room for disagreements about policy. They concerned the empirical magnitudes of some crucial structural parameters, the relative importance of nonpolicy demand shocks and policy variations themselves as sources of instability, the reliability and strength of stabilizing responses by private agents in decentralized markets, and the value weights attached to various dimensions of economic performance—inflation, unemployment, and output. The consensus on structure, within which these debates occurred, contained the following elements:

1. The nonagricultural business sector plays the central role in determining the economy's rate of inflation. In this sector, prices are marked-up labor costs, usually adjusted to normal operating rates and productivity trends. According to the standard "augmented Phillips curve" view, rates

of price and wage increase depend partly on their recent trends, partly on expectations of their future movements, and partly on the tightness (demand relative to supply at prevailing wages and prices) of markets for products and labor.

2. Variations in aggregate monetary demand, whether the consequences of policies or of other events, affect the course of prices and output, and wages and employment, by altering the tightness of labor and product markets, and in no other way. As a corollary, at least to a first approximation any mix of fiscal and monetary policies that yields the same aggregate demand has the same impact on inflation and real activity. Changing the mix cannot appreciably alter the short-run trade-off between inflation and employment. The proportions of fiscal and monetary stimulus or restriction can and must be decided on other grounds.

3. The tightness of markets can be related to the utilization of productive resources, reported or adjusted unemployment rates, and capacity-operating rates. At any given utilization rates, real output grows at a steady pace (then estimated to be 3.5 to 4 percent a year), reflecting trends in supplies of labor and capital and in productivity. According to Okun's Law, in cyclical fluctuations each percentage point of unemployment corresponds to 3 percent of GNP, a bit less than one year's normal growth.

4. Inflation accelerates at high employment rates because tight markets systematically and repeatedly generate wage and price increases in addition to those already incorporated in expectations and historical patterns. At low utilization rates, inflation decelerates, but probably at an asymmetrically slow pace. At the Phelps-Friedman "natural rate of unemployment," the degrees of resource utilization and market tightness generate no net wage and price pressures up or down and are consistent with accustomed and expected paths, whether stable prices or any other inflation rate.[1] The consensus view accepted the notion of a nonaccelerating inflation rate of unemployment (NAIRU) as a practical constraint on policy, even though some of its adherents would not identify NAIRU as full, equilibrium, or optimum employment.[2]

5. On the instruments of demand management themselves, there was less consensus. The monetarist counterrevolution had provided debate over the efficacy of monetary and fiscal measures, the process of transmission

of monetary policies to total spending, the proper indicators and targets of monetary policy, and the utility of active compensatory management.

Monetarism: The Two Waves

Monetarism has come in two waves, and I find it useful to distinguish their doctrines and policy implications, even though they have many commonalities and connections, both intellectual and personal. Monetarism-1 was principally, in the words of its most influential protagonist, "the monetary theory of nominal income."[3] This asserted the causal primacy of variations of money stock in fluctuations of aggregate dollar demand for goods and services. By the same token, it denied that pure fiscal policies, changes in overall expenditures and taxation that leave money stocks unaffected, have more than minor and transient effects on the path of nominal income. Likewise the doctrine attributed to instability of monetary supplies rather than to exogenous real shocks (that is, in capital productivity and thrift) responsibility for the major economic fluctuations of history. The major policy recommendation follows: keep money supply on a predictable stable path, without reference to recent or contemporaneous states of the economy or to the government budget.

By 1970 the debate triggered by these monetarist propositions had been raging for most of a decade—indeed, for much longer if disputes over the ancient quantity theory of money are counted. The 1960s conflict had been fought with theoretical and statistical weapons in professional media, and it had spilled into the public and political arena. At meetings of the Brookings panel, I believe, the majority view still rejected the strong proposition of the monetary theory of nominal income and favored the more eclectic modern Keynesian paradigm that had guided demand-management policies during the "new economics" years of the 1960s. According to this paradigm, monetary policies, fiscal policies, and nonpolicy shocks are all important determinants of aggregate demand. But by 1970 increasing attention was being paid, by macroeconomic analysts and model builders and by policymakers and central bankers, to measures of money supply, the "monetary aggregates." I comment below on this old debate. In 1980, however, it seems less fundamental than the challenge to the consensus view from the second wave of monetarism—Monetarism-2.

Keynesians and proponents of Monetarism-1 could disagree about the determinants of monetary demand but agree, at least qualitatively, on the structure that in the short run converts demand into output and prices. In fact Milton Friedman's candidate for what he called the "missing equation" of short-run macroeconomics served the same function as the short-run Phillips curve of the Keynesians.[4] Monetarism-2, the new classical economics, denies that systematic management of demand can alter the paths of real economic variables.

Real-World Challenges to the Consensus Model in the 1970s

No one foresaw in 1970 the main economic events of the decade or the formidable challenges those surprises would pose for macroeconomics and stabilization policy. We macroeconomists were caught unawares. It was not simply that our models, theoretical and econometric, now had to be applied to novel situations. Worse than that, the shocks of the 1970s required some fundamental rethinking and rebuilding. From an American perspective, the main events were of three kinds: the increased openness of the U.S. economy and the integration of U.S. financial markets with those overseas, the scrapping of the Bretton Woods system of adjustable exchange parities and its replacement by a regime of market-determined exchange rates with largely uncoordinated national interventions, and the predominance of price, supply, and demand shocks from sources other than government policies and the domestic industrial economy. These events all damaged the consensus framework sketched above.

Price and Supply Shocks
The main variable determinants of inflation in the past decade, particularly of the prices that concerned the public and worried their governments, were not those identified in the model. They were not domestic nonagricultural wages and prices. They were not prices in the fixprice sector but in the flexprice sector, food and raw materials. They were not mainly domestic prices, but prices of internationally traded goods. They were strongly influenced by foreign demands and supplies, and by foreign exchange rates. They were, most spectacularly, oil prices set by a cartel of foreign governments and the prices of other energy resources.

The consensus view did not prepare us, or our audiences in the public and in policymaking circles, for these developments. How do they influence the NAIRU or natural rate? How do they alter the short-run tradeoff? How long does the bulge in inflation rates following a major one-shot increase in a specific price last? How much and for how long does it raise the basic domestic wage-price inflation rate that was the centerpiece of our analysis?[5]

A central supposition of the "neoclassical synthesis" in macroeconomics was the separation of long-run supply trends from short-run demand fluctuations. Stated without great oversimplification, the view was that the trend of actual output is supply-determined, governed by the steady accretion of labor, capital, and technology. The trend represented equilibrium, analyzable and understandable by neoclassical tools focusing on the intertemporal choices of savers and investors. Short-run fluctuations around the trend were demand-determined disequilibria, analyzable and understandable by Keynesian tools upgraded and modernized. In practice the smooth trend could be fairly well estimated by "potential output," combining labor force and productivity growth; and Okun's Law captured the empirical regularities of employment-output responses to demand-determined deviations from potential.

In the 1970s it became impossible to rule out short-run variations in capacity supply and to take for granted that fluctuations in production were demand-driven. For example, how much of the decline in output in the 1974–75 recession was compelled by supply factors? How large were GNP "gaps" during the recovery of 1975–79? These were and are matters of doubt and dispute. Supply constraints, in this context, have three distinct meanings.

The first concerns the level and growth rate of the nation's capacity to produce, as measured by constant-price gross value added by U.S. factors of production. This is the concept underlying estimates by the Council of Economic Advisers of the economy's aggregate potential output at a standard rate of employment of the labor force. During the decade it became more difficult to identify potential output and to predict its path. In principle, increased costs of imported materials and final goods do not directly alter potential. But they may have had indirect effects. Toward the end of the decade, average productivity of labor virtually ceased to grow, for reasons not yet well understood. A related puzzle was the apparent decline in the Okun's Law coefficient from 3 percent of GNP per point of unemployment to around 2 percent.[6] After 1974 employment was surprisingly—disappointingly or pleasantly depending on point of view—high relative to GNP.

A second meaning is the volume of goods and services obtainable for final use by American resource inputs at a given rate of utilization. Potential in this sense was significantly reduced by adverse turns in U.S. terms of trade with the rest of the world. OPEC oil price increases were the most spectacular source, and in addition the dollar depreciated against other currencies by more than their inflation differentials.

A third sense of supply constraint refers to the markets for factors of production, particularly labor. The rise in real oil prices lowered the schedules of marginal productivity of factors complementary to petroleum and other forms of energy. If these factor markets were initially in equilibrium, with supplies positively dependent on real wages or quasirents, their employment would have to fall to restore equality of demand price and supply price. This phenomenon would be registered in potential GNP through the decline in labor force participation rather than in productivity. It is this scenario some observers have in mind in attributing post-OPEC shortfalls of GNP to supply rather than demand.[7] Another way to represent this scenario is to recall the old graphical summaries of short-run macroeconomic systems into aggregate demand and supply curves, each relating the absolute price level to output. An external or sectoral supply shock shifts the supply curve to the left.

Whatever the correct qualitative and quantitative answers to the questions raised, the basic macro models were ill-equipped to provide them. They were too focused on demand, too oriented to a closed economy, and too little disaggregated in both products and factors.

The New International Monetary Nonsystem
Even on its familiar turf, aggregate demand and its management, macroeconomics was not ready for the international developments of the 1970s. Theoretical models inherited from the 1960s were an inadequate guide. The United States is not exactly a small open economy that adapts to interest rates, prices, and demands determined overseas. Its monetary policies play a major role in determining international interest rates, and instruments denominated in different currencies are not such perfect substitutes that policies and events cannot create variable differentials in

rates. Asset stocks were unthinkingly ignored in earlier extensions of Keynesian flow models to open economies, but the recent concentration on stock equilibrium, with the slogan that the exchange rate is an asset price, did not do justice to entanglement of capital and current account transactions.[8]

The promise that floating rates would insulate economies from foreign shocks and allow national governments to pursue autonomous monetary policies never had solid theoretical foundation, and it was falsified by events. The faith that exchange speculation would be stabilizing was sorely tried by spasms that were independent sources of monetary and economic disturbance. The attacks on the dollar in 1974–75 and 1977–78 are examples. The decline in the dollar exceeded what could be attributed to purchasing power and cost parities or inflation differentials, or any sober assessment of longer run economic prospects. The mood that had seized the market in the fall of 1978 was quickly dissipated by President Carter's speech of November 1, but the speculators had forced the administration to change policy. In the climate of the 1970s there were no firm bases for estimates of future equilibrium exchange rates on which speculators could converge. Instead they often seemed to converge on unanchored opinions about other speculators' opinions. In these circumstances, a large element of macroeconomic policy is the making of announcements and the taking of measures that impress the foreign exchange markets; the intangible assets so purchased can depreciate rapidly.

Self-propelled, and at least temporarily self-justifying, speculation is not the only source of possible instabilities in the macroeconomic mechanisms of national economies with distinct currencies, linked by trade and financial transactions. The wealth effects of exchange rate adjustments are stabilizing when countries have long positions in assets denominated in other currencies, but can be destabilizing when they have foreign currency debts. The trade effects are stabilizing when the well-known elasticities conditions are met, but can be destabilizing when they are not. The so-called J curve is based on the perception that elastic demand and supply responses take time. If they are not foreseen in the exchange markets, "vicious" and "virtuous" cycles can acquire momentum. In a vicious cycle, depreciation raises domestic prices and inflation rates; initially the trade accounts move adversely; these impacts, magnified by currency speculation, bring further depreciation. In a virtuous cycle, everything goes right. These patterns provide one reason that weak currencies stay weak and strong currencies remain strong.

Open-economy models have important implications for demand-management policies. With floating rates, these measures manage exchange rates, too, and inevitably acquire a "beggar-my-neighbor" or *sauve qui peut* flavor. Expansionary monetary policies that gain export demand by exchange depreciation and tight policies that attract foreign funds and mitigate domestic inflation by appreciation are cases in point. One nation's fiscal stimulus, on the other hand, may spill, by higher interest rates and appreciation, into its partners' economies, with positive output and price effects that may or may not be welcome.

The first-approximation consensus that price-output paths are independent of the fiscal-monetary mix was impaired by the shift to floating exchange rates. Monetary easing offset by fiscal tightening lowers domestic interest rates and depreciates domestic currency. Assuming the depreciation feeds into domestic prices, this mixture raises the price level corresponding to any given aggregate output. This effect is less important for the United States than for more open economies, but here it has become an additional reason against relying on monetary stimulus in cyclical recoveries.

Supply-Side Macroeconomics and Stabilization Policy

I shall discuss three topics next: the macroeconomic consequences of OPEC and energy constraints, the short-run aggregate supply relationship between price level and output, and possible policies to increase supply in the short and long runs.

Oil and Macroeconomic Policy
I referred above to the question of whether the paths of output and unemployment after 1973 were supply-constrained, that is, OPEC-constrained, or demand-constrained. The 1974–75 recession and the low recovery path of 1975–78 cannot be attributed to the unavailability of oil. After OPEC-1 oil imports were elastically available to the United States at the higher dollar price. Even if oil consumption per unit of domestic value added was irreducible, the same potential output could be achieved by buying the same quantity of oil. The real loss to the country, in possible con-

sumption, could not in principle exceed the extra cost of the imports, about 1.5 percent of GNP. Substitutions for oil in production and consumption would diminish this loss.

OPEC made energy-guzzling capital goods—of both producers and consumers—obsolete in the sense that they would not be replaced by capital of similar design. But those that had not worn out did not suddenly become uneconomical to use. They would be scrapped in favor of energy-efficient models, Alfred Marshall told us, only if and when the total costs of buying and using the new were less than the variable costs of operating the old. In the interim, their quasi-rents would decline enough to signal that they are not worth replacing—a competitive story that has some difficulty coming through in a world of markup pricing in which consumers are asked to provide new capital in the quasi-rents of the old. Confusion on these elementary points seems to have led to some exaggerated estimates of the effects of OPEC on domestic aggregate supply.

There is no evidence of withdrawals of factor supplies because of their inability to earn the same real returns as before OPEC-1. Labor in the United States absorbed a 3.5 percent cut in real (deflated by the consumer price index) hourly wage rates during the year following the OPEC shock. In 1979 OPEC-2 chopped off another 3 percent. Real wage gains in the intervening three years fell far short of pre-1973 experience. Nevertheless, money wages did not accelerate. Labor force growth was so relentless that it was commonly blamed for the persistence of unemployment. By 1979 employment actually had risen 15 percent over 1973. Altogether the real cut in the 1975 wage bill, $32 billion (even without any allowance for normal growth of real wages), was more than enough to pay the extra cost of the oil imports. The same was true of the almost $45 billion cut in 1979. Moreover, the impact of the OPEC price increase on labor was diluted by internal price controls; domestic oil suppliers, forced to forgo part of the gains from the rise in the world price, in effect absorbed part of the national burden.

Adjustment to the OPEC shock without significant deviation from the tracks of potential output and employment was neither technologically infeasible nor inconsistent with market-clearing *real* wages. But it did require a big upward jump in paths of *money* prices. The real wage cuts occurred by price bulge, not by downward departure from the previous money-wage track. This is the scenario Keynes of the *General Theory* would have predicted. The oil shock shifted up and to the left the aggregate supply schedule, raising the nominal price level needed to induce any given real GNP. But, assuming the schedule was upward-rising in price-output $(p - Y)$ space, an accommodative policy moving the demand schedule up and to the right could hold the previous output path.

The drain of purchasing power to OPEC was, given the low short-run elasticity of U.S. demand for oil and the low propensity of the oil exporters to spend their receipts, a negative demand shock comparable to a domestic excise tax. The quasi-monetary effects depend on the distribution of the exporters' investments between dollar assets and other currencies, and on which dollar assets they choose. Dollar investments may account for more or less than the U.S. share of the oil exporters' current account surplus. An even balance, with an amount equivalent to our trade deficit to those countries channeled into U.S. government debt, would make the case the same as a comparable local tax devoted to reducing the supply of government debt. A greater OPEC preference for dollars over the currencies of other importers would appreciate U.S. currency, with possible negative effects on demand but favorable effects on prices. Among dollar assets, greater preference for equities and real assets, relative to money and government debt, would somewhat mitigate the primary contractionary effect of the "tax." The major point is that the price increase restricts aggregate demand in the importing countries as a group. Unchanged monetary and fiscal dial settings, a fortiori more antiinflationary dial settings, are bound to lead to contractions in real economic activity.

The first OPEC shock will probably be unique in several important macroeconomic respects. After the shocking increase of over 400 percent in 1973–74, the dollar price was raised little further until 1979. Inflation and exchange depreciation eroded the real price. For the United States it was 12 percent lower in 1978 than in 1974. Meanwhile, U.S. oil imports increased almost 50 percent from 1975 to their peak in 1977. In these circumstances oil imports were no barrier to recovery and expansion, beyond the tribute exacted by the foreign suppliers.

More serious problems arose when U.S. recovery and growth, and that of other oil importers, raised demand to the limits of the cartel's willing supply, a supply reduced by political events in the Middle East. The upsurge of spot prices triggered the second OPEC shock of 1979. With the price now clearing the market of supplies that evidently accord with the producing countries' intertemporal optimizations, the real price of oil cannot be expected to fall as it did between 1975 and 1979. Indeed, the real price should rise roughly at the real rate of interest that the producers can earn by extracting and selling the oil. Moreover, political mishaps and economic recalculations can change OPEC supply limits at any time.

The year 1979 made clear the macroeconomic consequences of encountering the OPEC supply ceiling, sharp boosts of oil prices and another bout of double-digit inflation. In a sense, contractionary macroeconomic policies, here and in other countries of the Organisation for Economic Co-operation and Development, can be seen as a means of containing oil demand through the income effects of slowing real economic activity. And in this indirect sense the current recession was triggered by an encounter with a supply constraint. But the decline of output will undoubtedly exceed what is needed to hold oil demand within current OPEC supply limits.

For the United States the macroeconomic difficulties of OPEC-2 were exacerbated by the vulnerability of the dollar to continued evidence of U.S. dependence on imported oil and of inflation rates that would trigger further escalation of OPEC dollar prices. This raised the specter of a vicious cycle of trade deficits, depreciation, oil price boosts, and inflation—a risk that undoubtedly helped motivate the Federal Reserve's restrictive policies of October 1979 and February 1980.

The clear lesson is that the United States and other oil-importing countries must find more efficient means of reducing oil demand than general recession and stagnation. Otherwise the 1979 crunch will recur whenever their growth at normal levels of economic activity collides with OPEC supply ceilings. And otherwise they will have no bargaining power vis-à-vis the cartel. This is the reason why decontrol of energy prices, and, indeed, even further increases in the relative prices of petroleum products to American consumers, make sense on macroeconomic as well as microeconomic grounds.

The Aggregate Supply Schedule

Long before the Phillips curve, short-run macroeconomic models included the aggregate supply schedule, relating the price *level* to real output. The Phillips curve shifted attention one derivative, relating the rate of change of prices to output. The two models are compatible. But it is the old aggregate supply curve that is the more relevant for supply-side macroeconomics.

At the classical pole this supply curve was vertical; at the vulgar textbook Keynesian pole, horizontal. The intermediate version attributed an upward slope to one or more of several short-run phenomena:

Money-wage rates are sticky, while the marginal productivity of labor diminishes with employment. As a result of rising marginal costs, markups rise along with capacity utilization. This effect, concealed by increasing utilization of hoarded labor during cyclical upswings, may appear only near the top of booms.

Capacity bottlenecks in particular industries and shortages of specific kinds of labor are encountered at all stages of expansions, with increasing frequency as the economy approaches aggregate potential.

Supply is price-inelastic in the short run in agriculture and other flex-price extractive industries. Expansion of aggregate demand, therefore, raises these prices sharply.

With a floating exchange rate, additional output means more imports relative to exports. This may mean exchange depreciation and higher domestic price indexes. However, as already observed, the effect of the expansion on the exchange rate depends on the mix of demand-management policies. Here, as in other respects, the apparatus breaks down in the sense that demand and supply price-output relations are not independent of each other.

Although procyclical movements of interest rates may, through the exchange rate, flatten the supply $p - Y$ curve, their direct effects on domestic prices is opposite. Mortgage interest rates go directly into the consumer price index. More fundamentally, heretics from the populist Texas Congressman, Wright Patman, to John Kenneth Galbraith have disputed the orthodox view that tight money policies are anti-inflationary, claiming that borrowers mark up interest charges like other costs.[9] An induced increase in velocity may accommodate such bootstrap inflation temporarily, but it cannot continue thereafter unless the Federal Reserve provides the money.

Nevertheless, the "Patman effect," a one-shot price adjustment to recover interest costs, may not be as silly as orthodoxy has said. In long-run equilibrium, firms earn enough to pay current interest rates on borrowed and invested capital. The adjustment mechanism that achieves this result usually runs in terms of investment and disinvestment, entry and exit, inspired by discrepancies between quasi-rents and capital costs. But it is at least possible that in imperfectly competitive industries firms anticipate the equilibrium condition by gearing markups to capital costs more or less continuously.

The $p - Y$ curves were features of macroeconomics before the Phillips curve. The implication of the supply curve was that prices would be higher the closer the economy was to its aggregate potential, but stable at each utilization rate. Movement from a lower output to a higher would bring a one-shot price increase. In an inflation-conscious era these changes look like accelerations. In Phillips curve equations, movements up or down the $p - Y$ supply schedule show up in the coefficient on first differences in unemployment, entangled with "speed limit" effects. These jumps in price level are hard for econometricians, policymakers, and private agents to distinguish from changes in the underlying inflation rate.

The aggregate supply schedule itself can shift, as from OPEC price increases and other supply shocks. Protection, farm price supports, minimum wage boosts, and other "self-inflicted wounds" so common in 1977 can also raise the schedule. Some policies, on the other hand, may shift it down. Arthur Okun and others have advocated reductions of indirect business taxes—sales taxes, excises, and payroll taxes—as a means of lowering the price level.[10] It is not obvious that a reduction of the tax wedge will lead to a fall in prices rather than a rise in wages or profit margins. The rationale of the recommendation is that money wages are conventionally or contractually sticky in the short run, while prices are determined by stable rule-of-thumb or competitive markups on per unit costs inclusive of indirect taxes. The same assumptions also support the view that factor prices will not move up in the short run even if the indirect taxes are replaced by direct taxes.

If successful, these policies achieve in the first instance a one-shot reduction in price level, which will be recorded as a temporary fall in the inflation rate. Will there be any lasting abatement? There will if money wage trends are formally or informally geared to the cost of living, but not if the dynamics of money wages are self-contained, independent of prices. The facts lie between these extremes, with the weight of U.S. experience on the wage-wage dynamic.

Supply-Increasing Policies

The currently popular meaning of "supply-side" refers to the productive capacity of the economy and to policies to increase its level and growth. Journalists love simple dichotomies: the Keynesians ignored supply and even, we are told, thought demand would create its own supply ad infinitum. Egged on by the media, economists and politicians have been flocking onto the bandwagon. Faddism, amnesia, and sloganeering are the least attractive characteristics of our profession. To borrow an aphorism of Paul Samuelson from another context, the Lord gave us two eyes to watch both demand and supply.

Here I find it necessary to set the record straight. Far from being wholly demand-oriented, the neoclassical synthesis paid a great deal of attention to the factors determining long-run growth and to policies that might raise the level and slope of the economy's full-employment path.[11] These included choosing a monetary-fiscal mix favoring capital formation relative to consumption, a subject discussed elsewhere in this paper; tax incentives for fixed investment, for example accelerated depreciation and tax credits; encouragement of public and private research and development; and investment in human capital by training and retraining on and off the job, and improvement of labor markets to reduce structural and frictional unemployment—both directed to reducing the natural rate of unemployment.

On all these fronts the federal government followed supply- and growth-oriented policies in the 1950s and 1960s, particularly I think in the early 1960s. If these efforts did not yield spectacular results, the main reason is that they are very hard to obtain. It is not that Keynesian economists and policymakers were blind to their importance.

Although we may be confident that increasing the ratio of investment to potential output will raise the capital-labor ratio and raise productivity, we know that the payoff is slow to come. Suppose, to take a not unrealistic numerical example, that business fixed investment is 12 percent of business gross product, that the stock of business capital is 1.5 times business gross product, and that capital consumption is 6 percent of the stock, 9 percent of gross product. The 3 percent of product devoted to net investment increases the stock at 2 percent a year. A sustained rise of 2 percentage points in gross investment would be a spectacular response to any imaginable combination of investment and saving incentives. Eventually, asymptotically, this would raise the capital-output ratio from 1.50 to 1.75. If the output-on-capital elasticity is one-third, this will raise gross output per effective worker by 8.33 percent, and net consumable income by 5.80 percent. But at the beginning, capital intensity is increasing at 1.33 percent a year, raising gross output by only 0.67 percent a year, and consumable income initially falls by 1.60 percent.

Welcome as these gains in productivity would be, they clearly do not produce a short-run solution for inflation. They do not lead to a long-run solution either. The growth in productivity bulges during the transition to greater capital intensity but gradually returns to the rate determined by technological progress, unless the investment-output ratio is repeatedly raised. To get a permanent increase in productivity growth, it is necessary to speed up technological progress, and nobody knows how to do that. If it happened, it would be its own reward, but there would not necessarily be a reduction of inflation. Productivity gains will raise real wages, but whether from higher money wages or lower prices our models say not. Countries with dramatically higher productivity growth than ours have sometimes had higher inflation rates, sometimes lower.[12]

An insistent supply-side chorus seeks remedy for the slowdown in business fixed investment in the 1970s in lower taxation of returns to capital. One theme of the diagnosis is that the nation's propensity to save is too low because the rewards for saving have been impaired by the combined impacts of taxation and inflation. I cannot undertake an evaluation here of these alleged effects or of the pro-saving consequences of income tax rate cuts and of liberalized tax treatment of capital gains and of retirement contributions. On the macro plane, the question is whether saving was the binding constraint on investment during the years of weak capital formation, notably 1975–78. The diagnosis assumes that a higher saving propensity would have been absorbed in extra investment rather than in a lower output path, and that increased thrift rather than higher real incomes than those actually experienced was the only source of extra saving. But if real incomes had been higher during the period, saving would surely have been higher, too. In the prosperous years of 1974 and

1979, business fixed investment was 11 percent of GNP, close to its postwar peak.

Alternatively, explanation for the slowdown of business capital formation in the 1970s may be sought in investment demand rather than in saving supply. In these terms the weakness of investment is quite understandable given the excess capacity and high cost of equity capital that characterized most of the period.[13] These in turn were in large measure the consequences of anti-inflationary policies, actual and anticipated. In this sense the failure of the country to solve its stagflation problem is damaging its long-run potential as well as its current performance. In this sense, too, short-run demand management affects long-run supply.

As supply-side economists have stressed, the taxation of nominal income leads to distortions during periods of inflation. The fact that some of these distortions are deterrents to investment is a rationale for compensatory tax concessions and incentives. Firms that use FIFO (first in first out) accounting pay taxes on fictitious inventory profits. But the law already invites them to shift to accounting practice that would virtually eliminate this burden. On plant and equipment, the problem is the overstatement of taxable earnings due to depreciation based on historical cost. On the other hand, the tax deductibility of full nominal interest payments is an investment stimulus, which is larger the higher the expected inflation rate. The balance of these two effects varies among firms and types of investment, depending on depreciation rates, debt-equity ratios, and the rate of inflation.[14] As nominal interest rates have risen along with inflation, corporations have shifted to debt financing. Moreover, some investment-oriented tax concessions were made in the 1970s; the high-bracket corporate income tax rate was reduced by 3.2 points and the investment tax credit was liberalized and made permanent. On efficiency grounds, a strong case can be stated for making the taxation of capital earnings more nearly neutral with respect to inflation, whether or not the balance of the distortions has been unfavorable to business fixed investment.

Likewise, considerations of efficiency—and equity, too—support reforms of individual income taxation that would spare savers taxation of the purely inflationary components of capital gains and interest income. But tax reductions of this kind would presumably be made up by increases elsewhere. The supply-side notion that uncompensated tax concessions to saving will increase the national supply of saving for private capital formation, as a fraction of GNP, is dubious. The fatal flaw is that such concessions are likely to lose more public saving than the private saving they promote unless the rate-of-return elasticity of saving (saving as a whole, not particularly favored assets) is much greater than any credible estimates.[15]

Another plank in the supply-side platform is the proposition that income tax cuts will bring forth vast increases in labor supply and productive effort. The supply elasticity would have to be incredibly large if the increased supply of goods were to exceed the increased consumption demand induced by the tax reductions. What is less relevant is that the elasticity would have to be even larger if tax revenues were not to diminish.[16]

Tax distortions of work-leisure choices and of choices among jobs have been around a long time. The relevant marginal tax rates are not significantly higher now than they were in the 1960s. They remain lower than in European countries whose superior productivity growth excites our envy and admiration.[17] Despite taxation, the absolute after-tax rewards to additional work are greater than in earlier periods, and greater in the United States than in almost all other countries. If the substitution effects are so important relative to income effects, why has a long-term trend toward leisure been associated with productivity growth? Why has work not increased as its marginal after-tax reward in consumption has progressively risen? An answer consistent with the alleged paramount importance of substitution effects requires a model in which the opportunity cost of work—in leisure off or on the job—rises commensurately with the productivity of work; an example is a model in which technological progress increases the utility of an hour of leisure as rapidly as the productivity of an hour of work.

Whether or not income taxation is in fact seriously depriving the nation of work and productivity, it is desirable to mitigate the distortions. Reduction of marginal income tax rates is not the only possibility. If people are working too little, what about taxing commodities complementary to leisure—hammocks, coffee, boats, skis?

At a time when labor force participation rates are setting records, it seems strange that anyone takes seriously the diagnosis behind the legislative proposals of Congressman Kemp and Senator Roth. Some rhetoric hints at an even more miraculous scenario, by which higher take-home wages induce the productivity that justifies them. The first Henry Ford profited from paying well above the market. Presumably he attracted the best and lifted their morale, a trick that cannot be generalized when everybody does it.

As economists have recognized for more than a decade, disincentive problems are acute at the bottom of the income distribution. The multiplication of income-conditioned assistance programs can imply confiscatory marginal taxation of earnings. The congeries of diverse national and state programs, some in kind and some in cash, also distort other choices —including location, family composition, and saving. Rational reform and integration of assistance with personal income taxation and social security could help to reduce both the NAIRU and the depreciation of human capital.

With respect to human capital, as well as to physical capital, demand management has important long-run supply-side effects. A decade of slack labor markets, depriving generations of young workers of job experience, will damage the human capital stock far beyond the remedial capacity of supply-oriented measures.

Monetarism and Stabilization Policies Today

The crucial issues of the day, as I already observed, are what happens when policies alter nominal GNP, the product of money stock and its velocity, MV, not how to change MV. In this light, the old monetarist debates about the monetary theory of nominal income are distinctly secondary. But as a veteran of those battles, I will offer some comments and try to clear away some residual debris.

Inflation and Accommodative Monetary Policy

Yes, of course, inflation is a monetary phenomenon, a pervasive reduction in the value of the monetary unit of account in terms of goods and services. Yes, of course, inflation means that the rate of growth of MV exceeds the rate of growth of real output. Yes, of course, the long-run sustainable growth of real output cannot exceed the trend of potential supply, limited by resources and technology. Yes, of course, a necessary condition of a stable price level is that the trend rate of growth of MV equal that of the economy's capacity to produce. But none of these tautological propositions reveal what will be the effects of changes of monetary policy, temporary or permanent.

Clearly the rate of inflation today would be much lower if the path of MV ever since 1960 or even 1970 had been fairly steadily held to, say, 4 percent a year. Clearly there are some paths of the monetary base or of the various monetary aggregates, M_i, that could have achieved that result. What is far from clear is that the paths of real variables—output, employment, investment—would have approached the paths actually realized, or even that current levels of those variables would be the same as their actual values. The Federal Reserve would not have accommodated the fiscal stimuli of the early 1960s, the fiscal excesses of the Vietnam War, the wage explosion of the early 1970s, the later shocks from increases in commodity prices and OPEC prices, and the inflationary pressures these events generated. Economists today differ, and historians doubtless will also, about the shape of such a counterfactual rerun of these two decades. I certainly cannot prove my suspicion that the path of real variables would have been disastrously worse.[18] I do think that it is disingenuous to give the impression, so prevalent today, that the whole inflationary experience could have been costlessly avoided by conservative demand management.

Throughout the 1970s accommodation has been the agonizing issue repeatedly facing the monetary authorities. The practice of describing monetary policy in terms of observed growth rates of M_i is misleading. It does not make sense to say that the policy was or is x percent money stock growth as if that number were something the central bank chooses arbitrarily and gratuitously. For one thing, the marksmanship of the Federal Reserve with respect to endogenous target variables, whether any M_i or a fortiori MV itself, is bound to be imperfect. More important, when the authorities have chosen policies supportive of continued inflationary growth of MV, they have not done so from ignorance of arithmetic, indifference to inflation, or, in my opinion, political pressure. They have done so, rightly or wrongly, mainly because of the perceived consequences of nonaccommodation on the real performance of the economy. The inertia of inflation in the face of nonaccommodative policies is the big issue. To discuss the roots of that inertia and the sources of nonmonetary pressures for accommodation—administered prices, contracts, collective bargaining, distributive conflict, supply shocks, OPEC—is not to commit any vulgar errors or to violate any of the identities stipulated above.

Real Money and Real Interest

A related diversion is the repeated charge that nonmonetarists erroneously assume that the government can alter the real quantity of money. Monetarists, in contrast, know that the authorities fix the nominal supply while the real quantity is independently determined by the public's demand. In long-run full-employment equilibrium, price flexibility makes this proposition true (though not quite, because the proportions in which various "outside" monetary assets are supplied to the public will determine their relative real quantities). But in the short-run context of stabilization policy, prices are not flexible enough to make the real quantity of any monetary aggregate independent of its nominal supply. Prices are one way, but not the only way, in which money demand adjusts to changes in money supply. Nominal interest rates are another. Figures 15.2 and 15.3 show the short-run congruence of changes in nominal and real monetary stocks, the monetary base, M_{1B}, and M_2. As in the case of MV (figure 15.1), variations in nominal and real stocks are strongly positively correlated, except during the periods dominated by external price shocks. Real quantities show the larger amplitude, contrary to the monetarist notion that endogenous price movements convert unstable nominal monetary supplies into stable real monetary demands.

Another extreme monetarist proposition is that the monetary authorities cannot alter the real rate of interest. Trying to do so by fixing a nominal interest rate will only lead to such monetary growth, actual and expected, as creates the inflation rate that converts the nominal interest rate into the economy's natural real rate. This is another proposition with a considerable quantum of truth for the long run. It falls short by failing to allow for what is sometimes called the Mundell effect, by which inflation lowers real rates by inducing substitution away from monetary assets with zero nominal interest.[19] It also makes no allowance for the nonneutrality of real-world taxes with respect to inflation rates, a point discussed above in connection with "supply-side" advocacy of fiscal reforms. In the 1970s after-tax nominal interest rates rose far less than the inflation rate. For example, the tax-exempt rate rose only 120 basis points from 1972 to 1979. Rates on Aaa corporate bonds rose about the same if the marginal tax rate effective in that market is assumed to be 50 percent. For

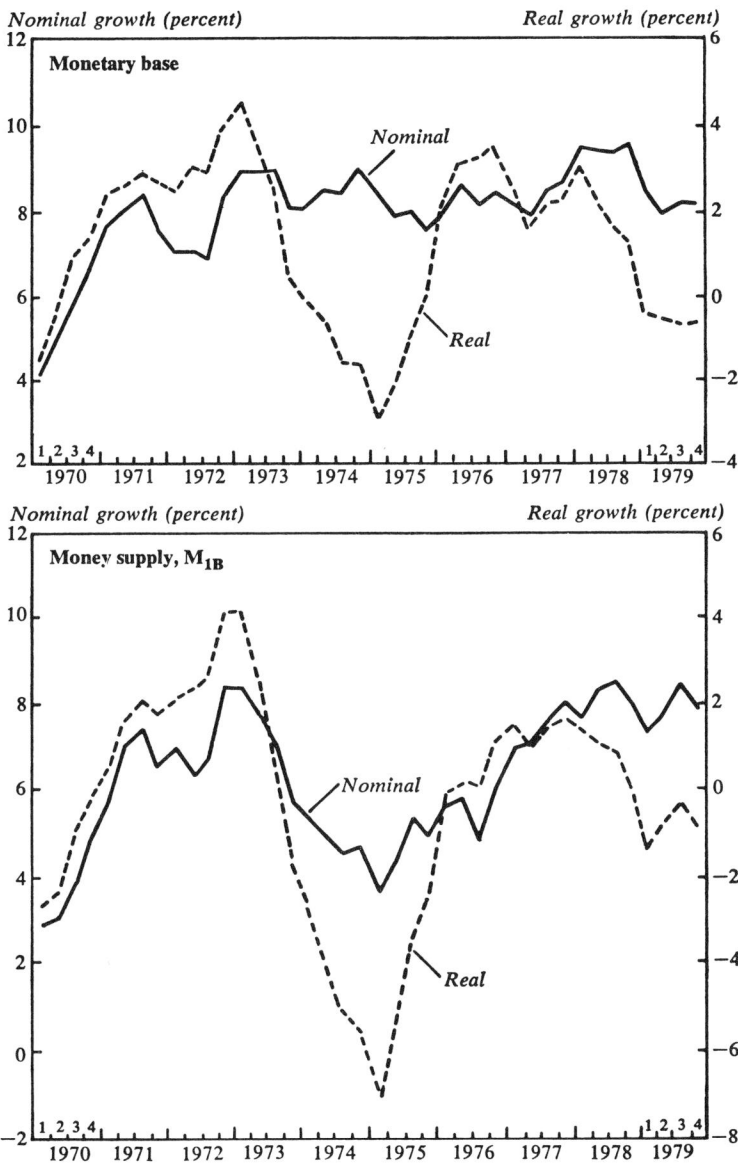

Figure 15.2
Rates of growth of the monetary base and M_{1b}, nominal and real, 1970:1–1979:4[a]

Source: Board of Governors of the Federal Reserve System.
a. Data are percent changes from a year earlier. The nominal series were deflated by the GNP deflator to obtain real series.

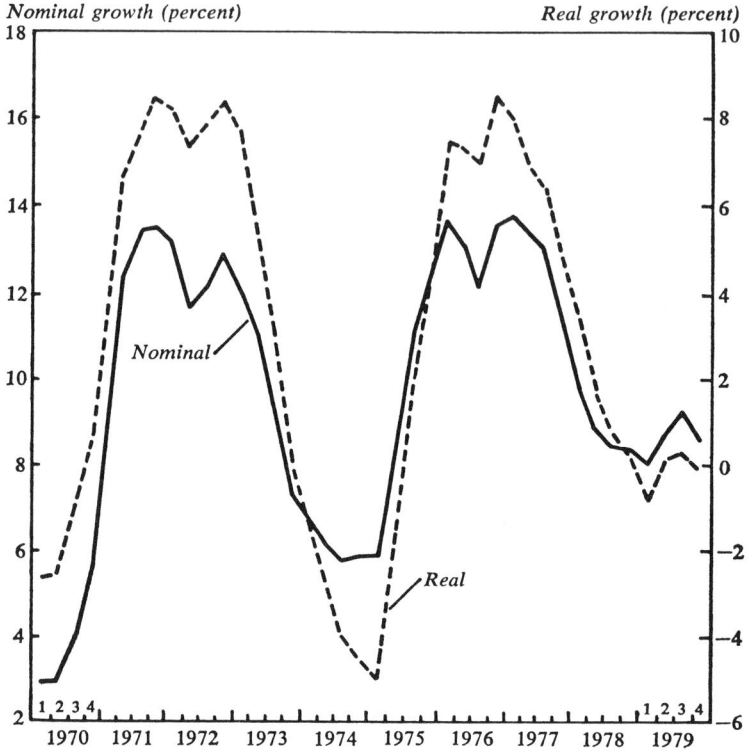

Source: Board of Governors of the Federal Reserve System.
a. Data are percent changes from a year earlier. The nominal series was deflated by the GNP deflator to obtain the real series.

Figure 15.3
Rates of growth of M_2, nominal and real, 1970–1979:4[a]

short-run stabilization policy, the important point is that, given the persistence and inertia of inflationary trends and expectations, the central bank can and does alter real rates of interest by measures that change the nominal rate. The notion that intertemporal substitutions in production and consumption are so perfect as to maintain constant real interest rates is one of the more bizarre propositions of this wild decade.[20] Figure 15.4 shows nominal commercial paper rates and "real" rates calculated in two ways, from the GNP deflator's inflation during the previous year and from the actual inflation during the coming half-year.

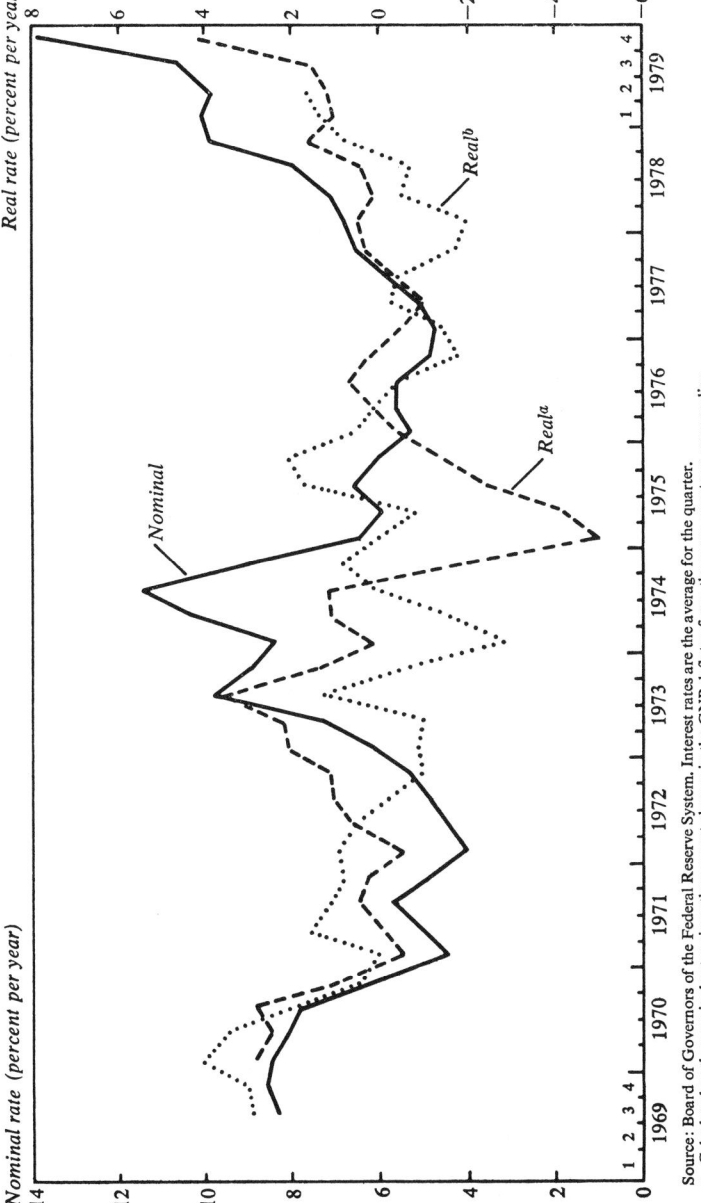

Figure 15.4
Interest rate on commercial paper, nominal and real, 1969:3–1979:4

Source: Board of Governors of the Federal Reserve System. Interest rates are the average for the quarter.
a. Calculated as the nominal rate minus the percent change in the GNP deflator from the same quarter a year earlier.
b. Calculated as the nominal rate minus the percent change (multiplied by two) in the GNP deflator over the next half-year.

Which Money Stock? Fundamental and Transactions Monetarism

A continuing theoretical and practical problem of monetarism has been the identification of the aggregate that is the monetary fulcrum of the economy, the exogenously supplied stock to which all endogenous variables of monetary dimension adjust. I discern two disparate approaches, which can be termed fundamental monetarism and transactions monetarism, respectively. The fundamental approach, motivated by the desire to find real-world counterparts for the variables of simple theoretical models, focuses on the monetary base, whose quantity is clearly under government control and is dollar for dollar net private wealth, unmodified by offsetting private debts.

The difficulties are manifold. What about other government obligations to the public, promises to pay the same base money in a few days or years or decades? The conditions on which they can be totally disregarded, as offset by taxpayers' estimates of future tax liabilities, are quite special and improbable. Indeed, some recent monetarists go to the other extreme, encompassing the entire interest-bearing debt in their concept of the monetary base. What about the fact that the government has lent, so to speak, its fiat to banks and guaranteed their demand liabilities, while keeping their total loosely connected to the monetary base? These and other complexities make the velocity of the monetary base quite variable. The fairly steady growth of the base in recent years has not prevented considerable variation in rates of increase of MV, prices, and real output.

Fundamental monetarism relies on the "classical dichotomy" and the neutrality of money. Transactions monetarism, a more pragmatic and empirical version, relies on the technology of transactions. It therefore emphasizes the key role of those dollar assets that are used in making payments and seeks to control the economy by controlling the supply of such media.

The endemic difficulties have been well known for a long time. The recent events that pushed the Federal Reserve to redefine the monetary aggregates were particularly striking examples. These included the spread of new transactions media, many bearing market-determined interest rates and many issued by nonbanks; the increased substitutability of interest-bearing assets for checking accounts; the availability of overdraft lines through credit cards, and so on. The recent definitional changes and extensions of reserve requirements are attempts by the Federal Reserve to cope with these explosions of financial innovation.

But the truth is that expenditures on goods and services are not limited by the stock of transactions media. Nor does expansionary monetary policy work by providing citizens, without their volition, more transactions money than they want, which they then spend because it is burning holes in their pockets.

The empirical upward trends in velocity of M_1, M_{1A}, and M_{1B} cannot be a law of nature. They reflect in imperfectly known and variable proportions the upward trend in nominal interest rates, presumably not a law of nature, plus innovative economies in cash management, some induced and some exogenous, some reversible and some not, plus liberalization of government regulations of banks and other financial institutions. When liabilities bearing market interest rates are included in the aggregates, the demand for the aggregates is surely not the same, or sensitive to market interest rates in the same degree, as when they were not.

Targets and Indicators

The use of targets for monetary aggregates to signal the intentions of the central bank has the advantage that changes in the targets tell in which direction the Federal Reserve will be trying to move the economy. The longer the horizon of the targets the more indicative the signals are, especially for economic agents outside the financial sector. Targets for a year ahead or longer may, for example, indicate a resolutely unaccommodating, but not wholly credible, stance toward shocks in prices and foreign exchange rates.

As Poole showed,[21] quantitative targets do not protect the Federal Reserve and the economy against "*LM*" surprises—which do occur, for example, "the case of the missing money."[22] They do defend moderately well against "*IS*" surprises, but not as well as a policy that would counteract the velocity changes induced by such surprises. It makes no sense to define as a "neutral" policy one that allows MV to respond endogenously precisely only to the extent that the public is induced by interest rate increases and other incentives to make economies of cash management. The institutions, habits, and technologies that determine those elasticities have little to do with the desirable degree of output and income response to fiscal measures or to exogenous changes in consumer, business, or foreign spending.

The money and financial markets have become obsessed with translating current information on deviations of actual aggregates from targets into information on future interest rates. Given the noise in weekly money stock reports and given that at times the Federal Reserve may have good reasons for moving the targets toward the actuals rather than vice versa—for example, in response to events in foreign exchange markets—this obsession probably puts more noise than rationality into interest rates and asset prices.

I think it would be preferable for the Federal Reserve to announce target ranges for MV growth a year ahead, indeed several years ahead. Alternatively, these could be expressed as two-dimensional brackets for GNP inflation and real GNP growth. This would leave the Federal Reserve free to follow policies consistent with these substantive targets without staking its credibility on hitting targets of only instrumental or indicative significance. The proposed targets would make clear the message the Federal Reserve has been trying to convey: that the economy's output path will be better when its wage and price performance improves. Disguised and confused in numbers for various esoteric M_i, this message does not now reach the audience that matters, especially when the accompanying rhetoric suggests that variations in these aggregates affect price inflation rates directly and costlessly regardless of the behavior of business and labor. The two-dimensional brackets are desirable because the Federal Reserve does not necessarily wish to hold the economy to a point-for-point trade-off between inflation and real growth. Ranges would allow not only for inevitable errors of forecast and control but also for flexibility in responding to shocks from international commodity and currency markets.

Coherent stabilization strategy requires that the Federal Reserve's targets be consistent with the economic assumptions and objectives of the federal budget. The present compartmentalized procedures, both in the executive branch and in the Congress, do not guarantee consistency or provide for conscious and deliberate decision about the fiscal-monetary mix. The Federal Reserve's objectives are expressed in the M_i, whose implications for economic outcomes are left vague and fuzzy. If they were expressed in prices and output, then the congressional oversight of monetary policy would blend into the congressional budget procedures, and the makers of monetary and fiscal policy would be forced to talk to each other seriously about their joint endeavor. The Federal Reserve Board probably finds the present dualism protective of its independence and of its advantage in having eight or more moves a year to the budget-makers' one. However, its chairmen regularly complain that Congress and the president saddle it with too much of the joint work of stabilization, and the unpleasant part at that. More Federal Reserve input in the budget process could produce a more balanced fiscal-monetary mix.

The Monetary-Fiscal Mix

In the 1950s and 1960s the neoclassical synthesis generated the doctrine that monetary and fiscal measures should be regarded as substitutes in supporting a given path of real GNP. Substitution of fiscal for monetary restraint would be a pro-growth or future-oriented policy, nudging the composition of national expenditure in favor of private capital formation and away from private or public consumption. This proposition depended on some empirical assumptions: that interest rate reductions and easing of credit stimulate investment more than they deter saving, while generalized tax increases or public expenditure reductions hit consumption more than investment. These are essentially the same grounds on which many people argue that expansionary fiscal measures crowd out capital investment. (A monetarist believer in 100 percent crowding out would not see any opportunity for offsetting the aggregate-demand consequences of monetary expansion or contraction by fiscal measures. And a believer in the Ricardo-Barro equivalence of postponed and current taxation would deny that any manipulations of public debt and taxes will affect national saving and investment.)[23]

The monetary-fiscal mix also affects the balance of payments or the exchange rate. Substitution of fiscal for monetary restraint is "bad" for a country trying to defend its currency, a chronic plight of the United States since 1960. In the 1960s defense of the overvalued dollar took precedence over the dedication of the demand-management mix to domestic growth; this was one reason for reliance on tax stimulus during the 1961–65 recovery. With the gold window closed and the dollar floating in the 1970s, this priority became less compelling. In principle a low interest rate and low exchange rate, offset by taxes bearing mainly on consumption, would be favorable to both foreign and domestic investment. But for many reasons, including the price effects mentioned above, such a policy was not feasible.

Even without foreign exchange considerations, the politics and administration of fiscal and monetary policy work against a growth-oriented mix. Fiscal expansion is the natural governmental response to recession and unemployment, and monetary restriction is the most available and acceptable weapon against inflationary booms. There is even some economic logic to this division of labor—the suspicion that while monetary restriction is very effective in cooling a hot economy, monetary ease is "pushing on a string" at the trough of a business cycle. In any case, a sequence of cycles with these asymmetries in policy creates a trend toward consumption at the expense of investment.

At least one more instrument is needed, and an obvious place to find it is in the structure of taxation. This indeed was the sophisticated rationale for the introduction of the investment tax credit in 1962, a specific stimulus for investment and only for domestic investment.

Addressing the same issues today and sharing widespread concerns about lagging capital formation, Martin Feldstein argues for a *tighter* monetary policy, along with new corporate tax reductions or tax incentives for investment.[24] His measure of monetary tightness is the after-tax long-term interest rate adjusted for inflation. He says this rate has been too low. The Federal Reserve, in keeping real interest rates *before* tax at levels comparable to those of previous prosperities, has, perhaps inadvertently, lowered the after-tax real interest rates that matter for investment and saving. Inflation, given that full nominal interest is taxable to creditors and tax deductible to debtors, is responsible for this outcome. Evidently he believes that this monetary policy, together with recent federal budgets, add up to an excessively expansionary and inflationary package of demand management. This judgment, whatever its merit, is separable from the proposition that the composition of the package errs in the direction of monetary ease.

On this point, the policy mix, Feldstein calls attention to the stimulus that the low after-tax real rates give to investment in owner-occupied homes, whose yields in service and capital appreciation are untaxed. Presumably the same low interest rates should be a stimulus to corporate investment in plant and equipment. But the argument is that such rates magnify the relative bias of the tax system in favor of residential investment. It may also be contended that housing is a particularly inflationary allocation of demand.

Given the aggregate real GNP available for private domestic disposition, there are three final uses among which it can be divided: consumption, residential investment, and nonresidential investment. The division can be affected by the mix of policies as among taxes bearing on the three uses and monetary measures. Feldstein wants to raise the share of nonresidential investment by specific tax concessions, obtaining the resources principally from residential construction. This is to be done by monetary tightening, which he argues will affect home building more adversely than fixed investment. But it will affect fixed investment too, working against the tax incentives. The two opposing levers will have to be worked very hard to obtain the desired allocational effect.

A better and surer way to shift resources out of residential construction would be to eliminate or diminish the tax favoritism for home ownership. Should not an economist recommend this route even if it is not politically feasible? Furthermore, it is not clear why more of the resources for business investment should not be obtained by taxes bearing principally on consumption. Is the mix of consumption and total investment, residential plus nonresidential, just right?

Fiscal Policy

Fiscal policy was in general a stabilizing influence during the 1970s. Certainly the "built-in stabilizers" damped the two recessions, in particular the severe downturn of 1974–75. The whopping deficits of the mid 1970s were mainly symptoms of their performance. Active counter-cyclical policies promoted recoveries from the two recessions. They also applied restraint in later stages of the recoveries, although critics would say too little and too late.

In figure 15.5, I show three measures of fiscal policy. One is simply the ratio of government purchases of goods and services to potential output. State and local purchases are included, on the grounds that their finance is so entangled with the federal budget that the total for all governments is more indicative than federal purchases alone. As figure 15.5 shows, this ratio has steadily declined over the decade and has not been a source of cyclical disturbance. The second measure is the high-employment federal

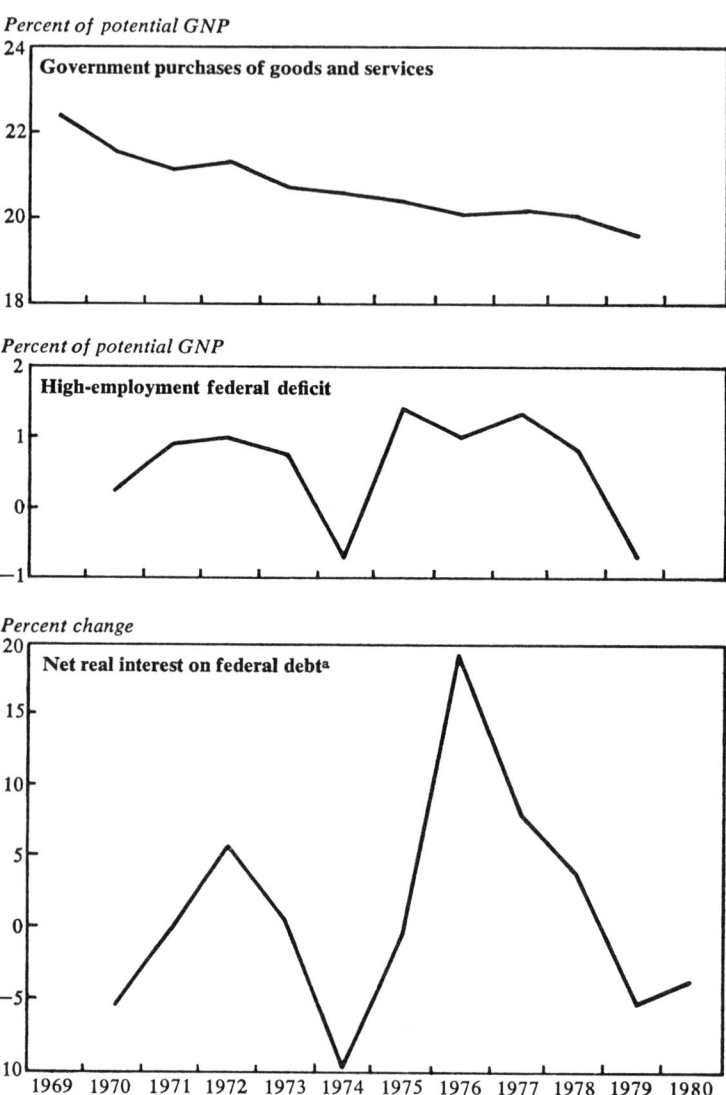

Figure 15.5
Measures of fiscal policy, 1969–1980

deficit as a percent of potential output. This has generally moved countercyclically, except for the 1974 shift to surplus.

The third series is a rough measure of changes in the real market value of outstanding federal nonmonetary debt. It measures net real interest payments to holders (other than federal agencies themselves) on the assumption that nominal interest rates on the securities were the same as in the base year, 1972. Thus the series excludes the increased interest payments due to the rise in nominal rates associated with inflation since 1972, most of which is in real terms repayment of principal. This real interest obligation has grown only by 11.4 percent since 1969, while real GNP has risen 33.7 percent, and potential GNP, 36.8 percent. Federal debt has declined relative to the economy. Its rate of change, as pictured in figure 15.5, has also been generally countercyclical.

Some trends in macroeconomic theory downgrade the importance of fiscal policies for good or ill. I do not refer just to the financial crowding-out propositions of Monetarism-1. A different source of skepticism is the proposition that current and planned consumption depends only on the present value of after-tax labor and property incomes, calculated over very long future horizons.[25] Changes in taxes and transfers, it is argued, affect these long-run calculations very little, if at all, especially if they are only temporary. I think that this argument carries to unrealistic extreme the valuable insights of permanent-income and life-cycle models of consumption. It ignores the liquidity constraints that shorten the horizons of many consumers. It does not recognize the role of the government as an intermediary between households with different present and future tax-and-transfer status, diverse liquidity positions and horizons, varying attitudes toward risk, and different intertemporal discounts and tastes.

Temporary and one-shot tax reductions and rebates are less stimulative than permanent cuts, no doubt. But they increase the liquid wealth of households with short horizons, who are likely to be especially numerous when the economy is depressed. Macroeconometric model simulations confirm the efficacy of the fiscal stimuli of 1975, and even the temporary tax surcharges of 1968.[26]

Why not rely solely on monetary measures to promote recovery from recessions? Fiscal stimulus in the form of direct spending on goods and services or transfers and tax reductions directed to private agents with high propensities to spend can be a surer way of increasing aggregate demand. Private spending may respond only weakly and slowly to the favorable interest rate and credit climate that monetary policy can produce. Moreover, the monetary authority is generally unwilling to push hard on the string, fearing that the liquidity created will be troublesome later.

My review of recent fiscal policy underlines the fact that this is the terrain of macroeconomics where the gulf between perceptions of the general public and economists' doctrines is the widest. Probably the most popular diagnosis of inflation is deficit spending, and the most common recipe for relief is balancing the federal budget.

Economists know that stabilization policy is logically and operationally separable from the size and balance of the budget. The demand stimulus of a larger budget can be neutralized by various mixtures of taxation and monetary restriction, and the demand stimulus of a deficit-increasing tax reduction can be offset by monetary restriction. What is occurring today is a concerted campaign to exploit popular discontent with inflation to reduce the relative size of the public sector and to reverse the income redistributions effected by government taxes and transfers. These objectives are legitimate political agenda, which deserve debate and decision on their merits. But they have nothing to do with inflation, and monetarist-conservatives (there is no logical necessity for this almost invariable combination) should be the first to point this out. Monetarists once reconciled opposition to deficits with their "money-is-all-that-matters" macroeconomics by alleging that political pressures force the Federal Reserve to print more money the larger budget deficits become. There is scant evidence for this effect these days.

Demand Management at the Stagflation Impasse

Even in happier times there were plenty of grounds for suspicion that price stability and full employment were incompatible objectives in modern capitalist democracies. Early in the game Abba Lerner, among others, pointed out that if Keynesian full employment were sustained the price level would be indeterminate, at the mercy of collective bargaining.[27] Sumner H. Slichter went further, observing that organized labor and central banks had switched roles, with unions determining the price level and central banks the volumes of output and employment. Graduate students of my generation told each other that of the three objectives—price stability, full employment, and freedom from wage and price controls—an economy like that of the United States could attain two at most.

Much of what we have learned since is simply the bad news that for "price stability" read "inflation rate stability" or more generally "stability of the expected path of prices," whatever its shape.

The Upward Drift of the "Natural Rate"

The relationships of prices and money wages to output and employment, and of all these variables to demand-management policies, were the big questions in 1970 and remain so today. Within the consensus framework, the questions focus on the terms of the short-run Phillips curve trade-off, both on the location of the NAIRU and the shape of the curve relating accelerations and decelerations to deviations from the NAIRU. More far-reaching issues concern the validity of the framework itself and its reliability as a guide to policy.

One regularity of Brookings panel meetings and papers has been the relentless rise in numerical estimates of the full-employment rate of unemployment.[28] Likewise the actions of policymakers reveal their implicit acceptance of ever higher normal unemployment rates. From 3 percent in the early 1950s, these explicit or implicit estimates of the natural rate seem to have risen successively to 4 percent in the 1960s, 5 percent in the early 1970s, then 6 percent. In the early 1980s, it is easy to predict, the magic number will not be lower than 7 percent.

Why is the unemployment rate so high, and even higher, at "full employment"? How are such high NAIRUs to be rationalized by theorists who associate the "natural" rate with an equilibrium in which unemployment represents voluntary choice and efficient search? These questions have occupied much time at this panel and many pages of *Brookings Papers*.

Explanations of the dismal trend fall in several categories.

1. The demographic composition of the labor force has shifted toward groups more prone to spells of unemployment between jobs or while entering, leaving, or reentering the labor force. Demographic shifts since 1965 can account for about a 1 percentage point rise in overall unemployment if each group is assumed to be permanently characterized by

its specific 1965 unemployment rate. (On the other hand, such calculations omit demographic trends, notably those toward more educational attainment and toward stronger attachments of women to working careers, which would have opposite effects.) Essentially the same upward shift of the NAIRU emerges from the observed increase in the overall unemployment rate relative to the rates for prime workers whose unemployment relative to available jobs is thought to be crucial in wage determination, or from calculations of a wage-weighted unemployment rate.[29]

2. Government policies—unemployment compensation, welfare benefits, and minimum wages—have raised the reservation wages of the unemployed relative to their marginal productivity in employment. Here again the main issue is the empirical magnitude of these effects, a subject that several Brookings panel papers have addressed.[30] My reading of them is that it would be hard to attribute more than a few tenths of a percentage point of unemployment to the *changes* in these institutions in this decade. In considering these policies as the *cause* of higher normal unemployment, it is relevant to remember that most of them were ex post responses to higher unemployment brought about by macroeconomic policies and events.

3. Normal rates of operation of capital capacity are now reached at higher rates of unemployment of labor than in the 1960s. In other words, the ratio of capacity to labor force has declined; recoveries encounter bottlenecks earlier; labor productivity falls and markups rise when unemployment is still high. The stagflation of the 1970s discouraged capital formation, and businesses positioned themselves to survive cycles of higher average unemployment.

As for the shape of the short-run trade-off, Murphy's Law of macroeconomics assures us that it is an L with the corner wherever we happen to be. Even less extreme nonlinearity has several significant implications.

One implication of Phillips curvature is that symmetrical cycles about a static NAIRU entail an accelerating drift.[31] A stable inflation trend requires a higher average unemployment rate the greater the amplitude of fluctuations. The natural rate so corrected may have increased in the recent unstable decade.

A second implication of asymmetry, connected with the first, is that managers of aggregate demand who desire a stable inflation outcome will regard the risks of positive errors as greater than the risks of symmetrical negative errors. They will aim for higher unemployment the larger their uncertainties about private demand, about the marginal effects of their own measures, and about the position of the NAIRU itself. These uncertainties have been larger in the 1970s and so perceived by the authorities.

A third implication is that the aggregate Phillips curve will shift up in periods of high intersectoral demand and supply shocks. Frictional and search unemployment will be greater when microeconomic reallocations dictate higher turnover. This may well have happened in recent years. It is picked up in part by the dispersion variable that George Perry and others have introduced in wage equations.

I conclude that little of the alleged increase of the NAIRU has been credibly explained in terms of the labor market itself, as voluntary leisure disguised as unemployment, or rational job search, or friction, or persistent misinformation. For the most part, the apparent rise of the NAIRU merely describes but does not explain the chronic acceleration of inflation itself.

Given the unprecedented external shocks that have contributed to acceleration in recent years, it seems particularly gratuitous to describe the phenomenon by saying that the natural rate of unemployment has shifted up once again. One might instead interpret the absorption of *real* wage reductions in 1974–75 and 1979, with only modest acceleration of money wages, as evidence that labor markets were not very tight even at unemployment rates below 6 percent. It is true that in labor market equilibrium the trend of real wages, in terms of workers' consumption, must reflect the adverse trend in the terms of trade in industrial America. But that adverse trend has so far come in jolts, and until the dust settles nobody really knows whether any more unemployment, and if any how much, is permanently necessary to reconcile American workers to it.

It is hard to resist or refute the suspicion that the operational NAIRU gravitates toward the average rate of unemployment actually experienced. Among the mechanisms which produce that result are improvements in unemployment compensation and other benefits enacted in response to higher unemployment, loss of on-the-job training and employability by the unemployed, defections to the informal and illegal economy, and a slowdown in capital formation as business firms lower their estimates of needed capacity. Conceivably the economy is moving to ever higher rates of unemployment that impose no greater discipline on wage increases. After another half-decade of stagflation, the fear of acceleration is likely to be as great an impediment to expansion at 7 or 8 percent unemployment as it has recently been at 6 percent.

An observer uncontaminated by the economists' consensus, vintages 1970 and later, unburdened by the natural rate or the NAIRU, might interpret the evidence quite differently. He might even conclude that money wage acceleration depends mainly on the direction the economy is moving rather than on its level. This conclusion would be consistent with the old-fashioned aggregate supply curve in $p - Y$ space discussed above. It is supported by the scarcity of high-employment recovery periods when wage inflation was abating. The decelerations that have occurred took place largely during recessions.[32]

It is possible that there is no NAIRU, no natural rate, except one that floats with actual history. It is just possible that the direction the economy is moving in is at least as important a determinant of acceleration and deceleration as its level. These possibilities should give policymakers pause as they embark on yet another application of the orthodox demand-management cure for inflation. The recession may bring disinflation, though at a frustratingly slow pace. The cumulative impact of a long and severe recession may eventually break the present core inflation. But will the economy ever be able to recover without accelerating wages and prices once again? This heretical view has policy implications quite different from the standard consensus. It questions the permanence of disinflationary gains from restrictive demand policies. It raises the value of stability in real economic outcomes, unlikely to be achieved by stability of policy.

Inertia, Expectations, and Structural Inflationary Bias

The original econometric versions of the accelerationist Phillips curve included as the augmentation term a distributed lag of past price or wage inflation rates, and either confirmed or assumed that the coefficients of the lagged variables added to unity. This augmentation variable, embodying lagged prices and wages, could be interpreted in two distinct ways. It could be a proxy for price or wage expectations, assuming these expectations are formed adaptively; because of this interpretation, equations of this specification were commonly called "expectations-augmented." It could represent the inertia of wage- and price-setting institutions: explicit or implicit contracts and patterns of emulation and catch-up.

The radically divergent policy implications of these two interpretations of the same statistical variable were only beginning to be appreciated in 1970. Today the distinction is the crucial issue in the controversy provoked by the new classical counterrevolution in macroeconomics (Monetarism-2).[33] This became clear as soon as rational expectations replaced adaptive expectations in theoretical specification of wage and price determination. Then expected policies rather than past inflation histories were doing the augmenting, and those policies were thereby deprived of the power to influence real outcomes, employment, and output. But if lagged prices and wages belong in the equation in their own right, representing institutional inertia and disequilibrium adjustment, then the qualitative conclusions of the 1970 consensus still stand.

I shall not resume this debate here. In the last paper of his I heard and read, Arthur Okun did a characteristically marvelous job of enumerating those observed facts of economic fluctuations which are not consistent with the misperceptions-equilibrium theories of the new classical macroeconomists.[34]

A battle of models is in progress concerning the extent to which, within the rational expectations framework, contractual inertia damages the strong policy-ineffectiveness propositions of the new wave of monetarists.[35] Common sense suggests that systematic feedback policies, based on information subsequent to that available when contractual commitments were made, will work and will be stabilizing. This seems to restore the effectiveness of policies. But Monetarists-2 then ask why rational parties do not make contracts covering in advance any contingencies to which the policy authorities could respond. The empirically relevant point is that actual contracts do not cover such contingencies; given that fact, no one has license to assume that the economy behaves as if they do. A reason that actual contracts do not cover contingencies, more specific than the practical difficulties of writing Arrow–Debreu contracts, is that compensatory policies are expected. If so, failure of the authorities to carry them out would be a surprise that puts both parties in less preferred positions. Moreover, I would remind the model builders, neither unemployed workers nor future entrants to the labor force are able to make contracts with anybody.

I expressed doubt above that the drift of the "natural rate" can be regarded as an equilibrium phenomenon. The alternative explanation is that most of the time labor markets are not in market-clearing equilibrium, that the disequilibrium adjustments to excess demand and excess supply are asymmetrical, that wages are mainly determined between employers and their existing employees with attention to mutual long-run commitments and to the maintenance of parities with other firms and workers, that except in extreme cases of economic duress the availability of unemployed workers has little effect on those determinations. This account implies that the economy has a structural bias toward inflation, even toward the acceleration of inflation. The structural bias means that inflation stability is not the same thing as equilibrium, that inflation stability generally requires aggregate excess supply in amounts that depend on the severity of the microeconomic and macroeconomic shocks to which the economy is subject, that inflation stability does not have the properties of allocational optimality associated with equilibrium.[36]

To state the issues in an overly simple but instructive way, there are two interpretations of U.S. inflationary history since 1965. One blames mistaken demand-management policies—they aimed at overfull employment, accommodated too readily existing inflation and inflationary shocks, intervened too promptly and energetically to arrest recessions and speed recoveries.[37] According to this thesis, correct policies can bring price stability plus realistically full employment.

The other interpretation depends on the view that the price- and wage-setting institutions of the economy have an inflationary bias. Consequently, demand management cannot stabilize the price trend without chronic sacrifice of output and employment unless it is assisted, occasionally or permanently, by direct incomes policies of some kind. According to this second thesis, there is little hope that monetary and fiscal disinflation alone will cure the current stagflation.

I believe that, while the first interpretation of events since 1965 contains important elements of truth, especially for the 1966–69 period of excess demand, it is very difficult to reject the hypothesis of structural inflationary bias.

But why is there a break in the postwar history of inflation around 1965? On the first interpretation this is easy to explain by the acceptance of Keynesian demand policies in the early 1960s. The second thesis must explain why the alleged structural bias did not generate more inflation before 1965.

The 1950s began with a successful application of wage and price controls during the Korean War. Thanks to these controls and to an austere fiscal policy, the speculative commodity price boom at the beginning of the war had no lasting inflationary effects. When the controls were removed, prices and price expectations were stable, with unemployment at 3 percent. There were three recessions in the decade of the 1950s. The recovery between the first and second took the inflation rate for gross business product as high as 5 percent, although unemployment barely edged below 4 percent. The succeeding recessions, responsible for the adage that it takes two recessions to expunge the inflationary legacy of one boom, left the Kennedy administration in 1961 with 7 percent unemployment and a 1 percent inflation rate. The recovery of 1961–65 raised inflation only to 2.5 percent while reducing unemployment to 4 percent. However, this was done with the help of the wage-price guideposts and of active if informal interventions by the federal administration in key wage bargains and pricing decisions.

There were other favorable factors that did not persist after 1965. The flexprice sector was generally neutral or counterinflationary in this period. Farm prices fell precipitously from 1951 to 1957 and were quite stable until 1965. The relative price of energy declined slightly. The country benefited from cheap imports from Europe and Japan; the overvaluation of the dollar hurt the U.S. net reserve position but was not reflected in dollar import prices while the exchange rate was pegged.

In summary, it can be argued that the structural bias toward inflation was there all along, but was held in check by a combination of frequent recessions, episodes of wage-price controls and guideposts, and favorable price inputs from flexprice and foreign sectors.

If the economy has an inflationary bias, if the NAIRU consists in significant proportion of involuntary unemployment, what can and should be done about it? The Galbraithian solution, permanent wage and price controls over the fixprice sector, entails all the familiar allocational inefficiencies. Probably it does not even solve the basic problem, namely to permit the economy to operate at higher rates of utilization without chronic inflationary pressure. The pressure would still be there bumping against the controls, and they would not survive.

The more fundamental solution is to diminish the asymmetry of wage and price response to excess supply and demand. This involves increasing the power of the economically disenfranchised outsiders, whose availability for work has so little impact on the wages paid the insiders or the prices set by their employers. A litany of procompetitive reforms has long been dutifully included in discussions of the trade-off dilemma.[38] It is a familiar list: antitrust; open union membership; labor market policies, among them training, retraining, and relocation; reform of unemployment insurance, public assistance, and minimum wage; repeal of Davis-Bacon and a host of other sacred cows. These things just do not get done.

A different approach is to use controls to mimic competitive behavior, for example to prevent wage increases by firms whose employment is decreasing at a time when qualified job seekers are available to them. Collective bargaining is carried out by the sanction of national legislation, and the public has the right to restrict the contents of contracts achieved under governmental protection. In similar vein, legal recognition could be withdrawn from collective bargaining contracts lasting more than one year. The quid pro quo from business would be the avoidance of price increases at times of declining sales and rising excess capacity. At the very least, such behavior should be a prima facie cause for attention from the antitrust division. The purpose of these proposals is to strengthen sectoral and economy-wide disinflationary responses to slack, diminishing the asymmetry that leads to inflationary bias.

Where Do We Go from Here?

In figure 15.6, I follow an old Brookings panel precedent of mine by presenting a simulation of the paths of unemployment and price inflation implied by a relentless policy of gradual monetary disinflation.[39] The policy is a specific version of the popular orthodox remedy for current inflation in the United States. The economy to which this policy is applied is a stylized version of the consensus view, with structural specifications and numerical coefficient values that embody conventional econometric consensus based on U.S. time series.

The story is as follows: beginning in 1980:1 the government takes monetary and fiscal measures that gradually reduce the quarterly rate of increase of nominal income, MV. It is reduced in ten years from 12 percent a year to the noninflationary rate of 2 percent a year, the assumed

STABILIZATION POLICY TEN YEARS AFTER

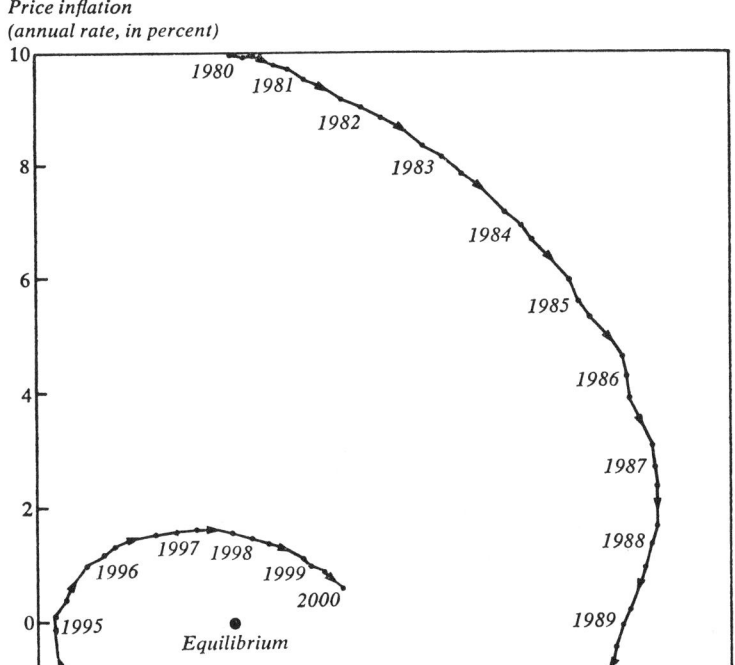

Source: Derived by the author. See text discussion.

Figure 15.6
Simulated effects of monetary disinflation on unemployment and inflation, 1980:1–2000:1

sustainable rate of growth of real GNP. The inertia of inflation is modeled by the average of inflation rates over the preceding eight quarters. The actual inflation rate each quarter is this average plus or minus a term that depends on the unemployment rate, U, relative to the NAIRU, assumed to be 6 percent. This term is $(6/U_{-1} - 1)$. It implies a Phillips curve slope of one-sixth a quarter, two-thirds a year at $U = 6$ and has the usual curvature.

At the start, real GNP is growing at its sustainable rate of 2 percent and unemployment is 6 percent. But the inflation rate is 10 percent. The development of unemployment is modeled by Okun's Law with a coefficient of 2.

Figure 15.6 shows that in this simulation a recession lasts until 1987, when unemployment reaches a peak of 10.3 percent and inflation has been reduced to 2.3 percent a year. In 1990, unemployment is 10.0 percent, and prices are stable.

The simulation illustrates another point. Steadiness in monetary policy, as registered in dollar spending on GNP, does not mean stability in economic outcomes. The cycle in figure 15.6 is damped, but it is wasteful and unnecessary. Clearly it would be preferable, and possible, to aim directly for the equilibrium (zero inflation, 6 percent unemployment) *before* the inflation rate crosses zero.

This is not a prediction! It is a cautionary tale. The simulation is a reference path, against which policymakers must weigh their hunches that the assumed policy, applied resolutely and irrevocably, would bring speedier and less costly results. There are several reasons that disinflation might occur more rapidly. When unemployment remains so high so long, bankruptcies and plant closings, prospective as well as actual, might lead to more precipitous collapse of wage and price patterns than have been experienced in the United States since 1932. Moreover, the very threat of a scenario like figure 15.6 may induce wage-price behavior that yields a happier outcome. A simulated scenario with rational rather than adaptive expectations of inflation would show speedier disinflation and smaller unemployment cost, to a degree that depends on the duration of contractual inertia, explicit or implicit.

One advocate of a policy like that of the simulation, William Fellner, argues that its effectiveness will be greatly enhanced if the intentions of the government are made credible to the public at the outset.[40] Consequently, he proposes that the government commit itself, ostentatiously and irrevocably, to the scheduled disinflation of monetary demand, whatever the outcome in employment, production, and profits. I agree that, if the authorities do in fact intend to follow such a schedule, they should make their intentions crystal clear in advance. I agree, too, that if the threat could in fact be made credible, the disinflationary response would be faster than implied by the conventional Phillips curve coefficient used in my simulation.

The question is how much. One obvious problem is that a long-run policy commitment can never be irrevocable, especially in a democracy. Important economic groups will not find it wholly credible, and some will use political power to relax or reverse the policy. Even assuming credibility and understanding by private agents, their responses are problematic. In the decentralized but imperfectly competitive U.S. economy, wage and price decisions are not synchronized but staggered. It is hard to predict how individual firms, employees, and unions will translate a threatening macroeconomic scenario into their own demand curves. If each group worries a lot about its relative status, each group will decide that the best strategy is to disinflate very little.

Finally, the problem is not simply unwinding an unpalatable inflation resulting from past monetary mistakes. The simulation reported in figure 15.6 does not allow for further inflationary shocks from OPEC, dollar depreciation, world shortages, or other events not now foreseen. Any of these could delay or prevent disinflation and raise the real costs of nonaccommodative policies, whether accompanied with a credible threat or not. It is far from certain that society has consensus on how the burdens of real economic reverses should be shared, or even on how such questions should be decided. An economic path anything like figure 15.6 will probably be politically and socially divisive.

For these reasons, I think it would be recklessly imprudent to lock the economy into a monetary disinflation without auxiliary incomes policies. The purpose of these policies would be to engineer directly a deceleration of wages and prices consistent with the gradual slowdown of dollar spending. Macroeconomic policy and wage-price guideposts or controls would be concerted. Instead of issuing a monetary threat to everyone in general and to no one in particular, the government would seek the consent and cooperation of organized labor and business in a five- to ten-year program to eliminate inflation at minimal cost in employment, production, and investment. The most promising incomes policy is to use tax-based incentives for complying with a sequence of gradually declining guideposts.[41]

This combination of controls and demand management would avoid the major pitfalls that have discredited previous episodes of controls. It would not try to restrain wages and prices in face of excess demand. At a macroeconomic level, this would be avoided by the consistent scheduling of monetary disinflation and guideposts. At a microeconomic level, compliance with guideposts would be induced by tax-based rewards and penalties, leaving individual firms flexibility to respond to the circumstances of particular markets. At the time the policy was ended, there would be no reason for anyone to be committed to or to expect wage or price increases greater than the final guideposts. Macroeconomic demand policy would be consistent with the actual inflation rate at the time.

At present there is no social consensus to support the combination of demand management and incomes policy just sketched. Yet public opinion polls again and again report latent majority support for controls, the direct remedy for inflation to which ordinary citizens instinctively turn. It will take more political leadership than the United States has seen for a long time to transform those sentiments into consensus for an effective policy. The importance of the project extends beyond the conquest of inflation to the real problems of resource allocation and wealth distribution that confront and divide us.

The people say that inflation is problem number one, and because they say so it is. "Inflation" has become the national obsession, the catchall scapegoat for individual and societal economic difficulties, the symptom that diverts attention from the basic maladies. Episodic efforts to control it, and constant anticipation that they will occur but achieve no more than transient success, severely damage the economy's real performance and future potential.

Yet despite the repeated rhetoric of firm resolution, the political leadership of the country does not adopt or even propose an effective program. This is partly because the economic and political establishment is beguiled by simplistic diagnoses and remedies, for which the economics profession bears no little responsibility. The government did it all—by spending too much, taxing too much, borrowing too much, and printing too much money. Let the government turn off all those spigots and there will be no more inflation.

It is not possible to do the job without effective wage and price controls of some kind. Demand management cannot do it alone. Without the leadership to develop a national consensus to face that truth, the prospects are for more stop-go, more muddling through. There could be worse prospects, and probably they include determined but unassisted monetary disinflation.

Notes

I am grateful to my colleagues at Yale and to members of the Brookings panel for comments on the original version, to Ray C. Fair also for the use of his model reported in the paper, and especially to members of the panel for many discussions of substance and for painstaking guidance of the revision. Bret Bertolin and Kathleen K. Donahoo provided efficient statistical and editorial assistance. Laura Harrison and other Cowles Foundation staff miraculously produced the typescripts under deadline pressures of my own making. The work was in part supported by the National Science Foundation and the Cowles Foundation.

In these notes *BPEA* refers to *Brookings Papers on Economic Activity*.

1. Milton Friedman, "The Role of Monetary Policy," *American Economic Review*, vol. 58 (March 1968), pp. 1–17; and Edmund S. Phelps, "Phillips Curves, Expectations of Inflation and Optimal Unemployment over Time," *Economica*, n.s., vol. 34 (August 1967), pp. 254–81.

2. Terminology of this kind apparently originated in Franco Modigliani and Lucas Papademos, "Targets for Monetary Policy in the Coming Year," *BPEA, 1:1975*, pp. 141–63.

3. Milton Friedman, "A Monetary Theory of Nominal Income," *Journal of Political Economy*, vol. 79 (March–April 1971), pp. 323–37.

4. Milton Friedman, "A Theoretical Framework for Monetary Analysis," *Journal of Political Economy*, vol. 78 (March–April 1970), pp. 221–22.

5. For analysis of "supply shocks" and inflation, see: Robert J. Gordon, "Alternative Responses of Policy to External Supply Shocks," *BPEA, 1:1975*, pp. 183–204; James L. Pierce and Jared J. Enzler, "The Effects of External Inflationary Shocks," *BPEA, 1:1974*, pp. 13–54; and Edward M. Gramlich, "Macro Policy Responses to Price Shocks," *BPEA, 1:1979*, pp. 125–66.

6. Peter K. Clark, discussion of George L. Perry, "Potential Output and Productivity," *BPEA, 1:1977*, pp. 55–58.

7. See, for example, Michael Bruno and Jeffrey D. Sachs, "Supply versus Demand Approaches to the Problem of Stagflation," forthcoming in *Weltwirtschaftliche Archiv*; and Jeffrey D. Sachs, "Wages, Profits, and Macroeconomic Adjustment: A Comparative Study," *BPEA, 2:1979*, pp. 269–319. For a review of the controversy, see Alan S. Blinder, *Economic Policy and the Great Stagflation* (Academic Press, 1979).

8. On these developments, see Pentti J. K. Kouri and Jorge Braga de Macedo, "Exchange Rates and the International Adjustment Process," *BPEA, 1:1978*, pp. 111–50; James Tobin and Jorge B. de Macedo, "The Short-Run Macroeconomics of Floating Exchange Rates: An Exposition," in John S. Chipman and Charles P. Kindleberger, eds., *Flexible Exchange Rates and the Balance of Payments: Essays in Memory of Egon Sohmen* (Amsterdam: North-

Holland, forthcoming); and Rudiger Dornbusch and Paul Krugman, "Flexible Exchange Rates in the Short Run," *BPEA, 3:1976*, pp. 537–75.

9. With an "Austrian" lag between inputs and outputs, there is an interest component in variable cost. This point has been emphasized in Lane Taylor, "IS/LM in the Tropics: Diagrammatics of the New Structuralist Macro Critique," in William R. Cline and Sidney Weintraub, eds., *Economic Stabilization in Developing Countries* (Brookings Institution, forthcoming); and Michael Bruno, "Stabilization and Stagflation in a Semi-Industrialized Economy," in Rudiger Dornbusch and Jacob A. Frenkel, eds., *International Economic Policy: Theory and Evidence* (Johns Hopkins University Press, 1979), pp. 270—89.

10. See, for example, Arthur M. Okun, "Efficient Disinflationary Policies," *American Economic Review*, vol. 68 (May 1978, *Papers and Proceedings, 1977*), pp. 348–52.

11. *Economic Report of the President, January 1962*, pp. 108–43.

12. Consumer price inflation in Japan exceeded that in the United States in 1951–54, when the Japanese rate was never below 5 percent. It also exceeded the U.S. rate every year but one from 1960 to 1977. In a similar comparison between France and the United States, France had the higher inflation rate in all but four years from 1950 to 1978. Compared with Germany over the same period, the United States had less inflation in 1955–56, 1960–66, and 1971–73. See International Monetary Fund, *International Financial Statistics Yearbook*, vol. 32 (IMF, 1979), pp. 58–59.

13. George M. von Furstenberg, "Corporate Investment: Does Market Valuation Matter in the Aggregate?" *BPEA, 2:1977*, pp. 347–97; and Peter K. Clark, "Investment in the 1970s: Theory, Performance, and Prediction," *BPEA, 1:1979*, pp. 73–113. .

14. John B. Shoven and Jeremy I. Bulow, "Inflation Accounting and Nonfinancial Corporate Profits: Financial Assets and Liabilities," *BPEA, 1:1976*, pp. 15–57, and "Inflation Accounting and Nonfinancial Corporate Profits: Physical Assets," *BPEA, 3:1975*, pp. 557–98.

Incidentally, the loss due to historical cost depreciation accounting cannot exceed the full tax benefit of depreciation no matter how high the inflation rate; hence the marginal loss from an extra point of inflation declines and approaches zero. On the other hand, the gain from deductibility of nominal interest is, given the debt-equity ratio, proportional to the inflation rate.

15. Suppose income is taxed at rate t, except that income saved is taxed only at $t - u$. Suppose that saving s is a linear function $s_y y_d + s_r r_d$ of disposable income and after-tax rate of return on saving, respectively $y(1 - t) + us$ and $r(1 - t + u)$. With pretax income y given and normalized to 1 and pretax return on saving given at r, $s(1 - s_y u) = s_y y(1 - t) + s_r r(1 - t + u)$ and $\partial s/\partial u = (s_y s + s_r r)/(1 - s_y u)$. This is positive for non-negative s, r, s_y, s_r, u and $s_y, s, u < 1$. However, if t is constant, the government is dissaving us. Does an increase in u bring a net increase in aggregate saving? Yes, if and only if $s_y + (s_r r/s)(1 - u) > 1$. s_y is the marginal propensity to save from disposable income. The second term is the elasticity of saving with respect to the rate of return net of the tax subsidy. It takes relatively high values of these parameters to make the subsidy pay off in aggregate saving.

16. Let $1/\beta$ be the elasticity of labor supply with respect to the after-tax wage. Let α be the output-on-capital elasticity in a two-factor Cobb-Douglas production function with constant returns to scale; α is also the elasticity of the schedule of marginal product of labor. Let γ be the percentage of after-tax income spent, for simplicity assumed to be identical for capital and labor income. Then a reduction in the tax rate t will reduce the supply of goods net of induced spending—and in this sense will be inflationary—unless t exceeds $(\alpha + \beta)/(1 + \beta) - [(1/\gamma) - 1]/(1 + \beta)$. It will reduce government revenue unless t exceeds $(\alpha + \beta)/(1 + \beta)$. For $\alpha = 0.3$, $\gamma = 0.8$, and $\beta = 3.0$, an improbably low value, the first limit is 0.760 and the second is 0.825.

17. The first three columns below give the percentage of an employee's gross earnings taken by national and local income taxes and social security contributions in selected countries in 1976 for three levels of earnings (100, 200, and 400 percent of the earnings of an average production worker in each country). The figures are for a two-adult, two-child family. In the first two columns all the earnings are due to the husband. In the third column, they are evenly divided between the two spouses. The figures are from Organisation for Economic Co-operation and Development, *The Tax/Benefit Position of Selected Income Groups in OECD Member Countries, 1972–1976*, a report by the Committee on Fiscal Affairs (Paris: OECD, 1978), table 16(c). The fourth column gives the corresponding marginal rate for an average production worker. The fifth column shows the maximum marginal personal income tax rates in 1976 (1974 for Japan). See ibid., table 6, and pp. 40–86. The U.S. rate on earned income is 50 percent. These figures refer only to central government taxation.

	Taxes and social security contributions, by income group			Marginal tax rate	Maximum marginal income tax rate
	100 percent	200 percent	400 percent		
Austria	13.3	20.8	23.4	28	62
Belgium	21.9	32.4	39.1	37	60
France	10.0	12.5	19.0	16	60
Germany	27.0	28.7	38.5	34	56
Japan	8.0	14.8	17.6	21	75
Netherlands	31.8	35.2	37.2	42	72
Sweden	35.0	53.0	54.0	63	57
United Kingdom	25.4	31.6	34.1	41	83
United States	17.0	22.0	29.0	32	70

18. I asked my colleague Ray Fair to check his macroeconometric model of the United States to see what would have happened if the Federal Reserve had rigorously followed a policy of 4 percent growth in M_1 beginning in 1961. The model balked after a few years at 4 percent but agreed to make a longer run with 5.4 percent. Even then it refused to go beyond 1973: 1, by which quarter the downward deviations from the historical path of real GNP, beginning in 1967 and turning into depression in 1970, had brought simulated output to two-thirds of its actual value. Disinflationary gains were minimal, partly because the model contains a strong "Patman effect," which translated astronomical interest rates into high prices. The offset in wage disinflation was surprisingly small, because the "discouraged worker" effect kept unemployment rates below 10 percent despite sharp declines in employment. Fair recognizes that this experiment strained his structural specifications, which were designed for more modest deviations from observed history. Moreover, both he and I are aware that so radical a difference of policy would have changed the whole structure and the whole history. He is not necessarily implicated in my conclusion that no one has the right to assume that a monetarist policy would have entailed no serious real cost.

19. Robert Mundell, "Inflation and Real Interest," *Journal of Political Economy*, vol. 71 (June 1963), pp. 280–83; and James Tobin, "Money and Economic Growth," *Econometrica*, vol. 33 (October 1965), pp. 671–84.

20. Eugene F. Fama, "Short-Term Interest Rates as Predictors of Inflation," *American Economic Review*, vol. 65 (June 1975), pp. 269–82.

21. William Poole, "Optimal Choice of Monetary Policy Instruments in a Simple Stochastic Macro Model," *Quarterly Journal of Economics*, vol. 84 (May 1970), pp. 197–216.

22. Stephen M. Goldfeld, "The Case of the Missing Money," *BPEA*, 3:1976, pp. 683–730.

23. Robert J. Barro, "Are Government Bonds Net Wealth?" *Journal of Political Economy*, vol. 82 (November–December 1974), pp. 1095–1117.

24. Martin Feldstein, "Tax Rules and the Mismanagement of Monetary Policy," *American Economic Review*, vol. 70 (May 1980, *Papers and Proceedings, 1979*), pp. 182–86.

25. Barro, "Are Government Bonds Net Wealth?" and Robert E. Hall, "Stochastic Implications of the Life Cycle-Permanent Income Hypothesis: Theory and Evidence," *Journal of Political Economy*, vol. 86 (December 1978), pp. 971–87.

26. Data Resources, Inc., "Fiscal Policy: The Scorecard Between 1962 and 1976," in Joint Economic Committee, *Economic Stabilization Policies: The Historical Record, 1962–76*, 95 Cong. 2 sess. (Government Printing Office, 1978), pp. 11–60.

27. Abba P. Lerner, "Money as a Creature of the State," *American Economic Review*, vol. 37 (May 1947, *Papers and Proceedings, 1947*), pp. 312–17.

28. Robert E. Hall, "The Rigidity of Wages and the Persistence of Unemployment," *BPEA*, 2:1975, pp. 301–35, and "The Process of Inflation in the Labor Market," *BPEA*, 2:1974, pp. 343–93; Michael L. Wachter, "The Changing Cyclical Responsiveness of Wage Inflation," *BPEA*, 1:1976, pp. 115–59; and Robert J. Gordon, "The Welfare Cost of Higher Unemployment," *BPEA*, 1:1973, pp. 133–95.

29. These adjustments of unemployment rates are discussed in George L. Perry, "Changing Labor Markets and Inflation," *BPEA*, 3:1970, pp. 411–41.

30. For an analysis of how length of unemployment is affected by the availability of unemployment insurance, see Stephen T. Marston, "The Impact of Unemployment Insurance on Job Search," *BPEA*, 1:1975, pp. 13–48. Martin S. Feldstein examines the relative importance of temporary layoffs; see his "The Importance of Temporary Layoffs: An Empirical Analysis," *BPEA*, 3:1975, pp. 725–44. The effect of an increase in the minimum wage on other wages, the possibility of disemployment, and the distribution of family income are examined in Edward M. Gramlich, "Impact of Minimum Wages on Other Wages, Employment, and Family Incomes," *BPEA*, 2:1976, pp. 409–51.

31. For example, suppose quarterly acceleration of inflation is $6(1/U - 1/U^*)$, where U is the unemployment rate in percent and U^*, the NAIRU, is 6. This implies that a year of 7 percent unemployment will reduce inflation by 56 basis points. A $U - \bar{U}$ cycle of the pattern 0, 1, 2, 1, 0, -1, -2, -1, 0, and so on will accelerate inflation by 18 basis points a year if $\bar{U}$ is equal to U^*. To avoid such acceleration requires a mean U some 25 basis points higher than U^*. This point was made in Martin Neil Baily, "Stabilization Policy and Private Economic Behavior," *BPEA*, 1:1978, p. 47.

32. Of the thirty overlapping two-calendar-year periods from 1949 to 1979, there are six in which the rate of wage increase fell while unemployment was also falling. These include 1952–53, during Korean wage-price controls, 1962–63 and 1963–64, the period of Kennedy-Johnson guideposts, and 1972–73, the period of Nixon controls. The other two are 1959–60 and 1976–77. There are seven recession biennia when wages decelerated and unemployment rose. The only period when there was acceleration of more than 50 basis points while unemployment was rising was 1974–75.

33. Robert E. Lucas, Jr., "Econometric Testing of the Natural Rate Hypothesis," in Otto Eckstein, ed., *The Econometrics of Price Determination*, A conference sponsored by the Board of Governors of the Federal Reserve System and Social Science Research Council (The Board, 1972), pp. 50–59, and "Econometric Policy Evaluation: A Critique," in Karl Brunner and Allan H. Meltzer, eds., *The Phillips Curve and Labor Markets*, Carnegie-Rochester Conference Series on Public Policy, vol. 1 (Amsterdam: North-Holland, 1976), pp. 19–46; and Thomas J. Sargent, "Rational Expectations, the Real Rate of Interest, and the Natural Rate of Unemployment," *BPEA*, 2:1973, pp. 429–72.

34. Arthur M. Okun, "Rational-Expectations-With-Misperceptions as a Theory of the Business Cycle," prepared for the American Enterprise Institute Seminar on Rational Expectations, February 1980.

35. For a review and discussion of the literature, see Bennett T. McCallum, "Rational Expectations and Macroeconomic Stabilization Policy: An Overview," prepared for the American Enterprise Institute Seminar on Rational Expectations, February 1980; and John B. Taylor, "Aggregate Dynamics and Staggered Contracts," *Journal of Political Economy*, vol. 88 (February 1980), pp. 1–23.

36. I discussed these points in my "Inflation and Unemployment," *American Economic Review*, vol. 62 (March 1972), pp. 1–18.

37. See William Fellner, *Towards a Reconstruction of Macroeconomics: Problems of Theory and Policy* (American Enterprise Institute, 1976).

38. See *Economic Report of the President, February 1970*, pp. 70–71; *Economic Report of the President, February 1971*, pp. 78–82; and Robert W. Crandall, "Federal Government Initiatives to Reduce the Price Level," in Arthur M. Okun and George L. Perry, eds., *Curing Chronic Inflation* (Brookings Institution, 1978), pp. 165–204.

39. James Tobin, "Monetary Policy in 1974 and Beyond" *BPEA, 1:1974*, p. 230.

40. William Fellner, "The Credibility Effect and Rational Expectations: Implications of the Gramlich Study," *BPEA, 1:1979*, pp. 67–78, and *Towards a Reconstruction of Macroeconomics*.

41. See Okun and Perry, eds., *Curing Chronic Inflation*. For an elegant alternative with the same properties of flexibility, see Abba P. Lerner, "A Wage-Increase Permit Plan to Stop Inflation," in ibid., pp. 255–69.

CHAPTER 16

MONETARY POLICY: RULES, TARGETS, AND SHOCKS

The proper conduct of monetary policy is now once again wide open to discussion. An immediate practical controversy concerns the role of central banks in recovery from the world depression. Underlying that debate are some unresolved fundamental issues regarding the responsibilities, goals, targets, and operating procedures of central banks.

Monetarism won the hearts and minds of many economists and most central bankers in the 1970s. Now it seems to be losing adherents and influence—partly because it is blamed for the severe depression, partly because regulatory, institutional, and technological changes have altered the meanings and velocities of monetary aggregates. Last summer Chairman Volcker and his Federal Reserve colleagues suspended their monetarist targets, to almost universal relief. The severity of the recession, the international debt crisis, and the pace of change in financial structure were all good reasons. It is doubtful, though possible, that money stock targets will regain their previous status. If not, what philosophy of monetary control, what framework for the conduct of policy, will replace them?

A host of monetary architects are ready to fill the vacuum. Some would restore the gold standard or make paper money convertible into other commodities. Some would replace intermediate monetary aggregates with other targets: the monetary base, nominal GNP or final sales, total domestic credit, price indexes or their rates of change, exchange rates. Some advocate irrevocable commitment to announced values of chosen targets; others contemplate revision of target values at regular or irregular intervals. Some propose simple rules and targets, not to be changed

The *Money, Credit, and Banking* Lecture at the Western Economic Association Meetings 1983. Reprinted by permission from *Journal of Money, Credit, and Banking* 15(4) (1983): 506–518.

during their tenure by reference to observed macroeconomic outcomes; others advocate complex feedback formulas describing how monetary instruments will respond to such observations. Some are willing to trust the judgments and priorities of the monetary authorities: let them look at the whole state of the economy and decide what to do without pre-commitments to any rules or formulas or targets. Hardcore monetarists would, of course, reinstate targets for M1 or other aggregates and tie the central bank more tightly to their realization.

Rules versus Discretion

"Rules versus discretion" denotes a long-standing debate on economic policy, especially monetary policy. Should policymakers consistently follow stable announced rules or should they have and use discretion in successive decisions? If they follow announced rules not subject to discretionary change from day to day or year to year, should the rules be fixed or reactive? A fixed, nonreactive rule sets the path of instruments or of intermediate targets under policy control independently of events and observations—policy is deliberately blindfold. A reactive rule alters the values of control variables according to feedback formulas exploiting up-to-date information on the state of the economy.

An example of a fixed rule is the celebrated recommendation of Milton Friedman that a chosen money supply, the control variable, be increased at a constant annual rate, 0 percent or 3 percent or k percent. Once the variable and its growth rate are chosen and announced, the authorities stick to it through thick and thin, depression and prosperity, deflation and inflation. An example of a reactive rule is one of Robert Hall's (1983) suggestions, that the central bank commit itself to the goal of holding the CPI to a preannounced target, and to adjust its securities portfolio so as to keep the CPI expected a year ahead on the futures market a quarter of the way from the actual current CPI to the target. Discretion, of course, allows policymakers to face each decision anew, unconstrained by rules of either kind.

The formal concepts and distinctions are hard to apply, for several reasons. First, note that fixed rules are rarely advocated for instruments directly under the authorities' control. Certainly no one in this day and age wants the Fed to peg permanently the federal funds rate or any other nominal interest rate, though a simple instruction to the open market desk is all it takes to do so. And no one, to my knowledge, favors literal freezing of the size of the Federal Reserve securities portfolio or of its rate of growth, another instrument under immediate and full control. That would not even fix the path of the monetary base—Friedman's (1984) latest preference, by the way, is to hold the base constant as an ultimate goal.

Advocates of fixed rules almost always have in mind intermediate targets, variables that are neither direct control instruments nor ultimate objectives. To control intermediate monetary aggregates, M's of any subscript, the Fed like any other gunner uses feedback information, correcting its aim by observing its misses in previous shots. Application of fixed nonreactive rules to variables under direct control, or very close to it, would be absurd even in the short run, because most of the factors generating noise in the transmission of open market operations have little monetary or economic significance. It would be an even greater absurdity over longer runs when changes in banking structure, financial technology, and regulations alter in unpredictable ways the linkages between control instruments and significant outcomes.

Thus the question is not whether reactive procedures will be used by the central bank. They inevitably will be. It is whether they are used for intermediate targets of little or no intrinsic importance, or for macroeconomic outcomes of ultimate significance, GNP, prices, unemployment.

Second, I think, effectively binding rules are bound to be simple, like fixed growth rates for intermediate monetary aggregates. Simplicity gives them their political appeal and power. The lasting strength of the budget balance norm is an example; it is impaired if confined to "full employment" conditions or waived for recessions. Likewise the once powerful imperative of gold convertibility at historic parity depended on *not* specifying in advance any circumstances in which the commitment might conceivably be repudiated.

It is not really feasible to spell out in advance what a central bank or government will and will not do in a long list of contingencies. One reason is political: no government or agency can bind its successors. Another is operational: formulas telling how the central bank will respond to statistics of unemployment, prices, and exchange rates, to budget and tax legislation, to OPEC extortions and Iranian revolutions, to Brazilian defaults and Soviet harvests, are on the same imaginary plane as private Arrow-Debreu contracts. If state-of-nature contracts were feasible and prevalent, we would not need money or monetary policy anyway.

In practice, then, any rule will be a simple fixed path of intermediate target variables, limiting responses to new information—prescribed or discretionary—to adjustment of instruments to achieve the path. Truly responsive policies will be discretionary, free to react to events, observations, and projections without formal constraints.

A currently popular theoretical notion is the concept of a policy régime, defined by the rules guiding the actions, reactive or nonreactive, of policymakers. Its significance arises from the belief that private agents adjust their behaviors to their understanding of the régime. For the reasons just given, I find the concept fuzzy in application: régimes and changes of régime are difficult to define and to discern.

The main contemporary issue is between some simple monetarist rule and discretionary countercylical policy. From 1950 to 1973, in most dimensions a period of remarkably stable and successful macroeconomic performance, the Federal Reserve was vague, responsive, and active. Most of the time its stance was "leaning against the wind." In the 1970s the Fed gradually became more monetarist and less responsive to the cyclical state of the economy. The climax of this development was the announcement in October 1979 of a program of relentless monetary disinflation, along with new operating procedures setting unborrowed reserves instead of overnight interest rates for periods between FOMC meetings. But the Fed, as its 1982 actions indicate, has never committed itself irrevocably to monetary aggregate targets independent of actual economic outcomes. Such a commitment would indeed be a régime change of great importance.

Simple fixed rules are often supported on the grounds that they minimize risk. Economists and central bankers, it is argued, know little about the effects of monetary measures, their size, their timing, even their direction. Action is at least as likely to do harm as to do good. "Fine-tuning" is more likely to destabilize than to stabilize. Countercyclical responses frequently have perverse consequences because of the "long and variable lags" between diagnosis and action and result. Activism confuses private agents and distorts the market signals on which they rely. The safest course is to do nothing.

However, as I have argued above, "doing nothing" is not well defined. Mariners would not define a fixed rudder angle rather than a fixed compass heading as conservatively "doing nothing." Monetary rules themselves require the authorities to adjust instruments to achieve intermediate targets. How fast they should try to return to track when events beyond their control, like winds, waves, and currents, throw them off is a consequential problem. Achieving intermediate targets, to whatever degree of precision, does not in any case achieve desired paths of macroeconomic variables that really matter. Your conclusion as to what is a minimum-risk strategy, or an optimal strategy, will depend on your model of the financial and economic system and on your objectives and priorities. It is unlikely to coincide with holding constant any of the instruments or variables directly under central bank control or any intermediate target paths. I shall return to these questions later in the lecture.

Real and Nominal Objectives

Should monetary authorities consider the real economic performance of their economies in setting policies? Should their objectives include real outcomes of national and international performance—production, employment, capital formation, trade—as well as nominal variables—prices, nominal incomes, exchange rates?

Today many economists and central bankers answer no. Monetary authorities' capabilities and responsibilities, they argue, cover only nominal variables. After all, they have only nominal instruments. Dedication of those instruments to real objectives has, they allege, not improved but if anything actually worsened real performance, while destabilizing prices and causing inflation. Chastened by the stagflation of the last fifteen years, central banks should be content to provide a stable, credible, predictable noninflationary nominal path and to accept whatever real outcomes come along that way. Devotees of the new classical macroeconomics assure us that those outcomes will be optimal. Knowing that the central bank will neither confuse them nor rescue them from the consequences of imprudent wage and price increases, private agents in free markets will achieve the natural equilibrium values of real variables, quantities, and relative prices.

The issue is an old one, and the answer has oscillated over the history of central banking. The primacy of nominal objectives was well established before the Great Depression. Central banks and governments were expected to place defense of a fixed parity of their currency with gold or foreign currencies ahead of domestic economic performance. Today some economists, statesmen, and commentators—frustrated by exchange rate instabilities these past ten years—advocate restoration of an international gold standard. They believe that the discipline of gold convertibility, available to individuals as well as to foreign governments, would create and maintain anti-inflationary expectations and behaviors.

Monetarists concur with the objective but prefer the discipline of nominal monetary rules to that of gold. Some would impose such rules by legislative or constitutional mandate. The purpose and effect are the same as intended by advocates of the gold standard. Monetary operations will be, and will be seen to be, independent of actual real economic performance.

I believe that purely nominalist monetary strategies are neither feasible nor desirable, for several reasons.

The first reason is political. The responsibility of the central government for real macroeconomic performance is strongly entrenched in the politics of democratic societies. This has been true at least since the Great Depression of the 1930s and especially after World War II. In the United States, for example, the Employment Act of 1946 and the Full Employment and Balanced Growth Act of 1978 ("Humphrey–Hawkins") commit the federal government, including the Federal Reserve System, to the pursuit of real economic goals. More important realistically, unemployment, real growth, and related variables are significant factors in public opinion and in electoral campaigns.

A purely nominal stance of monetary policy, willfully blindfold to real developments, is not likely to be credible. Sooner or later the central bank of a democracy will rescue the economy from the worst unintended real byproducts of a fixed nominalist line, just as Paul Volcker did last summer. Expectation that this will happen is bound to undermine policies whose effectiveness depends on public belief that it never will.

Central banks cannot stand aloof from objectives highly valued by the societies they serve. Central bankers and their constituencies frequently dismiss the priorities of elected officials, for example, reduction of unemployment, as "political" hence unworthy of respect. The legitimacy of such a value judgment is as doubtful as its welfare economics.

The second point is economic. The dichotomy between real and nominal policy operations, by which monetary instruments are classified as purely nominal, is not valid theoretically or empirically.

Nominal price and wage paths are sluggish, some more sluggish than others. Prices and wages which are administered or negotiated change less rapidly and readily than the prices of financial assets and of commodities traded in auction markets. Because of such inertia, fluctuations in aggregate nominal spending resulting from monetary operations have important real consequences over fairly long short runs. The 1980–83 recession and depression confirm this obvious fact once again. Nor is it confined to downturns. Cyclical recoveries, stimulated or at least accommodated by monetary expansions, generate real as well as nominal gains. It is disingenuous, to say the least, for central bankers to pretend that their actions have no effects on real interest rates, unemployment rates, and other variables of concern to the populace.

The claim that monetary policies, since they necessarily rely on nominal instruments, can have only nominal effects trades on an analogy between altering monetary stocks and changing the unit of account. Switching the unit of account from dollars to half dollars would, everyone agrees, have no real consequences. Why shouldn't doubling the stock of "dollars" by other means be likewise neutral? The analogy is false. Actual central bank operations do not, while units changes do, change the public's stocks of all nominal assets in the same proportion. Actual operations effect exchanges of some assets for others, usually obligations to pay currency on demand for obligations to pay currency in future. Since future currency is not a perfect substitute for present currency, these exchanges are not neutral. They generally affect real interest rates, real exchange rates, saving, investment, and other real variables. Price changes affect private wealth and its distribution. Changes in inflation rates and in the distribution of price expectations necessarily alter real rates of return on currency and other assets with fixed nominal interest, and therefore influence the whole structure of asset prices and returns.

Some of these nonneutral effects vanish, in principle, in long-run steady states. Others do not. Time will eliminate the inertia of price and wage adjustments. But there are no long-run steady states whose properties are independent of the paths by which they are reached. For example, depressions and high real interest rates may interrupt irreversibly the accumulation of physical and human capital.

I am arguing that monetary authorities should not, indeed cannot, escape responsibility for real macroeconomic outcomes. To avoid misunderstanding I stress that I certainly am not advocating that they disregard nominal outcomes, price levels, and inflation rates. Somewhere in the framework of monetary policy objectives and targets there must be nominal anchors that prevent unlimited accommodation and give due weight to the costs of inflation and society's distaste for it. Milton Friedman told us in his famous Presidential Address some fifteen years ago that monetary policy could not *peg* real variables like unemployment and real interest rates and should not try. If "peg" meant to seek a particular unchanging numerical value forever, I think no one wanted or wants to peg. Permanent pegging of unemployment is one thing. Taking account of the state of the labor market is quite another. Trying to move unemployment down in some circumstances, up in others, is not pegging.

We should be careful not to draw the wrong lessons from the 1970s. After 1965 there were three bursts of inflation, each followed by recessions deliberately provoked by anti-inflationary monetary policies. The first acceleration of inflation, associated with the Vietnam war, was a classic demand-pull episode. President Johnson, contrary to the advice of his own economists, loaded his increased war spending on to an already fully employed economy without raising taxes, and in retrospect the Federal Reserve was overaccommodative. The two bursts of inflation in the 1970s were associated with extraordinary supply and price shocks: the first in 1973–74 from food shortages, oil embargo, and OPEC's fourfold increase in the dollar price of oil; the second in 1978–80 from the Iranian revolution, restriction of Middle East oil supplies, and a further tripling of the OPEC price. These events happened to occur in the late stages of cyclical recoveries, to which conscious stimulative and accommodative policies in the United States and other countries had contributed.

The lessons pundits and policymakers commonly draw from these experiences are that recoveries are dangerous, especially if they are promoted by policy. Accordingly central banks are most reluctant now to adopt expansionary policies even when their economies are as severely depressed as they are today. But these are the wrong lessons if the frightening bursts of inflation were due not to recoveries per se or to policies that fostered them, but to the extraordinary exogenous shocks. Vietnam, OPEC, and the Ayatollah Khomeini were not the endogenous consequences of normal policy-assisted business cycle recoveries. Fear of recurrences should not paralyze our governments and central banks and consign our economies to chronic stagnation.

The serious question of macroeconomic policy today is how much unemployment and general economic slack to maintain as insurance against another acceleration of inflation. According to a widely accepted model, there exists at any time a minimum unemployment rate consistent with nonacceleration, sometimes called the natural rate of unemployment or more neutrally the non-accelerating-inflation-rate-of-unemployment (NAIRU). Here the unemployment rate is serving as a barometer of general slack, of the overall pressure of aggregate demand on productive capacity. Unfortunately no one knows what the NAIRU is. Current estimates for the United States vary from 8 percent to 5 percent. For policymakers this doubt is compounded by uncertainty about the translation of their instruments via aggregate demand into unemployment. The decision problem is to balance, given these uncertainties, the costs of unemployment and lost production against the risks and costs of accelerating inflation. Those costs and risks can be made commensurate by estimating the extra unemployment-years necessary to eliminate a bulge of accelerating inflation should it occur.

A conservative solution is to minimize expected unemployment subject to the constraint that the probability of trespassing the NAIRU threshold not exceed some epsilon, perhaps even zero. Thus if there were any nonnegligible probability that policies designed to bring expected unemployment down to, say, 9 percent would generate acceleration—either because the NAIRU may be at least that high or because the policies might actually bring a lower unemployment rate—then conservative policymakers would seek to keep unemployment higher than 9 percent. This solution is in the spirit of macroeconomic strategies prevailing today, and it is a recipe and rationale for stagnation.

An optimal cost-benefit solution would not apply so absolute a constraint. A marginal dose of stimulus is justified if and only if the expected gain from reduction in unemployment exceeds the expected loss due to inflation acceleration. The latter is the cost of the unemployment correction necessary to eliminate the acceleration multiplied by the probability that the NAIRU threshold will have been crossed. If, for example, the correction costs two unemployment points for every point by which the threshold was crossed, then the median estimate of NAIRU is the proper target of policy. A higher relative correction cost implies a higher unemployment target, a lower appraisal of the cost a more ambitious unemployment goal.

Monetary Rules and the Conversion of Shocks into Macroeconomic Outcomes

An important consideration in comparing competing frameworks for the conduct of monetary policy is how they combine with the structure of the economy to determine how unpredictable shocks are absorbed. Shocks generate deviations from the macroeconomic paths expected when the instruments are set or the intermediate target values are chosen. They arise from unanticipated external events, aberrations in behaviors of private agents, and imperfections in forecasting models. If policies are governed by irrevocably fixed rules, shocks and the deviations they generate lead to no new decisions. If targets can be revised periodically, policymakers can base their next move on the observations, influenced by the shocks, obtained in the interim. Between periodic revisions they may follow operating rules relating their instruments to observed variables.

Shocks are of several kinds. The most important are the following: *Real demand* shocks affect aggregate demand for goods and services. They may arise in consumer spending, investment, net exports, and government fiscal operations. *Financial shocks* affect demand for monetary assets relative to their portfolio substitutes. These two types may be correlated, for example, if increased demand for money or some other asset is also a symptom of greater saving. *Price* shocks affect current and expected prices of goods and services. They may arise in world commodity markets, in exchange rates, or in domestic wage and price settings by trade unions and businesses, for example, "cost-pushes."

The conversion of shocks into unexpected macroeconomic outcomes depends jointly on the structure of the financial and economic system and on the conduct of macroeconomic policies. Different monetary frameworks, in particular, distribute the various shocks differently as between macroeconomic variables, real GNP, real interest rates, exchange rates, and prices.

This mode of analysis has been well known at least since William Poole's celebrated article in 1970. Poole used standard *IS-LM* analysis and greatly simplified the problem. But the qualitative conclusions would survive in a more elaborate model. Reminding you of his analysis is a good way to emphasize some general principles.

Poole assumed that the central bank could fix either a monetary quantity M or an interest rate r, or alternatively adopt a supply function relating M to market-determined r. His M could be interpreted to be something closer to central bank instruments—the base or unborrowed reserves—than to an endogenous intermediate aggregate. His r is a short-term interest rate, nominal, but also real as he abstracted from price and inflation effects or he assumed inertia in those variables over the short period to which the analysis applies. The central bank's objective is a target value of GNP, but no information about this variable will be available during the period after the policy is decided. Interest rates, however, will be observed, making it possible to base the M-setting on them.

Poole showed that pegging the interest rate protected the economy from GNP deviations due to purely financial shocks but transmitted real demand shocks fully into GNP. A monetarist policy would convert both types of shocks partly into output and partly into interest rates. GNP would be less vulnerable to real demand shocks and more vulnerable to financial shocks than under the interest rate peg. A supply function relating M to r would in general dominate either of the two single-variable policies. The interest rate contains information, but the information is ambiguous because an upward deviation could be due to a positive shock either to real demand or to money demand. The supply formula that minimizes variance of GNP would be the more elastic the greater the relative probability of financial shocks, the smaller the interest- and income-elasticities of money demand, and the flatter the *IS* locus. Conceivably the optimal supply formula would be supermonetarist, namely one that changed M systematically in the opposite direction from observed interest rates. This might be required to convert a nonvertical natural *LM* curve into a vertical one, which would protect the economy completely from *IS* shocks, as would be appropriate if financial shocks were sure never to happen. In general, there is no justification at all for assuming that the optimal LM shape is the one that corresponds to a fixed M. The optimal rule could be either less or more accommodative than that. "Leaning against the wind" was usually somewhat more accommodative.

One characteristic monetarist proposition asserts the stability of money demand, the unimportance of financial shocks relative to real demand shocks. This calls for a vertical LM locus—if nature does not provide one, policy should. But the volatility of demand for any of the statistical measures of money, increasing in recent years, is evidence against this proposition and the prescription it implies.

Monetarist policy has made the LM curve more vertical in recent years. Structural changes are working in the same direction. Deregulation is allowing deposits to bear market-determined interest rates, which will move up or down with the rates depository institutions can earn on their assets. Thus the demand for deposits, however sensitive to the differential between open market rates and deposit rates, will be much less sensitive to the general level of rates. In short, this reform itself is making the economy's natural LM curve much steeper. If the pre-reform M–r rule was optimal by Poole criteria, it is no longer optimal. The rule should be changed in the accommodative direction—the more so if, as seems likely, the reform also increases the volatility of money demand. This seems likely because, once the two rates are so close, depositors will be less precise and prompt in moving funds between moneys and near-moneys. Professor Hadjimichalakis of the University of Washington here in Seattle has in a recent book (1982) explored thoroughly the implications for monetary policy of recent structural changes of this kind.

The Poole analysis can be extended to take explicit account of supply price shocks. The risk that price increases will be associated with upward deviations of GNP from the target path is, of course, a reason for gearing policy to a more modest real GNP objective. I discussed this problem earlier in the lecture. The possibility of a price shock uncorrelated with GNP is a different matter. Such a shock lowers real output and raises the price level. Steepening the LM curve accentuates the output fall and mitigates the price increase. For those concerned with price stability or with the danger that a one-shot price increase sets off a wage/price spiral in its wake, this is a reason for preferring a more monetarist structure. The OPEC crises of the 1970s delivered a positive supply price shock together with a negative real demand shock. If the *LM* curve, inclusive of the money supply rule, is close to vertical, there will be in such cases a much larger output loss but a smaller general price increase than if monetary policy is more accommodative. But in such cases the nature of the stagflationary shock is pretty obvious quite promptly, and it is unnecessary to respond as if interest rates are the only information.

The price shock just discussed is an increase in price level, present and future, leaving expected inflation unchanged. An increase in the expected inflation rate is a shock of a different kind. It is equivalent to a reduction in demand for money at a given real interest rate. The nominal interest rate rises relative to the real rate, and the real rate falls. Thus inflationary expectations are expansionary, like a negative shock to demand for money. If this seems strange in these times, it is because experience itself has led people to expect that monetary policy itself will become more restrictive on news of higher inflation.

The only reason in the Poole analysis for a rule relating a monetary quantity only to the nominal interest rate, if to that, is that other information regarding shocks is not available. In fact there is plenty of other information, even within the horizon before policy variables are reset.

Changes in endogenous money quantities themselves, relative to unborrowed reserves, are indicative of changes in money demand. By themselves, they are as ambiguous as interest rates in telling whether the source is transactions demand connected with increases in GNP or prices, or greater liquidity preference. A number of "reforms" have been proposed to limit variability in the money multipliers connecting the monetary base or unborrowed reserves to intermediate aggregates. These include indexation of the discount rate to market interest rates and payment of a similarly indexed rate on reserves. They are objectionable on the ground that they, like the deregulation of deposit interest, enhance the volatility of interest rates and the vulnerability of business activity to purely financial shocks. In addition, they suppress the information contained in deviations of endogenous monetary quantities from expectations.

Other information available monthly or more frequently covers personal income, credit volume, prices, retail sales, production, employment, inventories, and orders. These data should enable the Fed's experts to diagnose the shocks occurring and to advise whether they are types that should be accommodated or not. What usefulness monetary aggregates have comes from their informational content, not from their semantic monetary character. The informational content is limited. Central banks should ask their staffs to devote more effort to obtaining and utilizing alternative and supplementary information.

Monetary Objectives, Targets and Operating Rules: A Multistage Framework

Central bankers cannot hope for easy lives administering mechanical rules independent of actual and prospective economic conditions. In the end there is no substitute for stochastic dynamic models of the economy linking policy instruments to contemporaneous and future outcomes. Policymakers use at least implicitly their models of the way the world works; it is better to make them explicit. They can and should regularly consider and evaluate various feasible deviations from a "current policies" reference path. New information about exogenous variables, stochastic disturbances, and structural equations is always flowing in. New observations tell whether current instrument settings, targets, and operating rules are having their expected and intended effects.

Instrument settings, targets, and operating rules are not locked in forever. It is important that their subordination to fundamental objectives be generally understood. Periodically policymakers must reconsider whether their policies are achieving to the degree possible the desired mixture of basic economic objectives.

To simplify a complex decision process and to aid public understanding, the central bank could use a hierarchical, multistage structure. The objective for several years ahead could be described in ranges of outcomes sought in paths of variables of basic concern: unemployment, real GNP, prices, capital formation. Ideally these would be consistent with the multiyear budget and economic program of the Congress and the Administration, and the Federal Reserve would have considerable input to these joint projections.

For two years ahead, the intermediate target should be nominal GNP growth, or as Robert Gordon (1983) has suggested, nominal final sales. This would indicate how the policymakers would allow price and productivity shocks to affect output and employment, while allowing complete freedom to offset velocity-of-money surprises with money supplies.

Indeed the Fed might advertise this target as a velocity-adjusted monetary aggregate, a concept toward which it has been groping in these last turbulent years, explaining departures from monetary aggregate targets as corrections for identifiable changes in the "meaning" of the measures, that is, their relation to nominal income. For periods of a year or more, a nominal GNP or final sales target makes much more sense than any monetary aggregate, or the monetary base.

A nominal GNP or final sales target implies for the duration of its tenure a one-for-one trade-off between price and quantity. An upward supply price shock would mean commensurately smaller real GNP growth. These terms of trade may not accord with national priorities. Separate ranges for price and quantity would allow an extra degree of freedom. But a nominal GNP target range is easier to explain and understand. In any case it can be reset annually, taking into account price and wage developments, unemployment and excess capacity, estimates of sustainable real growth rates, and other circumstances.

For shorter periods, one or two quarters ahead, the central bank could indicate targets or operating rules relating to intermediate money stocks, bank reserves, and short-term interest rates. These would be consistent with the intermediate range nominal income targets, which in turn would be intended to implement the longer range program. For each short-term horizon the target ranges or rules would remain constant. The policymakers are thus deciding and announcing how, if at all, instruments will be changed in response to surprises that occur during the interval.

I have argued: that monetary policy cannot be governed by irrevocably fixed rules blind to actual economic developments; that policies responsive to events cannot be prescribed fully in advance but ultimately depend upon discretion; that monetary authorities cannot escape responsibilities for real economic outcomes of significance to the society, as exemplified by recovery from the world depression; that choices of targets and operating rules should be guided by the ways they interact with economic and financial structure to convert shocks of various kinds into macroeconomic outcomes and by the probabilities of the several kinds of shocks; that for periods long enough for velocity shocks to be identified and offset, a nominal GNP or final sales target is much preferable to any intermediate monetary aggregate. I have sketched a multistage framework for the conduct of monetary policy that embodies these ideas. I know that central bankers will object because explicit policymaking on these lines makes their responsibilities for important economic outcomes transparent. They prefer to hide behind less meaningful descriptions of what they are doing. But there is no reason for the rest of us to respect that preference.

A final remark. I have discussed the architecture of national monetary policy as if it were isolated from fiscal policy and from the macroeconomic policies of other nations. Those are serious omissions, which I do not have time or space or wit to remedy. Monetary strategies, targets, and projections should be consistent with those on which the federal budget is based. The two types of macroeconomic policy should not be made by separate governments which scarcely communicate with each other. The pessimal mix of the two policies from which we now suffer is in part the result of such compartmentalization. Likewise, the state of the world economy is testimony to the disarray among the policies of the major economic powers, those represented at the latest do-nothing summit festival in Williamsburg. Somehow surely they could manage greater coordination in macroeconomic policy.

Literature Cited

Friedman, Milton. "Monetary Policy for the 1980s." In *To Promote Prosperity: U.S. Domestic Policy in the Mid-1980s*, edited by John H. Moore. Stanford, Calif.: Hoover Institution, 1984.

Gordon, Robert J. "The Conduct of Domestic Monetary Policy." Prepared for the Bank of Japan Centenary Conference on Monetary Policy in Our Times. Tokyo, June 22–24, 1983.

Hadjimichalakis, Michael G. *Monetary Policy and Modern Money Markets: Fixed versus Market Determined Deposit Rates.* Lexington, Mass.: Lexington Books, 1982.

Hall, Robert E. "Macroeconomic Policy under Structural Change." Prepared for the Federal Reserve Bank of Kansas City Symposium on Industrial Change and Public Policy. Kansas City, August 25–26, 1983.

Poole, William. "Optimal Choice of Monetary Policy Instruments in a Simple Stochastic Macro Model." *Quarterly Journal of Economics* 84 (May 1970), 197–216.

CHAPTER 17

THE MONETARY AND FISCAL POLICY MIX

Aggregate Demand and Supply

In this lecture, I shall discuss the strategy of what economists call *demand management*—the policies of the government, including the Federal Reserve, that affect the aggregate spending of the population on goods and services and so act upon the economy. I refer to the economy as a whole, not to particular products or markets.

I distinguish *demand* from *supply* in the following sense: During business cycles the economy is not always constrained by its capacity to produce, its supply potential. Cyclical fluctuations reflect variations, for one reason or another, in the overall demand for goods and services, and thus for workers to produce them. In the long run, however, the output of goods and services in the country is clearly limited by the capacity of the economy to produce.

"Supply-side" economics concerns the growth of productive capacity. "Demand-side" economics, my main focus in this lecture, has to do with the management of the economy, not for accelerating its long-run capacity growth, but for stabilizing the business cycle and avoiding excesses of unemployment on the one hand and inflation on the other. The two "sides" are, however, related in a way that I will be discussing and trying to describe. Some strategies of short-run demand management are better for long-run growth than others.

In recent years, I think it is fair to say, the capacity of the economy to produce goods and services—potential output—has not been the binding constraint on the real output of the United States economy. Rather, the constraint has been the adequacy of aggregate demand to purchase the output of the economy. This has been true since 1980, when we fell into the first of two recessions that occurred in rapid succession. We began recovering from the second one at the end of 1982, but we haven't yet fully recovered. For more than two years the rate of utilization of the economy's potential has been flat; only 80 percent of industrial capacity has been utilized, recently even less. Normal capacity utilization in our economy in prosperity has been at 85, 86, or 87 percent. The unemployment rate of workers has been stuck for more than two years at 7 percent of the labor force, plus or minus a couple of tenths, more often plus than minus. There is no evidence that 7 percent is as low an unemployment rate as we can have today without setting off inflation. It's hard to find any bottlenecks or scarcities or shortages in this economy, or any tendency for wages to accelerate. The inflation rate has been extremely well-behaved, even after the end of the deep recession of 1981–82. This means that ever since 1979, demand management, or short-run stabilization policy, which is the main business of the Federal Reserve, has been the decisive determinant of unemployment, capacity utilization, and the growth of real GNP.

Demand Management, Fiscal and Monetary

Two major instruments of demand management are available to the central government in the United States and other advanced economies: on the one hand, monetary policy and, on the other, fiscal policy. Reference was made in the introductions to my service in Washington on the President's Council of Economic Advisers. At that time we on the Council were doing a teaching job. We had an important student, the President of the United States, John F. Kennedy, who seemed not to have absorbed a lot of economics in his undergraduate training. He was a good student and able to learn fast, and we were good teachers, I must say. We knew we were getting somewhere one day when he said "I think I now know the difference between monetary policy and fiscal policy. Monetary policy begins with an "M," and the chairman of the Federal Reserve is [William McChesney] Martin, so that's monetary policy. What we do in the budget must be fiscal policy." These two instruments of demand management policy are the ingredients I refer to when I speak of "the mix."

How does the use of these two instruments work on aggregate demand? Fiscal policy involves spending money. When the government spends more money directly on goods and services—mainly armaments these days—or transfers money to the beneficiaries of Social Security and other programs, aggregate demand for goods and services increases. You may or may not like particular programs, but how the money is spent doesn't matter for our immediate purpose. What matters is the additional overall spending on goods and services. If you don't believe that defense spending is stimulating, I invite you to come to Connecticut or Massachusetts to see that economies supplying defense-related products do prosper. Tax reductions work the same way. People generally spend a large fraction of their tax savings. For example, in 1981 we had a mammoth reduction in income taxes under the Economic Recovery Tax Act of 1981. To be sure, it was advertised by the Administration and in the press as a supply-side tax cut. Its philosophy was to increase incentives for working more, saving more, producing more, and taking more risk. Thus it was meant to be a policy to increase the capacity of the economy, its productivity, its potential output. In the immediate circumstances of the day, however, when the potential output of the economy was far above its actual performance, it worked to increase spending. The recipients of the tax cut didn't know that they weren't supposed to spend the proceeds, and so they spent them. Thus it worked as a demand-side stimulus.

Monetary policy generally works in ways that lower or raise interest rates and raise or lower market values of bonds, stocks, and other assets. Through these effects, monetary policy stimulates or restrains spending for investment goods—for house building, business plant and equipment, and inventories.

Exchange Rates and Aggregate Demand

There is one other mechanism by which monetary policy works to expand or restrict demand, a mechanism fairly new in American experience—and in world experience. Recent events have given a striking demonstration of its power. It works through the balance of exports and imports in foreign trade. Because of the floating exchange rate regime in which the United States and other countries have been operating since 1973, along with the amazing international mobility of funds, immense amounts of money can move rapidly across the exchange rates from, say, dollar assets into yen assets or vice versa, or into and out of pound-sterling, deutsche mark assets, or others. Recently we have had a textbook example of this mechanism, which, I must say to the credit of us economists, was well understood in theory before it actually occurred with such remarkable fidelity.

In the 1980s, thanks to our monetary and fiscal policies, interest rates in the United States were high, even higher than interest rates in other advanced economies. They attracted funds across the currency exchanges into dollar assets, often U.S. Treasury bills and bonds but into the whole range of dollar-denominated assets as well. Likewise, they deterred Americans from lending funds overseas. The result was a big demand for dollars relative to other currencies, which bid up the price of a dollar in yen and other major currencies. The dollar became costly to foreigners; other currencies became inexpensive to Americans. The further result was that people didn't buy many American goods, while we bought a lot of foreign goods at bargain dollar prices. We developed the massive surplus of imports over exports that is still reported every month.

Here, then, was a powerful mechanism by which a monetary policy that actively raised interest rates affected demand for U.S. goods and services. By reducing exports and raising imports, it diverted American demand to foreign goods instead of goods produced by American labor and capital. That supplemented the normal, old-fashioned way tight monetary policies and high interest rates work, by restricting residential construction and business investment.

The Fiscal/Monetary Policy Mix

In discussing the policy *mix*, I want to give the word a precise meaning. I am not talking about a mix-up between the two policies, although that may often occur. I am not referring to the two policies in a general way. I make a precise distinction between the total stimulus administered by the two policies and the relative contributions of each of the two policies to that total. It's as if you have two types of medicine: first you ask what is the total dose of the two medicines together; and second, how is the dose split between the two medicines. Right now I want to address the second question, how the dose is split between the two medicines—the mix.

THE MONETARY AND FISCAL POLICY MIX

Figure 17.1 relates the after-tax interest rate in the economy and the real (inflation-corrected) output of the economy. The horizontal axis represents output, real GNP, labeled "Y." The vertical axis is the interest rate after tax: $(1-t)r$, one minus the tax rate, that quantity times the interest rate. The "IS" curves, for investment and saving, tell how the interest rate has to move for given monetary and fiscal policies in order to induce the amount of spending that would buy exactly the output measured on the horizontal axis. Each IS curve is sloping down, because lower interest rates are needed to get people to spend more money. When interest rates are low, people spend more money on investment and borrow more for consumption as well. The down-sloping effect also comes through exports and imports, as I already explained. Lower interest rates mean the dollar is cheaper, and that helps our exports relative to our imports. All these effects together make an IS curve slope down, as shown.

This figure shows a whole family of IS curves. Some are higher than the others and further to the right. The position of a curve depends on government policies. (Other things too can affect the position, but for our purposes the point is that the position depends on policies.) Specifically, the position of an IS curve depends on fiscal policy. Each of the IS curves could be regarded as being drawn for a particular budget program, encompassing the federal tax system, the expenditure budget and the legislation determining transfer entitlements like Social Security. Curve IS_a is a relatively tight budget policy, whereas IS_b is somewhat looser, with more spending or lower taxes or both. IS_c and IS_d are even looser, even more stimulating. Think of the effects of the Reagan Administration's budgets from 1981 on as moving up to the right, shifting to higher IS curves by decreasing taxes and increasing defense expenditures.

Now consider the upward sloping LM curves, which are determined by our friends of the Fed. Any one such curve answers the following question: given a certain amount of money that the Fed is willing to provide to the economy, what will happen to interest rates if output should increase? The curve says the interest rate will go up. Why? Because banks have only so many reserves, and households and businesses have only so much money in the banks and in their pockets and tills. Higher outputs mean higher levels of business activity and more competition by borrowers for the limited amount of funds that the Fed is willing to supply. That

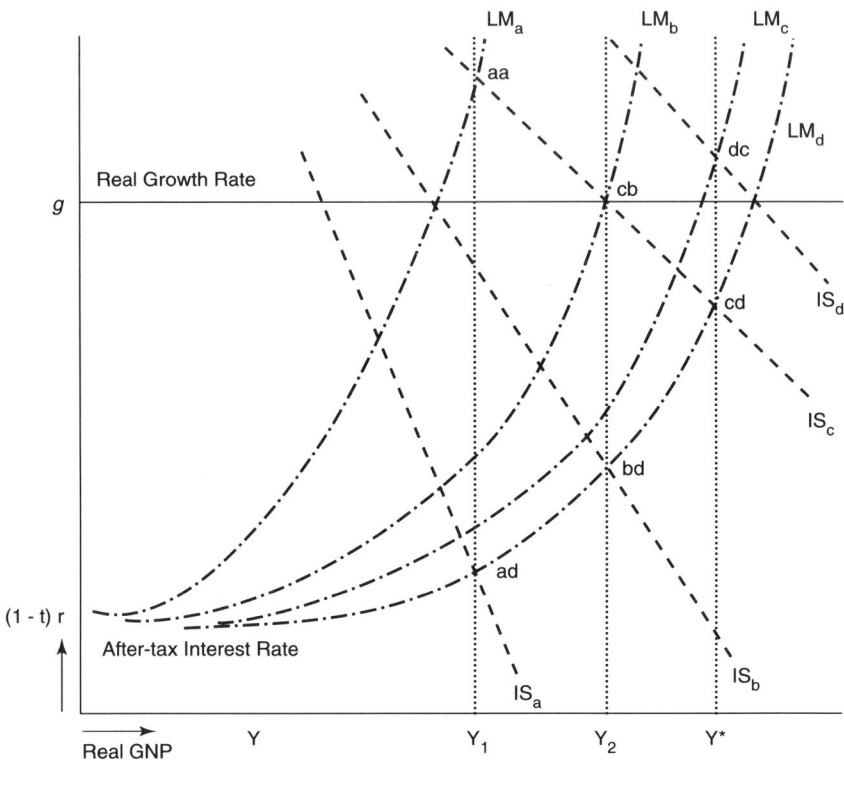

Figure 17.1
Policy mixes, interest rates, and GNP. The diagram shows how the same GNP values, Y_1 or or Y_2 or Y^* (full employment output), can be achieved by different mixes of monetary and fiscal policies. Fiscal policy determines which IS locus the economy is on; curves higher and to the right result from easier fiscal policies. Monetary policy determines which LM curve the economy is on; curves lower and to the right represent easier monetary policies. The horizontal line at g depicts the real growth rate of GNP. As discussed in the text, an after-tax interest rate above g means that federal debt grows explosively indefinitely.

competition will raise interest rates. Economists typically label this sort of relationship, "LM" for liquidity, money.

Just as there is a family of IS curves, so there is a family of LM curves. In this abstract representation, fiscal policy chooses a member of the IS family, as I already explained. Monetary policy chooses a member of the LM family. If the Federal Open Market Committee, which meets every six weeks in Washington, decides to be more generous to the economy in the amount of money it provides, it will move to an LM curve further to the right and down; any given output of income will be associated with a lower interest rate. Easier monetary policy moves the economy's LM curve to the right, and tighter monetary policy moves it to the left. As all economics students know, economists like intersections of curves, such as those that show the price of peanuts and the quantity bought and sold where a peanut demand curve crosses a peanut supply curve. Here we are interested in the intersection of an IS and an LM showing the interest rate and output generated by the corresponding fiscal policy and monetary policy. In Figure 17.1 there are lots of such intersections, indicating that there are several ways of achieving the same output, the same value of Y. All of these policy combinations deliver the same total dose, but the mixes differ. Different mixes of fiscal and monetary policy can generate the same aggregate demand, the same output, the same employment and unemployment, and the same capacity utilization rate. For example, the output represented by Y_2 can be created by the combination of monetary and fiscal policy designated by bd as well as by the combination marked cb. The higher intersection has a tighter monetary policy, and thus a higher interest rate and a relatively easier fiscal policy than bd. The intersection bd, on the other hand, has an easier monetary policy and a tighter fiscal policy, defined by an IS curve to the left.

Keeping Figure 17.1 in mind, let's think about what has happened in the United States during the last few years. Through a combination of policy decisions starting in 1979, we arrived at high intersections. That is, monetary policy was tight and fiscal policy was easy compared with mixes that could have produced the same output. The same Y could have been achieved with a different mix of policies.

Figure 17.2 makes the same point in another way. The horizontal axis represents fiscal policy. Moving to the right means easier budgets with

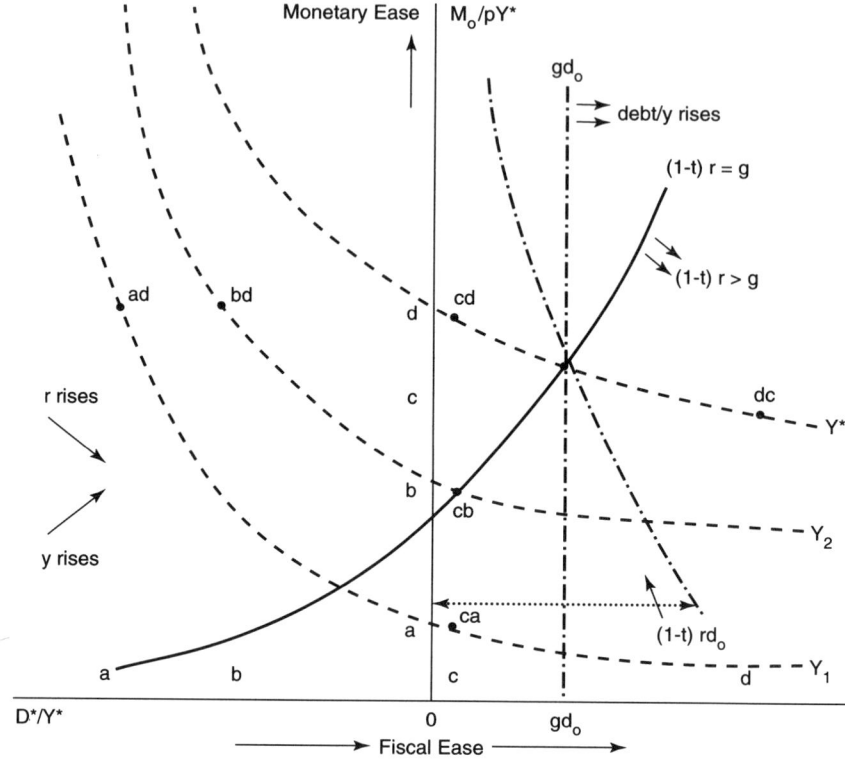

Figure 17.2
Fiscal and monetary policies and GNP outcomes. The information of Figure 17.1 is presented here in a different way. Monetary policy is measured by the ratio of the monetary base, in real terms, to potential output pY^*. Isoquants—combinations of the two policies that yield the same real GNP—are pictured for Y_1, Y_2, and Y^*. Points of intersection in Figure 17.1 are placed here also and labeled the same (ad, bd, etc.). The vertical line gd_o tells how big a deficit will keep the debt–GNP ratio at d_o, given GNP growth at rate g. The downward sloping curve $(1-t)rd_o$ is the interest cost of the existing debt d_o. The upward sloping curve $(1-t)r = g$ is the boundary between stable (above) and unstable (below) debt–GNP ratios, as explained in the text.

THE MONETARY AND FISCAL POLICY MIX

lower taxes, more spending, and bigger deficits. Monetary policy is on the vertical axis. Going up means easier monetary policy, with the Fed providing more money relative to total output. The dashed curves in this diagram are called isoquants (same quantity). All the points on the isoquant Y_1 are different ways of getting a given output Y_1. All the points on the next higher isoquant Y_2 represent policy combinations that produce the common result Y_2. The two Y_2 mixes we singled out in Figure 17.1 are both shown here, too, as cb and bd. One of them has easy fiscal policy and tight money and the other has tight fiscal policy and easy money. Then there is Y^*, which represents full capacity output—not the forced economic mobilization that occurred during World War II but the highest output a peacetime market economy can expect without having a resurgence of accelerating prices, rising inflation. (I don't know how large that is nor do I know what the corresponding lowest inflation-safe unemployment rate is. I was arguing with the local Fed people this morning about whether that figure is closer to 7 or to 6 percent or even lower than that now. As I said earlier, I am sure it's not as high as 7 percent.)

Prices vs. Quantities: The Common Funnel Theory

If our objective is just to determine output, our two policies evidently give us more degrees of freedom than we really need. We have at least two instruments—maybe more, considering that there are different kinds of taxes and expenditures, and several monetary tools. Since we have more tools than we need, why can't we achieve some other goal at the same time? We know that the the main constraint on demand, output, and employment is the danger of inflation. Why not use one instrument to control inflation and the other one to get a desirable level of output and employment? For example, why not keep inflation down by tight money while we push output up by easy budgets? Why not manipulate the mix of the policies to combat inflation and unemployment simultaneously? That would be ideal. Unfortunately, the world is not made that way—at least according to the strong belief of most macroeconomists.

This belief I call the "common funnel theory," illustrated in Figure 17.3. Fiscal and monetary policy together determine aggregate dollar spending for GNP. They do not, however, determine how dollar spending is divided between prices and quantities. The common funnel theory goes

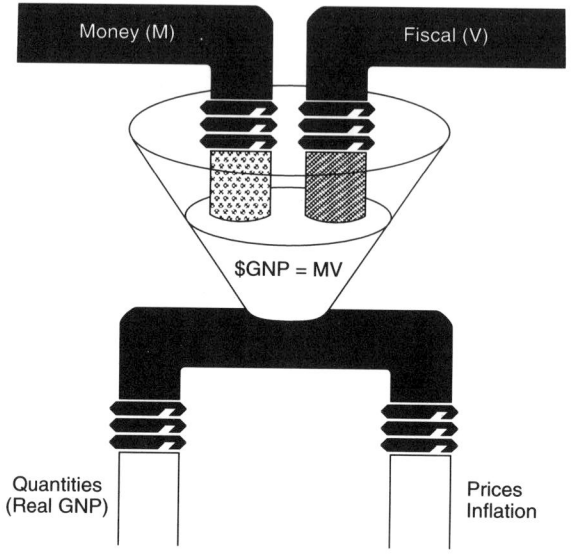

Figure 17.3
The common funnel theory. This schematic diagram illustrates the point that the mix of price/quantity outcomes is independent of the sources of aggregate dollar demand. Monetary policy affects the supply of money and fiscal policy its circuit velocity. It is the product MV (money supply times circuit velocity), which is equal to dollar GNP, which represents demand for goods, services, and labor and induces output and price responses from businesses and workers.

as follows: Consider an injection of spending in dollars into the economy. Its size matters for prices and quantities. But whether it comes from the Fed or the budget doesn't matter; it produces inflation and unemployment in the same combination either way. In Figure 17.3 we see that money is being provided by the Fed (M), while fiscal stimulus is being poured in (V). They go into a mixing pot. Then they come out in the form of prices and quantities. It doesn't matter from what source they came in, whether V or M, whether from fiscal stimulus or the Fed; they come out in the same proportions in changes in prices and changes in quantities.

Those proportions do depend on the state of the economy. If the economy is tight in terms of capacity utilization, then most of the demand goes into prices and little into quantity. If it is slack in terms of capacity utilization and labor employment, then the injections will show up mostly in quantities and only slightly in prices. The price/quantity outcome depends on the state of the economy, not on the sources of the demand or the policies that generated the demand.

Thus it is not true, according to the common funnel proposition, that the Fed has a particular handle on prices and the budget a particular handle on quantities. Some people in Washington thought that in 1981 or at least said that, but it flies in the face of most evidence and theory about how the economy works. We cannot solve the unemployment/inflation dilemma by mixing monetary and fiscal policy in different proportions.

Exchange Rates and Inflation

One necessary amendment to this discouraging proposition arises in international trade through the implications of floating exchange rates for macroeconomic policies, mentioned above. To understand this amendment let's go back to my previous story, in which tight money produces high interest rates and causes the dollar to shoot up in value relative to foreign currencies. This made foreign imports—Toyotas, Sonys, European vacations—cheap in dollars to Americans and helped our process of disinflation. The cheapness of foreign goods, which enter our price indexes in some proportion, gave us some relief from inflation in the early 1980s. That mechanism is now working in the opposite direction as the recent depreciation of the dollar becomes reflected in dollar prices of imports and exports.

This consequence of floating exchange rates is a point in favor of a tight money/easy fiscal mix. Relative to other mixes, it will have higher interest rates with the same outcome in employment and output, the same Y in Figures 17.1 and 17.2. This mix will be somewhat less inflationary, or more disinflationary, than a mix in which low interest rates are the result of easy money combined with a tight fiscal budget.

But there is a catch, as we are now learning: A high exchange rate obtained through higher interest rates is only temporary. We can't live with massive import surpluses forever. At some point—a point we recently reached in the United States—the exchange rate has to go down again, the dollar has to depreciate. As that happens, we have to give back the price reductions we earned earlier by artificial appreciation of the currency. After all, the same movements of exchange rates that made things cheap for us made things dear for other countries. This game is not one that all countries can play at the same time. One reason that Japan and Germany objected to the high value of the dollar is that it made not only American imports but also oil, which is invoiced in dollars, much more expensive in yen and deutsche marks.

For these reasons, I do not regard this qualification to the common funnel theory as a really important consideration in deciding on the monetary-fiscal mix. The gains in inflation control from choosing one mix rather than another to achieve the same output and employment are likely to be small and temporary for the United States.

Policy Mixes, Crowding Out, and Long-Run Growth

How do we decide the mix of policies? Assume that someone has decided on the total dose, that is, the path of GNP and unemployment. What is a socially rational choice of the mix of policies to support that decision? The mix does make a difference, much more for the long run than for the short run. At the beginning of the lecture, I pointed out that demand management strategy does affect the long-run capacity of the economy to produce. The policy mix makes that connection. The reason is that the *composition* of national output will be different with a different mix, even though *aggregate* GNP is the same with one mix as with another. The tight money and easy fiscal mix emphasizes consumption relative to investment—consumption by government and by private sector relative to future-oriented uses of national output. High interest rates deter investment, while an easy fiscal stance encourages consumption through tax cuts, high transfer payments, or high government current expenditure. True, government purchases are not always for consumption; if the government were running deficits to accumulate public capital which would enhance the productivity and capacity of the economy over the long run, this characterization would not be valid.

Recently the federal government has been financing current expenditures by deficit spending, and the Federal Reserve has countered the expansionary effects of this fiscal policy by high interest rates. The result is a larger consumption component of output than with a different policy mix. High interest rates have "crowded out" some domestic investment and a spectacular amount of foreign investment. By running big trade deficits, we are spending the overseas capital we previously acquired and going into debt to the rest of the world. This is just as damaging to the future prospects of Americans as failing to replace worn-out or obsolete capital equipment at home. Although our record of domestic capital formation in the last several years is not bad, we have financed it essentially by mortgaging productive assets to the rest of the world. That cannot be regarded as future-oriented activity. Whether domestic or foreign investment is crowded out, future generations pay the price.

Suppose we had achieved the same recovery since 1982 with a tighter budget and an appropriately easier, lower-interest-rate, monetary policy. Then we would not have suffered such big deficits in our balance of trade. We would have had as much, perhaps even more, domestic investment, and it would not be mortgaged to the rest of the world. That is one reason why I and many other economists have strongly preferred a mix easier in money and tighter in budget.

Stable and Unstable Policies

There is another reason for that preference. Freedom of choice among policy mixes is not unlimited. The mix chosen in the United States, at least until recently, is one that cannot be sustained. Let me explain: A substantial part of the federal budget is payment of interest on the national debt. Suppose that the interest rate the government has to pay on the debt is higher than the rate of economic growth. Suppose, realistically, that the Treasury's average interest rate is 7 percent, while the economy is growing in current dollar GNP at 6 percent per year, with 3 percent inflation and 3 percent real growth. Even if the budget is otherwise balanced, this disparity alone will make the debt grow by 7 percent while GNP will be growing by only 6 percent. As the debt grows faster than GNP, the interest burden will grow further, so that the deficit and debt become still larger relative to GNP. This accelerating process will continue year after year. This would be true even if the rest of the government budget were exactly balanced, but of course that has not been the case. A deficit in the "primary" budget—that is, exclusive of debt service—makes the process more explosive. The ratio of debt to GNP rises indefinitely, faster and faster, as does the deficit as a share of GNP. An even larger share of the population's saving is diverted from productive investment,

Table 17.1
Federal Fiscal History and Projections

	(As percent of GNP)				(Percent per Year)		(Percent)
	(1) Debt Beginning of Period	(2) Primary Deficit	(3) Total Deficit	(4) Real Deficit	(5) Net Real Interest Rate Assumed	(6) Growth of Real GNP	(7) Equilibrium Debt/GNP Ratio
1952–57	65	−0.6	0.3	−1.0	−0.7	2.8	−17
1958–66	48	−0.5	0.1	−0.8	−0.7	3.4	−12
1967–74	36	0.3	1.1	−0.5	−2.8	3.8	5
1975–79	23	1.4	2.5	−0.8	−2.8	3.5	22
1980–85	22	2.6	4.5	2.7	0.3	1.9	45
1986	38	2.7	5.2	4.0	3.4	3.0	Unstable
1991 A	35	−1.9	0.0	−1.4	1.5	3.0	−126
1991 B	35	−0.7	1.4	0.0	2.0	3.0	−70
1991 C	35	0.2	2.5	1.1	2.5	3.0	35

1991 A Balanced Budget, Gramm-Rudman-Hollings.
1991 B Balanced Budget, Correcting Interest for Inflation (4%).
1991 C Stabilizing Debt Relative to GNP.
Source: Author's calculations. Before 1980, originally presented in *Towards a Reconstruction of Federal Budgeting*, The Conference Board, 1983, pp. 51–59.

at home or abroad, into financing the federal government. As "crowding out" becomes more and more severe, the interest rate itself rises. The policy mix becomes a still tighter money, easier budget combination. The circle is really vicious.

Note the horizontal line g, "Real Growth Rate," in Figure 17.1 and the solid curve $(1 - t)r = g$ in Figure 17.2. These depict the boundary I have just been discussing; crossing it leads to the vicious circle just described. At this limit the interest rate becomes the same as the growth rate. If you go to mixes tighter in monetary policy and looser in fiscal policy, you enter the unstable territory of exploding debt.

The Policy Mix in the United States Today

Table 17.1 presents some data on the United States' federal debt and deficits since 1952. It shows the ratios of federal debt (to the public) to

GNP at the beginning of each of several periods. In 1952, for example, the public debt was 65 percent of one year's gross national product. As the Table shows, the ratio declined until 1980, to about 22 percent. The debt-GNP ratio actually started declining right after World War II, which had raised the ratio to 120 percent. While many people think the federal government has been following profligate fiscal policies continuously, as long as anyone can remember, at least since the Great Depression, the Table shows that this charge is far from true. The debt grew more slowly than GNP from 1946 to 1980.

Things changed radically in the 1980s. In the last five years the debt to GNP ratio has risen to 38 percent. That is a big increase, though 38 percent is still not a disastrously high number; we have had higher numbers before without disaster. Nonetheless, in the 1950s and 1960s the ratio was declining, while in the 1980s it has been rising.

Table 17.1 also shows the primary deficit in percent of GNP. This is the deficit we would have had if there had been no outstanding debt at the beginning of the period. For example, in the first period, 1952 to 1957, the primary budget showed an average surplus of 0.6 of one percent of GNP. It continued in surplus or close to balance in all periods through 1974. In 1986 prior to Gramm–Rudman, however, the primary deficit would have been 2.7 percent of GNP, the largest ever in peace time. The next column shows the total deficit, including interest payments on the debt, again in percent of GNP. The total deficit, which was very close to zero in the 1950s and 1960s, has risen to about 5 percent of GNP. Most of the increase occurred after 1980. Much of it, as the Table shows, is due to the tight money/easy fiscal mix, which brought high interest rates and in turn a tremendous surge of interest payments compared to the years before 1980.

Column 4 of Table 17.1 shows the "Real Deficit." Applying inflation accounting principles to the government budget and its debt means counting only real interest—the difference between the interest rate and the inflation rate—as a cost to the government. The implicit assumption is that the public's latent demand for government debt will cause people to save enough to maintain their holdings of the debt in real terms. In other words, people are assumed to understand that part of the high nominal interest they receive just pays for the loss in the real principal value of government securities due to inflation. Inflation accounting gives lower deficit figures, but the pattern shows a very sharp increase since 1980.

Columns 5 and 6 of Table 17.1 compare the real growth rate of the economy with the interest rate the government has to pay on its debt. I pointed out earlier the danger that confronts us if the interest that the Treasury has to pay (allowing for taxes) exceeds the growth rate of the economy. We were never close to that point until now; we crossed the line some time between 1980 and 1985. Before 1980 real GNP growth always exceeded interest cost by a wide margin—you get the same answer by comparing nominal interest rates and dollar GNP growth. But since then the comparison turned the other way, and these circumstances produced the unstable vicious spiral I described. This mix of monetary and fiscal policy simply cannot be allowed to continue indefinitely.

The last column is a bit more esoteric. It addresses the question: Is there a value at which the debt-GNP ratio would settle down permanently, as long as the parameters of the budget and the economy remained constant? If so, what is it? The answers depend on the values of three parameters: the primary deficit in ratio to GNP, x; the net (after-tax) interest rate $(1 - t)r$; and the rate of growth of GNP, g. The answer to the first question is "yes," if $(1 - t)r$ is less than g, as was true in every period except 1986. The answer is "no, unstable," if $(1 - t)r$ exceeds g, as in 1986. When a numerical answer to the question exists, it can be calculated for each period from the parameters of the period. Those numbers are shown in column 7. The negative numbers are especially hypothetical. Their significance is that the debt-GNP ratio would rapidly decline and, in principle, would settle down only if and when the government became a creditor rather than a debtor.

Three possibilities are shown for 1991 in Table 17.1. All of them assume that through fiscal year 1990 deficits will be reduced according to the Gramm–Rudman–Hollings schedule, enough to lower the debt-GNP ratio to 35 percent. The first scenario, A, assumes the Gramm–Rudman–Hollings target of a balanced total budget by conventional accounting will be met in 1991 and ever thereafter. As the applicable row of Table 17.1 shows, this is a very austere regimen, requiring a primary surplus of 1.9 percent of GNP, about $120 billion in 1991. A less austere policy

Table 17.2
National Saving and Investment as Percentage Shares of Net National Product, 1951–1985

	National Saving			Net Investment	
	Private	Government	Total	Foreign	Domestic
1951–60	8.4	−0.7	7.7	0.3	7.4
1961–70	9.2	−1.0	8.1	0.6	7.6
1971–80	9.7	−2.0	7.7	0.3	7.4
1981–85	8.6	−4.7	3.9	−1.3	5.2
1985	8.8	−5.4	3.4	−3.1	6.5

Source: Barry Bosworth, "Fiscal Fitness: Deficit Reduction and the Economy," *Brookings Bulletin*, Winter/Spring 1986, Table 1, p. 5.

would be to balance the budget calculated according to inflation accounting. The result is given in row B. The third possibility is to let bygones be bygones and be satisfied to maintain a 35 percent debt-GNP ratio. As row C shows, this could be approximated just by balancing the primary budget. The total deficit would then be 7 percent of the debt, 2.5 percent of GNP; the real deficit would be only 1.1 percent of GNP.

Table 17.2, borrowed from an article by Barry Bosworth in *Brookings Bulletin* of Winter/Spring 1986, offers additional relevant insights into our topic. Bosworth's numbers show for several periods national saving relative to net national product (NNP). (NNP is smaller than GNP by allowing for capital consumption.) National saving is composed of two parts, "private" (inclusive of state and local governments) and federal. In the 1950s private saving amounted to about 8.4 percent of NNP, but the government had a small deficit, and so national saving was 7.7 percent of NNP. Similarly in the 1960s and even the 1970s the national saving ratio was still close to 8 percent. Throughout these decades net national saving went both into domestic investment and, via trade surpluses, into increasing the nation's net claims against the rest of the world. Once again, the drastic change occurred in the 1980s. Federal dissaving offset more than half of private saving. Foreign investment, in consequence, turned strongly negative, and, even so, domestic investment fell relative to NNP.

These dismal outcomes are the result of the policy mix. The mix of fiscal and monetary policy we have drifted into in recent years is bizarre, extreme, and unprecedented. It has had very unfortunate consequences. This policy was meant, according to the rhetoric of 1981, to increase investment. It was supposed to be oriented toward using resources in ways that would increase productivity and long-term growth. The results are just the opposite. Fully 97 percent of the additional output the country has been able to produce since 1978 or 1979 has been consumed, either publicly or privately.

How did we manage to adopt such a bad policy mix? Tight monetary policies were used to bring down inflation after 1979, and real interest rates have never been the same. Then came the reckless budget policies of the 1980s—big tax cuts and rapid growth of defense spending.

Changing this policy mix is a high priority. We seem to be embarked upon a course that will tighten the budget under the gun of Gramm-Rudman. I do not myself believe Gramm-Rudman is a good way to correct our fiscal policy, and I think the target of balancing the conventional budget is overkill. I believe the federal government needs more tax revenue, but this is not the forum for arguing these points.

In any case, let me emphasize, fiscal correction is only half the needed remedy. The other half is up to the Federal Reserve, to whom I never fail to give advice, generally unheeded, when given the chance. As budget policy is tightened, monetary policy must be eased and interest rates substantially lowered. Otherwise, we will not achieve the same results in output and employment as under the present mix. Indeed, there is ample evidence now that the overall dose of stimulus from the two policies together is inadequate. It's not enough to keep the economy from outright recession. It needs to be rescued from stagnation. It is not enough to keep the unemployment rate near 7 percent and capacity utilization at 78 percent. The economy can do better than that without courting renewed inflation. In the present circumstances fiscal policy obviously can make no contribution to the resumption and completion of the recovery; it will instead be moving us the other way. Prosperity is the responsibility of the institution playing host to us today, the Federal Reserve System.

Appendix

The formulas used for the calculations reported in column 7 of Table 1 are as follows: Let $\dot{d}$ be the speed at which the ratio d is rising. The other symbols were defined in the text, p. 502. Then,

$$\dot{d} = x + [(1-t)r - g]d \tag{1}$$

This tells us immediately that d will be rising if neither x nor $[(1-t)r - g]$ is negative and if one or both of them is positive. We can also see, by putting $\dot{d}$ equal to zero, that the equilibrium or stationary ratio d* is $x/(r(1-t) - g)$. Therefore,

$$\dot{d} = [(1-t)r - g](d - d^*) \tag{2}$$

Equation (2) tells us that if $[(1-t)r - g]$ is negative d moves toward its equilibrium value d*. If $[(1-t)r - g]$ is positive, however, it moves away from d*, which is then an uninteresting unstable stationary point.

CHAPTER 18

THE MONETARY-FISCAL MIX: LONG-RUN IMPLICATIONS

Since 1981 the United States has faced, for the first time in history, the prospect that the federal debt would grow faster than the national product indefinitely. Economists have been prominent among the Cassandras deploring runaway public debt, but they have not been very specific about its hazards to the health of the nation. The usual story is "crowding out." The citizens' savings are limited. The more that the federal government borrows, the less are available for capital investments, the sources of productivity advances on which the living standards of the future depend. This is an unexciting story of slowdown in growth, and we are usually imprecise about magnitudes and speeds, and especially about whether, how, and when government borrowing leads to a catastrophic crisis.

The purpose of this paper is to present explicitly and precisely the crowding-out story, in a way that exposes the roles of the parameters of fiscal and monetary policies and the macroeconomic structure. The model is first presented algebraically, and then illustrated numerically by simulations assuming arbitrary, but, it is hoped, plausible parameter values.

For many sets of parameter values, these simulations do end in catastrophes, which can be precisely described and dated. I want to be clear at the outset that these are illustrative exercises, warnings—not predictions. They are, it is true, motivated by recent trends in the United States. But my prediction is that tax and/or expenditure policies will sooner or later be changed enough to stabilize the debt/GNP ratio. Indeed, those changes appear to be on the way already.

Reprinted by permission from *American Economic Review* 76(2) (May 1986): 213–218.

1 The Model: General Structure

Since I am here concerned with long-run trends, the structure of the model is borrowed from neoclassical growth theory. Full employment of an exogenously growing labor force is assumed. Gross output is produced by labor and fixed capital; it is divided between consumption and investment by the saving decisions of household members who are both workers and capitalists. The production function allows for variable proportions of the two inputs. The marginal productivity of capital determines the short-term interest rate.

Government debt *is* private wealth in this model. That is why it crowds out the alternative store of value, productive fixed capital. Ricardo-Barro equivalence effects, whatever their general validity, are not appropriate here. No one expects deficit-reducing tax increases or spending cuts when none have been put in place and the government denies or ignores their necessity. The message of this exercise is that they do need to be put in place so that people have credible reason to expect them.

Transactions with the rest of the world are not modeled in this exercise. In practice, as shown by recent experience, crowding out of net foreign investments (current account surpluses) mitigates the impact of budget deficits on domestic capital formation. But borrowing abroad cannot in general spare the economy the consequences of allowing government debt to absorb ever increasing shares of private saving. It could do so only if foreigners were willing to lend to us indefinitely at real interest rates below our economy's trend rate of real growth.

There is nothing new in studying long-run crowding out by use of neoclassical growth models. That is commonly done by comparative static analysis of steady states. Reduction in the fraction of national product saved and invested, resulting in the case at hand from governmental dissaving, moves the economy slowly from one steady-state path to another. The second path has a smaller capital-labor intensity than the first, therefore lower real wages and lower per capita consumption. Neither the transitional dynamics nor the differences between equilibrium paths are very dramatic. Students to whom this scenario of crowding out is exhibited yawn and wonder what all the shouting is about.

What is different in my simulations is attention to the possibility that, for quite realistic values of parameters, no steady states exist, or that the only one close to the initial conditions is an unstable equilibrium. In these cases an unstable vicious circle can lead fairly quickly to a dramatic crisis.

The key departure from the usual projections of deficits and debt growth and their effects is to make interest rates endogenous. Interest costs contribute to deficits and the growth of public debt. Increases in rates are the mechanism by which government borrowing squeezes capital investment.

Monetary policy enters the model via the fraction of public debt monetized by the central bank. Here I assume that the Federal Reserve holds the inflation rate constant and determines the degree of monetization accordingly. A higher inflation target slows down the pace of crowding out, because greater "seignorage" lowers the interest cost on total debt. In this full-employment model, there are no direct monetary effects on capital formation, which is governed wholly by saving. Given the fiscal parameters, the only way the central bank can alter policy is to change its inflation target.

There are two parameters of fiscal policy. The main fiscal parameter is the ratio of the *primary deficit*—the deficit exclusive of after-tax interest outlays—to *GNP*. Given this parameter, changes in the income tax rate make a difference in two familiar ways. Private saving depends on after-tax income, and both saving and money demand may depend on after-tax interest rates.

2 The Model in Detail

The nonfederal sector of the economy holds at all times a stock of wealth equal to a multiple μ of the *GNP*. Life cycle theory suggests that non-human wealth is a multiple, w, of after-tax labor income, which here is a constant fraction $1 - \alpha$ of *GNP*, where α is the elasticity of gross output with respect to capital in a standard two-factor Cobb-Douglas constant-returns-of-scale production function. Then, writing the federal proportional income tax rate as τ and letting $u = 1 - \tau$, we have

$$\mu_0 = wu(1 - \alpha). \tag{1}$$

Wealth demand may also be related to the after-tax interest rate uR. Here this relation is assumed linear; a nonnegative coefficient β represents the response of savings to interest.

$$\mu = \mu_0 + \beta u(R - R_0) = \mu'_0 + \beta u R. \tag{2}$$

(R_0 is introduced simply for calibration of the initial conditions of the simulations. Other variables similarly subscripted below play the same role.)

The wealth-*GNP* ratio μ is composed of the capital-*GNP* ratio k and the government debt/*GNP* ratio d:

$$k + d = \mu. \tag{3}$$

Debt takes two forms: nonmonetary, costing the government an after-tax real rate of interest r; and monetary, costing the government zero nominal interest, thus a real rate the negative of the inflation rate π. The stock of base money is a fraction h of *GNP*. The demand for base money, relative to *GNP*, depends on the nominal interest rate $r + \pi$. For a given inflation target π the central bank sets h to meet the demand:

$$\begin{aligned} h &= h_0 - \gamma(r - r_0) - \gamma(\pi - \pi_0) \\ &= h'_0 - \gamma(r + \pi). \end{aligned} \tag{4}$$

The nonnegative coefficient γ is higher the more sensitive are demands for base money to nominal after-tax interest rates.

The fundamental dynamic equation for d is

$$\dot{d} = x + d(r - g_y) - h(r + \pi). \tag{5}$$

Here x is the primary deficit in ratio to *GNP*. The growth rate of real *GNP* is g_y. Equation (5) says that the debt grows by the primary deficit if there is no outstanding debt at all (first term); that given an initial debt, it grows further by its net interest cost to the Treasury but declines relative to *GNP* by the economy's growth rate (second term); and that it declines by the amount of seignorage (third term).

In a steady state, real output can grow at its natural rate g. The gross marginal productivity of capital is α/k, and δ is the constant rate of capital depreciation:

$$R = \alpha/k - \delta. \tag{6}$$

The government's net interest cost of borrowing is lower than R for two reasons. One is that its creditors return part of their interest receipts in taxes on the interest—indeed on the nominal interest, a fact that saves the Treasury $\tau\pi$. The second is that the government can borrow with a credit-risk discount v from the after-tax return to capital equity. Thus

$$r = uR - v - \tau\pi. \tag{7}$$

The actual growth of *GNP* is

$$g_y = g + (\alpha/(1-\alpha))(\dot{k}/k). \tag{8}$$

Combining (5) and (3) yields a differential equation in k:

$$\dot{k} = \dot{\mu} - x - (\mu - k)(r - g_y) + h(r + \pi). \tag{9}$$

This is the fundamental dynamic equation of the model. The strategy for its solution is to express all the variables in (9) in terms of $\dot{k}$ and k and of the policy parameters (x, u, π) and structural parameters $(w, \alpha, \beta, \gamma, \delta, g, v)$. The other equations above enable this to be done.

Tedious algebra leads to the differential equation:

$$\dot{k} = Q(k)/V(k), \tag{10}$$

where $Q(k)$ is a cubic polynomial and $V(k)$ is a quadratic, with coefficients that depend on the parameters. If β and γ are both zero, the degrees of the two polynomials are reduced by one. This is a convenient reference case.

The more important of these two conditions is the assumed zero value of β. This implies that crowding out is unrelieved by any increase in saving induced by rise in interest rates. A positive value of γ, on the other hand, tends to make matters slightly worse than in the reference case. As interest rates rise and the demand for money falls, the central bank has to monetize less debt in order to meet its inflation target. In any case, for realistic values of h, seignorage is quantitatively small.

3 The Solution

Figure 18.1 depicts Q, V, and $k = Q/V$ for the reference case, all as functions of k. Since $d = \mu - k$ and $\dot{d} = \dot{\mu} - \dot{k}$, it also depicts $\dot{d}$ as a function of d. The quadratic Q has a positive intercept. Its roots are its intersections, if any, with the horizontal axis. In Figure 18.1 there are none. The denominator V is a negatively sloped line, which crosses the k axis at $\alpha\mu$. The vertical line at that point separates two quite different behaviors of $(\dot{k}, k)$. To its left, $\dot{k}$ is always positive, rising asymptotically to the dividing line. This part of the solution has no practical interest. The relevant region is to the right of the dividing line, where Q/V will have roots if and only if Q does. If these exist, they are steady-state values of k and thus also of d. The higher of the two is stable, the smaller unstable. If, as in Figure 18.1, Q has no roots, $\dot{k}$ is always negative in the relevant region; there is no steady state. Clearly, whether or not Q has real roots depends on the parameters. The general case, with β and γ nonzero, is qualitatively like the reference case but more complicated.

The economy is in trouble if there are no positive real roots of Q and thus no steady states. From whatever initial condition in the right region, k will steadily dwindle, at an ever increasing rate. The same trouble occurs even if roots and steady states exist, if the initial values of k and d are to the left of the lower, unstable root. The question is, what happens as k declines along the curve Q/V, according to which $\dot{k}$ goes to minus infinity. Gross investment cannot be less than zero; the capital stock cannot decline faster than the depreciation rate δ. Accordingly, the capital-output ratio k cannot decline faster than

$$\dot{k} = -(\delta + g)(1 - \alpha)k. \tag{11}$$

Equation (11), a line graphed in Figure 18.1, replaces (9) when Q/V is smaller than this number. The intersection of the two functions is the point of switching from regime I to regime II.

Although the rate of capital consumption is limited, the growth of debt continues. In regime II, $k + d$ exceeds μ. What gives? Assuming the structural and policy parameters remain the same, the natural adjustment is the valuation of the capital stock. In regime I, the value of q was implictly 1. But in regime II, when no gross investment is taking place, $q < 1$. Indeed such valuation is the neoclassical signal to agents that investment is an uneconomic use of output. The wealth constraint becomes

$$qk + d = \mu, \tag{12}$$

$$\dot{d} = -q\dot{k} - \dot{q}k + \dot{\mu}. \tag{13}$$

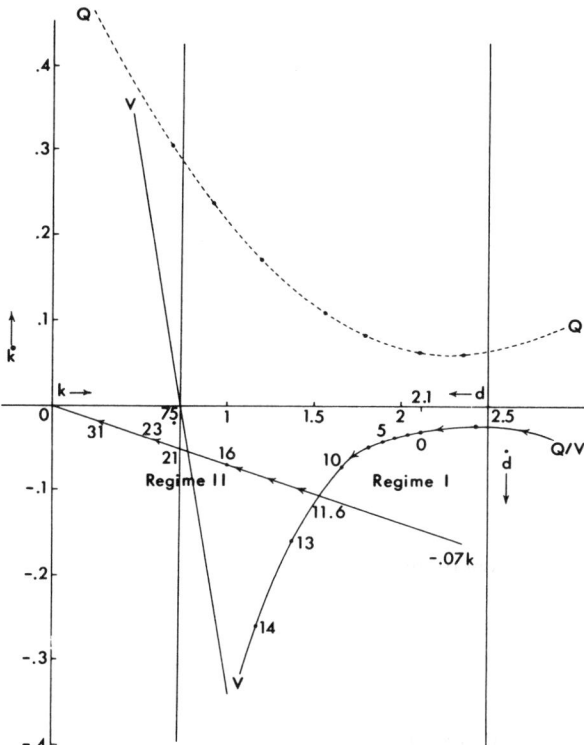

Figure 18.1
Simulation of the model (reference case)

Note: Numbers refer to numbers of years from "present." Regime I years 0–11.6, Crowding Out. Regime II years 11.6–, Capital Consumption.

The equation for the interest rate r is also different. Holders of public debt compare its return not with uR, but with $uR/q + \dot{q}/q$, what they can earn on equity. Thus (6) becomes

$$r = u\alpha/qk - u\delta/q + u\dot{q}/q - (v + \pi\tau). \tag{14}$$

The dynamics of regime II can be found by substituting (11)–(14), into (5), the same strategy used above for regime I. The result is an expression giving $\dot{q}$ as a function of q and k:

$$\dot{q} = Q(q,k)/V(q,k), \tag{15}$$

Table 18.1
Selected Simulation Results

	Regime Change	$q = 0$
T (Year)	11.6	23
$k(T)$ (Capital/GNP)	1.5	0.7
$d(T)$ (Debt/GNP)	1.0	1.8
$Y(T)/Y'(T)$ (GNP/Natural Growth GNP)	0.87	0.63
$C(T)/C'(T)$ (*Consumption*/Natural Growth C)	1.0	0.76

where, given k, Q and V are, respectively, quadratic and linear in q. In regime II the growth of debt "crowds out" q, pushing it down to zero, to make room for d within the wealth-income ratio.

IV Simulation Results

The parameter values used in the simulations are as follows:

Policy Parameters: x (primary deficit/GNP) = 0.03; τ (tax rate) = 0.20; π (inflation target) = 0.04.

Structural Parameters: α (capital share of GNP) = 0.30; δ (depreciation rate) = 0.07; g (natural growth rate) = 0.03; μ (private wealth/GNP) = 2.50; h (base money/GNP) = 0.05; β (savings/interest coefficient) = 0; γ (money demand/interest coefficient) = 0; ν (interest premium) = 0.01.

Initial Conditions: $d(0)$ (debt/GNP) = 0.40; $k(0)$ (capital/GNP) = 2.10; $R(0)$ (real interest rate (pre-tax)) = 0.073.

Table 18.1 exhibits selected results and Figure 18.1 shows the simulation graphically. The initial condition for $(\dot{k}, k)$ is the point marked 0 on the curve Q/V. From that point k declines, d increases, as shown on the curve for subsequent dates 5, 10, 11.6. At time 11.6, there is a regime switch. The regime II path is just a line from that point to the origin.

Figure 18.2 shows what happens in regime II. The upper left panel shows the decline in q and qk as d continues to increase, until, when q is zero at time 23, the debt absorbs all private wealth. The upper right panel tracks the amount by which debt plus capital stock valued at par exceeds the demand for wealth. The lower panel shows $\dot{q}$ over the same period.

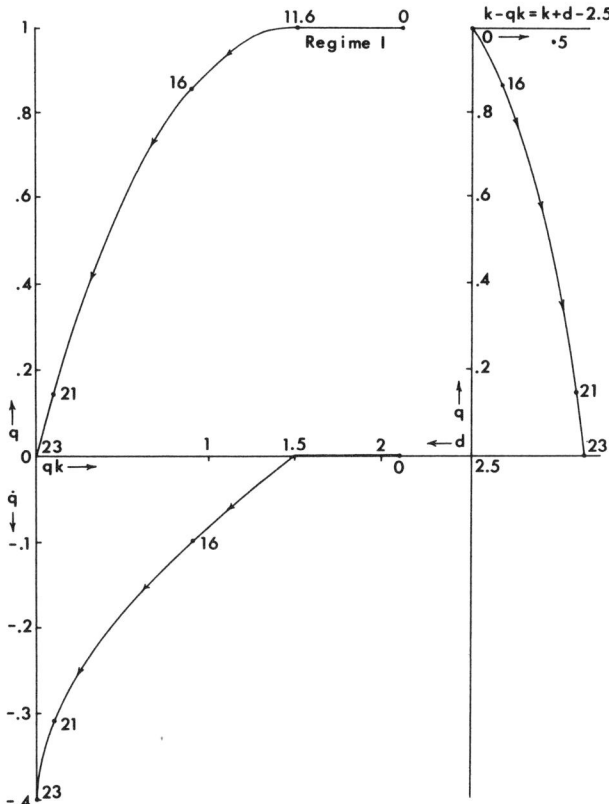

Figure 18.2
Simulation of the regime II (reference case)

Thus the debacle is the cessation of gross investment, followed by a decline in the stock market until the surviving capital stock is valueless.

Table 18.1 includes the simulated values of capital stock/GNP, debt/GNP, GNP itself, and national consumption (including government purchases) for the two critical dates, for regime shift and for $q = 0$. The GNP and consumption are measured relative to what they would have been had they grown steadily at the economy's natural rate of growth g. Note that before the regime change, the shortfalls of those variables are trivial; indeed consumption has not suffered, because the decline in national saving has offset the decline in capital intensity. As I remarked above, the

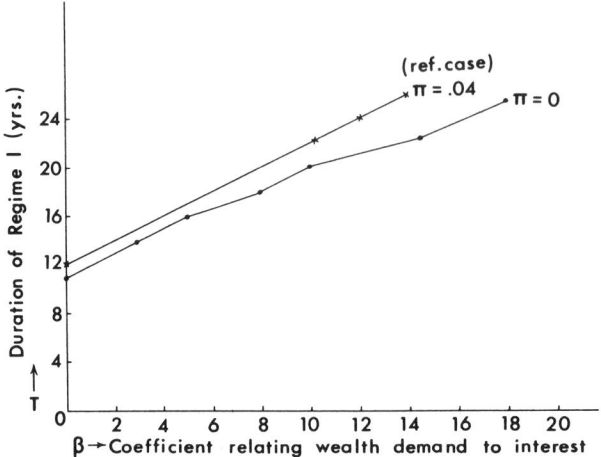

Figure 18.3
Effect of interest sensitivity of savings on duration of regime I (positive gross investment) for two inflation targets, .04 and 0.

Note: β's higher than plotted points prolong Regime I more than 25 years.

visible penalties of gradual crowding out are undramatic. The crunch comes in regime II, when losses of output and consumption become severe.

How do variations in the policy parameters affect the outcomes? The key fiscal parameter is x, the ratio of the primary deficit to *GNP*. With the other parameters the same as in the reference case, x must be below 0.00375 to make the system stable. But with x at that value, the steady-state values of k and d are, respectively, 2.37 and 0.13. The initial conditions (2.1, 0.4) are on the wrong side of that equilibrium. Hence k dwindles, but so slowly that the economy is still well inside regime I after 50 years. To have a steady-state equilibrium k of 2.1 or lower, x must be smaller than -0.001. In effect, a balanced primary budget is stable at or near the initial conditions. That is true in the reference case because the net real interest rate on federal debt, allowing for monetization, is very close to the natural growth rate. This choice of parameters and initial conditions was not accidental; it appeared to me that the U.S. debt/*GNP* ratio could be stabilized if the primary budget were balanced.

The inflation target makes a difference too. But in the reference case, with $x = 0.03$, it takes a 12 percent inflation to obtain a stable solution. Likewise, lowering the target from the reference value of 4 to 1 percent shortens the life of regime I by only one year.

I turn to the structural parameters. The most important one is β, the responsiveness of private demand for wealth to the real interest rate. In current macroeconomic theory, the interest elasticities of saving and wealth demand are key parameters, and there is a lively debate about their empirical magnitudes. In the reference case, perfect inelasticity is assumed. At the other extreme, perfect elasticity at the initial interest rate, clearly there would be no crowding-out problem at all.

An informative summary measure of the effects of varying a parameter is the duration of regime I, in years. In Figure 18.3, this measure is related to the value of β. To calibrate β, note that a value of 10 corresponds to an elasticity of about $1/4$. The figure assumes the reference case values of other parameters. Given so high an x, strict stability is not possible with any finite β. But positive values of β do slow down the crowding-out dynamics and prolong regime I. Values of 15 or higher make its duration longer than 25 years. The interest elasticity of money demand is less important. Introducing a γ of 0.25, which corresponds at initial values to an interest elasticity of money demand of about $1/4$, turns out to make very little difference.

I reiterate that these simulations are not predictions. They are designed only to illustrate why remedial policies should and will be adopted, and thus to make concrete the vague forebodings about runaway government debt.

Note

I thank Daphne Butler and Willem Thorbecke for valuable help in computations.

CHAPTER 19

FINANCIAL STRUCTURE AND MONETARY RULES

Monetary Policy and the Conversion of Shocks into Macroeconomic Outcomes

Rules governing the monetary policies of central banks determine the response of the economy to various macroeconomic shocks. The shocks are of several kinds. Three of the important are the following: *Real demand* shocks affect the aggregate demand for goods and services. They may arise from the spending behavior of consumers, from business investment, from exports, and from government fiscal operations. *Financial* shocks affect the demand for monetary assets relative to their close portfolio substitutes, whether by banks or by other private agents. *Price* shocks affect current and expected prices of goods and services; they may arise in world commodity markets, in exchange rates, or in domestic wage and price settings by trade unions and businesses. Monetary policies may be invariant to these shocks, at least for a time, because they cannot be discerned or anticipated or because on principle the authorities choose to ignore them. In any case the monetary rule distributes the shocks among several macroeconomic variables, of which the most important are real aggregate output, real interest rates, and prices. Different monetary rules distribute the various shocks differently. One important consideration, in choosing among competing rules, is evaluation of their conversions of shocks into the macroeconomic variables of social concern.

This mode of analysis has been well known at least since William Poole's celebrated article in 1970. Poole, using the standard IS-LM framework, compared a monetary policy fixing the interest rate (both real

Reprinted by permission from *Kredit und Kapital* 16 (January 1983): 155–171.

and nominal, as he abstracted from price and inflation effects) with one fixing the quantity of money. He assumed that the central bank could, if desired, respond quickly to observed interest rates but that output was not observed soon enough to be included in a monetary rule. He showed that pegging the interest rate protected the economy from output variation due to purely financial shocks but transmitted real demand shocks into output fluctuations. A monetarist rule, on the other hand, would convert both types of shocks partly into output changes and partly into interest rate changes. Output would be less vulnerable to real demand shocks and more vulnerable to financial shocks than under the interest rate rule.

These conclusions were based on the standard assumption that the Hicksian LM curve, taking account of the monetary rule, would be horizontal in conventional output/interest rate space under the interest-pegging policy and upward sloping under the monetarist rule. A vertical LM "curve" would protect the economy completely from fluctuation due to demand shocks, converting them entirely into interest rate volatility, while rendering output highly vulnerable to financial shocks. But a fixed-M policy would not insure a vertical LM curve unless the demand for that M were wholly interest-inelastic. Otherwise, to achieve a vertical LM curve and the shock distribution it would imply, would require a super-monetarist policy, namely one that changed the quantity of money systematically in the opposite direction from observed interest rates.

Figures 19.1, 19.2, and 19.3 picture graphically the three situations: pegged interest rate and horizontal LM curve; monetarist rule with upward sloping LM curve due to response of velocity or central bank or both to interest rates; vertical LM curve due either to inelasticity of velocity or to super-monetarist policy. In each case the expected outcome is point E and the shaded zones encompass outcomes with some $x\%$ probability given the joint distribution of real demand shocks displacing IS and financial shocks displacing LM, assumed uncorrelated in the illustration. The shapes of the zones, differing from diagram to diagram, show how the different LM shapes distribute the shocks differently as between output and interest rate deviations from E. In the extreme case of zero real demand shocks, outcomes are always on the central IS curve, solid in the diagrams; in the other extreme case, zero financial shocks, outcomes are always on the solid LM curve.

FINANCIAL STRUCTURE AND MONETARY RULES

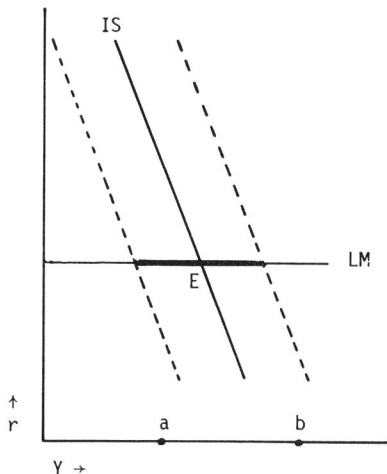

Figure 19.1
Pegged interest rate

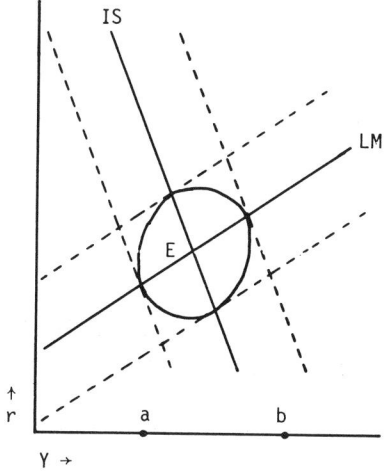

Figure 19.2
"Leaning against the wind"

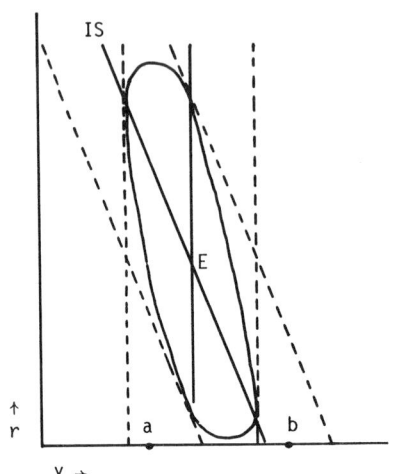

Figure 19.3
Super-monetarist

If a classical situation, with supply-determined output and flexible prices, is assumed instead of the Keynesian situation of the Poole article and of Figures 19.1–3, the Poole analysis is still applicable. Just reinterpret the horizontal axis in the IS-LM diagram to refer to price level rather than to real output. Because of the Pigou-Patinkin real balance effect, the IS curve will still be downward sloping.

One monetarist proposition asserts the stability of money demand, the unimportance of financial shocks relative to real demand shocks. This argues for a monetarist policy rule, as against a pegged interest rate, in the pursuit of output stability—and of price stability insofar as variations of real demand are absorbed in prices rather than quantities. But the logic of this monetarist argument would seem to call for a vertical LM curve, as in Figure 19.3. If nature does not provide one, then a super-monetarist policy would be in order. Nature would provide one according to the old-fashioned quantity theory of money, which denied or ignored the interest-elasticity of money demand. I have the impression that this view has been abandoned under the weight of theoretical logic and empirical findings. In general, the optimal shape of the LM curve depends on the joint distribution of LM and IS shocks, e.g. on their variances and covariance. This is true even if the objective is simply to minimize the variance of output (or price or some combination of the two) regardless of the variance of interest rates. There is no justification at all for assuming that the optimal LM shape is the one that corresponds to a fixed money supply. The optimal money supply rule could be either less accommodative than that, "super-monetarist," or more accommodative; by "accommodative" I mean in this context positively responsive to interest rates.

How the LM Curve Distributes Demand, Financial, and Price Shocks

The Poole analysis can be extended to take explicit account of supply price shocks along with the other two types. Here is a simple short-run model, from which may be derived the effects of each of the three kinds of shocks and the way in which these effects are altered by changing the slope of the LM curve.

$Y - E(Y, r, p) - u_1 = 0$ Goods and services (IS)   (1)

$r - lY + (l/k)(m - u_2)/P = 0$ Money (LM)   (2)

$p - S(Y) - u_3 = 0$ Price level   (3)

The symbols are the following: Y real output; r real interest rate; p price level; u_1 real demand shock; u_2 shock to excess demand for nominal money; u_3 shock to supply price of output; l slope of LM curve, account taken both of private agent's money demand response to interest rate and of the central bank's supply response; k income effect on money demand; m constant in money supply function.

The following are standard assumptions regarding:

the derivatives of the aggregate demand function E with respect to its arguments: $0 < E_Y < 1$; $E_r < 0$; $E_p \leq 0$ (the Pigou-Patinkin real balance effect);

the derivative of the aggregate supply function s: $S_Y > 0$;

the parameters of the LM relation: $l > 0$; $k > 0$; $m > 0$.

This is a Keynesian model, as equation (3) indicates. It is not possible to discuss nominal supply price shocks in a classical model where price is completely flexible and wholly endogenous. I spare you the standard comparative statics calculations which support the qualitative results

Table 19.1
Effects of Shocks on Macroeconomic Outcomes

	Variable		
Shock	Real Output	Real Interest Rate	Price Level
Excess Real Demand	+	+	+
Excess Money Demand	−	+	−
Increase in Supply Price	−	−	+

Table 19.2
Effects of Steepening LM Curve on Strength of Shock Effects (+ means absolute size if effect is increased)

	Variable		
Shock	Real Output	Real Interest Rate	Price Level
Excess Real Demand	−	+	−
Excess Money Demand	+	+	+
Increase in Supply Price	+	+	−

summarized in Tables 19.1 and 19.2.[1] These confirm those of the Poole analysis already discussed for the first two kinds of shocks. As one would intuitively expect, a positive price shock lowers real output and raises the price level. Steepening "LM" accentuates the output effect and mitigates the price effect. For those who are concerned more for price stability than output stability, this is a reason for preferring a more monetarist structure.

An external price shock, dramatically typified by the two OPEC crises of the 1970s, combines a positive supply price shock and a negative real demand shock. If the LM curve is close to vertical, there will be a much larger output loss but less of a general price increase than if monetary policy is more accommodative.

The price shock in the preceding analysis is an increase in price level, present and future, leaving expected inflation unchanged. An increase in the expected inflation rate is a shock of a different kind. It is indeed equivalent to a reduction in demand for money at a given real interest rate. The nominal interest rate rises relative to the real rate. But the result is that the real rate falls, as Table 19.1 says. The analysis indicates that inflationary expectations are expansionary. If this seems strange in these

FINANCIAL STRUCTURE AND MONETARY RULES 525

times, it is because the analysis assumes a fixed monetary rule while experience has led people to expect that monetary policy itself will become more restrictive on news of higher inflation. In the model, a positive expected inflation shock would be correlated with a positive shock to excess money demand. delivered by the central bank.

Reforms of Financial Structure and Their Macroeconomic Implications

The above review was intended to prepare the ground for the main point of the paper. Once policy is defined by a rule, it essentially modifies the structure of the system. Policy and structure become inextricably combined. Their joint product is what matters, as illustrated by the shape of the LM curve in the example above. One way to alter the operating properties of the system, specifically the way shocks are distributed among various outcomes, is to change the policy rule. Another way is to change the structure. Moreover, if structural reform occurs, whether for reasons connected with macroeconomic policy and performance or not, then most likely the policy rule should be changed too. That is, the rule that was optimal given the old structure will generally be no longer optimal under the new.

For example, suppose that changes in financial technology, institutions, and regulations twist the LM curve of Figure 19.2 toward the vertical one of Figure 19.3. Then if a monetarist rule was previously optimal, a more accommodative rule would now be optimal, with policy offsetting the nonaccommodative consequences of those structural changes.

The example is, it happens, realistic. Structural changes of the kind described are now occuring rapidly in the United States, and they are indeed the topical motivation of this paper. Financial deregulation is making the LM curve vertical. Quantity theorists were wrong in the past in arguing as if it already was, as if money demand were interest-inelastic. But now monetarists are in the front line of advocates of reforms of financial structure that will make the world over to their design. Let me explain in some detail.

The most important reform is that legal ceilings on interest rates on bank deposits are being removed. In only a few years even demand deposits will bear market-determined rates. Deregulation conforms to the spirit of the times. Economists instinctively support free price competition among banks as among airlines or trucks or dairy farmers. Monetarists are especially strong in free market instincts, but they have macroeconomic objectives as well. They wish to tighten the central bank's control of money supply, and to hold GNP more tightly to the money supply in the face of shocks to aggregate demand.

For these reasons, their agenda for "reform" include the introduction of flexibility in other interest rates too. They would have the Federal Reserve pay interest on banks' reserve balances, presumably at a rate indexed to market rates. They would index the Federal Reserve discount rate, making it equal a market rate plus a constant penalty. Along with contemporaneous reserve accounting, already in the process of adoption by the Federal Reserve, these reforms are designed to tighten the relation between the supply of unborrowed reserves and the deposit component of M1. In this monetarist vision, there will also be uniform reserve requirements in M1 deposits, which are transactions media, and none on other liabilities, which are not.

The pace of deregulation has recently accelerated. Banks and other depository institutions will, beginning this very month December 1982, be allowed to offer deposits payable on demand, with interest rates uncontrolled. Subject to a minimum balance requirement, $2,500, unlimited withdrawals on demand will be permitted, and these will include three automatic and convenient transfers to the depositor's other accounts in the same bank. Since the number of withdrawals by check will be limited to three per month, these deposits are not quite transactions media on the Fed's current M1 criterion, "checkable." Congress in 1982 rushed through the legislation authorizing these new deposits in order to enable banks and other regulated depository institutions to compete with money market mutual funds. The new deposits will be free of reserve requirements and will be insured by the federal government, an advantage over the funds.

More recently an even more decisive step was taken on the road to deregulation of deposit interest rates. Beginning in January 1982, banks and other depository institutions will be authorized to offer insured demand deposits with unlimited checking and pre-arranged transfer privileges. The only legal restrictions are a minimum balance requirement of $2,500 and the ineligibility of businesses to hold accounts of this type. These deposits are called "super-NOW" accounts. Regular "NOW" accounts have been available nationwide for non-business depositors, since January 1, 1981. They originated as interest-bearing savings deposits on which checks could be written provided they were called by another name, Notices Of Withdrawal. Like regular NOW accounts, super-NOW deposits are subject to reserve requirements and will be counted in M1.

As deposits come to bear competitive interest rates, monetary theory—models of money supply and demand and of the transmission of control measures and shocks through financial markets to the real economy—will have to be rewritten. Standard theory assumes that "money," whatever its other characteristics, bears an exogenously fixed nominal interest rate, set by law, regulation, or institutional convention. It may be zero, as it is on currency and has been on reserve balances and conventional demand deposits. It may be an effective ceiling above zero, as on passbook savings, on most time deposits, and in the United States on regular NOW accounts. Demand for monetary assets of these kinds is specified in our models to depend on the endogenous market-determined interest rates on substitute nonmoney assets and on other variables. The differential between those uncontrolled interest rates and the fixed nominal rates on monetary assets is compensated by the non-pecuniary services of money, which are thought to be inversely related to the real quantity held.

Consider how this traditional property differentiates "money" from assets with uncontrolled endogenous interest rates. When, for example, the supply of Treasury bills is increased, one adjustment that can induce people to buy and hold the new supply is the fall in the price of bills, the increase in their interest yield. This is not the only adjustment, but it is the obvious first-order vehicle of equilibration. For fixed-interest money, however, this first-order effect does not occur. If the supply of money is increased, the public has to be persuaded to hold it by changes other than in its own interest rate—notably other interest rates, transactions volumes, prices. Indeed in standard theory this is precisely the reason why monetary control powerfully affects nonfinancial variables. When market rates are paid on money too, the transmission mechanism will be significantly altered.

Currency, it is true, will continue to bear zero nominal interest. In the United States currency outside banks amounts to about one third of M1. One can imagine institutional arrangements for non-zero interest on currency—for example, letting holders annually exchange old bills for new ones plus some interest in coins. Maybe monetarists will propose this next! (Recall that Keynes discussed with some admiration Silvio Gesell's "crank" scheme to make interest on currency negative; the holder would have to buy and affix a stamp periodically to maintain the face value of bills.) Assuming that no arrangements of this kind will in fact be made, there will continue to be fixed-interest money. But our central bank does not control its supply, and cannot as long as the public is free to exchange currency for deposits and vice versa, and banks are free to make exchanges between currency and reserve balances held as deposits in Federal Reserve Banks.

The currency exception is probably not very important. Currency demand does not appear to be sensitive to interest rates when they are already very high. Moreover, interest-induced substitutions for or against currency are likely to be almost wholly with transactions deposits. Consequently when deposits come to bear market-determined rates it will not be a bad approximation in modeling money demand decisions to regard those rates as applying to the whole transactions money supply. Likewise when and if interest comes to be paid on reserve balances at the Federal Reserve, it will not be inaccurate to model bank demands for reserves inclusive of their currency holdings as dependent on that interest rate. In both cases, marginal adjustments will be made in interest-bearing form.

In the old regime, and in the standard model, the "market" for fixed-interest deposits is in disequilibrium. Depositors' demand is smaller than the amounts banks, individually and in aggregate, would like to supply at the controlled rates. Banks will gladly accept, on prevailing terms, any new funds the public would like to deposit; no one will be turned away. When rates are uncontrolled and competitively determined, they will clear the market. Banks will be supplying all the deposits they wish to offer. They will accept deposits to the point where their marginal cost, including interest, equals the marginal revenue expected from lending or investing the funds. Of course deposit interest rates will be, like loan rates now, administered prices. But, also like loan rates now and uncontrolled rates on certificates of deposit as well, they and the other terms of deposit agreements will be changed under competition. The United States system of banks and other financial institutions is, unlike the systems in most other countries, decentralized and competitive, though monopolistically competitive.

FINANCIAL STRUCTURE AND MONETARY RULES 529

In the new regime, the interest differential between bank assets and deposit liabilities would meet the costs of intermediation. These costs include the risk that deposit withdrawals and the accompanying reserve losses would impose extra costs, borrowing at a premium in the market or at the Federal Reserve discount window. A bank's choice of asset composition, as between illiquid loans and variable-price securities on the one hand, and excess reserves or other liquid assets on the other, would reflect that same risk. The marginal costs of intermediation are probably fairly constant over normal ranges of variation in the volume of bank deposits and assets. Thus the competitive deposit rate will be below the rates on bank loans and other assets by a fairly constant differential. The public's demand for deposits, on the other hand, depends principally on the interest differential and on transactions volume. If the differential becomes a constant, the demand for deposits will be independent of the *level* of interest rates. A rise in market interest rates will not reduce the demand for deposits as it does in the old regime and in the standard model, because the rate paid on deposits will rise too. The old monetarist assumption of interest-inelastic money demand will apply, though for a reason quite different from its original motivation.

Figure 19.4 pictures the new regime. It shows a family of deposit demand curves, for various transactions volumes proxied by money income Yp. The higher curves correspond to higher income levels. As indicated, deposit demand depends inversely on the interest differential. But given constant costs of intermediation, the banks' supply of deposits is perfectly elastic at the interest differential that meets those costs. Thus the equilibrium volume of deposits depends solely on the income level.

Equilibrium also requires demand = supply balance in reserves, as shown in the bottom panel of Figure 19.4. The supply of unborrowed reserves is determined by the central bank by its open market operations. (Actually these operations affect directly the unborrowed monetary base, only part of which takes the form of reserves. The remainder is currency outside banks. The Federal Reserve has to estimate, with some error, the public demand for currency.) The demand for unborrowed reserves has two components. Required reserves, as indicated in the diagram, are approximately proportional to deposits. From this demand must be subtracted *net borrowed reserves*, borrowings from the Federal Reserve less reserves held in excess of requirements. At present net borrowed reserves vary

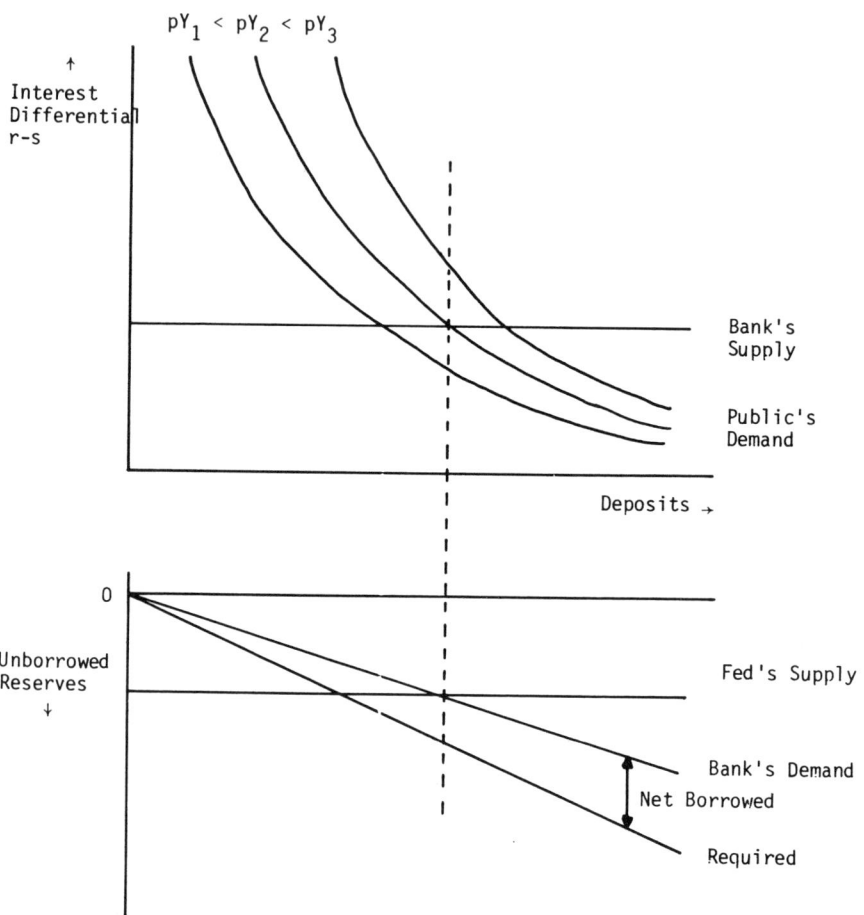

Figure 19.4

FINANCIAL STRUCTURE AND MONETARY RULES 531

directly, in the short run at least, with market interest rates. The discount rate charged by the Federal Reserve is constant, so that an increase in the market rates that can be earned on bank assets is an incentive to borrow and to economize holdings of excess reserves. Once interest geared to market rates is paid on reserves and interest charged on borrowing from the central bank is similarly indexed, this relationship will be nullified. Banks' net borrowed reserves will be essentially a constant fraction of deposits and required reserves, as pictured in Figure 19.4.

As a result, the central bank will control pretty tightly the volume of deposits by fixing the supply of unborrowed reserves. And thus the central bank will also determine quite closely the level of money income (pY_2 in the upper panel). These linkages will, moreover, not be loosened by variation of interest rate levels, as they are today. An interesting sidelight, pointed out by Michael Hadjimichalikakis (1982), is that innovations in financial technology which either raise transactions requirements for holding money or reduce costs of intermediation will reduce money income unless the central bank responds by increasing the supply of reserves.

The main outcome, as foreshadowed in my first section, is to fulfill the monetarist dream of a vertical LM curve.

Of course in the very short run the control of deposits and money supply via fixing unborrowed reserves will not be as tight as the Figure and accompanying text depict. As now, it will take action by the Federal Reserve, adjustment of reserve supply targets, to correct observed deviations from the desired track of monetary aggregates. But the corrections will be faster and the deviations smaller, because some of the adjustments that now require central bank action will occur automatically.

To appreciate the change, it is necessary to understand how the Federal Reserve operates in the present regime. The basic targets are, or at least were until recently, announced growth tracks of monetary aggregates, M1 in particular. Primary importance has been attached to meeting numerical targets announced in advance for money growth from the final quarter of one year to the final quarter of the next year. Interim targets for each quarter are also announced in the course of a year. These long- and short-range M-targets should be distinguished from the one-month operating instructions to the New York Federal Reserve Bank regarding open market operations. Since the celebrated announcement of October

1979, these instructions have been designed to obtain a supply of unborrowed reserves consistent with the short-run M targets. Suppose however that bank loans and deposits, and thus required reserves, rise beyond expectation. Money market interest rates will rise as banks scramble to meet their reserve tests. Banks will borrow more from their Federal Reserve Banks at the fixed discount rate and cut down their holdings of interest-free excess reserves. Monetary aggregates will rise above their desired tracks. Correction will come later, by downward adjustment of next month's reserve supply and possibly by upward adjustment of the discount rate.

In the new regime, if and when it is fully established in future, the adjustment will occur sooner by automatic increase in the discount rate. The same assumed shock will raise interest rates more and money supplies less than in the old regime.

This is one buffer or safety valve that the proposed structural reforms remove. The other one, more consequential in the longer run, is the increase in monetary velocity now induced by the rise in interest rates. This will be nullified as the rise in rates extends to money itself. There is no doubt some elasticity in the transactions velocity of money even at constant interest differentials. That is, households and businesses can find ways of handling increased economic activity with the same cash holdings, at least in the short run. As Akerlof and Milbourne (1979) have shown, depositors who follow an S-s strategy for their inventories of cash will handle larger transactions volumes with the same average cash holdings as long as they keep those S-s thresholds unchanged. They may change the thresholds when and only when they regard a new volume of transactions as permanent.

In the end the removal of these buffers will make the LM curve more nearly vertical in the short run and the longer run, given the same operating and targeting procedures by the central bank.

Dangers of Combining Monetarist Structure and Monetarist Policy

Monetarism has already steepened the LM curve considerably. Intermediate-run targets for monetary aggregates made money supply less responsive to demand than pegged interest rates in the forties or the "bill rate only" policies of the early 1960s or the "leaning against the wind" approach of other post-war years. The October 1979 change in operating procedures further removed the short-run accommodative buffers implicit in the previous practice of instructing the open market desk to hold the market interest on overnight interbank loans of reserves, "federal funds," within a narrow range decided periodically by Federal Reserve authorities. The new procedures substituted unborrowed reserve supplies for interest rates in these instructions. M1 targeting makes LM steeper than targeting on unborrowed reserves over a longer period, because it commits the Fed to reverse any lasting changes in the relation of required reserves to unborrowed reserves. The indexing of interest rates on reserves and discounts, as I have just explained, would automatize and accelerate such reversals. As we would have expected from Figures 19.1–3 and have already observed, monetarist targets and operating procedures have made interest rates much more volatile, and the fulfillment of the monetarist vision will make them more volatile still.

For several reasons, we could expect the location of the LM curve to be even more stochastic in the full monetarist regime than it is now. Once M1 deposits bear competitive market rates, depositors will have much less reason than now to "fine-tune" their allocation of funds between M1 deposits and other assets, including non-checkable deposits in banks and the new "money market" deposits with restricted checking and transfer privileges. Moreover, the transactions for which M1 balances are held are by no means solely GNP transactions. Indeed most debits to checking accounts are for other transactions, largely financial, and the two types are by no means perfectly correlated. The turnover of checking accounts for financial transactions is extremely high (more than four times a day, judging from New York "debits"). In the new regime, moreover, M1 holdings for financial transactions would be much larger, and GNP-velocity would be more seriously distorted by variability of finance-related holdings.

Another source of LM volatility is connected with intermediation and disintermediation, as these are influenced by borrowers' and lenders' perceptions of the relative risks of short and long commitments. As experience these last three years suggests, increased uncertainties about future interest rates lead borrowers and lenders to shift from long markets, where banks and other suppliers of checking accounts are not active on the demand side, to short markets, where they are active on both sides.

The shift increases the size of monetary aggregates that include the short liabilities of those intermediaries. Those bulges are not connected with positive "IS" shifts, but indeed possibly with the reverse. Ross Starr (1982) has documented this effect for M2. In the new regime, the effect could spill into M1.

When banks expand loans to their customers, they must somehow induce the public to hold more of their liabilities simultaneously. As borrowers expend the balances credited to their checking accounts, the direct and indirect recipients have larger balances. At least during the time it takes them to adjust, an M1 bulge accompanies an expansion of lending. When the loans are financing real investments, both are indicative of an IS shift which it is the purpose of M1 target policy to oppose. Sometimes, however, as observed in recent recessions, the loan demand reflects distress borrowing, designed to protect or rebuild liquidity for the borrower and his suppliers. It is a byproduct of a negative IS shift damaging to cash flow, rather than a positive one. In this case a constant M1 rule aggravates an undesired decline in income. This instability would be magnified in the new regime.

I have argued that in the new regime LM would be very steep even in the very short run. In my view IS is already very steep in the short run. That is, saving and investment decisions are interest-sensitive only with a lag. In a month or a quarter, expenditures on goods and services, investment and consumption both, are largely the execution of previous decisions, constrained only by current liquidity. Over a longer period, the decisions are reconsidered and remade, interest rates matter a great deal, and the IS curve is more gently sloped.

On the other hand, in our present monetary regime, and especially in our past monetary regimes, the LM locus has been significantly steeper in the longer run than in the short run. That is, the accommodative buffers previously discussed were allowed to operate for a while, but the central bank opposed with increasing strength lasting deviations from its targets for the economy or for the aggregates. The move to tighter targets, enforced more promptly, was motivated by the belief that cumulative inflationary movements in the economy got out of hand before the Fed could or would arrest them. But, as I think we have also seen, there is danger in moving too far in this direction. A restrictive non-accommodative policy, a steep LM curve, makes interest rates shoot up while having little immediate effect on GNP, as one would expect if IS is also steep in the short run. But the big rise of interest rates sows the seeds of subsequent collapse, as the high rates take their eventual toll.

During recession, moreover, the distress borrowing and liquidity syndromes previously described postpone the remedial decline in interest rates that should be the other side of the monetarist coin. As the present case illustrates, the collapse may be so great, the relief may be postponed so long, the real determinants of investment may become so unfavorable, that interest-sensitive expenditures are difficult to revive.

It is hard for me to believe that the Federal Reserve intended or anticipated that its M1 targets and operating procedures for 1981–82 would produce the dismal GNP history actually experienced. One reason they did, according to the Fed itself, was a positive financial shock, increasing the demand for M1. The test of intention would be whether the Federal Open Market Committee would accept—as I think they would with sighs of relief—a significant surprise burst of velocity growth over the next twelve months. Of course, it is for reasons of this kind that I favor gearing year-to-year Fed policy to more consequential economic variables like GNP, unemployment, and inflation rather than to any intermediate aggregate.

Whatever the Fed's targets, however, I advise caution in moving further toward a monetarist structure of the system. The buffers we have had, even those we still have, serve useful purposes. We can, it is true, have too many buffers and too much accommodation. Since demand (IS) shocks, financial (LM) shocks, and price shocks, are all likely, the optimal LM curve will be upward sloping, neither vertical nor horizontal, neither completely unaccommodating nor wholly accommodating. I suspect we have already made the LM curve steeper than optimal. We should not make it vertical. This means that if the structural changes I have described are adopted for microeconomic reasons—and I am by no means convinced they should be—then the central bank should offset their macroeconomic effects by adopting more accommodative operating procedures and targets.

Note

1. A further assumption, beyond the standard restrictions listed in the text, is required for the entries for Y and p in the third row of Table 19.2. It is that the Pigou-Patinkin effect E_p

is relatively weak. To understand it, imagine that (1) and (2) are solved to eliminate r and to derive an aggregate demand relation of p to Y, which will be negatively sloped. This, together with equation (3), the positively sloped aggregate supply relation of p to Y, determines p and Y. As in ordinary demand/supply analysis, an upward shift of the supply curve will lower Y and raise p. It will lower Y more and raise p less the gentler the slope of the demand curve. The question in Table 19.2 is how steepening LM alters the slope of the aggregate demand relation of p to Y. Two price effects on aggregate demand are present in the model. One is the Pigou-Patinkin effect: a price increase lowers real financial wealth and increases saving. This effect is smaller when LM is steeper, because it is offset to a greater degree by a decline in the interest rate. The other is the indirect monetary effect: a price increase lowers the real money supply and raises interest rates. Making LM steeper accentuates this effect. The first effect tends to make aggregate demand less sensitive to the price level, the second effect to make it more sensitive. The assumption of Table 19.2 is that the monetary effect dominates, so that the aggregate demand relation of p to Y becomes flatter. Technically, it is that $(m - u_2)/p$, the absolute value of the real money supply change due to a price movement, exceeds $-E_p/(1 - E_Y)$, the "multiplied" Pigou-Patinkin effect.

References

Akerlof, G. and Ross Milbourne (1979), "Irving Fisher on His Head: Part I," *Quarterly Journal of Economics*, Vol. 93, No. 2, pp. 169–187.

Hadjimichalikakis, M. (1982), *Monetary Policy and Modern Money Markets*, Lexington, Massachusetts: Lexington Books.

Poole, W. (1970), "Optimal Choice of Monetary Policy Instruments in a Simple Stochastic Macro Model," *Quarterly Journal of Economics*, Vol. 84, No. 2, May, pp. 197–216.

Starr, R. (1982), "Variation in the Maturity Structure of Debt and Behavior of the Monetary Aggregates: The Maturity Shift Hypotheses," Univ. of California, San Diego, Discussion Paper No. 82-9, March.

PART IV

INTERNATIONAL MACROECONOMICS

CHAPTER 20

ON THE INTERNATIONALIZATION OF PORTFOLIOS

1 Introduction

Portfolio theory has been an important component of open economy macroeconomic models. In such models, it is essential to distinguish between several categories of assets, both foreign and domestic, and to specify their demands and supplies. This framework has become increasingly relevant. Movements of capital across regional and national boundaries and currencies have exploded in volume, thanks to the dismantling of currency and exchange controls and other financial regulations and to revolutionary economies in technologies of communication and transaction. The globalization of financial markets was stimulated by the floating-exchange-rate regime established in 1973.

Figures 20.1 and 20.2 show the trends of internationalization of American owned wealth and foreign ownership of American assets respectively. The latter has been growing especially rapidly in the last ten to twelve years, a period when the U.S. net wealth position *vis-à-vis* the rest of the world deteriorated sharply and turned negative. Nevertheless, U.S. direct investments abroad and holdings of foreign equities grew sharply during the 1983–89 cyclical recovery. Evidently U.S. current account deficits were financed mainly in credit and bond markets. Figures 20.1 and 20.2 imply that internationalization in both directions remains quite modest. Americans, as private households and firms, have placed only 4% of their net worth in foreign assets. Foreigners' gross claims on Americans amount to about 7% of private net worth. However, projections of recent trends by Hamada and Iwata (1989) suggest that Japan and Germany will own one-

Reprinted by permission from *Oxford Economic Papers* 44 (1992): 553–565. Written with William C. Brainard. Originally presented at ETLA Conference, Helsinki, Finland, June 1991.

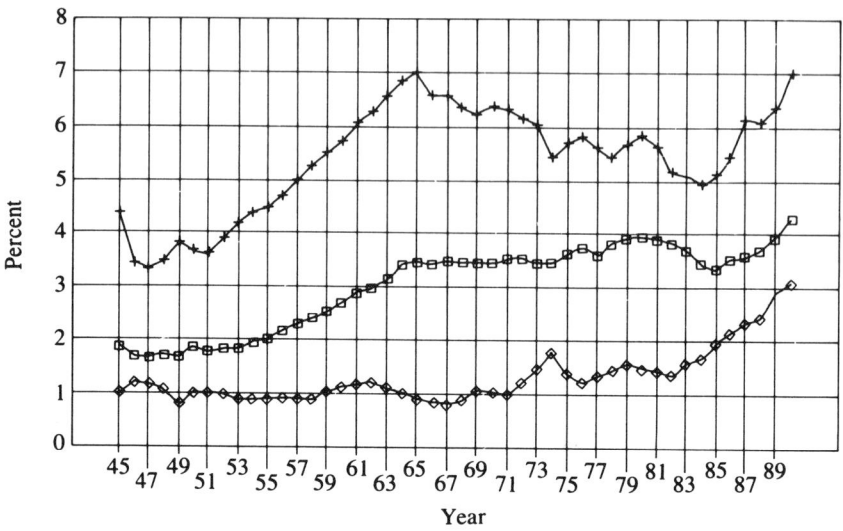

□–□ 1. All assets   +–+ 2. Real capital   ◇–◇ 3. Equities

Figure 20.1
U.S. private holdings of foreign assets (as percent similar U.S. total holdings).
Source: Board of Governors of the Federal Reserve System, *Balance Sheets for the U.S. Economy 1945-1990*, C.9 Balance Sheets Flow of Funds, March 1991.
Ratio 1: U.S. Private Holdings of Foreign Assets/U.S. Private Net Worth.
Numerator: Table for Net Foreign Assets (NFA), pp. 7–12: Line 2, Foreign assets owned by U.S. residents; Line 3, U.S. official foreign exchange and net IMF position; Line 14, U.S. government loans; Line 18, U.S. equity in IBRD, etc.; Line 19, U.S. government deposits.
Denominator: Table for National Net Worth (NNW), pp. 1–6: Line 19, Private net worth, consolidated.
Ratio 2: U.S. Direct Investment Abroad/U.S. Business Capital.
Numerator: NNW: Line 9, U.S. direct investment abroad.
Denominator: NNW: Line 4, Nonresident plant and equipment and Line 5, Inventories.
Ratio 3: U.S. Private Holdings of Foreign Equities/U.S. Nonfinancial Equities.
Numerator: NFA: Line 5, Foreign corporate equities.
Denominator: Table for Nonfinancial Corporate Business (NCB), pp. 31–36: Line 45, Market value of equities.

ON THE INTERNATIONALIZATION OF PORTFOLIOS

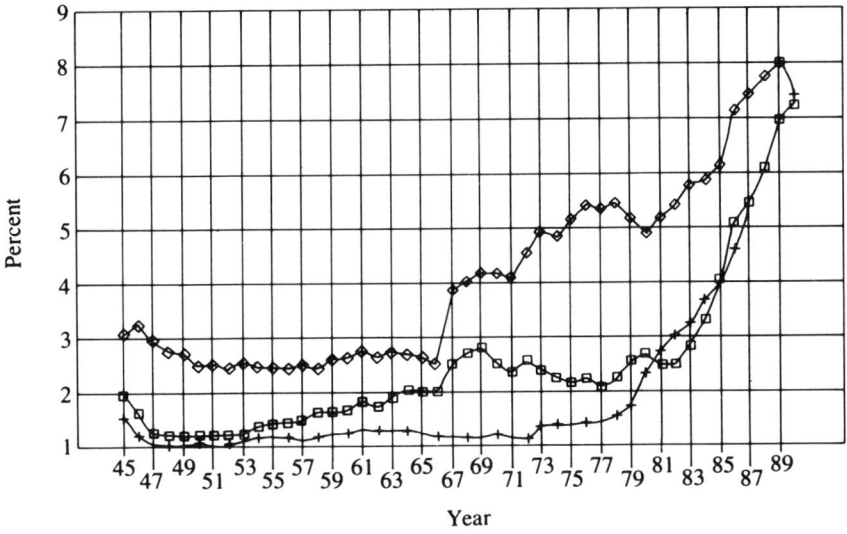

Figure 20.2
Foreign private holdings of U.S. assets (as percent of total similar U.S. assets).
Source: Federal Reserve Flow of Funds Balance Sheets, March 1991. See Figure 20.1.
Ratio 1: Foreign Privately Owned U.S. Assets/U.S. Private Net Worth.
Numerator: NFA: Line 22, U.S. assets owned by foreigners.
Denominator: NNW: Line 19, Private net worth consolidated.
Ratio 2: Foreign Direct Investment in U.S./U.S. Business Capital.
Numerator: NFA: Line 38, Direct investment in U.S.
Denominator: NNW: Line 4, Nonresident plant and equipment; Line 5, Inventories.
Ratio 3: Foreign Holdings of U.S. Equities/U.S. Nonfinancial Equities.
Numerator: NFA: Line 27, U.S. corporate equities (owned by foreigners).
Denominator: NCB: Line 45, Market value of equities.

third of the United States by 2010. Presumably these trends themselves are setting in motion adjustments that will cause them to slow down and even reverse.

Kuroyanagi, Hamada, and Sakurai (1989) are in the process of building a world asset and debt matrix from scattered sources; it is a difficult task. Some of their preliminary estimates are reported in Tables 20.1(A) and 20.2(A). Their numbers have been put in perspective by scaling them to the GNP. Shocks of wealth and capital are four to six times the GNP, so the numbers in Tables 20.1(B) and 20.2(B) would be much smaller if

Table 20.1
Foreign Assets and Debts, 1987

	1A. Billions of dollars			
	Assets	Debts	Net Assets	GNP
United States	1168	1536	−368	4527
Japan	1072	831	241	2369
Germany	584	436	148	1126
United Kingdom	1316	1149	167	667
	1B. Relative to GNP (percent)			
	Assets	Debts	Net Assets	
United States	25.8	33.9	−8.1	
Japan	45.3	35.1	10.2	
Germany	51.9	38.7	13.1	
United Kingdom	197.3	172.3	25.0	

Source: Assets and Debts figures from Kuroyanagi, Hamada, and Sakurai, (1989), Table 6. GNP figures from Statistical Abstract of the United States (1990), Table 1446, p. 840.

Table 20.2
Direct Foreign Investment Stock, 1986

	2A. Billions of dollars		
	From	To	Net Position
United States	260	220	40
Japan	58	7	51
Germany	49	31	18
United Kingdom	142	69	73
	2B. Relative to GNP (percent)		
	From	To	Net Position
United States	5.74	4.86	0.88
Japan	2.45	0.30	2.15
Germany	4.35	2.75	1.60
United Kingdom	21.29	10.34	10.94

Source: Kuroyanagi et al., (1989), Table 12. GNP as for Table 20.1.

scaled by those stocks. The tables decisively establish the primacy of the United Kingdom as an international lender, borrower, and investor; after all, the City and Whitehall have both been at it for a long time. The rest of us have a long way to go before our portfolios become as international as the British.

2 Exchange Rates and Portfolio Theory

The 1973 regime shift accentuated the interest of macroeconomists in explaining the determination of exchange rates. "The exchange rate is an asset price," a fashionable aphorism fifteen years ago, symbolized the centrality of asset markets, and thus of portfolio theory, in open economy macroeconomics. There is truth in the aphorism, but only half truth. The exchange rate is a factor (only one factor) in the price of an asset in any currency other than the one in which it is denominated. But it is also a factor in the external prices of goods and services.

The characteristic feature of portfolio theory in its macroeconomic applications is the assumption that assets are imperfect substitutes and that their relative prices and returns vary systematically as their relative quantities are varied by policies or other events. In contrast, models strongly influenced by finance theory often reduce the effective number of distinct assets by assuming perfect substitutability. These models are convenient for rational expectations methodology. However, the imperatives of empirical relevance and econometrics work in the direction of multi-asset models.

As usual in macroeconomics, a distinction can be made between short-run and long-run applications of portfolio theory. Short-run theoretical and empirical models concern cyclical fluctuations and demand management policies for counter-cyclical stabilization. In long-run trends of capital accumulation, growth, and terms of trade, real fundamentals can be expected to dominate.

3 Asset Markets in Short-run Open-economy Macroeconomics

Mundell–Fleming models—the open economy extensions of IS/LM—apply to single "small" economies to which the rest of the world is exogenous. They are useful, but some shortcomings of IS/LM are underscored and magnified by the extension. The IS/LM short-cut assumption, that all assets other than money are perfect substitutes for each other, is bad enough for a closed economy, but it worsens when the asset menu is expanded to embrace foreign assets. The rudimentary asset menu needs to be amended by recognizing foreign assets as distinct items. However, often this is not explicitly done, even when a "BP" curve is added in r–Y space purporting to show the locus of (r, Y) at which external payments in and out are balanced. This locus is horizontal unless foreign and domestic assets are imperfect substitutes, and if they are, then the stocks of those assets, not just their flows, are relevant and must be tracked.

Besides overdoing the assumption of perfect substitutability among assets other than money, the IS/LM model does not deal with asset stock accumulations. Although the solution of the model generally implies that capital and other assets are being accumulated, the effects of the accumulations are not explicitly modeled. The excuse is that the flows, during the period to which the model is relevant, are too small to alter the stocks significantly. This excuse is especially implausible for a country's stock of net foreign assets, which could be close to zero, small relative to current account flows within a year.

Over the years we have proposed an appropriate multi-asset stock adjustment framework (Brainard and Tobin (1968); Tobin (1982a, b)). The strategy is to specify, for each asset on the menu of portfolio choice, the desired end-of-period stock at the asset's current period price. This stock demand is a function of the vector of the rates of return for one period ahead (inclusive of expected capital gains or losses) for all the assets on the menu, national income, the commodity price level, and other non-financial variables. The list of variables is in principle the same for all the assets; each individual's portfolio demands are, in effect, a single decision. Stock demands will in general differ from the values, at the current period asset price, of the quantities of the asset carried over from the previous period. Flow demands for the period are considered to be fractions of these discrepancies plus a growth factor. Equation (1) illustrates the specification:

$$\alpha_i(A_i(t) - q_i(t)a_i(t-1)) + gq_i(t)a_i(t-1) = S_i(t) \qquad (1)$$

where α_i is the stock adjustment fraction, A_i is the function describing the desired end-of-period value of holdings of asset i, q_i is the price of asset i (usually related negatively to its rate of return), $a_i(t-1)$ is the quantity (not the value) of the asset carried over from the previous period, and g is the growth rate. The left-hand side of (1) is the flow demand in a period t, which is equated to the flow supply $S_i(t)$.[1]

For equities and direct investments in business capital, the S_i represent the increments in capital stocks evaluated at current replacement costs. For government obligations, base money, and interest-bearing debt, the S_i are the changes in outstanding supplies resulting from central bank and Treasury transactions with the public. These equal in total the government deficit. For claims on foreign countries, the S_i are supplies made available by the current account surplus. New asset supplies may contain exogenous elements, but they are generally not wholly exogenous. Domestic capital investments and government deficits are in part policy decisions and in part functions of other variables. The current account surplus or deficit, related to domestic and foreign economic activity and prices, and to exchange rates, is largely endogenous.

The demands and supplies, asset prices, rates of return, and growth rate in (1) can be defined either in nominal or real terms. The summation of equations like (1) across all assets, i, is the "IS" equation for the economy. The left-hand sides represent private saving and the right-hand sides record its absorption into net domestic investment, government deficit, and current account surplus. If there are n assets on the menu, the n independent asset demand = supply equations determine n variables. These variables include the rates of return and the rate on nominal base money. The latter rate is exogenously fixed, and others may be also, which is why the system can determine other variables, notably the Net National Product or the commodity price level.

Consider, for example, the simplest textbook closed economy model. There are only two distinct assets: (i) base money, the zero-interest monetary "debt" of the government; and (ii) other assets, notably government interest-bearing non-monetary debt and reproducible capital, assumed to be perfect substitutes for each other, bearing a common one period rate of return. The flow supplies of both assets add up to the government deficit (monetary + non-monetary) and capital investment. The two flow demands add up to private saving. (The conventional money demand = supply equation, "LM," is written in stocks rather than flows, in effect assuming full adjustment in one period.) There are two asset market-clearing equations and their summation is the IS equation. Any two of these three equations may be taken as the model; the conventional choices are IS and LM. In any case, because there is only one endogenous asset return to be determined, the system can also determine either Y or p, or some relation between them, and the aggregate demand "AD."

In a multi-asset open economy model, standard Mundell–Fleming one period multipliers for fiscal and monetary policies and internal and external shocks can be qualitatively confirmed using several assumptions. The most important are: (i) assets are gross substitutes for each other, in particular, an increase in wealth caused by a rise in the return on any asset does not raise the demand for holdings of any other asset; (ii) the private sector holds non-negative quantities of all assets, foreign and domestic (this does not exclude that the country is a net debtor internationally); (iii) expectations of future returns, inclusive of capital gains, on assets are not extrapolative, but are neutral or regressive. This means, in particular, that appreciation of the currency today does not lead portfolio managers to expect the currency to appreciate further tomorrow; and (iv) real net exports are increased by depreciation of the currency and reduced by appreciation (Tobin and Macedo, 1980; Tobin, 1982a, b).

However, the multi-asset approach does lead to different conclusions on some important issues. Our model does not, except in extreme cases, justify the proposition that fiscal policy is impotent in a floating-exchange-rate regime or that monetary policy is impotent in a fixed-rate regime. Furthermore, our model does not validate the extravagant claim that a floating rate insulates an economy from external demand shocks.

4 Models with More Than One Country Endogenous

The "small country" assumption that the rest of the world is exogenous is scarcely applicable to the relationships among the Group of Seven economies, particularly the three economic superpowers North America, the European Community, and Japan. In principle, a two-country or n-country model can be constructed from building blocks like those of the one-country model. An example for the two-country model of the United States and Japan follows.

ON THE INTERNATIONALIZATION OF PORTFOLIOS 547

In both countries assets are available to wealth owners and portfolio managers. (Some assets may be held in negative amounts. The notation is tedious because the identity of the asset, its country of origin, and the residence of asset holders must all be described.) Amounts of American assets are designated by a_i and amounts of Japanese assets by n_j. Holdings by Americans are denoted by ^{A} and those by the Japanese by ^{N}. Thus $a_i = a_i^A + a_i^N$ and $n_j = n_j^A + n_j^N$. The asset units are par values for nominally dominated securities and commodity units for equities or real properties. The American and Japanese steady-state growth trend rates are g_a and g_n respectively.

The prices of assets are q_{aj} and q_{nj}, in dollars or yen per asset unit respectively. These prices are related, normally inversely, to the rates of return r_{ai} and r_{nj}. In each country there is one asset, base money, with a value of 1 in local currency and a nominal return of zero or some other constant. The exchange rate is e dollars per yen.

The values of the desired asset holdings in the currency of the country of issue are, A_i^A and N_j^A for the Americans and A_i^N and N_j^N for the Japanese. In the currency of the holder they are A_i^A and eN_j^A, and $(1/e)A_i^N$ and N_j^N. The latter two are functions of the vectors and the rates of return (r_{ai}, r_{nj}), of prices and expected inflation rates, of the Net National Product (current and in principle future) in the investor's home country, and of the expected change in the exchange rate.

The flow demands for the various assets, expressed in dollars, are:

$$fA_i^A(t) = \alpha_i^A[A_i^A(t) - qa_i(t)a_i^A(t-1)] + g_a q_{ai}(t)a_i^A(t-1)$$
$$fA_i^N(t) = \beta_i^N e(t)\langle\{[1/e(t)]A_i^N(t)\} - [qa_i(t)/e(t)]a_i^N(t-1)\rangle$$
$$+ g_n e(t)[qa_i(t)/e(t)]a_i^N(t-1) \quad (2)$$
$$fN_j^A(t) = \alpha_j^A\{[e(t)N_j^A(t-1)] - e(t)qn_j(t)n_j^A(t-1)\} + g_a e(t)qn_j(t)n_j^A(t-1)$$
$$fN_j^N(t) = \beta_j^N e(t)[N_j^N - qn_j(t)n_j^N(t-1)] + g_n e(t)qn_j(t)n_j^N(t-1)$$

In each case, the first term is the stock adjustment and the second term is the flow required to make the holding increase at the rate of the economy's growth. The speeds of adjustment (α and β) are multiplied by the excess of desired holdings over the value of previous holdings at the prices of the current period. The flow demands for each asset—that is, $(fA_i^A + fA_i^N)$

and $[(fN_j^A + fN_j^N)/e]$ in local currencies—are to be equated with the new supplies.

Total wealth stocks and total private saving in both economies are implicit in the above equations. They equal the sum of stocks and flows for the wealth owners of the country. In steady states, with stock adjustments equal to zero, asset supplies and holdings and total wealth would be growing at rates g_a and g_n. There are two more supply = demand equations than there are endogenous asset prices (or corresponding rates of return). This is because the local prices of currencies and their nominal returns are fixed. And there is one more equation, the payments balance equation. It is natural to think of the equality of net capital flow to current account balance as determining the exchange rate, just as in the one-country framework sketched above. This is the payments balance equation (3), with the net capital inflow to the United States in dollars on the left-hand side and on the right-hand side the American current account deficit. This deficit has two parts: the trade deficit and the deficit in investment incomes. Here p and Y with superscripts are local price levels and Net National Products:

$$\Sigma_i fA_i^N - \Sigma_j fN_j^A = X^N(ep^N/p^A, Y^A) - eX^A(p^A/ep^N, Y^N)$$
$$+ \Sigma_i r_{ai} q_{ai} a_i^N - e\Sigma_j r_{nj} q_{nj} n_j^A \qquad (3)$$

What variables do the two extra equations determine? In some contexts these would be the two Ys and in others the two price levels. If aggregate supply equations—"AS curves"—were added for each economy, all four of these variables could be determined. Alternatively, two instruments of monetary policy, local interest rates or monetary bases, could be the free variables. The two price levels would be taken as predetermined in the short run and the two Ys would be those chosen by the monetary authorities. There are many other possibilities.

Models of this kind are designed to exploit imperfect substitutabilities among assets, to analyze the effects of variations in relative asset supplies, and to explain variations in differentials among asset rates of return. For these purposes, the crucial parameters are the partial derivatives of desired asset stocks with respect to the rates of return. It is intuitively natural to expect own partials to be positive, or at least non-negative. Furthermore, the gross substitutes assumption is convenient and plau-

ON THE INTERNATIONALIZATION OF PORTFOLIOS 549

Table 20.3
Illustrative Two-country Sectoral Portfolio Matrix

	American portfolios				Japanese portfolios				Total
	Hhs	Bus	Bks	Gov	Hhs	Bus	Bks	Gov	
American assets									
$ Base money	+	+	+						0
$ Deposits	+	+	−			+	+	+	0
$ Treas. debt	+	+	+	−	+		+	+	0
$ Hh debt	−	+	+						0
$ Bus. debt	+	−	+		+	+			0
Equity	+	−	−		+	+			0
Real property	+	+			+	+			+
A-owned A-assets	+	−	−	−					+
N-owned A-assets					+	+	+	+	+
Japanese assets									
YEN base money					+	+	+	−	0
YEN deposits		+	+	+	+	+	−		0
YEN treas. debt	+		+	+	+	+	+	−	0
YEN Hh debt					−	+	+		0
YEN bus. debt	+	+			+	−	+		0
Equity	+	+			+	−	−		0
Real property	+	+			+	+			+
A-owned N-assets	+	+	+	+					+
N-owned N-assets					+	−	−	−	+
Net worth	+	0	0	−	+	0	0	−	+

A, American; N, Japanese.

sible, though not mandated by rationality. High absolute values of cross partials indicate high substitutability between assets, and low values the reverse. Common vulnerabilities to certain risks make for high substitutability. Assets whose returns, including capital gains or losses, do not share the same risks, or move in opposite directions in response to the same shocks, will be poor substitutes. An example is given below, where it is argued that equities and real properties in two countries could be good portfolio substitutes for each other but poor substitutes for nominal assets in either currency.

Table 20.3 illustrates an accounting scheme for (2) and (3). In the matrix, the columns represent sectors of the two economies, America on the left and Japan on the right. Only four sectors of each economy are distinguished here. The rows represent assets, American at the top and

Japanese at the bottom. Seven asset categories are shown for each country. A plus sign in a cell indicates that the sector holds positive quantities of the asset, a minus sign implies that the sector is a debtor in this category of asset. The entries in a column, for both local and foreign assets, describe the sector's portfolio; they sum to the sector's net worth. The entries in a row show how the positive and negative holdings of a given asset are distributed amongst sectors in the two countries. The row sums, in the final column, are zero for all the assets that are obligations of one or more of the sectors. They are positive only for real property (capital) in the two economies. The sum of the values of the two capital stocks are equal to the sum of the sector net worths. Of course, one country—in present circumstances, Japan—may have a net worth greater than its own capital stock by the amount of its net claims on the other country.

Table 20.3 is a schematic balance sheet in which the entries are stocks. An analogous schema would describe the flows in any period, as in the model above. The illustration is for a two-country world, but the same format could be used for n countries. Obviously we are a long way from having data for such spreadsheets but Kuroyanagi, Hamada, and Sakurai (1989) have made a pioneering start.

In a two-country model, it is not possible to get definitive qualitative results like those reported above for a one-country open economy. This is true *a fortiori* for n countries. However, in a two-country floating rate model, the presumption is that expansionary fiscal policies and other positive "IS" shocks in one country will raise real outputs and/or prices in both countries. On the other hand, expansionary monetary policies and other positive "LM" shocks in one country will raise real outputs and/or prices in that country but lower them elsewhere (Tobin and Macedo, 1980).

5 Home Asset Preferences

International financial and capital markets determine simultaneously the prices of the various assets and currencies, as well as domestic commodity prices and/or incomes. Asset values will depend on their relative supplies and on the asset preferences of wealth owners. A common assumption is that wealth owners display a home currency preference, both on average and on the margin. That is, Americans hold most of their wealth in dollar assets and, at given rates of return and exchange rates, will place most of a given increment of wealth in dollars. They will require a premium over local rates of return to invest abroad.

As asset supplies and total wealth of the several countries evolve over time, so will their trade balances and current account deficits or surpluses. These depend on prices, exchange rates, interest rates, and domestic absorptions. Current account deficits equal capital inflows. The identity says nothing about causation, which can run either way. Monetary and financial shocks may lead to international asset transfers whose counterparts are current account imbalances; exchange rates may change in the process.

On the other hand, shocks of taste and technology that alter the competitiveness of nations in trade may lead to current account imbalances and shifts of wealth, which set in motion adjustments of prices, interest rates, and exchange rates along with international asset transfers. These adjustments are required because wealth owners differ in preferences. If those in a surplus country prefer local assets, their currency will become more valuable.

Home currency preference is by no means an implication of portfolio theory. The risks of nominal assets are those of commodity price fluctuation, interest rate variation, and default. Economies with different currencies, geographies, and central governments will be more independent of each other in these dimensions than, for example, the states of a central union.

Exchange risk may work either way. Here it is necessary to consider the correlations of deviations of exchange rates from expected trends with the other risks of nominal assets. If a foreign currency appreciates when home inflation increases and depreciates when foreign inflation is relatively high, foreign currency assets are a hedge. If the foreign currency depreciates when domestic interest rates move up, foreign securities are not a good hedge against capital losses on home bonds.

In the past, home asset preferences have been due less to risk-return calculus than to other factors: legal restrictions, transactions costs, and information gaps. These obstacles have all been diminishing. Institutional and individual portfolios are slowly becoming more international.

Equities and direct investments in real properties in foreign countries present opportunities and risks quite different from those of currency-denominated assets. Some of the geographical, political, legal, and informational reasons for home preference certainly apply to both. But one consideration that leads to home preference among currency-denominated assets, the avoidance of exchange risk in consuming the income or principal, applies with considerably less force.

Equities, and the real capital assets to which they are claims, are not entitlements to specified amounts of any currencies. An extreme view is that goods are goods, capital goods are capital goods, and factories are factories, wherever they are located. Earnings of multi-national companies come from worldwide sales in numerous currencies. Neither the earnings nor the value of the shares in any currency need be particularly correlated with the price of the currency of the country where the company is domiciled. Indeed, if a company is leveraged by debt in its home currency, owners of its equity are short in that currency.

Consider Japanese direct investments in the United States, say in particular the acquisition of facilities for producing internationally traded goods like automobiles. In the first instance, Japanese investors use dollars bought from Japanese exporters to buy or build a factory, instead of purchasing U.S. Treasury bonds or other nominal dollar assets. This substitution of American equity for bonds may be only transitory. Japanese investors' demand for nominal dollar assets should not decline by the full amount of their direct investments in the U.S. The reason is that an automobile factory in Ohio may well be a closer substitute for factories, properties, and equities in Japan and elsewhere than it is for future dollars *qua* dollars.

The international car market can be supplied from Tennessee or from Tokyo. The long-run real returns from owning a plant in Tennessee are not highly dependent on the dollar/yen exchange rate and not very vulnerable to the factors that might generate losses to Japanese holders of American bonds. U.S. inflation, for example, would raise the dollar earnings from operating the plant at the same time as it depreciated the dollar against the yen. Direct investment of this kind in the U.S. is a portfolio reallocation *vis-à-vis* Japanese plants, real properties, and equities more than *vis-à-vis* dollars *per se*. Indeed, scattering production for the world market over various locations may reduce risk by diversifying risks caused by national or regional productivity shocks.

When Japanese investments overseas are in real assets productive of nontraded goods, like office space in Rockefeller Center, they are not so obviously substitutes for similar real assets in Japan. But neither are they particular substitutes for U.S. bonds or other U.S. nominal assets. However, the principal location and legal and tax domicile of a business entangles its earnings with the domestic and exchange value of the currency. Equity in a country's businesses may be a closer substitute for home than for foreign debt securities.

6 Allowing for Risks to Consumption

A basic contribution to portfolio theory has been the recognition that what really concerns an individual saver and investor is the return on his total "portfolio," which includes nontradable assets (and possibly debts) as well as marketable assets. Indeed, human capital (the value of labor) is the major component of the wealth of the majority of us for most of our lives. The possibilities of selling or borrowing against it are strictly limited and the returns are uncertain. The returns are subject to their own idiosyncratic shocks, but also to many of the same shocks that affect the returns on tradable assets. It is this insight that led to "consumption-betas" in asset pricing models.[2]

Assuming that individuals are predominantly risk averse, they are willing to give up some mean expectation of portfolio return to reduce their risk. Applying this assumption to their total portfolios, inclusive of nontradable human capital, implies that they will give up some return on their market portfolios or accept some additional risk on them, to diminish their overall risk. Considerations of this kind suggest that a worker should not invest his retirement savings in the shares of the company that employs him and that a farmer should not invest in agricultural real estate subject to the same meteorological shocks as his own farm.

The same considerations may well suggest the reverse of home asset preference on the ground that domestic macroeconomic shocks affect capital and labor incomes in the same directions. If foreign assets are indeed useful hedges against major shocks to domestic wage incomes, then the small amount of international diversification observed is an even greater puzzle than it appears when only tradable-asset portfolios are considered. The puzzle leads to a forecast that global diversification has a long way to go.

Appendix A gives a simple example of the opportunities afforded by adding foreign assets to a portfolio. Using mean-variance analysis, risk-return frontiers are computed for two asset menus: (i) two tradable domestic assets, nominal bonds and equities; and (ii) the first menu augmented by two foreign assets, nominal bonds and equities. These frontiers show the minimum risk to the portfolio return for a sequence of required mean portfolio returns. It is shown that the addition of foreign assets to the menu improves the frontier.

Calculations are also made for the risks of a more inclusive "portfolio" inclusive of human capital yielding wages, a nontradable asset that the typical agent can neither buy nor sell. Taking into account this non-discretionary asset along with the menu of market assets whose holdings are discretionary makes a significant difference. When shocks to wages are correlated with those of other assets, the composition of efficient market portfolios will be quite different if the objective is to minimize total variance for a given mean return, rather than to minimize portfolio variance alone.

In the illustrative simulations of Appendix A, the several asset returns are affected in different ways and degrees by several domestic, foreign, and common shocks: shocks to productivity, inflation, nominal interest rates, world oil prices, and the nominal exchange rate. In the example, the availability of the foreign assets improves the frontier substantially, especially when account is taken of the covariances of wages with portfolio asset returns. The calculations also illustrate how different the efficient tradable portfolios are when efficiency is defined to be minimization of total risk rather than just risk on the portfolio of tradable assets.

The illustration does not give a full general equilibrium solution. It shows that there is "room for a deal." The home side would want a deal, and because foreign worker investors are in a symmetrical position, they would want a deal too. Of course, the deal would not be as good as the partial calculations suggest, because the reallocations of assets will change their rates of return.

7 Gains from International Asset Trades in the Long Run

This discussion has so far concerned relatively short horizons, when shocks to real and nominal aggregate demand and shocks to nominal interest rates are major sources of risks to domestic asset holdings. Likewise, exchange rate fluctuations induced by such shocks at home and abroad are major sources of risks in holding claims on foreigners. Over longer horizons, demand-side fluctuations in economic activity and nominal shocks to financial markets are less important sources of risk. Changes in levels and rates of growth of productivity, directly affecting the real value of a country's endowment of labor, land, and capital, are the basic domestic sources of risk. Shocks to the terms of trade a country faces in international commodity markets are likely to be the dominant external sources of risk. Although many investors appear to focus on short-run fluctuations in financial markets, over an individual's lifetime fundamental long-term risks are probably more important. For nations, this is *a fortiori* true.

Here, the long-run gains from international trade in assets are examined, an inquiry similar to the theory of gains from commodity trade. (If our model seems applicable to asset trade between individuals or households as much as between nations or regions, that is of course not surprising. So does the theory of trade in commodities, including the law of comparative advantage.) We investigate the importance of the basic risks identified above and the potential of international diversification to reduce them and thereby to improve welfare. Our illustrative model is simple and abstract; nevertheless it is not easy to analyze, and numerical simulations will be used.

A two-country competitive exchange economy is considered.[3] The two countries are mirror images of each other; there are two goods, one produced by each country, which are not perfect substitutes in consumption and are traded between the countries in a spot market in which the terms of trade are competitively determined. The representative agent in each country consumes both commodities but has a preference for home goods. In the simulations reported in Appendix B, the demand functions are contrived to imply a 20% share of imports when the price ratio between the two goods is unity. Agents have infinite horizons but discount the future. Preferences are intertemporally additive and display constant relative risk aversion. The demands in each period are derived from a CES "felicity"[4] function, with constant relative risk aversion for commodity bundles with any fixed composition of home and foreign goods. The felicity and utility functions for the two agents have the same elasticity of substitution, risk aversion, and time preference.

In this economy, an asset is simply a claim on current and future endowments. Each country is exogenously endowed each period with some quantity of its perishable consumption good. Over time the endowment of each country follows a Markov process, wandering around a mean level of one. The two processes are independent of each other. Specifically, in the simulations of Appendix B, a country with an endowment e_t in period t has either the same endowment, s percent more, or s percent less in period $t + 1$, with specified probabilities for the changes of state. These probabilities are not independent of the state. Movements of endowments away from their central value, 1, are limited by a floor and a ceiling. As the endowment approaches its floor, the probability of a downward move declines and that of remaining steady correspondingly increases. At the floor the probability of further decline is zero. The adjustment of probabilities near the ceiling is symmetric. The probability of a regressive movement is always the same. Although this process gives a stationary distribution of endowments, in the neighborhood of 1 it is approximately a random walk. Because the probabilities of movement up and down are symmetric in the sense described, no upward drift in endowments occurs.[5]

Because the purpose of this exercise is to investigate the importance of international portfolio diversification, we calculate equilibrium terms of trade, asset prices, rates of return, and risk premia for two asset menus. In the first, capital market autarky, residents of a country can hold claims only on their own country's endowments. They have no opportunity to diversify or to hedge on future changes in the terms of trade. Second, agents are allowed to hold claims for pro-rata shares of the foreign country's endowment in every future period. The optimal two-asset portfolio for each country's agents is computed and the effect of diversification on the rates of return and on welfare are calculated.[6]

Table 20.B1(a–e) reports, for all one-period states of the world (of which there are a finite number), the commodity price ratio, country 1's consumption of the two commodities, the marginal utilities of the home goods, and country 1's "felicity." In addition, the dependence of a country 1 agent's expected utility on the shares she owns of the future endowments in the two countries is calculated. Given the stochastic process assumed and the assumption that portfolios are unchanging over time, this expected utility is uniquely determined by the current state of the two countries' endowments. To indicate the magnitude of the gains from diversification, the certainty equivalent is also presented., i.e. that hypothetical sure permanent endowment which has the same utility as the actual uncertain claims. The simulations are made for a variety of assumptions about the elasticity of substitution between the two goods, varying from near perfect substitutability to near total inelasticity.

Each section of the table displays the outcomes under capital-market autarky and for various amounts of diversification (including the optimally diversified portfolio which maximizes utility). Our discussion will focus mainly on the gains from diversification to economies initially at the expected value of endowments (1, 1). To economize on computation, each "period" is taken to be five years, but the results are reported on an annual basis.

The near perfect substitutes case, shown in Table 20.B1(a), is the simplest to analyze. As expected, terms of trade are almost constant. Under autarky the marginal utilities of the two countries are essentially independent, but vary a great deal with the own countries' endowments. Endowment risk is important; the certainty equivalent of the uncertain future faced by an agent holding only domestic claims is 0.927, a 7.3% loss when the world is in state (1, 1). In the high substitutability case, the two representative agents have very similar preferences. Therefore, when trade between them in endowments is allowed, the optimal portfolio is essentially half domestic and half foreign claims. This cuts the risk discount from the certainty equivalent roughly in half, from 7.3% to 3.1%. Actually, much of this gain (2.2%) can be achieved with a portfolio of which only a quarter is invested in foreign claims.

Diversification changes the *ex post* distribution of consumption between countries. Just how it changes depends on the elasticity of substitution between the two consumption goods. If elasticity is > 1, favorable productivity draws in one country give a larger share of world income to foreigners the more they are diversified. Because foreigners spend a smaller share of their income on the good than domestic consumers, its relative price falls more than under capital-market autarky. Even in the near perfect substitutes case, this effect of diversification on the variance of relative prices can be seen. The variance of relative prices increases, but only very slightly, with increased diversification. These effects are reversed when the elasticity is < 1.

The more elastic the demands, the smaller are the variations of the terms of trade. A favorable endowment draw results in an offsetting deterioration in the terms of trade, but the offset is incomplete as long as the elasticity is > 1. As can be seen in Table 20.B1(b and c), this induces a correlation between the (home-good) marginal utilities in the two countries. Good outcomes in country 2 not only lower the marginal utility of good 2 in country 2, but also lower the marginal utility of good 1 in country 1.

In the elastic demand case, the gains from diversification are greater the higher the elasticity. For a substitution elasticity of 4, for example, the certainty equivalence of (1, 1) under capital market autarky is 0.932. The optimal portfolio, approximately 0.5–0.5, has a certainty equivalent of 0.965, a gain of 3.3%. When the substitution elasticity is 20, the certainty equivalent is 0.927 under capital-market autarky but 0.936 with optimal diversification (close to 0.5–0.5), a gain of 4.2%.

The possibility that endogenous adjustments in the terms of trade mitigate the gains from international diversification is shown most clearly in the case where the substitution elasticity $= 1$ (Table 20.B1c). In this case, terms of trade effects exactly offset the endowment changes. Owning a share of foreign endowment does not provide insurance against changes in the terms of trade; when home country endowment is low, the value of claims on foreign goods is also low. As a consequence, expected utility and certainty equivalent are insensitive to the share of wealth invested abroad.

With elasticities < 1, increases in the supply of a commodity decrease its share in world income. Hence, under capital-market autarky, positive endowment shocks make home agents worse off and improve the welfare of foreigners. This redistribution could, in principle, be quite dramatic. As shown in Table 20.B1(e), with an elasticity as low as 0.25, autarky is disastrous—the certainty equivalent for endowment state (1, 1) is < 0.04. (Agricultural countries and regions are familiar with this kind of disaster.) As can be seen in the table, the adjustments in the terms of trade generate a negative correlation of marginal utilities, suggesting substantial gains from even modest international diversification. Moving from a 0% claim on foreign assets to 5% raises the certainty equivalent of (1, 1) to 0.515. The optimal portfolio is very close to a hedging portfolio, a 20% portfolio share for foreign assets, corresponding to the assumed normal 20% share of imports (if only the farmers owned shares in the industries of their customers ...).

8 Asset Prices and Risk Premia

The computed competitive equilibria provide, for each single-period state of the two countries, values of *pro rata* claims on each country's future endowments in terms of the country's good in the current period. Such claims are referred to as equities, although they are unlike real-world equities in encompassing all claims on the country's resources. This model lumps profits, interest, and wages. Each equilibrium also determines the terms of trade, the price of country 2's good in terms of country 1's good. Thus, equity prices in home goods can be translated into foreign goods. Equilibrium in any period means that world consumption of each good is equal to the endowment of that good in the state of nature realized in that period. It also means that, at prevailing goods and asset prices, the demands of the agents for both countries' future endowments add up to the supplies.

Holding equity from one period to the next yields a share of the next period's endowment plus the value of the same claim in the state realized in the next period. Because the state of the world next period is uncertain, the return to holding equity from one period to the next is uncertain. Economists like to compare the expected one period return on equity to a one period risk-free rate of return, calling the difference between them the risk premium. This can be done here, but it is important to be clear about the concept of risk-free rate.

If an economy contains numerous agents with identical preferences and resources, there is no reason for trade among them. In autarky, for example, all agents would consume *pro rata* shares of their country's endowment and hold *pro rata* equity claims on its future. There would be no function for assets with different risk characteristics, in particular no reason for separate markets for risk-free real bills or bonds.

Nevertheless, from the state prices, implicit in the competitive equilibria described above, can be derived prices of any assets with specified state distributions of returns. Consider a promise to deliver one unit of commodity 1 next period, whatever the state of nature realized. This promise will have a price in terms of commodity 1 today, and from that price can be determined the risk-free rate of return. In a certain world or a world of risk-neutral agents, and in the absence of growth, this would simply be the rate of time preference, 4% in our simulations. In an uncertain world, risk-averse investors may be willing to buy a risk-free contract at a roughly different rate, lower or higher than their time preference rate.

Our simulations (Table 20.B2) show how opportunities for international diversification affect rates of return on the two assets—equity claims on endowments in the two countries. These returns are decomposed into risk-free return and risk premium. In our model, "consumption" consists of two consumption goods, combined in a Constant Elasticity of Substitution (CES) function. The "felicity" of composite consumption is given by a Constant Relative Risk Aversion (CRRA) function. Intertemporal choice is driven by the expected felicity of future consumption relative to present consumption. The risk-free return is the hypothetical amount by which consumption must be increased for certain, i.e. in every state of nature, to induce the consumer to give up one unit of present consumption.

Simulation results are tabulated (Table 20.B2) for three substitution elasticities, one above unity (viz. 20), one equal to unity, and one below unity (viz. 0.25). For each elasticity, results are shown for two portfolios. Optimal portfolio diversification lowers risk premiums, as would be expected. But it may seem surprising that it usually also raises the risk-free rate by more than the reduction in the risk premium, so that the rate of return on foreign equity also rises.

What is the reason for the rise in the underlying risk-free rate, notably, for example, in the top two panels, when the share in home equity is reduced from 1 to 0.5? The value of a risk-free asset depends on the expected marginal felicity of the extra future consumption it delivers for certain in the various states of nature. Assuming our CRR felicity function, the uncertainty of future consumption itself leads to a higher expected value of marginal felicity than would be the case if future consumption were certain. (This is a property of any felicity function with a positive third derivative.) The opportunity to diversify enables a risk-averse consumer to reduce risk and increase *total* utility. At the same time it lowers the *marginal* expected felicity of future consumption relative to present consumption. Consequently, the consumer would wish to shift consumption to the present. No such shift is possible—there are no stores of goods to draw down and endowments are exogenous. To make agents content not to shift, rates of return which govern intertemporal substitutions have to be higher. In the top panels of Table 20.B2 this effect is substantial, for both risk-free rates and total returns on foreign equity. Table 20.B2 reports the expected values and distributional characteristics of these two rates of return and of the risk premium for both economies, and tells how they are affected by widening the menu of assets to permit international diversification.

As already noted, when substitutability between the two goods is nearly perfect, variations in terms of trade are relatively inconsequential. Under capital market autarky, an agent's risk is almost entirely a reflection of the substantial volatility in the home country's endowments. The risk premium is 1.7%. Even though the response of terms of trade to relative supplies is small, it results in a slight positive correlation in the two countries' rates of return. That is, a good harvest in one country improves welfare in the other.

The composition of the optimal international portfolios held when diversification is allowed depends on the elasticity of substitution between the two consumption goods. In the near perfect substitutes case, agents will hold roughly equal quantities of each equity. This diversification cuts the variance of returns and risk premiums by about one half. With the same claims being held in both countries, the inter-country correlations of incomes and equity returns are high—nearly 0.6 in the case of equity returns.

When the elasticity of substitution is unity, changes in terms of trade suffice to accomplish efficient allocation of risks. There is little merit in opening up international asset markets; with or without them, asset returns in the two countries are highly correlated.

With low substitution, elasticity autarky entails large risks. With an elasticity as low as 0.25, fluctuations in equity prices are almost boundless. Even with 5% of portfolios in foreign equity, variations in asset prices are four times what they would be with unitary elasticity, and risk premia are correspondingly high. Positive home endowment shocks lead to losses of home income and gains in foreign income; thus equity returns in the two economies show a strong negative correlation.

In this case, the optimal portfolio enables the representative agent to hedge her position completely; portfolio shares mimic her consumption shares, in our simulations 80% domestic and 20% foreign. Given this degree of diversification, equity risks and risk premia fall dramatically to levels comparable to those of the case of unitary elasticity. The correlations between the two incomes become strongly positive instead of strongly negative.

9 Problems in Empirical Estimation

Current asset prices depend on expectations and on expectations of expectations. Portfolio choices involve comparisons of returns on many assets and thus involve expectations and joint probability distributions of large dimensions. The market prices that emerge today reflect choices by many diverse investors and depend on their estimates of the price vectors that similar market processes will generate in the future.

Unfortunately the relevant expectations are largely unobservable. Rational expectations theory confines price-determining expectations to those that will in fact be realized, at least actuarially. Those expectations are supposed to be anchored in a future equilibrium on which the views of investors converge. But econometricians, and presumably market participants too, have great difficulty in identifying such an equilibrium and much more in estimating it.

Our standard textbook theory of exchange rates says that a country's exchange rate is on a (singular) path towards an equilibrium rate. Its rate of change along that path is meanwhile making up for differences in national interest rates. A macroeconomic intervention, event, or news item can affect the current exchange rate by tilting the path (e.g. if the interest differential is changed) or by altering the expected future equilibrium rate (e.g. a change in expected fiscal policy). However, that equilibrium is hard to pin down. Purchasing power parity and zero current account balance are sometimes advanced as candidates for defining equilibrium, but they are treacherous. As for "ppp," the real exchange rate is generally dependent on the trade balance and reflects the imperfect substitutability of imports and domestically produced goods. As for current account balance, there is no reason to expect it in any practical long-run.

Moreover, the *nominal* exchange rate is not foreseeable on the basis of the real economic forces involved in projections of trade balances and terms of trade. We would have to model and estimate the monetary and fiscal policies of the several countries, their political and social tolerances of inflation and unemployment, the evolution of their price- and wage-setting institutions and of their financial systems, and many other phenomena relating to nominal variables and their interactions with real economic outcomes.

Observed flows of capital can reflect either or both of two conceptually distinct phenomena: reallocations of portfolio stock and allocations of new wealth in established patterns. Stock reallocations are one-shot effects that occur in response to changes in current and expected asset yields and in perceived risks. Because of transactions costs and other frictions, they do not take place instantaneously in response to news. They take time, but as they are completed and portfolios are reshaped they die out. In the absence of further changes of yields and risks, i.e. without news, these flows between markets and across frontiers and currencies become zero. Accretions to wealth, on the other hand, are a continuing source of capital flows.

For example, suppose U.S. assets are about 10% of fully adjusted Japanese portfolios. In stable circumstances 10% of the regular annual additions to these portfolios should be expected to flow to U.S. markets. Japan's wealth is estimated to be six times its GNP. Suppose that steady state growth for both Japanese wealth and Japanese GNP is in nominal terms 9% per year. Thus the steady flow into U.S. assets would be $0.10 \times 0.09 \times 6 \times \text{JGNP}$, about U.S.\$16 billion. In the recent decade, of course, Japanese holdings of U.S. assets have grown sharply in relation both to Japanese and U.S. wealth. One may infer that a stock adjustment has been occurring, and is ongoing. Obviously it must taper off sooner or later. But when?

The lags in portfolio adjustment make the econometrician's life difficult, because he or she cannot assume that observations reflect desired holdings. The long process of internationalization means that observations during the process are not good guides to investors' behavior once the reallocation is completed. The "bootstrap" method of calculating asset mean returns, variances, and covariances from market histories—

the same market histories the method is supposed to explain—is particularly likely to be misleading. A preferable approach may be to use "fundamental" data only (Tobin and Brainard, 1977; Brainard, Shoven, and Weiss, 1980; Tobin, 1984; Brainard, Shapiro, and Shoven, 1991). But, as already acknowledged above, it is difficult to identify the "fundamentals" of nominal variables.

Notes

In this paper we have adapted material from previous articles, in particular Brainard and Tobin (1968), Brainard and Dolbear (1971), and Tobin (1982a, b, 1990), as well as articles specifically cited.

1. A more general specification would allow the adjustment of desired stock to depend on discrepancies in other asset stocks, not just on the asset i (Brainard and Tobin (1968)).

2. An early paper with this perspective, distinguishing between tradable and nontradable assets and emphasizing social risk, is Brainard and Dolbear (1971). Golub (1990) has recently studied empirically opportunities for international diversification between the US and Japan. On the general use of "consumption betas," stressing covariances with consumption rather than with market, the basic references are Merton (1973) and Breeden (1979).

3. The model is in effect a two-country version of the model used by Mehra and Prescott (1985) to examine the equity risk premium. This paper was initially presented at an ETLA conference in Helsinki in June 1991. Subsequently we became aware of a similar analysis by Cole and Obstfeld (1991). The two most important differences are that in our model agents exhibit "home preference" and are allowed to have less than unitary elasticity or substitution between home and foreign goods.

4. It is convenient to call the utility generated by consumption in a single period "felicity" and to use the term "utility" to describe the properly weighted sums of period-by-period felicities over the consumer's horizon.

5. In our simulations, as explained in Appendix B, periods correspond to five years, and the steps s are 10%, approximately 2% at annual rates. Locally, the implied endowment growth process is essentially the same as the two state Markov process used by Mehra and Prescott (1985). They find that annual steps of 3.6% with a drift of 1.8% and a small amount of serial correlation mimic US data on real per-capita consumption for the period 1889–1978. As they note, allowing for serial correlation has only a minimal impact on the results because there is only small (negative) serial correlation in the observed consumption growth. Here, however, a time discount rate, rather than a declining marginal utility caused by trend growth, is the reason for a positive risk-free rate of interest.

6. It would be possible also to compute equilibria with a full set of Arrow–Debreu securities, i.e. one for each potential state of the world in each time period.

References

Brainard, W. C., Shoven, J. B., and Weiss, L. (1980). "Financial Valuation of the Return to Capital," *Brookings Papers on Economic Activity*, 2, 453–502.

Brainard, W. C. and Tobin, J. (1968). "Pitfalls in Financial Model-Building," *American Economic Review*, 58, 99–122.

Brainard, W. C., Shapiro, M., and Shoven, J. B. (1991). "Fundamental Value and Market Value," in *Macroeconomics, Finance and Economic Policy*, W. C. Brainard, W. D. Nordhaus, and H. W. Watts (eds), Cambridge MA: MIT Press.

Brainard, W C. and Dolbear, F. T. (1971). "Social Risk and Financial Markets," *American Economic Review*, 61, 360–70.

Breeden, D. (1979). "An Intertemporal Asset-Pricing Model with Stochastic Consumption and Investment," *Journal of Financial Economics*, 7, 265–96.

Cole, H. L. and Obstfeld, M. (1991). "Commodity Trade and International Risk Sharing," *Journal of Monetary Economics*, 28, 3–28.

Golub, S. S. (1990). "International Diversification of Social and Private Risk: the US and Japan," mimeo., Swarthmore College, PA.

Hamada, K. and Iwata, K. (1985). "The Significance of Saving Ratios for the Current Account: the US–Japan Case," mimeo., Yale University, CT.

Kuroyanagi, M., Hamada, K., and Sakurai, M. (1989). "Towards the Estimation of the World Asset and Debt Matrix", mimeo., Yale University, CT.

Mehra, R. and Prescott, E. (1985). "The Equity Premium Puzzle," *Journal of Monetary Economics*, 15, 145–61.

Merton, R. C. (1973). "An Intertemporal Capital Asset Pricing Model," *Econometrica*, 41, 867–87.

Tobin, J. (1982a). "Money and Finance in the Macro-Economic Process," *Journal of Money, Credit and Banking*, 16, 171–204.

Tobin, J. (1982b). "The State of Exchange Rate Theory: Some Skeptical Observations," in *International Monetary Systems under Flexible Exchange Rates: Global, Regional, and National*, Richard Cooper et al. (eds), Cambridge MA: Ballinger, 115–28.

Tobin, J. (1984). "A Mean-Variance Approach to Fundamental Valuation," *Journal of Portfolio Management*, Fall, 26–32.

Tobin, J. (1990). "Policies and Exchange Rates: a Simple Analytical Framework," mimeo., Center for Japan–US Business and Economic Studies, New York University.

Tobin, J. and Brainard, W. C. (1977). "Asset Markets and the Cost of Capital," in *Economic Progress: Private Values and Public Policy*, R. Nelson and B. Balassa (eds), Amsterdam: North Holland, 235–52.

Tobin, J. and De Macedo, J. B. (1980). "The Short-Run Macroeconomics of Floating Exchange Rates: an Exposition," in *Flexible Exchange Rates and the Balance of Payments*, J. Chipman and C. P. Kindleberger (eds), Amsterdam: North-Holland, 6–28.

Appendix A

The illustrative simulation involves two countries and four portfolio assets, U bonds and U equities in country U and J bonds and J equities in country J. Equities are pure and unlevered; leverage can be provided by negative holdings of bonds. All the assets yield stochastic real returns. Using mean-variance analysis, risk-return loci are computed for a representative investor in U. That is, for various levels of expected real portfolio return the portfolio with the minimum variance is determined. In the figures, the minimum standard deviations of portfolio return are plotted against the sequence of assumed levels of expected return. The locus for an asset menu confined to the two local U assets is compared with the locus for a four-asset menu, to show the potential gains from international diversification.

In some calculations, a fifth risky asset, human capital yielding stochastic real wages, is added. Unlike the four portfolio assets, this asset cannot be bought or sold. The mean-variance calculation is then to find the portfolio of market assets that minimizes the total variance, taking into account also the non-market asset, for each given expectation of total real return. The relative sizes of the wealth invested in the market portfolio and human wealth are invariant, in proportions 1 : y. Variation in total expected real return comes solely from variation in portfolio return. Portfolio variance is defined as

$$\sigma_R^2 = \Sigma_{ij} \sigma_{ij} x_i x_j \tag{A1}$$

where i and j run from 1 to n, the number of assets, σ_{ij} are variances and covariances, and x_i and x_j are the shares of the assets in the portfolio. This is to be minimized subject to two constraints.:

$$\Sigma_i x_i r_i = R \tag{A2}$$

for various values of R, the portfolio return. The r_i are the expected values of real returns on the assets i, and

$$\Sigma_i x_i = 1. \tag{A3}$$

Total variance, taking account of stochastic deviations from expectations for the non-market asset, wages w, as well as for portfolio assets, is:

$$\sigma_T^2 = \sigma_R^2 + y^2 \sigma_w^2 + 2\Sigma_i y x_i \upsilon \sigma_{wi} \tag{A4}$$

This variance can be calculated when σ_R^2 is minimized, or, as suggested above, σ_T^2 itself is minimized.

These minimizations are solutions of $n + 2$ linear equations, the n first order conditions and the two constraints, giving the nx_i and the shadow prices of the two constraints. To compute the overall minimum variance portfolio, the first constraint (A2) is omitted. A rational investor will not be interested in any portfolio with a mean return smaller than that available at overall minimum risk.

The calculations reported here allow negative values of x_i, borrowing or short-selling. It would be possible, of course, to impose constraints on negative positions.

Table 20.A1 lists the ten shocks here considered, their assumed standard deviations, and the participation of the five assets in those shocks. The two countries, U and J, are taken to be virtual mirrors of one another. The major assumptions in the assets/shocks matrix are the following:[1]

(i) Home productivity shocks hit home equities and wages positively. They have smaller negative effects on foreign equities. Foreign productivity gains benefit real wages, because they make foreign imports cheaper.

(ii) The two countries share world-wide interest rate shocks and are, in addition, vulnerable to idiosyncratic local interest rate movements. Interest rates, as the discount rate for capitalizing future payments, affect both bonds and equities.

(iii) Likewise, the two countries share world-wide inflation shocks and, in addition, are affected by local inflation shocks. Real returns on U bonds are affected negatively by J inflation, because worker-consumer-investors consume imports from J.

(iv) An oil shock is taken to be tougher on J equities than on U equities, but to have no effect on J inflation and thus on J bonds.

Table 20.A1
Shocks and Their Effects on Variability of Asset Returns

Assets	U bonds	U equity	J bonds	J equity	U wages	Std devs
Shocks						
U prod		1.5		−0.5	0.8	0.03
J prod		−0.5		1.5	0.2	0.015
World int.	−1	−1	−1	−1		0.02
U int	−1	−1				0.02
J int			−1	−1		0.02
World infl	−1		−1			0.025
U infl	−0.8					0.015
J infl	−0.2		−1			0.015
Oil	−0.5	−0.5		−1	−0.2	0.05
Exchge rate			1			0.03

Implied Variances and Covariances of Asset Returns

	U bonds	U equity	J bonds	J equity	U wages
U bonds	0.002203	0.001425	0.00107	0.00165	0.00025
U equity	0.001425	0.003506	0.0004	0.000806	0.001307
J bonds	0.00107	0.0004	0.00255	0.0008	0
J equity	0.00165	0.000806	0.0008	0.004031	0.000207
U real wages	0.00025	0.001307	0	0.000207	0.000685
Mean returns	0.02	0.06	0.02	0.06	

Note: Human capital (wages) assumed 5 times as large as discretionary portfolio. Variance/covariance matrix above not adjusted for this assumption.

(v) Finally, an increase in the nominal value of the yen, arising from speculative causes and not from any of the other listed shocks, is taken to increase the real payoffs of J bonds to U investors.

The variance/covariance matrix for the five assets, as derived from the shocks/assets matrix, is also displayed in Table 20.A1. In the final line of the table are shown the assumed mean returns for the four portfolio assets. The mean return on the fifth asset is irrelevant to the portfolio choices, although the variance of wages and their covariance with the market asset returns are relevant.

Table 20.A2 reports the solutions, for both two-asset and four-asset portfolios and for both minimands, "var R" and "total var." Here "stdev total" is $\sigma_T/6$, where σ_T results from (A4). The first column gives the calculated minimum risk portfolio, along with the portfolio R it implies. The remaining columns are solutions subject to the constraint that portfolio R be the required return of the first row.

Figures 20.A1 and 20.A2 show graphically that adding the two foreign assets to the menu improves the risk-return frontier. As Table 20.A2 shows, the four-asset portfolios that accomplish this improvement depend importantly on which variance is being minimized. In both cases, large positive holdings of J bonds and J equities, partly financed by borrowing in the U bond market, are efficient. This is especially true when it is total variance that is being minimized, and selling U equity short is also risk-reducing. This reflects the assumption that domestic productivity shocks have large positive effects on both the marginal productivity of capital and the wages of labor. J assets do not share this risk.

Table 20.A2
Risks and Returns: Comparing Portfolio and Total Risks for Two- and Four-asset Menus

Required Return	no req (min var)	0.030	0.040	0.050	0.060	0.070	0.080	0.090	0.100
Std Devs Return									
2 asset portfolios									
min var R									
stdev R	0.002	0.045	0.046	0.051	0.059	0.069	0.079	0.091	0.103
stdev total	0.026	0.026	0.027	0.029	0.031	0.032	0.034	0.036	0.038
min total var									
stdev R	0.012	0.045	0.046	0.051	0.059	0.069	0.079	0.091	0.103
stdev total	0.020	0.026	0.027	0.029	0.031	0.032	0.034	0.036	0.038
4 asset portfolios									
min var R									
stdev R	0.038	0.039	0.038	0.040	0.044	0.049	0.056	0.063	0.071
stdev total	0.025	0.025	0.025	0.026	0.027	0.028	0.029	0.030	0.031
min total var									
stdev R	0.110	0.084	0.084	0.085	0.087	0.089	0.093	0.098	0.103
stdev total	0.018	0.021	0.022	0.023	0.024	0.025	0.026	0.027	0.028
Portfolio Shares:									
2 asset portfolios									
min var R									
U bonds	0.728	0.750	0.500	0.250	0.000	-.25	-.50	-.75	-1.00
U equities	0.272	0.250	0.500	0.750	1.000	1.250	0.500	1.750	2.000
Portfolio R	0.031	0.030	0.040	0.050	0.060	0.070	0.080	0.090	0.100
min total var									
U bonds	2.577	0.750	0.500	0.250	0.000	-.250	-.500	-.750	-1.00
U equities	-1.577	0.250	0.500	0.750	1.000	1.250	1.500	1.750	2.000
Portfolio R	-0.043	0.030	0.040	0.050	0.060	0.070	0.080	0.090	0.100

4 asset portfolios

min var R							
U bonds	0.178	0.332	0.100	−.131	−.362	−.594	−.825	−1.060	−1.290
U equity	0.260	0.177	0.303	0.429	0.555	0.681	0.807	0.933	1.059
J bonds	0.406	0.418	0.400	0.381	0.362	0.344	0.325	0.307	0.288
J equity	0.155	0.073	0.197	0.321	0.445	0.569	0.693	0.817	0.941
Portfolio R	0.037	0.030	0.040	0.050	0.060	0.070	0.080	0.090	0.100
min total var							
U bonds	1.514	−.085	−.316	−.548	−.780	−1.011	−1.242	−1.473	−1.705
U equity	−1.611	−.739	−.613	−.487	−.361	−.235	−.109	−.017	−0.143
J bonds	0.964	0.835	0.817	0.798	0.780	0.761	0.742	0.724	0.705
J equity	0.132	0.989	1.113	1.237	1.361	1.485	1.609	1.733	1.857
Portfolio R	−0.039	0.030	0.040	0.050	0.060	0.070	0.080	0.090	0.100

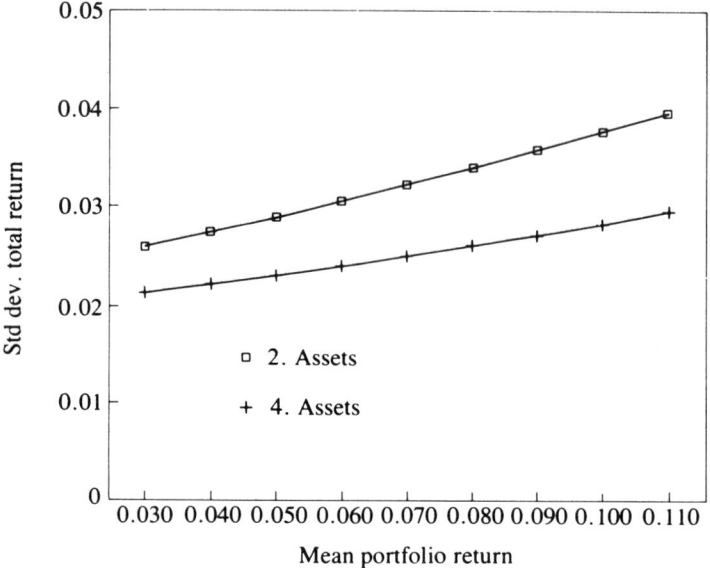

Figure 20.A1
Total risk-return frontiers (minimizing total variance)

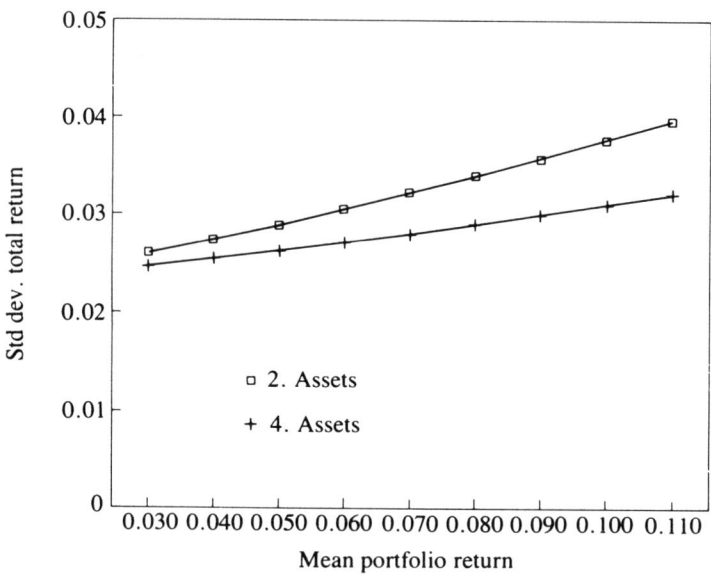

Figure 20.A2
Total risk-return frontiers (minimizing portfolio variance)

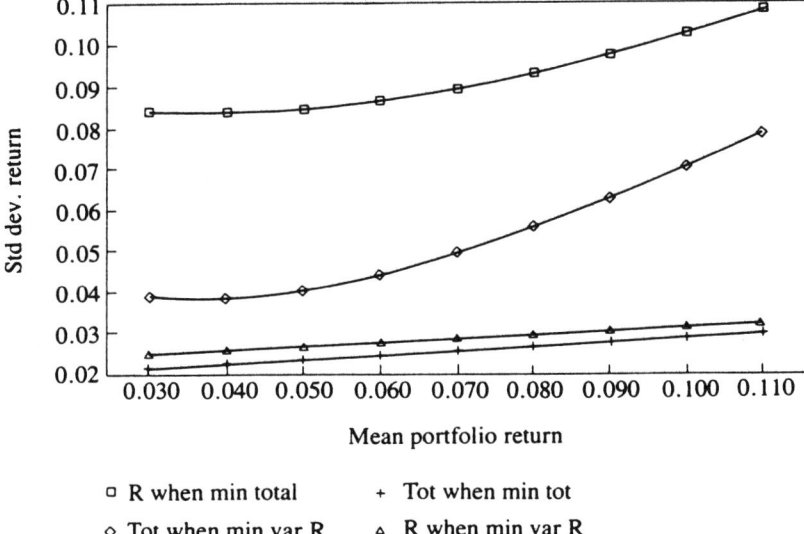

Figure 20.A3
Comparing risk-return loci (portfolio and total, two minimizations)

Figure 20.A3 makes the point that the choice of the minimand makes a big difference for the variance of portfolio return R (see the upper two loci in the Figure 20.A3). A high variance of R is efficient if the portfolios that produce it take advantage of covariances to reduce total variance. The bottom two panels of Table 20.A2 show radical differences in portfolio composition when the covariances of asset returns with wages are taken into account. Adding J assets to the menu provides these opportunities. The composition of the two-asset portfolios is, in this example, independent of the minimand. However, the differences in the two-asset minimum variance portfolios (first column) indicate that risk-shy investors worried about the variance of total return might stay out of equities or even sell them short.

Note to Appendix A

1. We have been guided to some extent by the empirical correlations reported by Golub (1990).

Appendix B

The model described in the text is a two-good two-country exchange economy. Each country is represented by a risk-averse agent with intertemporally additive preferences. The single period felicity function displays constant relative risk aversion (CRRA). Each agent $(i = 1, 2)$ maximizes:

$$U_i = \Sigma \beta^t u_i(C_{1i}, C_{2i}) \tag{B1}$$

where C_1 and C_2 are consumptions of goods 1 and 2, originating in countries 1 and 2. β is a time discount factor, and u_i is given by a CRRA–CES function:

$$u_i = [1/(1-\theta)][\alpha_i C_{1i}^\gamma + (1-\alpha_i) C_{2i}^\gamma]^{(1-\theta)/\gamma} \tag{B2}$$

In this felicity function, θ is the degree of relative risk aversion, the a_i are the CES 'share' parameters for the two countries, and γ determines the constant elasticity of substitution $\sigma \varepsilon = 1/(1-\gamma)$.

The two representative agents are assumed to have the same β and γ. In the simulations, the periods are meant to correspond to five years, but to promote understanding, our tables of simulation results report the parameters of the model on an annual basis. Thus, the β of 0.8 used in the calculations is approximately equivalent to a discount rate of 4.4% per year. Simulations were run for substitution elasticities, ε, of 0.25, 0.5, 2, 4, and 20. Agents have home good preferences, mirror images of each other. In the simulation, α_i is always chosen so that for a unitary ratio between the prices of the two goods the share of imports is 0.2.

Each country is exogenously endowed each (five year) period with only one good, which is perishable. Each endowment follows a Markov process. The two processes are independent. A country with an endowment e_t in period t has either the same endowment, 10% more, or 10% less in period $t+1$, except when its endowment is far from its central value of 1. In particular, for $1 < e_t < e_{\max}$:

$$e_{t+1} = 1.1 e_t \quad \text{with } P = P_{\text{out}}$$
$$e_{t+1} = 0.9 e_t \quad \text{with } P = P_{\text{in}} \tag{B3}$$
$$e_{t+1} = e_t \quad \text{with } P = 1 - P_{\text{in}} - P_{\text{out}}$$

The probabilities are reversed for endowments < 1. When the endowment $= 1$ it grows or shrinks with equal probability $(P_{\text{out}} + P_{\text{in}})/2$. $P_{\text{in}} + P_{\text{out}} = 0.5$ in the simulations. To confine the range of possible endowments to 11 for each country, the probability of moving out is reduced from P_{in} to 0.667, 0.333, and 0 times P_{in} in the three outermost states. The expected endowment is 1, the minimum is 0.62, and the maximum is 1.61. This process gives a stationary distribution of endowments, but in the neighborhood of 1.0 it is approximately a random walk.

The world economy can be in any of $11 \times 11 = 121$ states in any period. Competitive equilibria are calculated for each of these states using the following sequential procedure: First, the state-dependent terms of trade are calculated, using the condition that the current goods markets clear. These state prices depend, of course, on the incomes of the two country's agents, and hence on their portfolios as well as their endowments. The implied state-dependent consumptions of the two agents give state-dependent marginal utilities $[\lambda_1(s), \lambda_2(s)]$ for the home goods. These are shadow prices on the home endowments. The first order conditions corresponding to the fact that, in equilibrium, agents are indifferent between an extra unit of current consumption and an uncertain claim on future consumption, make it possible to compute the value of an asset with state-dependent future returns. The valuation of country 1's future endowment, for example, is obtained by solving the following recursive equation:

$$V_1(h) = \beta \Sigma \phi(h,j)(e_1(j) + V_1(j))\lambda_1(j)/\lambda_1(h) \tag{B4}$$

where $V_1(k)$ is the value of country 1's endowment in state k, $\phi(h,j)$ is the transition matrix giving the probability of the world's moving from state h to state j, and $e_1(j)$ is country 1's endowment in state j.

Table 20.B1a
Outcomes for Internationally Diversified Portfolios

Own consumption share = .8					elasticity = 20			relative risk aversion = 6.0	
share in home economy = 1.0									
end1	end2	price2/1	C11	C21	MU1	MU2	u1	Exp U1	Cert equiv
0.83	0.83	1.00	0.66	0.17	95.00	95.00	−15.7	−71.6	0.805
0.83	1.00	0.99	0.64	0.18	94.38	30.58	−15.6	−71.2	0.806
0.83	1.21	0.99	0.63	0.20	93.74	9.77	−15.5	−70.8	0.807
1.00	0.83	1.01	0.82	0.18	30.46	93.86	−6.1	−35.6	0.926
1.00	1.00	1.00	0.80	0.20	30.27	30.27	−6.1	−35.3	0.927
1.00	1.21	0.99	0.78	0.22	30.07	9.74	−6.0	−35.2	0.928
1.21	0.83	1.01	1.02	0.19	9.76	93.17	−2.4	−16.5	1.080
1.21	1.00	1.01	0.99	0.21	9.71	29.91	−2.4	−16.4	1.082
1.21	1.21	1.00	0.97	0.24	9.65	9.65	−2.3	−16.3	1.082
share in home economy = .9									
end1	end2	price2/1	C11	C21	MU1	MU2	u1	Exp U1	Cert equiv
0.83	0.83	1.00	0.66	0.17	95.00	95.00	−15.6	−67.7	0.814
0.83	1.00	0.99	0.65	0.19	83.66	33.80	−14.1	−61.4	0.830
0.83	1.21	0.98	0.64	0.22	72.07	11.82	−12.4	−54.9	0.849
1.00	0.83	1.01	0.81	0.17	33.73	83.20	−6.6	−35.5	0.927
1.00	1.00	1.00	0.80	0.20	30.27	30.27	−6.1	−32.5	0.943
1.00	1.21	0.99	0.79	0.23	26.66	10.77	−5.4	−29.5	0.961
1.21	0.83	1.02	0.99	0.18	11.78	71.70	−2.8	−17.4	1.069
1.21	1.00	1.01	0.98	0.20	10.75	26.51	−2.6	−16.1	1.085
1.21	1.21	1.00	0.97	0.24	9.65	9.65	−2.3	−14.9	1.103
share in home economy = .75									
end1	end2	price2/1	C11	C21	MU1	MU2	u1	Exp U1	Cert equiv
0.83	0.83	1.00	0.66	0.17	95.00	95.00	−15.6	−63.8	0.824
0.83	1.00	0.99	0.67	0.20	70.26	39.25	−12.2	−51.3	0.860
0.83	1.21	0.98	0.67	0.25	49.94	15.72	−9.2	−40.1	0.904
1.00	0.83	1.01	0.79	0.16	39.38	70.48	−7.6	−36.4	0.922
1.00	1.00	1.00	0.80	0.20	30.27	30.27	−6.1	−29.9	0.959
1.00	1.21	0.99	0.81	0.24	22.39	12.50	−4.7	−24.0	1.002
1.21	0.83	1.02	0.95	0.16	15.76	50.12	−3.5	−19.5	1.044
1.21	1.00	1.01	0.96	0.20	12.55	22.46	−2.9	−16.4	1.081
1.21	1.21	1.00	0.97	0.24	9.65	9.65	−2.3	−13.6	1.123
share in home economy = .6									
end1	end2	price2/1	C11	C21	MU1	MU2	u1	Exp U1	Cert equiv
0.83	0.83	1.00	0.66	0.17	95.00	95.00	−15.7	−61.9	0.829
0.83	1.00	0.99	0.68	0.22	59.60	45.78	−10.6	−44.9	0.884
0.83	1.21	0.97	0.69	0.29	35.72	21.15	−6.9	−31.2	0.951
1.00	0.83	1.01	0.78	0.15	46.00	59.84	−8.6	−38.5	0.911
1.00	1.00	1.00	0.80	0.20	30.27	30.27	−6.1	−28.7	0.967
1.00	1.21	0.99	0.82	0.26	18.99	14.59	−4.1	−20.6	1.033
1.21	0.83	1.03	0.92	0.14	21.22	35.79	−4.5	−22.7	1.013
1.21	1.00	1.01	0.94	0.19	14.66	19.07	−3.3	−17.4	1.068
1.21	1.21	1.00	0.97	0.24	9.65	9.65	−2.3	−12.9	1.134

Table 20.B1a (continued)
share in home economy = .5

end1	end2	price2/1	C11	C21	MU1	MU2	u1	Exp U1	Cert equiv
0.83	0.83	1.00	0.66	0.17	95.00	95.00	−15.7	−61.5	0.830
0.83	1.00	0.99	0.68	0.23	53.77	50.79	−9.8	−41.8	0.896
0.83	1.21	0.97	0.70	0.31	28.97	25.88	−5.8	−27.1	0.978
1.00	0.83	1.01	0.77	0.15	50.92	53.97	−9.4	−40.6	0.902
1.00	1.00	1.00	0.80	0.20	30.27	30.27	−6.1	−28.4	0.969
1.00	1.21	0.99	0.83	0.27	17.13	16.18	−3.8	−19.0	1.049
1.21	0.83	1.03	0.90	0.13	26.01	29.03	−5.4	−25.5	0.990
1.21	1.00	1.01	0.93	0.18	16.23	17.16	−3.6	−18.4	1.056
1.21	1.21	1.00	0.97	0.24	9.65	9.65	−2.3	−12.8	1.136

Notes:
end1, 2 = endowments in country 1, 2
price2/1 = price of country 2's good in terms of country 1's good
C11, C21 = consumption of goods 1 and 2 by country 1
MU1, 2 = marginal utility of good 1 in country 1, good 2 in country 2
u1 = the undiscounted felicity from consumption (C11, C21)
Exp U1 = present discounted value of expected utility for country 1
Cert equiv = the riskless consumption stream with the same utility as the uncertain claims on future endowments

Table 20.B1b
Outcomes for Internationally Diversified Portfolios

Own consumption share = .8   elasticity = 4   relative risk aversion = 6.0
share of home economy = 1.0

end1	end2	price2/1	C11	C21	MU1	MU2	u1	Exp U1	Cert equiv
0.83	0.83	1.00	0.66	0.17	76.49	76.49	−12.64	−56.69	0.808
0.83	1.00	0.97	0.65	0.19	73.74	25.33	−12.19	−55.00	0.813
0.83	1.21	0.93	0.63	0.21	71.09	8.30	−11.75	−53.21	0.818
1.00	0.83	1.04	0.82	0.18	25.24	73.20	−5.05	−28.65	0.926
1.00	1.00	1.00	0.80	0.20	24.37	24.37	−4.87	−27.75	0.932
1.00	1.21	0.97	0.78	0.23	23.50	8.07	−4.70	−27.00	0.937
1.21	0.83	1.07	1.01	0.19	8.28	70.52	−2.00	−13.51	1.076
1.21	1.00	1.04	0.99	0.21	8.04	22.32	−1.95	−13.12	1.082
1.21	1.21	1.00	0.97	0.24	7.77	7.77	−1.88	−12.80	1.088

share of home economy = .75

end1	end2	price2/1	C11	C21	MU1	MU2	u1	Exp U1	Cert equiv
0.83	0.83	1.00	0.66	0.17	76.49	76.49	−12.64	−51.72	0.823
0.83	1.00	0.95	0.67	0.20	57.93	31.09	−9.94	−42.17	0.857
0.83	1.21	0.90	0.67	0.25	42.69	12.35	−7.63	−33.58	0.897
1.00	0.83	1.05	0.79	0.16	31.26	58.21	−6.04	−29.36	0.921
1.00	1.00	1.00	0.80	0.20	24.37	24.37	−4.87	−24.32	0.957
1.00	1.21	0.95	0.81	0.24	18.46	9.91	−3.83	−19.82	0.997
1.21	0.83	1.10	0.96	0.16	12.42	42.89	−2.82	−15.68	1.044
1.21	1.00	1.05	0.96	0.20	9.96	15.55	−2.33	−13.25	1.080
1.21	1.21	1.00	0.97	0.24	7.77	7.77	−1.88	−11.04	1.120

ON THE INTERNATIONALIZATION OF PORTFOLIOS 575

Table 20.B1b (continued)
share of home economy = .6

end1	end2	price2/1	C11	C21	MU1	MU2	u1	Exp U1	Cert equiv
0.83	0.83	1.00	0.66	0.17	76.49	76.49	−12.64	−50.50	0.827
0.83	1.00	0.94	0.67	0.21	51.50	34.82	−9.00	−38.08	0.875
0.83	1.21	0.89	0.68	0.27	33.63	15.36	−6.23	−27.85	0.931
1.00	0.83	1.06	0.78	0.16	35.05	51.70	−6.66	−30.56	0.914
1.00	1.00	1.00	0.80	0.20	24.37	24.37	−4.87	−23.51	0.963
1.00	1.21	0.94	0.82	0.26	16.41	11.09	−3.47	−17.64	1.020
1.21	0.83	1.12	0.93	0.15	15.47	33.75	−3.39	−17.51	1.022
1.21	1.00	1.06	0.95	0.19	11.17	16.47	−2.57	−13.80	1.072
1.21	1.21	1.00	0.97	0.24	7.77	7.77	−1.88	−10.63	1.129

share of home economy = .55

end1	end2	price2/1	C11	C21	MU1	MU2	u1	Exp U1	Cert equiv
0.83	0.83	1.00	0.66	0.17	76.49	76.49	−12.64	−50.26	0.827
0.83	1.00	0.94	0.68	0.22	49.75	36.06	−8.74	−37.06	0.879
0.83	1.21	0.88	0.69	0.28	31.38	16.45	−5.88	−26.43	0.941
1.00	0.83	1.06	0.78	0.15	36.29	49.89	−6.85	−31.03	0.911
1.00	1.00	1.00	0.80	0.20	24.37	24.37	−4.87	−23.35	0.965
1.00	1.21	0.94	0.82	0.26	15.85	11.49	−3.37	−17.10	1.027
1.21	0.83	1.13	0.92	0.14	16.57	31.44	−3.60	−18.18	1.014
1.21	1.00	1.06	0.95	0.19	11.56	15.90	−2.64	−14.03	1.068
1.21	1.21	1.00	0.97	0.24	7.77	7.77	−1.88	−10.55	1.131

share of home economy = .50

end1	end2	price2/1	C11	C21	MU1	MU2	u1	Exp U1	Cert equiv
0.83	0.83	1.00	0.66	0.17	76.49	76.49	−12.64	−50.10	0.828
0.83	1.00	0.94	0.68	0.22	48.07	37.30	−8.49	−36.14	0.884
0.83	1.21	0.88	0.69	0.29	29.33	17.59	−5.55	−25.17	0.950
1.00	0.83	1.06	0.78	0.15	37.59	48.21	−7.06	−31.56	0.908
1.00	1.00	1.00	0.80	0.20	24.37	24.37	−4.87	−23.24	0.965
1.00	1.21	0.94	0.82	0.26	15.32	11.88	−3.27	−16.62	1.032
1.21	0.83	1.14	0.92	0.14	17.74	29.38	−3.81	−18.90	1.006
1.21	1.00	1.06	0.94	0.18	11.98	15.36	−2.72	−14.29	1.064
1.21	1.21	1.00	0.97	0.24	7.77	7.77	−1.88	−10.50	1.132

Table 20.B1c
Outcomes for Internationally Diversified Portfolios ($e = 1$)

Own consumption share = .8				elasticity = 1			relative risk aversion = 6.0		
share in home economy = 1.0									
end1	end2	price2/1	C11	C21	MU1	MU2	u1	Exp U1	Cert equiv
0.83	0.83	1.00	0.66	0.17	38.31	38.31	−6.33	−26.61	0.818
0.83	1.00	0.83	0.66	0.20	31.66	14.77	−5.23	−22.73	0.845
0.83	1.21	0.68	0.66	0.24	26.17	5.69	−4.33	−19.30	0.873
1.00	0.83	1.21	0.80	0.17	14.77	31.66	−2.95	−14.82	0.920
1.00	1.00	1.00	0.80	0.20	12.21	12.21	−2.44	−12.67	0.949
1.00	1.21	0.83	0.80	0.24	10.09	4.71	−2.02	−10.83	0.979
1.21	0.83	1.46	0.97	0.17	5.69	26.17	−1.38	−7.83	1.045
1.21	1.00	1.21	0.97	0.20	4.71	10.09	−1.14	−6.73	1.077
1.21	1.21	1.00	0.97	0.24	3.89	3.89	−0.94	−5.78	1.111
share in home economy = .75									
end1	end2	price2/1	C11	C21	MU1	MU2	u1	Exp U1	Cert equiv
0.83	0.83	1.00	0.66	0.17	38.31	38.31	−6.33	−26.61	0.818
0.83	1.00	0.83	0.66	0.20	31.66	14.77	−5.23	−22.73	0.845
0.83	1.21	0.68	0.66	0.24	26.17	5.69	−4.33	−19.30	0.873
1.00	0.83	1.21	0.80	0.17	14.77	31.66	−2.95	−14.82	0.920
1.00	1.00	1.00	0.80	0.20	12.21	12.21	−2.44	−12.67	0.949
1.00	1.21	0.83	0.80	0.24	10.09	4.71	−2.02	−10.83	0.979
1.21	0.83	1.46	0.97	0.17	5.69	26.17	−1.38	−7.83	1.045
1.21	1.00	1.21	0.97	0.20	4.71	10.09	−1.14	−6.73	1.077
1.21	1.21	1.00	0.97	0.24	3.89	3.89	−0.94	−5.78	1.111
share in home economy = .50									
end1	end2	price2/1	C11	C21	MU1	MU2	u1	Exp U1	Cert equiv
0.83	0.83	1.00	0.66	0.17	38.31	38.31	−6.33	−26.61	0.818
0.83	1.00	0.83	0.66	0.20	31.66	14.77	−5.23	−22.73	0.845
0.83	1.21	0.68	0.66	0.24	26.17	5.69	−4.33	−19.30	0.873
1.00	0.83	1.21	0.80	0.17	14.77	31.66	−2.95	−14.82	0.920
1.00	1.00	1.00	0.80	0.20	12.21	12.21	−2.44	−12.67	0.949
1.00	1.21	0.83	0.80	0.24	10.09	4.71	−2.02	−10.83	0.979
1.21	0.83	1.46	0.97	0.17	5.69	26.17	−1.38	−7.83	1.045
1.21	1.00	1.21	0.97	0.20	4.71	10.09	−1.14	−6.73	1.077
1.21	1.21	1.00	0.97	0.24	3.89	3.89	−0.94	−5.78	1.111

Table 20.B1d
Outcomes for Internationally Diversified Portfolios (e = 0.5)

Own consumption share = .8				elasticity = .50			relative risk aversion = 6.0		
share of home economy = 1.0									
end1	end2	price2/1	C11	C21	MU1	MU2	u1	Exp U1	Cert equiv
0.83	0.83	1.00	0.66	0.17	21.59	21.59	−3.57	−21.20	0.763
0.83	1.00	0.40	0.71	0.28	10.00	20.78	−1.65	−11.10	0.870
0.83	1.21	0.17	0.75	0.46	6.13	27.62	−1.01	−6.28	0.974
1.00	0.83	2.45	0.72	0.11	20.09	10.25	−4.02	−27.40	0.725
1.00	1.00	1.00	0.80	0.20	6.88	6.88	−1.38	−12.00	0.855
1.00	1.21	0.40	0.86	0.34	3.19	6.62	−0.64	−5.57	0.997
1.21	0.83	5.65	0.76	0.08	24.96	6.34	−6.04	−39.30	0.675
1.21	1.00	2.45	0.87	0.14	6.40	3.27	−1.55	−15.30	0.815
1.21	1.21	1.00	0.97	0.24	2.19	2.19	−0.53	−5.89	0.986
share of home economy = .90									
end1	end2	price2/1	C11	C21	MU1	MU2	u1	Exp U1	Cert equiv
0.83	0.83	1.00	0.66	0.17	21.59	21.59	−3.57	−14.90	0.819
0.83	1.00	0.61	0.67	0.22	16.20	9.56	−2.61	−11.60	0.861
0.83	1.21	0.37	0.68	0.28	12.70	4.48	−2.00	−9.27	0.901
1.00	0.83	1.62	0.79	0.15	9.58	16.34	−1.98	−9.38	0.899
1.00	1.00	1.00	0.80	0.20	6.88	6.88	−1.38	−7.10	0.850
1.00	1.21	0.61	0.81	0.26	5.16	3.05	−1.01	−5.51	1.000
1.21	0.83	2.63	0.93	0.14	4.47	12.83	−1.17	−5.88	0.987
1.21	1.00	1.62	0.95	0.19	3.05	5.20	−0.76	−4.32	1.050
1.21	1.21	1.00	0.97	0.24	2.19	2.19	−0.53	−3.24	1.112
share of home economy = .85									
end1	end2	price2/1	C11	C21	MU1	MU2	u1	Exp U1	Cert equiv
0.83	0.83	1.00	0.66	0.17	21.59	21.59	−3.57	−15.10	0.817
0.83	1.00	0.66	0.67	0.21	17.68	8.61	−2.83	−12.60	0.848
0.83	1.21	0.43	0.67	0.26	14.90	3.57	−2.32	−10.60	0.877
1.00	0.83	1.52	0.79	0.16	8.65	17.79	−1.80	−8.82	0.910
1.00	1.00	1.00	0.80	0.20	6.88	6.88	−1.38	−7.20	0.948
1.00	1.21	0.66	0.81	0.25	5.63	2.74	−1.09	−5.99	0.983
1.21	0.83	2.31	0.95	0.16	3.58	14.99	−0.94	−5.04	1.018
1.21	1.00	1.52	0.96	0.19	2.76	5.67	−0.69	−4.03	1.064
1.21	1.21	1.00	0.97	0.24	2.19	2.19	−0.53	−3.29	1.108
share of home economy = .8									
end1	end2	price2/1	C11	C21	MU1	MU2	u1	Exp U1	Cert equiv
0.83	0.83	1.00	0.66	0.17	21.59	21.59	−3.57	−15.30	0.815
0.83	1.00	0.68	0.66	0.20	18.74	8.11	−2.99	−13.30	0.838
0.83	1.21	0.47	0.66	0.24	16.61	3.13	−2.57	−11.70	0.860
1.00	0.83	1.46	0.80	0.17	8.11	18.74	−1.69	−8.57	0.915
1.00	1.00	1.00	0.80	0.20	6.88	6.88	−1.38	−7.33	0.944
1.00	1.21	0.68	0.80	0.24	5.97	2.58	−1.15	−6.39	0.971
1.21	0.83	2.14	0.97	0.17	3.13	16.61	−0.83	−4.65	1.034
1.21	1.00	1.46	0.97	0.20	2.58	5.97	−0.65	−3.92	1.070
1.21	1.21	1.00	0.97	0.24	2.19	2.19	−0.53	−3.36	1.104

Table 20.B1d (contd.)
share of home economy = .75

end1	end2	price2/1	C11	C21	MU1	MU2	u1	Exp U1	Cert equiv
0.83	0.83	1.00	0.66	0.17	21.59	21.59	−3.57	−15.50	0.813
0.83	1.00	0.70	0.66	0.20	19.57	7.78	−3.11	−13.90	0.831
0.83	1.21	0.49	0.65	0.23	17.99	2.86	−2.77	−12.60	0.848
1.00	0.83	1.43	0.80	0.17	7.73	19.48	−1.62	−8.43	0.918
1.00	1.00	1.00	0.80	0.20	6.88	6.88	−1.38	−7.46	0.941
1.00	1.21	0.70	0.80	0.24	6.24	2.48	−1.20	−6.72	0.961
1.21	0.83	2.04	0.98	0.17	2.84	17.94	−0.75	−4.41	1.045
1.21	1.00	1.43	0.97	0.20	2.46	6.21	−0.62	−3.85	1.074
1.21	1.21	1.00	0.97	0.24	2.19	2.19	−0.53	−3.42	1.099

Table 20.B1e
Outcomes for Internationally Diversified Portfolios (e = 0.25)

Own consumption share = .8   elasticity = 0.25   relative risk aversion = 6.0
share of home economy = 1.00

end1	end2	price2/1	C11	C21	MU1	MU2	u1	Exp U1	Cert equiv
0.83	0.83	1.00	0.66	0.17	13.80	13.80	−2.28	−5E+07	0.037
0.83	1.00	0.00	0.82	0.96	3.17	3E+09	−0.52	−2E+07	0.046
0.83	1.21	0.00	0.83	1.19	3.15	5E+10	−0.52	−6E+06	0.057
1.00	0.83	193.42	0.07	0.00	4E+07	3.24	−9E+06	−1E+08	0.031
1.00	1.00	1.00	0.80	0.20	4.40	4.40	−0.88	−4E+07	0.039
1.00	1.21	0.00	1.00	1.16	1.01	9E+08	−0.20	−1E+07	0.050
1.21	0.83	308.32	0.06	0.00	1E+08	3.21	−3E+07	−2E+08	0.027
1.21	1.00	193.42	0.09	0.01	1E+07	1.03	−3E+06	−7E+07	0.034
1.21	1.21	1.00	0.97	0.24	1.40	1.40	−0.34	−2E+07	0.044

share of home economy = .95

end1	end2	price2/1	C11	C21	MU1	MU2	u1	Exp U1	Cert equiv
0.83	0.83	1.00	0.66	0.17	13.80	13.80	−2.28	−165.24	0.463
0.83	1.00	0.03	0.77	0.48	4.69	138.60	−0.74	−55.14	0.577
0.83	1.21	0.01	0.78	0.62	4.45	97.75	−0.70	−19.69	0.709
1.00	0.83	29.73	0.52	0.06	129.41	4.80	−56.48	−279.21	0.417
1.00	1.00	1.00	0.80	0.20	4.40	4.40	−0.88	−97.35	0.515
1.00	1.21	0.03	0.94	0.58	1.49	44.16	−0.28	−29.86	0.652
1.21	0.83	68.72	0.57	0.05	103.02	4.54	−82.34	−373.13	0.393
1.21	1.00	29.73	0.63	0.07	41.23	1.53	−21.78	−149.83	0.472
1.21	1.21	1.00	0.97	0.24	1.40	1.40	−0.34	−48.12	0.593

Table 20.B1e (contd.)

share of home economy = .90

end1	end2	price2/1	C11	C21	MU1	MU2	u1	Exp U1	Cert equiv
0.83	0.83	1.00	0.66	0.17	13.8	13.80	−2.28	−14.54	0.753
0.83	1.00	0.15	0.72	0.29	7.70	12.16	−1.17	−8.11	0.846
0.83	1.21	0.05	0.73	0.39	6.62	7.54	−0.99	−5.57	0.912
1.00	0.83	6.17	0.71	0.11	11.97	7.84	−3.38	−16.36	0.735
1.00	1.00	1.00	0.80	0.20	4.40	4.40	−0.88	−7.70	0.855
1.00	1.21	0.15	0.87	0.35	2.45	3.87	−0.45	−4.01	0.974
1.21	0.83	18.43	0.81	0.10	7.67	6.74	−4.01	−18.12	0.721
1.21	1.00	6.17	0.86	0.14	3.81	2.50	−1.30	−8.37	0.841
1.21	1.21	1.00	0.97	0.24	1.40	1.40	−0.34	−3.65	0.993

share of home economy = .85

end1	end2	price2/1	C11	C21	MU1	MU2	u1	Exp U1	Cert equiv
0.83	1.00	0.34	0.68	0.22	10.98	6.00	−1.65	−7.97	0.849
0.83	1.21	0.13	0.69	0.29	9.62	2.71	−1.40	−6.71	0.879
1.00	0.83	2.85	0.78	0.15	6.04	11.07	−1.45	−7.10	0.869
1.00	1.00	1.00	0.80	0.20	4.40	4.40	−0.88	−5.00	0.932
1.00	1.21	0.34	0.82	0.27	3.50	1.91	−0.64	−3.85	0.982
1.21	0.83	7.41	0.92	0.14	2.76	9.72	−1.08	−5.28	0.922
1.21	1.00	2.85	0.94	0.18	1.92	3.53	−0.56	−3.37	1.008

share of home economy = .80

end1	end2	price2/1	C11	C21	MU1	MU2	u1	Exp U1	Cert equiv
0.83	1.00	0.47	0.66	0.20	12.99	4.84	−1.96	−9.01	0.829
0.83	1.21	0.22	0.66	0.24	12.52	1.78	−1.79	−8.28	0.843
1.00	0.83	2.14	0.80	0.17	4.84	12.99	−1.12	−5.81	0.904
1.00	1.00	1.00	0.80	0.20	4.40	4.40	−0.88	−4.93	0.935
1.00	1.21	0.47	0.80	0.24	4.14	1.54	−0.76	−4.39	0.957
1.21	0.83	4.59	0.97	0.17	1.78	12.52	−0.61	−3.40	1.007
1.21	1.00	2.14	0.97	0.20	1.54	4.14	−0.43	−2.70	1.055

share of home economy = .75

end1	end2	price2/1	C11	C21	MU1	MU2	u1	Exp U1	Cert equiv
0.83	1.00	0.54	0.65	0.19	14.23	4.40	−2.15	−9.94	0.812
0.83	1.21	0.29	0.64	0.22	14.82	1.46	−2.10	−9.71	0.816
1.00	0.83	1.86	0.81	0.17	4.35	14.19	−0.99	−5.48	0.915
1.00	1.00	1.00	0.80	0.20	4.40	4.40	−0.88	−5.10	0.928
1.00	1.21	0.54	0.79	0.23	4.54	1.40	−0.83	−4.90	0.936
1.21	0.83	3.49	0.99	0.18	1.43	14.81	−0.47	−2.85	1.043
1.21	1.00	1.86	0.98	0.21	1.39	4.52	−0.38	−2.54	1.068

Table 20.B2
Returns and Risk Premia

elasticity = 20

share in home economy = 1.0

end1	end2	SDev1	SDev2	SDev2p	corr	corrp	Rrf1	Rend1	Risk Prem	Prem2/1
0.83	0.83	0.050	0.050	0.049	0.004	0.025	0.014	0.036	0.022	0.13
0.83	1.00	0.050	0.036	0.036	0.007	0.021	0.014	0.036	0.022	0.10
0.83	1.21	0.050	0.041	0.041	0.006	0.019	0.014	0.036	0.022	0.11
1.00	0.83	0.036	0.050	0.050	0.007	0.018	0.014	0.031	0.017	0.13
1.00	1.00	0.036	0.036	0.035	0.000	0.029	0.014	0.031	0.017	0.10

share in home economy = .50

end1	end2	SDev1	SDev2	SDev2p	corr	corrp	Rrf1	Rend1	Risk Prem	Prem2/1
0.83	0.83	0.033	0.033	0.033	0.774	0.800	0.031	0.042	0.011	0.00
0.83	1.00	0.029	0.029	0.028	0.682	0.736	0.031	0.040	0.009	0.00
0.83	1.21	0.031	0.034	0.033	0.759	0.798	0.031	0.041	0.010	0.00
1.00	0.83	0.029	0.029	0.029	0.682	0.729	0.031	0.041	0.010	0.01
1.00	1.00	0.026	0.026	0.025	0.536	0.580	0.031	0.039	0.008	0.00

elasticity = 1

share in home economy = 1.0

end1	end2	SDev1	SDev2	SDev2p	corr	corrp	Rrf1	Rend1	Risk Prem	Prem2/1
0.83	0.83	0.042	0.042	0.033	0.215	0.799	0.022	0.039	0.017	0.03
0.83	1.00	0.043	0.031	0.027	0.210	0.934	0.022	0.039	0.017	0.01
0.83	1.21	0.043	0.036	0.030	0.250	0.906	0.022	0.039	0.016	0.02
1.00	0.83	0.031	0.043	0.032	0.210	0.795	0.022	0.035	0.013	0.03
1.00	1.00	0.032	0.032	0.025	0.151	0.913	0.022	0.035	0.013	0.02

share in home economy = .5

end1	end2	SDev1	SDev2	SDev2p	corr	corrp	Rrf1	Rend1	Risk Prem	Prem2/1
0.83	0.83	0.042	0.042	0.033	0.215	0.799	0.022	0.039	0.017	0.03
0.83	1.00	0.043	0.031	0.027	0.210	0.934	0.022	0.039	0.017	0.01

0.83	1.21	0.043	0.036	0.030	0.250	0.906	0.022	0.039	0.016	0.02
1.00	0.83	0.031	0.043	0.032	0.210	0.795	0.022	0.035	0.013	0.03
1.00	1.00	0.032	0.032	0.025	0.151	0.913	0.022	0.035	0.013	0.02

elasticity = .25

share in home economy = .95

end1	end2	SDev1	SDev2	SDev2p	corr	corrp	Rrf1	Rend1	Risk Prem	Prem2/1
0.83	0.83	0.142	0.142	0.563	-0.037	-0.758	-0.239	-0.086	0.152	83.87
0.83	1.00	0.095	0.222	0.964	0.538	0.578	-0.025	-0.027	-0.002	112.04
0.83	1.21	0.135	0.035	0.138	0.080	0.999	0.014	0.042	0.028	0.08
1.00	0.83	0.222	0.095	0.202	0.538	-0.949	0.056	0.175	0.119	-0.32
1.00	1.00	0.139	0.139	0.553	-0.003	-0.755	-0.239	-0.090	0.149	78.18

share in home economy = .82

end1	end2	SDev1	SDev2	SDev2p	corr	corrp	Rrf1	Rend1	Risk Prem	Prem2/1
0.83	0.83	0.045	0.045	0.102	0.215	0.853	0.018	0.035	0.018	0.00
0.83	1.00	0.047	0.031	0.112	0.279	0.836	0.016	0.036	0.019	0.00
0.83	1.21	0.048	0.034	0.111	0.335	0.859	0.015	0.036	0.021	0.00
1.00	0.83	0.031	0.047	0.096	0.279	0.780	0.020	0.032	0.013	0.00
1.00	1.00	0.032	0.032	0.106	0.215	0.792	0.018	0.031	0.014	0.00

Notes:

end1, 2 = endowments countries 1 and 2

Sdev1, 2 = standard deviations of returns on endowments, countries 1 and 2

Sdev2p = standard deviation of returns on endowment of country 2, valued in country 1's good

corr, corrp = correlation of returns on endowment, valued in home goods, valued in good 1

Rrf1 = the risk free rate of return on commodity 1 in country 1

Rend1 = expected rate of return on country 1's endowment

Risk Prem = difference between Rend1 and Rrf1

Prem2/1 = excess of what country 1 agents are willing to pay for claims on country 2 and their value in country 2

CHAPTER 21

POLICIES AND EXCHANGE RATES: A SIMPLE ANALYTICAL
FRAMEWORK

How do exchange rates, trade balances, and international capital movements react to national fiscal and monetary policies and to other events of macroeconomic significance? Divers answers to such questions may be heard in financial circles, political arenas, and academic conferences. All these propositions depend on models, implicit or explicit. Whether or not they would avow it, even practical traders in foreign-exchange markets have models in their heads, models probably borrowed unconsciously from economists. They interpret and act upon macroeconomic news in the light of their models or, more important, the models they think other traders depend on.

I propose here to set forth a simple open-economy macroeconomic framework, reflecting a model in the heads of many economists, though not all to be sure. It is certainly not a quantitative forecasting model. Economists are pretty poor at forecasting exchange rates, and evidently markets are not very good either. Here I am interested in a model that yields qualitative comparative static or dynamic results for policies and other exogenous shocks. It is also, I confess, what I teach undergraduate students. I have learned that what professors really believe, stripped of secondary complications and reservations, is what they teach.

Sometimes sharp students, more likely undergraduate than graduate, want to know what economists know that other people, including their roommates, do not. First of all, I tell them, are identities. From non-economists in public debate, and sometimes alas even from economists, we hear or read plenty of arguments that are fallacious because they

Reprinted by permission from *Japan, Europe, and International Financial Markets: Analytical and Empirical Perspectives*, eds. Ryuzo Sato, Richard M. Levich, and Rama V. Ramachandran, Cambridge: Cambridge University Press, 1993, pp. 11–25.

ignore identities. Likewise identities are frequently misused to imply causation. By themselves they do not, for example, tell us that government deficits generate trade deficits or that import surpluses finance themselves by inducing capital inflows or that business investments generate business profits. Those statements may be true, but you can't prove them by equations that are true by definition. Identities are only the beginning of wisdom.

I think open-economy macromodel builders can feel some intellectual satisfaction about the events of the past 20 years, especially the last 10. Fiscal and monetary policies under the floating-rate regime have worked out pretty much the way the textbooks said they would. Just as the IS/LM model, for all the hard knocks it has received from pure theorists, remains a good working approximation, so its international extension, Mundell-Fleming, has been a good guide. Thanks to that model, economists were prepared for the regime change in 1971–73. Qualitatively, that is. The quantitative extent of the open-economy effects of policies has exceeded our *ex ante* imaginations. But so, of course, have the experiments obligingly run by governments, particularly by the Reagan administration.

A Mundell-Fleming Model

Let's begin with three important identities. First, the output-expenditure identity for a single economy,

$$C + I + G - CAD = Y \tag{1}$$

which implies the identity of the sources and uses of national saving,

$$S^p - D^g = I - CAD \tag{1'}$$

where C is consumption, G government purchases, I net private domestic investment, CAD the current account deficit (if negative, a surplus), Y net national product, S^p private saving equal to $Y - TX - C$, TX taxes net of transfers, D^g government deficit (if negative, a surplus) equal to $G - TX$.

Second, the current account deficit equals the capital inflow,

$$CAD = F \tag{2}$$

Third, across countries both current accounts and capital flows sum to zero,

$$\sum CAD = 0 = \sum F \qquad (3)$$

Now I present a one-country model, motivated to apply to contemporary United States, running a current account deficit with "Japan" and borrowing in dollars to finance it.

The exchange rate is market-determined. The nominal value of the foreign currency, "yen," in terms of dollars is e. The real exchange rate E is ep^*/p, where p^* is the price of foreign goods in yen and p is the price of local goods in dollars.

The volume of U.S. exports in constant dollars depends on foreign economic conditions, in particular positively on foreign income Y^* and positively on the real exchange rate. Thus export volume is given by $X(\overset{+}{E}, \overset{+}{Y^*})$. Signs over the variables in functions indicate directions of effects. Real depreciation of the dollar makes U.S. goods more competitive and also has positive income effects, in that the command of given yen income over U.S. goods is increased.

The volume of imports of foreign goods in yen is $p^*IM(\bar{E}, \overset{+}{Y})$. Depreciation of the dollar makes foreign goods relatively less attractive and also has negative income effects on home demand for foreign goods. Converted into dollars, imports are $ep^*IM(E, Y)$. Thus dollar depreciation, while reducing import volume, might increase its dollar value.

The current account deficit CAD is the difference between imports and exports, both in dollars. The current account deficit includes also the net outpayments of investment income—interest, dividends, rents, etc. In the model, capital transactions take place in dollar assets bearing an interest rate r and priced, inversely to r, at $q(r)$. Let VF be the volume of such assets held by the Japanese, as valued at a standard interest rate $\bar{r}$ at which $q = 1$. Let ΔVF be the change in those holdings during the period; $q\Delta VF$ is the capital inflow at current asset prices. The net outpayments of investment income are $rqVF$. Thus the equality of the U.S. current account deficit to the capital inflow is the following:

$$CAD = ep^*IM(E, Y) - pX(E, Y^*) + rq(r)VF = q(r)\Delta VF \qquad (4)$$

The inflow $q\Delta VF$ increases the stock of external debt. Of course the aggregate value of the stock might also change because of changes in r, i.e., by $q'(r)VF\Delta r$.

From the viewpoint of the foreign holders of U.S. debt VF, its value in yen is what matters. That value is qVF/e. Appreciation of the dollar is a possible source of capital gains.

Suppose that Japanese wealth-owners hold VF at the beginning of this time period and wish to hold at the end of the period an aggregate of dollar assets of value p^*J in yen. They will buy ΔVF at price q such that $qVF/e + q\Delta VF/e = p^*J$. Thus

$$q\Delta VF = ep^*J - qVF \tag{5}$$

The desired real-yen amount J depends on their previous accumulations of yen and dollar assets and also on contemporary market outcomes at home and abroad. I model the latter dependences as $J(\overset{+}{s}, \overset{-}{r^*}, \overset{+}{Y^*})$. Here r^* and Y^* are local Japanese interest rate and income, while s is the expected yield to Japanese investors of dollar assets: $s = r -$ expected $\Delta e/e$.

Perfect substitutability between Japanese and American assets is *not* assumed. Note also that the nominal exchange rate appears here. The real rate that concerns Japanese investors is the difference between the yen yield of holding dollar assets and the *Japanese* inflation rate. The U.S. inflation rate is irrelevant to them except as a possible indicator of likely changes in the nominal exchange rate. They do not necessarily believe in purchasing power parity, and they should not if this model is correct.

In summary, the balance of payments equation in dollars is

$$\begin{aligned} CAD &= ep^*IM(E, Y) - pX(E, Y^*) + rqVF \\ &= ep^*J(s, r^*, Y^*) - qVF \end{aligned} \tag{6a}$$

In real dollars, this is

$$\begin{aligned} CAD/p &= EIM(E, Y) - X(E, Y^*) + rqVF/p \\ &= EJ(s, r^*, Y^*) - qVF/p \end{aligned} \tag{6b}$$

I shall not in this brief presentation consider price movements in the two countries. In the upper panel of Fig. 21.1, CAD is measured on the horizontal axis, and the nominal exchange rate e (or interchangeably for present purposes the real exchange rate E) is measured vertically. The curve XX shows their relationship as determined by trade in goods, imports and exports, for given values of the other relevant variables. As

POLICIES AND EXCHANGE RATES

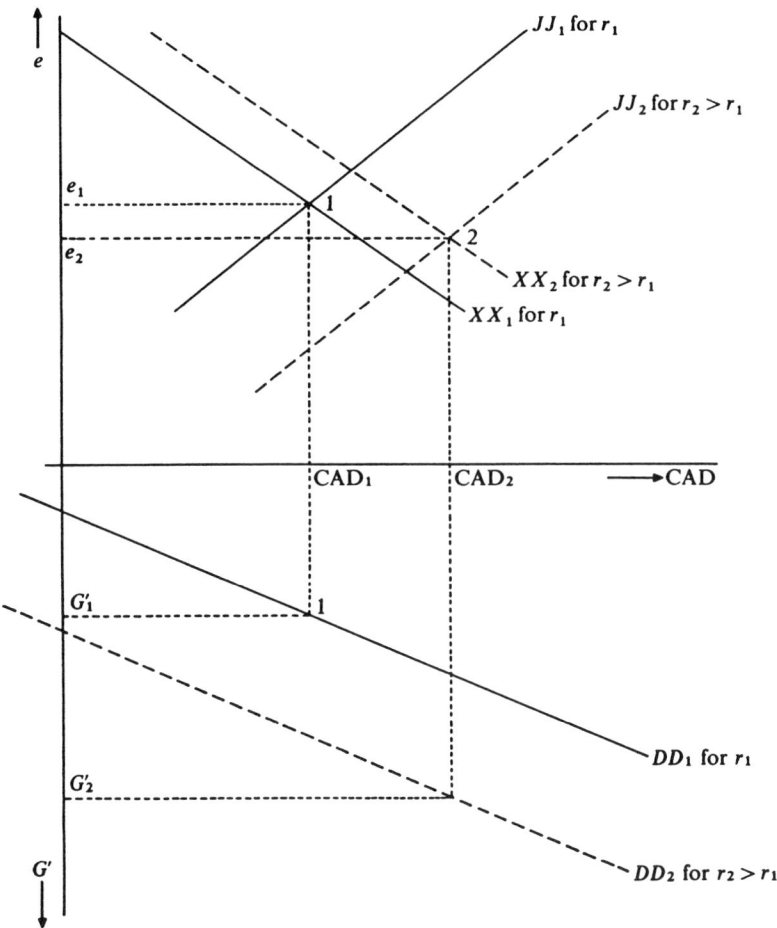

Figure 21.1
Determination of current account deficit and capital inflow by fiscal policy (see text for explanation)

drawn, *XX* assumes that depreciation of the dollar, increase in e, lowers the trade deficit. The slope would be positive if the import and export elasticities with respect to E were too low in absolute value to overcome the "*J* curve" effect of the higher dollar costs of imports. *XX* shifts right for increases in U.S. income Y and for increases in investment outflows, for example from increases in r.

Net capital inflows, $q\Delta VF$ as in Eq. (5), are depicted by *JJ*. It is upward sloping in Fig. 21.1 on two assumptions, both having to do with behavior of Japanese investors. First is a portfolio balance effect, implicit in the role of the exchange rate in Eq. (5): the higher is e, the lower is $1/e$, and the lower is the value in yen of Japanese holdings of dollar assets. This negative wealth effect increases the Japanese appetite for dollar assets, given interest rates in the two markets and exchange rate expectations. Second is a regressive expectations effect. The higher is e, the lower is expected $\Delta e/e$, and the higher is expected $\Delta(1/e)/(1/e)$, the better dollar assets look to Japanese investors. Extrapolative expectations are a different story. The higher is this period's e, the higher the expected $\Delta e/e$. This speculative response could reverse the slope of the *JJ* curve. In what follows I assume the standard shapes of *XX* and *JJ* as illustrated; the results depend on those assumptions.

A particular *JJ* curve assumes a given interest rate r in the U.S. A rise in the U.S. rate, holding the Japanese rate r^* constant, shifts *JJ* to the right, increases *CAD* and appreciates the dollar. *JJ* will also be shifted right, *CAD* increased, and e lowered by an autonomous increase in Japanese preference for dollar assets, whether by private investors or by the central bank.

The next step is to relate the U.S. *CAD* to the "IS" balance of aggregate demand and output in the U.S. The relevant equation is

$$D(r, Y) + [G - bT(Y)] - CAD = Y \tag{7}$$

where G is federal purchases of goods and services, $T(Y)$ is taxes net of transfers, b is the private marginal propensity to spend with respect to net taxes, and thus $G - bT(Y)$ is the aggregate demand effect of the budget deficit. Let us call this measure of fiscal policy G' for short. $D(\bar{r}, \overset{+}{Y})$ is the remainder of private demand for goods and services.

Here I assume, as I believe is realistic for the U.S. nowadays, that Y is chosen by the Federal Reserve. Monetary policy, here represented by r, is geared to achieve the Fed's desired path of Y. Given the Fed's target Y, Eq. (6) relates the three variables G', CAD, and r. This relation is illustrated by loci DD in the lower panel of Fig. 21.1, where CAD is again the horizontal axis and G' is measured vertically downward. As is illustrated, these two variables are positively related to each other for a given interest rate. If G' is increased, CAD must increase to keep aggregate demand constant at Y at the same interest rate. A higher interest rate allows a higher G' for the same CAD, DD_2 instead of DD_1.

A (short-run) equilibrium is illustrated by points 1 in the two panels of the figure, where DD_1, XX_1, and JJ_1 all correspond to the same U.S. interest rate r_1. Fiscal policy is G'_1. Another equilibrium, at point 2, corresponds to fiscal policy G'_2. The second policy is less austere than the first; therefore the CAD is larger, the interest rate is higher, and the dollar is appreciated. Although the higher interest rate shifts XX in the same rightward direction as JJ, because of the higher interest payments on outstanding foreign-held debt, the assumption in the figure is that the XX shift is relatively small. That is a safe assumption if the initial stock of debt is small; there would be no shift in XX if it were zero.

In this model, bad news about future fiscal policy should cause the dollar to rise, e to fall, on the grounds that the Fed will raise interest rates to stay on its desired path for output Y. One of the missing ingredients in this short-run model, however, is "Japanese" investors' views of the exchange rate e that will eventually be required in a sustainable current account equilibrium. If that should rise, expected $\Delta e/e$ will rise too, s will be lower for given r, JJ will move left and up; the current value of the yen e will rise and CAD will fall. A rise in the Japanese interest rate r^* would have similar effects.

Dispelling Some Myths about the Dollar

Let's put our simple model to work on some common misconceptions.

1. Eliminating the federal budget deficit will automatically eliminate the deficit in the U.S. external current account.

Imagine a political miracle. The President and Congress agree to a package of tax increases and spending cuts that balance the budget in fiscal year 1994, or even in fiscal year 1995. Will our $100 billion CAD

vanish simultaneously? Much rhetoric on the twin deficits seems to answer my question Yes. Common sense says No.

The dollar might strengthen in the exchange markets on news of a tough compromise budget package. That response might be rationalized on very general grounds of "confidence" in American political leadership strengthened by evidence that the President and Congress can jointly accomplish a mission they undertook for themselves. Yet it would be difficult to rationalize on macroeconomic grounds. The myth reflects a misunderstanding of the mechanics connecting fiscal deficits and external deficits. In fact, the way that fiscal austerity could eventually balance our trade is precisely by *depreciating* the dollar.

How would this come about? Via Federal Reserve policy. If the Fed tries to stay on the modest growth track along which its policy has steered the economy since mid-1984, then the Fed will ease money and credit and lower interest rates to counter the fiscal contraction in aggregate demand. As our model says, this will depreciate the dollar. Monetary policy is exchange rate policy.

Whatever happens to fiscal and monetary policies and to interest rates and exchange rates, correction of the trade deficit is not automatic. The nation has to earn an improvement in its net exports in competition with foreign producers. As we have seen over the last 8 years, the trade deficit responds quite slowly to changes in exchange rates, terms of trade, and other determining variables. Quick fiscal contraction, giving the Fed the opportunity to ease interest rates, would still leave us with a big and stubborn trade deficit. In terms of the figure, imagine XX to be nearly vertical in the short run. Although the JJ curve would be shifting left and raising E, CAD would respond very little in the short run. The decline in r might give some slight relief in outpayments of interest and profits.

2. Recession is the inevitable consequence and deserved punishment of America's profligacy, and its essential natural cure.

A decline in GNP would reduce our demands for imports. Assuming the marginal propensity to import is 0.25 or 0.2, it would take a $400 to $500 billion loss of GNP (8 to 10%) to wipe out a $100 billion trade deficit. That's not recession but depression. The moral is that, even with recession, we need some help from prices relative to those of our competitors, help provided by exchange depreciation.

Don't worry. A $100 billion fiscal package would reduce GNP by much less, $150 to $200 billion, and that only if the Fed refused to counteract it. Recession is not the inevitable result of fiscal tightening, especially if we phase in fiscal tightening gradually. But the Fed must pursue a low-interest-rate policy and allow the dollar to depreciate.

We could have a recession without any drastic fiscal correction. All it takes is for the Fed to heed the warnings that higher U.S. interest rates are needed to keep the dollar from falling.

Whether we Americans deserve recession for our macroeconomic sins, as our Asian and European critics say, is a question of ethics and justice, not of economic analysis. Those critics are not alone in believing this nation is undersaving. The victims of our binges of consumption and arms buildup are our own children and grandchildren. They will be helped if we save more of our prosperity incomes and accumulate capital assets for them, instead of debts. But increased thrift will not help them if it goes to waste in recession, unemployment, and idle capacity.

3. The United States can balance its external current account without an adverse shift in its real exchange rate.

A decline in the real value of the dollar in external trade—in the quantity of foreign goods obtainable by a given amount of our labor and other resources—is a decline in American real wages and other real incomes. It is bad news, for sure, but accepting it is essential if we are to avoid indefinite accumulation of ever more onerous foreign debt.

It would be wonderful to restore competitiveness and trade balance by a burst of American productivity, a favorite refuge of politicians. Alas, no one knows how to bring that about; certainly it can't be done in a hurry. Our foreign rivals may be better able to speed up cost savings and quality gains than we are.

There are two ways of bringing about a decline in our real exchange rate, i.e., a reduction in the costs and prices of U.S. goods relative to those of foreigners. One is depreciation in the nominal exchange rate, assuming it is not offset by increases in dollar wages and other costs. As argued above, the U.S. is in a good position to bring this off. The other is to have a domestic deflation, of prices, wages, and other costs in excess of the deflations of our competitors. We are not in a good position to win at this game. The Germans and Japanese already have near-zero inflation and are prepared to operate their economies with even more slack if need be.

A few years ago our government was quite justifiably chastising Japan and Germany and other European countries for the sluggishness of their macroeconomic performances since the second oil shock. They should stimulate their economies by fiscal and monetary policies. The resulting increases in their imports would help to correct the trade imbalances. Recently their growth rates have picked up, while the United States economy, having reached full employment, has turned sluggish. Anyway, faster foreign growth is not likely to be a major contribution to the solution. German and Japanese marginal propensities to import are not high enough to eliminate their surpluses.

Somehow there have to be relative price adjustments. The next time someone tells you devaluations do not work, are simplistic solutions, etc., etc., ask what the alternative solution is. Dollar appreciation?

4. The United States has to have high interest rates to induce foreigners to lend us the funds to finance our budget deficit and our excess imports.

We are being warned incessantly that we depend on foreigners—mainly Japanese banks, insurance companies, and pension funds—to buy U.S. Treasury bonds and other dollar assets. Their purchases both finance our budget deficit and provide us the foreign currencies we need to import Toyotas and Sonys. Should they decide not to buy dollar securities, the consequences, we are told, would be calamitous. That is why Washington must get its act together and follow policies of which these foreigners approve.

In terms of our model, the "calamity" we must avoid is a leftward shift of JJ. This will not by itself raise U.S. interest rates, which are under the Fed's control. Likewise, by assuring the liquidity of domestic financial intermediaries and markets the Fed can get the federal deficit domestically financed at prevailing interest rates. The natural result of a leftward shift in JJ is a higher e, a depreciation of the dollar. This would actually reduce CAD, per se a desirable outcome. However, if the U.S. economy is already at full employment, then in the absence of a fiscal correction there is no room in the economy for more exports or for substitution of domestic production for imports. Thus to prevent inflation, the Fed might have to react to a leftward shift of JJ by tightening credit and raising interest rates.

Obviously this obstacle would not be present if domestic aggregate demand were weakening, whether from fiscal contraction or private thrift.

In those circumstances, a fall in the dollar could correct the disequilibrium by taking the exchange rate to a more realistic level, from which the dollar could be expected to rise. It is a bad idea for the G-7 central banks to peg the dollar at a rate where the risk is all on one side, that it will go down. What we do not need is an exchange value of the dollar too high for timely and significant improvement in the trade position, too high for anyone even to entertain the possibility of appreciation. What we do not need, especially, is a U.S. commitment to defend an overvalued dollar with high interest rates, independently of domestic economic circumstances.

We frequently hear warnings of a "free-fall" of the dollar. I guess this means that exchange rate expectations become extrapolative instead of regressive. This can happen in any financial market. No one can tell when it might happen or what might trigger it or how far a price could move before more sober expectations took over. Our central bank cannot keep interest rates uneconomically high forever just to insure against this contingency.

International Capital Flows vs. Intercurrency Flows

My simple framework has numerous shortcomings, and I want to discuss some of them in this section and in the next and concluding sections.

Interregional trade occurs between geographical regions and their resident populations. It is international trade when the regions are those of national political jurisdictions. Balance-of-payments accounts refer to trade and capital transactions across national boundaries. We commonly regard those transactions as the ones that determine demands for and supplies of various national currencies and their exchange rates. That is, we identify transactions across boundaries with transactions across currencies.

The correspondence is imperfect. For one thing offshore currency markets—Eurodollars, for example—move exchange rates without being recorded in nationally based payments statistics, and without disturbing the accounting identities of current account deficits and capital account surpluses. Less obvious and more important is that some international capital flows may not really change relative demands for currencies or alter their rates of exchange.

Consider, for example, Japanese direct investments in the United States, in particular the acquisition of facilities for producing internationally traded goods like automobiles. In the first instance Japanese investors use dollars they bought from Japanese exporters to buy or build a factory, instead of purchasing U.S. Treasury bonds or other nominal dollar assets. This substitution of American equity for bonds may be only transitory. Japanese investors' demand for nominal dollar assets should not decline by the full amount of their direct investments in the U.S. The reason is that an automobile factory in Ohio may well be a closer substitute for factories, properties, and equities in Japan than it is for future dollars *qua* dollars.

The international car market can be supplied from Tennessee or from Tokyo. The long-run real returns from owning a plant in Tennessee are not very dependent on the dollar/yen exchange rate and not very vulnerable to the factors that might generate losses to Japanese holders of American bonds. U.S. inflation, for example, would raise the dollar earnings from operating the plant at the same time as it depreciated the dollar against the yen. Direct investment of this kind in the U.S. is portfolio reallocation vis-à-vis Japanese plants, real properties, and equities more than vis-à-vis dollars per se. When the investments overseas are in real assets productive of nontraded goods, like office space in Rockefeller Center, they are not so obviously substitutes for similar real assets in Japan. But neither are they particular substitutes for U.S. bonds or other U.S. nominal assets.

My model above, for these reasons, overstates the dependence of capital flows, specifically Japan to U.S., on nominal interest differentials and exchange rate expectations. For direct investments and equities, differences in net real marginal productivities are of prime importance. One should say, of course, *expected* differences. While these are not wholly independent of current differences in nominal interest rates and of expected movements of exchange rates, they mainly reflect longer-run estimates of the profitabilities of producing particular goods and services in different nations and jurisdictions.

Thanks to Reaganomics, the U.S. has been following loose-fiscal–tight-money policies for nearly a decade. Combined with a low rate of private saving, these policies created a nominal interest differential that attracted financial inflows, the more so because, partly in response to U.S. pressure, Japan had just relaxed restrictions on holdings of foreign assets by Japanese financial institutions. The policies kept the cost of capital high in the U.S., higher than in previous cyclical recoveries and higher than in other major economies. As domestic investment was crowded out, the marginal efficiency of capital was lifted, creating an opportunity for foreigners who could tap cheaper foreign sources of finance. In this light, the surge in Japanese direct investment in U.S. business is not surprising. What is perhaps surprising is that U.S. firms and Japanese lenders do not make more deals.

Stock Adjustments vs. Sustainable Flows

Observed flows of capital can reflect either or both of two conceptually distinct phenomena: reallocations of portfolio stock and allocations of new wealth in established patterns. Stock reallocations occur in response to changes in current and expected asset yields and in perceived risks. These are one-shot effects. Because of transactions costs and other frictions, they do not take place instantaneously in response to news. They take time, but as they are completed and portfolios are reshaped they die out. In the absence of further changes of yields and risks, i.e., without new news, these flows between markets and across frontiers and currencies become zero. Accretions to wealth, on the other hand, are a continuing source of capital flows.

For example, suppose U.S. assets are about 10% of fully adjusted Japanese portfolios. In stable circumstances we should expect 10% of the regular annual additions to these portfolios to flow to U.S. markets. Japan's wealth is estimated to be 6 times its GNP. Steady-state growth for both wealth and GNP is in nominal terms 9% per year. Thus the steady flows into U.S. assets would be $.10 \times .09 \times 6 \times$ GNP, about \$16 billion. In the recent decade, of course, Japanese holdings of U.S. assets have grown sharply in relation both to Japan's wealth and to U.S. wealth. I infer that a stock adjustment has been occurring, and still is. Obviously it must taper off sooner or later. But when? It's impossible to say. But catching up to target portfolio allocations is not the only force tending to slow down these capital flows. The increasing interpenetrations of loan markets, equity markets, and goods markets narrow the differentials between the two countries in both nominal interest rates and real costs of capital.

A Second-Approximation Model

The Mundell-Fleming style model presented above does not disaggregate the asset menus offered investors in the two countries. It does not model the two countries symmetrically. Neither does it distinguish between stock reallocations and steady flows. Here I can only sketch briefly some amendments to remedy these shortcomings.

Assets in both countries are available to wealth owners and portfolio managers in both countries. (Some assets may be held in negative amounts.) The notation is tedious, because the identity of the asset, its country of origin, and the residence of its holders must all be described. Amounts of American assets are designated by a_i, amounts of Nipponese assets by n_j. Holdings by Americans are denoted by superscript A, those by Japanese by superscript N. Thus $a_i = a_i^A + a_i^N$ and $n_j = n_j^A + n_j^N$. The units of assets are par values for nominally denominated securities and commodity units for equities or real properties. The economies' steady-state growth trend rates are g_a and g_n.

The prices of assets are q_{ai} and q_{nj}, in dollars or yen per asset unit. These prices are related, normally inversely, to rates of return r_{ai} and r_{nj}. In each country there is one asset, base money, whose price is identically 1 in local currency and whose nominal return is zero or some other constant. As before, the exchange rate is e dollars per yen.

The values of desired asset holdings in currency of the country of issue are for Americans A_i^A and N_j^A, for Japanese A_i^N and N_j^N. In the currency of the holder they are A_i^A and eN_j^A, $(1/e)A_i^N$ and N_j^N. These latter are functions of the vectors of rates of return (r_{ai}, r_{nj}), of prices and expected inflation rates, of NNP in the investors' home country, and of expected change in the exchange rate.

Here are the flow demands for the various assets, all expressed in dollars:

$$fa_i^A(t) = g_a A_i^A(t-1) + \alpha_i(A_i^A(t) - q_{ai}(t)a_i^A(t-1))$$

$$fa_i^N(t) = g_n e(t)[(1/e(t))A_i^N(t-1)] + \beta_i e(t)([(1/e(t))A_i^N(t)]$$
$$- (q_{ai}(t)/e(t))a_i^N(t-1)) \tag{8}$$

$$fn_j^A(t) = g_a[e(t)N_j^A(t-1)] + \alpha_j([e(t)N_j^A(t-1)] - e(t)q_{nj}(t)n_j^A(t-1))$$

$$fn_j^N(t) = g_n e(t)N_j^N(t-1) + \beta_j e(t)(N_j^N(t-1)) - q_{nj}(t)n_j^N(t-1))$$

In each case, the first term is the flow required to make the holding grow at the rate of the economy's growth. The second term is the stock adjustment. The α's and β's are the speeds of adjustment, which are multiplied by the excess of desired holdings over the value of previous holdings at the prices of the current period.

The flow demands for each asset—$f_{a_i}^A + f_{a_i}^N$ and $(f_{n_j}^A + f_{n_j}^N)/e$ in local currencies—are to be equated to the new supplies. For equities and direct investments in business capital, these are the increments in capital stocks, evaluated at current replacement costs or commodity prices. For government obligations, these are the changes in outstanding supplies resulting from central bank and Treasury transactions with the public. These equal in total the government deficit. New asset supplies need not be exogenous; domestic capital investments and government deficits are in part policy decisions and in part functions of other variables.

Total wealth stocks and total private saving in both economies are implicit in the above equations. They are just the sums of stocks and flows for the wealth owners of the country. In steady states, with stock adjustments zero, asset supplies and holdings and total wealth would be growing at rates g_a and g_n.

There are two more supply-demand equations than there are endogenous asset prices (or corresponding rates of return) to be determined. That is because the local prices of currencies and their nominal returns are fixed. And there is one more equation, the payments balance equation. It is natural to think of the equality of net capital flow to current account balance as determining the exchange rate, just as in the simple framework exhibited above. Here is the equation, expressed as the net capital inflow to the United States in dollars on the left-hand side and on the right-hand side the American CAD. This CAD has two parts, the trade deficit and the deficit in investment incomes.

$$\sum_i f_{ai}^N - \sum_j f_{nj}^A = X^N(ep^N/p^A, Y^A) - eX^A(p^A ep^N, Y^N)$$
$$+ \sum_i r_{ai} q_{ai} a_i^N - e \sum_j r_{nj} q_{nj} n_j^A \tag{9}$$

What variables do the two extra equations determine? In some contexts these would be the two Y's, or the two price levels. If aggregate supply equations, "AS curves," were added for each economy, all four of these

Table 21.1
Illustrative Two-country Sectoral Portfolio Matrix

	American portfolios				Japanese portfolios				Total
	Hhs	Bus	Bks	Gov	Hhs	Bus	Bks	Gov	
American assets									
$ Base money	+	+	+	−					0
$ Deposits	+	+	−			+	+	+	0
$ Treas. debt	+	+	+	−	+		+	+	0
$ Hh debt	−	+	+						0
$ Bus. debt	+	−	+		+		+		0
Equity	+	−	−		+	+			0
Real property	+	+			+	+			+
A-owned A-assets	+	−	−	−					+
N-owned A-assets					+	+	+	+	+
Japanese assets									
YEN base money					+	+	+	−	0
YEN deposits		+	+	+	+	+	−		0
YEN treas. debt	+		+	+	+	+	+	−	0
YEN Hh debt					−	+	+		0
YEN bus. debt	+		+		+	−	+		0
Equity	+	+			+	−	−		0
Real property	+	+			+	+			+
A-owned N-assets	+	+	+	+					+
N-owned N-assets					+	−	−	−	+
Net worth	+	0	0	−	+	0	0	−	+

variables could be determined. However, in the spirit of the simple model above, price levels would be taken as predetermined in the short run and the two Y's would be those chosen by the monetary authorities. The two free variables would be local interest rates r indicative of monetary policies, or, alternatively, values of the monetary base in each country.

Crucial parameters in a portfolio model of this kind are the partial derivatives of desired asset stocks with respect to rates of return, the r's. It is intuitively natural to expect the own partials, the responses to changes in the asset's own rate, to be positive, at least non-negative. Furthermore, a "gross substitutes" assumption is convenient and plausible, though not mandated by rationality. This says that cross partials, responses of a given asset demand to other rates of return, are non-positive and that the sum of all of them is not greater in absolute value than the own partial. High absolute values of cross partials indicate high substitutability between assets, low values the reverse. Common vulnerabilities to certain risks make for high substitutability. Assets whose returns, including capital gains or losses, do not share the same risks, or move in opposite directions in response to the same shocks, will be poor substitutes. I gave an example above, when I argued that equities and real properties in the two countries could be good portfolio substitutes for each other but poor substitutes for nominal assets in either currency.

Table 21.1 is a schematic illustration of the accounting underlying Eqs. (8) and (9). In the matrix, the columns represent sectors of the two economies, America on the left and Japan on the right. Only four sectors of each economy are distinguished here. The rows represent assets, American at the top, Japanese at the bottom. Seven asset categories are shown for each country. A plus sign + in a cell indicates that the sector holds positive quantities of the asset, a minus sign − that the sector is a debtor in this category of asset. The entries in a column, for both local and foreign assets, describe the sector's portfolio; they sum to the sector's net worth. The entries in a row show how the positive and negative holdings of a given asset are distributed among sectors in the two countries. The row sums, in the final column, are zero for all the assets that are obligations of one or more of the sectors. They are positive only for real property, capital, in the two economies. The sum of the values of the two capital stocks is equal to the sum of the sector net worths. Of course, one country—in present circumstances, Japan—may have a net worth greater than its own capital stock by the amount of its net claims on the other country.

Table 21.1 is a schematic balance sheet, in which the entries are stocks. An analogous schema would describe the flows in any period, as in the "second approximation model" above. The illustration is for a two-country world, but the same format can be used for n countries.

CHAPTER 22

THE STATE OF EXCHANGE RATE THEORY: SOME SKEPTICAL OBSERVATIONS

My friend Robert Triffin, for more than a quarter century my wise tutor in matters of international finance and money, constantly urged me to broaden the scope of my macroeconomic and monetary models beyond the convenient bounds of a closed economy. He understood very early the immense change that currency convertibility and internationalization of money and capital markets would bring. He foresaw the constraints these developments would impose on national macroeconomic policies and the necessity for orderly coordination of those policies, as well as for other dimensions of economic integration that would exploit the mutual benefits and minimize the hazards of international capital mobility. Never one to assume that institutions do not matter or that monetary arrangements are neutral and thus irrelevant, Triffin devoted his energy and his exceptional architectural talent to the design of international monetary institutions. The world has moved in the opposite direction this past decade, toward monetary anarchy rather than order. But this is not because the premises of Triffin's analysis were proved wrong or the institutions he designed and advocated were shown to be undesirable.

Having taken Triffin's advice too little and too late, I find myself puzzled by current theories of exchange rates and therefore uncertain whether institutional changes could yield results superior to our current international monetary anarchy. A few years ago I boldly advanced the hypothesis that foreign exchange markets were largely speculative, so that the signals they provided to private agents and the constraints they imposed on national policymakers were not conducive to economic efficiency.

Reprinted by permission from *International Monetary System under Flexible Exchange Rates: Global, Regional and National: Essays in Honor of Robert Triffin*, eds. R. Cooper et al., Ballinger Publishers, 1982.

Even more boldly, I proposed a solution—to throw sand in the all too perfect currency exchange mechanisms, in the hope of filtering out speculative noise and allowing national economies more macroeconomic independence (Tobin 1978). I share the attraction to "gimmicks" that Triffin once avowed, though I do not think he was attracted to this one of mine. Anyway, the hypothesis and the gimmick were admittedly speculation on my part.

Exchange Rates as Asset Prices

The theory of exchange rates has increasingly taken as its point of departure the observation that "an exchange rate is an asset price." The implication is that theories and models of portfolio choice and asset pricing can help us understand the determination of exchange rates. This shift of emphasis from the role of the exchange rate as an element in the relative prices of internationally traded goods was a natural response to the increasing international mobility of financial capital. Although the approach has grown in vogue in the 1970s during the floating rate regime, it is no less relevant to pegged rates. After all, the pegs were not forever frozen in granite or gold. Since they were adjustable—and often adjusted—portfolio managers had to consider the probabilities of devaluations and revaluations.[1] In the interims, asset demands and supplies had to be adjusted to clear the markets, and official interventions altered the supplies of assets denominated in different currencies to match the preferences of investors. Interventions, of course, occur with floating rates, too.

Exchange rates are not exactly asset prices. Rather, an exchange rate (say, Deutsche marks per dollar) is an element of the price to holders of one currency (dollars) of every asset denominated in a second currency (Deutsche marks). Likewise, the change in the exchange rate between purchase and sale or redemption is an element in the dollar rate of return on a DM-denominated asset.

Among other assets are the literal currencies—dollar bills and DM notes—and the exchange rate is their relative price. In a multi-asset world this fact is of limited significance. We should not expect the exchange rate to depend in any simple way on the relative supplies of national currencies or even of more broadly defined transactions moneys. The oversimplification, fostered by semantics, is analogous to a celebrated aphorism in closed economy monetary theory: "The [real] price of money is the reciprocal of the price level." Since everyone with even a smattering of economics finds it self-evident that the price of a commodity varies inversely with the supply, this definition of the price of money paves the way for the quantity theory. The semantics obscures the fact that variation of commodity prices alters the real values not only of currency and other transactions moneys but also of near moneys and a host of other promises to pay amounts specified in the monetary unit of account.

The Values of Fiat Currencies

Why fiat currency, intrinsically useless paper, has positive real value at all and how its value is determined are questions that continue to puzzle economic theorists (Kareken and Wallace 1980). *A fortiori*, determination of the relative prices of several fiat currencies seems to be a subject on which the utility-technology-resource-endowment paradigm of basic microeconomic theory has nothing to say.

Neil Wallace, John Bryant, and John Kareken have pointed out the essential arbitrariness of price levels and exchange rates in a world of fiat moneys (Wallace 1980; Bryant and Wallace 1979; Kareken and Wallace 1978). They find a function for fiat money, and a reason for its positive value, as a store of value for households with finite horizons in an infinitely lived economy with overlapping generations. The retired aged buy their consumption goods from the productive young. Given a foreseen path of money creation, intergenerational trade determines the path of prices and thus of real returns on money. The shape of the money path matters for real outcomes, but its scale does not. For example, the economy will have the same rate of deflation and the same consumption path with any constant quantity of money, whatever its size.

In this world there is no room for more than one fiat asset. Consequently, there can be only trivial differences between currency itself and promises of future currency payments by the issuing government; since government debt will be currency on maturity, it is essentially currency now. Likewise, there can really be only one fiat money—the one that promises the highest real return. If two or more currencies are being held simultaneously, they must be equivalent in nominal growth rates and real rates of return. Exchange rates between them simply preserve purchasing power parity. Exchange rates are just arbitrary conversions of units between equivalent fiat moneys, of no more significance than the exchange rates between dimes, quarters, and dollars.

Instructive and provocative as it is, the Wallace–Bryant–Kareken model, emphasizing the store of value function of money rather than the transactions function, does not do justice to the social convention that makes the national currency the generally accepted medium of transactions within the nation's boundaries. Neither foreign currencies nor any promises to pay the national currency not on demand but in future serve as equivalents. Other stores of value—land, capital, loans—are the principal vehicles of saving for retirement and bequest. Currency and promises to pay currency on demand are held for very short periods and circulate rapidly. They have positive real value because of their advantage in transactions, and the demand for them depends on this service yield plus the rate of change in their purchasing power. National currencies are far from perfect substitutes. They can and do coexist with widely different real rates of return. In the extreme, each nation holds no other currency but its own. If there are no other outside nominal assets, capital movements across exchanges are transfers of title to real property or the equivalent in private loans and debts.

These assumptions can support neutrality conclusions similar to those of the Wallace–Bryant–Kareken model. Real outcomes throughout the world are invariant to scalar changes in the paths of any or all currency stocks. These simply alter national price levels, to which exchange rates adjust as necessary to preserve purchasing power parity, without affecting intertemporal decisions. Saving, capital formation, and real international capital movements are unaffected. They imply current account imbalances, which in a multicommodity world in turn determine the real or relative prices that define purchasing power parity. Moneys are neutral in these abstract worlds, but they are not supernatural. The time shapes of currency supplies will in general affect saving, investment, international capital movements, and relative prices.

Neutrality amounts to nothing more than invariance to unit changes, like calling a dollar a new dime and ten dollars one new dollar. Models that reduce monetary policy essentially to splits of this kind naturally conclude that, like stock splits, they do nothing real. They merely alter prices and exchange rates in an obvious and trivial way. The all too common fallacy of misplaced concreteness is to identify real world monetary policies with unit changes. Money stock increases by open market operations or by printing currency to finance government expenditures are not neutral or trivial. They will in general change real interest rates and exchange rates.

Portfolio Balance across Currencies and Current Account Imbalances

The portfolio balance approach assumes that currency, future promises to pay currency, even by the government itself, and real assets are imperfect substitutes for each other and also that assets denominated in different currencies are imperfect substitutes. International financial and capital markets determine simultaneously the prices of the various assets and currencies, as well as domestic commodity prices or incomes. As shown in a previous article (Tobin and Macedo 1980), equations of asset demand and supply balance and intercurrency payments balance suffice to determine these variables.

Portfolio balance considerations suggest that asset values will depend *ceteris paribus* on their relative supplies and on the asset preferences of wealth owners. In the application of these considerations to the international scene, a key assumption is that wealth owners display home currency preference. At a given exchange rate between dollars and Deutsche marks, Americans will wish to hold a higher fraction of wealth, and of a given increment of wealth, in dollars than Germans will and a lower fraction in Deutsche marks.

As asset supplies and total wealth of the several countries evolve over time, so will their trade balances and their current account deficits or surpluses. These depend on prices, exchange rates, interest rates, and "absorption" of domestic outputs by consumption, investment, and government purchases. A country's portfolio allocations of new saving may, for example, favor accumulation of foreign assets over local capital investment and thereby generate a constellation of prices, exchange rates, and interest rates that leads to a current account deficit. Monetary and financial shocks may lead to international asset transfers whose counterpart is an imbalance in current account; a change in exchange rates is a likely, but not inevitable, part of the mechanism that brings this about. Shocks of taste and technology that alter the competitiveness of nations in trade may show up as shifts of wealth, accomplished by current account surpluses and deficits, which set in train adjustments of prices, interest rates, exchange rates, and international transfers of assets.

It is thanks to home currency preference that current account shocks move exchange rates at all (Kouri and Macedo 1978: 142–48; Dornbusch 1975). A U.S. deficit matched by a German surplus shifts wealth from U.S. to German portfolios, lowering demand for dollar assets and raising demand for DM assets. If asset supplies are unchanged, then they must change hands; Germans must buy some from Americans. The yields of dollar assets must rise or those of DM assets fall or both in order to maintain portfolio balance on both sides. All this will be accomplished by an increase in the dollar value of the Deutsche mark, an increase in the DM price of DM assets (lower interest rates), and a fall in the dollar price of dollar assets (higher interest rates), in some combination. In the absence of the difference in asset preferences, the current account imbalance could be financed without any change in the exchange rate.

How does the appreciation of the Deutsche mark help to equilibrate the system? It lowers the DM value of Germans' dollar holdings and induces them, in the interest of maintaining diversification, to channel some of the new wealth corresponding to their current account surplus into dollar securities. This inducement is powerfully reinforced in case German investors expect the dollar to rebound. These inducements do not apply to Americans, who because of their loss in wealth, reflected in the current account deficit, are willing to sell. Similarly, the incentive to sell DM securities provided by an increase in the dollar price of Deutsche marks— an incentive that is strengthened if the increase is expected to be temporary—applies to Americans but not to Germans. Concurrently with these asset shifts, appreciation of the mark may, given well-behaved elasticities, tend to eliminate the current account imbalance.

Empirically, the exchange depreciations associated with news of current account deficits seem larger than can be explained by the small shifts of wealth they entail. An alternative explanation is that unexpected weakness in current account is an indicator of competitive difficulties that will spell trouble later (Dornbusch 1980: 157–63). But what is the trouble? It is that current account deficits will shift wealth abroad and make exchange depreciation necessary. If actual wealth shifts are too small for the phenomenon they are supposed to explain, then are not the expected shifts also too small?

Home Currency Preference

Home currency preference is by no means an obvious implication of portfolio theory. To the contrary, it has been shown in a variety of models that risk can be reduced by diversification across currencies (Kouri and Macedo 1978: 118–26; Macedo 1981; Krugman 1981 and references therein). The risks of nominal assets are those of commodity price fluctuation, interest rate variation, and default. Economies with different currencies, geographies, and central governments will be more independent of each other in these dimensions than, for example, the states of a federal union.

Exchange risk may work either way. Here it is necessary to consider the correlations of deviations of exchange rates from expected trends with the other risks of nominal assets. If the foreign currency appreciates when home inflation accelerates and depreciates when foreign inflation is relatively high, foreign currency assets are a hedge. If the foreign currency depreciates when domestic interest rates move up, foreign securities are not a good hedge against capital losses due to interest rate increases at home. They offer some protection against domestic political difficulties and defaults, but expose the investor to risks of the same kind abroad.

In addition, exchange rates may move because of speculations unrelated to the properties of nominal assets relevant to owners of wealth. Even so, these independent movements would seem to offer opportunities for diversification, especially when nominal claims in home currency are subject to important inflation risk.

The great portfolio advantage of home currency assets is that they enable an investor to hedge against contractual obligations and predictable needs to pay out home currency in future. This advantage is eroded by uncertainty about future commodity prices, the more so the more distant the payments to be financed by disposition of assets. For this reason, we should expect foreign currency assets to play a bigger role in portfolios at times of high uncertainty about inflation.[2]

Home currency preference is probably due less to mean-variance calculus than to other dimensions of asset choice. Among these are that (1) information is more complete and less costly for home currency assets; (2) transactions costs, including not only costs of purchases and sales and currency conversions but also tax and legal complications, actual and contingent, are higher for foreign assets; and (3) foreign investments by institutions and intermediaries—savings banks, mutual funds, trusts, and pensions funds—are legally restricted. As in domestic financial markets, we should expect these obstacles to diminish as the basic portfolio investment advantages persist and become clearer. Eurocurrency markets, international banking, registration of foreign currency securities in domestic markets, mutual funds with international portfolios, multinational corporations, even the inclusion of foreign assets in university endowment portfolios—all testify to the growing internationalization.

Home currency preference is logically separable from geographical or political preference, though many of the reasons for one are also sources of the other. It is, of course, likely that shifts of wealth between countries bring in their wake shifts of preferences in equity investment. Wealth owners favor capital domiciled in their own countries. But the consideration that leads to home preference among currency-denominated assets—namely, that the investor thus avoids exchange risk in consuming the income or principal—applies with considerably less force.

Domestic Asset Supplies and Exchange Rates

Current account surpluses and deficits are, of course, by no means the only source of change in national asset demands and supplies. Indeed, they are minor compared to domestic asset creation. Wealth at the disposition of private agents grows with domestic capital formation and with public sector deficits and by capital gains on existing assets.

A U.S. government deficit increases the supply of Treasury obligations. Some of them may be bought by taxpayers as the best hedge against the taxes they foresee will be needed to service the debt.[3] But most likely there is a net increase in private wealth, and at prevailing interest and exchange rates, U.S. investors will not wish to absorb all of it in government bonds or even in dollar assets. An increase in the dollar interest rate on bonds and a decline in the dollar against other currencies will place some of the bonds overseas. This is a rationale for the time-honored conservative view that loose fiscal policy endangers or actually depreciates the currency. If public debt is rising faster relative to wealth in the United States than in Germany, that might be a reason for the dollar to fall against the Deutsche mark (Frankel 1979a, 1979b; Dornbusch 1980: 163–72).

But what of the assets that make up the difference? These are basically claims to the capital stock and its earnings, not to specified amounts of any currency. An extreme view is that goods are goods, capital goods are capital goods, factories are factories—wherever they are located. Earnings may in fact come from worldwide sales in numerous currencies. Neither the earnings nor the value of the shares in any currency is particularly correlated with the price of the currency in which the company is domiciled. If this is the nature of equity—a currency-diversified asset earning the world marginal efficiency of capital—then accumulation of wealth in this form does not satisfy the appetite of local investors for assets denominated in their home currency. By this argument, if Germany has high real investment and a low public deficit, while the United States has low real investment and high government deficit, the Deutsche mark should appreciate.

But the argument needs to be qualified on two counts. First, capital investment is typically debt financed, at least in part. If the Modigliani–Miller theorem applies, debt finance does not matter; the equity owners are in effect in debt to themselves. But the aggregation may be excessive and misleading. The equity owners could be at a corner. Risk-lovers seeking leverage, they have quite different portfolio preferences from their creditors, those risk-averse diversifiers who make the debt and exchange markets. To the latter, corporate debt issues are like government debt in the same currency. It may even be that high real investment throws so much private debt issue into the international market that the currency must depreciate to get it absorbed. In sum, it is not self-evident that public debt is an adequate or reliable measure of the supply of a currency to the asset markets.

The second point is that equity investments are not as currency-neutral as the extreme view suggests. The principal location and the legal and tax domicile of the business do entangle its earnings with the domestic and exchange value of the currency. For both foreigners and local investors, equity in the country's businesses may be a closer substitute for home debt than for foreign debt securities.

Expectations and Their Nebulous Anchor in Future Equilibrium

The price of an asset is the market's valuation of the future returns, in cash or in kind, sure or unsure, to which the owner will be entitled. Among those returns are the gains or losses from changes in the asset price itself. The current price thus depends on expectations of the price tomorrow, and that, in turn, depends on expectations of the day after tomorrow, and so on through the life of the asset or *ad infinitum*. New information about future prices, even those in the far distant future, affects the price today. In principle, the whole future is relevant even for investors or potential investors who intend to hold the asset only for a short time, because expectations of remote events will affect their capital gains or losses.

The situation is even more complex because portfolio choices involve comparisons of returns on many assets and thus involve expectations and joint probability distributions of large dimension. The market prices that emerge today reflect those choices by many diverse investors and depend on their estimates of the price vector that similar market processes will generate in the future. Thus expectations, and expectations of expectations, are crucial determinants of asset prices. But they are unobservable in practice and elusive in theory. These difficulties are acute for exchange rates.

If expectations can be anything, we have little to say about asset prices or about exchange rates in particular. Rational expectations theory confines price-determining expectations to those that will in fact be realized, at least actuarially. Those expectations are supposed to be anchored in a future equilibrium on which the views of investors, fully informed on both data and mechanism, converge. In the case of exchange rates, economists and econometricians, and presumably market participants too, have especially great difficulty in identifying such an equilibrium and much more in estimating it empirically.

Purchasing power parity and current account balance are sometimes advanced as conditions of equilibrium, but there are at least two reasons why they are inadequate and treacherous. First, equilibrium real terms of trade themselves depend on many features of the trading economies, some of them endogenous to the future paths of prices, exchange rates, and interest rates. The real exchange rate is not independent of the trade balance, except in those mythical one-good worlds that neglect all reasons for trade. Neither trade nor the current account as a whole is necessarily balanced at zero in any practical long run. Capital movements, transfers of technology, and other adjustments can continue for decades without wiping out the differences in marginal efficiencies of capital that induce them, and even then they may have to continue for decades more to maintain parity of real interest rates among economies whose effective supplies of labor and other local resources are growing at disparate rates.

The second reason is more devastating. Even assuming that an equilibrium of the real balance of payments and of the terms of trade could be foreseen, how could it be translated into expectations of exchange rates? One does not have to agree completely with Wallace *et al* to appreciate the force of their reminder that the relative price of two purely nominal "commodities" is quite arbitrary, certainly not deducible from the real economic forces involved in the difficult projections mentioned in the preceding paragraph. To guess at truly long-run equilibrium exchange rates, we would have to model the monetary and fiscal policies of the several countries, their political and social tolerances of inflation and unemployment, the evolution of their price- and wage-setting institutions and of their financial systems, and many other phenomena relating to nominal variables and their interactions with real economic outcomes.

Slow Portfolio Adjustment as a Source of Noise in Asset Prices

When news leads portfolio managers to revise their estimates of the expected future returns or risks of holding an asset at its prevailing price, they will wish to change their holdings. The portfolio adjustments will alter the prices of this and other assets, until they are aligned to the new information about expected returns and risks. If these price responses to news were discontinuous and instantaneous, then they could be distinguished from those continuous price movements that realize prior anticipations of expected returns and of entire probability distributions. An econometric investigator could then hope to recapture the determinants of portfolio choice from time series cleansed of unexpected capital gains and losses, identifiable as jumps in the price series.

In practice, unfortunately, the market rarely absorbs news so suddenly. Portfolio adjustments are strung out over considerable time, because of lags and costs in the diffusion of information and in decisions and transactions and because of liquidity and borrowing constraints. The result is that price movements reflecting adjustments of portfolios to news are inextricably tangled with those that reflect price paths anticipated in market price settings themselves.

Examples are numerous, both in domestic financial markets and in foreign exchange markets. Holding Treasury bills is an alternative to holding common stocks, and it is to be expected that the returns on the two will be positively correlated. News of higher bill rates—for example, because of tighter monetary policy, actual or expected—should lower the prices of equities in order to keep their subsequent yields inclusive of capital gains in line with bill yields. But if the adjustment of equity prices takes weeks or months, the investigator will see a negative *ex post* relationship between the two rates of return.

In a similar manner, portfolio adjustments generate confusing signals for the investigator of foreign exchange markets. The slide of the dollar in 1977–78 has been attributed to news that led international investors, including the managers of oil wealth, to believe that dollar assets were less secure and less remunerative than assets denominated in other currencies. The slide was sustained for at least fifteen months, and observations during that period certainly contribute, in any calculation that includes them, to the conclusion that dollar assets were less attractive in a multi-currency portfolio than they had been previously. To include observations during the portfolio shift in optimal portfolio calculations designed to support the hypothesis that rational portfolio adjustment to new information caused the decline in the dollar is to lift oneself by one's own bootstraps (as done by Kouri and Macedo 1978; and Dornbusch 1980).

The steady rise of the dollar from September 1980 to May 1981 is another example. Again, interest rate news appears to be responsible. Yet contrary to simple efficient market models, the response of exchange rates to the high positive differential between U.S. and European or Japanese interest rates was gradual. Since interest arbitrage kept forward exchange premiums in line with interest differentials, the forward rates predicted almost daily appreciations against the dollar that turned out to be wrong in sign. Both during this period and during the persistent swing against the dollar two years earlier, the market did not appear to be using information contained in the trend of the spot rate. If it had been used, if the differential interest rate news had been exploited all at once, then the dollar would have risen more sharply in 1980 and then depreciated at a pace consistent with the forward premium—that is, with the interest differential.

In sum, observations of multicurrency portfolios held during periods when *ex ante* exchange rate anticipations were so radically different from *ex post* realizations or when agents with expectations correct at least in sign were slow to act are not good data from which to infer the subjective probability distributions and risk preferences underlying portfolio choice. Likewise, sluggish and smooth adjustment to news casts doubt on theories that require prices to jump to that singular expectations fulfillment path that leads to equilibrium. This is an issue of some moment, for the rational expectations equilibrium in multi-asset markets is generally a saddle-point. Usually there is no continuous expectation-fulfilling path from the initial point to the newly displaced equilibrium.

The major alternatives to models of financial and asset markets that assume rational expectations and efficient use of information are models that assume slow adjustment periods and disequilibrium. Disequilibrium need not mean that markets are failing to clear, though it may take that form. It may be simply that portfolio investors are off their desired portfolios. They may be following rules of thumb that can be described as "bounded" rationality. Or they may be fully rational if market imperfections and costs of transactions and decisions are properly taken into account. In either event, the task of modeling their behavior is very difficult, perhaps beyond our present capacity, and the task of inferring behavior from market time series even more formidable. The slow adjustment disequilibrium approach does not finesse the problem of expectations formation. But while it does not necessarily imply stability of equilibrium, it does not make stability contingent on the market's jumping to a singular dynamic path, even to the extent of "overshooting" equilibrium.[4]

A possibly preferable approach to the calculation of the means, variances, and covariances relevant to portfolio choices and asset prices is to use "fundamental" data only. Capital gains and losses due to the movements of asset prices over the period of observation are excluded from the returns used in such calculations. It is a nonbootstrap approach in the sense that the market prices are not "explained" by market price observations themselves. The "fundamental" approach has been used to explain variations across firms in share prices, yielding some interesting results but leaving many puzzles unresolved, including variation over time in the general level of equity prices (Tobin and Brainard 1977; Brainard, Shoven, and Weiss 1980). For exchange rates, the analogous strategy would be to relate the prices of a cross-section of currencies to a set of underlying characteristics of their economies. But this approach requires specification of those "fundamental" determinants of nominal variables, precisely the subject on which we lack theoretical clarity and consensus.

One apparently robust conclusion of research on stock and bond prices is that their variability over time is far larger than the variability of their underlying fundamental determinants (Douglas 1969; Shiller 1979, 1981; Grossman and Shiller 1981). The markets appear to exaggerate the significance and permanence of bits of information, adding self-generated speculative risk to the basic risks of the securities. The same or perhaps even greater magnification is likely to occur in foreign exchange markets, given the elusiveness of the "fundamentals."

Concluding Remarks

Portfolio and asset-pricing models have not been very successful in explaining observed fluctuations of securities prices in domestic markets, and we should probably not expect them to do much better in empirical explanations of exchange rates. We know that an increase in interest rates in dollars, widening its differential above sterling or Deutsche mark interest rates, generally appreciates the dollar. We know that bad news about exports and imports usually depreciates the currency. Those regularities are roughly on a par with our empirical wisdom about stock markets, and maybe we cannot expect to do much better with currencies.

For reasons I have tried to explain, it is not really surprising that the portfolio and asset market approach to exchange rates turns out to have little to say about their levels and to concentrate on their changes in response to policies and other shocks. But that focus leaves us without an explanation of the expectational shocks that are probably responsible for more of the observed movements of exchange rates than those our theories do illuminate and without a soundly based way to distinguish the one kind of movement from the other. It leaves me where I came in, with the suspicion that a large part of the activity in foreign exchange markets is speculation on future speculation and with my proposal that governments cooperate to filter out the noise.

Notes

I am grateful to William Brainard, Stanley Black, and John Campbell for discussions enlightening me on the subjects of this chapter. An unpublished critical review of recent literature by Campbell, "Exchange Rates and the Current Account in a World of Capital Mobility," has been very helpful. Even more than usual, all errors and misunderstandings are my own.

1. Kouri (1976) has a model of the forward premium under adjustable and flexible rates.
2. This is borne out in the portfolios computed in Kouri and Macedo (1978: 129) and Macedo (1981).
3. The rationale for hedging of this kind is argued by Barro (1974). Reasons why it is incomplete are given by Tobin (1980).
4. These issues are clearly and usefully clarified by Burmeister (1980).

References

Barro, Robert J. 1974. "Are Government Bonds Net Wealth?" *Journal of Political Economy* 82 (November–December): 1095–117.

Brainard, William C., John B. Shoven, and Laurence Weiss. 1980. "The Financial Valuation of the Return to Capital." *Brookings Panel on Economic Activity* 2: 453–502.

Bryant, John, and Neil Wallace. 1979. "The Inefficiency of Interest-Bearing National Debt." *Journal of Political Economy* 87 (April): 365–81.

Burmeister, Edwin. 1980. "On Some Conceptual Issues in Rational Expectations Modeling." *Journal of Money, Credit, and Banking*, pt. 2 (November): 800–16.

Dornbusch, Rudiger. 1975. "A Portfolio Balance Model of the Open Economy." *Journal of Monetary Economics* 1 (January): 3–20.

———. 1980. "Exchange Rate Economics: Where Do We Stand?" *Brookings Panel on Economic Activity* 1: 143–86.

Douglas, George W. 1969. "Risk in the Equity Markets: An Empirical Appraisal of Market Efficiency." *Yale Economic Essays* 9, no. 1 (Spring): 3–46.

Frankel, Jeffrey A. 1979a. "The Diversifiability of Exchange Risk." *Journal of International Economics* 9 (August): 379–93.

———. 1979b. "On the Mark: A Theory of Floating Exchange Rates Based on Real Interest Differentials." *American Economic Review* 69 (September): 610–22.

Grossman, Sanford J., and Robert J. Shiller. 1981. "The Determinants of the Variability of Stock Market Prices." *American Economic Review* 71 (May): 222–27.

Kareken, John H., and Neil Wallace. 1978. "Samuelson's Consumption-Loan Model with Country-Specific Fiat Monies." Federal Reserve Bank of Minneapolis Staff Report No. 24, July.

———, eds. 1980. *Models of Monetary Economics*. Minneapolis: Federal Reserve Bank of Minneapolis.

Kouri, Pentti J. K. 1976. "The Determinants of the Forward Premium." Seminar Paper No. 62, IIES, University of Stockholm, August.

Kouri, Pentti J. K., and Jorge Braga de Macedo. 1978. "Exchange Rates and the International Adjustment Process." *Brookings Panel on Economic Activity* 1: 111–50.

Krugman, Paul R. 1981. "Consumption Preferences, Asset Demands and Distribution Effects in International Markets." NBER Working Paper No. 651, March.

Macedo, Jorge Braga de. 1981. "Optimal Currency Diversification for a Class of Risk–Averse International Investors." Working Papers in Economics No. 11, Woodrow Wilson School, Princeton University, May.

Shiller, Robert J. 1979. "The Volatility of Long–Term Interest Rates and Expectations Models of the Term Structure." *Journal of Political Economy* 87 (December): 1190–1219.

———. 1981. "Do Stock Prices Move Too Much to Be Justified by Subsequent Changes in Dividends." *American Economic Review* 71 (June): 421–36.

Tobin, James. 1978. "A Proposal for International Monetary Reform." *Eastern Economic Journal* 4, nos. 3–4 (July–October).

———. 1980. "Government Deficits and Capital Accumulation." In D. Currie and W. Peters, eds., *Contemporary Economic Analysis*, vol. 2, pp. 23–45. London: Coom Helm. Reprinted as Chapter III of *Asset Accumulation and Economic Activity*, Oxford: Blackwell, and Chicago: University of Chicago Press, 1980.

Tobin, James, and W. Brainard. 1977. "Asset Markets and the Cost of Capital." In R. Nelson and B. Balassa, eds., *Economic Progress: Private Values and Public Policy* (Essays in Honor of William Fellner), pp. 235–62. Amsterdam: North Holland.

Tobin, James, and Jorge Braga de Macedo. 1980. "The Short-Run Macroeconomics of Floating Exchange Rates: An Exposition." In J. Chipman and C. Kindleberger, eds., *Flexible Exchange Rates and the Balance of Payments: Essays in Memory of Egon Sohmen*. Amsterdam: North Holland.

Wallace, Neil. 1980. "The Overlapping Generations Model of Fiat Money." In John H. Kareken and Neil Wallace, eds., *Models of Monetary Economics*, pp. 49–82. Minneapolis: Federal Reserve Bank of Minneapolis.

CHAPTER 23

ARE THERE RELIABLE ADJUSTMENT MECHANISMS?

Once upon a time economics students of my generation learned the theory of international payments adjustment. We marveled at the natural mechanisms which, in principle at least, corrected the imbalances that triggered them. The subjects, even the words, still appear in modern textbooks (for example, Dornbusch [1980]), although they have been swallowed in "open economy macroeconomics," or in what might be called "multi-national macroeconomics"—were that subject advanced enough to merit a label. Both the world and the models economists build to model it are vastly more complex than students of my day were led to believe and did believe. Nevertheless, exploiting the license a keynoter has for imprecision and impressionism, I propose to review several possible adjustment mechanisms and to consider their applicability in today's world.

I shall in the end be skeptical that there are any reliable mechanisms. This conclusion, I suspect, is widely shared—if rarely voiced—among economists, and especially among practitioners and policy-markers in international finance. Perhaps it is a premise of this very conference. The universal call for coordination of national macroeconomic policies betrays a strong suspicion that absent such coordination the system will not equilibrate itself. The suspicion might be that the natural, automatic mechanisms are weak or perverse, or that they are frequently obstructed and perverted by unconcerted national policies.

With "endogenous politicians," in Assar Lindbeck's phrase, it may be difficult to distinguish policy responses from market responses. Several endogenous politicians are gathering at Venice this month, and effective coordination is not likely to be one of their responses. In the old days, in

Keynote paper presented at the Third International Conference of the Institute for Monetary and Economic Studies, Bank of Japan, June 1987. Reprinted by permission from *Bank of Japan Monetary and Economic Studies* 5(2) (September 1987): 1–12.

contrast, the mechanisms of payments adjustment were not thought to leave much room for discretionary national policies, concerted or disparate, for good or for ill.

I shall discuss both short-run and long-run adjustments, to both nominal and real shocks. The two distinctions are interrelated; nominal shocks and adjustments are relatively more important in short runs.

1 The Necessity of International Price Adjustments

In those old days to which I referred, the major short-run adjustments to payments imbalances were thought to occur through absolute price changes in deficit and surplus countries, which spelled relative price changes between those countries. Keynesian theory added, in the international context as in the analysis of closed economies, adjustments due to variations of output and effective demand. But for reasons of which I shall remind you below, this mechanism was thought to be inadequate by itself.

Emphasis was concentrated on the adjustments of current accounts, probably because capital movements—other than official settlements and short-term trade finance—were limited by national controls and other barriers. The problem was posed like this: Suppose trade imbalance arises because of changes in comparative advantage—differential changes in tastes, technologies, resources in the trading countries—or because of disparate changes in monetary stocks or velocities. What happens to restore balance?

The oldest and simplest story was the specie flow mechanism of the gold standard, with gold essentially a common international money. Gold would flow from the deficit country to its trading partners in surplus. According to the quantity theory of money, prices would fall in the former and rise in the latter. If the shock were real, the change in the countries' relative prices would shift international demands for goods and services from surplus countries to the deficit country. These shifts would eliminate the imbalance. If the shock were permanent, the new relative prices would be permanent. Once achieved, they would sustain a new equilibrium in international payments. This story assumes that the countries were producing different goods, imperfect substitutes.

The mechanism is essentially the same in fixed-exchange-rate systems in which governments, their central banks, and private banking systems augment money supplies beyond national quantities of gold or other international media. Recall the gold exchange system or Bretton Woods. However, the links to gold or international monetary reserves are looser. Banks and individual agents can substitute local paper money, and central banks and governments can allow or engineer such substitutions. Thus countries—especially and asymmetrically, surplus countries—can postpone or avoid the local price consequences of payments imbalances. "Rules of the game" arose to strengthen the price adjustment mechanism against the capacities and incentives of nations to weaken it. But the rules were informal and frequently honored in the breach.

Banking and central banking make monetary shocks possible. The price adjustment mechanism is supposed to work for them too. A local monetary expansion, or rise in velocity for that matter, raises local prices and generates a trade deficit, which drains gold or other international reserves. The local money supply is restricted until relative international prices are restored to their unchanged equilibrium. The local price increase is mostly, but not entirely, transient. When the adjustment is complete, prices throughout the world have all been raised in the same proportion, the amount necessary to absorb the increment to world money supply due to the initial local monetary shock.

This is essentially the "monetary theory of the balance of payments," even though its modern version was expounded for a one-good purchasing-power-parity world. (That assumption does not seem to me an attractive foundation for international payments theory. It provides no basis for international trade in the first place, except by excess "absorption" in one country and deficient absorption elsewhere. That phenomenon, as well as the neutral adjustment to monetary shock, can be treated without insisting on the "law of one price" in international trade.)

The price adjustment mechanism is also central to the correction of imbalances under floating, market-determined rates of exchange among fiat national currencies. The deficit country's currency depreciates against the surplus countries' currencies. The same changes in international relative prices occur in response to a real shock, possibly but not necessarily without any changes in nominal prices in the several economies. Likewise, in the case of a monetary shock, a local rise in prices robs it of any real domestic consequences, while the exchange depreciation preserves the equilibrium relation of the country's international prices to the rest of the world.

The key to the equivalence is, of course, the assumption that nominal monetary quantities, prices, and exchange rates are neutral; national moneys are veils; relative and absolute prices are perfectly flexible. It is hard to understand why anyone who believes that assumption—the "classical dichotomy," if you like—prefers one national or international monetary regime to another; cares whether adjustments of international relative prices are made, or prevented, by movements of local prices or of exchange rates; or worries about inflation and deflation.

To this, I am aware, can be voiced the objection that commodity money and fiat money differ. The equivalence just discussed would apply only to alternative regimes with fiat moneys. Under the gold standard, changes in prices of other commodities in one country or in the world do have real effects, via the relative price and production of gold. I think this is not a matter of important substance, except for gold-producing countries.

When classical or Walrasian assumptions supporting the irrelevance of nominal variables are dropped, choices among monetary regimes and international rules of the game become consequential. The case for floating rates was that changes in nominal exchange rates are the quickest and least painful way of bringing about equilibrating changes in international relative prices. The assumption is that the inertia of nominal wage and price paths allows nominal appreciations and depreciations to be real, while the same inertia slows or frustrates the same price adjustments in the fixed-parity regime. Even if discrete changes in parities can be made, they are crisis decisions inviting speculation before and after; they are usually too long delayed; they often undershoot and sometimes overshoot.

Tradeoffs there always are. Flexible rates can emit false as well as true signals. Speculative movements can change relative prices between countries when no change is basically called for, and the volatility of rates can leave traders confused about the relative prices which should enter their calculations and decisions on production, sales, and purchases. Unfortunately "variable peg" regimes, temporarily fixed rates, do not really eliminate these problems. A truly common international currency would do so, but we are far from the commonalities of institutions, laws, taxation, and politics that would make a universal money possible.

2 Obstacles to Price Adjustment Mechanisms

Under floating rates since 1973 nominal exchange rates have moved a great deal, and for the most part real exchange rates have moved with them. Nonetheless I shall argue that the major governments, the economic summit powers, are reluctant to let price adjustment mechanisms work, at any rate to work well enough to handle the tasks that now confront them. In the United States, West Germany (which calls the macroeconomic tune for the European Community and Monetary System), the United Kingdom, and Japan, governments and central banks are quite determined to stick to their nationally chosen paths of domestic price indexes.

The U.K. has for several years geared its monetary policy to hold an exchange rate that puts moderate disinflationary pressure on its prices. Both the big surplus countries, Germany and Japan, are unwilling to deviate from macroeconomic policies that have rewarded them with actual deflation. The U.S. authorities are afraid of a further depreciation of the dollar because dollar prices of imports and other internationally traded goods would rise.

These attitudes are by no means altogether new. They stood in the way of corrective devaluations and revaluations in the Bretton Woods era. For example, in the early 1960s the U.S. was running official settlements deficits, though its current account was in surplus. The U.S. inflation rate was only 2 percent per year, and the economy was not fully employed. Germany and other surplus countries were unwilling either to let their accumulations of reserves show up in higher prices or to revalue their currencies upward. Either course could have given the U.S. a larger trade surplus to match its capital outflows and unilateral transfers. The impasse was not resolved until a less auspicious time, when the Nixon Administration ran out of patience and killed the Bretton Woods system.

An important obstacle to international price adjustment is epidemic confusion between price levels and inflation rates. Once-for-all rises in price indexes do not necessarily spell continuing inflation or acceleration of prices. These one-shot increases often come from shocks that lift particular prices, supply shocks that alter relative prices. The oil price hikes of the 1970s, of unhappy memory, are major examples. Likewise, the recent declines when cartel discipline weakened made pleasant headlines. In both cases the events were not the kind that can regularly recur year after year. The transitional rates of inflation, or of disinflation in 1986, were bound to be temporary. Nonetheless the OPEC shocks of the 1970s were opposed by monetary restriction as if they were demand-pull inflations.

In 1981–85 the U.S. enjoyed the price-lowering effects of dollar appreciation. Those effects have to be reversed to correct the U.S. trade deficit, but the domestic price index increases due to exchange depreciation scare the Federal Reserve—even though they are once-for-all, even though the upward price adjustments are in effect repayment of downward adjustments borrowed from the rest of the world in the earlier 1980s. The likely policy consequence appears to be that the dollar is to be defended by higher interest rates, holding back an already sluggish economy. One objective is to offset the increases of import prices with extra domestic disinflation. A weightier objective is to guard against the risk that exchange depreciation and higher import prices trigger a price-wage-price spiral.

The examples of the 1970s show that this is not an unreasonable concern. However, running an economy on the assumption that price indexes can never be allowed to rise, regardless of the amount of slack in the economy, regardless of how low the underlying domestic wage and price inflation rates are, is a recipe for stagnation. Moreover, central bank sensitivities to these price shocks are asymmetric. Japan and Europe today, like the U.S. in 1981–85, accept external contributions to disinflation or deflation without engineering compensating expansionary measures. The ratchet effect is to hold down both world inflation and world expansion.

Policy stances are anticipated in the behavior of private agents. That is a lesson of experience as well as of modern economic theory. Financial markets react negatively when monthly inflation news is bad because they have learned that central banks tighten on such news. Indeed equity markets have become so obsessed by the prospect that central bank concern to prevent or arrest inflation will raise interest rates that they respond negatively to good news about real economic growth and profits, and positively to news of sluggishness and possible recession.

A principal argument for floating rates before 1971 was, as I observed above, that movements of nominal exchange rates would be, compared to movements of domestic nominal wages and prices, a quicker and less painful way of accomplishing necessary changes in international relative prices. This argument assumes, of course, that inertia in nominal wages and prices prevents or delays those adjustments at fixed exchange rates. The same inertia is expected to translate nominal exchange rate movements into effective adjustments in real exchange rates. Clearly this mechanism is disabled to the extent there are quick feedbacks from import prices (in domestic currency) into economy-wide wages and prices. Policies to avoid such feedbacks would improve the adjustment mechanism, just as policies to increase the sensitivity of local prices to market supply/demand conditions would improve the mechanism under fixed rates. Policies to stabilize wage and price paths, to avoid feedbacks from international prices, may be essential to successful devaluations or depreciations. Indexing should be minimized, and at the least exclude compensation for terms-of-trade effects. The case for incomes policies, for example, guideposts with sticks or carrots to induce compliance, is strengthened under floating rates.

3 Adjustments in Effective Demand and Absorption

International relative prices are one avenue of adjustment. Variations of output, real income, and employment are another. In the short run these arise from fluctuations in effective demand, given some inertia or stickiness in nominal wages and prices. A shock that unbalances trade lowers demand in the deficit country, and the consequent decline in income and output lowers imports. Likewise the positive impulse to demand in the surplus countries raises their imports. Elementary multiplier theory tells us that these adjustments are far from complete, even if monetary policymakers accommodate them by holding interest rates constant. That is, the multiplier is much lower than the reciprocal of the marginal propensity to import. Imports are only one of the leakages from spending flows; saving and taxes are also important.

What would it take to eliminate a U.S. trade deficit of $150 billion a year, 3 1/2 percent of GNP? Assuming a marginal propensity to import of 0.25, twice the average propensity, it would take a GNP contraction of $600 billion, 14 percent, and raise unemployment well into double digit rates. To add enough imports to erase its trade surplus, 3 percent of GNP and 20 percent of imports, Japan might need a 20 percent rise of GNP.

In medium and longer runs further equilibrating mechanisms may come into play. Current account imbalances transfer wealth from deficit to surplus countries; these transfers have both wealth and portfolio effects, some on trade and some on capital movements. Consumption stimulated by the accumulation of wealth leads the surplus country to import more. On the capital account side, the country's appetite for foreign assets diminishes, and the resulting appreciation induces some correction in the trade deficit. The reverse processes in the deficit country strengthen the adjustment.

However, current account imbalances could reflect long-lasting differences among economies in saving propensities, investment opportunities, and growth rates. In this case, there is no guarantee that they will go away, and possibly no economic reason they should. Consider the following scenario: Thrifty country J saves more than it needs for investment, that is, more than is needed to expand its capital stock, given the growth of labor force and the rate of technological progress. Profligate country U, however, needs J's excess saving.

To describe their difference another way, the desired wealth/income ratio in J exceeds its desired capital/output ratio, and the difference is its wealth-owners' demand for stocks of external assets. Both domestic and foreign components of wealth will grow at J's natural rate. On the other hand, in U the desired capital/output ratio exceeds the wealth/income ratio, the excess being capital owned abroad or in effect mortgaged to foreign creditors. If capital movements are not restricted, the returns to capital in the two countries must be equal (after allowing for trend in real exchange rate) or anyway stand in such relation that they meet portfolio preferences of savers and borrowers in the two countries. This relationship determines the capital stock in the two countries. The exchange rate path is determined such that a current account imbalance provides the flows that meet the saving and portfolio demands on both sides. The currency of the more rapidly growing country will be appreciating. It is conceivable that a high-saving fast-growing country eventually owns the whole capital stocks of less thrifty and more sluggish societies, but presumably the behaviors that destine this result would eventually be altered.

Rather than continue on this abstract and speculative line, which I don't really think represents the Japan/United States situation today, I turn to the concrete problems of adjustment we face right now.

4 The Adjustment Processes that Match Flows of Capital and Trade

The gross maladjustments of the 1980s have placed unparalleled burdens on the corrective mechanisms I have been discussing. The main sources of these burdens are first, the internationalization of wealth portfolios and asset markets, and second, the extreme, and extremely different, mixes of monetary and fiscal policies of the major countries. In the 1970s the sources of the international macroeconomic problems that beset those countries were mainly external and exogenous to them, shocks of unprecedented magnitude in peacetime. In the 1980s, the external environment has been benign; national policies and the failures of coordination are much more to blame for the generally poor economic performance of this decade.

Asset markets began to be internationalized as exchange controls and capital controls were gradually abandoned after World War II. The pace accelerated tremendously in the last decade. Communications and computer technologies facilitated international transactions and vastly lowered their costs. Multinational banks and financial enterprises multiplied. New international asset markets were born, new instruments and contracts were created, old and new national markets were linked. Deregulation of financial businesses in all countries allowed and encouraged, among other things, a burst of foreign activities. Off-shore money and credit markets in major currencies flourished. The floating exchange rate regime itself generated clients for managing positions in several currencies and countries, including speculators and arbitrageurs in cross-currency financial transactions. Finance in general became a go-go field, enlisting both the best and brightest of young technicians fresh from business schools and latter-day entrepreneurs and big-time operators; it even became an academic growth enterprise. International finance shared in the phenomenal expansion of the industry and the profession. The sun never sets on currency markets, in which the volume of transactions in New York alone is estimated to exceed $100 billion every business day. Japanese liberalizations of portfolio investment regulations were fateful.

As we all know, a country's capital outflow (inflow) must *ex post* equal its current account surplus (deficit). Market exchange rates, interest rates, and asset values move hour by hour and day by day to convert any *ex ante* deviations from this equality to their *ex post* identity. (Official capital movements, foreign exchange purchases or sales by central banks, may on occasion be factors in this equalization. They have been substantial in recent months, evidently of the same rough magnitude as the U.S. current account deficit.) Over longer short runs other macroeconomic variables, the ones discussed above, also play important roles.

Exchange rates, interest rates, and asset values can be moved by shocks to international demands for assets in various countries and currencies, as well as by shocks to trade and other current account items. This is the main point in discussing the current situation. Given the liquidity of financial assets in today's worldwide markets, given the intrinsic volatility of the expectations on which asset demands depend, capital account shocks can occur with much greater suddenness than changes in the determinants of trade in goods and services.

A nation's capital inflow or outflow depends positively on the expected returns on its assets relative to those in other currencies and on the expected appreciation of its exchange rate. (I remind you in passing that for an investor concerned ultimately with real returns in his or her own currency, it is the *nominal* interest differential plus the expected appreciation of the *nominal* value of the currency that matters. This reduces to concern for real returns and currency appreciation only if investors' expectations embody purchasing power parity.) The *level* of the exchange rate is much less relevant. We read in the business pages that foreign investors are buying American assets because they are bargains at the present low exchange value of the dollar. They are bargains only if the investors expect the dollar to rise. The level of the exchange rate matters only so far as its variation, like that of any asset price, alters the proportions of the portfolios of risk-averse diversifiers and induces them to shift from relatively appreciated assets.

In formulating exchange rate expectations, an investor with a long horizon will consider how the current rate differs from an equilibrium rate or path of rates. In that consideration, news about the present trade and current account imbalances is quite relevant. Anyone who thinks present U.S. current account deficits are unsustainable—presumably anyone who thinks—will have lowered his or her estimate of the future value of the dollar by observing the glacial pace of improvement of the U.S. trade position in response to the drastic dollar depreciation since mid-1985.

The list of determinants of capital account flows and stocks is different from the list of arguments a model-builder would put in functions explaining exports and imports of goods and services. For the current account, the level of the real exchange rate, in prices or labor costs, would appear, along with the national incomes of trading partners; stocks and returns on internationally held assets would determine the net flows of incomes on those assets.

Supply and demand are, Alfred Marshall taught us, some of us, blades of the same pair of scissors. Yet sometimes one blade may be the cutting edge, sometimes the other. That is the case in currency markets.

It is not too far-fetched to see the inflow of capital into dollar assets in 1981–85 as the driving force in the appreciation of the dollar. The inflow was attracted by relatively advantageous American interest rates, perhaps also by internationally contagious euphoria about the Reagan era. The inflow would have been reinforced, at least in the earlier years of the period, by the appreciation of the dollar itself. Eventually doubts of its continuation, even of its permanence, fed by ministers and central bankers at the Plaza hotel, overtook the markets.

Meanwhile the 1981–85 appreciation, together with the strong recovery of the U.S. economy relative to the stagnation in the rest of the world, brought a trade imbalance and a U.S. current account deficit matching the capital inflow. Qualitatively the events validated economists' textbooks; quantitatively, they exceeded everybody's prior imagination.

This story is consistent with the common accusation that U.S. trade and current account deficits mirrored its outsized federal budget deficit. However, the reconciliation is more complex than the accusing pundits generally recognize. True, the budget deficit made U.S. interest rates high. But this effect occurred indirectly, through Federal Reserve monetary policy. The Fed did not raise interest rates because the Open Market Committee members were appalled by the budget numbers they read. The chain of events, I think, was more like this: Defense spending and tax cuts stimulated demand and recovery. In order to hold the expansion to a path the Fed regarded as sound and inflation-safe, the Committee kept real interest rates from falling (from their 1980–81 highs) as low as they would have been in a normal pre-Reagan recovery period. Moreover, bond markets came to expect that the deficits were chronic, not just cyclical, and would eventually either lead to inflation or collide with prosperity private demands for capital. As a result long-term bonds yielded premiums above short rates that made them especially attractive to foreign financial institutions and portfolio managers.

When pundits say that budget correction would have avoided or shut off the capital inflow and the trade deficit, they are right if they add that the Federal Reserve would have had to lower interest rates to keep the economy on the same path of GNP and employment.

Today we face quite a different adjustment problem. The choices available in 1981–83 are not on the menu in 1987–88. The trade deficit is stubborn. Perhaps the J-curve lags are longer than we thought. Most of the J-curve scenario may still be ahead of us. Exporters to the American market have been willing to cut margins in their own currencies rather than lose market shares. In "customer markets," buyers are slow to shift to lower-cost suppliers. Perhaps the long period of dollar overvaluation has crippled U.S. export and import-competing industries. Some of the effects on competitiveness are irreversible, or anyway will take a long time to overcome. (Young economists are now enchanted by the fashionable newly discovered word "hysteresis.") Evidently some underlying adverse trends in American competitiveness have proceeded apace, unrelated to but obscured by the over-valuation. Finally, the accumulation of external debt itself is reducing U.S. net investment income from the rest of the world, which will soon become negative.[1]

Investors and portfolio managers throughout the world have, in any case, plenty of reasons to worry about the real exchange rate necessary eventually to cut the U.S. current account deficit to sustainable size. Given a large deficit that will be with us willy-nilly for some years to come, by what adjustment will the U.S. continue to attract the capital inflows to finance it? There are several possibilities.

(1) One is that U.S. borrows from foreign governments. After all, they like their trade surpluses and do not want to see the dollar fall in a manner that will eventually threaten their exports. They seem never to have learned how to obtain prosperity and growth driven otherwise than by export demands. Nevertheless, buying up dollars is not a way out that will appeal to the governments of surplus countries indefinitely. Like the creditors of Brazil and Mexico today, they will worry about the prospects of repayment. Nor will official borrowing on a grand scale appeal to the

U.S. government. Most important, this course will sooner or later turn off the private participants in the exchange markets. Their resources vastly exceed those of the governments. Once they are turned off, the dollar will fall.

(2) Second, the U.S. could "defend the dollar" by raising its interest rates to entice increasingly skeptical foreign lenders. The Federal Reserve has already moved cautiously in this direction, and is poised to do more. The consequence could be U.S. recession, which while curtailing American imports would have disastrous consequences throughout the world. Third World debtors would face both higher interest charges and diminished export markets.

(3) Third, the dollar could fall until it was low enough to convince investors that its subsequent rise would reward them for holding it. Although Paul Volcker and others are frightened of a "free fall," or "hard landing," overshooting of this kind is precisely the fantasy of rational-expectations economic theorists. Get the bad news over all at once. Markets do not seem to work that way. More likely, the fall occurs over an extended interval, during which expectations and fears of its continuation are destabilizing. No one has a rational basis for calculating the dollar's equilibrium value or the degree of overshooting that determines its floor. Nevertheless, a case can be made that, instead of trying to talk the market into supporting the dollar at its present rate, the officials of the several countries should welcome a rapid downward jump and intervene with rhetoric and money at a rate from which a rise in the dollar is credible.

Some combination of (2) and (3) seems the most probable chain of events.

The U.S. Government, as well as many unofficial commentators, have been urging Japan and Germany, the key European economy, to adopt policies to stimulate domestic demand. Given the slack in their economies and their low, even negative, inflation rates, expansionary policies are obviously desirable. They would benefit those societies themselves and the world as a whole. I have argued that the resulting increase in U.S. exports would be insufficient itself to correct the U.S. trade deficit. Improvement in U.S. competitiveness is essential and will probably entail further dollar depreciation, as well as considerable time.

Meanwhile, expansionary policies in Japan and Europe may or may not facilitate financing of the continuing U.S. current account deficit. Fiscal stimulus, such as Japan has recently announced, would raise interest rates and diminish demands for dollar assets. Monetary expansion would help to "defend the dollar," while retarding the dollar depreciation that may eventually be necessary to correct the trade imbalance. Nevertheless, from a global viewpoint, it is desirable not to raise interest rates in major economies. An attractive compromise would be monetary accommodation of expansions in Japan and Europe, whether fiscally driven or autonomous, holding interest rates outside the U.S. at current levels.

What about that U.S. budget deficit? Isn't it the culprit? Wouldn't its removal solve the problem? As long as the U.S. current account deficit is as stubborn as it now seems, correction of the budget would not avoid the country's need for foreign credit. It would, however, remove a major internal use of the borrowed funds. Here are some round numbers: At the moment U.S. nonfederal saving is $250 billion a year and net national borrowing (current account deficit) is $150 billion. Together they are financing a federal deficit of $180 billion and net private domestic investment of $220 billion. Without a federal deficit but with the same current account deficit and foreign borrowing, the U.S. would have to raise domestic investment and/or reduce internal saving by a total of $180 billion. How? Either by a drastic low-interest monetary policy fostering a mind-boggling investment boom, or by a recession deep enough to cut saving equally severely. (That is an over-statement, because the recession would also cut imports somewhat at the same time. Also, whatever the initial revenue and expenditure measures designed to correct the budget, some of the correction would be nullified by endogenous cyclical effects.) Anyway, the investment boom alternative seems quite unlikely, perhaps impossible. The recession alternative would be disastrous at home and abroad.

The moral is this: Substantial reduction of the federal deficit is an essential part of an ultimate solution, just as it was a major initial source of the problem. But now that the external current account deficit and the equivalent borrowing are more or less frozen into place for some years, it is not prudent to melt the budget deficit much faster than the external deficit can melt. Meanwhile it is, however, prudent to legislate a schedule of measures to be phased in gradually—in my view mainly revenue increases—that will in the end bring the budget deficit down, not to zero but to, say, 1 or 1 1/2 percent of GNP. This legislation would improve the market's view of the future of the dollar and help to attract the financing needed while the external deficit is being corrected.

Note

1. I am indebted to Paul Krugman and Richard Baldwin, "The Persistence of the U.S. Trade Deficit," forthcoming in *Brookings Papers on Economic Activity*, I, 1987.

CHAPTER 24

AGENDA FOR INTERNATIONAL COORDINATION OF MACROECONOMIC POLICIES

My friendship with Henry Wallich began almost fifty years ago when we were fellow graduate students at Harvard. It became much closer during the twenty-three years we were colleagues at Yale. We have often disagreed, but I have always enjoyed our arguments, learned from him, and respected him as an economist, teacher, and human being. Both in academia and in Washington, whether in learned journals or in popular media, he has always dedicated his mind and pen to our science's contributions to policy and to the general welfare. Henry has consistently asked the right questions and, undistracted by fashions and technicalities, has focused rare insight and wisdom on central issues, none more than monetary stability, national and international. Offering here some thoughts of mine on this subject, I am glad to see Henry's paper on international macroeconomic cooperation (Wallich, 1984).

* * *

Coordinate policies! So economists urge governments. Financiers, journalists, pundits, politicians take up the cry. Central bankers and finance ministers agree, as do presidents and prime ministers. They meet, they talk, they announce progress. It turns out to amount to very little. The need for coordination seems obvious from the imbalances of trade and gyrations of exchange rates in the 1980s. When no other appealing solutions are evident, "coordination" seems the natural panacea. But what is its specific content?

Reprinted by permission from *International Monetary Cooperation: Essays in Honor of Henry C. Wallich*, eds. P. Kenen and E. Truman, Princeton, NJ: Princeton University Press, 1987, pp. 61–69.

Coordination under Bretton Woods

Coordination is not a new subject. Long before Bretton Woods gave way to floating exchange rates, coordination was discussed and sought, but never successfully achieved. The major mechanism of coordination was thought to be international respect for certain "rules of the game." The rules concerned principally the obligations of surplus and deficit countries to take corrective measures. Some rules were actually prescribed in the Bretton Woods treaty, though with considerable ambiguity. Others were unwritten traditions that central bankers inherited from gold-standard days.

In those days, "surplus" and "deficit" usually referred to official reserve settlements. Under the fixed-parity regime, adjustment obligations referred to monetary policies; to official borrowing and lending, whether bilateral or through the International Monetary Fund (IMF); and to parity adjustments. In the 1960s, especially in policy discussions among the Group of Ten and in the Organization for Economic Cooperation and Development (OECD), fiscal measures were also considered instruments of international adjustment.

Surplus countries inevitably felt less compulsion to adjust than their opposite numbers, whose deficits could exhaust their reserves and international credit lines. For a deficit country, the first and principal defense of its parity was to take contractionary macroeconomic measures, especially to tighten domestic credit. Financial help from other countries and from the IMF was generally conditional on austere counterinflationary programs. Deficit countries were frequently pushed to the next line of defense, devaluation.

The United States occupied a special central position in the Bretton Woods system. Deficits did not impose reserve discipline on the United States until the 1960s. Other countries held U.S. dollar obligations as reserves. Thus financed, U.S. deficits did not lower U.S. gold reserves or alarm U.S. policymakers until the rest of the world began to distrust the U.S. Treasury's ability and willingness to maintain dollar/gold convertibility. At the same time, the reserve-currency role of the dollar foreclosed U.S. initiatives to devalue against other currencies. Eventually, the Nixon administration forced other countries to appreciate their currencies by telling them that their alternative was to buy dollars that might never be convertible into gold.

Surplus countries faced little pressure to adjust under Bretton Woods. They could enjoy their abundant and growing reserve positions, the export prosperity resulting from undervalued exchange rates, and the luxury of negotiating conditional credits to deficit countries from positions of superior strength and virtue. Although the Bretton Woods agreement gave lip service to symmetrical moral responsibilities, the IMF possessed almost no power over surplus members. That the United States had rejected the Keynes Plan, which would have been a better deal for deficit countries, became ironical when the United States itself turned into a deficit country with an overvalued currency.

Coordination under Floating Rates

Proponents of floating rates sometimes contended that free currency markets would achieve all the coordination needed, that consciously concerted policies and agreed "rules of the game" would be superfluous. Each country could pursue autonomously its national macroeconomic objectives. Official intervention in currency markets would be unnecessary and, indeed, harmful. Exchange-rate movements, replacing reserve settlements, would balance international payments. This did not mean, of course, that countries would be freed from the discipline of international markets. Discipline would be administered via terms of trade and of credit.

Experience has not borne out these optimistic claims but has instead validated the skepticism of Henry Wallich, who at the time expressed a preference for fixed rates (Wallich, 1969). Countries have not been happy with volatile market-determined exchange rates or with the accompanying imbalances of trade, current transactions, and capital movements. Those discontents inspire the current insistent cries for policy coordination.

Coordination has occurred when major central banks and governments all agreed on national and international policy priorities, most notably during the second oil shock in 1979–80. They unanimously and synchronously undertook severely restrictive monetary policies designed to wring the inflation of the 1970s from the economies of Western Europe, North America, and Japan. But policies have not been coordinated since late 1982; diagnoses and priorities have diverged once again. The United

States has criticized the caution of demand management in Europe and Japan. The whole world has condemned U.S. fiscal policy.

Nevertheless, even in the 1980s coordination of a kind has occurred on occasion, in the form of agreement on the desirable path or range of the dollar's value in terms of other major currencies. In September 1985, the Group of Five finance ministers meeting at the Plaza Hotel agreed that the dollar should fall from its heights and blessed the decline that was already under way. In 1987, major finance ministers and central bankers have agreed, beginning with the Louvre meeting in February, that the dollar has fallen far enough. They have made it clear by word and deed that they would back up this common view by official interventions in currency markets.

However, agreements on paths and ranges for exchange rates have not been accompanied by understandings on how the monetary and fiscal policies of the several countries would achieve them. Indeed, the economic summit in Venice in June 1987 failed even more obviously than its predecessors to reach any semblance of policy coordination. The cart has been put before the horse. Concerted *ad hoc* attempts to steer the exchange markets without agreement on the policies that affect and concern those markets are unlikely to succeed for long or to yield acceptable outcomes in more significant macroeconomic variables.

Some economists dissent from the general view that the unprecedented capital-account and current-account imbalances of the 1980s are pathological. Instead, they see the Invisible Hand at work worldwide—for example, the savings of thrifty Japanese are channeled to profligate U.S. consumers and taxpayers. Americans' optimal intertemporal plans, they say, appear to call for spending sprees in this decade. If both sides are optimizing, their plans presumably contemplate bulges of American saving and Japanese consumption in some future decade or century. Unfortunately, in the absence of long futures contracts in commodities, securities, and currencies, those bulges cannot be discerned. Meanwhile, less comforting hypotheses cannot be dismissed: that we in the United States are mistakenly assuming debt burdens we are unprepared to bear, and that Japanese savers are shortsightedly foregoing consumption and investment opportunities at home or elsewhere in the world.

Exchange rates today depend on expectations of exchange rates tomorrow and tomorrow's tomorrow. Rational expectations of real exchange rates depend on estimates of the real international terms of trade consistent with future current accounts, which in turn depend on the saving propensities and investment opportunities of the several nations. There is no presumption that current accounts should be zero along an equilibrium path. Nonzero current accounts must be financed by equivalent capital movements, in part induced by an appropriate structure of interest rates. Expectations of real exchange rates have to be translated into nominal rates by estimates of future price paths in the various countries. Estimates of national inflation rates, as well as of interest rates, require forecasts of monetary and fiscal policies.

The relationships just sketched are not, of course, sequential or recursive. They make up a complex system of dynamic interdependence that econometricians have not been able to estimate. I doubt that traders in the markets can do so either. I doubt they even try. The same complexities baffle policymakers, whether coordinated or not. While these complexities make coordination difficult, they also offer constructive opportunities to policy-makers to shape the expectations that guide the markets, even to make them more rational.

Floating rates have diminished the asymmetries of adjustment pressures on deficit and surplus countries. The logical counterpart of reserve accumulation under fixed rates is exchange appreciation under floating rates. But this is a handicap to export industries, by no means as welcome as building up reserves with an undervalued currency. In the past, moreover, countries often liked their currencies to be cheap, hoping to gain jobs at the expense of their foreign competitors—"beggar-thy-neighbor" macroeconomic policy. Now, however, there are symmetrical worries about depreciation and inflation because of the impact of exchange rates on the local-currency cost of imports and other goods whose prices are set in foreign currency. Thy neighbor may be beggared on prices instead of jobs. The 1981–85 appreciation of the dollar improved U.S. inflation statistics while generating a large trade deficit.

The primacy of price or inflation stability among macroeconomic objectives, a legacy of the 1970s, appears to be an obstacle to corrective adjustments today. Countries are reluctant to accept the local price increases incident to depreciation of their currencies. Despite continuing U.S. trade deficits, the Federal Reserve in 1987 has sought to prevent further decline of the dollar, largely for fear of the consequences for price indexes. In addition to talk, the Fed's moves have included increases in interest rates and sales of foreign currencies. During the preceding dollar appreciation, Japan and Europe continued along disinflationary paths, offsetting demand stimuli from exchange rates and U.S. recovery by domestic restraint of demand. Thus they succeeded in maintaining extraordinary slack in their labor and product markets.

The time-honored story of adjustments to payments imbalances assigns a decisive role to changes in relative prices between national economies. Under a gold standard or other fixed-parity regime, these changes occur internally consequent to movements of reserves—whether via automatic market forces or via acquiescent or active policy. With parity change or floating rates, relative prices change as exchange rates are translated into local prices. If these price adjustments are not allowed to occur, corrections of trade imbalances are delayed or frustrated.

Capital Mobility and International Interest Rates

The era of floating rates has coincidentally been the era of internationalization of money and capital markets. Advances in telecommunications and computers have made financial transactions throughout the world inexpensive and instantaneous. Deregulation has made most of them legal. New markets have opened, and the types of contracts traded have multiplied. Thousands of bright traders attend video screens and telephones watching for opportunities for speculation or arbitrage. The gross volume of transactions boggles the mind. With private funds as mobile as they have now become—and the end is not in sight—a return to fixed parities among currencies of major national or continental economies is probably not feasible: the political and institutional differences among those economies, the immobilities that still impede movements of goods and services, are too great.

In the absence of capital controls, money-market interest rates in different currencies, adjusted for exchange-rate expectations, cannot sharply diverge from equality. The same applies to longer-term nominal interest rates, though with less force because of the shortness of traded contracts in exchange-rate futures. Sometimes, as in Wallich (1984), interest-rate parity is alleged to apply to *real* rates. This assumes that exchange rates move with differences in inflation rates, an assumption so deviant from experience that no economist or trader could rationally rely upon it.

Capital mobility makes market interest rates converge, but to what? In the 1950s and 1960s, the answer could have been: to dollar interest rates under the control of the Federal Reserve. Not in the 1980s. The markets and monetary policies of the United States still weigh heavily in determining world interest rates, but so do the markets and central banks of other major countries. Only by accident will uncoordinated monetary policies produce a desirable average of world interest rates or a constellation of rates consistent with a viable structure of international capital and current accounts.

The world average of short interest rates is an obvious candidate for coordinated decision—subject, of course, to at least annual periodic review. Not every central bank would be expected to aim at the same interest rate. Deviations from the agreed average would reflect divergent expectations of, and targets for, inflation. They would also be calculated to induce appropriate exchange-rate paths and capital movements, that is, those capital movements consistent with feasible and mutually desired current accounts. First approximations would assume that each country is growing normally within its target ranges for unemployment and inflation.

Coordination of Demand-Management Policies

A quarter-century ago, the main substance of coordination appeared to be the use of monetary and fiscal policies to expand or contract aggregate demand in the several countries. Obviously, a surplus country with high unemployment and low inflation should pursue expansionary policies, while a deficit country with overfull employment and high or rising inflation should do the opposite. Appropriate policy was less clear for a surplus country in an inflationary boom or a deficit country in a noninflationary slump (like the United States in the early 1960s). Such imbalances were deemed "structural," requiring nonmacro policies lubricated by finance from surplus to deficit countries.

I published a "rules of the game" article for that era and that international monetary regime (Tobin, 1966), a precursor of this note. Even in those times, when full employment was a respected concept and an acknowledged responsibility of national governments, I doubted that countries could agree on each other's domestic unemployment, inflation, and growth targets. I suggested that each country, after discussions in the group, choose for itself and announce, at least to the group, the unemployment and price numbers that would determine its macroeconomic policy responsibilities—expansionary, neutral, or contractionary. I repeat that suggestion now. Naturally, these designations would not be forever; they would be for the next three years, say, and would be reviewed annually at group meetings. While they were in force, all members informed of current developments would know what policy responses to expect, and each member would be accountable to the others if these did not occur or were inadequate.

For reasons given above, price targets should be for indexes of domestic value added, excluding impacts of import prices. A country should not contract demand just because depreciation of its currency has raised the local prices of oil products, nor should it be expected to expand demand if appreciation has lowered them. If and when those price changes feed into domestic factor costs, they will become relevant to macroeconomic policy. Of course, every country should try, via domestic labor-market policies and other *micro*economic measures, to prevent such secondary effects. This rule of policy coordination would be an incentive to do so.

I will not conceal that I personally find outrageous the targets of demand management implicit in the persistent high unemployment rates and low rates of real growth accompanying low and declining inflation rates in Germany, Britain, and Japan. But Secretary Baker and Chairman Volcker could not persuade the leaders of their governments otherwise, and certainly I cannot. So let *them* bear the brunt of stating their targets explicitly to the world community and the obligation of sticking with them.

These demand-management obligations will contribute to corrections that involve reducing the trade and current-account surpluses of slack economies and the deficits of other economies, especially those with (self-defined) excess demand. Too much should not be expected. Marginal propensities to import are not big enough to remedy current trade imbalances without much larger relative changes in national aggregate demands than are desirable by anyone's criteria. Corrections of trade imbalances generally require real-exchange-rate movements as well.

How can these rules for demand management be reconciled with the coordination of interest rates and monetary policies proposed above? The mixes of fiscal and monetary policy in the various members of the group must come into play. A basic principle would be not to use monetary policy to beggar from neighbors either employment or price relief. Suppose, for example, that high unemployment hits an economy which, according to the first approximations of coordinated interest rates and capital movements, is assigned a relatively high interest rate. That country would be allowed to lower its interest rate below the assigned target by an amount commensurate to its shortfall in economic activity, but it would have to rely mainly on fiscal policy for active demand stimulus. A slack economy that normally has saving to export could obtain stimulus both from a low-interest-rate monetary policy and from fiscal policy. A fully employed economy threatened with inflation and short of domestic saving should correct its position by fiscal restraint rather than by high interest rates.

Difficulties Acknowledged and Unpleasant Alternatives Noted

Even if agreement in principle could be reached on meaningful coordination along these lines, I recognize that its implementation would be very difficult, both econometrically and politically. The attempt might be confined to the Group of Five; it certainly should involve no more than the Summit Seven. The OECD could be used as the technical secretariat, receiving information from the members of the group and preparing iterative medium- and short-term projections for discussion, negotiation, and decision.

The major political problem might be the inflexibility of fiscal policies dedicated to domestic interests and ideologies. Some national fiscal idiosyncracies would just have to be built into the estimates of national saving propensities assumed in projections and agreements. What is required is enough flexibility in short-run deviations from permanent fiscal policies so that monetary policies are not burdened with full responsibility for both domestic stabilization and international payments equilibrium.

I believe that coordination of macroeconomic policies would be somewhat easier if *international* measures were taken to diminish speculative and interest-sensitive short-term capital movements. To this end, I have proposed an internationally uniform tax on spot transactions across currencies (Tobin, 1978).

Coordination of macroeconomic policies is certainly not easy; maybe it is impossible. But in its absence, I suspect nationalistic solutions will be sought—trade barriers, capital controls, and dual-exchange-rate systems. Wars among nations with these weapons are likely to be mutually destructive. Eventually, they, too, would evoke agitation for international coordination.

References

Tobin, James, "Adjustment Responsibilities of Surplus and Deficit Countries," in William Fellner *et al.*, *Maintaining and Restoring Balance in International Payments*, Princeton, Princeton University Press, 1966, pp. 201–211.

———, "A Proposal for International Monetary Reform," *Eastern Economic Journal*, 4 (July/October 1978), pp. 153–159.

Wallich, Henry C., Remarks in "Round Table on Exchange Rate Policy," *American Economic Review*, 59 (May 1969), pp. 360–364.

———, "Institutional Cooperation in the World Economy," in Jacob A. Frenkel and Michael L. Mussa, eds., *The World Economic System: Performance and Prospects*, Chicago, University of Chicago Press, 1984, pp. 85–99.

CHAPTER 25

INTERNATIONAL CURRENCY REGIMES, CAPITAL MOBILITY AND
MACROECONOMIC POLICY

1 International Monetary Regimes

The structure of the international monetary system is once again a topic of great interest and controversy—among economists, business managers, financiers, and government leaders. Many members of all these groups are acutely dissatisfied with the floating-exchange-rate regime that succeeded the Bretton Woods system two decades ago. Within the European Community (EC) the Exchange Rate Mechanism (ERM) has re-established a regime of "adjustable pegs." After 1992 financial markets and institutions will cover the entire Community. The drastic further step of replacing national currencies with a single European currency is under way. These measures would still leave exchange rates among Japan, America, and the EC free to float in currency markets.

They would leave many other countries with choices among floating and fixing parities to one of the major currencies or to a basket of them. These are especially difficult choices for Eastern European countries and for the republics of the former Soviet Union. They also face the question how rapidly to relax restrictions on external financial transactions.

I shall distinguish two dimensions of the international monetary system. The first is the spectrum of exchange rate regimes, from single currencies to adjustable parities to freely floating market-determined rates. The second dimension is the degree of capital mobility across regions and political jurisdictions, from completely free movement of funds at one extreme to strict exchange controls at the other.

I begin by considering one extreme, permanent commitment to a single common currency by the people of one or several political jurisdictions.

Reprinted by permission from *Greek Economic Review* 15(1) (Autumn 1993): 1–4.

That has been true in the United States of America for two hundred years; the commitment was solidified when the Civil War was settled in 1865. It is inconceivable that the dollar will not always be the same in California as it is in New York State. The 1787 Constitution assigned exclusively to the federal government the right "to coin money and regulate the value thereof." The same Constitution also guarantees freedom to move funds and goods without hindrance between States and regions.

A single central monetary authority is a necessary implication of the combination of a single currency, capital mobility, and free trade. When the U.S. Federal Reserve System was set up in 1913, the authors of the legislation provided for twelve District Banks. They anticipated that the Banks could differ in monetary and credit policies and thus accommodate the special economic circumstances of their Districts. We still have twelve districts and twelve banks. But the idea that they could have separate interest rates, for example different in the Dallas District from what it is in the Boston District, disappeared long ago. A central national monetary policy is made in Washington, although the District Bank presidents participate in the Federal Open Market Committee along with the Board of Governors of the System. It is impossible to have more than one monetary and credit policy along with completely integrated financial markets.

This system, a single currency together with perfect capital mobility, has great advantages: gains from trade, economies of scale and scope, diversifications of risk. The disadvantages are the vulnerabilities of regions and sectors of the economy to shocks that reduce their competitiveness. When currency revaluations, capital controls, and trade restrictions are ruled out, other remedies have to be in place, both to alleviate the pains of transitions and to facilitate viable adjustments.

One remedy is, of course, just the natural response of competitive markets. Labor, capital, and commodities move across regions and sectors, encouraged by changes in job and profit opportunities and in relative prices and wages. In the United States we always have depressed areas, but they are not always the same. Mobility of labor and capital prevents areas from being permanently depressed. In addition, the federal government generally assists depressed regions and sectors, to ease the distress of transitions due to the natural shocks of economic development. Responses of both kinds are, I think, essential to make a single currency system work.

2 Capital Mobility, Speculation, and Macroeconomic Autonomy

Floating rates are the other extreme in this spectrum of currency regimes, that is, "clean" floating in which diverse currencies are allowed to assume market values without interventions by the various governments or central banks. That exchange rate system can be combined either with restraints on capital mobility and foreign exchange transactions or with free movement of capital. For any one member of the system, the gain from exchange controls or restrictions on capital movements is greater autonomy in the making of macroeconomic policy, monetary policy in particular. The disadvantages is the loss of many of the advantages of capital mobility in allocating savings to areas of highest marginal productivity.

Losses of national macroeconomic autonomy are of two kinds. First, capital mobility surrenders some autonomy to the rest of the world, specifically to the foreign policy-makers who determine world interest rates and the other attractions of external assets. Second, capital mobility gives considerable power to speculators who can generate excess volatility of exchange rates in the same way that they produce excess volatility of stock prices.

Clearly many international monetary regimes fall between the extremes. Most intermediate systems involve adjustable parities, rates that are fixed but not fixed forever. Under the Bretton Woods system the parities could be, and frequently were, changed by the country itself, almost always by devaluations. Although the International Monetary Fund in principle had the right to veto proposed changes in exchange rates, in practice it was impossible for the IMF to prevent a government from devaluing if it really wanted to do so.

The Bretton Woods system was quite asymmetric as between surplus and deficit countries. Countries had no choice but to devalue when they ran out of reserves and international credit, but there was nothing beyond pious words to stop surplus countries from accumulating positive reserves indefinitely. This kind of asymmetry is almost inevitable in any system of adjustable pegs. The European Monetary System is another example, a Bretton Woods system applied to a smaller area.

From a system of adjustable pegs it is not a big jump to "dirty" floating-rate systems. Consider, for example, the present-day regime of the Group of Seven, really of the Big Three, the EMS (mainly in practice Germany), the U.S., and Japan. The governments and central banks sometimes agree on ranges for the dollar vis-à-vis the yen and the deutsche mark, and these are enforced by central bank interventions. Thus, even though the system is in principle a floating rate system, in some short runs it approximates a fixed rate system. The ranges are adjusted by mutual agreement from time to time, and are not always effective. On occasion the central banks of G-7 lose control to private speculators.

Compromise systems, with fixed but adjustable rates or with ranges, do not seem to me to be as different in fact from floating rate systems as they are usually said to be. The reason is that the chosen parities are never irrevocable. There can be speculation against them, and we know there will be speculation against them, whenever funds are allowed to move across currencies. Speculation is not the same in a Bretton Woods system or within EMS as under market-floating. Instead of speculation on what the currency market will do tomorrow, speculation under Bretton Woods was on whether, when, under what circumstances, and how much country X would devalue its currency. In floating rate systems, speculation concerns both economic influences on rates and government interventions.

In contrast, there is no speculation in a single-currency system; no one is betting on changes in rates of exchange between the Connecticut dollar and the California dollar.

Speculation takes a different form in markets where the prices involved move continuously hour by hour and day by day, from speculation in markets where the prices move only in discrete jumps. The changes in exchange rates under a semi-fixed parity system are usually very traumatic. They are called *crises* every time they happen, and they draw much more attention than market rate changes day to day, which are more gradual and impersonal. Large discrete changes in exchange rates under government control are probably more disruptive of private business plans and transactions than the day-by-day fluctuations of floating-rate markets.

INTERNATIONAL CURRENCY REGIMES

3 A Single Currency?

Although in one sense a single currency is one end of a spectrum, it really differs dramatically—in kind, not just in degree—from any monetary system that has separate currencies. I do not think one can approach a single currency system by small steps. I do not think an optional common European currency, "ecus" that can circulate alongside national currencies, would be more than a symbolic step towards a single monetary unit. I doubt that Europe can gradually reap the gains of a single currency by moving progressively to greater fixity of rates among separate national currencies. A single currency is what Americans call a "brand new ball game."

The big monetary question for Europe is this: Can there some day be a unique European Currency? Can Europe establish the necessary preconditions? Can Europe replicate the structures that enable the system to work among the fifty states of the American Union? If so, when and how? I put the questions. I certainly do not know the answers.

It is not necessary to have a completely centralized government. We in the U.S.A. have fifty-one governments. The States do many things and do them quite differently. They have different taxes, regulations, and public services. Certain basic functions are centralized in the federal government, and it is those that are perhaps necessary to run a successful common currency system.

As I see it, the projected liberalizations in Europe in 1992 amount mainly to an increase in capital mobility. Europe already has a semi-fixed currency parity system, a baby Bretton Woods so to speak. Maybe somewhat greater commitments to fixed rates are involved in the 1992 liberalizations. but it seems that the existing exchange rate regime is going to be combined with a substantial increase in capital mobility. I also suspect, maybe wrongly, that the projected increase in capital mobility is much greater than the increases in mobilities of goods and services and of labor, which are already very mobile within the European Community.

Europe is making capital more mobile and financial markets more integrated, anticipating the advantages of a common currency and the associated central institutions. It will be interesting to see how well this partial movement towards currency integration will work.

4 Monetary Policy in a Currency Area

Where will the locus of macroeconomic control and policy reside in a system of this kind, i.e. in a fixed exchange rate regime with much greater capital mobility? If there are several independent centers of policy—governments or central banks—and if each is trying to conduct its own national monetary policy, who is responsible for the overall monetary policy of the group? The several centers jointly deploy enough instruments to determine all the exchange rates among their currencies plus the group's overall macro policy. But the latter will be an unintended and accidental by-product of the monetary strategies the several members of the group are playing in their game with each other. To put it in an illuminating but probably overly simple way of describing monetary policy, suppose each central bank is worrying about its interest rate relative to the interest rates of other members. Nobody among them is worrying about the average interest rate of the group or its average exchange rate vis-à-vis nonmembers.

How was overall policy determined in the pre-1914 gold standard? In the Bretton Woods System? How has it been done in the European Monetary System? In each of those cases, I think, one country was the decisive monetary policy-maker. It was the interest rate determined by the hegemony of that country which the other countries had to accept as the point of reference. From that international rate their own policies made deviations in response to local conditions, so far as the mobility of capital permitted deviations at all. The dominant country was Great Britain before the First World War and the United States in the Bretton Woods era, the first quarter century after the Second World War. It is the Federal Republic of Germany in the European Monetary System.

If after 1992 under the EMS the Bundesbank is still going to be essentially the European Central Bank, then one problem is solved. But another remains. Should one member of the Community set the tone for the whole European economy?

If the members of the EMS are going to permit more freedom of funds to move among their financial markets, then they are further reducing their monetary and macroeconomic autonomy. They are further reducing their room to differ from the policies of the Bundesbank in regard to interest rates and other macroeconomic variables.

5 Do Nominal Exchange Rates Matter?

Does it really matter whether exchange rates are fixed or floating? That is, does it matter for the real outcomes—production, consumption, relative prices, terms of trade—that determine economic welfare? In the classical tradition in economics, "money is a veil," obscuring for the uninitiated truly important economic events and fundamental magnitudes. Absolute or nominal prices—currency units per units of goods—are of only transient interest, in contrast to relative or real prices—units of one commodity per units of others. The exchange rate is doubly nominal, the price of one monetary unit in terms of another. Won't the real terms of trade, the volumes of exports and imports, and the performances of nations and regions be the same regardless of exchange rates? The classical answer is affirmative.

New classical macroeconomics has revived this doctrine, and since the 1970s it has been taken seriously by powerful governments and central bankers. It is commonly said, both by economic theorists and by central bankers, that there is no useful tradeoff between unemployment and inflation and no real social cost in following a monetary policy geared exclusively to price stability. The major European governments and central banks consequently took no active monetary or fiscal measures to stimulate demand to facilitate recovery from the 1979–82 recession. They had faith that their economies would return to equilibrium as natural adjustments of nominal wages and prices brought them back into line with normally growing money supplies. Do not adjust money and credit to prevailing nominal prices, rather count on the economy to adjust nominal prices to prevailing supplies of money and credit.

In practice these classical policies were little more successful in the 1980s than similarly complacent policies during the Great Depression. The United States, in contrast to Europe, enjoyed a full recovery in the 1980s—not because of Reagan's supply-side policies but because Volcker's Federal Reserve "fine-tuned" its monetary policies to bring about a demand-driven expansion.

On the international side, the classical recipe is similar. Do not adjust your exchange rate to your nominal wages and prices, rather count on your economy to adjust them to the exchange rate. This was certainly the theory of the gold standard, the basis for the claim that it prevented domestic inflation at no social cost. In similar vein, hitching the national currency to an external currency of proven stable purchasing power is a policy often adopted in recent years and still more often advocated. In some cases, no doubt, it is an effective way of disciplining the unions, businesses, consumers, and banks of an inflation-prone society. On the other hand, both history and recent events are full of cases where fixing and defending too high an exchange rate have entailed severe real costs. Nominal wages and prices just cannot adjust fast enough to escape those costs.

Recent British experience is a cautionary tale. The U.K. chose to adhere to the ERM at an extraordinarily high value of sterling. The Bank of England raised U.K. interest rates to double digits to boost the pound prior to formal adherence and then had to keep them high to sustain its parity. This policy may keep inflation under control, but it deters exports, employment, and growth. British enterprises and workers would be more competitive at a lower pound.

John Major's overvaluation of the pound is reminiscent of an earlier Chancellor of the Exchequer, Winston Churchill. In 1925 he returned to the gold standard at the 1914 parity. But after British inflation during the First World War the old parity overvalued sterling in dollars and francs. Consequently, Britain slid into depression several years before America and continental Europe. The Chancellor's decision inspired Keynes's polemic *The Economic Consequences of Mr. Churchill.*

Overvaluations of this kind can be corrected. Devaluation of sterling in 1931 put Britain on the road to recovery. The United States, in turn, did not begin to recover from the Great Depression until 1933, when President Roosevelt reversed previous policies and devalued the dollar against gold and sterling.

The monetary unification of East and West Germany, an ongoing experiment in creating a single currency, also contains some lessons. Freezing exchange rates, Herr Pohl of the Deutsches Bundesbank warned in retrospect, is not a step to be taken lightly. Conversions at wrong rates may cause considerable damage. In the German case, political imperatives understandably took priority. Monetary unification was symbolically important. From July 1, 1991 residents of the German Democratic Republic could convert limited quantities of their marks into deutsche marks at parity (1:1), although most asset conversions were at a rate of 2 ostmarks per DM. Most important for the economy, wages, salaries, and other recurrent payments were converted at full parity, not at the 2:1 rate the Bundesbank recommended.

Ex ante, 1:1 did not seem so unreasonable. GDR wages in marks had been about 1/3 of FRG wages in DM. Labor productivity was thought to be at least 1/3 of that of workers in West Germany. Therefore, East German businesses and workers should have been able to compete. It didn't turn out that way. The economy of East Germany collapsed. Industrial production fell 50 percent, it is estimated, and 30 percent of the work force lost full-time employment. Evidently prior estimates of East German productivity and competitiveness were far too optimistic.

In the best of circumstances, the economic transition of East Germany was bound to entail many difficulties and frustrations, and East German workers would be sorely tempted to move West. Yet if their DM wages had started 50% less, as the Bundesbank proposed, enterprises and workers would have had better chances to survive, while learning how to produce and compete in free markets. Unlike the adherence of Britain to the ERM, the marriage of the mark to the DM allows no divorce. Likewise, once lire, DM, francs, pounds, etc. are replaced by *ecus*, there will be no devaluations to rescue uncompetitive nations from unemployment.

6.1 International Policy Coordination: Fixed Exchange Rates

In a fixed exchange rate regime with funds highly mobile across currencies and frontiers, an individual country has little monetary autonomy. Its interest rates can differ very little from those in the outside world. It must rely on fiscal policies for countercyclical policies. But even so it may confront an impasse, a "fundamental disequilibrium," in the old jargon of the International Monetary Fund. Domestic full employment, given the fiscal policy required to sustain it, may imply chronic trade deficits and continuous drains of international reserves. One way out is devaluation, provided the nominal depreciation of the exchange rate succeeds in achieving a real depreciation, restoring competitiveness. If this way out is excluded, the country must somehow contrive to have very flexible prices and wages.

The role of policy coordination, worldwide or regional, is to prevent collectively counterproductive jockeying for macroeconomic advantage.

When national central banks are focusing on interest rate differentials, as they must do in a world of capital mobility, the overall average of interest rates will be nobody's business. It may end up too high for general prosperity, or too low to keep inflation at bay. The world interest rate level, or the European interest rate level, requires international coordination. Likewise coordination is needed to define permissible national deviations from the agreed average.

A country whose economy is underemployed can reasonably have relatively low interest rates, while those of a country with an overheated economy should be relatively high. These criteria of under- and overemployment and production must necessarily be each country's own. But they must be declared in advance and consistently adhered to, used in the joint decisions both on average interest rates and on the national deviations.

6.2 International Policy Coordination: Floating Exchange Rates

Policy coordination is also necessary in a floating exchange rate regime. Experience the last twenty years has refuted the extravagant claims of some advocates of floating rates, that national monetary policies could proceed without external concerns, leaving the currency markets to reconcile the policies and macroeconomic performances of the several economies. National monetary policy is a more effective tool of domestic demand management than in fixed rate regimes. But it works by moving the exchange rate, depreciating it to shift demand from foreign to domestic goods or appreciating it to shift demand in the opposite direction. It can be a "beggar-thy-neighbor" policy for employment and output in the first case, and for inflation in the second. Differential interest rate movements, actual and anticipated, are the mechanisms by which national monetary policies move exchange rates. As in the fixed-rate regime, the world average interest rate level may become an accident of national game-playing in the absence of coordination.

However, floating rates add some degrees of freedom. Interest rate differentials of importance for domestic demand management can be sustained in international money markets by compensating expectations of currency appreciations and depreciations. Thus a country in need of demand stimulus from interest rates lower than the rest of the world—like the United States in 1991—could in principle carry out this policy with an appropriately low exchange rate which is rationally expected to appreciate gradually.

An adjustable-peg exchange rate regime does not possess these same degrees of freedom. As long as a central bank is defending its parity, it is constrained by its international reserves and their domestic monetary effects. In these circumstances it is not possible for markets or central banks to arrive at estimates of probabilities of depreciation or appreciation that would compensate for deviations from world interest rates. Nor could any such estimates be confirmed and reinforced by the actual paths of exchange markets.

Policy coordination must pay attention not only to short-run demand stabilization but also to trends in current accounts. The desired future pattern of current accounts should be estimated in the light of the various national domestic saving and investment balances. Currency values should be low but rising for countries with excessive current account deficits, high and falling for countries with excessive surpluses. To make these developments possible, fiscal policies should be tight in the former countries and easy in the latter countries.

Naturally, the appropriate directions of fiscal policies for long run current account equilibrium will be taken into account in determining the target pattern of interest rates. For example, in recession or incomplete recovery an economy like the United States needs low interest rates both for short-run demand management and for an exchange depreciation to correct its balance of trade. At full employment, however, the United States could expect to have a relatively low interest rate only for the second reason and only if it were following a policy of fiscal austerity, because otherwise there would be no room in the economy for an improvement in net exports.

Policy coordination of this kind is not easy, either intellectually or politically. Governments have not been notably successful in establishing effective monetary and macroeconomic policy coordination. The G-7 is supposed to play a coordinating role among the major OECD Countries. So far "coordination" seems to have been directed less to policy than to one of the outcomes of policy, namely exchange rates. The Group has sometimes been able to agree on temporary ranges of currency rates but not on the fiscal and monetary policies that would validate them. If a financially more integrated European Community chooses not to leave monetary policy to the Bundesbank, it will have to develop some institutions for policy coordination.

7 Speculation and Taxing Transactions

Speculation on currencies is a serious problem in any regime short of a single currency. Greater freedom of capital movements brings important advantages, but at the cost of enhanced speculative opportunities. There is more scope for bubbles and for false signals from financial markets. Governments and central banks lose some autonomy to the market. Markets have whims which the authorities might not, should not, always like to follow. The markets have developed extremely efficient technologies of transactions and information. It is so easy and so cheap to make financial transactions, and the amount of private funds that can quickly be mobilized to support fashionable market opinion is so large, that countervailing official interventions have difficulty controlling exchange rates and interest rates.

I take credit, or confess guilt, for having suggested quite a few years ago a radical proposal for international monetary reform. I proposed to put "sand in the wheels" of the excessively efficient currency markets. These markets are engines that work all too well technically but do not work all that well economically, especially macroeconomically. The sand in the wheels would take the form of transactions taxes, which direct traders' attention to long-run fundamentals and away from transient contagious market sentiment.

Suppose you have to pay, let's say, a one percent tax every time you make spot transactions in foreign exchange markets (or for that matter in domestic securities markets). If you intend to hold the asset purchased for 30 years, the tax is one percent going in now and one percent coming out 30 years later. The calculation of the rate of return that induced you to make the transaction is negligibly influenced by the tax. If it was a socially worthwhile allocation of saving, within or between national economies, the tax would not interfere with it. But if you are a "day trader," in this morning and out this afternoon, for example buying sterling with dollars and then reversing the transaction the same day, that one percent tax each way eats up any gain in the value of sterling pretty fast.

"Sand in the wheels" deters traders from acting on short-run views of investments, either international or domestic. Transactions taxes would diminish excess volatility. They would focus investors' attention on longer-run fundamentals. Maybe they can secure the benefits of increased mobility without some of the costs. The intent is to slow down capital movements, not commodity trade. But even if it were not possible to exempt *bona fide* commodity transactions, the tax would be too small to be a significant trade barrier. In any case, it would have to be imposed by all countries and would not affect export-import balances.

At the same time, a tax on currency transactions would create room for greater national autonomy in monetary policy. A two percent tax on a round trip to another currency wipes out an eight point differential in per annum interest rates on three-month bills. The tax thus makes viable differences in local-currency interest rates that would otherwise be erased by arbitrage.

Let me be clear about "sand in the wheels." There's good sand and there's bad sand. Saying that a little sand in the wheels may be a good thing does not mean that every monopolistic restriction of entry into financial industries is justified, or that every fixing of interest rates by administrative decree is beneficial. Intervention which is impersonal, constant, and automatic, like the fixed transactions tax I suggested, will do its job in an efficient manner, compared with the usual *ad hoc* interferences with mobility of capital, either internal or international. The transactions tax might actually make it easier to clear up some counterproductive monopolistic and restrictive financial practices.

J. M. Keynes in 1936 pointed out that a transactions tax could strengthen the weight of long-range fundamentals in stock market prices, as against speculators' guesses of the short-range behaviors of other speculators. The same is true for the foreign exchange markets. Vast resources of intelligence and enterprise are wasted in financial speculation, essentially in playing zero-sum games. Transactions taxes might re-allocate some of these resources. To the extent that they do not, they will at least produce needed government revenues without bad side-effects. It is estimated that as much as $1000 billion gross foreign exchange transactions occur every business day. Since the currency transactions tax would have to be international, the proceeds might appropriately go to the World Bank.

8 Conclusion

The international integration of financial markets is a trend that cannot be stopped. The wonders of modern telecommunications and computers assure its continuation. Even if they wanted to, governments would not be able to impose effective barriers on movements of funds across currencies and borders. Goods and services and labor are becoming more mobile also, but at a much slower pace. National governments can still impose barriers on their movements, and they do. These discrepancies create grave problems in macroeconomic management. They are not easily solved by any international monetary regime.

A single currency, superseding national currencies, has great merits, but they can be realized only with other common economic, political, and social institutions, for all of which a basic sense of community is essential. Perhaps this can be achieved in Western Europe, and perhaps early agreement on a common currency will even help to create the requisite sense of community.

A system of fixed but adjustable exchange parities among national currencies does not achieve the benefits of a single currency. Those benefits depend on the permanence of the arrangement and on the confidence of the people of all the regions in its permanence. If adjustment of parities is a distinct possibility, speculation on its probability can bring large changes in the allocation of international reserves among countries. The potential volume of speculative capital movements has become enormous as money markets and securities markets have been internationalized.

In an adjustable-peg system, defense of reserve positions and parities becomes the primary concern of governments and central banks of deficit countries. No counterpart adjustment responsibilities are felt by surplus countries. The pre-1914 gold standard conveyed the sense of a durable single-currency system for the world as a whole until World War I and its aftermath, when Britain, the key country, could not maintain the old parity of sterling with gold without overvaluing the pound against other currencies. Likewise the gold-dollar standard of the Bretton Woods era could not survive the cessation of gold-for-dollar convertibility in 1971. Like Britain in the 1920s and early 1930s, the United States in the 1960s and early 1970s needed to depreciate its currency against other currencies. In both cases, when the surplus countries refused to appreciate their currencies significantly against the key currency, they made the continuation of the system too costly for the key country. Once the adjustable-peg system is loose from its anchor, the regime delivers neither the advantages of a permanent single currency nor those of a flexible floating rate system.

While a floating rate system by no means assures painless automatic adjustments to disturbances in trade and capital transactions among countries or to idiosyncratic differences among nations in economic policies and developments, it does have important virtues. Official reserves do not command high priority in macroeconomic policy decisions. Exchange rate movements take the place of international transfers of reserves, and their consequences are shared more symmetrically. Expectations of exchange appreciations and depreciations may provide additional degrees of freedom in reconciling diverse national monetary policies, because those expectations can compensate for departures from interest rate parities across national money markets.

International policy coordination is needed in any system that preserves national currencies and national monetary policies, whether adjustable pegs or floating rates. The speculative opportunities created by the technologies of modern financial markets and financial institutions are a threat to rational policies, both national and international. A modest international transactions tax may be useful in focusing financial investors on long-run fundamental prospects rather than short-run gains.

PART V

ECONOMICS AND ECONOMISTS

CHAPTER 26

A REVOLUTION REMEMBERED

Fifty years ago, I was about to be a sophomore in Harvard College and returned to Cambridge early to attend the Tercentenary. A wide-eyed midwestern beneficiary of President James Bryant Conant's incipient national scholarships, I wasn't going to miss the pageantry of the celebration. It was worth getting wet in the rain. It was marvelous to be a member of an institution to which the whole world was paying homage, and of a family that included, of course, the President of the United States.

FDR was my political hero; I knew he was "that man in the White House" to most of his fellow alumni, and I loved hearing him remind them that Harvard men didn't like Jackson in 1836 or Cleveland in 1886. "Now, on the three hundredth anniversary," he whispered, "*I* am President." *The Lampoon's* Tercentenary issue contains a barbed spoof of the WPA, the New Deal's massive workfare program. I recall a later Harvard pageant, the alumni parade on Class Day of my Commencement in 1939, in which the 25th reunion class, 1914, wore only suspended barrels bearing the legend "A Harvard Man Did This to Us."

At the Tercentenary, the Governor of the Commonwealth, James Michael Curley, was neither Harvard man nor popular among Harvard men. But he and his audience suspended hostilities, although he could not resist reminding the assemblage, in a less suave manner than Roosevelt's, that the U.S. Presidents at Harvard anniversaries were always Democrats. I won't forget his Boston Irish accent as he said, "Shakespeare unquestionably anticipated this institution when he penned the line that reads 'How far that little candle throws its beams, so shines a good deed in a naughty world.'"

Presented September 1986 at Harvard University *350th Symposia* in celebration of Harvard's birthday. Reprinted by permission from *Challenge Magazine* 31(4) (July/August 1988): 35–41.

Harvard awarded 62 honorary degrees that day, all to scholars and scientists. Three of them were economists: Wesley C. Mitchell, "noted for his study of the business cycles which, despite all efforts, still revolve"; Douglas B. Copland, "... a successful practitioner of theoretical economics ... who has applied his knowledge most fortunately for the recent history of Australia"; and Dennis H. Robertson, "An academic man who has thought deeply about industrial and banking problems, his writings have left their mark on modern economic theory." Three other honors were tangentially related to economics, those to the historian J. H. Clapham and the statisticians Corrado Gini and R. A. Fisher.

The choice of Mitchell, among economists resident in America, still looks good. Joseph A. Schumpeter was ineligible as one of Harvard's own. Today we would probably choose Irving Fisher. But at the time he probably struck the Harvard jury as an unsound crank; anyway Yale was already represented by two eminent historians. The interesting choice is Robertson, Keynes's younger friend and rival at the other Cambridge. Keynes's *Treatise on Money* (1930) had not succeeded in his purpose of establishing his claim to be a scholar, as well as a commentator on current events and a man of affairs. *The General Theory* was published in February 1936, and was getting a frosty reception in the profession. The Harvard jury would not yet have absorbed its message and appreciated its impact, and wouldn't have liked them anyway.

Destiny in the Wings

Yet Harvard was destined to become very soon the bastion of Keynesian economics in the New World. Paul Samuelson, my revered elder, participated actively in the process. I viewed it from the worm's eye of an undergraduate, starting shortly after the Tercentenary. My tutor that year, also my introductory economics (Ec A) instructor, was an eccentric graduate student, Spencer Pollard. He decided that for tutorial he and I, mainly I, should read "this new book from England. They say it may be important." So I plunged in, being too young and ignorant to know that I was too young and ignorant. It was fun, my first taste of an intellectual, theoretical battle parallel to a battle over policy and politics. It was easy to side with the forces of enlightened revolution against entrenched and irrelevant orthodoxy. "Let not moss-covered error moor thee by its side, as the world on truth's current glides by," so it says in *Fair Harvard*, the ode written for the Bicentenary in 1836.

Thanks to Spencer Pollard, I became an early undergraduate expert on the multiplier, liquidity preference, involuntary unemployment, and other themes of *The General Theory*. What I missed was what Paul Samuelson says he picked up as an undergraduate at Chicago, a solid grounding in the theories against which Keynes was revolting. Harvard's undergraduate economics curriculum was not Keynesian in my years of concentration; it simply didn't pay much attention to any brand of what we now call macroeconomics. The introductory course was solidly under the control of the permanent department chairman, Professor Harold Hitchings Burbank, a political and ideological conservative and an exponent of simplistic orthodox economics. The young section leaders insinuated heresies on their own, increasingly Keynesian as the revolution spread. Even in my year, it is true, we read extensively in Harvard's own Professor Sumner Slichter's *The American Economy*, a pragmatic and empirical pre-Keynesian text with an account of business fluctuations along somewhat Keynesian lines. Slichter was eclectic and institutional; he did not erect formal theories from his insights. His heresies were never explicit enough to damage his considerable reputation in the business community.

Chamberlin Remembered

Our undergraduate theory course was taught by Edward Chamberlin. It was standard classical and Marshallian theory, plus monopolistic competition, Chamberlin's own claim to revolutionary fame, *The Theory of Monopolistic Competition* (1933). Monopolistically competitive with Joan Robinson in Cambridge, England, he had argued in the early 1930s that pure competition among agents with no control over their prices should not be, could not be, the central paradigm of microeconomic theory. That revolution withered from neglect, not from refutation. Chamberlin did not push it, because he was temperamentally orthodox; Mrs. Robinson did not push it, because she had bigger and more heretical fish to fry. Neoclassical theorists ignored it, because it was annoyingly intractable in general equilibrium models. Keynes and his followers, both in America and Britain, ignored it and attempted to ground their new macroeconomics on the standard microeconomic foundations of pure competition, hoping to win their ball game on their opponents' home field. That strategy backfired 30 or 40 years later. Although Keynesians of my generation sincerely say that they always had imperfect or monopolistic competition in mind as their micro-foundations, only recently have serious theoretical attempts begun to formalize this vision.

Professor Chamberlin was my tutor in my senior year. I was writing my honors thesis on a central problem in Keynesian theory—maybe *the* central problem—the determination of money wages and their relation to unemployment. Chamberlin knew nothing about the subject and cared less. We had a pleasant year and became good friends, discussing every week such topics as Catholic agrarianism (small is beautiful), a movement he believed in.

In our theory class, Chamberlin's main heckler was my classmate Marion Levy, who had learned Veblen and institutionalism in his freshman year at Texas. (Marion, now Professor of Sociology at Princeton, became a hard-nosed orthodox theoretician in his later years.) One of the most popular advanced undergraduate economics courses—and one of the best—was on the economics of socialism, taught jointly by Paul Sweezy, a Marxist, and Edward Mason, who told us the first day he had once been a socialist but had learned better.

Among undergraduates there was lively and usually highly political debate about the great world economic crisis of the times. Mostly it concerned the future of capitalism: whether it would survive; whether it deserved to survive. That the Great Depression was the ultimate convulsion of a dying system was, of course, a widely accepted view. To many of my friends, the live alternatives to Adam Smith and Alfred Marshall were Marx and Veblen, not Keynes.

Keynesian economics was, in the context of those times, essentially conservative. The message was that capitalism was not doomed; its major failing, chronic large-scale unemployment, could be remedied fairly easily, by intelligent use of the fiscal and monetary instruments governments already had at their disposal. This message was not welcome news to Marxists committed to the view that the system was no longer structurally capable of prosperity and progress.

There were, of course, attempts to marry the Marxist and Keynesian critiques. Intellectually, I think, the best of them was the 1940 article that appeared in the *Review of Economic Studies*, "Mr. Keynes and Mr.

Marx," by Sidney Alexander, then a graduate student. *An Economic Program for American Democracy*, by seven Harvard and Tufts economists, created quite a stir—even among noneconomists—when it was published in 1938. The authors were all young Turks. Some, like Paul and Maxine Sweezy, were Marxists; others were just Keynesians. The message that came through was Keynesian and indeed Hansenian, but with the remedies tilted to egalitarian redistribution.

In my observation, this was the usual outcome when anyone tried to reach a coherent synthesis of the two doctrines: the Marxism was crowded out, and the result was liberal Keynesianism rather than socialism. Among young economists around Harvard in those days, the exceptions would be Paul Sweezy and Paul Baran. In England, the powerful leadership of Joan Robinson created a Keynesian tradition with strong Marxist or left-wing components. No similar movement thrived in the United States.

Conservatism Reigned

At the time of the Tercentenary, the senior Harvard economics faculty was quite orthodox and conservative. Its grand old man, F. W. Taussig, an American Marshall, had just retired; the nth edition of his *Principles* was still the major text of Ec A. Seven members of the department had joined in publishing in 1934 a critical assessment of the New Deal, *The Economics of the Recovery Program*. Schumpeter explained that depressions have happened before, that they perform necessary economic functions, and that recoveries occur on their own. He did concede the existence of "widespread suffering and needless waste" and saw some role for temporary public "expenditure to blot out the worst things without injury to the economic organism." Chamberlin provided a primer on Say's Law. Other chapters took after NRA, AAA, and other regulatory innovations, which goodness knows offered plenty to criticize.

Roosevelt's reflationary gold and monetary policies, indispensable for recovery, did not deserve the condemnations they received here and elsewhere from other Harvard authors, and from the vast body of professional economists—with the honorable exception, I am happy to say, of Yale's Irving Fisher. Likewise, the New Deal reforms of financial institutions and markets deserved more favorable reception. Harvard did not have even a strong Chicago monetary theory type, who could have followed the logic of the quantity theory to advocate more expansionary measures than the Fed took before 1933.

After *The General Theory* appeared, Harvard's flagship economic periodical, the *Quarterly Journal of Economics*, published in November 1937 a symposium on the book featuring a largely negative review by Jacob Viner of Chicago. D. H. Robertson, the Tercentenary honoree, agreed with Viner in contesting Keynes's liquidity preference as an obstacle to classical interest rate equilibration of saving and investment. Taussig gently chided Keynes for giving apparent priority to employment ahead of output. Harvard's brilliant young mathematical theorist, Wassily Leontief dismissed on pure neoclassical grounds the whole idea that real variables like employment and output could have monetary determinants in equilibrium. His short article anticipates 50 years of subsequent criticism of Keynes on this point. In the next issue, Keynes replied to all this graciously and uncombatively. The article—his last serious contribution to macroeconomic theory—is much admired; many believe it to be a better explanation of his thinking than the book itself.

Arrival of Hansen

The decisive change in Harvard economics began in 1937. In the Tercentenary year, Lucius Littauer gave Harvard $2 million for instruction and research in public administration, part of which endowed the Littauer chair in Political Economy. Alvin Hansen of the University of Minnesota was appointed to the chair. So far as I know, no one in Cambridge had reason to suspect that the 50-year-old man they were recruiting from Minnesota would turn out to be the most influential apostle of Keynesian economics in the United States.

Professor John H. Williams, Dean of the new Littauer School, was the decisive voice in inviting Hansen to the Littauer chair, according to both President Conant and Williams. Although Williams himself wrote in 1976 that Hansen "was already widely known as the leading disciple of John Maynard Keynes, about whose theories I had doubts," there was at that time no such evidence in Hansen's writings. Hansen had been very critical of Keynes's *Treatise*, against which he scored some important points. He had reviewed *The General Theory* unenthusiastically. Whatever his macroeconomic views when he received and accepted Harvard's invitation, he had ample credentials for the new chair; he was a strong and prolific general economist, keenly and practically interested in using public institutions and policies to ameliorate social ills.

Hansen's change of heart and mind about Keynes's new book altered the climate at Harvard in academic year 1937-38. Hansen shared with John Williams the teaching of graduate Money and Banking, and there the graduate students found a Keynesian mentor.

John Williams was skeptical of all theories. He always could see, and tell us, the arguments on both sides. Yet he was simultaneously a vice president of the Federal Reserve Bank of New York, and one presumes he must have been decisive as a policy adviser. Even prior to *The General Theory* and to the coming of Hansen, Williams always included in his syllabuses a prize-winning book by Foster and Catchings, two amateur economists who claimed to have found the fatal underconsumption flaw in capitalism, *Business without a Buyer* (1928). They were regarded by the profession as kooks. Williams said he couldn't find the flaw in their argument and challenged students to locate it; nevertheless, he was sure there was one. The fact was that, like other heretics, Foster and Catchings had a muddled misunderstanding of matters that Keynes and Hansen later set straight.

I took the undergraduate Money and Banking course that year. Williams was away most of the time, and Hansen lectured to us only once, at the end, giving a most impressive exposition of the essence of *The General Theory*. We were well prepared for it, because the bulk of the lectures had been given by Richard Gilbert, one of the young authors of *An Economic Program*, an enormously gifted economist and teacher. Rereading my notes recently, I was struck by how clear, thoughtful, and complete his lectures were and how much they anticipated later developments, even today's. Our profession lost a great prospect when Gilbert was diverted after World War II from an academic to a business career. He died in 1986.

The Fiscal Policy Seminar, also shared by Hansen and Williams, was exciting for the participants and fruitful for economics and for the nation. It was really a research institution, whose latest products were presented and discussed at its weekly meetings. Those products were presentations by Williams and Hansen, graduate student papers, chapters of dissertations, or reports from visitors, many of whom were alumni on the firing line in Washington. Junior participants like me felt the seminar connected us both to the latest scientific developments and to federal policymaking. In 1939 Hansen himself was busy educating Washington by his testimony to the Temporary National Economic Committee of the Congress, much of which he tried out at the seminar.

Thanks to Hansen, Harvard was the locus of development of Keynesian fiscal theory. Although Keynes saw the importance of fiscal policy, via the multiplier, he did not work out the details. This was done mainly at Harvard and mainly by Hansen and Hansen-trained economists, among them Robert Bishop, Robert Bryce, Emile Despres, Richard Gilbert, Richard Goodwin, George Jaszi, Griffith Johnson, Lloyd Metzler, Richard Musgrave, Harvey Perloff, Paul Samuelson, Walter Salant, William Salant, Alan Sweezy, Arthur Smithies, Lorie Tarshis, and Henry Wallich. The methods and substance of this work are still the routine foundations of macroeconometric models and of the practical work of the Office of Management and Budget, the Congressional Budget Office, and of many other public and private agencies in this country and elsewhere.

Hansen had one loyal ally among the Harvard senior faculty—Seymour Harris, an indefatigable and enthusiastic crusader for Keynesian ideas. I do not know when and how his conversion occurred. That a conversion was necessary is indicated by his chapter, "Higher Prices," in *The Economics of the Recovery Program*, where he deplored the Roosevelt Administration's "inflationary" gold and monetary policies. In the late 1930s and the 1940s, the books Harris edited and the *Review of Economics and Statistics* under his editorship were ready media for the output of Keynesians at Harvard and elsewhere. On the campus, his Dunster House Forum presented the lively issues of theory and policy to Cambridge audiences. Harris himself wrote prolifically.

Gottfried Haberler was a dedicated and accomplished neoclassical theorist. He was an open-minded and fair-minded economist, thoughtful and undoctrinaire. In the 1930s, the League of Nations engaged him to write a systematic survey of theories of economic fluctuations; at the same time the League commissioned Jan Tinbergen to do an empirical statistical study, which turned out to be the first macroeconometric model of the United States. The first edition of Haberler's report, *Prosperity and Depression* (1937), was written before *The General Theory*. The second edition (1939) added a long chapter on that book and the discussion it set off. It was a thoughtful, critical, and balanced exegesis. The third edition (1941) added another chapter, which contains—besides the first citations I know of my first published article—what later became known as the real balance or Pigou or Patinkin effect, an important abstract argument against Keynes's claim for underemployment equilibrium. In the give-and-take on the Harvard campus, Haberler was an active and erudite participant, coming down on the anti-Keynesian side more often than not, despite or perhaps because of the outbursts from Samuelson that always followed.

The Alumni Revolt

The reputation Harvard acquired in the late 1930s and 1940s as *the* Keynesian economics department was based on a small number of senior faculty, mainly Hansen, and on a larger number of junior faculty and graduate student teachers, important in undergraduate instruction. The Keynesian influence was already waning when, in the late 1940s, an alumni campaign against Harvard's "leftist" economics department broke out. Keynesian economics was indiscriminately lumped with socialism as a leftist threat to American free enterprise. The essential conservatism of the Keynesian message was not appreciated. The most extreme attacks came from a right-wing group of Harvard alumni who styled themselves the Veritas Foundation. More serious problems arose from the Board of Overseers.

In 1948 the Overseers withheld their approval of the promotion of J. Kenneth Galbraith to a professorship. This was an exercise of the Overseers' constitutional prerogative roughly comparable to a veto by the House of Lords. It has happened only one other time in modern history. The Board changed its mind a year later, after President Conant threatened to resign. Galbraith had several distinguished claims to heresy offensive to conservative members of the Board. Certainly one of them was his sympathy for Keynesian ideas, although he had not been a Hansen protegé and was not primarily a macroeconomist.

In 1951 a Harvard Overseers Visiting Committee chaired by Clarence Randall, CEO of Inland Steel and an intellectual who participated actively in national policy discussion, solemnly complained to the President and Fellows of the Keynesian bias of the department. Conant was seriously disturbed and took a year to prepare his response. Although he rejected Randall's charges, he did conclude that the economics department could use more of the case study methodology of the Business School. He established a joint professorship to bring this about. So far as I can tell, this chair was never filled in a way that satisfied Randall's hopes or Conant's intent. Anyway, the revolt withered away.

Macroeconomics Comes of Age

Macroeconomics as a distinct subject of theory and empirical research did not really exist before 1936. After World War II it flourished, and its initial identification with Keynes was gradually diluted. That is to say, the mainstream embraced and absorbed Keynes. Economists were busy modifying, elaborating, extending, refining, replacing, testing, and estimating relationships, models, and hypotheses. Under Paul Samuelson's leadership, the so-called "neoclassical synthesis" of orthodox and Keynesian principles was developed and applied to national fiscal and monetary policy. Laurence Klein at the Cowles Commission in Chicago, following Tinbergen, built Keynesian macroeconometric models, from which most of the many models around today are descended. Mathematical theorists built dynamic and stochastic models of business fluctuations with Keynesian features. Monetary theory and policy were rescued from the undeserved, and unintended, neglect occasioned by the prewar stress on fiscal policy. International transactions, in goods, services, and assets, were incorporated in macro models.

Harvard, it must be reported, did not have much to do with these postwar developments. Harvard-trained economists were very much involved, but few were at Harvard. Not that Harvard economics became anti-Keynesian—it simply stressed subjects other than macroeconomics. Was this because of the Overseers' revolt?

There were, of course, important exceptions. James Duesenberry, a Michigan Ph.D., was in the middle of the early postwar reappraisal of the consumption function, contributed to monetary theory and research, and was one of the architects of the Brookings econometric model. Thomas

Schelling, a graduate school contemporary of mine at Harvard after the war, wrote a definitive textbook on multiplier macroeconomics, a fine theoretical synthesis of much previous work. This came out while he was at Yale; after he was recalled to Harvard, he moved on to other topics and was not doing macroeconomics. Dale Jorgenson advocated, formulated, and estimated "neoclassical" investment functions, important in macro theory and macro models—and not particularly anti-Keynesian. Arthur Smithies for a while continued his work on government budgeting. Of the alumni of the Fiscal Policy Seminar, Richard Musgrave, the leading public finance economist of his generation, was recalled to Cambridge from exiles at Hopkins, Michigan, and Princeton. The late Otto Eckstein drifted into macroeconomics from industrial organization, first contributing to theory and empirical research on price formation and inflation, and then of course presiding over the first big commercial macroeconometric model at the firm he founded, Data Resources Incorporated.

The President's Council of Economic Advisers owes its founding by Congress in 1946 to the Keynesian revolution. Four members of the Council have been drawn from the Harvard faculty. Two, Duesenberry and Eckstein, served Democratic Presidents. Hendrik Houthakker advised a Republican President, Nixon. Martin Feldstein was chairman of Reagan's Council, 1982–84. We know that Feldstein advised against the Administration's budgets, demand stimuli masquerading as supply-side measures and so extreme as to be caricatures of Keynesian fiscal policies. We know that his advice was not taken. Loyalty to my present university tempts me irresistibly to tell you that the leading academic source of Council members has not been Harvard, but Yale, which boasts six—plus two who came to Yale after their Council stints.

Counterrevolutions

And now? In the world at large and in the economics profession, Keynesian macroeconomics, even the neoclassical synthesis, has lost much of the acceptance it enjoyed 20 years ago. The Keynesian revolution of the 1930s is the victim of several counterrevolutions: monetarist, supply-side, and "new classical." Pre-1936 orthodoxy is highly respectable once again.

Although Harvard has not been particularly prominent in the more theoretical aspects of these counterrevolutions, it has been the locus of an influential attack on Keynesian economics and policies, led by Martin Feldstein. Like Hansen in the 1930s and 1940s, Feldstein has been the leader of a series of fertile research programs seeking empirical findings relevant to public policy.

Feldstein and his colleagues have questioned the priority given by Keynesians to full employment. They contend that since World War II, unemployment has been largely voluntary, frictional, and temporary; therefore less of an economic problem for society than inflation and inadequate capital accumulation. They view complacently the high unemployment rates of postwar recessions and the general upward trend in rates of unemployment.

Feldstein and company mounted and executed an ambitious program of research on the effects of taxes, Social Security and other transfers, and other fiscal measures on saving and investment. The enterprise seems comparable to the old Fiscal Policy Seminar in its productivity, excitement, and close connection to national policy. But its theme and message were quite different. The conclusions added up to a sophisticated version of supply-side economics, with great emphasis on the disincentives to saving and investment arising from taxes on capital income. Feldstein also argued that the prospect of Social Security benefits drastically diminished private saving, at the same time as the government was spending the corresponding payroll taxes for current purposes. While most economists agree that taxes and transfer programs have effects in the directions indicated, there is considerable doubt as to their empirical magnitudes.

Feldstein blames Keynesians for a pro-consumption bias fostering the anti-saving and anti-investment policies of which he complains. Paul Samuelson and I protest, because our "neoclassical synthesis" stressed that the objectives of Keynesian demand management could be achieved by monetary and fiscal measures favorable to capital accumulation. We were members of a Keynesian team who during the Kennedy Administration practiced our preachings by introducing the Investment Tax Credit and other pro-investment incentives.

Happily, I observe in younger members of the Harvard department today some stirrings of the concerns and interests that moved many of us 50 and 40 and 20 years ago. They give me hope.

CHAPTER 27

NEOCLASSICAL THEORY IN AMERICA: J. B. CLARK AND FISHER

The intellectual breakthroughs that mark the neoclassical revolution in economic analysis occurred in Europe around 1870. The next two decades witnessed lively debates in which the new theory more or less absorbed or was absorbed in the classical tradition that preceded and provoked it. In the 1890s, according to Joseph A. Schumpeter (1954, p. 754) there emerged "a large expanse of common ground and ... a feeling of repose, both of which created, in the superficial observer, an impression of finality—the finality of a Greek temple that spreads its perfect lines against a cloudless sky." Of course the temple was by no means complete. Its building and decoration continue to this day, even while its faithful throngs worship within.

American economists were not present at the creation. To a considerable extent they built their own edifice independently, designing some new architecture in the process. They participated actively in the international controversies and syntheses of the period 1870–1914. At least two Americans were prominent builders of the "temple," John Bates Clark and Irving Fisher. They and others brought neoclassical theory into American journals, classrooms, and textbooks, and its analytical tools into the kits of researchers and practitioners. Eventually, for better or worse, their paradigm would dominate economic science in this country.

1 The Founding of the AEA: The Failed Rebellion

The neoclassical triumph was far from clear in 1885, when the American Economic Association was founded. The founders were young economists

Reprinted by permission from *American Economic Review* 75(6) (December 1985): 28–38.

rebelling against the long dominant classical tradition of Ricardo and John Stuart Mill. Several of the organizers, notably the main entrepreneur, Richard T. Ely, had absorbed in Germany historicist and institutionalist views of methodology, along with reformist and statist ideas of policy. The profession, small as it was, was badly split. Some of the elders, among them Simon Newcomb and William Graham Sumner, declined to join.

The new Association's constitution (AEA, 1987) contained a Statement of Principles "... accepted as a general indication of the views and the purposes of those who founded the ... Association, but ... not to be regarded as binding upon individual members." The quoted note was favored even by some participants in the organizing meeting who were sympathetic to the Statement, in order to make it possible for economists otherwise minded to become members. The first two of the four principles were:

1. We regard the state as an agency whose positive assistance is one of the indispensable conditions of human progress.

2. We believe that political economy as a science is still in an early stage of development. While we appreciate the work of former economists, we look not so much to speculation as to the historical and statistical study of actual conditions of industrial life for the satisfactory accomplishment of that development.

An echo of the second principle survives in the present charter as the first of the "objects of the society," adopted in 1888:

The encouragement of research, especially the historical and statistical study of the actual conditions of industrial life.

At the same 1888 meeting the original Statement of Principles was dropped, and to the initial purpose of "encouragement of perfect freedom of economic discussion" was added assurance that the Association will "take no partisan attitude, nor will it commit its members to any position on practical economic questions" (AEA, 1889, p. 86). This language too remains in the current charter. No doubt these catholic amendments made it possible for the Association to flourish.

As the marginalist revolution took root in America, it dealt a more decisive blow to the old orthodoxy, though not to its *laissez faire* implications, than the Germanic ideas inspiring Ely and his friends. The deductive method, "speculation," survived after all, indeed received a new and long lease on life. Pure theory was alive and well on this continent. Classical economics was demoted, as the rebels had hoped, but it was in an important sense revitalized, transformed from obsolescent tradition into exciting inquiry engaging the best analytical minds. This development in no way crowded out historical and statistical research or inhibited the policy interests and advocacies of American economists.

2 The Early American Neoclassical Economists

In Schumpeter's review of the American troops 1870–1914 (1954, pp. 863–877), the three superstars are Clark, Fisher, and Taussig. Frank W. Taussig (1859–1940) belongs in the triumvirate less for his own theoretical contributions than for his applied studies of international trade and tariffs, his distinguished public service, and his celebrated Socratic teaching of theory to generations of Harvard graduate students. He was a statesman of the profession. His theoretical ideas are scattered through his applied writings and through his *Principles of Economics* (1911, 1939) where they are integrated with his considered interpretation and exposition of accumulated knowledge. This popular text, still used in Harvard's introductory course when I took it as a sophomore in 1936–37, was like Marshall's *Principles* a wise man's serious attempt to expound the whole field as he saw it. Alas, the days of books like that are past. Taussig's views and attitudes were Marshallian also: reverence for the classical elders, undiminished by acceptance of many of the amendments to their doctrines compelled by the neoclassical revolution; and unwillingness to carry theory, especially mathematicized theory, to extremes untempered by common sense, history, and observation.

I shall concentrate on Clark and Fisher, referring to their contemporaries, including Taussig, and predecessors only when their works are particularly relevant to my main task. Time and space do not allow me to recognize even in that degree several eminent theorists, among them: Thomas N. Carver (1865–1961), like Clark a distribution theorist; Frank A. Fetter (1863–1949), an effective neoclassical critic of Marshall; and Fred M. Taylor (1855–1932), a theorist of market socialism anticipating Oskar Lange and Abba Lerner. I cannot pretend to completeness in this review of the contributions of our early leaders to neoclassical theory.

A Clark and His Conversion

John Bates Clark (1847–1938) was the most influential theorist and the most revered economist of the era in America. He was a founder of the Association and its third President 1894–95. In his time and ever since, he has been identified as the leading apostle of "marginalism" in general and of the marginal productivity theory of distribution in particular. *The Distribution of Wealth* (1899) is a genuine classic.

His standing in his time can be seen in Paul Homan's *Contemporary Economic Thought* (1928), where the first essay, all eighty-five pages of it, is devoted to Clark. "He is," the author says, "certainly the American theorist who during the past generation has made the most original and impressive contributions to abstract economic theory. Of international reputation, he has been classed by Professor Alfred Marshall as among the three or four great theoretical writers of the early twentieth century." Homan goes on to report the judgment of Edwin R. A. Seligman (1861–1939), another founder of the Association and later Clark's colleague at Columbia, placing Clark in the rarefied company of Ricardo, Senior, John Stuart Mill, Jevons, and Marshall (Homan, 1928, p. 17).

I recounted above the multi-faceted controversy that attended the founding of the Association in 1885, at the same time German versus English economics, historicism and institutionalism versus classical theory, and state intervention versus *laissez faire*. I pointed out how the issue was largely resolved by the triumph of an unforeseen third force, neoclassical economics. In 1885 Clark was definitely on Ely's side, although he was among those who favored stating the "principles" moderately enough not to discourage membership. Like Ely and Seligman, Clark had been greatly influenced by his studies at Heidelberg under Karl Knies.

Clark's personal intellectual journey over the next fifteen years sums up what happened to the profession at large. His first book, *The Philosophy of Wealth* (1886) reflects his German training and the spirit of 1885. It contains an attack, albeit gentle and respectful, on the premises of classical theory: on its dismissal of human motives other than material self-interest; on its assumption that the economy is competitive and its glorification of competition; on its extreme individualism and neglect of the organic whole of society. The Ricardian system is described as "the apotheosis of selfishness." Clark proposes public interventions to restrain industrialists' economic power, to achieve through arbitration justice in distribution between capital and labor, to supplant competition and conflict by cooperation, and in general to subject economic processes to control by the higher morality of the community.

During the next ten years Clark became absorbed by the intellectual challenges of the theory of (functional) distribution. A series of papers paved the way to his *magnum opus* (1899). Homan says, "When ... after years of patient thought and preparation, he published *The Distribution of Wealth*, the logical beauty and precision of the system of theory there displayed was like an illumination from Heaven to many of those whose goal for economic science was the reduction of economic life to terms of law and order" (1928, p. 34). However that may be, Clark had certainly discovered and embraced neoclassical economics; he completely reversed his earlier positions. Dramatic conversions are rare events at any age, and Clark's at fifty is as remarkable as Alvin Hansen's conversion to Keynesian economics at the same age in 1936.

Clark now finds that competition among self-interested individuals is the vehicle of social cooperation and justice he had found lacking thirteen years before. It now turns out that the organic whole of society is served by competition, because the market valuations of commodities and factors as derived from individuals' marginal utilities are their values to society as well. In later writings (Clark, 1901, 1904, 1912), it should be noted, Clark urged vigorous government intervention, not to supplant competition but to enforce it by antitrust policies.

B Fisher, the Theorist Born not Made

Today we look back on Irving Fisher (1867–1947) with awe and admiration, but he was not fully appreciated by his contemporaries. Today Fisher leads other old-timers by wide and increasing margins in journal citations. In column inches in the *Social Sciences Citation Index* (1979, 1983), Fisher led his most famous contemporaries, Wesley Mitchell, Clark, and Taussig in that order, by rough ratios $5:3:1:1$ in 1971–75 and by $9:3:1:1$ in 1976–80. Much more than the others, moreover, Fisher is cited for substance rather than for history of thought.

Yet Homan's 1928 survey does not include Fisher. (Besides Clark, it covers Veblen, Marshall, Hobson, and Mitchell.) Today theorists would almost unanimously substitute Fisher's name for Clark's in the encomiums quoted above. Fisher was twenty years younger than Clark, and some of the contributions on which his current reputation is based came in the 1920s and 1930s. Nevertheless he had ample claim to recognition before the First World War, and certainly before 1928.

Time has thus substantiated Schumpeter's prediction that "some future historian may well consider Fisher as the greatest of America's scientific economists up to our own day" (1954, p. 872). Few would challenge that ranking in *our* own day, especially if we exclude immigrants like Schumpeter himself and candidates still living.

Schumpeter gives two reasons for the lukewarmness of contemporary opinion of Fisher. His zealous and almost cranky espousal of his many causes, some economic like the compensated dollar and 100% reserves, some non-economic like prohibition, eugenics, vegetarianism, and hygiene, distracted attention from his scientific achievements. His mathematical and analytical methods, the very features that appeal to modern readers and enabled Fisher to anticipate many later developments, were uncongenial departures from the prevailing styles of doing economics at the time.

To these two factors might be added that unlike Taussig and Clark, whose cohorts of admiring students spread their fame throughout the profession, Fisher had few students and disciples. From personal experience I can also add that if Fisher was a prophet with insufficient honor in the profession, he was totally without honor in his own university outside the economics department. His crank causes were remembered, and also his incautious public and personal optimism about the stock market and the economy in 1929 and after, when he lost his family's fortunes and the university had to save his house for him.

Fisher was not involved in the controversies of 1885. Although he visited Germany during a post-doctoral academic Wanderjahr in Europe, he certainly was not subject to the Germanic influences on the Association's founders. He reflected on those old controversies and on the German influence on early American economics in his 1918 Presidential address to the Association, a strange speech greatly colored by the war just concluded (Fisher, 1919). He referred to "the curiously interesting fact that this Association largely owes its birth to German economics [which] brought us a new and altruistic impulse. In particular, we received from Germany the idea ... of making economics of service to 'the state.' But ... the war's revelations have made us realize that 'the state' served by German economists ... was simply the Hohenzollern dynasty.... Some among the very group of teachers who stirred the enthusiasm out of which this Association grew ... helped to lay the foundation for the war," which Fisher identified as "predatory economics." He noted that his own "revered master," Sumner, was among those who declined to join the new Association.

Fisher came to economics at Yale, where his whole life was spent from freshman year on. His mentors were Sumner, primarily a social theorist, J. Willard Gibbs, the great mathematical theorist of thermodynamics, and Arthur T. Hadley, an economist whom Schumpeter includes among six "who prepared the ground" (1954, pp. 865–66). Young Fisher's interests and talents were universal. By the time he finished his doctorate he had written and published poetry, political commentary, book reviews, a geometry text together with tables of logarithms, and voluminous notes on mathematics, mechanics, and astronomy for the benefit of students he was teaching or tutoring in order to support himself, his widowed mother, and his younger brother. Later Fisher published an introductory economics text (1910 and 1911); its graceful exposition of sophisticated theoretical material will impress a modern connoisseur, but it was too difficult for widespread adoption. Some of it survived in a leading introductory text of the 1920s and 1930s, by the younger Yale economists Fairchild, Furniss, and Buck (1926).

From the beginning Fisher was quite naturally and enthusiastically a mathematical economist, really the first one in the United States. Walrasian economics was the natural grist for his mill. But Fisher was never one to rely solely on deduction or "speculation," of which the insurgents of 1885 were so suspicious. He was as committed to "historical and statistical study of actual conditions" as any of them could have wished. Nor was he detached from policy and advocacy—quite the reverse, as already noted.

3 General Equilibrium: Value, Distribution, Capital, and Interest

There are several threads interwoven in the neoclassical fabric: "marginalism" in general, i.e. the calculus of maximization; marginal utility in particular, and the subjective theory of value; the marginal productivity theory of distribution; general equilibrium; and in some cases the mathematical method. Of course, none of these was entirely absent from pre-1870 economics. Marshall and Taussig could make a persuasive case for progressive continuity rather than radical innovation. Nevertheless the conjunction of these themes in the works of Jevons, Menger, and Walras—followed by Edgeworth, Böhm-Bawerk, Wicksell, Pareto, Clark, Fisher, and many others—generated discernible new style, scope, and substance in economic analysis.

The distribution of income and wealth, and in particular the sources, determinants, and social rationales of interest and other returns to private property, were obsessive topics in economics, in both Europe and North America, both before and after 1870. One reason, especially important in the intellectual environment of Europe, was the Marxist challenge to the legitimacy of property income. Answering Marx was a strong motivation for the Austrian school, in particular for the capital theory of Böhm-Bawerk and his followers. In positive as well as normative theory, neoclassical economics was in a much better position than classical economics to respond to the Marxist challenge. The labor theory of value, which Marx borrowed from the great classical economists, neither explains relative prices as commonly observed nor justifies functionally or ethically incomes other than wages. The contortions to which Smith, Ricardo, and Mill and their successors had to resort in order to remedy these failings were embarrassing. Solution of these long-standing problems was one great promise of the subjectivist-marginalist revolution of 1870.

These topics engaged the best efforts of Clark and Fisher, and each in his own way sought the answers in general equilibrium systems. Their methods were quite different. Clark did not use mathematics, and even diagrams are few and far between in his work. Fisher used mathematics and diagrams profusely.

A Clark's Marginal Productivity Theory of Interest

The Distribution of Wealth is an ambitious undertaking, inspired by the vision of integrating into a single theoretical system consumption and production, capital and labor, interest, wages, and rents, marginal productivity and marginal utility. Clark limits his ambition to the analysis of stationary states. He distinguishes statics from dynamics. Acknowledging that the latter is more important as well as more difficult, he says that the static foundations must be laid first and, like many of us since, he defers the dynamics to later times and other theorists.

Clark is remembered most for the marginal productivity theory of distribution. Thünen, was there long before, in 1826, as Clark recognizes (Thünen, 1826). But no one paid attention, and in America and elsewhere the discussion of distribution was preoccupied with Ricardian rent theory and its implications for wages, with wages-funds, and with arguments over what incomes were residual claims. Clark contends that Thünen did not understand that payments of marginal productivity to intra-marginal workers did not exploit them, because all homogeneous workers are marginal, and that Thünen therefore did not appreciate the ethics of marginal productivity distribution. He claims also that Thünen did not understand that marginal productivity payments precisely exhaust the total product. Clark himself intuitively understood this theorem to depend on constant returns to scale, but he gave no proof. More important, Clark was seeking not only a common principle to explain all factor payments but also a distribution theory which, in combination with the marginal utility theory of consumption, would generate a competitive equilibrium, indeed an equilibrium with socially optimal properties.

Another independent discoverer or rediscoverer of marginal productivity theory was an American contemporary of Clark, Stuart Wood (1853–1914). A paper of his on the theory of wages (Wood, 1889) was presented at the very same session of the Association as one of Clark's early papers on the same subject. Modern readers would find Wood's paper the clearer and more precise, especially his treatment of labor/capital substitution. George Stigler recalled Wood to the attention of the profession (Stigler, 1947). In a series of remarkable papers Wood "discovered for himself a whole Walrasian system with variable production coefficients" (Schumpeter 1954, p. 869). Clark's 1899 opus does not cite Wood.

Clark's own approach was not Walrasian; it was quite aggregative. He assumes that both "interest," meaning the return to capital, and wages will be equalized across sectors. Competition and mobility achieve these equalizations, but in the equilibrium he is describing there is "mobility without motion"—a pretty phrase. For his purpose Clark needs a factor of production *capital*, homogeneous both across the whole economy and over time. He distinguishes this capital from capital goods.

Capital goods differ from industry to industry and from time to time. They are specific and transient embodiments of the general and permanent factor capital. This is the fund accumulated by the economy's savings up to date. (However, Clark takes land to be a part of the homogeneous capital stock, an awkward and unnecessary shortcut that destroys the equality of capital to accumulated savings and dismisses all Ricardian and Malthusian problems in one fell swoop.) In a stationary state the fund is constant, though the capital goods in which it is embodied may change with depreciation and replacement and with interindustry shifts. In these respects capital is like labor, which also is homogeneous and remains in constant supply while individuals enter and leave the labor force and their occupations change.

It is these two factors that produce aggregate output with constant returns to scale and have marginal productivities dependent on their relative supplies. It is these marginal productivities that determine interest and wages. The marginal productivity of a factor declines as its relative employment increases.

In describing marginal productivity as a function of inputs, Clark is at pains to distinguish between variations of labor relative to existing capital goods and variations relative to a constant stock of capital with capital goods appropriately adjusted to each situation. Clark calls the returns to existing capital goods, including land, rents. They will be equal to interest, the marginal productivity of capital, in full equilibrium, when the capital-goods composition of capital is appropriately adjusted. For durable but mortal capital goods these rents seem to be like Marshallian quasi-rents. But for natural and immortal land Clark ignores the fact that value must adjust since supply cannot and the resulting problems. Clark reserves the term "profits" for the temporary entrepreneurial surpluses of transitional dynamics.

Clark's model of aggregate production is essentially the same as that of the one-product two-factor "neoclassical" growth models of Roy Harrod (1939) and of several authors in the 1950s and 1960s, e.g. (Solow, 1956 and 1969). These models generalized Clark's stationary state to paths of steady growth. Of course modern neoclassical growthmen did not subscribe to Clark's case for the ethical justice of marginal productivity distribution. His stress on this normative argument nevertheless was the reason the revival of his model aroused the passionate fire it drew in the "war of the two Cambridges" in the 1950s and 1960s.

In referring to Clark's *model*, I slipped into modern parlance. Like most theorists of those days, Clark did not regard himself as building a model or telling a "story" or spinning a parable, as a theorist does today. In Fisher's more abstract modes, he thought of himself as a model-builder; indeed he actually constructed a hydraulic-mechanical model of general equilibrium (1892). Most theorists at the time, however, regarded themselves as discoverers of natural laws, like physical scientists. Their propositions, however derived and however, if at all, tested on observations, were meant to be taken seriously as accounts of the real world, not as logical exercises about hypothetical economies. Thus Clark regarded the diminishing marginal productivity of capital, as he defined it, as a law of nature. He did not—we know now after the heated capital controversies of the 1950s and 1960s, "double-switching" and all that, he could not— prove this was the case, either by deducing it from more primitive assumptions or by verifying it empirically.

The authors who revived the model a half century later did so in quite a different spirit. They were careful to specify the strict though unrealistic assumptions necessary to derive the model, and they did not regard either the assumptions or the model as incontrovertible law. But neither did they regard their theory of growth as an exercise of no relevance to the real world. Their justification was the rough congruence between the theory's implications and the "stylized facts" of economic history. They could not and did not deny that other models might "explain" those same facts.

Clark did not discover a natural law or an ethical justification for the functional distribution of income in capitalist societies. But his model of production and distribution remains the approximation of first choice for very many economists when they are confronted with such practical problems as accounting for observed growth rates over time and between different nations (Denison, 1967 and 1974), or estimating the consequences of tax incentives for saving and investment (Summers, 1981) or of public deficits (Gramlich, 1984) or of pay-as-you-go social security (Feldstein, 1974).

Clark's system has a demand side, where marginal utility is supposed to play a role analogous to that of marginal productivity on the supply side. Clark has been credited with independent discovery of marginal utility, a claim of which Paul Samuelson said, "To learn *for yourself* a new theory ten years or more after it has been widely published is to invite from the jury an indictment for negligence rather than an award for brilliance" (1967, p. 18). Clark's version does gain some original twists by recognizing that a given commodity might be a package of several different "utilities" provided in different proportions by other commodities. The idea is awkwardly suggestive of later formulations (Strotz, 1957 and Lancaster, 1966) where utility is generated by characteristics possessed by commodities rather than directly by the commodities.

Clark's utility theory is inadequate for his system because it does not encompass future consumption and does not explain saving. The size of the permanent fund of capital in the stationary state is left hanging in the air. Clark criticizes "waiting" and "abstinence" as theories of interest by pointing out that no waiting is needed to obtain the consumable product of capital in the stationary equilibrium. That is true, but only because the saving to build up the stock has already been done, and of course because saving is by definition zero in the equilibrium. Why don't consumers try to eat up the fund? Had Clark applied here his "mobility without motion" insight regarding equilibrium, he would have seen that he was missing one of the scissor blades necessary to have a theory of interest. As it is, he is left without a platform from which to comment on Böhm-Bawerk and other participants in the controversies of the day regarding the sources of interest incomes.

B Fisher: General Equilibrium with Intertemporal Choices and Opportunities

Throughout his career Fisher was fascinated by the same set of problems that engaged Clark. Fisher came back to them repeatedly. He attacked them in a more elegant, abstract, mathematical, general, and ethically neutral manner than Clark or Böhm-Bawerk, and at the same time in a clearer, simpler, and more insightful way than Walras. His first try was *Appreciation and Interest* (1896). This was Fisher's second substantial professional publication in economics. He returned to the subjects in 1906, 1907, and finally in 1930.

Fisher's first contribution to economics was his doctoral dissertation (1892). This is a masterly exposition of Walrasian general equilibrium theory. Fisher, who was meticulous about acknowlegments throughout his career, writes in the preface that he was unaware of Walras while writing the dissertation. His personal mentors in the literature of economics were Jevons (1871) and Auspitz and Lieben (1889).

The book describes the ingenious physical model noted above, which makes Fisher a precursor of a current Yale professor, Herbert Scarf (1973), and other practitioners of computing general equilibrium solutions. Fisher was greatly impressed by the formal analogies between the thermodynamics of his mentor Gibbs and economic systems, and he was able to apply Gibbs's innovations in vector calculus.

Fisher expounds thoroughly the mathematics of utility functions and their maximization, and he is careful to allow for corner solutions. He uses independent and additive utilities of commodities in his physical model; later he was to show how this assumption could be exploited to measure marginal utilities empirically (1927). But the general formulation in his dissertation makes the utility of every commodity depend on the quantities consumed of all commodities. At the same time, he states clearly that neither interpersonally comparable utility nor cardinal utility for each individual is necessary to the determination of equilibrium. Fisher's list of the limitations of his analysis is candid and complete. The supply side of Fisher's model is, as he acknowleges, primitive. Each commodity is produced at increasing marginal cost, but neither factor supplies and prices nor technologies are explicitly modeled.

Finally, Fisher provides in appendices a survey and bibliography of applications of mathematical method to economics. From this beginning to his participation as elder statesman in 1933 in the founding of the Econometric Society, Fisher was a crusader for this methodological cause.

Fisher's general equilibrium system did not encompass capital and interest, but he attacked the subject soon after. His first contribution, one that should not be underestimated, was to get straight the concepts and accounting. This he did in 1896 and 1906 with clarity and completeness that have scarcely been improved upon. It's all there: continuous and discrete compounding; nominal v. real rates; the distinction between high prices and rising prices, and its implications for observations of interest rates; the inevitable differences among rates computed in different *numeraires*; rates to different maturities and consistency among them; appreciation, expected and unexpected; present values of streams of in- and out-payments; and so on. Schumpeter calls this work "the first economic theory of accounting" and says "it is (or should be) the basis of modern income analysis" (1954, p. 872).

Perhaps the most remarkable feature is Fisher's insistence that "income" is consumption, including of course consumption of the services of durable goods. In principle, he says, income is psychic, the subjective utility yielded by goods and services consumed. More practically, income could be measured as the money value, or value in some other *numeraire*, of the goods and services directly yielding utility, but only of those. Receipts saved and invested, for example in the purchase of new durable goods, are not "income" for Fisher; they will yield consumption and utility later, and those yields will be income. To include both the initial investment and the later yields as income is, according to Fisher, as absurd as to count both flour and bread in reckoning net output. This view naturally led Fisher to oppose conventional income taxation as double taxing of saving, and to favor consumption taxation instead. His views on these matters are loudly echoed today.

Fisher published his theory of the determination of interest rates in *The Rate of Interest* (1906). A revised and enlarged version was published in 1930 as *The Theory of Interest*. One motivation for the revision was that Fisher's many critics apparently did not understand the 1906 version. They typically concentrated on the "impatience" side of Fisher's theory of intertemporal allocation and missed the "opportunities" side. It was there in 1906 already; the theory is much the same in both versions.

In 1930 Fisher is at pains to label his theory the "impatience and opportunity" theory. "Every essential part of it," he acknowleges, "was at least foreshadowed by John Rae in 1834." He does claim originality for his concept of "investment opportunity." This turns on "the rate of return over cost, [where] both cost and return are differences between two optional income streams" (1930, p. ix). As Keynes acknowledged, this is the same as his own "marginal efficiency of capital" (1936, p. 140).

In these books Fisher extended general equilibrium theory to intertemporal choices and relationships. His strategy was different from Walras's. Walras tried to extend his multi-commodity multi-agent model of exchange to allow for production, saving, and investment. This maintained his stance of full generality but was also difficult to expound and to understand. Fisher saw that intertemporal dependences were tricky enough to justify isolating them from the inter-commodity complexities that had concerned him in his doctoral thesis. Therefore he proceeded as if there were just one aggregate commodity to be produced and consumed at different dates. This simplification enabled him to illuminate the subject more brightly than Walras himself.

The methodology of Fisher's capital theory is very modern. His clarifications of the concepts of capital and income lead him to formulate the problem as determination of the time paths of consumption—that is, income—both for individual agents and for the whole economy. Then he divides the problem into the two sides, tastes and technologies, that are second nature to theorists today. One need only read Böhm-Bawerk's murky mixture of the two in his list of reasons for the agio of future over present consumption to realize that Fisher's procedure was not instinctive in those times.

Fisher's theory of individual saving is basically the standard model to this day. He stated clearly what we now call the "life cycle" model, explaining why individuals will generally prefer to smooth their consumption over time, whatever the time path of their expected receipts. But he was not dogmatic, and he allowed room for bequests and for precautionary saving. Where Fisher differed from later theorists, and especially from contemporary model-builders, was in his unwillingness to impose any assumed uniformity on the preferences (or expectations or "endowments"—the latter term was not familiar to him though the concept was) of the agents in his economies, and in his scruples against buying definite results by assuming tractable functional forms. In general, many of the advances claimed in present-day theory appear to depend on greater boldness in these respects.

On the side of technology, Fisher's approach was the natural symmetrical partner of his formulation of preferences, equally simple, abstract, and general. He assumed that the "investment opportunities" available to an individual (not necessarily the same for everybody) and to the society as a whole can be summarized in the terms on which consumption at any date can be traded, with "nature," for consumptions at other dates. In modern language, we would say that Fisher postulated intertemporal production possibility frontiers, properly convex in their arguments, consumptions at various dates.

All that remained for Fisher, then, was to assume complete intertemporal loan markets cleared by real interest rates, count equations, and show that in principle the equalities of saving and investment at every date determine all interest rates and the paths of consumption and production for all individuals and for the society. Like hundreds of mathematical theorists since, he set the problem up so that it conformed to a paradigm he knew, in this case the Walrasian paradigm of his own doctoral dissertation. A more rigorous proof of the existence of the equilibria Fisher was looking for came much later, from Arrow and Debreu (1954). As we know, the problems of infinity, whether agents are assumed to have infinite or finite horizons, are much more troublesome than Fisher imagined.

In any event, Fisher had an excellent vantage point from which to comment on the controversies over capital and interest raging in his day. His formulation of "investment opportunities" seems to allow for no factor of production one could call "capital" and enter as argument in a production function. For that matter, he doesn't explicitly model the role of labor in production either, or of land. Strangely, in Fisher's insistence that interest is *not* a cost of production, he seems to say that labor is the only cost, evidently because labor and labor alone is a source of disutility, the loss of utility from leisure, the opportunity cost of the consumption afforded by work. Proceeding in the same spirit, he postulates that, from a position of equality of present and planned future consumption a typical individual will require more extra future consumption than present consumption as compensation for extra work. The difference, the agio, is interest, whether or not it is a "cost." Fisher attributes the agio to "impatience," at the same time scorning the notion that interest is the cost of securing the services of a factor of production called "abstinence" or "waiting."

In the 1890s and 1900s Knut Wicksell, discovering marginal productivity independently of Clark, was modeling production as a function of labor and land inputs with the output also depending on the lags between those inputs and the harvests (1934, vol. I, pp. 144–66). Similarly Taussig amended marginal productivity theory to discount wages and rents for the interest over the lag from input to output (1939, vol. II, pp. 62–66). These are "Austrian" formulations, akin to Böhm-Bawerk's examples of trees and wine, in which time itself appears to be productive. Fisher rightly objects to any generalization that waiting longer increases output. His own intertemporal frontiers are, to be sure, sufficiently general to encompass such technologies. They can also accommodate Leontief input-output tables and Koopmans-Dantzig activity matrices with lags, Hayekian trianglular structures with inventories of intermediate goods in process, Solow technologies with durable goods and labor jointly yielding output contemporaneously or later. The only common denominator of these and other representations of technology is that they relate consumption opportunities at different dates to one another, though not necessarily always in the convex tradeoff terms Fisher assumed. There does not appear to be any summary scalar measure to which the productivity of a process is generally monotonically related, whether roundaboutness, average period of production, or replacement value of existing stocks of goods.

Fisher describes himself as an advocate of "impatience" as an explanation of interest, though he realizes there are two sides of the saving-investment market, and though he acknowledges that real interest rates can at times be zero or negative. He does appear to believe that in a stationary equilibrium with constant consumption streams, consumers will require positive interest, and that only those technologies and investment opportunities affording a "rate of return over cost" equal to this pure time preference rate would be used. He does not face up to Schumpeter's 1911 argument that in such a repetitive and riskless "circular flow" rational consumers would not care whether a marginal unit of consumption occurs today or tomorrow (1936, pp. 34–36). Like Böhm-Bawerk, Fisher appeals to the shortness and uncertainty of life as a reason for time preference. For life-cycle consumers, however, time preferences are entangled with age preferences, and it is hard to defend any generalization as to their net direction. Fair annuities take care of the uncertainty.

Both John Bates Clark and Irving Fisher enlarged and improved the neoclassical temple, as Schumpeter described the structure in the passage I quoted at the beginning. The importance and quality of their contributions to theories of general equilibrium, capital, and distribution are shown by their absorption into the corpus of theory and their continued usefulness to economists today. Fisher's contributions have proved the more durable, and the more useful as foundations for further advances in theory. On a remarkable range of topics, modern theorists adopt and build upon Fisherian ideas, sometimes unknowingly. Fisher's methodologies, not just his use of mathematics but his explicit formulations of problems as constrained optimizations, is the accepted style of present-day theorizing. Those are the reasons that, of the two giants of theory in the early days of American economics, Fisher is accorded in fuller measure the esteem of his successors.

4 Fisher as Monetary Theorist and Macroeconomist

Although it may be questioned whether theories of money and of business fluctuations, macroeconomics in modern jargon, are neoclassical, I shall conclude this essay with remarks on this branch of theory. Here too Irving Fisher was the major American theorist of the early decades of this century, indeed until the early 1930s. An account of Fisher the theorist would be incomplete without some reference to this part of his work. Here especially Fisher combined theorizing with empirical research, both historical and statistical. The problems he encountered led him to invent statistical and econometric methods—index numbers and distributed lags are important examples—to apply for the purposes at hand to the data he and his assistants compiled. (He even studied the turnover of cash and checking accounts of a sample of Yale students, professors, and employees.) But I leave it to others to report and appraise Fisher's econometric innovations and his empirical applications.

Money was a big subject in American economic literature in the nineteenth century, before Fisher came on the scene. The monetary events of the times—the inconvertible greenbacks issued during the Civil War, their redemption in gold in 1879, the demonetization of silver, the rapidly increasing importance of banks—stimulated research and controversy. Fisher's major treatise (1911) refers to works of Simon Newcomb (1885), Charles F. Dunbar (1901), Alexander Del Mar (1902), J. Laurence Laughlin (1903), Wesley C. Mitchell (1903), David Kinley (1904), and Edwin M. Kemmerer (1909).

Most of these are historical and empirical. In monetary theory, Fisher's most important predecessors are Newcomb (1835–1909), Del Mar (1836–1926), and Laughlin (1850–1933). Newcomb is a celebrated figure in American astronomy. He was also a mathematician and economist. He was one of the conservatives who shunned the Association in 1885, and most of his writings in economics were *laissez faire* propaganda. But he anticipated Fisher's Equation of Exchange and modeled the circular flows of goods and money that the equation summarizes (1885). Spiegel (1971) would cast him as America's first mathematical economist, but if that term is used in anything like its modern meaning the honor clearly belongs to Fisher.

Del Mar (1885) concluded, as did Fisher later, that money supply changes are wholly absorbed in prices after about ten years. His observations of transitional adjustments also anticipated Fisher in stressing the differences among individual prices in their rigidities, the relative stickiness of money wages, the cyclical movements of velocity due to changing expectations, and the roles of these phenomena in cyclical fluctuations. Del Mar was not an academic, but he was a great scholar, as his monumental work *A History of the Precious Metals* (1880, 1892) testifies.

Laughlin was the first of the series of distinguished monetary scholars and teachers at the University of Chicago. He was not an enthusiast for the quantity theory, largely because he saw that the money supply of any one nation was endogenous under the international gold standard (1903, 1905). Fisher saw the point and included it in his list of sources of variation of the American money supply, but he apparently thought the damage to his quantity theory was minor. Laughlin has recently been admiringly rediscovered (Girton and Roper, 1978).

For all its theory, statistics, and index numbers, *The Purchasing Power of Money* is a tract supporting Fisher's proposal for stabilizing the value of money. This came to be known as the "compensated dollar," the gold-exchange standard combined with a rule mandating periodic changes in the official buying and selling prices of gold inverse to changes in a designated commodity price index. In 1911 Fisher proposed that the gold price changes be uniform and synchronous in the currencies of all countries linked by fixed exchange parities, in proportional amounts related to an international price index. Later he was willing to accept as second best that the United States adopt the scheme on its own. Keynes proposed a similar but less formal rule for the United Kingdom (1923). The proposal is an early example of a policy *rule*, another Fisherian idea ahead of its time, more likely to be popular among economists today than it was with Fisher's contemporaries. Indeed some rules recently proposed are quite Fisherian, for example (Hall, 1985).

The "compensated dollar" is but one of several proposals Fisher advanced over the years for stabilizing price levels or mitigating the effects of their unforeseen variation. In the 1911 book he also writes favorably of the "tabular standard," which meant no more operationally than facilitating price-indexed contracts. In the 1920s he launched a crusade for 100% reserves against checkable deposits, culminating in *100% Money* (1935). This idea is also beginning to resurface in the 1980s as a preventive defense against the monetary hazards of bank failures. In Schumpeter's view, Fisher's zeal for monetary reforms lost him some of the attention and respect his scientific contributions to monetary economics deserved, and made him come across more monetarist than his own analysis and evidence justified (1954, pp. 872–73).

The Purchasing Power of Money is a monetarist book. Fisher asserts the quantity theory as earnestly and persuasively as Milton Friedman. There are two species of quantity theories. One is a simple implication of the "classical dichotomy." Since only relative prices and real endowments enter commodity and factor demand and supply functions, the solution values for real variables in a general equilibrium are independent of scalar variations of exogenous nominal quantities. Walras exploited this implication of general equilibrium theory. Surprisingly Fisher does not. In any case, it does not quite apply to a commodity-money system like the gold standard, which Fisher was analyzing. Fisher's theory is of the second kind, based on the demand for and supply of the particular nominal assets serving as media of exchange.

Starting from his Equation of Exchange, elaborated to distinguish the quantities M and M' of the two media currency and checking deposits and their separate velocities V and V', Fisher argues: that the real volume of money-using transactions T is exogenous; that the velocities are determined by institutions and habits and are independent of the other variables in the Equation; that the division of the currency supply, the monetary base in current terminology, between currency and bank reserves is stable and independent of the variables in the Equation; that banks are fully "loaned up" so that deposits M' are a stable multiple of reserves, determined by the prudence of banks and by regulation; that exogenous changes in currency supply itself are the principal source of shocks, which, given the preceding propositions, move price level P proportionately. The many qualifications for transitional adjustments are conscientiously presented, but the monetarist message is loud and clear.

The argument is familiar to modern readers, but certain features deserve notice:

(1) Fisher gives the most illuminating account available of the institutions and habits that generate the society's demand for transactions media relative to the volume of transactions. He rightly emphasizes the fact that, and the degree to which, receipts and payments are imperfectly synchronized. He seeks the determinants of velocity in such features of social and economic structure as the frequency of wage and bill payments and the degree of vertical integration of firms. His belief that these institutions change only slowly supports his contention that velocities are exogenous constants.

(2) Much ink has been spilled on the difference between Fisher's velocity approach to money demand and the Cambridge (England) "k" formulation. The latter, like Walras's *encaisse désiré*, directs attention to agents' portfolio decisions. To Fisher's critics that seems behavioral, while velocity is mechanical. The issue is overblown; the same phenomena can be described in either language. Fisher himself discusses hoarding. Fisher's explicit attention, in discussing economy-wide demand for circulating media in distinction to other stores of value, to the fact that money "at rest" soon takes "wing" to fly from one agent to another seems to me to be a merit of his approach.

(3) As already noted, Fisher resolved a question current in his day, whether banks' creation of deposit substitutes for currency should be regarded as increasing the velocity of basic money or as enlarging the supply of money. His choice of the latter course compels attention to the structure, behavior, and regulation of banks. He could not be expected to foresee that the proliferation of future candidates for designation as "money" would create the monetarist ambiguities we see today.

(4) Fisher's T covers all transactions, those for intermediate goods and financial assets as well as those for final goods counted in national product. His transactions velocity is correspondingly larger than circuit or income velocity. For the most part later writers have not followed his example. It is hard to attach meaning to the *real* volume of financial transactions, and therefore to see why a T that includes them should be

constant or exogenous with respect to the Equation. On the other hand, modern students of money demand tend simply to forget transactions other than those on final payments.

(5) Fisher ignores the possibility that other liquid assets can serve as imperfect substitutes for money holdings because they can be converted into means of payment as needed, though at some cost. Partly for this reason, he ignores interest rate effects on demand for transactions media. In his day there may have been more excuse for these omissions than there was later. But they are still surprising for an author who elsewhere pays so much attention to the effects of interest rates and opportunity costs on behavior.

The quantity theory by no means exhausts Fisher's ideas on macroeconomics. His views were much more subtle than straightforward monetarism, but they are scattered through his writings and not systematically integrated. Consider the following non-neutralities emphasized by Fisher:

(1) Although the famous "Fisher equation" for nominal interest, real interest, and inflation is frequently cited nowadays in support of complete and prompt pass-through of inflation into nominal interest rates, Fisher's view throughout his career was quite different. From (1899) on he believed, and confirmed by sophisticated empirical investigation, that such adjustment takes a very long time. In the interim, inflation would lower real rates, as nominal rates would adjust incompletely. The effect was symmetrical; he attributed the severity of the Great Depression to the high real rates resulting from price deflation. Moreover, Fisher was always quite explicit about the effects of these movements of real interest rates on real economic variables, including aggregate production and employment, and their role in business cycles.

(2) An assiduous scholar of price data, Fisher knew that some prices were more flexible than others, that money wages were on the sticky side of the spectrum, and that the imperfect flexibility of the price level meant that the T on the right-hand side of his Equation would absorb some of the variations of the left-hand side. In the early 1930s he came to a very modern position. Real variables like production and employment are independent of the level of prices, once the economy has adjusted to the level. But they are not independent of the rate of change of prices; they depend positively on the rate of inflation. He even calculated a "Phillips"

correlation between employment and inflation (1926). He was just one derivative short of the accelerationist position (Friedman, 1968); in a little more time he would have made that step, aware as he was of the difference between actual and expected inflation. Anyway, his policy conclusion was that stabilizing the price level would also stabilize the real economy.

(3) In the early 1930s, observing the catastrophes of the world around him, which he shared personally, Fisher came to quite a different theory of the business cycle from the simple monetarist version he had espoused earlier. This was his "debt-deflation theory of depression" (1932), summarized in the first volume of *Econometrica*, the organ of the international society he helped to found (1933). The essential features are that debt-financed Schumpeterian innovations fuel a boom, followed by a recession which can turn into depression by an unstable interaction between excessive real debt burdens and deflation. Note the contrast to the Pigou real balance effect, according to which price declines are the benign mechanism that restores full employment equilibrium. The realism is all on Fisher's side. This theory of Fisher's has room for the monetary and credit cycles of which he earlier complained, and for the perversely pro-cyclical real interest rate movements mentioned above. Fisher did not provide a formal model of his latter-day cycle theory, as he probably would have done at a younger age. The point here is that he came to recognize important non-monetary sources of disturbance. His practical message in the early 1930s was "Reflation!" He was right.

These insights contain the makings of a theory of the determination of economic activity, prices, and interest rates in short and medium runs. Moreover, in his neoclassical writings on capital and interest Fisher had laid the basis for the investment and saving equations central to modern macroeconomic models. Had Fisher pulled these strands together into a coherent theory, he could have been an American Keynes. Indeed the "neoclassical synthesis" would not have had to wait until after the Second World War. Fisher would have done it all himself.

Note

The assistance of Peter Mathews, a Yale economics graduate student, was invaluable to me in the preparation of this essay. I am deeply indebted to him, but the opinions expressed here are my own reponsibility and all errors are my fault, not his.

References

American Economic Association, "Report of the Organization of the American Economic Association," *Publications*, *1*, 1887

———, "Report of the Third Annual Meeting," *Publications*, *4*, 1889, 86

Arrow, Kenneth J. and Debreu, Gerard, "Existence of an Equilibrium for a Competitive Economy," *Econometrica*, July 1954, *22*, 265–290

Auspitz, Rudolf and Lieben, Richard, *Untersuchungen uber die Theorie des Preises*, Leipzig: Duncker und Humboldt, 1889

Clark, John Bates, *The Philosophy of Wealth*, Boston: Ginn & Co., 1886

———, "The Possibility of a Scientific Law of Wages," *Publications of the American Economic Association*, March 1889, *4*, 39–69

———, *The Distribution of Wealth*, New York: Macmillan, 1899

———, *The Control of Trusts*, New York: Macmillan, 1901. (Second enlarged edition with J. M. Clark, 1912)

———, *The Problem of Monopoly*, New York: Macmillan, 1904

Del Mar, Alexander, *A History of the Precious Metals*, London: George Bell, 1880, and New York: Cambridge Encyclopedia Co., 1902

———, *The Science of Money*, London: George Bell, 1885

Denison, Edward F., *Why Growth Rates Differ*, Washington: Brookings Institution, 1967

———, *Accounting for United States Economic Growth 1929–1969*, Washington: Brookings Institution, 1974

Dunbar, Charles F., *Theory and History of Banking*, second edition edited by O. M. W. Sprague, New York and London: G. P. Putnam, 1901

Fairchild, Fred R., Furniss, Edgar S., and Buck, Norman S., *Elementary Economics*, 2 vols., New York: Macmillan, first edition 1926, fifth edition 1948

Feldstein, Martin S., "Social Security, Induced Retirement, and Aggregate Capital Accumulation," *Journal of Political Economy*, September–October 1974, *82*, 905–26

Fisher, Irving, *Mathematical Investigations in the Theory of Value and Prices*, New Haven: Connecticut Academy of Arts and Sciences, *Transactions 9*, 1892 (Reprinted, New York: Augustus M. Kelley, 1961)

———, *Appreciation and Interest*, American Economic Association *Publications 11*, no. 4, 1896 (Reprinted, New York: Augustus M. Kelley, 1961)

———, *The Nature of Capital and Income*, New York: Macmillan, 1906

———, *The Rate of Interest*, New York: Macmillan, 1907

———, *Introduction to Economic Science*, New York: Macmillan, 1910

———, *The Purchasing Power of Money*, New York: Macmillan, 1911

———, *Elementary Principles of Economics*, New York: Macmillan, 1911

———, "Economists in Public Service," *American Economic Review*, March 1919, *9*, 5–21

———, "A Statistical Relation between Unemployment and Price Changes," *International Labour Review*, June 1926, *13*, 785–792

———, "A Statistical Method for Measuring 'Marginal Utility' and Testing the Justice of a Progressive Income Tax," in J. H. Hollander ed., *Economic Essays Contributed in Honor of John Bates Clark*, New York: Macmillan, 1927

———, *The Theory of Interest*, New York: Macmillan, 1930

———, *Booms and Depressions*, New York: Adelphi, 1932

———, "The Debt-Deflation Theory of Great Depressions," *Econometrica*, October 1933, *1*, 337–357

———, *100% Money*, New York: Adelphi, 1935

Friedman, Milton, "The Role of Monetary Policy," *American Economic Review*, March 1968, *48*, 1–17

Girton, Lance and Roper, Don, "J. Laurence Laughlin and the Quantity Theory of Money," *Journal of Political Economy*, August 1978, *86*, 599–626

Gramlich, Edward M., "How Bad Are the Large Deficits?" in Gregory B. Mills and John L. Palmer eds., *Federal Budget Policy in the 1980s*, Washington: The Urban Institute, 1984, 43–68

Hall, Robert E., "Monetary Policy with an Elastic Price Standard," in *Price Stability and Public Policy*, Federal Reserve Bank of Kansas City, 1985, 137–160

Harrod, Roy F., "An Essay in Dynamic Theory," *Economic Journal*, March 1939, *49*, 14–33

Homan, Paul T., *Contemporary Economic Thought*, New York: Harper, 1928

Jevons, William Stanley, *The Theory of Political Economy*, London: Macmillan, 1871

Kemmerer, Edwin M., *Money and Credit instruments in their Relation to General Prices*, New York: Holt, 1909

Keynes, John Maynard, *A Tract on Monetary Reform*, London: Macmillan, 1923

———, *The General Theory of Employment, Interest and Money*, New York: Harcourt Brace, 1936

Kinley, David, *Money*, New York: Macmillan, 1904

Lancaster, Kelvin, "A New Approach to Consumer Theory," *Journal of Political Economy*, April 1966, *74*, 132–157

Laughlin, J. Laurence, *Principles of Money*, New York: Scribner, 1903

———, "A Theory of Prices," *Publications of the American Economic Association*, February 1905, *6*, 66–83

Miller, John Perry, "Irving Fisher of Yale," in William Fellner *et al*, *Ten Economic Studies in the Tradition of Irving Fisher*, New York: Wiley, 1967, 1–16

Mitchell, Wesley C., *A History of the Greenbacks*, Chicago: University of Chicago Press, 1903

Newcomb, Simon, *Principles of Political Economy*, New York: Harper, 1886, 315–347

Rae, John, *The Sociological Theory of Capital*, 1834, reprinted New York: Macmillan, 1905

Samuelson, Paul A., "Irving Fisher and the Theory of Capital," in William Fellner *et al*, *Ten Economic Studies in the Tradition of Irving Fisher*, New York: Wiley, 1967, 17–38

Scarf, Herbert, *The Computation of Economic Equilibria*, New Haven: Yale University Press, 1973

Schumpeter, Joseph A., *Theory of Economic Development*, translated from German edition 1911 by R. Opie, Cambridge: Harvard University Press, 1934

———, *History of Economic Analysis*, edited by Elizabeth B. Schumpeter, New York: Oxford University Press, 1954

Social Sciences Citation Index, *Five Year Cumulation*, 1971–75 and 1976–80, Philadelphia: Institute for Scientific Information, 1979 and 1983

Solow, Robert M., "A Contribution to the Theory of Economic Growth," *Quarterly Journal of Economics*, February 1956, *70*, 65–94

———, *Growth Theory: An Exposition*, Oxford: Oxford University Press, 1969

Spiegel, Henry W., *The Growth of Economic Thought*, Englewood Cliffs: Prentice-Hall, 1971

Stigler, George J., "Stuart Wood and the Marginal Productivity Theory," *Quarterly Journal of Economics*, August 1947, *61*, 640–49

Strotz, Robert H., "The Empirical Implications of a Utility Tree," *Econometrica*, April 1957, *25*, 269–280

Summers, Lawrence H., "Taxation and Corporate Investment: A q-Theory Approach," *Brookings Papers on Economic Activity*, 1:1981, 67–127

Taussig, Frank W., *Principles of Economics*, first edition 1911, fourth edition, New York: Macmillan, 1939

Thunen, John Heinrich von, *Der isolierte Staat in Beziehung auf Landwirtshaft ynd Nationalokonomie*, vol. 1, Hamburg: Perthes, 1826

Wicksell, Knut, *Lectures on Political Economy*, translated by E. Classen from the second Swedish edition 1911, London: George Routledge & Sons, 1934

Wood, Stuart, "The Theory of Wages," *Publications of the American Economic Association*, *4*, 1889, 5–35

CHAPTER 28

IRVING FISHER

Irving Fisher was born in Saugerties, New York, on 27 February 1867; he was residing in New Haven, Connecticut at the time of his death in a New York City hospital on 29 April 1947.

Fisher is widely regarded as the greatest economist America has produced. A prolific, versatile and creative scholar, he made seminal and durable contributions across a broad spectrum of economic science. Although several earlier Americans, notably Simon Newcomb, had used some mathematics in their writings, Fisher's dedication to the method and his skill in using it justify calling him America's first mathematical economist. He put his early training in mathematics and physics to work in his doctoral dissertation on the theory of general equilibrium. Throughout his career his example and his teachings advanced the application of quantitative method not only in economic theory but also in statistical inquiry. He, together with Ragnar Frisch and Charles F. Roos, founded the Econometric Society in 1930; and Fisher was its first President. He had been President of the American Economic Association in 1918.

Much of standard neoclassical theory today is Fisherian in origin, style, spirit and substance. In particular, most modern models of capital and interest are essentially variations on Fisher's theme, the conjunction of intertemporal choices and opportunities. Likewise, his theory of money and prices is the foundation for much of contemporary monetary economics.

Fisher also developed methodologies of quantitative empirical research. He was the greatest expert of all time on index numbers, on their theo-

---

Reprinted by permission from *The New Palgrave*, Vol. 2, eds. John Eatwell et al., London: Macmillan Press, Ltd., 1987, pp. 369–376. Much of this chapter repeats parts of Chapter 27. Both chapters are reprinted in full nevertheless, in order to preserve the integrity of each essay. The essay was reprinted in *New Palgrave Capital Theory*, eds. John Eatwell et al., New York: Norton, 1991, pp. 161–177.

retical and statistical properties and on their use in many countries throughout history. From 1923 to 1936, his own Index Number Institute manufactured and published price indexes of many kinds from data painstakingly collected from all over the world. Indefatigable and innovative in empirical research, Fisher was an early and regular user of correlations, regressions and other statistical and econometric tools that later became routine.

To this day Fisher's successors are often rediscovering, consciously or unconsciously, Fisher's ideas and building upon them. He can be credited with distributed lag regression, life cycle saving theory, the "Phillips curve," the case for taxing consumption rather than "income," the modern quantity theory of money, the distinction between real and nominal interest rates, and many more standard tools in economists' kits. Although Fisher was not fully appreciated by his contemporaries, today he leads other old-timers by wide and increasing margins in journal citations. In column inches in the *Social Sciences Citation Index* (1979, 1983), Fisher led his most famous contemporaries, Wesley Mitchell, J. B. Clark, and F. W. Taussig in that order, by rough ratios $5:3:1:1$ in 1971–75 and $9:3:1:1$ in 1976–80. Much more than the others, moreover, Fisher is cited for substance rather than for history or thought.

For all his scientific prowess and achievement, Fisher was by no means an "ivory tower" scholar detached from the problems and policy issues of his times. He was a congenital reformer, an inveterate crusader. He was so aggressive and persistent, and so sure he was right, that many of his contemporaries regarded him as a "crank" and discounted his scientific work accordingly. Science and reform were indeed often combined in Fisher's work. His economic findings, theoretical and empirical, would suggest to him how to better the world; or dissatisfaction with the state of the world would lead him into scientifically fruitful analysis and research. Fisher's search for conceptual clarity about "the nature of capital and income" led him not only to lay the foundations of modern social accounting but also to argue that income taxation wrongly puts saving in double jeopardy. Fisher turned his talents to monetary theory because he suspected that economic instability was largely the fault of existing monetary institutions. His "debt-deflation theory of depression" was motivated by the disasters the Great Depression visited upon the world.

Economics was not the only aspect of human and social life that engaged Fisher's reformist zeal. He was active and prolific in other causes:

temperance and Prohibition; vegetarianism, fresh air, exercise and other aspects or personal hygiene; eugenics; and peace through international association of nations.

Fisher was an amazingly prolific and gifted writer. The bibliography compiled by his son lists some 2000 titles authored by Fisher, plus another 400 signed by his associates or written by others about him. Fisher's writings span all his interests and causes. They include scholarly books and papers, articles and popular media, textbooks, handbooks for students, tracts, pamphlets, speeches and letters to editors and statesmen. They include the weekly releases of index numbers, often supplemented by commentary on the economic outlook and policy, issued for thirteen years by Fisher and assistants from the Index Number Institute housed in his New Haven home.

Fisher was the consummate pedagogical expositor, always clear as crystal. He hardly ever wrote just for fellow experts. His mission was to educate and persuade the world. He took the trouble to lead the uninitiated through difficult material in easy stages. Whenever he was teaching or tutoring students, he wrote handbooks or texts for their benefit—in mathematics and science when he was still a student himself, in the principles of economics when he was the professor responsible for the introductory course. Fisher's economics text was published in 1910 and 1911. Its graceful exposition of sophisticated theoretical material will impress a modern connoisseur, but it was too difficult for widespread adoption. Some of it survived in a leading introductory text of the 1920s and 1930s, by the younger Yale economists Fairchild, Furniss and Buck (1926).

A Brief Biography

Irving Fisher grew up and attended school successively in Peace Dale, Rhode Island; New Haven, Connecticut; and St Louis, Missouri. His father, a Congregational minister, died of tuberculosis just when Irving had finished high school and was planning to attend Yale College, his father's *alma mater*. Irving was now the principal breadwinner for himself, his mother and his younger brother. He did have a $500 legacy from his father for his college education. The family moved to New Haven, and together managed to make ends meet. Irving tutored fellow students during term and in summers.

Fisher was a great success in Yale College, ranking first in his class and winning prizes and distinctions not only in mathematics but across the board. He was also determined to make good in the extra-curricular college culture so important in those days. His efforts won him election to the most prestigious secret senior society, Skull and Bones, the ultimate reward senior campus leaders bestowed on members of the class behind them.

Awarded a scholarship for graduate study, he stayed on at Yale. Graduate Studies were not departmentalized in those days, and Fisher ranged over mathematics, science, social science and philosophy. His most important teachers were Josiah Willard Gibbs, the mathematical physicist celebrated for his theory of thermodynamics, William Graham Sumner, famous still in sociology but at the time also important in political economy, and Arthur Twining Hadley, a leading economist specializing in what is now known as Industrial Organization.

As the time to write a dissertation approached, Fisher had still not chosen his life work. Young Fisher's interests and talents were universal. In the seven years at Yale before he finished his doctorate, he had written and published poetry, political commentary, book reviews, a geometry text together with tables of logarithms, and voluminous notes on mathematics, mechanics and astronomy for the benefit of students he was teaching or tutoring. If he had specialized in anything in six years at Yale, it was mathematics, but even in his graduate years he had spent half his time elsewhere.

Sumner put him on to mathematical economics, and in his third year of graduate study, he finished the dissertation that won him worldwide recognition in economic theory. Fisher's 1891 PhD was the first one in pure economics awarded by Yale, albeit by the faculty of mathematics. Although the university, thanks to Sumner, Hadley and Henry W. Farnum, was strong in "political economy," there was no distinct department for the subject, let alone for "economics." This was generally the case in American universities. Venturing into mathematical economic theory, Fisher was very much on his own; and his route into economics was quite different from that of most American economists of his era.

The dominant tradition in American political economy was imported from the English classical economists, mainly Smith, Ricardo and John Stuart Mill; it was just beginning to be updated by Marshall. This tradition Fisher's mentors at Yale had taught him well. But the neoclassical developments on the European continent from 1870 on, the works of Walras and Menger and Böhm-Bawerk, or even those of their English counterparts Jevons and Edgeworth, had been little noticed at Yale or elsewhere in America.

At the time, the main challenge in America to classical political economy was coming from quite a different direction. The American Economic Association was founded in 1886 by young rebels against Ricardian dogma and its *laissez-faire* political and social message. They included Richard T. Ely, J. B. Clark, Edwin R. A. Seligman and other future luminaries of American economics. Many of them had pursued graduate studies in Germany. In the German emphasis on historical, institutional and empirical studies they found welcome relief from implacable classical theory, and in the German faith in the state as an instrument of socially beneficial reform they found a hopeful antidote to the fatalism of economic competition and social Darwinism. Sumner was prominent among several elders who refused to join an Association born of such heresy; he did not relent even though the AEA very soon became sufficiently neutral and catholic to attract his Yale colleagues and other initial holdouts. Fisher, a bit younger than the founding rebels and educated solely at one American university, was not involved. It was his reconstruction, rather than their revolution, that was destined eventually to replace the classical tradition in the mainstream of American economics.

Fisher stayed at Yale throughout his career. He started teaching mathematics, evidently even before he received his doctorate and was appointed Tutor in Mathematics. His first economics teaching was under the auspices of the mathematics faculty, an undergraduate course on "The Mathematical Theory of Prices." In 1894-5 during his Wanderjahr in Europe, this young American star was welcomed by the leading mathematically inclined theorists in every country. On his return he became Assistant Professor of Political and Social Science and began teaching economics proper. He was appointed full Professor in 1898 and retired in 1935.

Fisher was struck by tuberculosis in 1898. He spent the first three years of his professorship on leave from Yale and from science, recuperating in more salubrious climates. His lifelong crusade for hygienic living dates from this personal struggle to regain health and vigour. The experience powerfully reinforced his determination to gain "a place among those who have helped along my science" and his ambition "to be a *great man*," as he wrote to his wife (I. N. Fisher, 1956, pp. 87–8). After his recovery the books and articles began flowing from his pen, never to stop until his death at the age of 80.

Fisher participated actively in teaching and in university affairs until 1920. Thereafter his writings and his myriad outside activities and crusades preoccupied him. He taught only half time and had little impact on students, undergraduate or graduate. Thus Fisher had few personal disciples; there was no Fisherian School. The student to whom Fisher was closest, personally and intellectually, was James Harvey Rogers, a 1916 PhD who returned to Yale as a professor in 1930. His career was prematurely ended by his tragic death in a plane crash in 1939 at the age of 55.

Fisher was, on top of everything else, an inventor. His most successful and profitable invention was the visible card index system he patented in 1913. In 1925 Fisher's own firm, the Index Visible Company, merged with its principal competitor to form Kardex Rand Co., later Remington Rand, still later Sperry Rand. The merger made him wealthy. However, he subsequently lost a fortune his son estimated to amount to 8 or 10 million dollars, along with savings of his wife and her sister, when he borrowed money to exercise rights to buy additional Rand shares in the bull market of the late 1920s.

More than money was at risk in the market. Fisher had staked his public reputation as an economic pundit by his persistent optimism about the economy and stock prices, even after the 1929 crash. His reputation crashed too, especially among non-economists in New Haven, where the university had to buy his house and rent it to him to save him from eviction. Until the 1950s the name Irving Fisher was without honour in his own university. Except for economic theorists and econometricians, few members of the community appreciated the genius of a man who lived among them for 63 years.

Irving Fisher's marriage to Margaret Hazard in 1893 was a very happy one for 47 years. She died in 1940. They had two daughters and one son, his father's biographer. The death of their daughter Margaret in 1919 after a nervous breakdown was the greatest tragedy of her parents' lives. Their daughter Carol brought them two grandchildren.

General Equilibrium Theory

Fisher's doctoral dissertation (1892) is a masterly exposition of Walrasian general equilibrium theory. Fisher, who was meticulous about acknowledgements throughout his career, writes in the preface that he was unaware of Walras while writing the dissertation. His personal mentors in the literature of economics were Jevons (1871) and Auspitz and Lieben (1889).

Fisher's inventive ingenuity combined with his training under Gibbs to produce a remarkable hydraulic-mechanical analogue model of a general equilibrium system, replete with cisterns, valves, levers, balances and cams. Thus could he display physically how a shock to demand or supply in one of ten interrelated markets altered prices and quantities in all markets and changed the incomes and consumption bundles of the various consumers. The model is described in detail in the book; unfortunately both the original model and a second one constructed in 1925 have been lost to posterity. Anyway Fisher was a precursor of a current Yale professor, Herbert Scarf (1973) and other practitioners of computing general equilibrium solutions. In his formal mathematical model-building too, Fisher was greatly impressed by the analogies between the thermodynamics of his mentor Gibbs and economic systems, and he was able to apply Gibbs's innovations in vector calculus.

Fisher expounds thoroughly the mathematics of utility functions and their maximization, and he is careful to allow for corner solutions. He uses independent and additive utilities of commodities in his first mathematical approximation and in his physical model; later he was to show how this assumption could be exploited to measure marginal utilities empirically (1927). But the general formulation in his dissertation makes the utility of every commodity depend on the quantities consumed of all commodities. At the same time, he states clearly that neither interpersonally comparable utility nor cardinal utility for each individual is necessary to the determination of equilibrium. Fisher's list of the limitations of his analysis is candid and complete. The supply side of Fisher's model is, as he acknowledges, primitive. Each commodity is produced at increasing marginal cost, but neither factor supplies and prices nor technologies are explicitly modelled.

Finally, Fisher shows his enthusiasm for his discovery of mathematical economics by appending to his dissertation as published an exhaustive survey and bibliography of applications of mathematical method to economics.

General Equilibrium with Intertemporal Choices and Opportunities

The distribution of income and wealth, and in particular the sources, determinants and social rationales, of interest and other returns to private property, were obsessive topics in economics, both in Europe and North America, at the turn of the century. One important reason, especially in Europe, was the Marxist challenge to the legitimacy of property income. Answering Marx was a strong motivation for the Austrian school, in particular for the capital theory of Böhm-Bawerk and his followers. Neoclassical economics was in a much better position than its classical precursor to respond to the Marxist challenge. The labour theory of value, which Marx borrowed from the great classical economists themselves, neither explains nor justifies functionally or ethically incomes other than wages.

These topics engaged the two leading American economists of the era, John Bates Clark and Fisher. Clark (1899) set forth his marginal productivity theory of distribution, arguing that a generalized factor of production, capital, the accumulation of past savings, has like labour a marginal product that explains and justifies the incomes of its owners.

Fisher attacked these problems in a more elegant, abstract, mathematical, general and ethically neutral manner than Clark, and than Böhm-Bawerk. At the same time, his approach was clearer, simpler and more insightful than that of Walras.

The general equilibrium system of Fisher's dissertation was a single-period model. No intertemporal choices entered; hence the theory was silent on the questions of capital and interest. But Fisher took up these subjects soon after.

His first contribution, one that should not be underestimated, was to set straight the concepts and the accounting. This he did in (1896) and (1906) with clarity and completeness that have scarcely been surpassed. It is all there: continuous and discrete compounding; nominal versus real rates; the distinction between high prices and rising prices, and its implications for observations of interest rates; the inevitable differences among rates computed in different *numéraires*; rates to different maturities and consistency among them; appreciation, expected and unexpected; present values of streams of in- and out-payments; and so on. Schumpeter calls this work "the first economic theory of accounting" and says "it is (or should be) the basis of modern income analysis" (1954, p. 872).

Perhaps the most remarkable feature is Fisher's insistence that "income" is consumption, including of course consumption of the services of durable goods. In principle, he says, income is psychic, the subjective utility yielded by goods and services consumed. More practically, income could be measured as the money value, or value in some other *numéraire*, of the goods and services directly yielding utility, but only of those. Receipts saved and invested, for example in the purchase of new durable goods, are not "income" for Fisher; they will yield consumption and utility later, and those yields will be income. To include both the initial investment and the later yields as income is, according to Fisher, as absurd as to count both flour and bread in reckoning net output. This view naturally led Fisher to oppose conventional income taxation as double taxing of saving, and to favour consumption taxation instead. His views on these matters are loudly echoed today.

Fisher published his theory of the determination of interest rates in *The Rate of Interest* (1907). A revised and enlarged version was published in 1930 as *The Theory of Interest*. One motivation for the revision was that Fisher's many critics apparently did not understand the 1907 version. They typically concentrated on the "impatience" side of Fisher's theory of intertemporal allocation and missed the "opportunities" side. It was there in 1907 already; the theory is much the same in both versions.

In 1930 Fisher is at pains to label his theory the "impatience and opportunity" theory. "Every essential part of it," he acknowledges, "was at least foreshadowed by John Rae in 1834." He does claim originality for his concept of "investment opportunity." This turns on "the rate of return over cost, [where] both cost and return are differences between two optional income streams" (1930, p. ix). As Keynes acknowledged, this is the same as his own "marginal efficiency of capital" (Keynes, 1936, p. 140).

In these books Fisher extended general equilibrium theory to intertemporal choices and relationships. This strategy was different from Walras. Walras tried to extend his multi-commodity multi-agent model of exchange to allow for production, saving and investment. This maintained his stance of full generality but was also difficult to expound and to understand. Fisher saw that intertemporal dependences were tricky enough to justify isolating them from the intercommodity complexities that had concerned him in his doctoral thesis. Therefore he proceeded as if there were just one aggregate commodity to be produced and consumed at different dates. This simplification enabled him to illuminate the subject more brightly than Walras himself.

The methodology of Fisher's capital theory is very modern. His clarifications of the concepts of capital and income lead him to formulate the problem as determination of the time paths of consumption—that is, income—both for individual agents and for the whole economy. Then he divides the problem into the two sides, tastes and technologies, that are second nature to theorists today. One need only read Böhm-Bawerk's murky mixture of the two in his list of reasons for the agio of future over present consumption to realize that Fisher's procedure was not instinctive in those times.

Fisher's theory of individual saving is basically the standard model to this day. Undergraduates learn the two-period "Fisher diagram," where a family of indifference curves in the two commodities consumption now c_1 and consumption later c_2 confront a budget constraint $c_1 + c_2/(1+r) = y_1 + y_2/(1+r)$, where the y's are exogenous wage incomes in the two periods and r is the (real) market interest rate. From the usual tangency can be read the consumption choices and present saving or dissaving. This is indeed a Fisher diagram, but of course he went much beyond it.

He stated clearly what we now call the "life cycle" model, explaining why individuals will generally prefer to smooth their consumption over time, whatever the time path of their expected receipts. But he was not dogmatic, and he allowed room for bequests and for precautionary saving. Where Fisher differed from later theorists, and especially from contemporary model-builders, was in his unwillingness to impose any assumed uniformity on the preferences (or expectations or "endowments"—the latter term was not familiar to him though the concept was) of the agents in his economies, and in his scruples against buying definite results by assuming tractable functional forms. In general, many of the advances claimed in present-day theory appear to depend on greater boldness in these respects.

On the side of technology, Fisher's approach was the natural symmetrical partner of his formulation of preferences, equally simple, abstract and general. He assumed that the "investment opportunities" available to an individual (not necessarily the same for everybody) and to the society as a whole can be summarized in the terms on which consumption at any date can be traded, with "nature," for consumptions at other dates. In modern language, we would say that Fisher postulated intertemporal production possibility frontiers, properly convex in their arguments, for consumptions at various dates.

All that remained for Fisher, then, was to assume complete intertemporal loan markets cleared by real interest rates, count equations, and show that in principle the equalities of saving and investment at every date determine all interest rates and the paths of consumption and production for all individuals and for the society. Like hundreds of mathematical theorists since, he set the problem up so that it conformed to a paradigm he knew, in this case the Walrasian paradigm of his own doctoral dissertation. A more rigorous proof of the existence of the equilibria Fisher was looking for came much later, from Arrow and Debreu (1954). As we know, the problems of infinity, whether agents are assumed to have infinite or finite horizons, are much more troublesome than Fisher imagined.

In any event, Fisher had an excellent vantage point from which to comment on the controversies over capital and interest raging in his day. His formulation of "investment opportunities" seems to allow for no factor of production one could call "capital" and enter as argument in a production function. For that matter, he doesn't explicitly model the role of labour in production either, or of land. Strangely, in Fisher's insistence that interest is *not* a cost of production, he seems to say that labour is the only cost, evidently because labour and labour alone is a source of disutility: the loss of utility from leisure being the opportunity cost of the consumption afforded by work. Proceeding in the same spirit, he postulates that, from a position of equality of present and planned future consumption a typical individual will require more extra future consumption than present consumption as compensation for extra work. The difference, the agio, is interest, whether or not it is a "cost." Fisher attributes the agio to "impatience," at the same time scorning the notion that interest is the cost of securing the services of a factor of production called "abstinence" or "waiting."

In the 1890s and 1900s Knut Wicksell, discovering marginal productivity independently of Clark, was modelling production as a function of labour and land inputs with the output also depending on the lags between those inputs and the harvests (Wicksell [1911], 1934, vol. I, pp. 144–66). This is an "Austrian" formulation, akin to Böhm-Bawerk's examples of trees and wine, in which time itself appears to be productive. Fisher rightly objects to any generalization that waiting longer increases output. His own intertemporal frontiers are, to be sure, sufficiently general to encompass such technologies. They can also accommodate Leontief input–output tables and Koopmans–Dantzig activity matrices with lags, Hayekian triangular structures with inventories of intermediate goods in process, Solow technologies with durable goods and labour jointly yielding output contemporaneously or later. The only common denominator of these and other representations of technology is that they relate consumption opportunities at different dates to one another, though not necessarily always in the convex trade-off terms Fisher assumed. There does not appear to be any summary scalar measure to which the productivity of a process is generally monotonically related, whether roundaboutness, average period of production, or replacement value of existing stocks of goods.

Fisher describes himself as an advocate of "impatience" as an explanation of interest, although he realizes there are two sides of the saving-investment market, and although he acknowledges that real interest rates can at times be zero or negative. He does appear to believe that in a stationary equilibrium with constant consumption streams, consumers will require positive interest, and that only those technologies and investment opportunities affording a "rate of return over cost" equal to this pure time preference rate would be used. He does not face up to Schumpeter's argument in 1911 that in such a repetitive and riskless "circular flow," rational consumers would not care whether a marginal unit of consumption occurs today or tomorrow (Schumpeter [1912], 1934, pp. 34–6). Like Böhm-Bawerk, Fisher appeals to the shortness and uncertainty of life as a reason for time preference. For life-cycle consumers, however, time preferences are entangled with age preferences, and it is hard to defend any generalization as to their net direction. Fair annuities take care of the uncertainty.

Monetary Theory: The Equation of Exchange and the Quantity Theory

Irving Fisher was the major American monetary economist of the early decades of this century; the subject occupied him until the end of his career. Here especially Fisher combined theorizing with empirical research, both historical and statistical. The problems he encountered led him to invent statistical and econometric methods—index numbers and distributed lags in particular—to apply for the purposes at hand to the data he and his assistants compiled. (He even studied the turnover of cash and checking accounts of a sample or Yale students, professors and employees.)

Money was a big subject in American economic literature in the 19th century, before Fisher came on the scene. The monetary events of the times—the inconvertible greenbacks issued during the Civil War, their redemption in gold in 1879, the demonetization of silver, the rapidly increasing importance of banks—stimulated research and controversy. Nevertheless, monetary theory was relatively undeveloped and unsystematized, both in Europe and in America. Fisher's treatise (1911a) was an ambitious attempt to organize with the help of theory a large body of historical and institutional information.

Yet for all its theory, statistics and index numbers, *The Purchasing Power of Money* is a tract supporting Fisher's proposal for stabilizing the value of money. This came to be known as the "compensated dollar," the gold-exchange standard combined with a rule mandating periodic changes in the official buying and selling prices of gold inverse to changes in a designated commodity price index. In 1911 Fisher proposed that the gold price changes be uniform and synchronous in the currencies of all countries linked by fixed exchange parities, in proportional amounts related to an international price index. Later he was willing to accept as second best that the United States adopt the scheme on its own. Keynes proposed a similar but less formal rule for the United Kingdom (1923).

The proposal is an early example of a policy *rule*, another Fisherian idea ahead of its time, more likely to be popular among economists today than it was with Fisher's contemporaries. Indeed, some rules recently proposed are quite Fisherian, for example Hall (1985).

The "compensated dollar" is but one of several proposals Fisher advanced over the years for stabilizing price levels or mitigating the effects of their unforeseen variation. In the 1911 book he also writes favourably of the "tabular standard," which meant no more operationally than facilitating price-indexed contracts. In the 1920s he launched a crusade for 100 percent reserves against checkable deposits, culminating in *100% Money* (1935). This idea is also beginning to resurface in the 1980s as a preventive defence against the monetary hazards of bank failures. In Schumpeter's view, Fisher's zeal for monetary reforms lost him some of the attention and respect his scientific contributions to monetary economics deserved, and made him come across as more monetarist than his own analysis and evidence justified (Schumpeter, 1954, pp. 872–3).

The Purchasing Power of Money is a monetarist book. Fisher asserts the quantity theory as earnestly and persuasively as Milton Friedman. There are two species of quantity theories. One is a simple implication of the "classical dichotomy": since only relative prices and real endowments enter commodity and factor demand and supply functions, the solution values for real variables in a general equilibrium are independent of scalar variations of exogenous nominal quantities. While Fisher mentions this implication of general equilibrium theory, he does not dwell upon it as one might expect. Anyway, it does not quite apply to a commodity-money system like the gold standard, which Fisher was analysing. Fisher's theory is mainly of the second kind, based on the demand for and supply of the particular nominal assets serving as media of exchange.

Fisher is usually given credit for the Equation of Exchange, although Simon Newcomb, a celebrated figure in American astronomy as well as an economist, had anticipated him (1885, pp. 315–47). The Equation is the identity $MV = PT$, where M is the stock of money; V its velocity, the average number of times per year a dollar of the stock changes hands; P is the average price of the considerations traded for money in such transactions; and T is the physical volume per year of those considerations. It is an identity because it is in principle true by definition. Actually Fisher, of course, recognized the heterogeneity of transactions by writing also $MV = \Sigma p_i Q_i$, where the p_i and Q_i are individual prices and quantities. His interest in index numbers was substantially a quest for aggregate indexes P and T derived from the individual p_i and Q_i in such a way that the two forms of the equation would be consistent. Much of the book (1911a), both text and technical appendices, is devoted to this quest.

Here and in later writings, particularly (1921) and (1922), Fisher was looking for the "best" index number formula. He postulated certain criteria and evaluated a host of formulas, investigating their properties both *a priori* and from applications to data. Since the criteria inevitably conflict, there can be no formula that excels on all counts. Although Fisher was mainly interested in measuring movements of the aggregate price level, naturally he wanted a price index P and a quantity index T to have the property that $P_1 T_1 / P_0 T_0 = (\Sigma p_1 Q_1)/(\Sigma p_0 Q_0)$, where the subscripts represent two time periods at which observations of p's and Q's are available.

This and various other desirable consistency properties are not hard to meet. The difficult question is the choice of weights in the two indexes, especially when a whole series of consistent period-to-period comparisons is desired, not just one isolated comparison. For a price index, should the quantity weights be those of a fixed base year, yielding what we now call a "Laspeyres" index $(\Sigma p_1 Q_0)/(\Sigma p_0 Q_0)$? Or should the weights be those of the ever-changing current period, yielding a "Paasche" index $(\Sigma p_1 Q_1)/(\Sigma p_0 Q_1)$? The indicated correlate quantity indexes would be the opposites, respectively "Paasche" and "Laspeyres." In 1911 Fisher opted for the Paasche price index. He also seemed to approve the idea of chain indexes, in which the period 0 of the above formulas is not fixed in calendar time but is always the prior period, even though these violate one possible desideratum, that the relative change between two periods should be independent of the base used. He also wrote favourably of the practical advantages of an entirely different procedure, namely taking the median of an expenditure-weighted distribution of percentage price changes from one period to the next.

In 1920, however, Fisher proposed as the "Ideal Index" a candidate he had not ranked high in 1911, namely the geometric mean of the Laspeyres and Paasche formulas. This formula has the pleasant property that the correlate of an Ideal price index is an Ideal quantity index. Correa Walsh, another index number expert, on whose comprehensive treatise (1901) Fisher relied heavily from the beginning of his own investigations, reached the same conclusion independently at about the same time (Walsh, 1921).

These index number issues do not seem as important to present-day economists as they did to Fisher. Knowing that they are intrinsically insoluble, we finesse them and use uncritically the indexes that government statisticians provide. But Fisher's explorations have been important to those practitioners.

In Fisher's Equation of Exchange (1911a) the T and the Q_i are measures of all transactions involving the tender of money, intermediate goods and services as well as final goods and services, old goods as well as newly produced commodities, financial assets as well as goods. The corresponding velocity is likewise comprehensive, much more so than the "income" or "circuit" velocity preferred by some monetary theorists, notably Alfred Marshall and his followers in Cambridge (England), who count only transactions for final goods, for example for Gross National Product.

Fisher elaborated the equation to distinguish the quantities M and M' of the two media currency and checking deposits and their separate velocities V and V': $MV + M'V' = PT$. This was a bow to the rising importance of bank deposits relative to currency as transactions media. Previous practice counted only government-issued currency as money, in modern parlance high-powered or base money, and regarded bank operations as increasing its velocity rather than adding to a money stock.

How does the quantity theory come out of the Equation of Exchange? Fisher argues that the real volume of money-using transactions T is exogenous; that the velocities are determined by institutions and habits and are independent of the other variables in the equation; that the division of the currency supply, the monetary base in current terminology, between currency and bank reserves is stable and independent of the variables in the equation; that banks are fully "loaned up" so that deposits M' are a stable multiple of reserves, determined by the prudence of banks and by regulation; that exogenous changes in currency supply itself are the principal source of shocks, which, given the preceding propositions, move price level P proportionately. The many qualifications for transitional adjustments are conscientiously presented, but the monetarist message is loud and clear.

The argument is familiar to modern readers, but certain features deserve notice:

IRVING FISHER 715

(1) Fisher gives the most illuminating account available of the institutions and habits that generate the society's demand for transactions media relative to the volume of transactions. He rightly emphasizes the fact that, and the degree to which, receipts and payments are imperfectly synchronized. He seeks the determinants of velocity in such features of social and economic structure as the frequency of wage and bill payments and the degree of vertical integration of firms. His belief that these institutions change only slowly supports his contention that velocities are exogenous constants.

(2) Much ink has been spilled on the difference between Fisher's velocity approach to money demand and the Cambridge (England) "k" formulation. The latter, like Walras's *encaisse desiré*, directs attention to agents' portfolio decisions. To Fisher's critics that seems behavioural, while velocity is mechanical. The issue is overblown; the same phenomena can be described in either language. If the other variables in the equation are defined and measured the same way, then V and k are just reciprocals each of the other. Fisher himself discusses hoarding. Fisher's explicit attention, in discussing economy-wide demand for circulating media in distinction to other stores of value, to the fact that money "at rest" soon takes "wing" to fly from one agent to another seems to be a merit of his approach.

(3) As already noted, Fisher resolved a question current in his day, whether banks' creation of deposit substitutes for currency should be regarded as increasing the velocity of basic money or as enlarging the supply of money. His choice of the latter course compels attention to the structure, behaviour and regulation of banks. He could not be expected to foresee that the proliferation of future candidates for designation as "money" would create the monetarist ambiguities we see today.

(4) For the most part later writers have not followed Fisher in his preference for a comprehensive concept and measure of transactions volume. It is hard to attach meaning to the *real* volume of financial transactions, and therefore to see why a T that includes them should be a constant or exogenous term in the equation. On the other hand, modern students of money demand tend simply to forget transactions other than those on final payments.

(5) Fisher ignores the possibility that other liquid assets can serve as imperfect substitutes for money holdings because they can be converted

into means of payment as needed, though at some cost. Partly for this reason, he ignores interest rate effects on demand for transactions media. In his day there may have been more excuse for these omissions than there was later. But they are still surprising for an author who elsewhere pays so much attention to the effects of interest rates and opportunity costs on behaviour.

(6) When Fisher was writing, the United States was on the gold standard; the exchange parities of the dollar with sterling and other gold-standard currencies were fixed. Fisher discusses in detail the implications of foreign transactions for the elements of the Equation of Exchange and for the quantity theory. He recognizes that tendencies towards purchasing-power parity, even though imperfect, make money supplies in any one country endogenous, tie prices to those of other countries and enhance quantity adjustments to monetary shocks in the short run. Much of the 1911 book applies, therefore, to the gold standard economies in aggregate. Indeed, Fisher finds the increase in gold production after 1896 to be the main cause of price increases throughout the world.

Macroeconomics: Business Fluctuations and the Great Depression

The quantity theory by no means exhausts Fisher's ideas on macroeconomics. His views were much more subtle than straightforward monetarism, but they are scattered through his writings and not systematically integrated. Consider the following non-neutralities emphasized by Fisher:

(1) Probably Fisher's principal source of fame, especially among non-economists, is his equation connecting nominal interest i, real interest r and inflation $\pi: i = r + \pi$. It is frequently misused. Like the Equation of Exchange, it is first of all an identity, from which, for example, an unobservable value of r can be calculated from observations of the other two variables. More interesting, certainly to Fisher, is its use as a condition of equilibrium in financial markets; for this purpose π must be replaced by expected inflation π^e, another unobservable. In a longer run, as Fisher recognized, steady-state equilibrium would also be characterized by equality of actual and expected inflation: $\pi = \pi^e$.

The Fisher equation is frequently cited nowadays in support of complete and prompt pass-through of inflation into nominal interest rates.

Fisher's view throughout his career was quite different. For one thing, neither Fisher's theory of interest nor his reading of historical experience suggested to him that equilibrium real rates of interest should be constant. Moreover, from (1896) on he believed that adjustment of nominal interest rates to inflation lakes a very long time. This he confirmed by sophisticated empirical investigations, regressions in which the formation of inflation expectations was modelled by distributed lags on actual inflation. During the transition, inflation would lower real rates; nominal rates would adjust incompletely. The effect was symmetrical; he attributed the severity of the Great Depression to the high real rates resulting from price deflation.

Moreover, Fisher was quite explicit about the effects of these movements of real interest rates on real economic variables, including aggregate production and employment. In *The Purchasing Power of Money* these transitional effects are mentioned, but minimized in the author's zeal to convince readers of the importance of stabilizing money stocks. But in Fisher's writings on interest rates, the transitions turn out to be long. In his accounts of cyclical fluctuations in business activity, and especially of the Great Depression, they play the key role.

(2) An assiduous student of price data, Fisher knew that some prices were more flexible than others, that money wages were on the sticky side of the spectrum, and that the imperfect flexibility of the price level meant that the T on the right-hand side of his Equation of Exchange would absorb some of the variations of the left-hand side.

In the early 1930s he came to a very modern position. Real variables like production and employment are independent of the level of prices, once the economy has adjusted to the level. But they are not independent of the rate of change of prices; they depend positively on the rate of inflation. He even calculated a "Phillips" correlation between employment and inflation (1926). He was just one derivative short of the accelerationist position (Friedman, 1968); in a little more time he would have made that step, aware as he was of the difference between actual and expected inflation. Anyway, his policy conclusion was that stabilizing the price level would also stabilize the real economy.

(3) During the Great Depression, observing the catastrophes of the world around him, which he shared personally, Fisher came to quite a different theory of the business cycle from the simple monetarist version

he had espoused earlier. This was his "debt-deflation theory of depression" (1932), summarized in the first volume of *Econometrica*, the organ of the international society he helped to found (1933). The essential features are that debt-financed Schumpeterian innovations fuel a boom, followed by a recession which can turn into depression via an unstable interaction between excessive real debt burdens and deflation. Note the contrast to the Pigou real balance effect, according to which price declines are the benign mechanism that restores full-employment equilibrium. The realism is all on Fisher's side. This theory of Fisher's has room for the monetary and credit cycles of which he earlier complained, and for the perversely pro-cyclical real interest rate movements mentioned above.

Fisher did not provide a formal model of his latter-day cycle theory, as he probably would have done at a younger age. The point here is that he came to recognize important non-monetary sources of disturbance. These insights contain the makings of a theory of a determination of economic activity, prices, and interest rates in short and medium runs. Moreover, in his neoclassical writings on capital and interest Fisher had laid the basis for the investment and saving equations central to modern macroeconomic models. Had Fisher pulled these strands together into a coherent theory, he could have been an American Keynes. Indeed the "neoclassical synthesis" would not have had to wait until after World War II. Fisher would have done it all himself.

His practical message in the early 1930s was "Reflation!" When his Yale colleagues and orthodox economists throughout the country protested against public-works spending proposals and denounced Roosevelt's gold policies, Fisher was a conspicuous dissenter. He was right. Characteristically, he crusaded vigorously for his cause—in speeches, pamphlets, letters and personal talks with President Roosevelt and other powerful policy-makers. Characteristically too, as his letters home (I. N. Fisher, 1956, p. 275) disclose, he saw clearly and unapologetically that in lobbying for what was good for the country he was also hoping to rescue the Fisher family finances.

Addressing the President of Yale shortly after Fisher's death, Joseph Schumpeter and eighteen colleagues in the Harvard economics department wrote, "No American has contributed more to the advancement of his chosen subjects.... The name of that great economist and American has a secure place in the history of his subject and of his country." According to his son, this is the eulogy that would have pleased Irving Fisher the most (I. N. Fisher, 1956, pp. 337–8). Today, four decades later, economists can confirm the judgement and prediction of that eulogy.

Note: Fortunately Fisher's son, Irving Norton Fisher, preserved the memory of his father in two indispensable publications, a biography and a comprehensive bibliography (1956, 1961). I have also relied extensively on Professor John Perry Miller's biographical essay (1967) and Professor William Barber's account (1986) of political economy at Yale before 1900. My review of Fisher's contributions to general equilibrium theory, the theory of capital and interest, monetary theory and macroeconomics draws heavily and often literally on a recent essay of my own (Tobin, 1985) (Chapter 27 above).

Selected Works

1892. *Mathematical Investigations in the Theory of Value and Prices*. New Haven: Connecticut Academy of Arts and Sciences, *Transactions 9*, 1892. Reprinted, New York: Augustus M. Kelley, 1961.

1896. Appreciation and interest. *AEA Publications* 3(11), August, 331–442. Reprinted, New York: Augustus M. Kelley, 1961.

1906. *The Nature of Capital and Income*. New York: Macmillan.

1907. *The Rate of Interest*. New York: Macmillan.

1910. *Introduction to Economic Science*. New York: Macmillan.

1911a. *The Purchasing Power of Money*. New York: Macmillan.

1911b. *Elementary Principles of Economics*. New York: Macmillan.

1921. The best form of index number. *American Statistical Association Quarterly* 17, March, 533–7.

1922. *The Making of Index Numbers*. Boston: Houghton Mifflin.

1926. A statistical relation between unemployment and price changes. *International Labour Review* 13, June, 785–92.

1927. A statistical method for measuring 'marginal utility' and testing the justice of a progressive income tax. In *Economic Essays Contributed in Honor of John Bates Clark*, ed. J. H. Hollander, New York: Macmillan.

1930. *The Theory of Interest*. New York: Macmillan.

1932. *Booms and Depressions*. New York: Adelphi.

1933. The debt-deflation theory of great depressions. *Econometrica* 1(4), October, 337–57.

1935. *100% Money*. New York: Adelphi.

Bibliography

Arrow, K. J. and Debreu, G. 1954. Existence of an equilibrium for a competitive economy. *Econometrica* 22(3), July, 265–90.

Auspitz, R. and Lieben, R. 1889. *Untersuchungen über die Theorie des Preises*. Leipzig: Duncker & Humblot.

Barber, W. J. 1986. Yale: the fortunes of political economy in an environment of academic conservatism. In W. J. Barber, *Economists and American Higher Learning in the Nineteenth Century*, Middletown, Conn.: Wesleyan University Press.

Clark, J. B. 1899. *The Distribution of Wealth*. New York: Macmillan.

Fairchild, F. R., Furniss, E. S. and Buck, N. S. 1926. *Elementary Economics*. 2 vols, New York: Macmillan. 5th edn, 1948.

Fisher, I. N. 1956. *My Father Irving Fisher*. New York: Comet Press.

Fisher, I. N. 1961. *A Bibliography of the Writings of Irving Fisher*. New Haven: Yale University Library.

Friedman, M. 1968. The role of monetary policy. *American Economic Review* 58(1), 1–17.

Hall, R. E. 1985. Monetary policy with an elastic price standard. In *Price Stability and Public Policy*. Federal Reserve Bank of Kansas City, 137–60.

Jevons, W. S. 1871. *The Theory of Political Economy*. London: Macmillan; 5th edn, New York: Kelley & Millman, 1957.

Keynes, J. M. 1923. *A Tract on Monetary Reform*. London: Macmillan.

Keynes, J. M. 1936. *The General Theory of Employment, Interest and Money*. New York: Harcourt, Brace.

Miller, J. P. 1967. Irving Fisher of Yale. In *Ten Economic Studies in the Tradition of Irving Fisher*, ed. William Fellner et al., New York: Wiley.

Newcomb, S. 1885. *Principles of Political Economy*. New York: Harper.

Rae, J. 1834. *The Sociological Theory of Capital*. Reprinted, New York: Macmillan, 1905.

Samuelson, P. A. 1967. Irving Fisher and the theory of capital. In *Ten Economic Studies in the Tradition of Irving Fisher*, ed. William Fellner et al., New York: Wiley.

Scarf, H. (With T. Hansen.) 1973. *The Computation of Economic Equilibria*. New Haven: Yale University Press.

Schumpeter, J. A. 1912. *Theory of Economic Development*. Trans. from the 2nd German edn of 1926 by R. Opie, Cambridge, Mass.: Harvard University Press, 1934.

Schumpeter, J. A. 1954. *History of Economic Analysis*. Ed. E. B. Schumpeter, New York: Oxford University Press.

Social Sciences Citation Index. 1979, 1983. *Five Year Cumulation*, 1971–5 and 1976–80. Philadelphia: Institute for Scientific Information.

Tobin, J. 1985. Neoclassical theory in America. *American Economic Review* 75(6), December, 28–38.

Walsh, C. M. 1901. *The Measurement of General Exchange Value*. New York and London: Macmillan.

Walsh, C. M. 1921. *The Problem of Estimation*. London: King & Sons.

Wicksell, K. 1911. *Lectures on Political Economy*. Trans. E. Classen (from the 2nd Swedish edn), London: George Routledge & Sons, 1934; New York: A. M. Kelley, 1967.

CHAPTER 29

GROWTH AND DISTRIBUTION: A NEOCLASSICAL KALDOR-ROBINSON EXERCISE

Retrospect: Kaldorian Distribution Theory

In 1956 Nicholas Kaldor published his "Keynesian" theory of the distribution of output between labor and property incomes, and in 1960 I published a short spoof of his article.[1] I was a brash young American. In reprinting that note in a collection of my essays in 1971, I wrote:

> Chapter 7 is an irreverent spoof of a distribution theory advanced by Nicholas Kaldor and others..... [It] is a footnote to the running controversy between neoclassical growth theory and its opponents. Neoclassical theory would have the division of full employment output between investment and consumption depend on the society's propensity to save. If property owners and wage earners differ in their saving behavior, the distribution of income between them would help to determine the share of investment in national output. The income distribution, in turn, depends, in neoclassical theory, on the marginal productivities of capital and labor. Kaldor rejected marginal productivity theory and needed an explanation of factor shares in its place. He regarded the investment share of total output as independently determined by technology and entrepreneurship—something to which the national saving propensity must adapt, rather than vice versa.... I would like to record here my judgment, which the reading lists of my courses confirm, that Mr. Kaldor has made many outstanding contributions to economic theory. He should be excused this aberration.[2]

Nicky Kaldor was unperturbed by my note, although he did bother to reply.[3] Fortunately, we subsequently became good friends and were usually on the same side of macroeconomic controversies. I had the opportunity to express my esteem for him in his presence both at the

Reprinted by permission from *Cambridge Journal of Economics* 13(1) (March 1989): 37–45. Corrected and revised version published here was Cowles Foundation Discussion Paper No. 934, Vol. 3, December 1989.

celebration of the centenary of Keynes's birth at Kings in 1983 and at Yale when Lord Kaldor gave the first set of Okun Memorial Lectures in 1983.[4]

For this symposium in his memory, I return to the subject of our disagreement three decades ago.

I was not criticizing the proposition that saving propensities might differ for incomes of different types, as well as for incomes of different magnitudes. After all, one important strand of mainstream saving theory, the life cycle model, also focuses on the difference between human and nonhuman wealth. More important, businesses, especially corporations, may not be acting just as agents of convenience for individual shareowners when they plow back profits. They may be instead institutionalizing that compulsion for accumulation which Marx—and Joan Robinson, Kaldor, and other post-Keynesians—have regarded as central to capitalism.

In this institutional spirit, Kaldor himself applied his differential propensities to sources of income, labor or property, rather than to classes of persons, workers and capitalists. For this reason he could not get excited about the long-run implications of recognition that both classes save and accumulate wealth, the discussion triggered by the Pasinetti process.[5] Empirically, it has not been possible to prove that business saving is just a one-for-one substitute for household saving.

Kaldorian saving propensities can easily be built into Swan-Solow–type neoclassical growth models where, like other saving functions, they help to determine a stable steady-state capital intensity and corresponding stable values of other variables. Indeed the classical saving function, a popular extreme form of the Kaldorian hypothesis—nothing is saved from wages and nothing is consumed from profits—leads to the "Golden Rule" optimum, the steady state with maximum consumption per worker. In that equilibrium investment equals profits and, in a Swan-Solow model, the marginal productivity of capital is equal to the growth rate. However, the weight of evidence is against the view that national saving and investment are as large as capital incomes.[6]

Moreover, if Kaldorian saving propensities are built into a one-good neoclassical growth model, they will help to determine the distribution of income and wealth. The steady-state capital stock is endogenous, dependent on saving behavior. Therefore the marginal productivities of capital and labor and, except in the special case of the Cobb-Douglas production function, the relative shares of labor and capital incomes are likewise endogenous and dependent on saving behavior. But differential saving propensities are not, except in the special case of the Leontief production function, *necessary* to determine distributive shares. Almost any saving function, for example the primitive assumption that a constant fraction of income of all kinds is saved, will determine the steady-state capital/labor ratio and thus also marginal productivities and factor shares.

What did bother me thirty years ago? First, I found it hard to believe that factors' returns had nothing to do with their productivities, and my note made fun of some implications of that belief. Second, in relation to macroeconomic theory, my problem was this: If marginal productivity is dropped as an explanation of income shares and the consumption function is drafted to replace it, how is aggregate output to be explained? I was shocked to see a "Keynesian" model that apparently assumed output to be independent of aggregate demand even in the short run. And given full employment, I thought, the role of the consumption function is to help to determine investment as equal to saving, which it cannot do if it is assigned the burden of determining wages and profits. To me, a model with investment wholly exogenous was both unKeynesian and unpalatable.

Of course, marginal productivities are indeterminate, within limits, when factors are fully employed and technology requires them to be used in constant proportions. Maybe differential saving propensities can help in these circumstances. What determines investment and output remains a problem. Animal spirits? Perhaps, in short run business cycles. In those circumstances there is no mechanism to ensure that capital capacity and labor supply stand in the correct proportions to each other. Whether capacity is and is expected to be short relative to labor supply or redundant is surely important in investment decisions. In the long run, capital capacity is adjusted to the requirements of exogenous growth in effective labor supply and of technology.

I take my cue from Joan Robinson:

The rate of investment ... can be accounted for in two ways which do not seem to be connected with each other. Investment is determined, in one sense, by profit expectations, the 'animal spirits' of entrepreneurs which incline them to take the risks of investment, and the state of supply of finance, which may be subsumed under the head of the level of interest rates.

In another sense, the rate of investment that can be maintained over the long run depends on technical conditions and the supply of labour. According to this view, the rate at which the effective supply of labor is growing ... limits the rate at which capital can accumulate, because there would be no point in bringing capital goods into existence when there is not going to be labour to operate them.[7]

Factor Shares and Saving in a Growth Model with Leontief Technologies

I provide here a simple example of a model in which the distribution of income between wages and returns to capital ownership cannot be explained by marginal productivities, because they are not determinate. The reason is that the technological input/output coefficients are constant à la Leontief. Kaldorian differential saving propensities are shown to be a natural way to close the model, to determine factor shares, and to equate aggregate saving to technologically required investment. But other consumption/saving functions may also do the trick. The primitive uniform constant propensity to save, the same for wages and profits, can make excess consumption demand a function of the profit rate. The reason is that the relative price of capital goods depends on the profit rate and therefore so does aggregate net income in terms of consumption goods.

Of course, a workable neoclassical alternative is to equate the profit (interest) rate to a constant rate of time preference (augmented in a non-stationary model by a term for decline in the marginal utility of growing per capita consumption.) But the specification that saving is supplied perfectly elastically with respect to the interest rate depends on infinitely long horizons for consumption and saving decisions and other implausible assumptions.

A technology consists of two activities; one produces consumption goods, the other capital goods. The two goods are not the same; the price of capital goods in terms of consumption goods is endogenous. Each activity uses labor and capital services. I shall analyze steady states in which total quantities of labor and capital are fully employed in the two activities. The labor supply is exogenous, growing in effective units at a constant rate, determined by natural increase and/or Harrod-neutral progress. The steady-state capital stock, relative to the labor force, is determined by the technology. The output of capital goods—gross investment—is what is needed to offset depreciation and to equip the increment in labor supply. Capital goods are used in both activities. In production, the capital goods used in the consumption goods activity are the same as those used in the capital goods activity itself. In use, they are different, both in the labor required to operate them and in their speed of depreciation.

Available to the economy are two or more technologies, each defined by the four input/output coefficients describing the consumption and investment activities and by the two depreciation rates. The economy may choose one among whole technologies, but it cannot mix activities. That is, for example, the consumption activity of technology I cannot coexist with the investment goods activity of technology II. The nature of the investment goods produced and used might determine the differential productivities of those goods and of labor in making the two kinds of goods. I believe this assumption is in the spirit of some of Joan Robinson's representations of technology.[8] The all-or-nothing choice of technology gives rise to the possibility that different technologies will be chosen at high and low profit rates.

I assume that the economy will be on its factor-price frontier, along which the activities in use break even and it is not possible to increase either wages or rates of return to saving, both measured in consumption goods, without reducing the other factor's earnings. The break-even conditions for the two activities determine two prices in terms of consumption goods: the wage and the price of capital goods. They determine these prices *given the profit rate*. The equations do not determine the profit rate. That is the essential indeterminacy, traceable to the fixed-coefficient technology, the vacuum that the Kaldorian saving function may fill.

The two factor prices are the wage (in consumption goods per worker per period) and the profit rate net of depreciation (pure number per period). Total net capital income, in consumption goods, is the profit rate multiplied by the value of the capital stock. This capital income and the wage bill are the factor incomes that add up to the value of total net output. And it is those factor incomes to which the Kaldorian consumption or saving coefficients apply. Within each technology, the price of capital goods, and therefore the value of the capital stock, depend endogenously on the profit rate.

A neoclassical theorist might argue that the consumption/saving decision depends on the profit rate as well as, or even instead of, aggregate profits measured in consumption goods. This dependence would represent the intertemporal substitution effect, Irving Fisher's interest incentive for saving. This is certainly not what Kaldor had in mind. I have not allowed for it in the present model.

For each technology, the steady-state input balance equations determine outputs of consumption goods and investment goods (per effective worker). These are technologically determined, independent of wages, capital goods prices, and profit rates.

"Reverse switching" is quite possible. That is, a lower-consumption technology can be on the factor-price frontier at higher wages and lower profits. Of course, the other direction of switching, which seems more normal, is also possible.

I find this "switching" implication preferable to the usual examples, which involve curiously rigid alternative sets of time lags between labor inputs and outputs.[9] In the present example, there are no such lags (although they could be added) and the emphasis is on fixed rather than working capital. Another advantage of the present model is that the steady-state output of investment goods is determined quite naturally to meet the requirements of technology and growth.

The Formal Model

Here is the model: First, the equations for a technology for the outputs of consumption goods C (activity a) and investment goods I (activity b):

$a_L C + b_L I = 1$ (Labor demand = supply, normalized to 1)   (1)

$a_K C = K_C,\ b_K I = K_I$ (Capital in each industry)

$a_K(n+d)C + b_K(n+d+s)I = I$ (Steady state gross investment)

$a_K(n+d)C + (b_K(n+d) - (1 - sb_K))I = 0$ (Investment goods demand = supply)   (2)

Here n is the growth rate, and d, $d + s$ (≥ 0) are the depreciation rates in the consumption goods and investment goods activities. Equations (1) and (2) may be solved for the steady-state outputs C and I. Let A be the determinant of the input/output coefficients, $a_L b_K - a_K b_L$, and let $v = (1 - sb_K)$. Then:

$$C = (b_K(n+d) - v)/(A(n+d) - va_L),$$
$$I = -a_K(n+d)/(A(n+d) - va_L) \tag{3}$$

The factor-price frontier can be found from the "dual" of the system (1)–(2). The price of consumption goods, the numeraire, is normalized to 1. The wage rate is w. The price of investment goods is p. The profit rate is r. Thus the gross rental cost of capital services is $p(r+d)$ in the consumption goods activity and $p(r+d+s)$ in investment goods production. The break-even equations for the two activities are:

$$a_L w + a_K p(r+d) = 1 \quad \text{(Consumption goods activity)} \tag{4}$$

$$b_L w + (b_K(r+d) - (1 - sb_K))p = 0 \quad \text{(Investment goods activity)} \tag{5}$$

These two equations are to be solved for w and p, given r. The solutions are:

$$w = (b_K(r+d) - v)/(A(r+d) - va_L), \quad p = -b_L/(A(r+d) - va_L) \tag{6}$$

By inspection, comparing (3) and (6) gives the standard "Golden Rule" result that $w = C$ when $r = n$.

The wage equation in (6) is the factor-price frontier. Its slope is:

$$\partial w/\partial r = -va_K b_L/(A(r+d) - va_L)^2 \tag{7}$$

This slope is negative. If A is negative—the investment goods activity is more capital-intensive than the consumption-goods activity—the frontier is concave to the origin. This is also true if A is positive but the expression $(A(r+d) - va_L)$ is negative. The frontier is convex to the origin if A and that expression are both positive. If A is zero—both activities are equally capital-intensive—the frontier is a line with slope $-b_K/va_L$. In that case the wage for $r = 0$ is $1/a_L - b_K d/va_L$ and for $r = -d$ is just $1/a_L$, the productivity of labor in the consumption goods activity; and the profit rate for $w = 0$ is $(1 - (d+s))/b_K$, the net productivity of capital in capital goods production.

The value of the capital stock is:

$$pK = a_K b_L v/[(A(r+d) - va_L)(A(n+d) - va_L)] \tag{8}$$

The slope of a $(w - r)$ frontier is supposed to be a measure of capital intensity. For example, in the Swan-Solow model—one product, two

Table 29.1
Assumed Parameter Values and Key Results in Illustration (labor supply normalized to equal 1)

	Technology I	Technology II
a_L	2	0.05
a_K	1	2
b_L	0.9	2
b_K	2	0.02
d	0.035	0.47
s	−0.025	0.1
n	0.03	0.03
C	0.485	0.482
I	0.034	0.488
K	0.55	0.97
price when $r = n$	0.47	0.97
first switch pt, r	0.026	0.026
first switch pt, w	0.486	0.486
second switch pt, r	0.366	0.366
second switch pt, w	0.289	0.289

factors, etc.—the slope is equal to the negative of the capital/labor ratio. Here too, as can be seen from (7) and (8), the two are closely related, and are equal when $r = n$.

The same calculations can be made for a second technology, indeed for every available technology, each one defined by values of a_L, a_K, b_L, b_K, d, and s. The growth rate n is also exogenous, but it is assumed to be independent of technology. Here a two-technology numerical illustration is presented.

Table 29.1 tells the numbers assumed in this illustration and reports some of the calculations.

Figures 29.1A and 29.1B show illustrative factor-price frontiers for two technologies. One is convex to the origin, the other concave. The example has been contrived to exhibit switching. There are two switch points. Both are shown in Figure 29.1A, but only the first one in Figure 29.1B. Technology II has the lower steady-state consumption, but is used in preference to Technology I at very low and very high profit rates. The "reverse" switch shown in Figure 29.1A occurs at a profit rate lower than the growth rate. It is not surprising that wasteful over-capitalization occurs at such low profit rates.

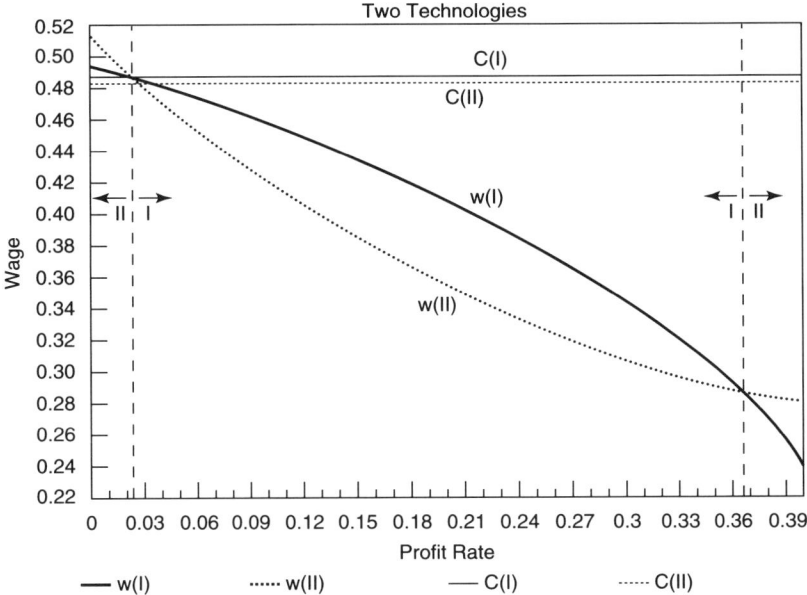

Figure 29.1A
Factor prices and consumption (two technologies). The factor-price frontier for Technology I, $w(I)$, is concave to the origin; the frontier for Technology II, $w(II)$, is convex to the origin. Switch points are at profit rates of 0.026 and 0.366. Consumptions for the two technologies, each independent of the profit rate, are shown as $C(I)$ and $C(II)$. $C(I)$ is the larger. In each technology wage and consumption are equal when the profit rate is equal to 0.03, the assumed growth rate.

Indeed it is not hard to see that a reverse switch can occur in this model only at profit rates below the growth rate. A switch point is a profit rate r^* at which $w(I) - w(II) = 0$. From the wage formula in (6), it is clear that the difference $w(I) - w(II)$ is a quadratic function of r, call it $Q(r)$. Likewise, because $C = w$ at $r = n$, the difference $C(I) - C(II)$ is $Q(n)$. As in the example, suppose that $Q(n) > 0$. Consider a reverse switch point, such that $Q(r) < 0$ for $r < r^*$, while $Q(r^*) = 0$. Clearly n cannot be smaller than, or even equal to, r^*. But $r*$ could be smaller than n. Of course a reverse switch point may not occur at any non-negative profit rate.

The second switch in the example is "normal" in the sense that a higher profit rate entails lower consumption as well as a lower wage.

Figure 29.2 shows the capital stocks, valued in terms of consumption goods, in relation to profit rates in the two technologies. Technology II is

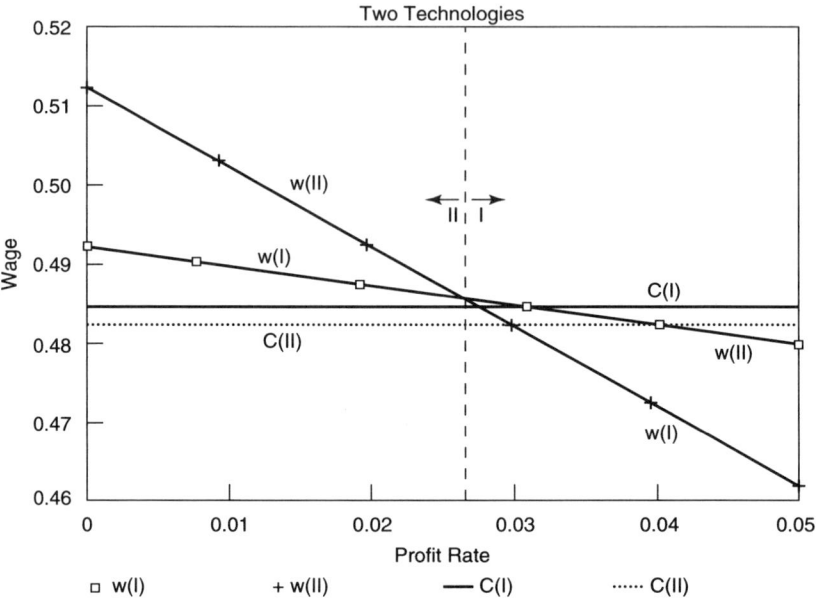

Figure 29.1B
Factor prices and consumption (two technologies). The upper left-hand corner of Figure 29.1A, the vicinity of the first switch point.

relatively capital-intensive, in particular in the consumption goods activity. However, Technology II capital depreciates rapidly.

All that is needed now is to superimpose a consumption function on Figure 29.1A or 29.1B. If nothing is saved from wages and nothing is consumed from capital income, the profit rate is equal to the growth rate, and the wage is equal to the consumption afforded by the technology in use at that profit rate. In general, consumption demand C^D is equal to $c_L w + c_K r p K$, where c_L and c_K are the propensities to consume from labor income and capital income respectively. In equilibrium consumption demand must equal consumption supply C^S, the consumption corresponding to the dominant technology.

In the two technologies of the example, net investment npK is small relative to net output $w + rpK$ (equal to $C + npK$—remember that p depends on r), between 1.5 and 7 percent for profit rates between 0 and

GROWTH AND DISTRIBUTION

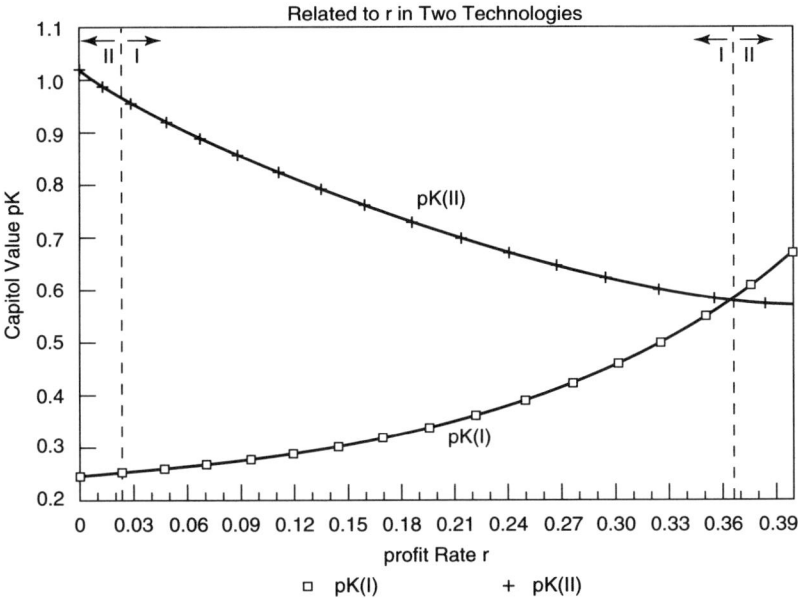

Figure 29.2
Value of capital stock (related to r in two technologies). In each technology the steady-state capital stock is constant in units of that technology's capital goods. But the price of capital goods varies with the profit rate, positively in Technology I, negatively in Technology II. At the two points where technologies are switched, the value of capital stock jumps. At the second switch point, capital stock values in the two technologies differ very little, but they are not equal.

0.5. Likewise capital incomes never exceed 6 percent. Therefore, the average propensities to consume in aggregate and from wage incomes have to be quite close to 1 in order to have any equilibrium at all.

Figure 29.3 continues the illustration of Figure 29.1B. C^S is shown, jumping at the profit rate where the two factor-price frontiers cross in Figure 29.1B. The downward-sloping continuous but kinked curve, designated by the wage w, is the factor-price frontier, taking account of both technologies and the switch from one to the other. The curve for C^D, consumption demand, takes consumption propensities to be 0.96 and 0.5 for labor and capital incomes respectively. In equilibrium consumption demand must equal consumption supply. In the example depicted in Figure 29.3, this happens to occur to the left of the first switch point, at a

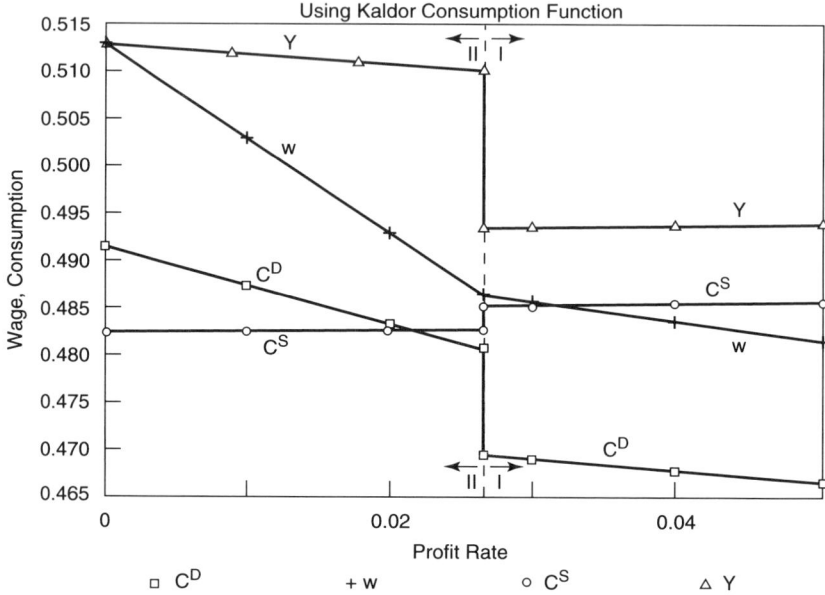

Figure 29.3
Determining wage and profit rate (using Kaldor consumption function). As in Figure 29.1B, the region in the vicinity of the first switch point is shown. The downward-sloping w curve (+), kinked at the switch point, is the frontier. Consumption supply C^S (○) jumps from $C(II)$ to $C(I)$ at that point. Consumption demand C^D (□), with propensities of 0.96 for wages and 0.5 for profit incomes, can be equal to supply only at the switch point. The top locus is aggregate net income $Y(\triangle)$, equal to $w + rpK$, which would be consumption demand if the propensity were 1.0 from both kinds of income. Because of the dependencies of p on r shown in Fig. 29.2, this locus declines before the switch point, jumps down, and then rises slowly.

profit rate of 0.02. With higher consumption propensities the intersection of C^D and C^S could be moved to or beyond the switch point.

At the switch point itself the "intersection" would generally be an overlap of the vertical jumps of C^D and C^S. This would not be a full equilibrium, because in neither of the two possible technologies would the value of C^D at the common prevailing wage and profit rate be equal to the corresponding value of C^S. At the same time, it would be true that to the left there would be excess consumption demand, and to the right excess supply. A way to obtain a switch-point equilibrium, in which both the zero-profit conditions and the consumption equation are satisfied, would

GROWTH AND DISTRIBUTION

be to allow the operation of both technologies simultaneously in suitable proportions.

Note that the wage frontier itself would be consumption demand if workers spent all their wages and capitalists saved all their profits. The equilibrium would be at a profit rate equal to the growth rate 0.03, with technology I and its consumption.

Note also that it is *not* strictly essential to have different propensities for the two types of income. The reason is that the variations of r and of p bring some variation in the functional distribution of income even in these fixed-coefficient technologies. In Figure 29.3, the top locus is Y, aggregate net income per worker, equal to $w + rpK$. It is initially declining with r, then jumps down at the switch point, where the price of capital goods falls drastically. Thereafter net income rises with r, almost imperceptibly in the figure. The changing distribution of income can be seen by comparing net income and the wage as the profit rate varies. A consumption function with the same propensity for each type of income would be just the net income locus shifted down proportionately. For example, a common propensity of 0.984 would support the "golden rule" equilibrium.

However, that equilibrium would be unstable by Kaldor's criterion, in the sense that if the profit rate were lower consumption demand would be less than supply, and the excess supply would cause the profit rate to fall further. That is because in Technology I net income per worker, wage plus profit, measured in consumption goods, rises with the profit rate r. However, stable equilibria with common consumption propensities are also possible. In this exercise they could occur in the domains of Technology II, where net income falls with r.

In this exercise, I have tried to place certain insights of Lord Kaldor and Joan Robinson in a context where their purpose and relevance may be understood and appreciated by a wider audience. Are there morals to the story? Competitive markets are most likely to exist and to perform well when local incremental decisions are possible. However, societies frequently face all-or-nothing decisions, choices among lumpy alternatives, often difficult or impossible to reverse. The ordinary tools of neoclassical economics are much less useful for the second class of problems than for the first.

Notes

This paper is a corrected version of a paper of the same title published in the *Cambridge Journal of Economics* Volume 13, Number 1, March 1989, pp. 37–45. Offprints were distributed as Cowles Foundation Paper No. 730. I am indebted to Professor Ian Steedman of Manchester University for pointing out to me a serious error in the original paper. His comment will be published in the *Journal*. I apologize for this error, and I especially regret making the error in an issue of the *Journal* devoted wholly to celebrating the contributions to economics of the late Nicholas Kaldor.

My mistake was to state factor-price frontiers as relations of the wage to the rental price of a unit of capital rather than to the profit rate, i.e. to rp rather than to r, where r is the profit rate and p is the price of capital goods in terms of consumption. This would be relatively innocuous within a specification of a single technology and type of capital, where the two measures of capital cost would be uniquely related. But—as Professor Steedman points out and as I once understood but forgot—it makes no sense in comparing the frontiers for two technologies, which differ as to the nature of capital and as to the relation of p to r.

For anyone who is interested, the present version of the paper corrects the error.

1. N. Kaldor, "Alternative Theories of Distribution", *Review of Economic Studies*, Volume XXIII 1955–56, 83–100.

   J. Tobin, "Toward a General Kaldorian Theory of Distribution: A Note", *Review of Economic Studies*, Volume XXVII 1960, 119–20. Reprinted in Tobin, *Essays in Economics: Volume 1, Macroeconomics*, Chicago: Markham Publishing Co., 1971, Chapter 7.

2. Tobin, *Essays in Economics: Volume 1. Macroeconomics*, p. 3.

3. N. Kaldor, "A Rejoinder to Mr. Atsumi and Professor Tobin", *Review of Economic Studies*, Volume XXVII 1960, 121–23.

4. See my "Comment" on Lord Kaldor's paper "Keynesian Economics after Fifty Years" at the 1983 conference, in D. Worswick and J. Trevithick, editors, *Keynes and the Modern World*, Cambridge: Cambridge University Press, 1983. See also my Preface to the Okun Lectures, N. Kaldor, *Economics without Equilibrium*, Armonk, N.Y.: M. E. Sharpe Inc., 1985.

5. L. L. Pasinetti, "Rate of Profit and Income Distribution in Relation to the Rate of Economic Growth, *Review of Economic Studies*, Volume, XXIX, 1962, 267–79. In the course of the debate provoked by this seminal article, Kaldor, in "Marginal Productivity and Macroeconomic Theories of Distribution", *Review of Economic Studies*, Volume XXXIII, 1966, 309–19, said

   > ... I have always regarded the high savings propensity out of profits as something which attaches to the nature of business income, and not to the wealth (or other peculiarities) of the individuals who own property. It is the enterprise, not the particular body of individuals owning it at any one time, which finds it necessary ... to plough back a proportion of the profits earned.... Hence the high savings propensity attaches to profits as such, not to capitalists as such.

6. A. Abel, N. Mankiw, L. Summers, and R. Zeckhauser, "Assessing Dynamic Efficiency: Theory and Evidence," National Bureau of Economic Research Working Paper No. 2097, 1986.

7. J. Robinson, "The Theory of Distribution", in her *Collected Economic Papers*, Volume II, Oxford: Blackwell, 1960, 146. The author says that the paper is "an amended version of a paper published in French in *Economie Applique*, Oct.–Nov. 1957."

8. See J. Robinson, *The Accumulation of Capital*, London: Macmillan, 1966, especially Chapter 10, "The Spectrum of Techniques." Here she introduces discrete constant-

GROWTH AND DISTRIBUTION

proportion techniques for labor and fixed capital. However, she does not explicitly model technologies with distinct activities for consumption goods and investment goods.

J. Robinson and J. Eatwell, *An Introduction to Modern Economics*, London: McGraw-Hill, 1973, 183–195 sets forth a multi-sector Sraffa type input/output model and derives from it a wage/profit-rate frontier. A uniform mark-up rate is applied to the cost of every intermediate input in the pricing of all intermediate and final outputs. Evidently this corresponds to a uniform one-period lag between inputs and proximate outputs. But no such lag and markup apply to labor inputs and wages. In any case, this model does not handle fixed capital, or even inventories other than those implicit in the work in progress during the one-period lag.

The general model of alternative "blueprints," each involving an indivisible technology using different kinds of capital goods that produce together with labor both the capital goods themselves and consumption goods has been discussed in, for example, L. L. Pasinetti, "Switches of Technique and the 'Rate of Return' in Capital Theory," *Economic Journal*, Volume 79, 1969, 508–531. The general model is so complex that points of interest depend greatly on simple illustrations, like the one in my text.

9. In her Chapter 10 of *The Accumulation of Capital*, "The Spectrum of Techniques," Mrs. Robinson discusses switching as "A Curiosum," pp. 109–113. See P. A. Samuelson, "A Summing Up," *Quarterly Journal of Economics*, Volume 80, 1966, 568–583, for a review of reswitching possibilities in models with input/output lags.

CHAPTER 30

ARTHUR M. OKUN

Arthur Okun was born in Jersey City, New Jersey, on 28 November 1928. He died suddenly in Washington, DC, on 23 March 1980.

Okun received his BA, ranked first in his college class, in 1949 and his PhD in economics in 1956, both from Columbia University. He started teaching at Yale as Instructor in 1952, and advanced up the ladder to the rank of Professor in 1963. From September 1961 to January 1969 Okun was, except for two academic years 1962–4, on leave from Yale at the President's Council of Economic Advisers (CEA) in Washington, first as a staff member, then as a Council Member 1964–8, and finally as Chairman 1968–9. When Administrations changed in 1969, Okun joined the Brookings Institution as a Senior Fellow, an appointment the held the rest of his life.

Prior to his public service in the 1960s Okun was not well known outside Yale. Those who knew him personally appreciated his extraordinary talents and virtues. He was a great and generous teacher, both in the classroom and out. His open-door office was the place for students and colleagues to get things straight, confusions dispelled, errors corrected, models repaired. A thinker of natural integrity and inexhaustible curiosity, he pursued matters in depth, unsatisfied until logic was tight and facts fell into place. His teachings of policy-oriented macroeconomics created an oral tradition that many beneficiaries remember with deep gratitude. But little of it was published, because Art Okun was unduly modest and perfectionist about putting his wisdom into print.

At the CEA Okun found another metier, macroeconomic analysis directly related to the policy issues of the day. It began when President

Kennedy's Council, of which one Member was from Yale, enlisted Okun as a consultant. The Council wanted to convince the President, his White House staff, the Congress, and the public that reduction of unemployment from 7 percent to 4 percent would yield economy-wide benefits much greater than moving from 93 to 96 percent employment superficially suggested. Okun was asked to estimate the gains of real Gross National Product associated with unemployment reduction. The answer became famous as Okun's Law, one of the most reliable empirical regularities of macroeconomics. Okun found that a reduction of one percentage point of unemployment was associated with a gain of 3 percent in real GNP. His research, later published (1962), also provided a methodology for estimating Potential GNP, the real output the economy can produce at a full-employment or "natural" rate of unemployment, and the "Gap" between actual and potential output.

These concepts are central to estimates of the "high-employment" or "structural" federal budget deficits implied by tax and spending policies, as distinguished from actual deficits, which depend also on the performance of the economy as indicated by the Gap. The entire apparatus was displayed in the 1962 *Economic Report of the President*, and was a mainstay of subsequent *Reports* for twenty years. Okun himself was a major contributor to all the *Reports* 1962–70.

Okun was the Council's principal forecaster and estimator of the consequences of alternative policies. As he won the confidence of Council Chairmen, White House staff, Presidents, and even Treasury Secretaries, he became the obvious choice for President Johnson to appoint Council Member and then Chairman. The period 1966–9 was difficult for the CEA and for Okun personally. The 4 percent unemployment target had been achieved in 1965, with negligible cost in higher inflation. Then came the acceleration of Vietnam spending, overheating the economy and lifting the inflation rate three percentage points by 1969. At the beginning of 1966 Gardner Ackley, CEA Chairman, and Okun urged President Johnson to ask Congress to raise taxed. He would not do so until too late, and even then the temporary income surtax of 1968 had disappointingly small effects. When Okun left the government in 1969, the unemployment-inflation nexus became the foremost problem on his research agenda for the rest of his career.

From 1969 much of his energy and leadership went into his brainchild, the Brookings Panel on Economic Activity, which enlisted able economists from Brookings and elsewhere for research on the major macroeconomic developments and policies of the times. The papers are published in *Brookings Papers on Economic Activity*, which under the painstaking editorship of Okun and George Perry quickly became one of the most admired professional journals in economics. The editors put the contents of every issue in perspective with their analytical summaries of the papers and discussions.

Okun had nearly completed a major treatise on macroeconomics (1981) when he died; it was edited and finished by his colleagues at Brookings. The book is a culmination of his thinking and writing over many years, his search for a coherent model of an advanced capitalist economy in a democratic society, based on his understanding of how businesses, workers, and consumers behave and relate to one another. Okun did not believe that the economists' favourite paradigm, purely competitive markets cleared by flexible prices—Adam Smith's "invisible hand"—provided realistic foundations for macroeconomics. He was impressed by the informal reciprocal expectations and obligations that characterize repeated dealings between sellers and customers or employers and workers. A creative phrase-maker, Okun called this web of implicit contracts the "invisible handshake." His "customer markets" are in many ways efficient substitutes for price-cleared auction markets, but they are also the source of endemic macroeconomic difficulties.

Okun saw no easy resolution of the cruel dilemma policy-makers face in the trade-off between unemployment and inflation. All too often, and especially in the 1970s, fiscal and monetary demand management could achieve acceptable outcomes in one of these two dimensions only at the cost of unacceptable results in the other. Okun had no use for the monetarist view that inflation could be easily prevented or conquered if only the central bank mustered sufficient will and wisdom. Nor did he share the simplistic view of some theorists of various schools that inflations are neutral and innocuous, devoid of real consequences. He advocated structural anti-inflation policies, including wage and price guideposts strengthened by tax-based incentives for compliance, to diminish the unemployment costs of anti-inflationary monetary and fiscal measures (1978).

The intellectual climate of professional macroeconomics was inhospitable to *Prices and Quantities* when it was published. "New classical" models relying on "invisible hand" microfoundations were the dominant fashion. They are theoretically appealing but have trouble explaining the commonly observed facts of business fluctuations. No one knew those facts better than Okun, whose last published paper (1980) is a masterful litany of the many ways new classical business cycle theories fail to fit them. Fashions change and controversies fade. Okun's macroeconomics will be an important component of whatever new synthesis emerges from contemporary debate.

Arthur Okun was not only an effective adviser and participant in the making of economic policy; he was also a scholar and scientist of *political economy*—the ancient name for our discipline suggests a broader scope of inquiry and concern than most economists essay today. Okun's reflections on the role of the academic policy adviser in government and on the politics and economics of macroeconomic management, published shortly after he returned to private life, are the most thoughtful of the genre (1970).

For his Godkin Lectures at Harvard (1975) Okun chose the broadest and most basic question of political economy: how democratic societies do, can, and should balance the ethical desirability of mitigating inequalities of well-being against the practical utility of the inequalities arising in free markets as incentives for efficient economic performance. Okun coined the metaphor "leaky bucket" for losses in aggregate wealth incident to government interventions to transfer wealth from rich to poor. Citizens will disagree on the tolerable degree of leakage, he says, but both liberals and conservatives should face the trade-offs realistically. They should be able to agree on measures to plug leaks, exploiting opportunities to diminish inequality without impairing incentives (even if such reforms are not Pareto optimal). Okun suggests an agenda of such opportunities, focusing on measures to assure greater equality of opportunity. The book has already become a classic. In its erudition, logic, lucidity, and wisdom, and above all in its humanity, it truly reflects the qualities of its author.

Selected Works

1962. Potential GNP: its measurement and significance. *Proceedings of the Business and Economic Statistics Section, American Statistical Association*, Washington: ASA, 98–103. Reprinted in (1983), 145–58.

1970. *The Political Economy of Prosperity.* Washington, DC: Brookings Institution.

1975. *Equality and Efficiency: The Big Tradeoff*. Washington, DC: Brookings Institution.

1978. A reward TIP. In Senate, Banking, Housing and Urban Affairs, *Anti-Inflation Proposals*, Hearings 95 Congress 2 Session, Washington: Government Printing Office, 15–28. Reprinted in (1983), 67–75.

1980. Rational-expectations-with-misperceptions as a theory of the business cycle. *Journal of Money, Credit and Banking* Part 2, 12(4), November, 817–25. Reprinted in (1983), 131–41.

1981. *Prices and Quantities a Macroeconomic Analysis*. Washington, DC: Brookings Institution.

1983. *Economics for Policymaking: Selected Essays of Arthur M. Okun*. Ed. J. A. Pechman, Cambridge, Mass.: MIT Press; with editor's preface.

CHAPTER 31

ROBERT TRIFFIN

President Daughdrill, Dr. Bies, Mr. and Mrs. Seidman, ladies and gentlemen. I am proud to introduce to you my long-time mentor and colleague Robert Triffin. The pride I feel is that of bringing to you a friend for whom I have great admiration and affection, an extraordinary human being whom I know you will appreciate and like.

Robert, let me also introduce to you this audience. Memphis is a long way from Brussels, not even that close to Washington, New York, New Haven, and Boston. But, as you and Lois are finding out, your new friends here are not only extremely hospitable, but also deeply interested in political economy and political economists, for whom their tastes are sophisticated and discriminating.

Our paths, Robert's and mine, have often joined or crossed these past fifty years. He was a student generation ahead of me at Harvard, graduate student when I was an undergraduate, instructor when I was a graduate student. His generation was a spectacular group, making new economics while studying and teaching both old and new. (You have previously honored two other members, Galbraith and Musgrave, and I imagine you might have honored Samuelson if Stockholm had delayed doing so.) Robert Triffin's Wells Prize dissertation, making theoretical sense of Chamberlinian monopolistic competition, was on our reading lists as soon as it was published in 1940. No wonder my peers and I looked on Robert and his contemporaries with considerable awe.

Robert and I went different ways during the war—I refer to *our* war, the Second World War. He went to Washington, and from research and

---

Introduction of the 1988 Recipient, Robert Triffin, and Presentation of the Award, The Frank E. Seidman Distinguished Award in Political Economy, Rhodes College, Memphis, TN, September 15, 1988.

practical experience developed the interest that would dominate his career, international monetary economics. We had occasional contacts here and there, but our close association and long friendship began when Robert came to Yale in 1951, a year after my arrival. Robert's appointment was a great coup, which, together with the recruitment of Henry Wallich, William Fellner, and the Cowles Commission in the space of four years, brought the Yale department up to world-class status.

Robert was a marvelous citizen of the department and the university—loyal, humane, wise, and tolerant. I had many reasons to be grateful for his presence and his counsel.

Robert's contributions to the university are less evident to the outside world than his publications and his public service. Let me mention just two. First, Robert founded and fostered a program to train economists sent by foreign governments for a year or two of graduate work, oriented to economic development and international economic relations. The program continues, and its alumni—many of them personally taught and inspired by Robert—occupy positions of importance and influence in central banks, ministries, and international organizations all over the world.

Second, Robert was Master of Berkeley College, one of Yale's twelve undergraduate residences, for years. He and Lois dedicated themselves to their 300-odd adopted adult children, who revered them with great affection. Robert's Mastership covered the era of student unrest and revolt, but Robert's sympathetic understanding of students' concerns and values, exemplified by the altruistic undertakings of his own sons, was an important factor in maintaining peace and civility in his college and throughout our campus.

I return to my personal narrative. In 1961 I joined President Kennedy in Washington as a member of his Council of Economic Advisers. When the three of us Advisers divided special responsibilities among ourselves, one of my subjects turned out to be international economic policy. I was not an expert; one could say I knew almost nothing. My first move was to prevail on Walter Heller to call in Robert Triffin as a consultant.

Back at Yale, Robert had taught me, as he was teaching students, colleagues, members of Congress, bankers, and anyone who would listen, about the inherent instability of the gold-dollar Bretton Woods monetary system. He called it right, well in advance. Other central banks, and private citizens, would not forever hold dollars as if they were as good as gold, while the gold backing of the dollars steadily diminished. Triffin's message was that we needed concerted *international* action to meet the world's growing needs for liquidity.

Messengers who bring bad news are often unwelcome, and those who were managing the *status quo* didn't want to hear Triffin's message and didn't want anyone else to hear it either. As the Kennedy Administration began, the United States was beginning to feel the pains of payments deficits and gold losses, but the U.S. Treasury was certainly not ready for Triffin. The Cassandra who says the world is justifiably losing confidence in the dollar is working for the U.S. government?!

We did have some little successes—Robert, Dick Cooper, and I—and I certainly learned a lot of international economics. We know of course that Robert has had plenty of success in other theaters. He was a major architect of the European Payments Union, and of the European Monetary System.

In broader scope, Robert has always been a European, like his friends Jean Monnet and Robert Marjolin a builder of transnational European institutions. He's still at it, no doubt helping with the arrangements for the bold move scheduled for 1992. But Robert has never favored an inward-looking protectionist Europe. He would like to see a world-wide central bank, and other global institutions, particularly devoted to improving the lot of the Third World. And above all, Robert seeks world peace, disarmament, détente.

I have known very few people who believe so deeply in what they are doing and pursue their interests with such passion. Robert has always been in great demand, and supply, as a consultant to governments and international institutions. In one of his books he appended the word "regrettably" to the customary prefatory warning that the views expressed were not those of his employers and clients.

Robert has made powerful intellectual and scientific contributions throughout his career. But almost all the time his work has been geared to policy, to designing, repairing, and improving institutional architecture, in forms attractive to the disparate interests of the parties involved. I once heard Robert defend himself against the charge that his work consisted in inventing "gimmicks." Sure, he said, those are what we need, workable and salable gimmicks. (I recall one he urged on Mossadegh in Iran: let the landowners assess themselves for property taxes, provided only that they must sell their land to anyone, including the government, who offers to buy it at assessed value.)

Inevitably Robert has been a student of politics and history as well as economics. No one could be better qualified for the Seidman Award, for "an economist who has distinguished himself or herself *internationally* (my emphasis) ... to the interdisciplinary advancement of economic thought as it applies to the implementation of public policy."

Robert, old friend, it's for me a great honor and privilege to present to you the 1988 Frank E. Seidman Distinguished Award in Political Economy.

CHAPTER 32

WALTER W. HELLER

Few economists, indeed few scholars of any discipline, influence significantly and positively the events and public policies of their times. Few academicians earn intellectual renown in their professions mainly by contributions incident to policy-making while in government service. Walter Heller did both.

Heller burst onto the national scene in 1960 at the age of forty-five when President-elect Kennedy chose him to be Chairman of the Council of Economic Advisers (CEA). Kennedy liked him when he met him in Minneapolis during the campaign, and Senator Hubert Humphrey strongly recommended him. At the time Heller was not a national figure, although he was a professor at the University of Minnesota, a respected scholar in his fields of taxation and public finance, and an active participant in the affairs of his university and his state government. He was to become a leader in his profession, an economist-statesman known and admired throughout the world, and a writer, speaker, and adviser eagerly sought by businesses, governments, and universities.

The CEA is a small agency in the Executive Office of the President. The Employment Act of 1946 set it up to help the President propose and execute federal policies to achieve the objectives of the act, "maximum production, employment, and purchasing power." The agency's influence, prestige, and success have varied greatly over its forty-four years and nine presidents.

Walter Heller served as Council Chairman under Presidents Kennedy and Johnson for four years (1961–64). His influence continued well beyond his tenure, after which he returned to the University of Minnesota.

Reprinted by permission from *Proceedings of the American Philosophical Society* 135(1) (March 1991): 101–107.

His successors at the council had been his colleagues; he remained close to them and to President Johnson through 1969.

I am not a dispassionate observer, because I was one of the other two council members in 1961–62 and continued to play on Heller's team after I returned to academia. But I think there is wide agreement that the 1960s were the best years of CEA's life, that under Heller's leadership the CEA achieved greater standing with the president, the rest of the federal government, the Congress, the press, the economics profession, and the general public than at any other time. During the 1960s the small CEA staff (about 15 professional economists) certainly reached unrivaled heights of quality, dedication, and *esprit de corps*. Heller and his fellow council members recruited to the CEA staff such economists as Kenneth Arrow, Arthur Okun, and Robert Solow.

Heller's achievement in the early 1960s was to engineer a revolution in federal macroeconomic policy. He persuaded president, Congress, and Federal Reserve to dedicate fiscal and monetary policies not to traditional narrow rules of thumb but to the stability and growth of the national economy. He argued that balancing the budget should not be an objective for its own sake, and that the Treasury and Federal Reserve should not tie themselves to interest rate or money stock targets independently of economic circumstances. Although these ideas about the theory and practice of macroeconomic policy suffered some hard knocks in the 1970s and 1980s, they are currently enjoying a comeback and stand a good chance of winning out in the end.

In 1961 the doctrines of the Heller CEA were mostly mainstream ideas among economists. They went back to John Maynard Keynes's great 1936 book *The General Theory of Employment, Interest and Money*. Some Keynesian ideas had been espoused by President Truman's CEA under chairman Leon Keyserling. In the 1940s and 1950s a number of theorists—some of whom (Paul Samuelson, Robert Solow, James Tobin) were later to work with Heller in the 1960s—modified Keynes's heresies and tried to reconcile them to orthodox neoclassical economics. Yet the Heller message seemed novel to Washington and to the lay public in 1961. The media called it "The New Economics."

The 1962 *Economic Report of the President*, written by Heller and his colleagues under Heller's direction, is the manifesto expounding the CEA's theory of the economy and of government policy to Congress, the general public, and the economics profession. (It has recently been reprinted, along with its 1982 counterpart, the manifesto of Reaganomics.)[1] It could be regarded as Heller's *magnum opus*, with worthy sequels in his three subsequent *Reports*.

The 1962 *Report* is a statement of the mainstream synthesis of Keynesian and neoclassical economics, sharpened by the generality of its audience and by its essential political and pragmatic focus. It also contains a number of important innovations in economic analysis and policy design: the empirical relation of GNP and unemployment, which as "Okun's law" proved to be one of the most durable regularities of macroeconomics; proposals for automatic triggering of spending increases and tax cuts, to augment the "built-in fiscal stabilizers" cushioning the economy against recessionary shocks; the investment tax credit as an instrument to serve the double purpose of stabilizing demand and increasing capital formation for long-term growth; the "guideposts for noninflationary wage and price behavior," designed to avert possible inflationary effects of economic expansion; the theory of "policy mix," showing how choices between fiscal and monetary policies to achieve and maintain full employment could be guided by other objectives, the balance of payments and long-run growth.

Heller's message encountered great resistance at first. President Kennedy himself was skeptical, and reluctant to risk political goodwill on unorthodox economic strategies. But Heller was a great teacher. In conversations, lectures, or writings, Heller had an unmatched talent for finding the revealing examples, instructive jokes, and colorful metaphors that made his points succinctly, convincingly, and accurately. JFK turned out to be a keen student. The president's 1962 Yale commencement address showed how well he had learned his lessons.

Most members of Congress, most reporters and pundits, and almost all businessmen and financiers were at first suspicious or hostile. With humor and good humor, Heller patiently and persuasively brought them round. He gained tolerance and support for his ideas and his proposals, and he won appreciation and affection for himself as a person.

The Kennedy-Johnson tax cut was the ultimate victory. Taxes were cut in 1964—eighteen months later than Heller had wanted—not as in the past just to relieve and reverse a cyclical recession but to keep an ongoing recovery from stalling short of full employment. The budget outcome was deliberately subordinated to the macroeconomic health of the country.

Thanks to the tax cut and to a series of previous but less visible demand management policies from 1961 on, the American economy enjoyed a full recovery from the recession of 1960–61, reducing the unemployment rate from 7 percent to the administration's objective, 4 percent, by early 1965. This recovery raised real GNP at an average annual rate of 4.9 percent. It was virtually free of inflation; consumer prices rose only 1.2 percent a year. In the spirit of the wage and price guideposts, the president and his administration actively pressed trade unions and business managements to hold down wages and prices. The Federal Reserve was persuaded to accommodate the recovery; its monetary policies kept long-term federal bond yields below 4.2 percent during Heller's four years.

Heller and his colleagues and successors were two-sided Keynesians. When in 1966 LBJ's escalation of the Vietnam war threatened to overheat the economy, they urged tax *increases*. But LBJ did not take their advice until 1968, too late to prevent inflation from ratcheting to nearly 5 percent per year. Even so, the decade of the 1960s was in most dimensions of macroeconomic performance an unparalleled success.

Although the council's primary responsibility and Heller's primary interests were in macroeconomic events and policies, Heller and his council advised their presidents on the whole range of economic policies. An important example is the "War on Poverty," a campaign initially and successfully urged on JFK in 1963 by Heller and carried forward by LBJ. Heller's January 1964 *Economic Report* contains a chapter (to which CEA staff member Robert Lampman of the University of Wisconsin made major contributions) outlining the economic case for the "war" and the strategies to be followed.

Heller had long been an advocate of sharing federal revenues with state and local governments. His advocacy was instrumental in LBJ's appointment of a task force to work out the details. Eventually Congress enacted the plan, after President Nixon also recommended it in 1972. The purpose of revenue sharing was to use the federal taxing power to meet national needs and to overcome some of the inequalities in taxable capacities among states and localities. Unfortunately revenue sharing was essentially killed by the Reagan and Bush Administrations.

I would like to tell what it was like serving with Walter Heller on the Council of Economic Advisers, drawing on remarks I made at the memorial service in Minneapolis June 26, 1987.

When I was recruited as a council member, JFK and Walter both promised that the council would work as a team, not as in some previous—and subsequent—administrations as a hierarchy. They kept the promise. That came naturally to Walter, characteristically generous and thoughtful in relations with friends and associates. He made sure that Kermit Gordon, the other council member, and/or I frequently went with him or on our own to the Oval Office, to the meetings of the Troika (Walter's term for Council-Budget Bureau-Treasury) or the Quadriad (his term for Troika plus Federal Reserve), to hearings on the Hill, to international groups in Paris, and to other strategic affairs.

Walter presided informally over a family of like-minded, dedicated, capable, and enthusiastic men and women, old friends and new, within which lines of authority and rank—chairman, members, staff—were blurred. In spite of, or because of, a certain anarchy, great things were done. They were what Walter wanted to get done, but by leadership in his own style.

Walter liked to think out loud, to work and even to write gregariously. He scheduled few internal meetings. Yet many were the hours we sat in his office: Kermit Gordon and I, usually also Bob Solow and Art Okun, who became council members de facto, often Joe Pechman, not on our payroll but Walter's trusted friend from student days on, more Washington-savvy than any of us, occasionally Paul Samuelson in from Cambridge. Other staff members would come and go as needed or spontaneously.

Walter would bring us up to date on goings-on in the White House, on the Hill, in the press. We would hash over our strategies: our responses to White House requests or to the latest outrages of Treasury, Federal Reserve, labor, *Time* magazine, the French government; and our—mostly Walter's—next moves in the battles for the minds of the president, Congress, reporters, businessmen, the general public. And yes, we would talk about how the economy was doing and what federal policies we should be pushing for. There were plenty of envelopes with backs on which to scribble the sums.

Very often we were collectively writing or rewriting something—the draft of a presidential message to Congress (how important it was to do the first draft, and the last!), one of the many speeches Walter was giving to educate the country, testimony for Congress, key parts of our *Economic Report*, and most frequently a memo. The most important memos were for JFK. Walter knew how to get them read. He made friends with Ken O'Donnell, gate-keeper to the Oval Office, who would slip Walter's memo into the weekend Hyannisport briefcase. Walter had made it easy to read—short, pointed, colorful, and studded with the figures of speech that were the Heller trademark. The Treasury's thirty pages of bureaucratic prose were no competition.

Meanwhile Walter went on with his own calendar. The man loved the telephone: there were phone calls in—he was always there for the White House and the press—and phone calls out. There were recesses to keep appointments, which very likely he had forgotten. Never mind. During interruptions we could advance the subject at hand, contrive some needed language for the draft on the table, or catch up individually on other work. The interruptions themselves were likely to introduce a new subject for the group. You couldn't call these sessions orderly.

We didn't always agree. We argued. But the values we shared, our common view of the world, the unspoken reasons we were all there, almost always moved us to consensus. There was usually no formal bottom line, but in his gentle way Walter made sure we left the room knowing what we were going to do.

Often these gatherings kept us from dining at home—it was a relief if Walter had an embassy dinner—and we continued over sandwiches or at a nearby restaurant, then returned to the office. There were a few all-nighters. Walter was an indefatigable night owl. Not also an early bird, fortunately—the morning was when the rest of us did the essential work to prepare for the next evening. Walter was probably on the phone at home.

Morale was high. Serving on Walter's council, we were a band of brothers and sisters, and the bonds of common purpose and experience lasted our lifetimes.

Walter Heller was born in Buffalo but grew up mainly in Milwaukee. He went to Oberlin College, from which he was graduated in 1935. Thanks to the leadership of Professor Ben Lewis, this small college produced many fine professional economists in the late 1930s, 1940s, and 1950s. Heller went to graduate school at the University of Wisconsin, receiving his Ph.D. in 1941. The progressive tradition was strong in Madison in those days, in state politics, in the university, and in the economics department. Professor Harold Groves was training and inspiring a generation of scholars of public finance. Two of the most notable products were Walter Heller and his contemporary Joseph Pechman (who died in 1989).

Young men and women in the 1930s went into economics with the conviction that as economists they could help solve the appalling problems of the day. They enjoyed the subject for its own sake, to be sure, but they expected it to pay off in improving the world. Having a considerable and perhaps a naive faith in the power of knowledge and truth, they did not doubt that government could be an instrument of economic and social progress. Oberlin and Wisconsin reinforced these attitudes in Walter Heller. Certainly they stayed with him for the rest of his life.

After completing his degree, Heller lectured for a year in Madison and then went to the United States Treasury as a fiscal economist, 1943–46. He could not serve in the armed forces because of poor eyesight. After the war he continued to serve the federal government as a consultant; he was chief of internal finance for the U.S. Military Government in Germany 1947–48 and a member of a State Department mission on German Fiscal Problems in 1951.

In 1946 Heller was appointed to the faculty of the University of Minnesota. Heller was naturally a mainstay of any institution that attracted his loyalty, and he loved the university. He was a prime mover in the build-up of its economics department in the 1950s, before and during his tenure as its chairman, 1957–60. Likewise he was a proud and enthusiastic citizen of the Twin Cities and the state. To their economics and politics he could contribute not only his energy and intellect, but also his special knowledge in public finance. He was co-author of a book on state income taxes, and he was fiscal adviser to the governor of Minnesota. He little knew that his experience in advising Minnesota Democrats would one day launch him on the national scene.

After his Washington career, Heller continued to be a major national and international player in discussions of macroeconomic events and policies.

Together with George Perry of the Brookings Institution, an alumnus of the CEA staff, he wrote a monthly economic forecast and commentary, distributed by a Minneapolis bank. Many of his lectures and essays were reflections on economic policy-making, drawing on his Washington experience, among them his 1966 Godkin lectures at Harvard, published as *New Dimensions of Political Economy* (Harvard University Press). He entered the lists of macroeconomics debate, as in his dialogue with Milton Friedman, *Monetary vs. Fiscal Policy*, 1969. (The book was mistitled. Friedman denied fiscal policy any role in economic stabilization and argued against active monetary policy too, contending that the best the Federal Reserve could do was to make the money supply grow at a constant rate whatever the prevailing macroeconomic conditions. Heller characteristically argued for the active use of both policies in judicious combination.)

In 1965 Heller resumed his active role back home in Minnesota, in the university and in his department. He took on the introductory economics course and lectured enthusiastically to thousands of students, entertaining and enlightening them with "war stories" from Washington. Ironically his department was gaining international distinction as a center for "New Classical Macroeconomics," a school of thought antagonistic to what Heller had believed, taught, and practiced throughout his career. But Heller respected intellectual quality of any brand and took pride in his department's newfound distinction. His belief that scientific achievement and promise were the criteria for academic appointments was by no means new. As a graduate student in Madison in the late 1930s Heller had organized a protest against the Wisconsin department's failure to keep Milton Friedman on its faculty.

He was in great demand outside the university. He gave speeches and lectures all over the world. He was on *Time's* Board of Economists. He wrote regularly for the op-ed page of the *Wall Street Journal*. He was a favorite guest on "Meet the Press" and other public affairs programs on television and radio. He was consultant to business, nonprofit institutions, and government agencies in Minnesota, Washington D.C., and abroad. He was a director of eight companies.

Honors came thick and fast. His university made him a Regents' Professor. He was president of the American Economic Association in 1974. He was awarded eight honorary degrees; those from Oberlin and Wisconsin meant the most. Joe Pechman organized a Heller festschrift in 1982, *Economics in the Public Service* (W. W. Norton), to which Heller himself contributed an essay, "Kennedy Economics Revisited."

Walter Heller married Emily Karen Johnson in 1938. She died in 1985. From about 1955 on she suffered the disabilities of lupus, but courageously functioned normally nonetheless. In her later years, Walter helped to found, and obtain national support for, the Lupus Foundation. The Hellers had three children: Walter P., now a professor of economics at the University of California, San Diego; Eric J., a professor of chemistry at the University of Washington; and Kaaren L., a homemaker in Mercer Island, Washington.

Heller listed his "hobbies and sports" as travel, wood chopping, and clam digging. The truth is that his only hobby was work until after he left the government. As for travel, his profession was the occasion for most of it. Wood chopping and clam digging came with his acquisition in 1967 of property on Hood Canal in Washington state, on which he built a vacation and retirement home. He loved the Pacific Northwest. In his boyhood he had spent his summers in Seattle with his uncle. When Walter Heller suffered his sudden fatal heart attack at his Hood Canal home, he was busy digging a channel from his beloved lagoon to the sea.

Note

1. James Tobin and Murray Weidenbaum, eds., *Two Revolutions in Economic Policy*, Cambridge, Mass.: MIT Press, 1988.

CHAPTER 33

THE OPTIMAL CASH BALANCE PROPOSITION: MAURICE ALLAIS'S PRIORITY

Maurice Allais's well-deserved Nobel Prize fortuitously brought to our attention an injustice inadvertently done him, to which we were unknowing accessories. For years the literature has ascribed to us the parentage of the transactions-cost model of optimal cash balances, with its notorious square-root formula derived from inventory theory.[1] Recently, we found that its essence is contained in Allais' 1947 Economie et Intérêt *(pp. 238–41). As Jacob Viner used to say, no matter to what source the origin of an economic proposition is ascribed, someone is sure to come up with an earlier one.*

In any event, here is a translation of the pertinent passages. Allais describes the model in footnotes (11) and (12) to the following text (pp. 238–41):

One may note that the value of the benefits obtained from an additional [money] balance of 100 francs when the average balance is already 10,000 francs is much less than when that balance is zero. If, for example, a consumer carelessly invests all his funds he will almost certainly have trouble meeting his basic needs, of which some will perhaps be essential and for which he will not even have the time to have recourse to credit. Holding the mere sum of 100 francs will by itself avoid for him a thousand petty inconveniences by permitting him to have lunch, go home on the bus, buy a newspaper, give a tip, etc., and maintenance of this balance could provide him a yield of much higher value, say 500 francs, for example, representing a liquidity premium of 500 percent. In contrast, when his average balance is already high, say 10,000 francs, for example, an additional 100 francs would evidently have a very low value, of the order tenths or hundredths. (footnote 11)

Reprinted by permission from *Journal of Economic Literature* 27 (September 1989): 1160–1162. Written with William J. Baumol.

It is then easy to see how the amount of the average balance held in equilibrium by an economic agent is determined. In effect, to the extent that the marginal liquidity premium l_m of the average balance is higher than the pure interest rate, it is in the agent's interest to keep his capital in the form of a money balance. This balance is only superficially "sterile," because in reality it brings, each time period, advantages equal in value to the liquidity premium. When, on the other hand, the liquidity premium becomes smaller than the pure interest rate, investment of disposable capital becomes more advantageous than keeping it in the form of money balance. *The optimal situation in equilibrium obtains when the size of the balance is such that its marginal liquidity premium is equal to the pure rate of interest* [emphasis in original]. (footnote 12)

Thus, one sees that the service of money is advantageous but that no price is paid for it directly. Its cost comes *indirectly*, from gain forgone because of the loss of interest that would arise from investment of the money balance. Equilibrium occurs when the marginal value of liquidity, the service rendered by money, is precisely equal to the interest lost, and the money balance is increased or diminished as the marginal liquidity premium is higher or lower than the market interest rate.

The footnotes follow: We begin with Allais's footnote 11.
(11) It is in fact easy to make precise via a particular example these intuitive, but obviously rather fuzzy, ideas.

Consider, for example, an economic agent who has a continuous inflow of net receipts equal to R per unit of time (Figure 33.1) and suppose that he only invests the money received in this way at intervals of time of length T, when his balance reaches some certain value. In these circumstances the curve representing his balance as a function of time will be made up of a series of linear segments and will oscillate between zero and RT, so that its mean value will be

$$M = \frac{RT}{2}. \tag{1}$$

If one then used $F(V)$ to represent the [transactions] cost of investing an amount equal to V in value, the transactions cost per unit of time will be equal to $F(RT)/T$, that is, to $RF(2M)/2M$. If the average balance increases by ΔM, the cost saving per unit of time, which is equal to the

THE OPTIMAL CASH BALANCE PROPOSITION

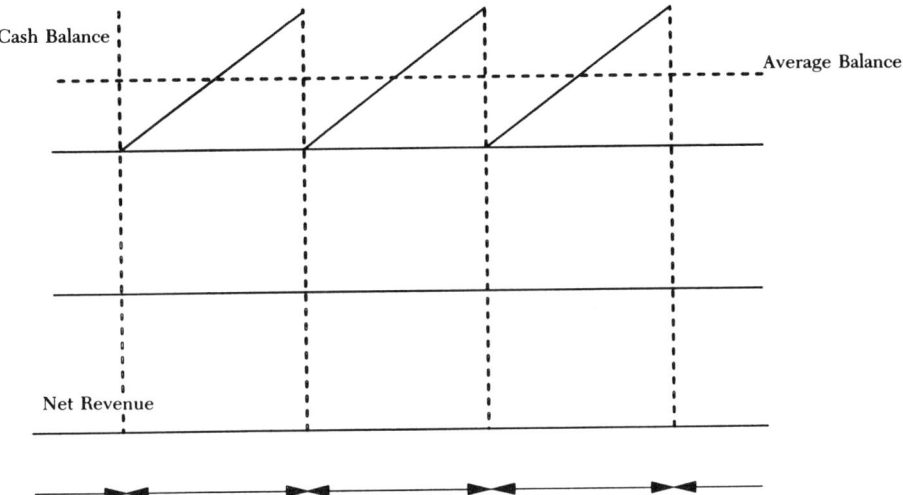

Figure 33.1

marginal liquidity premium of the average balance, will equal the derivative of the quantity, so that one will have

$$l_m = -R \frac{d}{dM} \frac{F(2M)}{2M}. \tag{2}$$

If F is constant one then obtains

$$l_m = \frac{RF}{2M^2}, \tag{3}$$

a function decreasing in the average balance, M.

This extremely simple example has the advantage of making it easy to understand how things work out and of showing how a rigorous and general theory of liquidity can be constructed.

Here we proceed to Allais's footnote 12.

(12) In the example of note (11) the balance, M_E, held in equilibrium is determined naturally by the relation

$$-R \frac{d}{dM} \frac{F(2M)}{2M} = i. \tag{4}$$

It is, as a matter of fact, easy to derive this relationship directly. Let C be the amount of capital held by the agent under consideration. At the end of each period, T, one has

$$\Delta C = iTC_0 + RT - F(RT), \tag{5}$$

where C_0 represents the capital held at the beginning of period T. This relation yields

$$\frac{\Delta C}{T} = iC_0 + R - R\frac{F(2M)}{2M}. \tag{6}$$

One may be tempted to use the rate $\Delta C/T$ as a first approximation to the derivative dC/dT, but such an approximation amounts to the assumption that the income R is invested in a continuous manner, whereas in fact it is invested only discontinuously. This assumption would attribute to dC too high a figure for the amount of interest earned on the balance during each period, T, an excess approximately equal to the product, iM, of its average value, M, and the market rate of interest, i. In fact, it is clear that one should write

$$\frac{dC}{dt} = iC + R - R\frac{F(2M)}{2M} - iM. \tag{7}$$

The optimal balance is then attained when capital accumulates most rapidly, that is to say, when the sum

$$R\frac{F(2M)}{2M} + iM \tag{8}$$

attains its minimum, a result that is realized when one sets

$$\frac{d}{dM}\left(R\frac{F(2M)}{2M} + iM\right) = 0. \tag{9}$$

In the case where F is a constant, the size of the balance is determined by the relation

$$\frac{RF}{2M^2} = i.$$

Thus, if $R = 100{,}000$ frs, $F = 200$ frs and $i = 5\%$, one obtains $M = 14{,}000$ frs. One sees in this way that even an investment transactions cost that is relatively modest can imply a substantial value for the average balance. Because

$$\frac{M}{R} = \sqrt{\frac{F}{2iR}}$$

one sees that in the case considered the relationship of the average balance to annual income is weaker the higher is this income. This result continues to hold if F increases with income R, but less rapidly than the latter. This is a state of affairs that seems to prevail quite generally.

Note

1. The inventory-theoretic derivation goes back to 1925–27 when it was independently contributed by some half-dozen authors. This was described in Baumol (1952) on the basis of information obtained from Thomson Whitin who had first called the literature to Baumol's attention. On the early literature see Whitin (1953, chapter 2, esp. p. 32, footnote 4).

References

Allais, Maurice. *Economie et Intérêt*. Paris: Imprimerie Nationale, 1947.

Baumol, William J. "The Transactions Demand for Cash: An Inventory Theoretic Approach," *Quart. J. Econ.*, Nov. 1952, *66*, pp. 545–56.

Tobin, James. "The Interest-Elasticity of Transactions Demand for Cash," *Rev. Econ. Statist.*, Aug. 1956, *38*, pp. 241–47.

Whitin, Thomson M. *The Theory of Inventory Management*. Princeton: Princeton U. Press, 1953

CHAPTER 34

WILLIAM S. VICKREY

President Daughdrill, Mr. Seidman, ladies and gentlemen, it is an honor for me to introduce to you William Spencer Vickrey, McVickar Professor of Political Economy Emeritus at Columbia University, currently President of the American Economic Association. I am proud to have served on the Seidman Award selection committee that enthusiastically recommended Professor Vickrey to the Board of Trustees.

Bill Vickrey has been at Columbia University, with some interruptions, since 1935. Few economists, few academics, have such long careers at a single institution. He went to Columbia for Ph.D. study in economics just after graduating from Yale—a wise move, I believe, given the state of economics at the time at those two institutions. It was a particularly happy choice for Vickrey and for the profession, because his 1947 dissertation under Robert Murray Haig, a leading public finance authority, was a classic work, republished as such in 1964. And Vickrey carried on, embodied, and strengthened Columbia's traditional eminence in public finance.

Bill, let me in turn introduce to you this audience. Memphis is a long way from New York and New Haven. But as you are finding out, your new friends are not only extremely hospitable but also deeply interested in political economy and its practitioners, for whom their tastes are sophisticated and discriminating. With the leadership of the Seidman family, expressed in the Award and in numerous other ways, Memphis is connected to the whole world of political economy.

Introduction of 1992 Recipient, William S. Vickrey, and Presentation of the Award, The Frank E. Seidman Distinguished Award in Political Economy, Rhodes College, Memphis, TN, September 24, 1992.

The eighteen previous recipients of this Award have, each in his own way, made a significant contribution to the science, the art, and the practice of political economy. Bill Vickrey's contributions are equally distinguished, and they too have taken forms reflecting the recipient's unique interests and talents. I have long admired Bill's work, unhappily from a moderate distance (Yale and Columbia are separated by all of 75 miles) and without many personal contacts. I did not have the good fortune to be his student or colleague. In connection with this Award, I discovered that Vickrey's contributions to economic theory and its applications were even more original, penetrating, and extensive than I had previously appreciated.

Indeed many economists of all ages agree that Bill Vickrey deserved much more recognition, much earlier in his career, than he received. The American Economic Association, which only recently chose him as its President, fourteen years ago honored him as one of its few Distinguished Fellows. The citation on that occasion expresses well the belated appreciation of his profession, and I would like to quote from it.

"Many of us have had the experience of thinking we were the first to publish this or that new proposition in economic theory only to find that William S. Vickrey had done it earlier—and whereas our "original contribution" contained ... error, Vickrey had done it correctly. Some great scholars receive recognition from the beginning, but, inscrutably, with others it takes a little longer. His numerous works contain many seminal contributions, and many more that would have been seminal but for the fact that the profession was not yet ready for his ideas.... We are proud to recognize the creative, inspirational, and persistently operational character of William S. Vickrey's contributions to economic theory and economic policy."

As a theorist, Bill Vickrey has been original, insightful, and elegant. He thinks more deeply than almost anyone else about the meanings and implications of the basic assumptions of economic theory. He uses whatever mathematics is useful for himself, his students, and his readers; after all, he majored in math at Yale. But he has never regarded mathematics *per se* as a substitute for logical thought, economic intuition, and common sense. His famous course in theory at Columbia was a gem, or rather a series of gems, opening the eyes and minds of generations of graduate students. Those lectures were the bases for Vickrey's two volumes on theory, micro and macro. They too are classics. Graduate students today, and their teachers, would learn more durable lessons from them than from fashionable contemporary literature.

Maybe Bill Vickrey could be described as a theorist's theorist, and some of his achievements, like an article on auction "markets" singled out in the full text of the 1978 AEA citation, do require experts to appreciate them fully. But pure theory was never Bill's main objective. He is an economist's theorist, certainly an applied economist's theorist, as well as a theorist's supplied economist. He seems always to have believed that the principles and analytical tools of economists can be put to work in the social interest. His mind is always on potential applications—in policy making, legislation, administration, and institutional architecture. The AEA citation rightly describes his work as "persistently operational."

Bill Vickrey is definitely not a simple admirer of *laissez faire* who regards the proper work of economists to be explaining to a skeptical populace how the invisible hand of free market competition harnesses self-interested economic behavior to the maximum welfare of society. He knows it takes a lot of hard thought and hard work and ingenuity to design institutions that yield reasonably fair and efficient outcomes. Bill takes seriously theoretical conditions of economic optimality, like marginal cost pricing, and he tries to think of institutions that would approximate those conditions.

An example is his painstaking 1952 work on the fare structure of the New York subway system. Vickrey knew that the flat rate fare (a nickel at the time) could not be optimal. For efficiency, the fare should take account of the extra congestion a passenger causes. A passenger who rides to or from a heavy-traffic station during rush hours imposes more costs on the system and on other passengers than one who rides between remote stations in the middle of the day or at night. Vickrey was not content to point out this principle of welfare economics. He went into the specific details of the New York system and its traffic. He even worked out the engineering details of implementing a more rational system of fares related to marginal costs. Technology has caught up with him now. His suggestions would be much easier and cheaper to implement than in the 1950's. Vickrey also observed that it might save money to collect no fares at all at certain stations at certain times. Incidentally, Vickrey believed that it is not optimal to make the riders pay the full fixed costs of the system.

Vickrey has also been ahead of his time in advocating that users who congest roads and streets pay the costs they impose. At least twenty years ago he proposed tolls for driving in congested areas at peak times and worked out the engineering mechanics of recording such use by tamper-proof meters in each vehicle. They would be officially read at intervals, and the registered owner of the vehicle would be billed. Here, too, modern electronics and telecommunication technologies make his plan much more feasible. Some cities in Europe are beginning to charge tolls for entering downtown areas.

The bulk of Vickrey's contributions have been on taxation, the field of his Ph.D. thesis, published as *Agenda for Progressive Taxation*, the classic I mentioned at the beginning. His work in design of taxes is at the same time one of the most theory-intensive and the most practical of economists' prescriptions. He has treated extensively the taxation of income, expenditure, wealth, capital gains, business profits, and inter-generational transfers of wealth.

Let me just tell you one of his great ideas. Vickrey favors progressive taxation as a matter of equity, but he worries about the fact that progressive rate structure means that the same total income over several years will be taxed more if it is concentrated in one tax year than if it is spread evenly. This is unfair, and it creates uneconomic incentives to move income, at least in appearance, from one tax year to another. For this reason, tax codes generally allow some averaging. Vickrey's proposal goes further. The IRS would keep for each taxpayer a cumulative account of income and tax paid. Each year you would be liable for a tax on your total income up to that point, and your previous tax payments would be credits against this liability. The ingenuity and simplicity of this idea are breathtaking. As soon as you hear it you are likely to say, yes of course. You will think of some problems, but you may be sure that Bill long ago thought them through.

In his own vita, Vickrey mentions with obvious pride an honorary degree Doctor of Humane Letters from the University of Chicago, and adds the following about himself: "The award that is posted on the door of his office, however, is the 'Rip van Winkle' award from the Center for Advanced Study in the Behavioral Sciences 'for deep and uninterrupted concentration while attending seminars.'" Spies at Columbia tell me that Bill attends numerous seminars throughout the university and rests with closed eyes for much of the time. However, he always does perk up, and then he at once offers the most cogent comment or blockbuster question of the whole discussion. Rip van Winkle, in contrast, was ignorant of what had gone on while he slept. Some say that Vickrey does sleep but keeps his eyes closed when he wakes up just long enough to capture the gist of the paper and discussion and to formulate his intervention. Perhaps only he knows, perhaps nobody knows, the truth.

Well, Bill that time has come. I have the honor and privilege to present to you the 1992 Frank E. Seidman Distinguished Award in Political Economy.

CHAPTER 35

PAUL SAMUELSON: MACROECONOMICS AND FISCAL POLICY

The Young Keynesian at Harvard

When the Keynesian Revolution burst upon Cambridge, Massachusetts in 1936 Paul Samuelson, all of twenty years old, had been a graduate student at Harvard for less than a year. Ten years later he recalled the invasion [1946, II, Chap. 114, p. 157].[1]

I have always considered it a priceless advantage to have been born as an economist prior to 1936 and to have received a thorough grounding in classical economics. It is quite impossible for modern students to realize the full effect of ... "The Keynesian Revolution" upon those of us brought up in the orthodox tradition.... To have been born as an economist before 1936 was a boon—yes. But not to have been born too long before!

Bliss was it in that dawn to be alive
But to be young was very heaven!

I was born a year too late, alas. I began studying economics as a Harvard sophomore in 1936, and my tutor, Spencer Pollard, blithely suggested we start by reading a new book from England. Unlike Paul, who as an undergraduate at Chicago studied under Simons, Knight, Viner, Director, and company and consorted with graduate students named Stigler, Wallis, Hart, and Friedman, I didn't really know what I was rebelling against. But maybe the classically educated old-timers like Paul didn't either, for later he often said and wrote that there was no clear, explicit, classical macro-model prior to the Keynesian challenge. Anyway, the virus that, as he recounts, so rapidly conquered the young economists of Cambridge was in turn transmitted by them to us undergraduates in

Reprinted by permission from *Paul A. Samuelson and Modern Theory*, eds. E. Cary Brown and R. M. Solow, New York: McGraw-Hill, 1983, pp. 189–201.

classes, seminars, tutorials, and common rooms. And so, though he was never formally my teacher, I began learning from Paul Samuelson in those exciting years, and I'm still at it.

Samuelson's program at Harvard was not conventional graduate study. He had anticipated much of that at Chicago, and at Harvard he was soon liberated from requirements by appointment to the Society of Fellows. He undertook the ambitious and searching formal investigation of economic theory ultimately compiled in his *Foundations*. A theorist so gifted in the calculus of optimization and market clearing and so fascinated by the elegance of neoclassical equilibrium and welfare results might have been immune to the Keynesian virus. As many general equilibrium theorists have done then and since, he might have thrown up his hands at the messy problems and untidy techniques of macroeconomics. Samuelson chose to work both sides of the street.

A big reason was certainly Cambridge itself, the American scene of intense debate over the world economic crisis and the crisis of world economics. Haberler, Hansen, Harris, Schumpeter, and Williams were in the thick of battles fought in an unceasing sequence of classes, seminars, forums, papers, and conversations. So was an unparalleled band of eager, talented, junior faculty and graduate students, among them the Sweezys, the Salants, Metzler, Goodwin, Galbraith, and Gordon. Academic economics seemed terribly important, both for understanding the Depression and for overcoming it.[2]

In this setting Samuelson became a Keynesian as well as a Walrasian, though he says [1964, II, Chap. 114] it took him and everyone else at least eighteen months and help from the equations of Hicks, Lange, Meade, and Harrod to understand the *General Theory*. A brash *enfant terrible*, Paul amazed and delighted his contemporaries and us youngsters by puncturing the classical fallacies of senior professors and unwary visitors or exposing their shaky grasp of new truth.

What if Paul had stayed at Chicago? What if he had gone to Columbia, as his Chicago mentors urged? Would he have eschewed macroeconomics? Would he have become a monetarist? Probably even he cannot be sure. My own guess is that he would sooner or later have come to terms with Keynesian macroeconomics in much the same way that he in fact did. Given his insatiable appetite for all economics, given his real-world curiosities and concerns, he was bound to give Keynes most serious attention. As a microeconomist, he was never so bewitched by the miracle of the Invisible Hand as to regard market failure as per se implausible. Moreover, his early articles display a general interest in stability of equilibrium and a generous admiration for the pragmatic pre-Keynesian dynamic models of Frisch and other European mathematical economists.

But only at Harvard could he have become friends with Alvin Hansen, the major personal association and example attracting Samuelson to Keynes and to macroeconomics. Hansen's integrity, shown by his public 180-degree change of mind about the *General Theory* at age 50, his evident conviction and seriousness of purpose, his lack of pretension, and his collegial treatment of students and junior faculty—all earned him affection, admiration, and influence among young scholars. Samuelson expresses these feelings in several tributes [1959, II, Chap. 84; 1975, IV, Chap. 287; 1976, IV, Chap. 285]. From his young friend Samuelson, Hansen asked and received theoretical and technical help and collaboration, including the famous accelerator-multiplier model, Paul's first published contribution to macroeconomics [1939, II, Chap. 82].

The Coverage of this Chapter

In this appreciation of Paul Samuelson as macroeconomist I shall concentrate on his contributions to the methodology and substance of macromodel building and to the positive and normative theory of stabilization, with emphasis on fiscal policy. This was Samuelson's own emphasis in his first twenty-five years, both in his pathbreaking early papers on multiplier statics and dynamics and in his crystallization of the neoclassical synthesis after the Second World War. But at no stage was Samuelson a "fiscalist," and I shall point out the important role money and monetary policy played in his macroeconomics from the beginning. More thorough reviews of his contributions to the theory of money and finance are provided by Don Patinkin and Robert Merton elsewhere in this volume in honor of Samuelson.

There are several other overlaps, reflecting connections of Samuelson's macroeconomics to his many other interests and fields of contribution. This chapter of that volume concerns income determination in the short run and stabilization policy, but these topics necessarily intersect Samuelson's work on capital theory and long-run economic growth, treated in Robert Solow's chapter. Likewise Samuelson was a student of public finance theory in general, not just fiscal macroeconomics, as will be evident both here and in Richard Musgrave's review.

Samuelson's model of intergenerational consumption loans [1958, I, Chap. 21] is treated elsewhere in the book. It has turned out to be an amazingly insightful construct, with implications for basic monetary and macroeconomic theory that have only recently begun to be fully exploited. Its overlapping-generations setup is the simplest major competitor to the classical simplifying assumption that economic agents have infinite horizons. On the differences between infinite and finite horizons turn such issues as the elasticity of the economy's ultimate demand for wealth, the absorption of saving by government deficits financed by interest-bearing debt, the displacement of capital by money, public debt, and unfunded social insurance, the long-run neutrality of inflation and monetary growth, and the optimality of monetary saturation. Both Keynes and Samuelson understood a crucial macroeconomic fact—savers and investors acquire assets that last longer than they do. I do not expatiate here on these fruits of a paper written twenty-three years ago. I simply marvel at the prescience and genius they confirm.

I cannot do justice to several well-known unusual aspects of Samuelson's voluminous writings. His feeling for economics as an evolving science with history and tradition is rare, all too rare, among modern economists. He learned the history of doctrine in every field he wrote about and wrote perceptively about the major contributions and contributors of the past. Notable for macroeconomics are his essays on Keynes and Hansen cited above, and on Wicksell [1959, II, Chap. 120]; Harris [1975, IV, Chap. 284]; Schumpeter [1951, II, Chap. 116]; and Lerner [1963, III, Chap. 183]—all marvelous examples of intellectual and personal biography. His substantive papers are full of illuminating reference to the histories of their subjects, placing his own results in perspective for the less learned reader.

What other high-powered mathematical theorist except Irving Fisher has written a running commentary on the events, outlooks, and policies of his years? As I read again a sequence of Samuelson's pieces in this genre, I saw how the Wunderkind from Gary added wisdom to logic, fortunately never sacrificing brashness to maturity. Samuelson has always been a voracious consumer and efficient distiller of the profession's research output, whether theory, empirical findings, or big-model forecasts. To a far-reaching network of informants within the profession he added over the years contacts in business, finance, and government throughout the world. His comments on current events and issues make good use of inputs from all sources. I have not tried to assess Samuelson's forecasting success, and I suspect he has been too canny to leave an easily tested record. There is the danger that inspection would reveal him to be another Sumner Slichter, who often figures in Samuelson's writings as an economist reputed for successful forecasting but by undisclosed and unreplicable methods.

A final and somewhat personal introductory comment. As a member of the Kennedy economic team, I knew, as my colleagues did, that our analysis and strategy were not nearly as "new economics" as the media label suggested. I did not know, more charitably did not remember, how much of our doctrine, as expounded for instance in the 1962 *Economic Report*, Samuelson had written down long before. To mention only two examples, Samuelson coined the concepts of potential output and its growth [1953, II, Chap. 99] and stated then that the objective of countercyclical policy was not just to smooth fluctuation and stabilize employment and output, but to minimize departures from full employment equilibrium and the trend of potential output. Other long-standing Samuelson contributions to our new economics will be clear in my review below of the neoclassical synthesis. By 1961 these ideas had become second nature to us, the public domain of our intellectual heritage. Samuelson was a member, one might better say coach, of that team. But he certainly didn't remind us that ideas we were so excitedly developing and propagating had appeared in his writings ten or fifteen years earlier.

The Statics and Dynamics of Income Determination

In Cambridge in the late 1930s and early 1940s Paul Samuelson undertook a fundamental inquiry into the sources of operationally meaningful propositions in economic theory. By happy chance this inquiry coincided with the ferment triggered by Keynes's *General Theory*. By still happier chance the new macroeconomics was grist for Samuelson's mill; it was the natural subject matter for developing many of the methodological points he sought to make. These concerned the properties of whole systems:

the meaning of equilibrium and disequilibrium; statics, stationarity, and dynamics; stability and instability; hysteresis. According to the young Samuelson [1941, I, Chap. 40], it was Ragnar Frisch who, a decade earlier, had engineered a "revolution of thought" in economics, one comparable to "the transition from classical to quantum mechanics." This was a shift from "statical to dynamical modes" of analysis.

It may seem paradoxical that Samuelson, given this methodological stance, found Keynesian macroeconomics a fertile field to plow. The *General Theory* itself was thoroughly in the statical mode. So were those formalizations by Hicks and others that alone, according to Samuelson's own testimony, made the book comprehensible. The paradox is, of course, resolved by his celebrated and controversial correspondence principle, summarized in his dictum "One interested only in fruitful statics must study dynamics" [*Foundations*, p. 5].

Samuelson found two sources of meaningful propositions in economic *theory*. One is that relations among observable variables reflect agents' solutions of optimization problems like maximization of utility or profits or wealth. First- and second-order conditions could then restrict signs and magnitudes in comparative static analyses, for example, of the effect of variations of taste, technology, or taxes. However, Samuelson was definitely not sanguine about the power of this principle for relations aggregated over many agents. He was therefore skeptical of its usefulness in generating systemwide propositions. Given the inevitable differences among agents, anything could happen in aggregate and still be consistent with individual optimizations. These misgivings, which foreshadow much later, the rigorous proofs of similar negative results by Sonnenschein, McFadden, Mantel, and others, contrast with a popular current fashion among macroeconomic theorists, who achieve the appearance of rigor by assuming away troublesome heterogeneities among agents. In any case, it led Samuelson to emphasize his second theoretical source of meaningful propositions, the correspondence principle.

According to the principle, a general hypothesis of dynamic stability restricts the parameters of a system of relationships [*Foundations*, p. 5]. With and only with these restrictions can meaningful comparative static propositions about the equilibrium position or motion of the system be obtained. A famous and simple example concerns the Keynesian multiplier: If and only if the marginal propensity to spend is less than one is the equilibrium stable and the multiplier formula usable for predicting the ultimate effect of an exogenous change in investment or government purchases. Initially Samuelson seemed prepared to assert stability as an empirical hypothesis, and thus in the example to say that the marginal propensity to spend must be less than one because otherwise the system would be unstable. After all, he said, unstable systems don't generate many observations—"How many times has the reader seen an egg standing upon its end?" [*Foundations*, p. 5]. I recall Joseph Schumpeter's rebuke to this line of reasoning, "Who could ever claim that capitalism is stable?"

Later, after prodding by Donald F. Gordon in 1955, Samuelson retreated, admitting that observations might be generated by a process different from the proposed model under analysis, even by a slowly divergent dynamic system, so that the quantitative information about particular parameters implied by his principle was seriously limited [1955, II, Chap. 128]. Moreover, the same static equations may be the equilibrium of a host of dynamic models, so that the stability restrictions are themselves ambiguous. The canon of consistency for theorists of course survives: Don't do comparative statics with dynamically unstable systems.

In [1941, I, Chap. 38] Samuelson illustrated the correspondence principle by applying it to several simple models. One of them was a Keynesian-IS-LM model with three endogenous variables—income, interest, and investment—and three exogenous parameters—consumption, investment, and money. Like the other examples, this one was methodologically instructive. But the ambiguities in the results—even when several behavioral partial derivatives were signed a priori—also show the limitations of the method.

The young Samuelson's belief that the future of economic theory lay in Frisch's footsteps, in explicit dynamical models, and in comparative dynamics as well as in proper comparative statics, has not been confirmed in quite the way nor to the degree that he anticipated. For one thing, such systems easily become too complicated for closed analytical results. This is especially true of nonlinear systems, and Samuelson admitted he was too optimistic about the usefulness of linear models. Moreover, without and probably also with the restraints of optimizing assumptions, dynamic specifications of behavior equations contain an embarassing abundance of free parameters on whose values the model-builder has few clues.

Distributed lag structures are a good example. Of course, modern computers permit a great deal of numerical analysis and simulation. Macroeconometric models are nonlinear dynamic systems, and comparative dynamics is their routine stock in trade. But for better or worse their parameter restrictions do not come from theory. They are squeezed from data by econometric estimation or are imposed by model-builders' intuitions. Whether the new dynamic economics connected with rational expectations, replacing past initial conditions with future terminal conditions, will realize the Frischian revolution remains an open question.[3]

As the years wore on, Samuelson himself tended to use the statical mode and keep the associated dynamics and stability analysis implicit. Even with respect to the multiplier, he found that the most important lessons came from Keynes's static version rather than from sequential processes of the Kahn, Robertson, or Swedish types. His neoclassical synthesis of macroeconomic theory, discussed below, is essentially a comparative static analysis of the equilibrium effects of policy variations.

In any event, Samuelson taught a generation of economists about difference equations, dynamic process analysis, and stability conditions and immensely clarified their conceptions of equilibrium, disequilibrium, and comparative statics. Most of this brilliant instruction was in the context of macroeconomics. Armed with his metatheoretical methodology, Samuelson produced a remarkable series of papers [1939, II, Chaps. 82 and 83; 1940, II, Chap. 85; 1942, II, Chap. 86; 1943, II, Chap. 90; 1948, II, Chap. 91; 1952, I, Chap. 41] ringing all the changes on investment and fiscal multipliers and laying the formal basis for Keynesian fiscal theory. He cut through the confusions of the day regarding sequential processes versus equilibrium outcomes; saving-investment identities, schedules, and equilibrium equalities; exogenous tax variations versus endogenous responses of revenues; one-shot versus continued multiplicands; pump-priming versus stable multiplier scenarios. He showed that with any linear lagged spending function the ultimate multiplier for a permanent unit injection is the same as the cumulative sum of income increases due to a single unit injection. He offered as a theorem, quite relevant today, that fiscal stimulus could not pay for itself in augmented tax revenues (thus overlooking the classroom *curiosum* that this can happen in a stable model if some spending, presumably for investment, is induced by before-tax rather than after-tax income). The balanced budget multiplier escaped Samuelson's notice at first, and by his own report he was initially dubious [1943, II, Chap. 108, p. 1446]. Nevertheless, he must be counted as one of the several independent discoverers of this celebrated, probably overcelebrated, theorem, a history of which he has given [1975, IV, Chap. 274].

Perhaps more remarkable for early multiplier papers, Samuelson did not neglect other macroeconomic effects. He explained how monetary, interest, and price responses could affect the parameters, processes, and outcomes. One paper shows how interest rates will evolve during fiscal stimulus, depending on the proportions in which the additional deficit is financed by public debt, low-powered money, and high-powered money. Clarity about stocks and flows was of course characteristic of all his writings, worth noting only because of the confusions in other discussions at the time.

The accelerator-multiplier model, an analysis suggested by Hansen in connection with the 1937–1938 recession, was pathbreaking in substance and methodology. Of course it was not the first mathematical business-cycle model, but it was more closely and directly tied to current macroeconomic concepts and literary theory than earlier exercises of Frisch and others. It was the progenitor of Metzler's classic inventory-cycle models; inventories were more suitable for the acceleration principle than fixed capital. The Hansen-Samuelson model suffered from relating induced investment to movements of consumption rather than total output, a misspecification easy to remedy. All models are parables, and Samuelson always made their morals explicit. Here the lesson was that various literary theorists of the cycle were mistaken to believe that nonlinearities were necessary to explain upper and lower turning points. Samuelson did not recognize at the time the defect of linear models as cycle theories, namely that if the model parameters imply cyclical fluctuations at all they either explode or die out except for singular values of the parameters. Evidently Samuelson sided with Keynes in thinking that exogenous investment shocks rather than intrinsic mechanisms were responsible for the persistence of fluctuations. He rather discounted the durable importance of accelerator-induced investment, because it would eventually have no effect on the capital stock, compared with the more basic determinants of demand for capital emphasized by Keynes and Hansen.

These exercises in the determination of output by effective demand were carried out by a neoclassical price theorist, but he found unproblematic the failure of prices, wages, and interest rates to eliminate excess supplies. Introducing a second and more thoughtful discussion of the accelerator-multiplier model than the original version [1939, II, Chap. 83], Samuelson simply refers to frictions and imperfections as evident justifications for proceeding. Indeed Samuelson never found the existence of excess-supply disequilibrium in the labor market a surprising departure from Walrasian equilibrium worthy of defense or of theoretical investigation. Looking for the essential Keynesian contribution ten years after the *General Theory* [II, chap. 114], he singled out not nominal wage stickiness but Keynes's insight that capital markets would not be cleared by interest rates, asset valuations, and other financial adjustments without movements of real income.

Probably for similar reasons, Samuelson could never muster much enthusiasm for the controversy about the Pigou or real-balance effect, the *riposte* to the claim of the *General Theory* that involuntary unemployment could characterize a true equilibrium in the classical sense [1963, II, Chap. 115]. Evidently Samuelson agreed all along that in principle competitive markets could not be in Walrasian market-clearing equilibrium with excess supplies of labor. He has been much interested, as a matter of pure theory and the logic of Walrasian systems, in the issues raised by Patinkin concerning the neutrality of outside money—or moneys, including government debts—and the classical dichotomy [1968, III, Chap. 176]. Samuelson certainly recognized a wealth effect on demand, emphasizing very early the link from asset revaluation to consumption as a more powerful effect of monetary policy than that of interest rates on investment. But he cites Pigou and quotes a 1935–1936 remark of Leontief—"If wages are low enough, this dime in my hand will employ everyone in the nation"—more as curious examples of a principle carried to uninteresting extreme that as serious macroeconomic argument [1964, II, Chap. 115, p. 1536]. Samuelson did not regard the actual economy as perfectly competitive. He thought frictions and imperfections made automatic market adjustment slower than the volatile fluctuations of investment demand associated with Keynes's "state of long-term expectation." He commented, again long before expected price inflation or deflation was so central a theoretical issue and practical concern, that such expectations are quite possibly more important determinants of aggregate real demand than are price levels [1940, II, Chap. 88].

From early postwar years on, Samuelson was skeptical that full employment and price stability were compatible objectives in the absence of good luck or wage and price controls.[4] It did not occur to him to define full employment by the unemployment rate consistent with price or inflation stability. He certainly regarded Keynesian fiscal policies, and monetary policies, too, as two-sided weapons, to be used against excess demand as well as excess supply. His article with Solow [1960, II, Chap. 102], suggesting that Phillips curves represent tradeoffs for policymakers, has been much maligned, cited as the prototypical example of Keynesian error of the 1960s. Actually it is quite guarded and sophisticated in distinguishing long-run effects from short-run and worrying about expectations induced by policies and experience. It certainly does not say that expansion of monetary demand can purchase any desired rate of employment and capacity utilization indefinitely at finite cost in inflation.

Samuelson's early macroeconomic writings concern the demand side of fiscal policy. Many of his later writings concern the supply side and therefore have particular relevance today. His contributions to public finance are reviewed elsewhere in this volume. Therefore, I shall simply note that in the 1950s and 1960s Samuelson clearly analyzed the effects of accelerated depreciation, investment tax credits, preferential treatment of capital gains, and deductibility of interest. A 1964 paper [III, Chap. 179] proves the neutrality of proportional taxation on accrual of true economic income to capital, with respect to rates of return. Regarding concessions going beyond such neutrality he said, "If we call spades spades, let's call bribes bribes," even if we decide as a matter of national policy to offer them. He could repeat verbatim in 1981 much earlier testimony to this effect.

The Neoclassical Synthesis

Paul Samuelson's greatest contribution to macroeconomics was the neoclassical synthesis, of which he was the principal architect [1951, II, Chap. 98; 1953, II, Chap. 99; 1955, II, Chap. 100; 1963, II, Chap. 115]. This *Weltanschauung* reconciled the classical and Keynesian strands of his thinking and that of many of his contemporaries. It became orthodox doctrine for a generation of economists and for many of their students.

Certainly in the profession it was the mainstream Keynesian tradition in North America.

Of course there has always been strong dissent in both directions. From the older Cambridge, Joan Robinson and her colleagues and disciples attacked the synthesis as a heretical perversion of Keynes's true message. American post-Keynesians echo the charge. This battle is intimately entangled with the war of two Cambridges over capital and growth theory, reviewed elsewhere by Robert Solow.

On the other side of Samuelson's middle ground, Walrasians have always questioned the basic consistency of the market failures assumed or alleged in Keynesian theory with rational behavior. Recently this challenge has dramatically regained professional attention and support from the new classical macroeconomics and the theory of rational expectations. Robert Lucas, the leader of this counterrevolution, pays Samuelson and his partners in crime the high compliment of making the neoclassical synthesis the heresy become orthodoxy that Lucas is rebelling against.[5]

As I interpret it, Samuelson's exposition of the neoclassical synthesis contains both positive and normative propositions. The positive propositions, baldly stated, are as follows:

Market-clearing equilibrium provides a tolerably good description of long-term trends. Market adjustments *and countercyclical policies* will over the decades keep macroeconomic outcomes close to full employment on average; anyway, there will be no tendency for relative margins of underutilization to rise secularly. In this sense, long-run growth tracks equilibrium supplies of labor, capital, natural resources, and—most decisive for labor productivity and living standards in Samuelson's view—knowledge.

These tracks are fairly smooth and cannot account for observed short-run volatility in economic performance. Fluctuations about the trends reflect mainly shocks to aggregate effective demand, to which prices, wages, and interest rates cannot and do not respond rapidly enough to preserve equilibrium. Movements of output and income are therefore intrinsic to the economy's responses to shocks, and in the absence of stabilizing policies the mechanisms of quantity adjustment can produce cumulative swings of large amplitude.

At bottom these short-run disequilibria reflect adjustment costs and lags, market imperfections, and discrepancies of information and expectation. The shocks that generate cyclical fluctuations may be governmental in origin, but there are many other sources as well. As noted above, Samuelson accepted Keynes's view that investment, dependent on business expectations and confidence regarding a long and uncertain future, was naturally erratic. For this combination of reasons, there is plenty of room for fiscal and monetary measures of stabilization to hold the economy closer to its equilibrium path.

The neoclassical synthesis cleansed Keynesian economics of some mistakes of content, context, or emphasis, mistakes not so much intrinsic to the *General Theory* as Depression-bound simplifications and extrapolations by Keynes's followers in the thirties and forties. Among these were:

1. The view that consumption demand would inevitably become weaker with the advance of productivity and the secular-stagnation pessimism to which it led. Samuelson anticipated [1943, II, Chap. 108] the agonizing postwar reappraisal of the consumption function, arguing that upward shifts in the short-run function would prevent secular decline of the average propensity to consume;

2. The view that monetary policy was inconsequential because of very high interest elasticity of demand for money or very low interest elasticity of investment;

3. The connected view, certainly not Keynes's own but inherited from the accelerator and perpetuated by Harrod-Domar growth theory, that capital-output ratios are frozen. Samuelson was at pains to disavow both this extreme and the "implicit 'classical' axiom that motivated investment is *indefinitely expansible or contractable* so that whatever people try to save will always be fully invested" [1946, II, Chap. 114, p. 1523];

4. The exclusive stress on government purchases, like public works, as vehicles of fiscal stimulus. Of course Samuelson had long recognized tax and transfer multipliers;

5. The assumption of textbook convenience that nominal prices or wage rates or both would remain constant in the face of fluctuations of aggregate demand—all that is really needed is that they are not perfectly flexible.

The normative and policy propositions follow easily, and in Samuelson's mind they were the most important part of the message. After all, as much as he relished all aspects of economics, he loved welfare economics most of all. Neoclassical welfare calculus, he found, far from being rendered irrelevant by Keynesian economics, applies not only to resource allocation in equilibrium but also to the choice of measures to restore and maintain full employment. Essentially resources are scarce even when some are temporarily unemployed. There are always socially valuable ways to employ them; make-work projects—like Keynes's burying coins for treasure seekers to dig up—are always unnecessary and wasteful.

The size of government and the amount of public consumptions and investments should be in principle determined by equating their returns in social utility on the margin with the values of the private uses of resources they displace. Fiscal and monetary policy can always generate the private purchasing power to reemploy the resources in private consumption and investment, which thus become the opportunity cost of exhaustive public expenditures. This principle—Samuelson called it the new look [1955, II, Chap. 100]—is consistent with the use of fiscal policy, discretionary or built-in, for stabilization, because stimulus can be provided or withdrawn by adjusting taxes and transfers as well as purchases. Samuelson was careful to point out [1951, II, Chap. 98], taking issue with a number of proposed formulas for countercyclical policy, that the principle does not imply that government purchases should be cyclically constant at their optimal levels for an economy in sustained macroequilibrium. If recession or depression reflects weakening of the marginal efficiency of private investment or of the marginal utility of current private consumption, then it is a proper social response to channel some of the released resources into public programs whose marginal social values remain high. The reverse would be true in booms.

Furthermore, Samuelson argued, monetary and fiscal measures are within wide limits substitute techniques of stabilization. Their mixture can be adjusted to achieve socially desired allocations of output, as between consumption and investment Rational stabilization policy does not consist, as many Keynesian enthusiasts continued to believe even after the Depression, in throwing all instruments together into high or reverse gear. It consists in choosing, among those combinations that achieve stabilization objectives, one that also meets social criteria of allocational efficiency. If these criteria dictate, as they appeared to in 1961 and again in 1981, shifting the composition of output in favor of capital formation, this can be achieved without changing overall macroeconomic balance by combining tighter fiscal policy with easier monetary policy. In the 1960s application of this recipe was largely inhibited by interest rate floors designed to stem gold outflows. In the 1980s it is inhibited by official dedication to monetarist and supply-side nostrums.

It is relevant to the 1981 bandwagon rush to offer tax concessions to encourage private saving and business investment that Samuelson added distributional equity to the goals of stabilization and allocation that could be achieved by judicious choice of fiscal and monetary measures. We don't have to suffer extremes of inequality in order to achieve full employment and high capital intensity. Neither does prosperity require that we channel purchasing power to workers and to the poor, as underconsumptionists before and after Keynes contended. In summary, Samuelson told Congress [1955, II, Chap. 100, p. 1330]:

A community can have full employment, can at the same time have the rate of capital formation it wants, and can accomplish all this compatibly with the degree of income-redistributing taxation it ethically desires.

Samuelson consistently recognized that the one goal that fiscal and monetary policies may be unable to marry, probably permanently, with full employment is price stability. Even so, he surely overstated the case. In a more elaborate exposition Samuelson would recognize the limits on substitutions among policy instruments imposed by economic behavior and by other constraints or goals such as international trade and capital movement.

To my mind his optimisim is nevertheless much closer to the truth than the reverse doctrines popular in 1981, that prosperity and progress are imposslble without smaller government and greater inequality. But then I am a partner in crime, so dubbed in a cherished inscription by PAS on the flyleaf of Volume I, and I think the neoclassical synthesis was the great achievement of postwar macroeconomic theorizing.

Notes

1. Citations of Samuelson's *Collected Scientific Papers* give year of original publication, volume in roman numerals, chapter, and sometimes specific pages.
2. Samuelson's own reminiscences are in [1972, IV, Chap. 278].

3. On the methodological issues of this paragraph see Lucas (1980).
4. An early example is [1953, II, Chap. 99, pp. 1294–5, 1307].
5. Lucas (1980).

References

Lucas, Robert E., Jr. (1980): "Methods and Problems in Business Cycle Theory," *Rational Expectations*, A Seminar Sponsored by the American Enterprise Institute for Public Policy Research, *Journal of Money, Credit and Banking* vol. 2, (Nov.).

Samuelson, Paul A. (1939): "Interactions between the Multiplier Analysis and the Principle of Accleration," *Review of Economics and Statistics* 21 (May); *Collected Scientific Papers*, II, chap. 82.

——— (1939): "A Synthesis of the Principle of Acceleration and the Multiplier," *Journal of Political Economy* 48 (Dec.); *Collected Scientific Papers*, II, chap. 83.

——— (1940): "The Theory of Pump-Priming Reexamined," *American Economic Review* 30 (Sept.); *Collected Scientific Papers*, II, chap. 85.

——— (1941): "Concerning Say's Law," *Econometrica* 9 (April); *Collected Scientific Papers*, II, chap. 88.

——— (1941): "The Stability of Equilibrium: Comparative Statics and Dynamics," *Econometrica* 9 (April); *Collected Scientific Papers*, I, chap. 38.

——— (1942): "The Stability of Equilibrium: Linear and Nonlinear Systems," *Econometrica* 10 (Jan.); *Collected Scientific Papers*, I, chap. 40.

——— (1942): "Fiscal Policy and Income Determination," *Quartely Journal of Economics* 56 (Aug.); *Collected Scientific Papers*, II, chap. 86.

——— (1943): "Full Employment after the War," in S. E. Harris, ed., *Postwar Economic Problems*, New York, McGraw-Hill; *Collected Scientific Papers*, II, chap. 108.

——— (1943): "A Fundamental Multiplier Identity," *Econometrica* 11 (July–Oct.); *Collected Scientific Papers*, II, chap. 90.

——— (1948): "The Simple Mathematics of Income Determination," in L. A. Metzler et al., *Income, Employment and Public Policy: Essays in Honor of Alvin Hansen*, New York, Norton; *Collected Scientific Papers*, II, chap. 91.

——— (1948): "Dynamic Process Analysis," in Howard Ellis, ed., *A Survey of Contemporary Economics*, vol. I, Philadelphia, Blakiston; *Collected Scientific Papers*, I, chap. 41.

——— (1951): "Principles and Rules in Modern Fiscal Policy: A Neo-Classical Reformulation," in *Money, Trade and Economic Growth: Essays in Honor of John Henry Williams*, New York, Macmillan; *Collected Scientific Papers*, II, chap. 98.

——— (1951): "Schumpeter as a Teacher and Economic Theorist," *Review of Economics and Statistic* 33 (May); *Collected Scientific Papers*, II, chap. 116.

——— (1953): "Full Employment versus Progress and Other Economic Goals," in Max Millikan, ed., *Income Stabilization for a Developing Economy*, New Haven, Yale University Press; *Collected Scientific Papers*, II, chap. 99.

——— (1955): "Comment on 'Professor Samuelson on Operationalism in Economic Theory,' by Donald F. Gordon," *Quarterly Journal of Economics* 69 (May); *Collected Scientific Papers*, II, chap. 128.

——— (1956): "The New Look in Tax and Fiscal Policy" in Joint Committee on the Economic Report, 84th Congress, 1st Session, *Federal Tax Policy for Economic Growth and*

Stability (Nov. 9, 1955), Washington, U. S. Government Printing Office; *Collected Scientific Papers*, II, chap. 100.

――― (1959): Book review of Torsten Gardlund, *The Life of Knut Wicksell* in *Review of Economics and Statistics* 41 (Feb.); *Collected Scientific Papers*, II, chap. 120.

――― (1959): "Alvin Hansen and the Interactions between the Multiplier Analysis and the Principle of Acceleration," *Review of Economics and Statistics* 41 (May); *Collected Scientific Papers*, II, chap. 84.

――― (1960): with R. M. Solow, "Analytical Aspects of Anti-Inflation Policy," *American Economic Review* 50 (May); *Collected Scientific Papers*, II, chap. 102.

――― (1964): "The General Theory," in Robert Lekachman, ed., *Keynes' General Theory: Reports of Three Decades*, New York, St. Martin's Press; *Collected Scientific Papers*, II, chap. 114.

CHAPTER 36

SEYMOUR HARRIS

Biographical Note (by John McCutchan)

One of America's leading twentieth-century economists, Professor Harris typified the vitality of academic life. A teacher of economics for fifty years at Princeton, Harvard, and the University of California, San Diego, Dr. Harris was Chairman of the Department of Economics at Harvard and at UCSD. He was author of fifty-one books and an early and leading exponent of the New Economics. As a teacher and advisor to Presidents and presidential candidates, consultant to the Department of the Treasury and the Senate Finance Committee, as well as numerous federal, state, and international agencies and foreign governments, Dr. Harris had an important impact on recent national and international economic policy. A prolific and disciplined writer, he was editor of *The Review of Economics and Statistics* and contributed articles to a wide number of publications, among them *The New Republic*, the *Wall Street Journal*, the *Washington Post*, and *Commentary*. In 1968, he was presented the Alexander Hamilton Award by Treasury Secretary Henry Fowler in recognition of his long service to the Department of Treasury. A much sought-after expert witness on Capitol Hill, he became John F. Kennedy's first economic advisor in 1952 and continued to serve him into the Presidency.

Dr. Harris retired from Harvard in 1963 to become Chairman of the Department of Economics at UCSD in La Jolla, a post he held until 1970. Though retired from teaching, Professor Harris continued to write daily and had just completed his fifty-first book—an analysis of rising medical costs—prior to his death in 1974.

This chapter originally appeared in a book privately published by John McCutchan in memory of Seymour Harris, 1975. The Tribute had been delivered at the Memorial Service at Harvard in 1974.

Tribute

I speak of Seymour Harris with the affection, admiration, and gratitude of a generation younger than his own, his students who became his friends.

Seymour was a generous and thoughtful friend and patron of younger scholars. In my own case, he was a constant source of encouragement, instruction, help, and counsel—from the time of our first meeting when I was a Harvard freshman. Seymour was Senior Tutor of Dunster House. My roommate and I visited him during the annual rites by which freshmen applied to Houses and Houses selected freshmen. We were among the earliest barbarian immigrants to Harvard College, brought from the Midwest by Conant's national scholarship plan, and we were looking for the cheapest rooms. We were not greeted everywhere with enthusiasm (Eliot, for example). But Seymour, perhaps partly because he could spot me even then as a future economist, rolled out the crimson carpet and made us feel like the prize pair of the class of 1939. We ended up at Lowell—a mistake for which Seymour never ceased to twit me—but our friendship began, and Seymour went out of his way to keep in touch with me throughout my college career and afterward.

Years later, at the end of the Second World War, a deciding point in my own career, it was natural to write Seymour about the chances of returning to Harvard as a teaching fellow, and he convincingly urged me to forsake the attractions of Washington for academia. Many were the other doors he helped to open, some known to me and doubtless others unknown.

Carl Kaysen, Frank Sutton, and I collaborated with Seymour on a book in the late 1940's. We were ruthless in tearing up each other's drafts, and Seymour was not immune from the youthful arrogance of his junior collaborators. He took it with marvelous grace and modesty, resorted to no egotistical defense of his prose or seniority, and cooperated fully and industriously in the common design.

The thirties were an exhilarating time to discover economics, and Harvard was an exciting place. Young students, even undergraduates, could feel the rare convergence of intellectual revolution and instant relevance. It seemed that the ideas hammered out in this Cambridge, as in the older one, were actually solving the problems of nation and world. And Seymour Harris was one big reason for confidence that economics really made a difference.

Seymour, himself, was a prominent bearer of the new Keynesian standard, and he joined the fray with the zest of a happy warrior. Seymour loved friendly competition, between Keynesians and anti-Keynesians, Harvard and Yale, Dunster and Lowell, Democrats and Republicans, Treasury and Federal Reserve. Always the entrepreneur and educator, he was a participant in and a catalyst for memorable confrontations of ideas and policies. Under his leadership, Dunster was a center of economic ferment, indeed, of general ferment, over world affairs. It was no accident that Dunster had a stellar cast of economics tutors, of all ranks and ages, or that the House attracted more than its share of the liveliest undergraduates majoring in economics. Seymour also promoted Dunster House Forums, and the dining hall was filled to hear Sweezy tilt with Schumpeter, or Hansen with Haberler, or union leaders with Boston bankers.

At Littauer, Seymour and his close friend, but ideological opponent, Haberler brought to their seminar a parade of thinkers and doers in international economics, many of them former students reporting back from some firing line. Hansen and Williams, in similarly amicable disagreement, were doing the same for fiscal and monetary policy, and Seymour usually attended those seminars as well.

Under Seymour's editorship the *Review of Economics and Statistics* enjoyed a golden age probably unique for professional journals, in which high scientific standards in theory and empirical research were combined with lively discussion of pressing policy issues. It did not just happen. It happened because Seymour was an active, foresighted, and irresistibly persuasive editor—organizing symposia, soliciting articles, scouting the profession for relevant research.

Seymour brought a formidable mixture of energy, entrepreneurship, imagination, dedication, and loyalty to every institution he served, whether it was Dunster House, the *Review*, Harvard University, the Economics Department, the Democratic Party, or the U.S. Treasury. There was also a measure of historical curiosity, as his economic histories of various of these institutions indicated. My last sustained contacts with Seymour were on the New Frontier, when he was special senior adviser to Secretary of the Treasury Douglas Dillon. Seymour helped educate the Secretary and other Treasury officials. And, with his usual flair, he periodically called the best economists of all views to Washington to discuss the issues with the Secretary and others concerned with economic policy.

These consultants' meetings, a most constructive institution, were never so well focused and informative as under Seymour's original leadership. In those days we on the Council of Economic Advisers did not always see eye to eye with the Treasury. But Seymour was an effective agent for understanding and conciliation.

Seymour's prodigious record of publication is, for all of us from whom words flow on to paper with less facility, an awesome example of productivity. He always had the foresight to recognize an important problem, the initiative to assemble all the relevant information, and the industry to get the book written and produced. And so, time and time again, he led the profession into fields where its tools have been able to make productive and relevant contributions.

We shall not see his like again. But today let us not mourn Seymour Harris; let us not mourn the passage of time; let us rejoice together in our memories of a human life richly fulfilled.

INDEX

Aaa corporate bond rates, 382
Abel, A. B., 286, 287
Accelerated Cost Recovery, 369
Accounting framework, 70–74
Agents' behavior
  finite vs. infinite horizons, 275–276, 284–288, 300, 772
  new classical macroeconomic theory, 226–227
  policy changes affecting, 622
  rich vs. poor, 312, 317
Aggregate demand
  demand shock and changes in, 177
  exchange rate and, 489–490
  fiscal policy affecting, 489
  inadequacy of, 488
  monetary policy affecting, 489–490
  price level and, 187–188, 189–193
  real vs. nominal, 173–174
Aggregate production model, 682–683
Aggregate supply schedule, 402, 431–434
  factors affecting, 433
  Phillips curve, 431–432
  p-Y, 433
Akerlof, G., 532
Alexander, Sidney, 665
Allais, Maurice, 757–761
Allen, R. G. D., 6
American Economic Association, 673–675, 703
ANCAP, 147, 148
Anti-inflation policy, 222–223
Appreciation and Interest (Fisher), 684
"Are Government Bonds Net Wealth?" (Barro), 258
Arrow, Kenneth J., 9, 16, 27, 688, 709
Arrow-Debreu contract, 153
Arrow-Debreu general equilibrium specifications, 274
Asako, K., 304

Aschauer, D. A., 295–296
Asset accumulation models, 69
  empirical, 72–73
  theoretical, 71
Asset demands, 39–40
  determinants of, 42–44
  estimation, 104–105
  gross substitutes assumption, 40–41
  short-run functions, 87
  specification, 85–87
Asset exchanges, 310–315
Asset markets model, 543–546
Asset prices
  exchange rates as, 602–603
  in foreign investments, 559, 611–614
  liquidity preference and, 167–168
  models, consumption-betas in, 553
Assets
  disaggregation of, 24
  financial vs. real, 67
  with fixed nominal interest rates, 53–54
  gross substitutability, 40–41
  international transactions, 55
  supply sources, 32–34
Automatic overdraft privileges, 130

Backus, David, 105
Balanced budget multiplier, 263, 776–777
Balanced budget norm, 232, 473
  constitutional amendment, 254
Balance-of-payments accounts, 593
Ball, Lawrence, 173
Banking Act of 1935, 135
Banks
  adjustment coefficients, 95–96
  asset demand specification, 98–99
  inside assets, 52
  interest rate responses, 94
  nationally chartered, 148
  state chartered, 147

Baran, Paul, 665
Barro, Robert J., 258, 279, 283, 289, 291, 292, 316, 408
Barro effect, 336
Barsky, R. B., 308
Barter, 139, 140
Barth, J. R., 295
Base money, 33
 demand function for, 52–53
 rate of return, 56
 United States, 145
Baumol, William J., 12, 166, 243–244
Beggar-thy-neighbor policy, 428, 637, 652
Benninga, S., 312–313
Bequests, 282, 336
 optimal, 285
 retirement savings and, 349
Bernheim, D. B., 286–287, 297
Beveridge curve, 390–391
Bill market equilibrium model, 306
Bimetallism, 142
Black, John D., 7
Blinder, A. S., 265
Bondist policy, 316
Bonds
 Aaa corporate rates, 382
 after-tax real rate, 382
 interest rates, vs. real GNP growth rate, 291
 neutrality, 282
 steady-state solution, 56–58
Bootstrap approach, 168, 563–564
Borrowing against future earnings, 127
Boskin, M. J., 278
Bosworth, Barry, 503
Brady, Dorothy, 338
Brainard, William, 13–14, 25, 105, 404–405
Bretton Woods monetary system, 619, 621, 634–635, 645–646, 744–745
Brock, W. A., 300
Brookings Panel on Economic Activity, 738–739
Bryant, John, 603
Buchanan, James, 257
Budget deficit
 bond-financed, 316
 current account deficit and, 589–590
 financing of, 35–38, 57
 impacts of, 69–70, 316–321
 inflationary impact, 316, 319–321
 real, 501–502
 structural vs. actual, 738
Buiter, W. H., 265, 266, 288, 292, 317

Burbank, Harold Hitchings, 663
Business cycles
 as demand fluctuations, 178–179
 theory of, 152, 227, 387, 408

Cagan, Philip, 337
Capital accumulation
 productive, claims to, 34
 steady-state equilibrium, 56–60
Capital assets
 in foreign countries, 552–553
 pricing model, 167
Capital flow
 adjustment processes affecting, 625–631
 determinants of, 625–627
 international vs. intercurrency, 593–595
 stock reallocations and, 563, 595
Capital formation
 displaced by social security wealth, 344–345
 factors affecting, 34–35
 full employment and, 783
 investment demand and, 436
Capital gains, prototype model, 107
Capital goods
 vs. capital, 681–682
 profit rate and price of, 725–726
Capital markets, 115
 forms of, 119
 perfect, 288–290
Capital mobility, international, 645, 647–648
 interest rates and, 638–639
Capital stock criterion, 257–258
Capital theory, 686–688, 708
Cargill, T. F., 309
Carmichael, J., 288, 307
Catholic agrarianism, 6
Central bank, 644
 blind vs. feedback rules, 473
 credit, 132
 expansionary policies, 478–479
 purpose of, 132–133
 real economic outcomes, 477–478
 social and political responsibilities, 476–477
Chamberlin, Edward, 2, 6, 663–665
Chamley, C., 310–311
Clark, John Bates, 676–677, 689
 marginal productivity theory, 680–684, 706
Classical dichotomy, 153–155, 159, 210, 259, 444, 692
Cleared vs. uncleared markets, 81–82
Cobb-Douglas utility function, 278

INDEX

Cohen, D., 303
Collective bargaining, government policy toward, 460
Commodity money, 141, 144
  vs. fiat money, 146–147, 151, 152–153
  value of, 151
Commodity standard, 147
Common funnel theory, 401–403, 495–497
Comparative statics, 774–777
  of balanced-budget equilibrium, 266
  sign structure, 49
Competition
  monopolistic, 121, 663–664
  non-price, 120–121
Competitive equilibrium, 206
Conant, James Bryant, 1, 2, 661, 669–670
Consolidated approach, 294
Constant Elasticity of Substitution (CES) function, 560
Constant Relative Risk Aversion (CRRA) function, 304, 560
Consumption
  equilibrium condition, 299
  lifetime income and, 10
  liquidity constraints, 342
  tax policy affecting, 280, 291
Contemporary Economic Thought (Homan), 676
Copland, Douglas B., 662
Correspondence principle (Samuelson), 774–775
Countercyclical response vs. monetarist rule, 474
Cowles Commission for Research in Economics, 8–9
Credit rationing, 288–289
Crowding in, 112, 270–271
Crowding out, 112, 269, 277–278, 316, 507
  fiscal-monetary mix affecting, 498–499
  through higher future interest rates, 280
  interest rate and, 500
  long-run, 508
  neoclassical growth model, 508–517
  policy parameters affecting, 515–516
  of private capital formation, 270–271
  social security and, 344
CRRA. *See* Constant Relative Risk Aversion (CRRA) function
Curley, James Michael, 661
Currency speculation, transactions taxes, 654–655
Current account balance, 585
  exchange rate and, 605–606, 628–629

expansionary policies reducing, 630
international policy coordination, 653
macroeconomic shocks to, 625–626
price adjustment mechanisms and, 619
transfer of wealth through, 624

Darby, M. R., 319
Debreu, Gerard, 688, 709
Debt financing, 378, 436
Debt management, 69–70
Debt neutrality, 258–259, 279–282
  conditions for, 284–298, 313
  future research, 297–298
  infinite horizons and intergenerational transfers, 284–288
  with limitless debt, 291–292
  lump-sum taxes and, 289, 290–291
  overlapping generations model, 282
  testing of, 292–295, 321
Debt-deflation theory of depression (Fisher), 695, 700, 718
Debt/GNP ratio, 499–500, 501, 502–504
Deficit, federal budget
  nominal vs. primary, 267
  reduction, Gramm-Rudman-Hollings schedule, 502
Deficit financing, 259
  fiscal and monetary policies determining, 68
  infinite-horizons models, 290
  liquidity constraints, 290
  macroeconomic theory, 232
  with money, 298–309
  with non-monetary debt, 277–293
Deficit spending, 256–257
  cumulative effects, 263–266
  expansionary effects, 406–407
  interest rates and, 407, 498–499
Deflation
  expected, 189–190
  unemployment and, 393
Deflationary gap, 394
Del Mar, Alexander, 690–691
Demand management
  fiscal-monetary mix, 488–489, 641
  with income controls, 464
  inflationary effects, 458
  instruments of, 401–404, 422–423, 488–489
  international coordination, 639–641
  objectives of, 401
  policy from 1971–79, 417–421
  stagflation and, 452–465
  targets, 640

Denomination, convenient, 123–124
Deposits
  creation, 128–129
  demand vs. interest rate levels, 529
  insurance, 133–134
Deposit rates
  ceilings, 113
  controlled, 53
  deregulation of, 525–526
  and M-1, 533–534
  regulation Q ceilings, 112
Deregulation, 136
  of deposit interest rates, 525–526
Derivative monetary media, 144, 145
Diamond, D. W., 124
Dillon, Douglas, 790
Discount rate
  impact of inflation on, 376–377, 381
  indexing, 526
Disequilibrium
  in asset markets, 613
  theory, 176–177, 183
Disinflation
  credible threat policies, 227–228
  unemployment and, 393
Disintermediation, 135
Disposable resources, calculating long-run, 42
Distribution of Wealth, The (Clark), 677, 680–684
Distribution theory, 677
  Kaldorian, 721–726, 733
Dollar
  appreciation of, 622, 627
  compensated, 691, 692, 711–712
  defending, 629, 630, 637–638
  depreciation of, 591–592, 608–609
  effect of budget balance norm on, 589–590
  free-fall fear, 593, 629
  prices and value of, 622
  trade balance and, 591–592
Domar, Evsey, 13, 266
Dornbusch, R., 300, 617
Drazen, A., 285, 300–301
Duesenberry, James, 670, 671
Dybvig, P. H., 124
Dynamic analysis, 265
Dynasties, 287

Eckstein, Otto, 671
Econometric Society, 699
Econometrics, teaching methods, 7
Economic activity models, 69

  empirical, 72–73, 80–85
  theoretical, 71, 75–80
Economic policy
  objectives, 409–414
  qualitative vs. quantitative goals, 408–409
  stability and expectations in, 193–194
Economic Program for American Democracy, An, 4, 665
Economic Recovery Tax Act of 1981, 369, 489
Economic Report of the President (1962), 748–749
Economic statistics
  cross-section observations, 8
  teaching methods, 7
Economic theory
  of accounting, 685–686
  Anglo-American tradition, 6
  socio-political factors, 203–205
Economics of the Recovery Program, The, 665, 668
Economists
  mathematical, 679, 699
  neoclassical, 675–679
Edgeworth, F. Y., 6
Effective demand
  constraints on, 175–178
  fluctuations in, 623
  principle of, 172–175, 214
Efficient markets hypothesis, 305–306
Eisner, Robert, 268
Elasticity of substitution, 278
  constant, 560
  in internationally-diversified portfolios, 557–558, 561–562
  nominal interest rate and, 303
Elmendorf, D. W., 295
Ely, Richard T., 674
Empirical model of U.S. economy, 72–73
  asset demand specification, 85–87, 104–106
  balance equations, 80–83
  financial block simulation, 106–113
  government sector, 83–84
  household sector, 99–104
  intermediaries, 83, 87–99
  nonfinancial sectors, 83
  within-period endogenous variables, 81–82
Employment. *See* Unemployment
Endowments
  dated, 133
  and risks, 556, 557
Equation of Exchange (Fisher), 217–218, 691, 692–694, 712–716, 717

INDEX 795

Equilibrating mechanisms, 174
Equilibrium business cycle theory, 178–179, 180
Equities, 33
  foreign, 552–553, 559
European Community
  Exchange Rate Mechanism, 643
  single currency, 647
European Monetary System, 648
Exchange market
  value of money in, 149–151
  vicious and virtuous cycles, 427–428
Exchange rates. *See also* Floating exchange rate; International coordination
  adjustable pegs, 653, 656
  aggregate demand and, 489–490
  appreciating, 231–232
  as asset prices, 543, 602–603
  capital mobility and, 594–595, 645, 647
  current account balance and, 591–592
  domestic asset supplies and, 608–609
  between equivalent fiat moneys, 604
  expectations, 594–595, 610–611, 626, 636–637
  fiscal-monetary mix and, 447–448
  fixed, 634, 648, 651–652
  inflation and, 497–498
  international capital movements and, 46
  long-run equilibrium, 611
  nominal, 621–623, 649–651
  path to equilibrium, 562–563
  reaction to exogenous shocks, 583
  wealth effects of adjustment, 427
Exchange risk, home currency preference and, 551, 607
Expansionary policy
  classical variant, 50–51
  effectiveness of, 49–50
  inflation and, 58, 59
  multipliers, 50
Expectations, 26–27, 68. *See also* Rational expectations
  of asset prices, 48
  diverse interest, 166
  in new classical macroeconomics, 225–226
  policy, 193–194
  in portfolio theory, 610
  state of long-term, 213
Expectations-augmented wage and price equations, 456–457

Fama, E. F., 305–306
Federal Deposit Insurance Corporation, 133
Federal Reserve Act of 1914, 148

Federal Reserve system
  defending the dollar, 629, 637–638
  district banks, 644
  foundation of, 148
  monetary policy, 414, 444, 474, 531–532, 534–535, 627–628
  responsibility for economic recovery, 504
  target setting, 445–447, 484–485, 531–532, 534–535
Feldstein, Martin, 286, 291, 292–293, 295, 671
  anti-Keynesian views, 672
  monetary policy, 369, 448
  and social security, 338–339, 343, 344–345
Fellner, William, 11, 166, 462–463
Fiat money, 144
  vs. commodity money, 146–147, 151, 152–153
  neutrality of, 209–210, 276
  value of, 150, 208–209, 603–605
FIFO. *See* First-in-first-out accounting convention
Financial intermediaries, 52–54, 120–122
  functions of, 122–125
  government surveillance, 134–135
  long-term customer relations, 121
  portfolio decisions, 86, 136–137
  quantitative rationing, 121–122
  regulations and innovations affecting, 70
  risk-taking, 130
  theoretical model, 76–77
Financial markets, 118–120
  entry, branching, and merging, 136
  functions of, 122–125
  informal, 120
  non-price competition, 120–121
Firms
  demand-constrained, 176–177
  retirement taxes and contributions, 350
First-in-first-out accounting convention (FIFO), 371, 383, 436
Fiscal multiplier theory, 262–263
Fiscal policy
  affecting aggregate demand, 489
  causing currency depreciation, 608–609
  constant, open market operations and, 323
  downgrading of, 451
  instruments of, 404
  measures of, 1969–1980 period, 449–452
  recession and tightening of, 590–591
  saving and investment effects of, 672
Fiscal-monetary policy mix, 258, 401–404, 488–489, 490–495
  easy vs. tight, 402, 403, 493–495, 497–499

Fiscal-monetary policy mix (cont.)
  exchange rate and, 447–448
  favoring capital formation, 434
  history and projections, 500–504
  inflation control, 497–498
Fischer, Stanley, 186
Fisher, Irving, 6, 146–147, 303, 662, 665, 673, 677–679, 719, 725. *See also* Equation of Exchange (Fisher); Fisher effect
  biographical information, 700–704
  capital theory, 686–688, 708
  doctoral dissertation, 684–685, 702
  Equation of Exchange, 691, 692–694, 712–716
  general equilibrium theory, 684–690, 705–711
  interest equation, 156, 159, 182–183, 686, 694–695, 716–717
  investment opportunity concept, 688, 707, 709
  life cycle model, 687, 708
  inside loan markets, 122–123
  macroeconomic theory, 694–695, 716–719
  monetary theory, 160–161, 690–694, 711–716
  quantity theory of money, 154, 712
  wealth redistribution effect, 189, 192
Fisher effect, 190, 304–309, 322–323
Fixed rules, 472–473, 474, 691–692
  and conversion of shocks into macroeconomic outcomes, 480–484, 519–524
Fixprice sector, 183
  macroeconomic shocks, (1970–1979), 420
Floating exchange rates, 427, 539, 657
  vs. adjustable pegs, 643
  beggar-thy-neighbor policy, 428
  clean, 645
  dirty, 420, 646
  domestic price effects, 432–433
  inflation and, 497–498
  as an international adjustment mechanism, 620
  international policy coordination, 652–654
  two-country model, 550
Foreign currency assets, 33
  demands for, 55
  government holdings, 37
Formal disequilibrium macroeconomics, 216–217
Free market money, 147–149
Frenkel, J. A., 300
Friedman, B. M., 271
Friedman, Milton, 11, 13, 17, 158, 308
  monetary theory, 160, 218, 226, 237–240, 472–473
  natural rate (Presidential Address of 1967), 219–220, 385–386, 395n, 478
  permanent income theory, 10
  quantity theory of money, 154, 259
Friedman, Rose, 338
Frisch, Ragnar, 7
Full employment, 219, 222–223, 386, 672
  capital formation and, 783
  equilibrium, 223
  price/wage flexibility and, 180
Functional finance theory, 257

Galbraith, John Kenneth, 432, 669
Gale, D., 291
Garbade, K., 306
General equilibrium theory, 23, 27, 679–684, 705–706
  formal, 151
  hydraulic-mechanical analogue model, 705
  with intertemporal choices and opportunities, 686–690, 706–711
  mathematical models, 6–7
  modern, 206
  value of money in, 208–211
General Theory of Employment, Interest and Money, The (Keynes), 2–3, 23, 187–188, 662–663
  Harvard critique of, 666
  market failures in, 212–214
Germany
  economic policy, 621, 640
  monetary unification of East and West, 650–651
Gilbert, Richard, 667
Gold standard, 142–143, 151, 618, 649–650
  advocates of restoration, 476
  elimination of, 145, 146
  supply-side view, 229
Goldberger, Arthur, 8
Golden rule, 300. *See also* Phelps's golden rule
  capital intensity, 247
  for dynamic efficiency, 281
  equilibrium, 733
Goldsmith, Raymond, 117–118
Goodhart's law, 406
Gordon, Donald F., 775
Gordon, Kermit, 16, 751
Gordon, Robert, 484
Government debt. *See also* Budget deficit
  as currency substitute, 271

INDEX 797

effects of, 69–70
monetary and non-monetary, 36, 260
steady-state equilibrium, 58–60
Government financing
choices, 255–256
intertemporal budget constraints, 281
macroeconomic theory, 261–272
non-tax, 309
requirements, 45–46
Government regulations
of banks and financial intermediaries, 131
macroeconomic effects, 70
of stock trading, 130
Government transfers, effectiveness of, 451–452
Gramm-Rudman act, 501
Gresham's law, 142
Gross national product
to debt ratio, 499–500, 501, 502–504
rates of growth (1970–1979), 417–419
Gross substitutes assumption, 41, 49, 548–549
Grossman, S., 313
Group of Five, international coordination, 636
Group of Seven, 546
exchange rate, 646
Groves, Harold, 753
Growth dynamics of public debt, 266
Growth rate, natural, 35
Growth theory, 13
Gurley, J. G., 126

Haberler, Gottfried, 2, 668–669
Hadjimichalakis, Michael G., 482, 531
Haliassos, M., 301–302
Hall, Robert, 147, 472
Hamada, K., 539, 541, 550
Hansen, Alvin, 2, 4, 179, 262, 666–669, 777
Harris, Seymour, 4, 668, 787–790
Harrod, Roy, 13, 266
Harvard College
alumni revolt, 669–670
development of Keynesian theory, 668, 769–771
economics program, 2, 665–669
Tercentenary, 661–662
Hayek, F. A., 211
Heller, Walter W., 16, 17, 747–755
Hicks, John R., 4, 6, 26, 215
IS/LM model, 14, 24
High-powered money. *See* Base money

Historical cost effect, 370
Homan, Paul, 676
Home asset preference, 550–553
Home currency preference, 605, 606, 607–608
exchange risk and, 607
Horizons
defining, 45
finite vs. infinite, 275–276
household, length of, 42
relevant to current economic behavior, 68–69
Household sector
empirical model, asset demand specification, 99–104
saving behavior, 33
theoretical model, 71, 75–76
Houthakker, Hendrik, 7, 671
Hubbard, R. G., 290
Human capital, 42–43
Hume, David, 155
Hyperdisinflation, 321

Iden, G., 295
Illiquid assets, 125
Income
as consumption, 686–688, 707
explicit vs. inflationary taxation of, 242–251
lifetime, 10
Income redistribution, 680
leaky bucket, 740
neoclassical theory, 207–208
Income tax cuts
consequences of, 435
supply-side effects, 437
Incomplete markets, 213
Index Number Institute (Fisher), 699–700
Index Visible Company (Fisher), 704
Infinite horizons, debt neutrality and, 284–288
Inflation. *See also* Anti-inflation policy
accommodative monetary policy and, 438–440
accounting, 268, 502
cost-push, 222, 224, 390
demand-pull, 478
effects of monetary restriction on, 318–319
exchange rates and, 497–498
expansionary policy affecting, 58, 59
expectations, 48, 51, 261, 483
history (1950–1980), 458–459
interest rate response to, 315–316, 524

Inflation (cont.)
  international price adjustment and, 621–622
  investment incentives and disincentives, 376–383
  Keynesian theory, 219, 221–224
  long-run, capital formation and, 242–251
  monetary theory of, 218, 226
  money demand and, 319–320, 483
  nominal rate of return and, 307
  optimal, 240–242
  short-run, 240–242
  social costs of, 411–412
  structural bias toward, 458–460
  tax, 268–269
  taxable inventory gains attributed to, 371–376
  unemployment and, 219–220, 221–225, 402–403, 717, 739
  Vietnam War associated, 478
Inflationary gap, 179, 394
Inside money, 52
  substituting for outside, 128
Insider power, 184
Insurance
  federal deposit, 148
  of home mortgages, 134
  unemployment, 176
Interest. *See also* Nominal interest rate
  elasticity of U.S. saving, 278–279
  impatience theory, 689, 710
  marginal productivity theory, 680–684
  on outstanding debt, 267
  sensitivity, two-period life-cycle model, 278
Interest rate. *See also* International interest rate
  after-tax, 448, 491–493
  ceilings, 135–136
  controlled, 53
  deficit spending and, 407
  deposit creation and, 128–129, 525–526, 528, 529
  differentials, 652
  expectations, 166
  Fisher's interest equation, 156, 159, 182–183, 686, 694–695, 716–717
  fixed, 53–54, 491–493, 519–520
  on government debt, 498–500
  government vs. private lenders, 289
  indexing, 533
  to induce foreign investment, 592–593
  long-term, 182, 448
  market-determined, 54, 135

  monetary velocity and, 532
  nominal vs. real (1969–1979), 440, 443
  pegging, 481, 520, 521
  real money balances and, 190
  as stabilizer for demand shocks, 179–183
Intergenerational consumption loans, model of, 772
Intergenerational transfer
  age differences, 301
  debt neutrality and, 284–288
Intermediation, marginal costs of, 529
International coordination
  under Bretton Woods system, 634–635
  of current accounts, 653
  of demand management policies, 639–641
  fixed exchange rates, 651–652
  floating rates, 635–638, 652–654
  of macroeconomic policy, 641–642
International diversification, 554
  asset prices, 559–560
  long-run gains, 555–559
  rates of return, 560
  to reduce risk, 555
  risk premiums, 560–562
  substitutability of goods, 557–558, 561–562
International interest rate
  capital mobility and, 638–639
  U.S. role in, 426–427
International Monetary Fund, 645
International monetary system, 643–646
  adjustable parities, 645, 656
  reform of, 654–655
  single currency, 643–644, 646, 647
International price adjustments, 617–631
  inflation and, 621–622
  problems with, 621–623
International trade
  Mundell-Fleming model, 584–589, 596–599
  one-country-model, 585
  substitution between goods, 561–562, 586
Internationalization
  of American owned wealth, 539–543
  of money and capital markets, 638
Interregional trade, 593
Inventory
  accounting conventions, 371–376
  fixed investment and, 370
  overtaxation of profits, 371–376, 383
Investment. *See also* International diversification
  demand, capital formation and, 436
  inventories and fixed, 370

INDEX 799

Investment incentives
  fiscal-monetary policy affecting, 448
  with inflation-distorted taxes, 376–383
  international, 592–593
Investment tax credit, 381, 404, 448, 672
Invisible hand, 186, 205–208, 636, 739
Irrelevance results, 312, 323
IS curve, 75, 534–535
IS/LM model, 14, 24
  of aggregate demand, 261–264
  assumption of perfect substitutability, 544
  of fiscal-monetary policy, 491–495
  of foreign assets, 543–544
  of monetary policy, 519–520
  stocks in, 44–45
  three-asset, 270–271
  two-asset, 270
ITC. *See* Investment tax credit
Iwai, Katsuhito, 186
Iwata, K., 539

Japan
  direct U.S. investment, 594–595
  economic policy, 621, 630, 640
  U.S. trade, two-country model, 546–550, 565–581
Jevons, W. S., 147
Johnson, Lyndon B., 16–17, 478, 749–750
Jorgenson, Dale, 671
Judd, K. L., 290

Kahn, R. F., 262–263
Kaldor, Nicholas, 721–726, 733
Kareken, John, 603
Katona, George, 337
Kennedy, John F., 15–16, 747, 749, 751
Keynes effect, 188, 190
Keynes, John Maynard, 2–3, 23, 662. *See also General Theory of Employment, Interest and Money, The*; Keynesian economics
  vs. classical economists, 4–5
  horizon of analysis, 45
  liquidity preference curve, 11
  speculative motive, 12
  on transactions taxes, 655
Keynesian economics, 171–175. *See also* Neoclassical synthesis
  applied to labor market, 5
  building blocks, 10
  counterrevolutions, 671–672
  diverse interest expectations, 166
  liquidity preference, 165–168, 181

market failure, 211–214
Marxism and, 664–665
mistakes of, 781
vs. monetarism, 218
multiplier formula, 774–775
opposition to, 204–205
principle of effective demand, 172–175
short-run model, 263–266
speculative motive, 165–168
uncleared markets, 386–387
Klein, Laurence, 670
Kochin, L. A., 292
Koopmans, Tjalling, 9
Kormendi, R. C., 294–295
Kowalewski, Kim, 342
Kuroyanagi, M., 541, 550
Kydland, F. E., 408

Labor theory of value, 680, 706
Laffer curve, 229
Laissez faire policy, 411
Laitner, J. P., 286
Last-in-first-out accounting convention (LIFO), 371
Last-resort lending, 132–133
Laughlin, J. Laurence, 690, 691
Leontief technologies, 724–725
Leontief, Wassily, 2, 7, 166, 666
Lerner, Abba, 257, 258, 452
Levhari, D., 300
Levy, Marion, 664
Life cycle model, 278, 687, 708, 722–723
LIFO. *See* Last-in-first-out accounting convention
Lindbeck, Assar, 184
Lintner, J. H., 12–13, 167
Liquid assets, 125, 129–130
Liquidity preference, 165, 166
Littauer, Lucius, 666
LM curve, 533–535
  intermediation and volatility of, 533–534
  optimal shape, 522–523
  response to macroeconomic shocks, 523–524, 525
  vertical, 520, 522, 531
Loans, 53
  demand for, prototype model, 107–108
  functions of inside markets, 122–123
  maturity shifting, 124–125
  prime rate convention, 121–122
  as uncleared market, 82
Lucas critique, 407–408

Lucas, Robert E., 220, 224, 255, 385–386, 780
Lump-sum taxation, 289, 290–291

M-1 interest rate, 533–534
McCallum, B. T., 309, 316
McGovern, George, 17
Macroeconometrics
  Lucas critique, 255
  models, 670
Macroeconomic models, 23
  accelerator-multiplier, 777–778
  of asset markets, 13–14
  classical variant, 50–51
  comparative dynamics, 776
  consensus, 1970s, 421–428
  continuous vs. discrete time, 46–47
  dynamics and long-run steady states, 55–61
  financial intermediation, loans, and inside money, 52–54
  government budget constraints, 45–46
  Keynes-Hicks, 24–25
  Keynesian variant, 48–50
  mixed, 51–52
  monetary policy in, 25
  multi-asset, 32–52, 269–272
  Mundell-Fleming, 543–544, 546
  short-run, 272
  stocks, flows, and specific saving functions, 44–46
  substitutability, aggregation, and estimation, 54
Macroeconomic policy
  aggregate supply schedule, 431–434
  development of, 400–401
  international coordination, 414–415, 641–642
  oil and energy constraints, 428–431
  supply-increasing, 434–438
Macroeconomic shocks, 480, 519
  price and supply, 424–426
  types of, 480, 519
  unexpected outcomes, 480–484, 519–524
Macroeconomics. *See also* Formal disequilibrium macroeconomics; New classical macroeconomics
  with constrained effective demand, 175–178
  critics of, 272–274
  foundations of, 3–4
  history, 23
  money and, 159–162

postwar development of, 670–671
synthesizing with neoclassical tradition, 10–15
Major, John, 650
Mandatory retirement saving
  life cycle model vs. dynastic model, 336
  liquidity view, 336–337
  macroeconomic effects, 335–337
  motivation for, 340–341
  redistributive effects, 342–343
  self-discipline issues, 341
  simulation analysis, 346–364
  vs. voluntary saving, 340–343
Mankiw, N. Gregory, 171, 173
Marginal opportunity cost, 157–158
Marginal productivity of money, 157
  nominal interest rate and, 159
Marginal productivity theory, 185, 676, 688
  of distribution, 706, 710
  of interest, 680–684
Marginal utility theory, 683–684
Marginalism, 676, 679–680
Mariano, R. S., 293–294
Market adjustment mechanisms
  in economy-wide markets, 186–187
  interest rates, 179–183
  Keynesian vs. classical view, 174
  nominal wages and prices, 183–189
  to restore full employment equilibrium, 174
Market clearing, 172, 385–386, 780
  adjustment mechanisms, 186
  in new classical macroeconomics, 255
Market failure, 172, 211
  macroeconomic theory, 173, 212–214
  neoclassical theory, 207
Markowitz, Harry, 12, 166–167
Marschak, Jacob, 9
Marshall, Alfred, 6, 160–161, 429
Marxism
  challenge to property income, 680, 706
  Keynesian theory and, 664–665
Mason, Edward S., 7, 664
Maximization of expected utility, 284
Methodology of positive economics, 208
Meyer, R. A., 309
Microfoundations, 26, 274–275
Milbourne, Ross, 532
Mitchell, Wesley C., 662
Modigliani, Franco, 10–11, 257–258, 295
Modigliani-Miller theorem, 122, 275
Monetarism, 11, 204, 217–220. *See also* Quantity theory of money
  combining structure and policy, 532–535

INDEX   801

fundamental, 444
vs. Keynesian theory, 218
macroeconomics and, 160–161
policy regime concept, 474
recession and, 471
transactions, 444–445
Monetarism-1, 218, 423, 451
Monetarism-2. *See* New classical macroeconomics
Monetary aggregates, 423
targets for, 445–446
Monetary base
rates of growth, 1970–1979 period, 441–442
velocity of, 444–445
Monetary disinflation, 460–464
Monetary policy, 309–321. *See also* Structural reform
accommodating unpredictable shocks, 480, 519–524
with corporate tax reductions, 448
counter-cyclical, 254
effect on capital investment, 14
equilibrium allocations, 323
in fixed exchange rate systems, 648
fixed interest rate vs. fixed money supply, 519–520
hierarchical, multistage structure, 484–486
inflation and, 438–440
instruments of, 403–404
LM curve effects, 482
macroeconomic outcomes, 25, 480–484
monetarist vs. bondist policy, 316
objectives, 475–480, 484–486
parameters of, 37–38
real consequences of, 210–211
stochastic dynamic model, 484
targets and operating rules, 484–486
tightening, 448–449
Monetary rules, 691–692, 711–712
vs. discretion, 414, 472–475
Monetary theory
of balance of payments, 619
history, 690–691
of nominal income. *See* Monetarism-1
Money. *See also* Commodity money; Fiat money
choosing, 141
definitive, 144
dominated in real rate of return, 312
exchange value, 149–151
functions of, 143–146
in general equilibrium theory, 208–211

high-powered vs. low-powered, 128
macroeconomic theory and, 159–162
as means of payment, 143–144
neutrality of, 151–153, 156, 159–160, 210, 778
non-pecuniary yields, 260
precious metals as, 141–143
price of, 156–159, 160–161
privatization, 147–149
representative, 144, 145
societal value, 139–141, 149
unit of account, 208
value function, 143–144, 153, 604–605
veil metaphor, 152, 209, 273, 385, 649
Money demand
Allais-Baumol-Tobin model, 158
Baumol cash inventory analysis, 243–244
business cycles and fluctuations in, 178–179
equals supply equation, 160, 161
expected inflation rate and, 483
interest elasticity of, 181, 516–517
interest rate sensitivity, 11–13, 528
nominal interest rates and, 440
real, inflation and, 319–320
speculative motive, 165–168
vs. wealth demand, 248–251
Money illusion, 184, 212, 394
Money markets, 119
Money stock, increasing, 259
Money supply
fixed, 519–520, 522–523
public debt and, 609
Money velocity, interest sensitivity, 11–13, 532
Money-wage stickiness, 186, 399, 432, 433
Monopolistic competition, 663–664
Multi-asset stock adjustment framework, 544–546
Multi-commodity-multi-agent exchange model, 686, 707–708
Multiplier theory, 176–178, 671
Mundell effect, 49–50, 298, 440, 442
Mundell, R. A., 159
Mundell-Fleming model, 543–544, 546, 584–589, 596–599
Mundell-Tobin effect, 160
Musgrave, Richard, 671
Mutual funds, open-end, 129–130

NAIRU. *See* Non-accelerating inflation rate of unemployment (NAIRU)
National income accounts, 31, 33, 36

National product equation, 75
National wealth, 115
Natural rate of unemployment, 394–395, 422
  deviation from, 385–386
  tests of, 305
  upward trends, 453–456
Negative income tax, 17
Nelson, C. R., 306
Neoclassical synthesis, 215–217, 425, 670, 672, 779–783
  normative and policy propositions, 781–783
  opposition to, 780
Neoclassical theory, 211–214
  anatomy of market failure, 207
  vs. Keynesian theory, 10–15
  marginalism, 679–680
  response to Marxism, 680, 706
  in the United States, 673–695
Net financial investment, empirical model, 80
Net worth
  personal, 116
  private, 116–118
Neutrality of money, 151–153, 156, 159–160
  outside, 778
  criticism of, 273–274
  fiat, 209–210, 276
  in Keynesian theory, 214
  new classical macroeconomic model, 226
New classical macroeconomics, 204, 218, 273, 408, 423–424, 457, 754
  agents' behavior, 226–227
  market clearing, 255
  rational expectations, 255
New economics, 16, 748
New Keynesians, 173
Newcomb, Simon, 674, 690–691, 712
Nixon, Richard M., 17
Nominal income, taxation of, 436
Nominal interest rate
  and money demand, 440
  elasticity of substitution and, 303
  fixed, 260, 527–528
  inflation and, 315–316
  and marginal productivity of money, 159
  uncontrolled, 527–528
  zero floor, 182
Nominal prices
  adjusting exchange rate to, 649–650
  degree of flexibility, 183

equilibrating mechanisms, 174
inertia, models of, 186
vs. nominal exchange rate, 622–623
response to demand shocks, 183–189
unemployment and, 388–389
Nominal wages
  adjusting exchange rate to, 649–650
  vs. nominal exchange rate, 622–623
  vs. real, cuts in, 183–184
  response to demand shocks, 183–189
  unemployment and, 388
Non-accelerating inflation rate of unemployment (NAIRU), 391, 392, 394, 422, 479–480
  upward shift, 453–456
Notices of Withdrawal. *See* NOW accounts
NOW accounts, 526–527
Numeraire, 143, 151, 208, 213

O'Connell, S. A., 291
O'Donnell, Ken, 752
Office of Price Administration and Civilian Supply, civilian supply division, 7
Okun, Arthur, 9, 16, 186, 433, 457, 737–740
Okun's Law, 422, 425, 462, 738, 749
OLS adjustment matrix, 105
OPEC. *See* Organization of Petroleum Exporting Countries (OPEC)
Open market operations, 112
  constant fiscal policy and, 323
  with staggered portfolio adjustments, 315
  system response to, 107
Ophelimity index, 409, 413
Optimal cash balance, 757–761
Optimal debt, 282–283
Optimal time path of money supply, 237
Optimization, 26
  individual, 206
  new classical theory, 226–227
Organization of Petroleum Exporting Countries (OPEC), 420, 478–479
  macroeconomic consequences, 428–431
Output, supply-determined, 425
Outside assets, substituting inside for, 125–127
Outside money, substituting inside for, 128
Overlapping generations model, 61, 150
  for debt neutrality proposition, 282
  with two-period lifetimes, 275
Over-taxation, stagflation and, 369, 383
Overvaluations, 650
Own-currency preferences, 55
Own-rates of interest, 58

Paper currency, 144
Pareto optimization, 206
Partial adjustment assumption, 108
Partial equilibrium analysis, 6
Patinkin, Don, 153, 188, 189, 259, 300, 778. *See also* Real balance effect
Patman effect, 432–433
Pechman, Joseph, 753, 755
Peled, D., 311–312
Pension and insurance funds
  adjustment coefficients, 92–93
  asset demand specification, 98
  interest rate responses, 91
Perry, George, 754
Phelps, Edmund S., 13, 239
Phelps's golden rule, 281, 300. *See also* Golden rule
Phillips curve, 191–192, 219, 221, 388, 389–390, 395–396n
  augmentation variable, 456
  Lucas interpretation, 220
  macroeconomic model, 222–223
  microeconomics of, 391–392
  short-run trade-off, 453–456
  sources of, 390
Philosophy of Wealth, The (Clark), 676–677
Pigou, Arthur Cecil, 188, 211. *See also* Real balance effect
Pigou effect. *See* Pigou, Arthur Cecil
Plosser, C. I., 296–297
Pohl, Herr, 650
Polemarchakis, H., 311
Policy instruments, 404–408
Pollard, Spencer, 2–3, 662–663, 769
Poole, William, 445, 481–482, 483, 519, 523
Portfolio adjustments
  price movements reflecting, 611–612
  response to foreign exchange markets, 612–613
  staggered, 315
Portfolio choices, 311. *See also* International diversification
  asset prices, 559–560
  across currencies and current account imbalances, 605–607
  empirical estimation, 562–564
  of financial intermediaries, 136–137
  fundamental data approach, 613–614
  household, 44
  optimal international, 561–562
  risky, 12
  short- vs. long-run applications, 543
  staggered, 301–302
Portfolio theory, 12, 14, 166–167, 404–405, 539
  balance effect, 588
  covariance complementarity, 41
  expectations in, 610
  two-country model of U.S. and Japan, 546–550, 565–581
Poterba, J. M., 289, 297
Prescott, E. C., 408
President's Council of Economic Advisers
  foundation of, 671
  Kennedy-Johnson years, 747–752
Price adjustment mechanisms
  Phillips curve, 191–192
  stability of, 190–191
Price of money, 602–603
Price shocks, 480, 519
  GNP deviations with, 482–483
Price/quantity outcome, 497
Prices. *See also* Nominal prices
  deviation from equilibrium values, 388–389
  greater flexibility in, 192
  indexing, 712–714
  rigid-price Keynesian, 192, 193
  set in monetary unit of account, 213–214
  target, excluding import prices from, 640
Prices and Quantities (Okun), 739–740
Price-setting mechanisms, 213–214
Principles of Economics (Marshall), 6
Principles of Economics (Taussig), 675
Probit analysis, 8
Production function, backyard, 123
Productivity growth
  income taxation and, 437–438
  inflation and, 435
Property investment
  foreign, 552–553
  home ownership, tax favoritism, 449
Prosperity and Depression (Haberler), 668–669
Protopapadakis, A., 312–313
Public debt
  burden, 256–257
  interest on, 36
  money supply and, 609
Purchasing Power of Money, The (Fisher), 691, 692, 711, 712, 717
Purvis, Douglas, 105

q-ratio. *See* Tobin's q
Quantity theory of money, 154, 155–156, 217–218, 259, 522, 692–694, 712
  foreign transactions and, 716
Quarterly Journal of Economics, 5, 666

Rae, John, 686, 707
Randall, Clarence, 669
Ratchet effect, 622
Rate of return
  inflation and nominal, 307
  money dominated in, 312
  steady-state solution, 56–57
  on unfunded retirement insurance, 343–345
Rational expectations
  vs. adaptive, 457
  contractual inertia and, 457
  dynamic solutions, 55–61
  equilibrium in multi-asset markets, 613
  future equilibrium, 562, 610–611
  in new classical macroeconomics, 255
Rational stabilization policy, 782–783
Reaganomics, 203, 204, 627–628
Real balance effect, 188–189, 259–260, 669, 695, 718, 778
Real demand shocks, 480, 519
Real wages
  deviation from equilibrium values, 388–389
  effect of unemployment on, 455–456
  vs. money wages, 187
Recession, fiscal tightening and, 590–591
Regressive expectations effect, 588
Replacement costs, normal, 34–35
Representative agent model, 275
Reserve requirements, 128–129, 131–132, 532
  interest rates and, 109
  one-hundred percent, 133–134
  simulation, 108
Reserves, 130–131
  correcting positions, 132
  demand for unborrowed, 529, 531
  net borrowed, 529, 531
Retention of earnings, empirical model, 80
Retirement saving plans. *See also* Mandatory retirement saving
  adverse selection, 341
  firm contributions, 350
  insurance aspect, 341
  unfunded, low return on, 343–345
Revenue sharing, 750
Reverse switching, 726, 729

Review of Economics and Statistics, 789
Ricardian equivalence. *See* Ricardian neutrality
Ricardian neutrality, 258, 267, 279–281
Risk, 129–130
  pooling, 124
  premia in foreign investments, 559
Risk aversion, 12, 553
  Brainard theory, 405
  international diversification, 555
Robertson, Dennis H., 155, 662, 666
Robinson, Joan, 3–4, 663, 665, 723, 725, 780
Rogers, James Harvey, 704
Romer, David, 173
Roosevelt, Franklin D., 154, 661, 718
  economic recovery program, 3, 4, 665
Rotemberg, J. J., 314
Runs, 131, 133

Sakurai, M., 541, 550
Samuelson, Paul A., 10, 15, 215, 224, 663, 684, 751
  anti-inflation policy, 222–223, 224
  at Harvard, 2, 7, 662, 769–771
  macroeconomic theory, 434, 771–779
  neoclassical synthesis, 670, 672, 779–783
  writings, 772–773, 779
"Sand in the wheels," 654–655
Sargent, T. J., 224, 305, 312, 317, 320, 322–323
Sargent-Wallace model, 321
Saturation, capital vs. monetary, 237–240
Saving. *See also* Life cycle model; Mandatory retirement saving
  behavior, models of, 10–11
  growth model with Leontief technologies, 724–733
  to income ratio, 1935–1936 and 1972–1973 periods, 337–339
  individual, 27, 31
  total, 38–39
Savings institutions
  adjustment coefficients, 89–90
  asset demand, 87, 97–98
  interest rate responses, 88
Scarf, Herbert, 685, 705
Schelling, Thomas, 670–671
Schumpeter, Joseph A., 2, 6, 7, 124, 207, 662, 665
  on Irving Fisher, 678, 718–719
  on neoclassical economics, 673, 675

INDEX 805

Schwartz, A, 308
Schwert, G. W., 306
Seater, J. J., 293–294
Securities and Exchange Commission, stock trading regulations, 130
Seignorage, 145–146, 239, 319–321
 on base money, 268–269
 modern, 259–260
Seligman, Edwin R. A., 676
Separation theorem, 12, 167
Sharpe, W. F., 12–13, 167
Shaw, E. S., 126
Shoeleather costs, 277, 298
Shubik, Martin, 150
Sidrauski, Miguel, 238, 299, 300
Siegel, J. J., 302
Simultaneity bias, 292
Simultaneous equations systems, 47
Single-currency regime, 647, 656
 speculation in, 643–644, 646
Slichter, Sumner H., 452, 663, 773
Smith, Adam, 5, 205
Smith, B. D., 312
Smith, Gary, 105, 316, 342
Smithies, Arthur, 671
Social discount rate, inflation and, 241
Social Security, 339–340
 displacement of capital formation by, 344–345
 early retirement and, 343
 households' expectations, 348
 private saving and, 339–340, 672
Social welfare function, 409–410
Solow, Robert M., 13, 16, 222–223, 224, 265, 751
Sorenson, Ted, 15
Speculation, 675
Spiegel, Henry W., 691
Spot transactions, uniform tax on, 642
Stability, expectations and, 193–194
Stabilization policy, 411
 from 1971–1979, 417–421
 international constraints, 419–420
Stabilizers, built-in, 263
Stagflation, 369, 417
 causes of, 382
 demand management and, 452–465
 Keynesian macroeconomics and, 220–225
Starr, Ross, 534
Steady-state consumption
 evaluating, 241–242
 monetary and capital intensity, 244–246
 private and collective, 247–251

Steady-state debt/GNP ratio, 269
Steady-state solutions, 55–61
Stebbing, P. W., 307
Sterling, A., 295
Steuerle, Eugene, 382
Stickiness of money wages, 394, 432, 433, 778
Stigler, George, 681
Stiglitz, J. E., 289
Stochastic macroequilibrium, 391–393, 484
Stock
 capital flow and reallocation of, 595
 financial and real assets, single-period model, 74–75
 in macroeconomic models, 44–45
 observed capital flow and reallocation of, 563
 steady-state solution, 56–58
Stock market intervention, 111, 130
Stock-flow dynamics, 14
Stone, Richard, 8
Strategic complementarity, 177
Structural reform
 combining with monetarist policy, 532–535
 macroeconomic implications, 524–532
Substitutability, 54
 among assets, 40–41
 assumption of perfect, 544
 of government debt for currency, 271
 imperfect, 112
 intertemporal, 297
Summers, Lawrence H., 278, 289, 297, 308–309, 371, 383
Sumner, William Graham, 674, 679, 702, 703
Supermonetarist policy, 522
Superneutrality, 156, 159, 238, 260, 276–277, 302
 defense of, 299
 empirical tests, 304–309, 322
 with infinite horizons, 322
 steady state, 298–304
Super-NOW accounts, 526–527
Supply/demand analysis, 388
 asymmetry of wage/price response, 454–455, 460
 non-linearity of response, 392
Supply-side economics, 204, 228–231, 434–438
 vs. demand-side economics, 487
 distributional effects, 230
Sweezy, Maxine, 665
Sweezy, Paul, 664, 665

Tabular standard, 147, 692, 712
Tanner, E. J., 292
Tanzi, V., 307
Taussig, Frank W., 665, 666, 675, 688
Tax Reform Act of 1986, 369–370
Taxation. *See also* Lump-sum taxation
  explicit vs. inflationary, 242–251
  optimal timing, 283
  progressive, 766
Taxes
  asset demand and, 43–44
  discounting, debt neutrality and, 293
  inflationary effects, investment and, 376–383
  lowering rates, 229
  marginal, inflationary effects, 381–382
Taylor, John, 186
Thatcherism, 203
Theil-Goldberger mixed estimation technique, 104
Theoretical model of U.S. economy, 71, 75–80
Theory of Interest, The (Fisher), 686, 707
Time inconsistency, 412–413
Tinbergen, Jan, 7, 399–400, 408, 409–410, 411, 414–415, 668
Tobin, James, 159–160
  on Cowles Commission, 8–9
  at Harvard, 1–7
  influence of Keynes on, 1–5
  policy and public service experience, 15–18
Tobin effect, 277, 298–299, 301
Tobin's q, 14–15
Tokens, 142, 144
Trade
  vs. barter, 139
  current account imbalance and, 626
  multilateral, 139–140
Trade deficit
  currency devaluation and, 651
  fiscal-monetary policies affecting, 590
Traditional financial and fiscal orthodoxy, 204, 232–233
Transaction taxes on currency exchanges, 654–655
Transactions media, 131, 145
  inventory theory of management, 11–12, 26
Transfers, asset demand and, 43–44
Treasury View, 233
Treatise on Money (Keynes), 662
Triffin, Robert, 601–602, 743–746

Uncleared markets, 386–387
  vs. cleared, 81–82
  unemployment in, 389
Underemployment
  equilibrium, 5
  interest rates affecting, 652
Undersaving, intergenerational effects, 591
Unemployment
  coexistence of vacancies with, 390–391
  demographic shifts, 453–454
  effects of monetary disinflation on, 460–463
  eliminating involuntary, 5
  frictional, 387, 391
  government policy, 454
  inflation and, 219–225, 240–242, 402–403, 717, 739
  insurance, 176
  involuntary, 179, 387
  Keynesian theory, 175–176, 221–224
  pegging of, 478
  real wages and, 176
  revisionist view, 230–231
  voluntary, 176
  wage inflation and rate of, 393, 394
Unit of account, 143
United Kingdom
  boosting the pound, 650
  economic policy, 621, 640
United States
  foreign ownership of assets, 539–543, 594–595
  internationalization of portfolios, 539–543
  Japanese trade, two-country model, 546–550, 565–581, 586
  monetary base, 145
  saving behavior, 411
Utility
  with constant relative risk aversion, 304
  in economic policy choices, 410–411
  maximization model, 167

Vickrey, William S., 763–767
Viner, Jacob, 666
Volcker, Paul, 476, 629

Wachtel, P., 306
Wages. *See also* Real wages
  theory of, 681
  unemployment and inflation of, 393, 394
Wage-setting mechanisms, 213–214
Waldo, D. G., 315
Wallace, Neil, 310–311, 312, 317, 320, 603

Wallich, Henry, 633, 635, 638
Walras, Leon, 6, 7, 211, 684, 686, 707–708.
  See also *Numeraire*
  general equilibrium theory, 207, 216, 217, 692, 705
Walras's Law, 25
Walsh, Correa, 713
War on poverty, 17, 750
Wealth. *See also* National wealth
  accumulation, household portfolios, 44
  human, 284
  non-human, age-weighted average, 127
  private, sources of new supplies, 32–34
  redistribution, 189
Wealth demand
  life-cycle saving theory, 239–240, 246
  vs. money demand, 248–251
Wealth/GNP ratio, 509–510
Webb, D. C., 289
Weiss, A., 289
Weiss, L., 313
Welfare economics, second-best, 239
Wicksell, Knut, 34, 129, 688, 710
Williams, John H., 666, 667
Withdrawals of deposits, 130
  reserve requirements and, 132
Wood, Stuart, 681
Work-leisure choices, tax effects, 437–438
World asset and debt matrix, 541–543

Yale University, 744
  approach to monetary and financial theory, 14
  Cowles Commission for Research in Economics, 9
  economics program, 702–703

Zeldes, S. P., 291